STRIKING BACK

A HISTORY OF COSATU

STRIKING BACK

A HISTORY OF *COSATU*

JEREMY BASKIN

Ravan Press — Johannesburg

Published by Ravan Press (Pty) Ltd
PO Box 31134, Braamfontein
2017 South Africa

First published 1991

Index compiled by Sharon Rubin of SM Rubin Indexing Services

Cover design and illustration by Jonathan Shapiro

ISBN 0 86975 410 6

Printed and bound by Sigma Press (Pty) Ltd, Pretoria

To Carol

shopstewards for jumpcuts

CONTENTS

Preface

THE Congress of South African Trade Unions (Cosatu), South Africa's largest-ever trade union federation, has been in existence for little over five years. Its history, although brief, has been eventful and politically significant. Certainly it has been rich enough to justify a book, even if it is only an interim account. I have tried to record and assess the key elements of Cosatu's history, tell the story of the federation and reflect a little on its past. It need hardly be said that this work is not the final word on the subject, and is presented to the reader for discussion, debate, improvement and, hopefully, enjoyment.

What follows is not a history of the whole trade union movement in South Africa, but only of its major component, Cosatu. Other trade unions or federations are referred to in passing, insofar as they affect Cosatu. This is by no means an attempt to diminish the relative historical importance of some of these organisations.

This work is not a comprehensive history of Cosatu, but an overview. Many aspects dealt with in a paragraph could, in time, become the subject matter of a book or thesis. Cosatu, with its regions and locals, its affiliates and its more than one million members is a subject begging further historical study.

Cosatu's leadership, membership and affiliates have co-operated extensively in the writing of this work. But it is not an official history, and the views expressed are my own, not those of the federation.

Throughout the period covered in this book, I have been a trade unionist active in one of the Cosatu affiliates. I participated in the federation's structures at all levels, and held and expressed views on major and controversial issues. This personal involvement has given me insight into Cosatu. But, it can be argued, it also makes me a biased observer. I have attempted to be self-conscious of this problem throughout. On issues where there was debate within Cosatu, I have tried to present all viewpoints with fairness, especially those with which I disagreed at the time.

I set out to write a critical history and hope that I have succeeded. Nevertheless, I make no apologies for the deep sympathy which I have for Cosatu. While I have tried, therefore, to be as 'objective' as possible, my own inclinations will undoubtedly colour the history as a whole, and the interpretation of specific events.

I have relied heavily on the internal documents of Cosatu for source material, as well as interviews and discussions – both formal and informal – with key figures in the union movement. Not all of them wish to be acknowledged. The result is that the ideas and perspectives of a wide number of people have been absorbed and incorporated into this book. It has not always been possible to distinguish where the ideas are my own, or those of a colleague. Perhaps this is inevitable in an organisation where discussion and debate play so large a role. But naturally, I take final responsibility for the views expressed.

It has become customary in books on South Africa to add a note on 'the use of racial terminology.' Where racial oppression exists then racial labelling, unfortunately, follows close behind. I have followed the common practice of calling all those South Africans who are not white, black. I have at times referred to African, coloured and Indian sections of the oppressed black population, but only when this is more accurate or contributes to a better understanding of the issue at hand.

The South African trade union movement is a minefield of acronyms. With unions launching, merging and dissolving, even the most active trade unionists have problems remembering the full names of all organisations. For those unable to tell their AAWU's from their LBWU's, a complete list of abbreviations and acronyms found in the text is included.

Finally, a word of thanks to all those who assisted in making this book a reality. The ordinary workers and unionists who have helped me understand something of trade unionism over the years are too numerous to thank by name. They know who they are. In addition, the following people have been particularly helpful and deserve special mention: Gay Seidman, Howie Gabriels, both Jay Naidoos, Karl von Holdt, Sydney Mufamadi, Carol Steinberg, Alec Erwin, Sipho Kubheka, Eddie Webster, Jane Barrett and Gwede Mantashe. They have all helped in various ways, from emotional support, to reading through earlier drafts of the manuscript, to helping me understand critical issues. The staff of the *South African Labour Bulletin* were particularly generous with their facilities and support, and deserve special gratitude. So too do Lael, Jobi, Karen, Steve and Johnny, all of whom assisted me at various times with research, and Sue Kramer who helped track down and select the pictures. I must also thank both Rev Frank Chikane of the South African Council of Churches, and the Friedrich-Ebert-Stiftung, for their help. Their generosity enabled me to take a year's leave, thereby giving me the opportunity to write the bulk of this manuscript.

Jeremy Baskin
June 1991

Acronyms and abbreviations

AAC	Anti-Apartheid Conference
Aato	All-Africa Teachers Organisation
Abwu	Amalgamated Black Workers Union
Actwusa	Amalgamated Clothing and Textile Workers Union of South Africa
Acusa	Amalgamated Cleaners Union of South Africa
AFCWU	African Food and Canning Workers Union
Aftu	African Federation of Trade Unions
AHI	Afrikaanse Handelsinstituut
Amwu	African Mine Workers Union
ANC	African National Congress
Arahwu	African Railway and Harbour Workers Union
Assocom	Association of Chambers of Commerce
Atasa	African Teachers Association of South Africa
Azactu	Azanian Confederation of Trade Unions
Azapo	Azanian Peoples Organisation
Bamcwu	Black Allied Mining and Construction Workers Union
Bawu	Black Allied Workers Union
BC	Black Consciousness
BCAWU	Building, Construction and Allied Workers Union (Cusa and Nactu affiliate)
BCAWU	Brick, Clay and Allied Workers Union (NFW and Cosatu affiliate)
Bifsa	Building Industries Federation of South Africa
Blatu	Black Trade Union (on the railways)
BMR	Bureau for Market Research
BMWU	Black Municipality Workers Union
Cast	Civic Association of the Southern Transvaal
Cawu	Construction and Allied Workers Union
CB	Conciliation Board
Ccawusa	Commercial, Catering and Allied Workers Union of South Africa
CCOBT	Consultative Committee of Black Trade Unions
CDF	Conference for a Democratic Future
CDWU	Commercial and Distributive Workers Union
CEC	Central Executive Committee
CIWW	Council of Industrial Workers of the Witwatersrand
CLC	Canadian Labour Congress
Cnetu	Council of Non-European Trade Unions
Cosas	Congress of South African Students
Cosatu	Congress of South African Trade Unions

CSAWU	Cleaning Services and Allied Workers Union
CTMWA	Cape Town Municipal Workers Association
CTUC	Commonwealth Trades Union Congress
Cusa	Council of Unions of South Africa
CWIU	Chemical Workers Industrial Union
Detu	Democratic Teachers Union
DPSC	Detainees Parents Support Committee
Eawu	Engineering and Allied Workers Union
ECC	End Conscription Campaign
Elptu	East London Progressive Teachers Union
EPG	Eminent Person's Group
Exco	Cosatu's National Executive Committee
Fawu	Food and Allied Workers Union
FBWU	Food and Beverage Workers Union
FCI	Federated Chamber of Industries
FCWU	Food and Canning Workers Union
Fedcraw	Federal Council of Retail and Allied Workers
Fedsaw	Federation of South African Women
FFF	Five Freedoms Forum
Fofatusa	Federation of Free African Trade Unions of South Africa
Fosatu	Federation of South African Trade Unions
Gawu	General and Allied Workers Union (dissolved 1987)
Gawu	Garment and Allied Workers Union (launched 1988)
GFWBF	General Factory Workers Benefit Fund
GMSA	General Motors of South Africa
GNP	Gross National Product
GST	General Sales Tax
GWIU	Garment Workers Industrial Union
GWU	General Workers Union
Gwusa	Garment Workers Union of South Africa (merged with NUTW)
Gwusa	General Workers Union of South Africa (associated with Macwusa)
Harwu	Hotel and Restuarant Workers Union
Hawu	Health and Allied Workers Union
IAS	Industrial Aid Society
IC	Industrial Council
ICFTU	International Confederation of Free Trade Unions
ICU	Industrial and Commercial Workers Union
ILC	Interim Leadership Committee (of the ANC)
ILO	International Labour Organisation
IMF	International Metalworkers Federation
Imssa	Independent Mediation Services of South Africa
ITF	International Transport Federation

ITS	International Trade Secretariat
IUF	International Union of Foodworkers
IWA	Industrial Workers of Africa
JCI	Johannesburg Consolidated Investments (mining house)
Ledcom	Local Education Committee
LMG	Labour Monitoring Group
LRA	Labour Relations Act
LRAA	Labour Relations Amendment Act
LRAB	Labour Relations Amendment Bill
LRS	Labour Research Service
LWC	Living Wage Campaign
Macwusa	Motor Assemblers and Component Workers Union
Mawu	Metal and Allied Workers Union
MDM	Mass Democratic Movement
Micwu	Motor Industries Combined Workers Union
Mgwusa	Municipal and General Workers Union
MK	Umkhonto we Sizwe (Spear of the Nation)
Mwasa	Media Workers Association of South Africa
Mwusa	Municipal Workers Union of South Africa
Naawu	National Automobile and Allied Workers Union
NAC	National Action Council
Nactu	National Council of Trade Unions
Nafcoc	National African Chamber of Commerce
Napawu	National Post Office and Allied Workers Union
NBF	National Bargaining Forum (auto industry)
NBIU	Natal Baking Industrial Union
NDM	National Democratic Movement
NECC	National Education Crisis Committee
Nedcom	National Education Committee
Nehawu	National Education, Health and Allied Workers Union
Neusa	National Education Union of South Africa
NFW	National Federation of Workers
Ngwusa	National General Workers Union of South Africa
NICISEMI	National Industrial Council for the Iron, Steel, Engineering and Metallurgical Industry
NICPRINT	National Industrial Council for the Printing Industry
Nismawu	National Iron, Steel and Metal Workers Union
NMC	National Manpower Commission
NOW	Natal Organisation of Women
NSRAIEU	National Sugar Refining and Allied Industries Employees Union
NUCW	National Union of Clothing Workers
Nudaw	National Union of Distributive and Allied Workers

NUFAW	National Union of Furniture and Allied Workers
NUGW	National Union of Garment Workers
NULCDW	National Union of Laundry, Cleaning and Dyeing Workers
NUM	National Union of Mineworkers
Numsa	National Union of Metalworkers of South Africa
NUNW	National Union of Namibian Workers
Nupawo	National Union of Printing and Allied Workers
NUR	National Union of Railwayworkers
Nusas	National Union of South African Students
NUTW	National Union of Textile Workers
NUWCC	National Unemployed Workers Co-ordinating Committee
OATUU	Organisation of African Trade Union Unity
OFS	Orange Free State
OVGWU	Orange-Vaal General Workers Union
PAC	Pan Africanist Congress
Pawu	Plastic and Allied Workers Union
Pebco	Port Elizabeth Black Civic Organisation
Popcru	Police and Prisons Civil Rights Union
Potwa	Post and Telecommunications Workers Association
Ppwawu	Paper, Printing, Wood and Allied Workers Union
PSSC	Public Sector Co-ordinating Committee
Pwawu	Paper, Wood and Allied Workers Union
PWV	Pretoria, Witwatersrand, Vereeniging area
Rawu (CT)	Retail and Allied Workers Union – Cape Town-based
Rawu	Retail and Allied Workers Union – Pretoria-based and linked to Ngwusa
RC	Cosatu's Regional Congress
REC	Cosatu's Regional Executive Committee
Redcom	Regional Education Committee
RMC	Release Mandela Committee
Saawu	South African Allied Workers Union
SAB	South African Breweries
SABC	South African Broadcasting Corporation
SACC	South African Council of Churches
Saccola	South African Consultative Committee on Labour Affairs
SACL	South African Confederation of Labour
SACP	South African Communist Party
Sactu	South African Congress of Trade Unions
Sacwu	South African Chemical Workers Union
SADF	South African Defence Force
Sadtu	South African Democratic Teachers Union
Sadwa	South African Domestic Workers Association
Sadwu	South African Domestic Workers Union
Safnetu	South African Federation of Non-European Trade Unions

Samwu	South African Mineworkers Union (dissolved 1987)
Samwu	South African Municipal Workers Union (launched 1987)
Sansco	South African National Students Congress
SAP	South African Police
SAPAIF	South African Printing and Allied Industries Federation
Sarhwu	South African Railways and Harbour Workers Union
Sastawu	South African Scooter, Transport and Allied Workers Union
Satawu	South African Textile and Allied Workers Union
Sats	South African Transport Services
Sayco	South African Youth Congress
Seifsa	Steel and Engineering Industries Federation of South Africa
SFAWU	Sweet, Food and Allied Workers Union
Soyco	Soweto Youth Congress
SRC	Students Representative Council
Tasa	Teachers Association of South Africa
Tawu	Transport and Allied Workers Union (Cusa and Nactu affiliate)
Tawu	Textile and Allied Workers Union (breakaway from NUTW)
T&LC	Trades and Labour Council
TFC	Teachers Federal Council
TGWU	Transport and General Workers Union
Tuacc	Trade Union Advisory Co-ordinating Council
Tucsa	Trade Union Council of South Africa
TUI	Trade Union International
TWIU	Textile Workers Industrial Union
UAW	United Automobile Workers
UDF	United Democratic Front
UIF	Unemployment Insurance Fund
Ummawosa	United Mining, Metal and Allied Workers of South Africa
UPE	University of Port Elizabeth
Utasa	United Teachers Association of South Africa
UTP	Urban Training Project
Uwusa	United Workers Union of South Africa
WCL	World Confederation of Labour
WCOTP	World Confederation of Organisations of the Teaching Profession
Wectu	Western Cape Teachers Union
WFTU	World Federation of Trade Unions
Wosa	Workers Organisation for Socialist Action
WPGWU	Western Province General Workers Union (later GWU)
WPGWU	Western Province Garment Workers Union (merged to form Gawu)
WPWAB	Western Province Workers Advice Bureau
ZCC	Zion Christian Church

Introduction

WHEN Popo Molefe, the first general secretary of the United Democratic Front (UDF), stepped ashore in Cape Town following his release from Robben Island in December 1989, he had spent almost five years in one prison or another. He had kept himself informed of developments, in the ways that political prisoners do. But, inevitably, prison had isolated him from the details and texture of the anti-apartheid struggle.

As a key figure in the mass democratic movement, Molefe was well-placed to provide a 'before and after' perspective. One of his first impressions, he told a reporter from the *Cape Times*, was the massive growth of the trade union movement. When he had been arrested in early 1985, unions had formed a relatively small part of the democratic movement. On his release he found them to be a central pillar.

The five years stolen from Molefe's life were, essentially, the first years of Cosatu. This book tells the story of those years. Part One looks briefly at the long history of the South African union movement. It explores the difficult process of the 'unity talks' and the various strands which were woven together to form Cosatu.

Part Two deals with Cosatu's first year and the wave of enthusiasm and mass struggles which accompanied it. The decline of the Trade Union Council of South Africa (Tucsa) and the launch of the United Workers Union of South Africa (Uwusa) and the National Council of Trade Unions (Nactu) are also examined, as are the early debates over political policy and the devastating effects of repression.

Part Three examines the massive strike wave of late 1986 and early 1987, including the largest-ever strike by South Africa's mineworkers. It explores the process of merging unions to create 'one industry, one union', and the related political differences underlying Cosatu's adoption of the Freedom Charter.

Part Four explores Cosatu's most difficult period, from mid-1987 to mid-1988, when the federation almost collapsed. Restrictions, debilitating repression, and hardline employers exacerbated Cosatu's own internal disunity. Only the serious threat of a new labour law, and Cosatu's successful stayaway action in response, encouraged the rebuilding of unity.

Part Five traces this process of rebuilding, and the increasingly unified political and organisational perspectives adopted by Cosatu's affiliates. Cosatu showed its ability to survive. The campaigns around the Labour Relations Amendment Act (LRAA) and a living wage provided a basis for a period of further union growth, and Cosatu's 1989 congress reflected this consolidation. This section includes chapters which examine the violence in Natal, the position of women in the unions, and the period of intense mass action which preceded the release of Nelson Mandela.

The final section of the book looks at developments in the current period. It examines the key issues facing Cosatu and the impact of political changes on the union movement since the unbanning of the African National Congress (ANC) in February 1990. It also reflects on the strengths and weaknesses of the federation, and some of the challenges which face it in the coming years.

Some common misconceptions

There are four widely-held misconceptions about Cosatu which should be clarified at the outset.

Firstly, Cosatu is a federation of trade unions and not a trade union itself. It acts as the umbrella body of its affiliated unions, as a national trade union centre. It is, therefore, not strictly correct to write, as I do, of Cosatu's million-strong membership. Those million workers are members of the various unions affiliated to the federation. Cosatu is the sum of its affiliated parts but is also more than that. It has an organisational dynamic of its own. Unorganised workers looking for a union usually ask for Cosatu and are only then directed to the appropriate affiliate. While this book looks mainly at Cosatu as an organisation, it also explores the dynamic relationship between its component affiliates.

A second misconception views Cosatu as an organisation riven by internal division. In 1987 and 1988 in particular, this became a popular theme in the media. Splits were forecast, and sometimes hoped for, between 'workerists' and 'populists'. Certainly there have been differences within Cosatu. But differences are not the same as divisions. This is a position often stated by Cosatu's leadership, but too easily dismissed by observers. For all its internal differences, that which unites Cosatu is far greater than anything dividing it.

Thirdly, Cosatu's affiliates are not monolithic. While unions have different positions dominant within them, their ranks frequently contain the entire range of views found within Cosatu. This is not necessarily divisive. Where it has caused serious splits, as in the case of the Commercial, Catering and Allied Workers Union of South Africa, this will be made clear. However, it is a useful shorthand to record that NUM proposed this or CWIU that. The reader should be aware that this simply expresses the dominant view of that union.

Fourthly, Cosatu's public profile has been almost entirely political, leading many observers to see it primarily as a political organisation. However, Cosatu is first and foremost a mass organisation of employed workers. Both it and its affiliates are concerned with the organisation of workers and their day-to-day problems. Ninety percent of Cosatu's activities relate directly to this less-glamorous and frequently-repetitive work. While the importance of these activities are hard to overestimate, it is difficult to give them full due in a book of this sort.

Even this routine organisational work is political, or has political implications. As Friedman points out in his account of the union movement, it has frequently 'given powerless people a chance to wield power for the first time in their lives.'[1] A large part of Cosatu's task has been to develop this basic organisational consciousness into more directed political involvement.

Underlying assumptions

In assessing Cosatu's achievements and failures, there must be some yardstick, some measure of what the tasks of the trade union movement should be. The union movement has, I believe, three basic strategic tasks in the apartheid era: firstly, to organise unorganised workers; secondly, to fight for the improvement of the material conditions of its members in particular, and workers generally; and thirdly, to ensure the maximum involvement of workers in the national democratic struggle. Cosatu's ability to achieve these three tasks is the measure of its success.

Within the unions there is total agreement on the need for political involvement. Cosatu has, from the outset, been compelled to take a stand against the many injustices of South African society. Its members have experienced starvation wages, poverty, imprisonment, racism in the workplace, repression and even death. They have, in short, been on the receiving end of apartheid.

The issue of apartheid invades every page of this book. That is unavoidable. But the black working class is not simply confronted by discrimination and lack of equal rights. It is also faces poverty engendered by the capitalist system. Black workers suffer both oppression as a race and exploitation as a class. This is common cause within Cosatu.

It is true that South African society is defined in terms of race. But to understand the society fully, and to understand Cosatu, we must dig beyond the surface to the social realities which lie below. Apartheid has led to the oppression of all black South Africans, but all have not experienced this oppression equally and to the same degree. Class and ethnic divisions also operate. Similarly, all white South Africans reap some fruits from apartheid, but not in a uniform way. The result is a political dynamic of class, race and nationalism which has hotly-debated implications for the strategies adopted by the liberation movement.

Debates on these matters have focused not on whether there is a connection between 'apartheid and profit' but on the relationship between national liberation and democracy, on the one hand, and the struggle for socialism and social justice, on the other. Mark Shope of Sactu expressed that relationship well as far back as 1964, when he addressed a solidarity conference in Ghana:

> (I)t must never be forgotten that apartheid and racial discrimination in South Africa...has an aim far more important than discrimination itself: *the aim is economic exploitation*. The root and fruit of apartheid and racial discrimination is profit.[2]

Notes

1. Steven Friedman, *Building Tomorrow Today. African Workers in Trade Unions 1970-1985*, Johannesburg, 1987, 6.
2. Ken Luckhardt and Brenda Wall, *Organize...or Starve. The History of the South African Congress of Trade Unions*, London, 1980, 35.

Part One

Before Cosatu

1

Unions before Cosatu

Planting the seeds

BLACK unions have existed in South Africa for over 70 years, and have a long and proud history. Cosatu has been a student, a prisoner, a judge and a product of that history. 'Our Congress has been founded on the heroic sacrifices of our comrades before us – from the ICU to Cnetu to Sactu.' The words are Jay Naidoo's in his first speech as Cosatu's general secretary.

This chapter reveals some of the influences and lessons which the past has taught the present generation of unionists. Some of the issues which emerge from the earlier history of unionism are the key role played by members of the Communist Party; the long-term weaknesses of unions centred on an individual leader; the inability to unite black and white workers despite the predominance of non-racial perspectives; the importance of plant-based unionism as a vehicle for making gains and a shield for withstanding repression; and the inevitability of political unionism in South Africa.

The Industrial and Commercial Workers Union

The origins of unions for black workers lie in the establishment of the Industrial and Commercial Workers Union of Africa (ICU) in Cape Town in 1919. Prior to this there were other unions. But these invariably catered for white workers and were modelled on, and often branches of, the craft unions of Britain. There were also small beginnings in 1917 when the Industrial Workers of Africa (IWA) attempted, with limited success, to organise workers on the Witwatersrand.

The ICU began by recruiting among Cape Town's dockworkers. Strike action by over 2 000 workers led to some early successes which saw wages double. Thereafter the union, under the leadership of the charismatic Clements Kadalie Muwamba, began to grow rapidly. It drew in membership across industries and was, in effect, a general union. In Natal the union grew particularly strongly during the mid-1920s under the leadership of AWG Champion, while in the Orange Free State Selby Msimang emerged as a key organiser.

As the ICU developed it drew in members from a range of classes, including teachers, small traders, and rural farmworkers and labour tenants. It resembled, at times, a mass movement of the dispossessed more than a union.

At its height, in 1927, membership was 100 000.[*] But the ICU leadership was, by and large, cautious, and discouraged strikes. A 1928 edition of its newspaper, *Workers Herald*, noted that the strike weapon had only been used on three occasions. Members who went on strike spontaneously were often not supported by the union.

Communist Party members played a central role in building the ICU, and many held key positions. They attacked the leadership of Kadalie, accusing him of corruption and inefficiency, and criticised his unwillingness to organise disciplined industrial unions, introduce democratic elections by the membership and democratic control of funds, and actively pursue strike action.

Under the influence of British liberals, Kadalie fought for and achieved the expulsion of key communists in 1926. This deprived the ICU of some of its most capable and militant leadership – men such as Gomas, La Guma, Khaile and Mbeki. A further split followed between Kadalie and the corrupt Natal branch under Champion. From 1927 the ICU went into steady decline, hastened by government restrictions on some of its leaders. By 1930 it was dead in all but name.

The influence of the ICU was vast. Many individuals went on to organise the unions which emerged after the ICU. Its ability to become a mass movement wielding real power showed the potential of mass organisation of the working class. The ICU also established a tradition of black worker resistance. An ICU member wrote that:

This, and other union membership claims, should be treated with caution as they are often unreliable or exaggerated. Indeed, Cosatu's obsession with 'paid-up' membership reflects an attempt to introduce accuracy into the statistics.

Although the (organisation's) initials stood for a fancy title, to us it meant basically: when you ill-treat the African people, I See You; if you kick them off the pavements and say they must go together with the cars and the oxcarts, I See You... When you kick my brother, I See You.[1]

The ICU had many shortcomings. Its collapse highlighted the weakness of general unionism; it failed to build working-class leadership and proper structures for democratic control; and related to this, it allowed the development of individual leadership and personality cults.

As the ICU declined, attempts were made to organise new unions along industrial lines. Communist Party members, including those expelled from the ICU, were particularly active. In 1928, the South African Federation of Non-European Trade Unions (Safnetu) was launched on the Witwatersrand. It consisted of five unions representing 10 000 black workers. Historians Luckhardt and Wall have noted that although the Communist Party called for non-racial trade unions 'as the ideal, the reality was that black workers first needed to solidify their collective strength against not only capital but also white workers firmly committed to the industrial colour-bar.'[2]

Safnetu did not last long. Police repression disrupted its activities, as did the onset of the world economic depression in the late 1920s – massive unemployment made unionisation extremely difficult. Additional disruption was caused when squabbles in the communist movement spilled over into the trade union movement, and many key Safnetu organisers, including Ben Weinbren, TW Thibedi, Gana Makabeni and Solly Sachs, were expelled from the Communist Party.

Revival in the mid-1930s

During the early years of the depression, the Communist Party initiated the African Federation of Trade Unions (Aftu), but initially this met with limited success. Unionism only began reviving in the mid-1930s, at the same time as massive urbanisation was underway. Thousands of small farmers, peasants and their families – both black and white – tried to escape the growing poverty of the rural areas. Industry was developing rapidly, and the manufacturing sector began to challenge the economic dominance of mining. Employers increasingly needed machine operators and semi-skilled workers for the production line, and this led to tensions between the established, mainly white, craft unions and the newer industrial unions.

Union organisation was most obvious in three regions from the mid-1930s to the early 1940s. In Natal, Communist Party militants took the lead in organising workers. Between 1936 and 1945 at least 27 unions for black workers were organised. Most brought together African and Indian workers.[3]

In the Western Cape, Communist Party militants led campaigns to organise workers in the clothing, milling and other industries. In the transport sector, Afrikaner nationalists were attempting to expel all black workers from the railway union, and in October 1936 black railway workers launched the South African Railways and Harbour Workers Union (Sarhwu) in Cape Town. By the early 1940s it had expanded to all provinces and claimed a membership of 20 000.[4] The Food and Canning Workers Union (FCWU), formed in February 1941 under the leadership of Ray Alexander, was another key union. Its focus on factory-floor organisation and militant struggles for wages and recognition enabled it to survive, even through the dark years of the 1960s, and in 1985 it was to be one of the founder unions of Cosatu.

The communist-led unions, organised into Aftu, continued their work in the Transvaal. In another organising initiative a number of unions were launched around the central figure of Max Gordon, a Trotskyite and opponent of the Communist Party. Organisationally a pragmatic unionist committed to cautious practices, Gordon's favoured strategy was to make representations to the government wage board, calling on it to improve minimum wages paid to African workers. This strategy was supported by the Department of Labour, which was concerned about the political potential of African unions and the role being played by communists in them.

In a number of industries Gordon's unions achieved significant progress. Gains made at wage board hearings were used to recruit members, and by 1939 eleven unions with 20 000 members had formed the Joint Committee of African Trade Unions, with Gordon as secretary. Gordon, who was white, unfortunately did little to build shopfloor structures or create a skilled leadership corps. This brought him into conflict with a number of the African organisers who insisted on more power for themselves and the affiliated unions. When Gordon was interned in 1940 for his opposition to the war, the Joint Committee unions went into rapid decline.

Friedman has convincingly argued that Gordon's unions benefitted from 'the relative freedom to move' and their willingness to use the space and 'the rights offered by the government.' But their excessive reliance on the wage board strategy made them organisationally weak. While it gave the unions 'a platform', it was no substitute for negotiation or organisation. The result was that 'it was Gordon's expertise, not the organised strength of their members, which won them their gains.' The union became 'an advice office which could solve problems' for workers.[5]

A second initiative in the Transvaal revolved around Gana Makabeni and a number of other black unionists. Largely excluding whites and communists from their activities, they organised workers in a number of sectors, culminating in 1940 with the formation of the Co-ordinating Committee of African Trade Unions.

Unity talks between the Joint Committee and Co-ordinating Committee unions took place in 1938, but were unsuccessful. The two blocs remained, divided in turn from the unions organised under the Aftu banner and those developing in the Cape and Natal.

Throughout this entire period African unions, while not illegal, were excluded from labour law. Only white, coloured and Indian workers were allowed to form and join registered unions. By a peculiar anomaly, African women were not excluded from registered unions, although few worked in industry at the time. This legal loophole was closed in the following years.

War and the formation of Cnetu

The outbreak of war in 1939 opened enormous opportunities for the union movement to grow, with a war economy stimulating the development of local substitution of previously-imported products. The labour force increased dramatically as industry grew and the demands of a war economy had to be met.

Black South Africans were not allowed to carry weapons, even in the struggle against Nazism, and this prevented large-scale recruitment of black soldiers. Thousands of white male workers, many of them employed in skilled jobs, left for the battlefronts of Europe and North Africa. With no alternative, employers were increasingly forced to use black workers in more skilled positions. With the economy booming, this gave black workers more power than ever before, and their unions grew rapidly.

In 1941 the Transvaal section of the ANC called a conference to discuss the formation of a mineworkers union. This led to the launch of the African Mineworkers Union (AMWU) under the leadership of JB Marks, a member of both the ANC and Communist Party.

Following unity talks between sections of the union movement later in the same year, the Council of Non-European Trade Unions (Cnetu) was formed with Makabeni as president and ANC member Dan Tloome as vice-president. Structured as a coalition of unions rather than a unified organisation, Cnetu was a loose federation comprising many weak industrial unions together with a few which were better organised.

A strike wave in 1942 lead to relatively high wage increases for workers in a number of sectors. In response the Smuts government introduced War Measure 145, which outlawed strikes. At the same time the government tried to ensure a more reasonable level of wage increases in an attempt to avoid strike action. The policy was a mixed success. A number of illegal strikes occurred, many forcefully repressed, but the overall incidence of strikes decreased.

Unions achieved a considerable amount during the war years. Real wages increased by over 50% between 1941 and 1946 and unionisation grew dramatically. But the war presented black trade unions with a dilemma. It gave them greater opportunities to organise and gain permanent trade union rights for the first time. However, after the German invasion of the Soviet Union, union leaders began supporting the war effort, and many discouraged strike action, arguing that strikes should be used only as a last resort. A minority, most notably the Progressive Trade Union group caucus, opposed this position within Cnetu.

Similar arguments took place in most colonial countries at this time. Many within both the nationalist and left movements saw the defeat of Hitler and the defence of the Soviet Union as their main objective. Others, particularly within the ANC and liberal ranks, supported Britain in its fight against Germany. And some argued that worker and nationalist organisations should take advantage of the war between the European powers, and use the opportunity to strengthen their claims. The ANC and Communist Party rejected this last view, arguing that the African people should only advance their claims within the context of support for the Allied war effort.

There were certainly opportunities to win formal recognition of black trade unions during 1942 and 1943. But this would have required concerted pressure from Cnetu, which it was not prepared to exert. Cnetu tried to maintain good relations with the government, even inviting Labour Minister Madeley to open its conferences. Madeley asked for patience: 'Recognition of unions will come about,' he said, 'but you must rely on me.'[6]

Cnetu grew rapidly during the war years. By 1945 it claimed a membership of 158 000 workers organised into 119 affiliates. It is unclear why Cnetu encouraged such a multiplicity of unions rather than developing a few stronger national affiliates. This weakened its chances of survival in the post-war years.

In 1946 the African Mineworkers Union (Amwu) called a strike demanding improved conditions for black mineworkers. The action was sparked off by the Chamber of Mines' repeated refusal to negotiate, meet the union or even reply to its correspondence. In mid-August 76 000 workers, mainly on the Witwatersrand, responded to the union's call. The action lasted for a week, but was crushed when police drove workers underground using massive force. At least 12 workers died and over

1 200 were injured. Fifty union and Communist Party leaders were arrested and charged with sedition as a result of the strike. Cnetu had not been able to offer the miners any meaningful support.

The harsh response to the miners' strike reflected the post-war government's attitude to the union movement. With the war over it no longer had to tolerate relatively strong unions. In an increasingly hostile environment, Cnetu went into rapid decline.

In the immediate post-war years, South African society witnessed a battle for the fruits of victory over fascism. Struggles over union rights were accompanied by conflicts over land, housing and political rights. Racism, the credo of the Nazis, had been defeated in Europe. But in South Africa it remained alive and well.

The National Party gave most militant expression to this racism. They promised a South Africa with 'die kaffir op sy plek en die koelie uit die land.'[*] When the white electorate voted a National Party government into office in 1948, this marked the beginning of a particularly dark period for the trade unions, the liberation movement, and black South Africans as a whole.

Sactu and the 1950s

In 1950 the National Party government outlawed the Communist Party. Many individuals, both communists and non-communists, were forcibly removed from their positions in the union movement in terms of the prohibitive restrictions of the Suppression of Communism Act. These developments were accompanied by the extension of racist legislation to most aspects of society. The 1950s saw the enforced breaking up of unions into separate racial branches; the intensification of legalised job reservation whereby certain jobs were reserved for whites; and a government declaration that it would never recognise black trade unions.

All these initiatives were met with resistance. The ANC became the centre of mass mobilisation against the extension of apartheid, and thousands flocked to its ranks. But resistance was less than total on the trade union front. Most established unions were members of the Trades and Labour Council (T&LC) whose national executive decided in 1950 that it would support the call for the exclusion of African trade unions from membership.

This was the beginning of a major re-alignment within the union movement. The T&LC rapidly disintegrated. The bulk of its members

---

[*] *'Kaffir' and 'koelie' are racist terms used to describe Africans and Indians respectively. The National Party election call was for the 'kaffirs' to be put 'in their places,' and the 'koelies' to be sent back to India.*

went on to form the Trade Union Council of South Africa (Tucsa), a body which vacillated over the years between total rejection of African trade unions and attempts to control them. Others within the T&LC joined forces with the ultra-right Afrikaner nationalist unions, fighting for white worker privileges and racial segregation in the factories. In time, these unions established the South African Confederation of Labour (SACL).

Progressives within the T&LC united with the rump of the Cnetu unions, and in 1955 launched the South African Congress of Trade Unions (Sactu) with 19 affiliates and a claimed membership of 20 000. It was a small beginning but thereafter its membership rose steadily. Sactu's organised strength rested heavily on three unions – the FCWU and its counterpart, the African Food and Canning Workers Union (AFCWU), the Textile Workers Industrial Union (TWIU), and the National Union of Laundry, Cleaning and Dyeing Workers (NULCDW).

Sactu adopted a higher political profile than any of its predecessors. As the chairperson of its inaugural conference argued,

> You cannot separate politics and the way in which people are governed from their bread and butter, or their freedom to move to and from places where they can find the best employment, or the houses they live in, or the type of education their children get.[7]

This position was made more explicit in a statement of policy adopted at Sactu's first annual conference in 1956:

> Sactu is conscious of the fact that the organising of the mass of workers for higher wages, better conditions of life and labour is inextricably bound up with a determined struggle for political rights and liberation from all oppressive laws and practices. It follows that a mere struggle for the economic rights of all the workers without participation in the general struggle for political emancipation would condemn the Trade Union movement to uselessness and to a betrayal of the interests of the workers.[8]

Sactu cemented its political involvement by joining the ANC-led Congress Alliance, participating actively in the mass political campaigns of the 1950s and the drafting of the Freedom Charter. Despite intensive state repression and the government's adoption of harsh anti-union policies, Sactu grew steadily, both in membership and in the quality of its organisation. By 1959 it had 46 000 members organised into 35 affiliates,[9] and had attempted, with some success, to build strong factory-based unions.

Sactu promoted organisation through a number of mass campaigns. The best-known of these was the 'pound-a-day' campaign, the forerunner of the living wage campaigns of the 1980s. The campaign was launched at a national workers' conference at the beginning of 1957, where over 300 union delegates established campaign committees and called for a work stayaway in Port Elizabeth and the Witwatersrand on 26 June. The campaign received ANC backing and massive working-class support, with an estimated 70-80% of workers in Johannesburg, Vereeniging and Port Elizabeth staying away. It also had an effect on workers' wages as employers and government conceded real wage increases for the first time in years.[10]

The following year Sactu intensified the campaign. A far larger workers' conference resolved on a three-day stayaway around two main slogans – 'Forward to Pound-a-Day Victory!' and 'The Nats Must Go!'. The ANC again supported this call, giving particular emphasis to the second demand. The stayaway was timed to coincide with the white general elections. This time, however, the state and employers mobilised to ensure that there would be no repeat of the 1957 stayaway.

One day into the stayaway, after a mixed response to the call, the ANC's national leadership called off the action. This provoked strains between the ANC and Sactu, which asked why the ANC had suspended a Sactu call. Dan Tloome, a leading unionist, argued that the slogan 'Defeat the Nats' was misleading and had possibly caused people to believe that the Congresses favoured the opposition United Party with its slightly more liberal model of racism.

Despite the strains, the alliance between the ANC and Sactu remained strongly in place. Indeed, Sactu members often constituted a significant proportion of the ANC's membership in various branches and regions. In addition the apparent determination of the government to crush both the nationalist and trade union movements made unity a necessity for both.

A turning point came with the Sharpeville massacre in 1960, and the banning of the ANC and its recently-formed rival, the PAC. The ANC tried to continue legal resistance. It called for a national convention and organised mass action and a stayaway under the banner of the National Action Council (NAC). When these failed to move the state by even an inch, calls within ANC ranks for an armed struggle became irresistible. The relative failure of the stayaway, Nelson Mandela argued, had closed a chapter in the strategies of resistance. On 16 December 1961, the ANC and SACP launched Umkhonto we Sizwe (MK), the 'Spear of the Nation', and initiated the armed struggle against the apartheid state. announced The high command of MK announced:

The time comes in the life of any nation when there remain only two choices: submit or fight. That time has now come to South Africa... The government policy of force, repression and violence will no longer be met with non-violent resistance alone.[11]

Hundreds of ANC members, including almost the entire Sactu leadership, were recruited into MK. However, the government succeeded in infiltrating MK networks, and mass arrests followed. In his history of Sactu, Rob Lambert has noted that 'since the Sactu leadership at all levels formed the majority of the MK cadres, the union movement suffered severely as a result of mass arrests.'[12] Unionists not involved in MK work continued to organise, but they too faced massive repression. By 1965 Sactu as an internal federation of unions was effectively dead. It continued to operate from exile.

The Sactu experience remains hotly debated. Differing interpretations of its history directly informed the strategies and approaches of the union movement which re-emerged in the 1970s. For some, including many in what would become the Fosatu tradition, Sactu's 'close identification with the Congress Alliance and its campaigns was the cause of its demise in the 1960s.'[13]

Friedman's major work on the re-emergence of trade unions in the 1970s argues that Sactu was a 'captive of the nationalists', concentrating on the campaigns of the Congress Alliance to the detriment of factory organisation. Sactu's 1957 stayaway call for a pound-a-day had been a success, but the 1958 stayaway was a failure partly because the ANC dominated it. 'Congress leaders did not value a worker movement as an end in itself,' although they valued its ability to mobilise workers. For Friedman, 'Sactu's submission to the nationalist movement reached its logical conclusion' when scores of officials abandoned union work to take up arms. From this perspective the lessons of Sactu for the new unions were

● organise a factory base first;
● consider open political involvement later;
● and if the unions do get involved in politics it should be 'independent worker politics' not 'populist nationalism'.[14]

Sactu was still a legal mass organisation. It was, therefore, undoubtedly a fatal error for union leaders to become active participants in armed struggle. But Friedman is wrong to see this as an inevitable consequence of the ANC-Sactu alliance.

Lambert's in-depth study of Sactu paints a complex picture which contradicts many of Friedman's conclusions. Lambert found that Sactu concentrated heavily on grassroots organisation and the building of factory committees. While in the Transvaal 'unions were viewed as little more than the economic wing of the ANC,' this was not the dominant view in other parts of the country.[15] 'Sactu grew most rapidly in Natal and in the Eastern Cape where the relationship between the unions and the ANC was the closest.' Politics did not divert Sactu from its union tasks. Rather, argues Lambert, 'engagement in the Alliance actually strengthened workplace organisation.'[16]

In addition, argues Lambert, Sactu influenced the ANC as much as the reverse. The working class 'came to exert an increasingly powerful influence on the content of nationalist politics.'[17] Lambert concedes that the turn to armed struggle and the subsequent mass arrests 'unintentionally destroyed (Sactu's)...organisational foundation that was becoming so effective in the resistance.'[18] But in the post-Sharpeville historical context it is hard to see what alternatives existed to the introduction of armed struggle into the arsenal of the liberation movement.

Sactu's lasting achievements, according to official Sactu historians Luckhardt and Wall, included 'planting the roots of non-racial trade unionism in the soil of apartheid South Africa' and its commitment to 'the revolutionary struggle for political emancipation.'[19]

As the union movement re-emerged during the 1970s and 1980s the influence of Sactu was often felt. Some held it up as a model to be emulated, while others saw in its history mistakes to be avoided. It was no accident, however, that sections from the preamble to Sactu's constitution were incorporated into the preamble to the Cosatu constitution. And its guiding motto – 'an injury to one is an injury to all' – would become the new federation's official slogan.

The dark decade

By the mid-1960s political, military and trade union resistance to apartheid had been effectively crushed. This opened the way for the government to implement of some of the most totalitarian measures ever seen in South Africa.

Repressive legislation intensified, giving almost unlimited powers to the security police. Thousands were imprisoned, many receiving life sentences on Robben Island. Others, including Sactu activists, were executed. The bantustan system was implemented in earnest, with all Africans divided into separate ethnic groups. In the cities, Africans were told they could expect no rights. They were simply temporary workers, *gastarbeiters* from their tribal homelands. Labour laws were tightened further with the twin aims of controlling workers and channelling their labour to meet the requirements of the employers. Real wages for black workers declined. For almost ten years strikes were virtually unheard of. For the unions, and the entire opposition, it was a dark decade.

As conditions for black people worsened and controls became tighter, the economy boomed. Once it had become clear that the apartheid government was not about to fall, foreign investment poured into the country, as did white immigrants from Europe in search of a place in the sun. During the 1960s South Africa's Gross National Product (GNP) grew at an average of 6% per annum – with Japan, the highest growth rate in the world at the time. The manufacturing sector expanded dramatically, much of its growth being capital intensive. Large monopolistic companies, such as Anglo American, Barlow Rand and Gencor, grew in size and influence. Profits and white living standards increased dramatically.

The black working class saw very few of the fruits of this economic 'miracle'. State expenditure financed a growing military apparatus as well as the ambitious social engineering projects of grand apartheid. But the economic boom also had its unplanned consequences, creating the conditions for a new wave of worker resistance and trade union organisation.

The 1973 strikes

Those few African unions which survived the dark decade remained largely under the influence of Tucsa. But in 1969, with African unionism apparently crushed, Tucsa bowed to government pressure and expelled African unions from its ranks.

Tucsa reversed its 1969 decision four years later, and readmitted African unions. This was a direct result of the strike wave which swept the Durban area at the beginning of that year.

The Durban strikes were not entirely unexpected. There had been rumblings from workers the previous year when Putco bus drivers in the Transvaal had stopped work demanding higher pay. But after police had arrested 300 of them, and under threat of dismissal, they had returned to work. Then, in October 1972, 4 000 dockworkers in Durban and Cape Town took action demanding higher wages. Workers were flexing their muscles.

In Durban, African workers were earning an average of R13 per week, and it was here that these initial rumblings of discontent became a thunderstorm. On 9 January 1973 about 2 000 workers at Coronation Brick downed tools and demanded a pay rise. They won a small increase. Within weeks thousands of textile workers in Pinetown and Hammarsdale also downed tools. They were soon joined by municipal workers and thousands of others. Police reinforcements were brought in. Wage increases, mostly of about R2 per week, were implemented and the strike wave started to subside. The first three months of 1973 saw

61 000 workers on strike – more than the total for the previous eight years.[20]

Some observers labelled the strike wave as 'spontaneous', but no strike lacks organisation completely. The Natal actions involved informal organisational and leadership networks which exist in every workplace. Most strikers refused to elect leaders to present demands, although employers favoured this procedure. Often the entire workforce would chant demands in unison, to avoid 'ringleaders' being identified. Nevertheless government officials soon began blaming the strike wave on agitators. One member of parliament declared that 'the Bantu of Natal' did not 'have it in them to come together and agree that a thousand of them should strike.' And the Minister of Labour, Marais Viljoen, blamed 'agitators' and 'inciters' for the strike wave.

The government responded by banning a number of individuals involved in attempts to revive union organisation. And it introduced a new law which claimed to give African workers a channel to communicate grievances while still not recognising their right to form trade unions. These liaison committees, explained Minister Viljoen, would deprive 'Bantu trade unions' of 'their life's blood and any necessity for existence.' In later years workers referred to these committees, usually foisted on them by management, as 'dogs without teeth'.

The Natal strikes were not an isolated episode. In September 1973 police opened fire on miners protesting against the rejection of a wage demand at Anglo American's Western Deep. Twelve were killed. Sporadic strikes continued throughout the remainder of the year and into 1974. Apart from Natal, strikes occurred in East London, Johannesburg and on the mines. The rebirth of black trade unionism was underway.

Unions re-emerge

The rebuilding of the union movement began in the early 1970s, even before the 1973 strikes. Organising efforts started almost simultaneously in Durban, Cape Town and on the Witwatersrand.

Durban workers flocked to join the General Factory Workers Benefit Fund (GFWBF) when it was established in 1972. During 1973 it felt confident enough to launch two unions, Mawu and NUTW, operating in the metal and textile industries respectively. The launch of the Chemical Workers Industrial Union (CWIU) and the Transport and General Workers Union (TGWU) followed in 1974. These Durban-based unions became known as the 'Tuacc group', after their umbrella body – the Trade Union Advisory Co-ordinating Council (Tuacc) – was formed in 1973. They experienced massive growth in the aftermath of the 1973 strikes, but were unable to sustain this organisationally. Nevertheless, the

Tuacc unions could claim almost 14 000 members by early 1976, although less than a third of these were fully paid-up.[21]

In Cape Town the first steps at rebuilding organisation came with the launch of the Western Province Workers Advice Bureau (WPWAB) in 1972. WPWAB set out to organise workers' committees in various factories and co-ordinate these in an embryonic council structure. By 1976 it claimed a membership of 5 000.[22] In time WPWAB changed its name and become the Western Province General Workers Union (WPGWU), the forerunner of the General Workers Union (GWU).

On the Witwatersrand three separate initiatives deserve mention. The earliest of these was the Urban Training Project (UTP) formed in 1970 by ex-Tucsa officials who had been involved in organising African workers. UTP helped service a number of existing unions expelled from Tucsa and encouraged the formation of new unions. These included the Transport and Allied Workers Union (Tawu), set up after the 1972 Putco drivers' strike; the Sweet, Food and Allied Workers Union (SFAWU) and the Paper, Wood and Allied Workers Union (Pwawu), formed during 1974, and the Building, Construction and Allied Workers Union (BCAWU), which was set up in 1975. Some of the unions formed by UTP, such as the SA Chemical Workers Union (Sacwu) and the Commercial, Catering and Allied Workers Union (Ccawusa), were launched with the help of registered Tucsa unions.

By 1977 the UTP unions had established the Consultative Committee of Black Trade Unions (CCOBTU), although this was initially little more than a forum in which union general secretaries could meet. The CCOBTU unions claimed a signed-up membership of 19 000 in early 1976.

A less-successful organising effort involved the Black Allied Workers Union (Bawu), established in 1971. Formed by Drake Koka with the backing of the black consciousness movement, Bawu's focus on 'conscientisation' rather than organisation met with little success. Its problems were compounded when Koka was banned.

By 1977 Bawu claimed 6 000 members, only 1 000 of them paid-up.[23] It suffered repeated splits in the late 1970s, giving rise to the South African Allied Workers Union (Saawu), the General and Allied Workers Union (Gawu) and the National Federation of Workers (NFW). Those who retained the Bawu name moved into an uneasy political alliance with Inkatha in the 1980s.

The third organising effort on the Witwatersrand centred around the Industrial Aid Society (IAS). Formed in 1974, the IAS assisted the Tuacc unions, and Mawu in particular, in setting up Transvaal branches. These unions formed the Council of Industrial Workers of the Witwatersrand (CIWW), but their organising efforts only began in earnest in late 1975.

Those who helped rebuild the union movement

Many individuals were responsible for the rebirth of the union movement.[24] In the early 1970s they saw that conditions were ripe for the re-emergence of unions, and acted on that realisation. Broadly, they fall into five different groups although in practice these were not always divided so neatly, and some, notably Barney Dladla, at the time Minister of Labour in the KwaZulu homeland government, cannot be placed in any of these categories.

Firstly, there were the Sactu and ANC activists. Some had been lying low since the early 1960s, while others had been released from prison after serving long sentences. This group also included younger recruits wanting to rebuild the ANC. Prominent amongst the Sactu/ANC group were Zora Mehlomakhulu, Oscar Mpetha, Elijah Loza (who died in detention in 1987), Barnett Ntsodo and Alpheus Ndude in Cape Town; Bhekisisa Nxasana, Masobiya Mdluli (killed in detention in 1976), Aaron Masango, Alpheus Mthethwa and Albert Dhlomo in Durban; and Elliot Shabangu, John Nkadimeng, Phindile Mfeti (who disappeared mysteriously in the late 1980s and was presumably eliminated), Robert Manci and Miriam Sithole in the Transvaal.

The second group consisted of a few of the earliest worker recruits to the emerging unions. They saw beyond the 'bread-and-butter' demands of the unions and were committed to building a strong union movement. Some, but not all, had been ANC members in the 1950s, or linked up with ANC networks after emerging first as worker leaders. Prominent individuals included 'Baba K' Makhama, Lydia Kompe, Piet Pheku, Elison Mothlabe and Sipho Kubheka in the Transvaal; Moses Ndlovu, June-Rose Nala, Obed Zuma, John Makatini, Azaria Ndebele and Jabulani Gwala in Natal; and 'Storey' Mazwembe (who died in detention in 1976) and Wilson Sidina in Cape Town.

A third group was made up of white university students and intellectuals. Spurned by black students who were joining the growing black consciousness movement, some turned to Marxist class theory, and became convinced of the need to organise the working class. Many operated from the wages commissions established by the National Union of South African Students (Nusas). Their ranks in the early 1970s included Jeanette Curtis (later killed by a bomb while in exile) and Gavin Anderson in Johannesburg; Halton Cheadle, Dave Davies, Dave Hemson, Pat Horn, Alec Erwin and John Copelyn in Natal; and Gordon Young in Cape Town.

Fourthly, individuals from within the established union movement, mainly Tucsa, saw the need to build unions. This group included Loet Douwes-Dekker and Eric Tyacke, formerly of Tucsa's African Affairs

Department, who were instrumental in establishing UTP. In Durban Harriet Bolton helped the emerging unions. Others within the established unions, such as Emma Mashinini, were called on to establish new unions. Yet others conducted their own rebellions within Tucsa and smaller unaffiliated unions. These included Joe Foster, Les Kettledas, Brian Fredericks and Fred Sauls, who campaigned to 'clean-up' the motor unions of the Western and Eastern Cape with the slogan 'the union should belong to the workers.'[25]

Finally, and those with least impact, were individuals from the black consciousness movement, most notably Drake Koka. In the early 1970s the black consciousness movement gained ground politically. Dominated by black intellectuals and black university students, its union organising activities – at least in the early 1970s – were given low priority. This was perhaps not surprising given its then widespread hostility towards 'class analysis'. Many from BC ranks later became active unionists, although most first broke with the BC tradition.

Rebuilding the unions

The first few years were not easy. Almost all organising initiatives began as advice offices rather than unions. The pioneers were aware of the hostility of the state and employers, and decided to test the waters by concentrating on the few remaining legal rights which black workers then had. Thus, for example, WPWAB stressed that it was organising African workers to achieve their legal right to a factory-based works committee. Sactu activists, operating largely illegally, were especially conscious of the dangers of repression. Some died as a result of their activities while others were imprisoned.

Most of the organising attempts met with early, if limited, successes which were soon followed by major reverses. The Durban unionists benefitted from the 1973 wave of worker militancy but as the strike wave receded, so did membership. Workers had joined in the expectation of quick benefits, but many of the unionists soon realised that the key to success was organisation and not promises. In the early years the unions had little to offer their members except the threat of victimisation, hard work, protracted battles, and the expectation of improved conditions at some future date.

The most fruitful initiatives concentrated on organising factory by factory and achieving small incremental gains. The Tuacc unions were especially successful in this. Together with WPWAB, they stressed the need for workers in each plant to elect their own leaders. This slow approach required great patience and was the key to making progress. Workers would stand by the union through thick and thin only if they were well organised. Only a strong leadership in each plant would make it difficult for repressive measures to succeed. The slogan 'the union is not the office' and the concentration on building 'worker leadership' – rather than emphasising union officials – both date from this period.

Almost all the emerging unions were politically inactive. They took help from where they could, including sympathetic individuals within Inkatha and the coloured Labour Party. But this low profile was a political decision. Most of the key founders were politically conscious individuals. Many were supporters of the banned ANC and SACP. Others were committed Marxists. But almost all the emerging unions accepted the argument, at that stage, that the major political task was to build union organisation. Open, explicit politics would come later. Developing a political profile too soon, most unionists argued, would be suicidal.

Union organisation developed slowly with small gains, many defeats, and a gradual building of worker self-confidence. Some of the defeats would, in time, persuade many employers that repression of unions could not be a long-term policy. The strike at Barlow Rand's Heinemann Electrical plant was a key example. Mawu's Transvaal branch had begun organising Heinemann in October 1975, using the intensive organising methods of Tuacc. Organisers met daily with workers to discuss ways of building the union. Organisation expanded in layers. First, only the most trusted contacts were spoken to. Then a slightly wider layer was approached and this process continued until a majority of workers had joined Mawu. Union organisers met, away from the factory premises, to develop strategies with the union committee in the plant, and encourage and advise them.

After four months the workers felt strong enough to make a move. They persuaded the company-appointed liaison committee, most of whose worker members had joined the union, to resign. Workers then boycotted management's attempts to hold further elections and presented a petition calling for union recognition. Management refused. Only one company in the whole country had at that stage formally recognised an emerging African union. Management then moved to crush the union. On 25 March it fired 20 workers, including three shop stewards, and when workers sprang to their defence it dismissed another 400.

Matters did not end there. The union and workers had prepared for this eventuality. The following Monday they gathered outside the factory gates and asked to speak to the managing director. Instead a large police contingent with pickaxes, batons and dogs ordered them to disperse. As workers were dispersing, police attacked them. Many were injured, some seriously. The Mawu organisers were later charged with inciting workers to strike, and the workers were only re-employed on an individual basis if they agreed to support the company's liaison committee.[26]

The Heinemann strike demonstrated that union success demanded more than strong organisation and a vaguely 'liberal' employer. But it also showed employers that the costs of refusing to accommodate workers' demands could be ongoing disruptions, strikes, dismissals and lost production.

Three months after the Heinemann strike the political face of South Africa changed dramatically. A massacre of protesting Soweto school students on 16 June 1976 resulted in a countrywide uprising. Hundreds were killed. Millions of workers joined student and community organised stayaways protesting police action and demanding political rights. Trade unions played little or no part in these actions, not because they opposed them but because they were politically cautious. In addition, the centre of organisation for the stayaways involved townships, not factories.

Their caution provided little protection. When the government responded to the uprising by detaining some, arresting others and implementing a general policy of repression, the unions found that they were not exempt. In November 1976, 26 individuals associated with the emergent unions received five-year banning orders from the government. They included the organisational leadership of the National Union of Textile Workers (NUTW) and Mawu in both Transvaal and Natal, UTP officials, and students associated with WPWAB. This action was an attempt to choke the emerging unions, but the intensive organisational work paid off. Despite all problems the unions survived and, from 1977, grew.

Survival and growth in the 1970s

One of the unions affected by bannings was the Food and Canning Workers Union, formerly the jewel in Sactu's crown. FCWU had survived the dark decade, one of the few Sactu affiliates to do so. But it did so as a shadow of its former self, maintaining organisation in only a few factories in the rural areas of the Western Cape.

From 1976 onwards Jan Theron, a young Cape Town university graduate, together with Oscar Mpetha and Liz Abrahams, two Sactu stalwarts, began rebuilding the union. They concentrated on plants which had once been union strongholds and FCWU and AFCWU slowly began to grow again.

The emerging unions continued their strategy of fighting for recognition. They made informal gains but few companies were prepared to grant formal recognition, and as late as 1979 emergent unions were recognised at only four factories.[27] The state and employers intensified their promotion of liaison committees and works committees as alternatives to unions. By 1978 there were 2 600 liaison committees and over 300 works committees nationally.[28]

Even when the emergent unions attempted to use official channels they were defeated by a hostile alliance of state and employers. In late 1976 workers at Armourplate, a subsidiary of the British company Pilkingtons, managed to negotiate a legal obstacle course and embark on South Africa's first-ever legal strike by African workers. Despite their attempts to use official channels the strikers were dismissed within hours and many were arrested and interrogated by security police. Only in 1981 did an emergent union again decide to tread the legal path. By then hundreds of strikes had taken place, illegally. If legal strikes carried no advantage, argued unionists, then why give employers advance notice of an impending action?

There was every indication that the struggle for union recognition would be long and hard. However, a number of other factors were causing both employers and the state to rethink their strategies. The crushing of the 1976 uprisings had been achieved at great cost to the state, and had not destroyed resistance. Thousands were flocking to join the ANC, and the activities of its military wing, Umkhonto we Sizwe, had increased dramatically. A spirit of defiance was increasingly evident, particularly among the youth. The ruling class was aware that it would have to combine reforms with repression to maintain control.

On the labour front the unions were causing employers problems with their campaigns for recognition. Companies were losing production and profits in an effort to avoid relatively straightforward union demands. A few leading employers began to argue that some accommodation could be made. International pressure on both the state and employers, especially multinational companies, was also growing. It was in this context that the government appointed Professor Nic Wiehahn to head an investigation into the country's labour laws in 1977.

Few in the emerging union movement expected anything meaningful to come from the Wiehahn Commission. They continued their efforts to organise workers, and slowly met with some success. A number of foreign firms, more susceptible to international pressure than locally-owned ones, were targetted for organisation. Some were forced into informal recognition of unions. At the same time there were increasing rumblings within Tucsa's ranks as the motor unions disaffiliated, charging that Tucsa was doing nothing to organise African workers.

There were also signs of a new type of unionism, using new methods of mobilisation and tactics of struggle.

In 1979 the FCWU called on traders and consumers to boycott Fattis & Monis products in an effort to have dismissed workers reinstated and win union recognition. After a protracted battle the company gave in. The lesson seemed to be that unions did not have to rely on worker power alone. They could, in the right circumstances, call upon community support.

In the same year workers at Ford's Cortina plant in Port Elizabeth went on strike after management dismissed Thozamile Botha, a Ford worker and leader of the Port Elizabeth Black Civic Organisation (Pebco). The strike spread beyond Ford to other factories in the Port Elizabeth area, and the company eventually reinstated Botha. But workers strongly criticised their own union, the United Automobile Workers (UAW), for being too tame.

The criticism hurt: UAW was one of the emergent unions and a part of the Federation of South African Trade Unions (Fosatu). It showed all emergent unions that even they were not exempt from criticism if unresponsive to worker demands.

The Ford strike signalled the beginning of a new type of unionism, linked to the community and with a more militant political profile.

During the late 1970s the unions showed an ability to survive, and indeed slowly gained ground. Talk about union unity began to be heard. In March 1977 most of the emergent unions attended a meeting in Johannesburg to discuss the possibility of launching a federation of unions, and protracted talks followed.

Tensions ran high between the CCOBTU/UTP unions and the CIWW bloc, each accusing the other of poaching members. Both Cape-based unions, WPGWU and FCWU, felt that moves towards forming a federation were premature. The Tuacc unions, fearing organisational isolation, were strongly in favour of such a move. They also anticipated that the Wiehahn Commission would open up new possibilities and new dangers with which only a federation would be able to deal.

The talks between the various union blocks finally resulted in the formation of the Federation of South African Trade Unions (Fosatu) at Hammanskraal in April 1979. This brought together some 20 000 workers organised in 12 unions.[*] These included three registered unions formerly within Tucsa, two of which later merged to form the National Automobile and Allied Workers Union (Naawu); the Tuacc bloc of unions; and three CCOBTU/UTP unions which broke away to join Fosatu: Pwawu, the Glass and Allied Workers Union, and the Engineering

---

* I am indebted to Alec Erwin for pointing out that Fosatu's paid-up membership at the time of its launch was only 20 000, rather than the more-frequently cited figure of 45 000.

and Allied Workers Union (Eawu). A fourth union from this group, SFAWU, joined shortly afterwards. Alec Erwin was elected Fosatu's first general secretary and John Mke president.[*]

Fosatu was established as a tight federation with strongly centralised decision making, and policies binding on affiliates. It pioneered the principle of direct worker control in South Africa, with worker delegates constituting a majority in all structures of the federation. It also developed the system of union branch executive committees composed of delegates from every factory, rather than a branch executive which was elected at an annual general meeting. Other key Fosatu principles involved non-racialism, shopfloor organisation, a stress on developing shop stewards, and worker independence from political organisations. It favoured intensive organising, based on the targeting of key plants.

As the first federation of the re-emergent unions, Fosatu was well placed to respond to the government announcement which accompanied the release of the Wiehahn report.

Wiehahn and union recognition

On 1 May 1979 the first of the Wiehahn reports was released. It recommended recognition of the right of African workers to form and belong to trade unions – something no South African government had hitherto agreed to. The report noted that the unions were growing. By leaving them outside the official system they would escape control.

Friedman has summarised the main aspects of the Wiehahn report in the following terms:

> The unions' potential strength meant they must be controlled – their present weakness...meant this should be done soon... It would, the report argued, be 'far healthier' to allow the unions to register at an 'early stage'... This would counter 'polarisation', ensure 'a more orderly process of bargaining' and expose African unions 'more directly to South Africa's trade union traditions and the existing institutions thus inculcating a sense of responsibility to the free market.'[29]

---

* Mke was also president of UAW. His authority as Fosatu president was seriously undermined in the wake of the Ford strike, and he was replaced by Chris Dlamini at Fosatu's second congress in 1982. Other figures prominent at Fosatu's launch and who would later be prominent in Cosatu were Ronald Mofokeng, John Gomomo and Andrew Zulu. Mofokeng was elected Fosatu's treasurer and became Cosatu's national treasurer in 1989. Gomomo was chairperson of Fosatu's Eastern Cape region and in 1989 was elected Cosatu's second vice-president; and Zulu became chairperson of Cosatu's vast PWV region.

Despite this cynical reasoning, the bottom line remained that Wiehahn had proposed official recognition of black trade unions. The voices calling for recognition had come not only from trade unions. Some employers had begun to believe that co-option of the unions would be less costly than repression. The township uprisings gave added impetus to their argument that if the unions' basic economic demands were not accommodated they would be driven in a revolutionary direction. Until then the unions had been relatively a-political, at least publicly. It was important to remember, the argument went, that the 1976 uprising had started over the relatively minor issue of opposition to Afrikaans language education. The inability to accommodate the demand for English as language of instruction had politicised many students and driven them into the revolutionary camp. An early recognition of African trade unions would, it was hoped, prevent a similar process amongst workers.

A host of arguments followed. Determined to include extensive controls in any proposed legislation providing for recognition, the government proposed that unions would not be allowed to recruit 'contract' workers, and that 'foreign' workers would be excluded from any new labour dispensation. Both suggestions would have involved the unions discarding almost half of their members in return for the spurious pleasures of registration. 'Contract' workers, or migrants, formed the backbone of many unions. They were often migrants simply because the pass laws prevented them from living permanently in the cities and confined them to single-sex hostels. And talk of 'foreigners' has always had an ominous ring in South Africa, where newly arrived (white) English immigrants were afforded every legal citizenship right, while millions of indigenous Africans were deemed 'foreigners' and consigned to one or other 'independent' homeland.

The emerging unions declared that they would not register under such conditions, while on the shopfloor unionisation received a massive boost. Ordinary workers saw the government conceding on union recognition, and increasing numbers joined up. Employers, largely unable to distinguish between their employees let alone identify contract workers from others, started to bow to the inevitable.

Under pressure the government also began to retreat. It could not simply overlook union objections; after all it was trying to co-opt the emerging unions into the system. Union rights were granted to all Africans but, under pressure from the racist unions, other controls – including a bar on racially 'mixed' unions – were retained.

This new government response split the union movement over the question of registration. Fosatu decided its affiliated unions would apply for registration but added that unless granted 'non-racial' registration they would refuse to enter the system.

Fosatu's decision caused a stir amongst the emerging unions. Several, notably the WPGWU, argued against registration, claiming that the controls would far outweigh the benefits and the unions would lose their autonomy for the sake of official bargaining rights. Even these bargaining rights were unacceptable, argued WPGWU. The official system was bureaucratic and favoured the dinosaur mentality of the established unions. Unions which joined it would be corrupted.

The disagreement was fundamental. Fosatu felt the WPGWU argument reflected a lack of self-confidence. Official bargaining rights were a victory, not something to be feared. Certainly they held dangers, but so did all bargaining relationships, which necessarily involved both limits and possibilities. A gap had opened up, argued Fosatu, and it should be exploited. The CCOBTU unions, from a more conservative perspective, also decided to register. WPGWU was left largely isolated. But not for long.

Saawu and the community unions

The consumer boycotts and the Ford strike of 1979 signalled the emergence of a new breed of unionism which also rejected registration, arguing that it involved collaboration with state structures. Sactu backed this position.

These new unions emerged in many different forms. The most notable was the South African Allied Workers Union (Saawu) which began life in East London in March 1980 under the leadership of Thozamile Gqweta. Saawu grew dramatically as workers throughout the city joined and took militant action in support of their demands. By October 1980 its membership was 15 000, a remarkable achievement for a relatively small city.

In Port Elizabeth, UAW dissidents at the Ford plant formed a breakaway union, the Motor Assemblers and Components Workers Union (Macwusa), and went on to form the General Workers Union of South Africa (Gwusa) for workers in other industries. In the Transvaal the Black Municipality Workers Union (BMWU), led by the charismatic Joe Mavi, was launched in June 1980. A month later it led a strike by 10 000 Johannesburg municipal workers. In time Macwusa spread to the Transvaal where it gained some support in Pretoria's motor plants. Saawu and other unions also began to establish themselves in other parts of the country.

These unions differed organisationally and politically from the more established emerging unions. Many styled themselves as 'community unions', believing it impossible to separate workers' factory demands from their township problems. They aligned themselves closely to, indeed often formed the core of, township civic organisations, and were seen as more 'political' than the other emerging unions. In contrast to most of the other emerging unions, their leadership was often drawn from the more educated layers of the workforce. Most of the unions in this group aligned themselves more or less openly with the ANC's political perspectives, and affiliated to the United Democratic Front (UDF) when it was launched in 1983.

Organisationally, the 'community unions' frequently had a different approach to other emerging unions. They moved rapidly, mobilising workers across a broad front, and relied on extensive organising and mass campaigning in contrast to the intensive methods of the Fosatu bloc. They were more at home with the rally and the mass meeting than the gradual development of shop steward structures.

The 'community unions' experienced two main problems – state action and organisational weaknesses. Saawu in particular faced extreme repression. It was banned by the Ciskei government, under whose rule most of its members lived. Its leadership was repeatedly detained, harassed and tortured. The security police and East London employers followed a well-planned strategy, ensuring that it was refused recognition in the factories. This seriously weakened the union.

Many of the 'community unions' showed a capacity for militant action and dramatic growth followed by an equally dramatic fall. Too little effort was put into consistent and patient organisational work and preparations for major conflicts. In many respects their experience was similar to that of the Tuacc unions in the wake of the 1973 Durban strikes. They rode the crest of a wave and then fell heavily. Their organisational structures were unequal to the task of maintaining a massive post-strike membership or the winning of effective economic gains.

The spread of organisation

As the 'community unions' rose and fell, Fosatu affiliates grew and consolidated their organisational strength. They focused on achieving recognition at plant level, and by the end of 1981 Fosatu was the largest union bloc with 95 000 members in 387 organised factories.[30] Its affiliates were winning recognition in many plants and achieving concrete improvements by challenging unfair dismissals and low wages.

Many innovative tactics were adopted. CWIU, a Fosatu affiliate, pushed for a legal strike demanding recognition at Colgate – the first by African workers since the abortive effort at Armourplate in 1976. After 98% of workers voted for strike action, Colgate backed down. Fosatu affiliates also began experimenting with the industrial court and won several landmark cases.

A number of realignments took place in the post-Wiehahn years. Most of the 'community unions' affiliated to the UDF, which was launched in 1983. They developed loose structures of co-operation with each other as well as links with Sactu's structures in exile. The close ties between WPGWU (soon simply GWU) and the 'community unions' were shortlived. They had united around an anti-registration position, but their reasons, politics and organisational approach were different, as will be seen in the following chapter. GWU's hostility to registration gradually diminished as it saw Fosatu making major gains without sacrificing its independence.

There were also realignments in the CCOBTU camp. In September 1980 all its unions, except Ccawusa and the four which had earlier left to join Fosatu, launched the Council of Unions of South Africa (Cusa), which started life with nine affiliates and 30 000 members.[31]

Cusa rejected non-racialism in favour of 'black leadership' charging, with some justification, that there were too many whites in influential positions within Fosatu. It also organised itself as a 'loose federation', leaving affiliates largely to their own devices. The result was that it combined a handful of stronger unions with many which remained extremely weak.

Cusa grew dramatically during the early 1980s. But its unions were generally far weaker than Fosatu's, and less likely to embark on strike action. Its impact on the labour scene was significantly less.

One of its initiatives must, however, be mentioned in a history of Cosatu. In 1982 Cusa took the lead in trying to organise black mineworkers when it launched the National Union of Mineworkers (NUM). This was the first such effort since the defeat of the 1946 strike. Cusa appointed Cyril Ramaphosa, then employed in its legal department, to head the initiative and provided the resources to make the organising work possible. By June 1983 NUM had 20 000 members. By the end of 1984 it claimed 110 000.* This made Cusa at least as large as Fosatu. But from early on NUM was an unhappy affiliate, and matters came to a head over the question of the trade union unity talks in the early 1980s.

Meanwhile Fosatu was absorbing some of the lessons of the 'community unions'. Mass mobilising methods were not to be scoffed at. It was the subsequent consolidation of organisation that was the challenge. Unions could not turn members away, but at the same time needed to ensure that organisational and democratic standards were maintained.

---

* Fosatu had also seen the need to organise miners. It approached the question using its low-profile and gradualist organising methods. Miners were organised under the auspices of Mawu, and this was seen as a first step towards launching a miners' union. But these tactics were inappropriate to the industry and the early 1980s, and NUM easily outflanked Mawu's organisational efforts.

Fosatu shop stewards began establishing locals or shop steward councils in the Transvaal and Natal. These were an attempt to take the membership beyond a plant-level consciousness, and ease the pressure on organisers unable to cope with the flood of workers wanting to join Fosatu.

The locals brought together workers from a particular township or industrial area, such as KwaThema or Wadeville. Inevitably they began to take up more general problems. Workers on strike would receive support from their colleagues in neighbouring factories. Community problems, such as the demolition of shacks, were also taken up and the relevant community councils confronted. The local shop steward councils were one of Fosatu's most important legacies to the trade union movement. They marked the beginning of a more active engagement of Fosatu's members in political issues.

Fosatu faced growing pressures from its membership to take a higher political profile. But its leadership, or most of it, remained cautious. Fosatu took up the 1983 and 1984 campaigns against the government's proposed new tricameral constitution, but did so in isolation from the broader campaign conducted by the UDF and others. Fosatu's leadership argued the need for working-class autonomy from other interests, and was fearful of entering alliances with what it termed 'populists'. This cautious approach was finally challenged by Fosatu's Transvaal shop stewards in November 1984. It was a tribute to Fosatu's structures and principles that this challenge took place through the federation's local and regional structures, rather than outside of them.

Union issues in the early 1980s

Despite organisational and political differences the emerging unions all saw a need for greater unity. But during the early 1980s a number of key issues repeatedly emerged as points of difference. Registration – at root a debate around non-collaboration and the merits of entering the post-Wiehahn labour relations structures – and the tactics of political involvement were strongly debated. Cusa, and to a lesser extent Fosatu, adopted a relatively abstentionist political profile. But this was itself a political decision, and many argued that it was an inappropriate tactic for the 1980s.

In addition there was the question of organising methods and the relationship between organisation and mobilisation. This, in turn, linked to the question of structures and worker control. Fosatu argued strongly that workers on the shopfloor should dominate all union structures and control union officials, and insisted on mandates, report-backs and worker control. But critics differed, claiming that Fosatu's obsession over 'mandates' and downplaying of the role of union officials prevented speedy and effective decisions. These differences in perspective emerged repeatedly in the unity talks of the early 1980s.

Notes

1. Luli Callinicos, *Working Life, 1886-1940. Factories, Townships and Popular Culture on the Rand*, Johannesburg, 1987, 114.
2. Luckhardt and Wall, *Organize...or Starve*, 49.
3. Luckhardt and Wall, *Organize...or Starve*, 57.
4. Luckhardt and Wall, *Organize...or Starve*, 52-3.
5. Friedman, *Building Tomorrow Today*, 17-22.
6. Luckhardt and Wall, *Organize...or Starve*, 62.
7. Luckhardt and Wall, *Organize...or Starve*, 97.
8. Luckhardt and Wall, *Organize...or Starve*, 97.
9. Lacom, *Freedom from Below. The Struggle for Trade Unions in South Africa*, Durban, no date, 108.
10. Lacom, *Freedom from Below*, 132-3.
11. Francis Meli, *South Africa Belongs to Us. The History of the ANC*, Harare, 1988, 145-6.
12. Rob Lambert, 'Political Unionism in South Africa. An Analysis of the South African Congress of Trade Unions', unpublished PhD thesis, Department of Sociology, University of Witwatersrand, 1989, 462-3.
13. Rob Lambert and Eddie Webster, 'The Re-emergence of Political Unionism in Contemporary South Africa', in (ed) William Cobbett and Robin Cohen, *Popular Struggles in South Africa*, London, 1988, 21. This quotation does not relect Lamber and Webster's viewpoin.
14. Friedman, *Building Tomorrow Today*, 31.
15. Lambert, 'Political Unionism', 470.
16. Lambert, 'Political Unionism', 472.
17. Rob Lambert, 'Trade Unions, Nationalism and the Socialist Project in South Africa', in (ed) Glenn Moss and Ingrid Obery, *South African Review 4*, Johannesburg, 1987, 236.
18. Lambert, 'Political Unionism', 462-3.
19. Luckhardt and Wall, *Organize...or Starve*, 441.
20. *The Durban Strikes 1973. 'Human Beings with Souls*, Durban/Johannesburg, 1976.
21. Friedman, *Building Tomorrow Today*, 113, 136.
22. Lacom, *Freedom from Below*, 158.
23. Friedman, *Building Tomorrow Today*, 61.
24. Hundreds were involved in rebuilding the union movement, and it is impossible to list them all in a work of this nature. Those mentioned are a selection – by no means complete – of some of the more prominent and long-serving unionists who were involved in the 1970s. They are drawn from my own knowledge, Friedman's *Building Tomorrow Today*, and discussions with various trade unionists including Sydney Mufamadi, Joe Foster, Sipho

Kubheka, Alec Erwin, John Nkadimeng, Bhekisisa Nxasana and John Makatini.
25. Author's interview with Joe Foster, Cape Town, 3 August 1990.
26. Friedman, *Building Tomorrow Today*, 114-6.
27. Friedman, *Building Tomorrow Today*, 147.
28. Lacom, *Freedom from Below*, 161.
29. Friedman, *Building Tomorrow Today*, 156.
30. Friedman, *Building Tomorrow Today*, 243.
31. Friedman, *Building Tomorrow Today*, 197.

2

The trade union unity talks

All for one

EVERY birth is accompanied by blood and pain, and the birth of Cosatu was no exception. These experiences influenced both the shape of Cosatu today, and its attitudes towards unions which did not participate in the launch of the new federation.

The union unity talks took place between 1981 and 1985. Those 'four solid years of painstaking deliberations', as Cosatu's assistant general secretary Sydney Mufamadi labelled them, were marked by mistrust and conflict. Differences of interest, of political outlook, of organisational methods and of personality had to be overcome before Cosatu could be born.

August 1981: the Langa summit

A number of the emerging unions had started informal discussions about co-operation as early as 1979. But unity talks began in earnest during August 1981, when over 100 representatives from 29 unions met at Langa, Cape Town. This meeting, convened by GWU, was attended by all the major emerging unions including the Cape-based FCWU/AFCWU and GWU, the newly-formed Saawu, and the affiliates of both Fosatu and Cusa.

This was a time of rapid growth for the unions. Saawu, with 20 000 members, was taking the East London area by storm. A wave of industrial action had hit the Border region as workers flocked to attend Saawu's general meetings and join its ranks. Fosatu, launched as a federation in 1979, was experiencing slower but nevertheless steady growth. With 54 000 members, it was the largest bloc amongst the emerging unions, and some of its affiliates had developed into national industrial unions. FCWU/AFCWU* was beginning to break out of its Western Cape base, to which it had been confined since the repression of Sactu during the early 1960s.

The Langa summit aimed to develop a united response to the newly introduced labour laws which had emerged from the Wiehahn report. The emerging unions were conscious that these provisions aimed to divide and control them while at the same time extending rights previously denied to black unions.

The summit, chaired by Saawu's Thozamile Gqweta, agreed to establish regional solidarity committees to co-ordinate solidarity action on a regular basis. It condemned the detention of unionists and the harassment of unions by Ciskei authorities. After a brief discussion of registration under the new labour law, a unanimous resolution was adopted. 'We resist and reject the present system of registration insofar as it is designed to control and interfere in the internal affairs of the union,' proclaimed the public statement issued after the meeting. But this concealed deep differences which would haunt the unity talks for years to come. The carefully-worded resolution aimed to accommodate both those opposed to registration and the large Fosatu and Cusa blocs which intended to register and use the space created by amendments to the law. It reflected opposition to registration under the new law, but concealed deep divisions over the tactics of registration.

The Langa conference succeeded in placing unity on the agenda. Although it ended with nothing more than the promise of future co-operation through the solidarity committees, it was undoubtedly the beginning of the long process culminating in the launch of Cosatu.

The death of Neil Aggett

Within months of the Langa summit one of its participants, FCWU/AFCWU organiser Neil Aggett, died while in police custody. Reports of serious torture of detainees – including Aggett – had been

---

* The Food and Canning Workers Union had two components: the registered FCWU for non-African members, and the unregistered AFCWU for African members. In practice they operated as one and the acronyms are used interchangeably.

filtering through to unions for a while, and when Aggett died on 5 February 1982 at John Vorster Square, Johannesburg's police headquarters, a shocked union movement decided to arrange a protest action. If unity meant anything, it should include a united response to atrocities such as this.

All union members were called upon to stop work for 30 minutes on 11 February. A hundred thousand workers responded, the majority of them members of Fosatu affiliates and FCWU/AFCWU itself. The action involved over two-thirds of Fosatu's membership, while only a handful of Saawu and Macwusa-organised plants, and hardly any Cusa members, responded to the call.

The Aggett stoppage was a limited action when compared to some of the massive stayaways which occurred subsequently. But it was the first union-organised initiative attempting to mobilise workers nationally at their places of work, over an issue going beyond the factory floor. This event influenced the unity talks for years to come. Fosatu's confidence in its mobilising skills grew, as did its reputation for being able to 'deliver the goods' in mass actions.

The effects of the Aggett stoppage were felt at Fosatu's second national congress, held early in April 1982. In an obvious reference to those unions whose members had not participated in the action, general secretary Joe Foster criticised unions where 'radical political positions are adopted' but which make 'little headway into the power of capital.'

While praising the unity talks for creating 'unity out of apparent disunity,' Foster felt that this unity would decline in significance as it was basically 'ad hoc'. Unity would have to involve 'more and more concerted and concrete actions unless it merely wants to be the source of endless press statements.' These actions would require a more permanent organisational link, demanding a process for making democratic and equitable decisions. This could take the form either of a 'loose federation such as Tucsa,' or a tight federation of industrial unions. Fosatu felt the latter course, involving 'disciplined unity', was the only path that could unite the trade unions and build a working-class movement.

This was, in effect, a proposal that the unity talks should be aimed at forming a new trade union federation with structures similar to those of Fosatu, and the congress resolved that Fosatu was prepared to disband in the interests of forming a new federation. Two weeks after the Fosatu congress, the second unity summit began at Wilgespruit on the West Rand.

April 1982: Wilgespruit

Discussion at the Wilgespruit meeting focused on the idea of a new federation, with delegates arguing heatedly over the principles that would form the basis of union unity. Macwusa and Gwusa claimed that the decision of the Langa summit on registration had not been carried out, and indicated that they were not prepared to co-operate with registered unions or unions which participated in industrial councils. They argued that the Langa summit had agreed to deregister, yet Fosatu and Cusa unions had chosen to register. Macwusa/Gwusa then left the meeting, calling on other unregistered unions to join them. None did.

The 'registration debate' generated a lot of heat which, in retrospect, seems difficult to understand. It mirrored political debates between the 'non-collaborationist' and the 'participationist' traditions of resistance politics. The anti-registration faction warned that registration held many dangers. The new labour laws, and the pressure to register, were yet another trick of the regime aimed at more subtle control. Registered unions would be drawn into a web of rules and regulations, political involvement would be impossible, and unions would become economistic and reformist. The anti-registrationists were also fearful that the participationists were simply justifying an attitude to state institutions which would lead them in the direction taken by organisations like Inkatha.

By contrast, the registration faction claimed to be aware of the dangers of co-option. But, they argued, the registration option had only emerged because of growing worker pressure on the state and employers. The new Wiehahn labour dispensation was itself a product of struggle, and it would be wrong not to utilise the space it offered to expand union organisation.

Despite these arguments, the Wilgespruit summit reached an in-principle agreement to work towards a new trade union federation. The summit also exposed differences within the anti-registration camp.

less prepared to work and even unite with registered unions. Unions such as Macwusa and Gwusa opposed registration in principle, believing that it involved collaboration and acceptance of state control. They wanted a federation of unregistered unions. Wilgespruit saw relations begin to cool between AFCWU and GWU, on the one hand, and the other unregistered unions, on the other.

Many of the unregistered unions, the 'community unions' as they were known, were unhappy with the approach of Macwusa/Gwusa. Following the Wilgespruit summit, at least three 'informal meetings' of this group took place, with seven unions participating: Saawu, Gawu,

BMWU, SA Transport and Allied Workers Union (Satawu), Orange-Vaal General Workers Union (OVGWU), Macwusa and Gwusa. This group agreed to counter the 'opportunistic manoeuvres' of Fosatu which was 'trying to use us in its attempts to form a federation on its terms.' At the same time, 'we acknowledge our obligation in terms of striving to see to it that the federation, if formed, should have a progressive basis.' The Macwusa/Gwusa walk-out from the Wilgespruit summit was felt to be a 'reactionary' move. Macwusa and Gwusa disagreed, arguing that they saw no point in sitting at a table with 'reactionaries.' But they were eventually prevailed upon to attend the next summit, and the seven unions agreed that 'no union from our ranks should stage a walk-out.'[1]

Deadlock in Port Elizabeth

The third summit was held in Port Elizabeth during July 1982. The group of seven 'community' unions raised objections to registration and participation in industrial councils, which Macwusa and Gwusa alone had focused on at Wilgespruit. Their criticisms were directed mainly at Fosatu and Cusa, most of whose affiliates were registered. They also put forward seven 'non-negotiable' principles which, they argued, should be the basis of any new federation: non-registration, shopfloor bargaining, federation policy binding on affiliates, worker control, non-racialism, participation in community issues, and rejection of reactionary bodies nationally and internationally.

Other unions also put forward principles they saw as the basis for unity. Fosatu, FCWU and GWU felt that worker control, non-racialism and industrial unionism were non-negotiable. The CTMWA agreed, but felt that a new federation could include both industrial and general unions. Cusa stood for black worker control, industrial unionism and a loose federation.[2] Cusa's delegation included, for the first time, a young lawyer who would soon make his mark in the union field – Cyril Ramaphosa.

This Port Elizabeth meeting turned into the most bitter of all the summits. The only principle that all agreed on at the time was 'worker control', and even this was qualified by Cusa accepting only 'black worker control'. The seven community unions declared their principles non-negotiable, and said they could not work with unions which did not share all seven principles. Others disagreed, arguing that co-operation was more important than principled stands. But after lengthy arguments it became clear that the summit was deadlocked.

The meeting ended with a terse press statement: 'It was decided that there is no basis for the formation of a federation of all unions represented at this stage. No further meeting is planned.'[3]

The Port Elizabeth deadlock was a serious blow to the search for unity, and it was nine months before the unions met again. After the meeting Fosatu announced that it would continue talks with 'like-minded unions.' Macwusa and Gwusa continued to raise the possibility of launching a federation of unregistered unions. GWU tried to mediate between the group of seven and the other unions. But, according to a GWU official, the seven 'were entirely unbending – they wouldn't make any compromises which might bring the two sides closer together and we were forced to give up.'[4] Unity initiatives continued but the talks themselves were dead. GWU decided to proceed with talks with 'unions like Food and Canning Workers Union, Fosatu, the Cape Town Municipal Workers' Union, Mwasa and Cusa...those unions that want unity.'[5]

The Port Elizabeth summit saw the hardening of blocs within the union movement. The group of seven unions had taken a united stand, and became known to their adversaries as the Magnificent Seven, an ironic allusion to the film classic of the same name. These seven 'community-based unions' later affiliated to the UDF. The Port Elizabeth summit saw GWU and FCWU/AFCWU move closer to the Fosatu bloc and away from their earlier close working relationship with Saawu. The summit also saw tensions grow between Fosatu and its allies, on the one hand, and Sactu, and to a lesser extent the ANC, on the other. Political suspicions between Fosatu and Sactu had deepened following Joe Foster's speech to Fosatu's 1982 congress, and these increased further with their differences over the political complexion of any proposed new federation.[*]

April 1983: Athlone

The need for unity meant that talks would have to continue, sooner rather than later. GWU took the initiative and called the fourth summit, stressing that the meeting was to discuss the practicalities of forming a federation. The summit, held in Athlone, Cape Town, was well-attended with large worker delegations.

Fosatu discussed its position extensively beforehand. An editorial in the March 1983 edition of *Fosatu Worker News* commented that:

---

[*] *Sactu exerted influence over, and was itself influenced by, the 'community-based unions', with many key leaders among the latter being Sactu activists. Sactu supported the stance taken by these unions at the Wilgespruit summit, particularly the hardline stance against registration and industrial councils. Once Sactu's stance changed in 1984, it played a significant role in changing the direction of the unity talks.*

it is impossible to build unity if any one union or group of unions insists on dictating the terms of unity... However,...there are two crucial policies which we can never sacrifice... WORKER CONTROL and NON-RACIALISM.

The group of seven unions retreated from their earlier position. They accepted a proposal to form a federation including unions with differing policies. This was a major breakthrough, but differences emerged over the steps needed to establish a federation. Prior to the meeting OVGWU had circulated a utopian, even anarchistic, proposal to all unions. It suggested that the plan for forming a new federation, whilst admirable, 'is premature and misconceived. The task of unifying the trade union movement can never be solved by organisational manoeuvres at leadership level...' It called instead for local solidarity action committees to be formed which would unite workers. This would create the basis for later regional and then national co-ordination. OVGWU's phrases sounded democratic: unity should be built organically from the bottom-up. Its position was supported, to differing degrees, by the rest of the group of seven unions as well as Cusa.

For Fosatu and its allies, OVGWU's position sounded like the indefinite postponement of all discussion over the launching of a federation. Fosatu delegates called for immediate practical steps to form a new federation. Workers, they argued, had given the go-ahead for this. In any event unity would develop more effectively within the structures of a federation. If the emerging unions were to organise and act effectively they would need to pool their resources within one federation. Furthermore, the idea of solidarity action committees had been agreed at the Langa summit in 1981. In practice, argued Fosatu and its allies, these committees had been ineffective.

These two positions were hotly debated. Finally all the unions present, except for OVGWU, undertook to participate in the formation of a new federation, or seek a mandate to participate. The meeting ended with agreement to set up a feasibility committee to discuss practical proposals.

The feasibility committee meets

The first meeting of the feasibility committee, held in Athlone during July 1983, examined three issues but took no decisions:
● the form of a new federation was discussed, and Fosatu's proposal for a tight structure considered;
● Cusa and Fosatu argued that foreign funding would be needed to assist in launching an effective federation, although it would have to be proper-

ly controlled. However, FCWU/AFCWU, supported by CTMWA and Ccawusa, claimed that outside funding would lead to dependence and loss of control by worker membership;

● demarcation was also discussed, and participating unions agreed to inform each other where they were organising.

The discussions were concrete and fruitful. But the optimism engendered by the Athlone meeting was premature, and it did little to stop an increasing number of conflicts between unions competing for the same membership.

The unity talks deadlocked again when the steering committee met in Johannesburg during October. Macwusa, Gwusa, Saawu, Gawu and the Cusa affiliates failed to provide the membership information needed to continue demarcation discussions. A number of the others – Fosatu, GWU and FCWU/AFCWU in particular – felt this indicated that they were not serious about unity, and began growing impatient with what they perceived to be delaying tactics.

The atmosphere grew sour and suspicious, and allegations of poaching flowed thick and fast. GWU accused Saawu of disorganising its members in the East London and Durban docks. Ccawusa claimed Saawu was organising workers at a branch of a chain store they had organised. The emerging unions were competing for membership. The question was whether demarcation agreements could solve the problems, as FCWU proposed, or whether they would more easily be solved within the framework of one federation composed of national industrial unions. This raised the more fundamental problem of how the general unions could transform themselves into industrial unions, and at what pace.

The unity talks nearly broke down during the October meeting. Only a proposal by Cusa to resume the meeting in November postponed the inevitable split. Even then Fosatu, the largest bloc, warned that it might not attend. Within its internal structures it was debating the value of continuing with the talks, and requested a postponement of the November meeting. Fosatu felt little immediate pressure to form a new federation. Its affiliates had a rapidly-growing membership and were benefitting from being in a highly-organised federation. There was a strong feeling within its ranks that the unity talks were a waste of time. Those who wanted unity, argued many within its central committee, were welcome to affiliate to Fosatu. GWU and FCWU/AFCWU, by contrast, were feeling increasingly isolated. They needed to belong to a federation.

At its central committee meeting held in October 1983, Fosatu decided to begin bilateral unity talks. It chose a delegation to meet with 'like-minded' and 'more pragmatic' unions, such as FCWU/AFCWU, the Cusa affiliates, CTMWA, GWU and Ccawusa, all of which seemed to believe that unity with the group of seven 'community' unions was unlikely.[6] Organisationally, the group of seven were considered weak at building and consolidating shopfloor structures. Politically, the seven had affiliated to the recently-launched UDF, while the other unions had decided not to. Practically, the seven seemed to be using delaying tactics and appeared half-hearted in their commitment to industrial unionism. However, there was support for the holding of one further unity meeting. Ccawusa agreed to convene it.

March 1984: Johannesburg

FCWU/AFCWU threw down the gauntlet when the meeting opened: talks could continue only if it was clear who was ready to join a new federation. Three criteria would have to be satisfied by unions or federations wanting to continue unity discussions:
● that a clear and unconditional decision to join a new federation had been taken;
● that all federations had taken a clear decision to disband in favour of a new federation;
● that general unions were in the process of dividing themselves into industrial components.

Those unions unable to satisfy all three criteria should be given observer status, said FCWU/AFCWU, but could rejoin the talks once they met the criteria. This position was accepted by Fosatu, Cusa, CTMWA, Ccawusa and GWU. The Municipal and General Workers Union (Mgwusa), Saawu and Gawu objected and refused to accept observer status. They were told to accept this or leave the meeting.*

'Unions which are not demarcated along industrial lines...are not ready to join a federation. These unions did not accept the offer of observer status and left the meeting,' said the feasibility committee in a statement issued after the meeting. 'No union has the right to decided who should and who should not have observer status,' countered Gawu's Sydney Mufamadi at a later date. 'We were kicked out of the unity talks...because we had to walk out when we were only given observer status.'

The meeting continued in the absence of Mgwusa, Saawu and Gawu, and concentrated on structures for a new federation. Those remaining, representing some 300 000 workers, committed themselves to forming the new federation during the course of 1984.

---

* The Johannesburg-based Black Municipality Workers Union had recently changed its name to Mgwusa. Macwusa and Gwusa were absent from this meeting; OVGWU had not attended since the Athlone meeting of April 1983.

The feasibility committee met again on a number of occasions without the UDF-affiliated unions, becoming the powerhouse and central focus of the unity initiative. But it was still not clear how united those remaining were. Political differences remained and the issue of non-racialism versus racial exclusivity was still unresolved.

There were also signs that the country was about to be rocked by the largest popular uprisings ever to confront apartheid, and major realignments – particularly within Fosatu and Cusa – were beginning to take place.

The 1984 uprisings

The newly-formed UDF gained momentum during 1984. Students were boycotting classes in growing numbers, and by mid-year conflicts over high rentals were developing in a number of townships. Political and community organisations, together with the trade unions, began campaigning against the election for a new tricameral, racially-based parliament, scheduled for August and September 1984.

As the elections neared, conflict increased. Unrest erupted in the Vaal Triangle townships in September. Unpopular councillors and mayors were called on to resign, their homes were petrol-bombed, and some were killed. The protests spread countrywide as township residents rejected undemocratic councils and rent increases, and presented a variety of local grievances. In response the state moved troops into the townships.

This impacted on the unions from the highest leader down to the most ordinary member. Large numbers of union members started participating in mass action, stayaways and consumer boycotts. Most of these were led by the UDF or its affiliates, and the UDF unions gained in prestige as the uprising grew. However, most workers still joined more established unions such as the Fosatu affiliates, which were better organised and more effective on the shopfloor. But Fosatu remained politically aloof. It took up the campaign against the tricameral elections but did so in isolation from other organisations.

Cusa was also affected by developments. Most of its unions had a poor reputation at shopfloor level. Its leadership combined the a-political, and even the pro-Inkatha, with an influential number of people inclined towards black consciousness. During 1984 its mining affiliate, NUM, grew so rapidly that its membership exceeded that of all the other affiliates combined. Increasingly, however, NUM diverged from Cusa's leadership, and began believing that Cusa was not serious about union unity. In mid-1984 the NUM conference decided to join the new federation even if Cusa did not.

The year also witnessed a number of new unions in the black consciousness tradition initiating their own unity process, and forming the Azanian Confederation of Trade Unions (Azactu).

Unity discussions could not proceed in a vacuum, isolated from the growing uprising in the townships. The events leading up to the November 1984 stayaway showed this clearly. In mid-September the Fosatu-affiliated Sweet, Food and Allied Workers Union (SFAWU) launched a consumer boycott against Simba chips after the dismissal of 450 of its members. In the explosive political climate the boycott campaign rapidly took root in black communities, particularly on the Witwatersrand.

In October, the Congress of South African Students (Cosas), a powerful organisation of school students, began discussions with parents and workers over increased support for school boycotts, the demand for equal education and the right to form student representative councils. Students, they argued, supported worker struggles such as the ongoing Simba boycott. But their parents – the workers – did not understand or support student struggles. In a widely-distributed pamphlet, Cosas listed examples of the similarity between student and worker struggles. Faced with a government which was closing large numbers of schools to try and break the boycott, Cosas argued that the

> boycott weapon is not strong enough against our common enemy, the bosses and their government. Workers, we need your support and strength in the trade unions. We students are ready to help your struggle against the bosses in any way we can. *But today we need your support.*

Workers from the Springs township of KwaThema responded first. On 22 October 1984 almost the entire black workforce of Springs stayed away in response to a call from the students and their local union leadership. Within a week a Transvaal regional stayaway committee had been formed. It included student, community and civic bodies. Importantly, it also included unionists from both Fosatu and Cusa, as well as UDF-affiliated unions. The committee began mobilising for a two-day stayaway planned for 5 and 6 November. Issues to be raised included the education crisis, removal of troops from the townships, rent increases and the reinstatement of the Simba workers.[*] Both Inkatha and Azapo condemned the stayaway call.

---

[*]*Simba management, under pressure from a strong consumer boycott, rapidly retreated and announced the reinstatement of the dismissed workers even before the stayaway began.*

The Transvaal regional stayaway

Fosatu's participation was not without internal tensions. Many established leaders argued that the federation was bowing to populist pressures. But these leaders were losing their tight grip on the federation. Even within Fosatu's central committee there was growing pressure for a more engaged approach. This reflected rank-and-file impatience, particularly in the Transvaal, with what was perceived to be Fosatu's political hostility towards mass action.[7]

To its credit, Fosatu was flexible enough to accommodate the changing situation and respond to these pressures. It mandated Mawu's Moses Mayekiso to represent the interests of the federation on the stayaway committee, where he sat with activists from the Soweto Youth Congress (Soyco), the Release Mandela Committee (RMC) and UDF-affiliated unions. The response to the stayaway call was overwhelming, with 800 000 workers from the Witwatersrand and Vaal Triangle absenting themselves from work on 5-6 November.[8]

Meanwhile the practical aspects of the new federation were progressing smoothly, but without the participation of the 'community unions'. The feasibility committee continued to meet and a draft constitution was circulated. But the spirit of the unity talks could not remain unaffected by the changing political climate.

Following the November stayaway, Sactu circulated a carefully-worded letter giving its position on the unity talks.[9] It urged the general unions 'to hasten the process of industrialisation' but felt that the feasibility committee should not make this 'a condition for participation' in the talks. Giving some unions observer status 'might create an element of mistrust.' Sactu urged the feasibility committee to assist the general unions to industrialise, and re-open the talks to all unions. 'Sactu shall be happy with the formation of a one democratic trade union federation, based on the principle "One Industry, One Union,"' it concluded.

Behind the scenes Sactu worked to persuade the UDF-affiliated unions to resume their participation in the unity talks. 'We told them they should not be complacent,' recalls Sactu's general secretary John Nkadimeng. 'They should go in, accept decisions and criticise. They should not simply rely on movement (ie ANC) support and avoid building strong industrial unions on the ground. There should be no excuses but they should go in.'[10]

There were also pressures within Fosatu to include the UDF unions in the talks again. In early 1985 first Fosatu's executive and then its central committee called for the re-opening of the talks. Although some unions in the feasibility committee were unhappy about this they agreed to Fosatu's proposal. But they received an assurance from Fosatu that re-opening the talks would not delay progress towards launching the new federation, and that progress made since the walkout/expulsion of the UDF unions would not be reversed.

Why did Fosatu, the union bloc most sceptical of the UDF unions, back their re-entry into the unity talks? Fosatu leadership had perceived the need to respond to the changing political climate within the country. A well-attended meeting of Transvaal shop stewards held in early 1985 had proposed the re-inclusion of the UDF unions in unity talks, and Fosatu regional leaders had been meeting with a number of representatives of the UDF-affiliated unions. Fosatu's powerful Transvaal region, as well as Chris Dlamini, the federation's president, were beginning to challenge Fosatu's political direction, and were a force which could not be ignored.

The more far-sighted of Fosatu's national leaders realised that it would be counter-productive to form a new federation without the co-operation and support of the ANC and Sactu. In addition, both Fosatu and the increasingly-powerful NUM wanted a federation of all unions. 'We thought', recalls Fosatu's Joe Foster 'that if you can't bring in all the unions then you will achieve nothing.'[11]

Ironically, it was Naawu general secretary Fred Sauls, with his reputation of hostility towards the UDF, who put the case for re-opening the talks to the UDF-affiliated unions. He argued, recalls Alec Erwin, that 'it was a mistake to isolate ourselves from the nationalist movement.'[12]

June 1985: Ipelegeng

Unity talks were re-opened both to UDF unions and groups like Azactu, which had emerged since the Langa summit. A wide range of unions accepted invitations from the feasibility committee to a final summit meeting to be held at Ipelegeng, Soweto, on 8-9 June 1985. All unions were asked to bring their national executive committees to the meeting.

It was soon clear that the road would be rocky. Prior to the meeting the invited unions were asked to comment on the draft constitution for a new federation. Azactu's Pandelani Nefolovhodwe suggested that the feasibility committee 'must be prepared to listen to us as equals... There must be a new beginning and all previous decisions must be suspended.' It was not clear whether this included decisions taken before the launch of Azactu only months beforehand, or whether Azactu felt that each time a new union was formed unity talks should start afresh! Gawu's Mufamadi felt that if the UDF unions were to return to the talks 'the feasibility committee would have to be enlarged and we cannot rule out the possibility of having to rewrite the constitution.'[13]

Mufamadi also claimed that the general unions had made progress towards industrialising and noted their role in setting up Sarhwu. Donsie Khumalo of the Retail and Allied Workers Union (Rawu), a breakaway of Macwusa/Gwusa in Pretoria, argued that 'the unity talks must take cognisance of the real strengths of the general unions,' but agreed that 'an acceptable starting point for negotiations is the dismantling of general unions.' On the equally divisive issue of UDF affiliation, opposed by members of the feasibility committee, Mufamadi believed that this 'should not be a problem. We are prepared to enter the federation with other unions not affiliated. Discussions about affiliation and other policy matters should take place within the federation.'

There was great excitement as the 400 delegates packed into the hall at Ipelegeng. NUM's Cyril Ramaphosa, who chaired the gathering, noted that the Ipelegeng summit was not simply a re-opening of the talks. It also aimed at ratifying the work of the feasibility committee.

Union delegates at Ipelegeng were asked to set out their standpoint on two issues – the draft constitution, which proposed a tight federation, and five unifying principles which were the cornerstones of the new federation: non-racialism, one union one industry, worker control, representation on the basis of paid-up membership, and co-operation at national level. Azactu affiliates, not surprisingly, took a hostile approach. Their main spokespersons, Nefolovhodwe and Cunningham Ngcukana, objected to the constitution in its entirety as Azactu had not been involved in its drafting. They also spoke out against the principle of non-racialism, and counterposed the concept of 'anti-racism'. Non-racialism, they argued, was a liberal concept associated with the Congress and Freedom Charter tradition. While this stand implied that Azactu would not participate in the launching congress of a new federation, other delegates at Ipelegeng stressed that the door would remain open for Azactu to join at a later stage.

The surprise of the meeting was provided by the Cusa affiliates. Some stood up to support Azactu's stand on non-racialism. A majority said they knew nothing about the unity talks and had not been consulted or represented at them. They had seen a draft of the constitution for the first time that day. These statements shocked the other feasibility committee unions. After all, Cusa had participated in all the unity meetings. Cusa's Piroshaw Camay had even played a major role in drafting the constitution. This lent credence to NUM's claims that Cusa was not committed to worker control or trade union unity. It soon became apparent that only Cusa's black mineworkers would join the new federation.

All the other participants in the feasibility committee reaffirmed their support for the draft constitution and the five underlying principles, with one exception: the Jewellers and Goldsmiths Union, a tiny Fosatu affiliate with less than 1 000 members. As a craft union, the JGU was concerned that the broad definition of 'industry' excluded them, and would result in their dissolution.

The UDF affiliates supported the five principles. They made much of the fact that they had not been party to drafting the constitution, and wanted to know why, as they put it, they had been kicked out of the unity talks the previous year. They were also hostile to the feasibility committee. But their ranks included both hardline and conciliatory elements, those dwelling on the past and those looking to the future. It became clear that the UDF unions, or most of them, wanted to be part of the new federation.

A meeting of the UDF unions after Ipelegeng highlighted these tensions. A minority argued that a national federation was needed and that the political differences could be solved. A majority felt there was no point in participating in the new federation. Only concerted efforts by the ANC and Sactu in the closing months of 1985 persuaded the UDF unions to reconsider their position.[14]

Nevertheless, their support for the new federation was not wholehearted. The feasibility committee unions were dominated by 'reactionary leadership', argued one document emanating from the UDF union bloc in the Transvaal. It was essential to move into the new federation 'to strengthen the move towards a progressive direction within these unions... Our aim is to win over the entire federation onto the side of progress, of peace and of liberation.'[15] Despite these arguments, a few individuals within the UDF bloc, including some from Saawu and Gawu, remained implacably opposed to joining a new federation.

Could Cosatu have accommodated Cusa and Azactu? A union federation, as a mass structure, is generally inclusive rather than exclusive. However, insufficient organisational work had been done amongst Cusa's affiliates to persuade them of the long-term benefits of a merger programme aimed at building industrial unionism. This had been left to Cusa's representatives at the unity talks, despite indications that they were not all preaching the unity message with vigour.

Other unions represented on the feasibility committee had never expected all of Cusa's affiliates to join a new federation. A number of its unions were run as personal fiefdoms and would never have accepted merging with other industrial unions. However, a number of affiliates were expected to join, not only NUM.

The feasibility committee had done very little preparatory work among Azactu affiliates. This was more understandable given that Azactu was formed only months previously. But there was a deeper political problem. The new federation would inevitably adopt political positions, and this required a relatively unified perspective. This had to take account of the political and organisational dominance of the non-racial ANC/UDF tradition. Black consciousness and, to a lesser extent, Africanist views were common within Azactu and Cusa ranks, and they could not accept the dominance of the non-racial tradition.

It would have been relatively simple to make the minor change in the wording of the principles from 'non-racialism' to 'anti-racism'. But when Azactu delegates to Ipelegeng explained their views, it became apparent that more than semantics was at stake. They objected to being in a federation dominated by the politics of the 'non-racial democratic' tradition. Azactu and Cusa could have been accommodated within the new federation if they been prepared to work democratically within its structures. But this pattern of division on political grounds has occurred in all mass structures in South Africa from unions to women's organisations and even to broad fronts.

The Ipelegeng summit saw Cyril Ramaphosa, NUM's general secretary, rise to prominence. His patient and good-humoured handling of a difficult meeting gained him the respect of all participants, even his adversaries. It revealed a level of diplomacy and firmness which was to make him the unanimous choice as convenor of Cosatu's launching congress.

The different traditions

Ipelegeng divided those unions wanting to be part of the launching congress from those staying out. But the unity of unions moving towards the launching congress was comprised of a number of distinct strands.
● The eight Fosatu affiliates had a reputation for being effective at shopfloor level and having consolidated their structures, although not all were evenly developed in this respect. Politically, Fosatu was divided between the bulk of its established leadership, suspicious of what they termed 'popular politics', and a growing number of officials and workers who favoured the political direction of the UDF. The former viewed 'national' and 'popular' politics as 'petty bourgeois', laid great stress on working-class autonomy and avoided any alliances with UDF in particular. The latter wanted working-class engagement with the ongoing uprisings in the township, and were often members of, or sought alliances with, the UDF in particular. The majority of Fosatu's approximately 140 000 ordinary members, while extremely loyal to the organisation, were not strongly allied to any particular political formation.
● Some of the unaffiliated unions, such as GWU and FCWU/AFCWU, were also respected for their shopfloor organisation but had suffered because of their isolation from any federation. Although they had both recently expanded significantly from their bases in the Western Cape,

their perspectives and leadership were still largely moulded by developments in that area. Politically the leadership of both FCWU/AFCWU and GWU were, by this stage, close to Fosatu, although they had a more open approach to the question of alliances with other organisations. In FCWU's case this was in part a consequence of its past as a Sactu affiliate.[16]

● The CTMWA, based entirely amongst municipal workers in the Western Cape, had a reputation for poorly-developed shop steward structures, and of being unable to take militant action. Some in its leadership were sympathetic to UDF while others had roots in the Unity Movement tradition.

● NUM and Ccawusa had both emerged from the UTP/Cusa tradition, although Ccawusa had never been a Cusa affiliate. In its short existence, NUM had emerged as the largest union in the country, with developed shaft steward structures. Ccawusa, with a longer history, had become the major union of commercial workers, with strong support especially in the Transvaal. Politically the leadership of both unions contained both black consciousness and UDF-oriented individuals. Within NUM the latter position was dominant, while in Ccawusa the line-up was more finely balanced.

● The UDF-affiliated unions, such as Saawu, Gawu, Macwusa/Gwusa, Sarhwu, and a cluster of tiny unions making up the National Federation of Workers (NFW), were generally small and poorly organised at shop-floor level. Saawu was an obvious exception, with membership in all corners of the country, but particularly in East London. Its membership was, however, not well consolidated. In addition Saawu was a divided union, with its 'Njikelana' faction participating in the launch of Cosatu, and its Natal-based 'Kikine' faction abstaining. Politically the UDF grouping was strongly linked to the growing mass movement, and hence it drew on a working-class sympathy and enthusiasm in excess of its organised factories. It was also internally divided between its more pragmatic wing, fully committed to a new federation, and a group sceptical of the politics and credentials of its future partners in the federation.

Preparing to launch

After the Ipelegeng summit it was clear who was going to participate in the new federation. The feasibility committee, expanded to include the UDF unions, but without Cusa delegates, continued meeting. It discussed credentials and practical arrangements for the launching congress. Tensions still remained, particularly between the older feasibility committee members and the UDF unions. Major issues were left unresolved, to be finalised within the structures of the new federation.

The original target of launching in October could not be met. Some unions wanted the date postponed to the following year but a majority, growing impatient and sensing the political urgency, insisted that 1985 be the year of unity. Eventually the last weekend of November 1985 was chosen to launch the new federation. The venue was to be the University of Natal in Durban, with Fosatu in charge of practical arrangements.

Meanwhile Cusa and Azactu, claiming that they had been kicked out of the unity talks, met on 2 November. While Azactu saw this as the first step towards a rival federation, Cusa's Camay dismissed conjecture that the talks foreshadowed the establishment of formal links. The talks, he said, were aimed at nothing more than 'the development of working relationships.'[17]

During the final feasibility committee meetings delegates felt that a tentative name for the new federation was needed. Proposals included, Sactu, Saftu, Fotusa and Cosatu – all based on some combination of the words 'federation' or 'congress' of South African trade unions. Most delegates did not feel strongly about any particular name. Some argued that 'Cosatu' had a nice ring to it, and would go well in songs and slogans. 'Federation' was a more accurate description of the new organi-sation. 'Congress', on the other hand, reflected an association with the 'Congress' tradition of the ANC. Eventually Mandla Gxanyana, a dele-gate from FCWU, stood up and said that as long as the word 'Congress' was included in the name, he was happy. Most delegates agreed with the sentiment. Cosatu was about to be born.

'The fact that it took so long to unite,' said Mufamadi after the launch, 'can be attributed to differences of opinions and differences in our assessments of many events or developments... differences that can be ironed out through discussions and comradely persuasion.' Similar views were expressed by Moses Mayekiso some years after the launch:

> It was political differences that had stood in the way of worker unity. While the debates were not always very easy, at least it was a start and there were debates. Cosatu is alive today because we aired all our suspicions then. It was worth it because most of our suspicions were over nothing.[18]

Notes

1. Notes on unity talks, in author's possession.
2. Notes on Port Elizabeth summit, in author's possession.
3. Notes on Port Elizabeth summit, in author's possession.
4. Friedman, *Building Tomorrow Today*, 305.

5. *Phambili Basebenzi*, GWU newsletter, December 1982, reproduced in *South African Labour Bulletin*, 8(4), February 1983.
6. Fosatu, 'Unity Briefing, unpublished Fosatu internal document, 5 March 1984.
7. See, for example, 'Worker in the Community', paper presented at the University of Witwatersrand by a panel of shop stewards from Fosatu's Springs local in 1983; and unpublished notes from Fosatu policy workshops held in 1984.
8. See the report of the Labour Monitoring Group on the November 1984 stayaway, *South African Labour Bulletin*, 10(6), May 1985.
9. Letter dated 12 December 1984, Fosatu archives, file C6.12, Cullen Library, University of Witwatersrand.
10. Author interview with John Nkadimeng, Johannesburg, 17 October 1990.
11. Author interview with Joe Foster, Cape Town, 3 August 1990.
12. Author interview with Alec Erwin, Johannesburg, 24 January 1991.
13. Ingrid Obery, 'Long Road to Unity', *Work In Progress*, 37, June 1985.
14. Author interview with Mike Roussos, Johannesburg, 23 August 1990.
15. 'Why are we going into the new federation?', Inter-union project document, 1985.
16. Devandiren Pillay, 'Trade Unions and Alliance Politics in Cape Town, 1979-85', unpublished D.Phil thesis, Department of Sociology, Essex University, September 1989.
17. *Weekly Mail*, 29.11.85.
18. Lacom, *Comrade Moss*, Johannesburg, 1989, 98.

3

The launch of Cosatu

A giant has risen

O N the last weekend in November 1985 worker delegates gathered
at the sports hall of the University of Natal. Durban was typically
hot and humid as 760 delegates from 33 unions, representing
over 460 000 organised workers, moved into the hall. Many workers
were singing. Behind the platform hung a banner proclaiming 'Workers
of the World Unite!', and an enormous panelled painting produced by
Fosatu's Port Elizabeth local stood to one side.

Cyril Ramaphosa, general secretary of NUM, had been chosen earlier as convenor of the launching congress, and he shared the platform
with two recording secretaries. In the foyer latecomers registered and
were given congress documentation. Each delegate was also handed a
cheap portable radio and headphones, used to allow simultaneous trans-
lation into four languages – Zulu, Sotho, English and Afrikaans.

Worker marshals struggled to keep a large contingent from the local
and foreign media at bay. The mood was excited but nervous. Had there
been sufficient preparation for this launch? Tensions had run high at the
final preparatory meetings. Although the constitution had been agreed in
principle and there was general enthusiasm for the name Cosatu, many
key issues remained unresolved. Would Cosatu be politically aligned?
What international policy would be best? Who would be elected as office bearers? But the date for the launch had been set. There was no

going back. At 11 am on 30 November 1985 the launching congress opened with the singing of South Africa's unofficial national anthem, *Nkosi Sikelel' iAfrika*.

In retrospect it seems strange that Cosatu was launched with so many issues unresolved. However, there was a sense of urgency, and a widespread belief that the time was right to launch a new federation. In the townships mass mobilisation and uprisings continued despite the government's declaration of a partial state of emergency only months beforehand. The union movement needed a vehicle, a federation, to respond to these developments effectively.

Most leading unionists felt that differences could be debated endlessly. But the resolution of differences required decisions and their acceptance, and the best way to achieve this was within the democratic structures of a federation. Postponing Cosatu's launch would only delay the resolution of differences. There was also concern that rank-and-file membership was growing impatient over delays in uniting.

Ramaphosa sets the tone

Cyril Ramaphosa opened the congress with a short address. 'The formation of this Congress represents an enormous victory for the working class in this country,' he said. 'Never before have workers been so powerful, so united and so poised to make a mark on society ... We all agree that the struggle of workers on the shop floor cannot be separated from the wider political struggle for liberation in this country.' But what, asked Ramaphosa, would be the political role of the new federation?

> If workers are to lead the struggle for liberation we have to win the confidence of other sectors of society. But if we are to get into alliances with other progressive organisations, it must be on terms that are favourable to us as workers... When we do plunge into political activity, we must make sure that the unions under Cosatu have a strong shop floor base not only to take on the employers but the state as well... In the next few days...we will be putting our heads together not only to make sure we reach Pretoria but also to make a better life for us workers in this country. What we have to make clear is that a giant has risen and will confront all that stand in its way.[1]

Founding unions of Cosatu and delegations at the launch[2]

Affiliate	Delegates Present/ Delegates Entitled	Paid-up membership
Abwu	5 / 5	1 000
BCAWU	4 / 5	748
Ccawusa	70/70	50 345
CDWU	5 / 5	1 600
CSAWU	3 / 5	850
CTMWA	22/22	11 097
CWIU	41/41	20 700
FCWU	46/46	26 455
Gawu	38/38	19 076
GWU	20/20	20 000
Gwusa	5 / 5	2 905
Hawu	5 / 5	1 111
Mawu	57/57	38 789
Macwusa	6 / 6	3 100
Mwusa	18/18	9 249
Naawu	40/40	20 338
Ngwusa/Rawu	10/12	6 037
Nismawu	5 / 7	976
Napawu	5 / 5	2 163
NUTW	43/43	23 241
NUM	120/120	100 000
Pwawu	22/24	11 856
Rawu (CT)	8 / 8	3 830
Saawu	45/45	25 032
Sadwa	9 / 9	4 500
Samwu	6 / 6	3 029
Sarhwu	16/16	8 220
Sastawu	9 / 9	4 700
Satawu	5 / 5	1 900
SFAWU	39/39	19 596
Satwu	5 / 5	581
TGWU	22/22	11 000
Ummawosa	6 /16	8 335

Constitution and structures

The first task of the launching congress was to adopt a constitution. This took longer than anticipated as numerous amendments to the agreed draft were proposed, mainly by the UDF-affiliated unions. But the larger unions generally adhered to agreements made in the earlier rounds of unity talks, and only one significant amendment was agreed to: approved by 435 votes to 326, it established the post of assistant general secretary.

Summary of Cosatu Structures

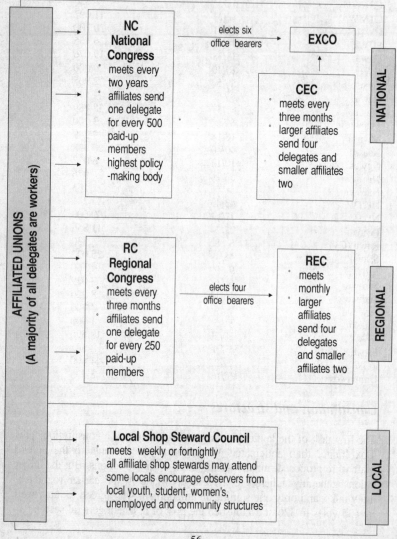

AFFILIATED UNIONS (A majority of all delegates are workers)

NC National Congress
- meets every two years
- affiliates send one delegate for every 500 paid-up members
- highest policy-making body

elects six office bearers →

EXCO

CEC
- meets every three months
- larger affiliates send four delegates and smaller affiliates two

NATIONAL

RC Regional Congress
- meets every three months
- affiliates send one delegate for every 250 paid-up members

elects four office bearers →

REC
- meets monthly
- larger affiliates send four delegates and smaller affiliates two

REGIONAL

Local Shop Steward Council
- meets weekly or fortnightly
- all affiliate shop stewards may attend
- some locals encourage observers from local youth, student, women's, unemployed and community structures

LOCAL

Even this move caused some resentment. A minority of delegates, deeply suspicious of the UDF-affiliated unions, felt that it was wrong to change what had been agreed upon previously. They believed that the accommodation being urged by the majority amounted to horse-trading and the creation of positions for individuals. The majority argued that the issue was not one of principle, that an assistant general secretary might indeed be needed to assist with the workload, and that it was important to be accommodating rather than exclusive at the founding conference. The heated tone of this debate revealed the tensions and unresolved issues which unions were bringing to the congress.

After lengthy debates a constitution was eventually agreed upon. This determined the basic structures of the federation. Cosatu would be a disciplined and active federation with structures at national, regional and local levels (see diagram).

The central theme of the constitution was that all structures would contain a majority of worker delegates. This principle was aimed at preventing union officials from dominating Cosatu structures. In addition, large worker-controlled meetings and congresses were seen as central to ensuring mass participation in decision making.[*]

At the national level there would be a national congress (NC) every two years with affiliated unions represented by one delegate for every 500 paid-up members. The NC would be the highest decision-making body. Between congresses a central executive committee (CEC) would meet every three months. It would be made up of four delegates from each of the larger affiliates and two from each of the smaller affiliates. In addition an executive committee (Exco), made up of the six elected national office bearers plus four additional members elected by the CEC, would meet monthly.

Regionally, there would be a congress every four months made up of one delegate for every 250 paid-up members which an affiliate had in

* The terminology of South African trade unions differs from that of many other union movements internationally. The key distinction in South Africa is between 'workers' and 'officials'. Cosatu has 'office bearers' elected on a regular basis at national, regional and local levels. They hold standard positions such as chairperson/president, vice-chairperson, treasurer and secretary. The only positions which can be occupied by 'officials' – ie full-time employees – are those of the national and regional secretaries. All Cosatu affiliates follow this 'worker/official' distinction to a greater or lesser degree, in an attempt to ensure that workers rather than full-time functionaries control their own organisations; and that elected leadership remains rooted on the shopfloor and in touch with its base. It is also an attempt to limit the tendency towards bureaucratisation of unions. In practice, the distinction does not always work, a question discussed elsewhere in this book.

that region. A regional executive committee (REC) would meet monthly. The launching congress determined that ten regions should be established, although this was later changed to nine.[*]

At local level, structures would be established to unite workers from a particular town or township. These Cosatu locals would be open to all shop stewards living or working in the area. Locals were the basic unit of organisation, aiming to advance Cosatu's interests at grassroots level.

These structures have, with one important exception, remained largely unchanged since the formation of Cosatu. However, the second national congress held in 1987 agreed to restructure the national executive committee (Exco), which now consists of Cosatu's elected office bearers plus two delegates from each affiliate. This had been the original intention during the unity talks, but the large number of affiliates, and their vastly differing sizes, made it impractical. It was only possible to implement this amendment once the programme of mergers was underway.

Policies adopted at the launch

The extended time spent in debating the constitution meant that many resolutions adopted at the launch were not adequately discussed. The congress called for one union to be established in each industry within six months. Delegates also voted for the launch of an education programme and a newspaper.

Another resolution examined exploitation and discrimination against women. Most women could only find employment in 'a limited range of occupations' and had to do 'boring and repetitive work with low and often unequal pay.' They experienced 'sexual harassment' and often lost their jobs when falling pregnant. Cosatu should take up these problems, the congress decided. Progress in implementing the resolution should be monitored by a special 'worker-controlled sub-committee' of Cosatu's education department.

Resolutions called for the lifting of the state of emergency, withdrawal of troops from the townships, release of political prisoners and unbanning of all restricted individuals and organisations. Delegates also agreed, in defiance of the law, that all forms of international pressure,

---

* The nine Cosatu regions are: Southern Natal, Northern Natal, Eastern Cape, Western Cape, OFS/Northern Cape, Western Transvaal, Northern Transvaal, Highveld and Witwatersrand. Some of these are inaccurately named since Highveld includes the Lowveld and the entire Eastern Transvaal; Western Transvaal centres on the Vaal Triangle and the Northern OFS; Western Cape includes the Southern Cape and Namaqualand; and Eastern Cape includes the Border area and Transkei/Ciskei.

'including disinvestment or the threat of disinvestment', were essential and should be supported.

Resolutions demanded the right to strike and picket, and called for the CEC to determine a national minimum living wage. The congress condemned the bantustan system and the 'super-exploitation occurring in these areas,' and delegates declared their determination 'to organise in plants based within the bantustans.' Congress resolved that the migrant labour system, 'including pass laws and influx control', should also be scrapped. Workers had a right to live in 'proper housing' with their families and 'near their place of work.'

The congress decided that the official colours of Cosatu would be red, black and yellow. Delegates also debated Cosatu's official logo. A number of designs had been solicited beforehand and these were on display. Two designs were popular – one depicting a red star rising over a map of Africa, and another depicting three workers marching alongside an industrial-type wheel. Although there were objections that the three workers were all male, the design proved to be the popular choice when it was amended to include a woman worker with a baby strapped to her back.

A number of resolutions, including the key one on political policy, were referred to the first meeting of the CEC. This left only the difficult issue of elections. Cosatu's leadership would have to face enormous tasks. The organisation had been launched but still had to be built. A leadership capable of weaving together the various strands of the union movement which had come together to form Cosatu was needed. To do this they would have to enjoy overwhelming support. Any hint of acrimony would limit their ability to perform their tasks adequately. For these reasons the elections were extensively caucused outside the congress hall. Union delegations huddled together to discuss prospective leaders, and emissaries shuttled from one caucus to another trying to achieve consensus.

After much discussion between the unions Elijah Barayi was elected president, Chris Dlamini vice-president and Makhulu Ledwaba second vice-president. Maxwell Xulu was chosen as treasurer, while Jay Naidoo and Sydney Mufamadi were elected general secretary and assistant general secretary respectively. All except Ledwaba who stood against Robert Gqweta of Saawu, receiving 488 votes to Gqweta's 261, were elected unopposed. All were men.

'You must know that a lion has been born,' Barayi told delegates after his election.

To the South African government I say your time is over... We do not apologise for being black. We are proud of it. As from today Mandela and all political prisoners should be released. PW Botha, you have failed in your duties so release Mandela.

In his speech Dlamini emphasised the need for all unions to work together. From now onwards, he stressed, there should be no talk of UDF unions or Fosatu unions. 'We are all just unions.'

Profiles of office bearers

What sort of people were those elected to lead Cosatu? All except Barayi were relatively young. They combined, nevertheless, a wealth of union and political experience.

Elijah Barayi was the 55 year-old vice-president of NUM and a personnel assistant at Blyvooruitzicht mine. Born in 1930 in the Eastern Cape town of Cradock, he was the youngest of ten children. His father, a municipal worker, and his mother, a domestic, encouraged his education. Barayi completed his matric at the Healdtown Institution in 1949, but his family was unable to pay for him to continue his studies at Fort Hare University. In 1951 he obtained his first job as a clerk in the Department of Native Affairs at Cradock.

The post-war period was one of enormous growth and revival for the ANC, particularly in the Eastern Cape. In 1952 Barayi joined it, under the influence of the Rev Calata, a former ANC secretary general. 'He taught me politics,' recalls Barayi. It was the time of the Defiance Campaign and Barayi joined in with enthusiasm. He remembers a group of volunteers marching without papers to the local police station, in defiance of curfew regulations barring Africans from being on the streets at night. 'We were not prepared to carry documents in the land of our forefathers.' Barayi and the others were arrested, refused to pay any fines, and served one month in prison. 'I was delighted to go to jail,' recalls Barayi, and on his release he took part in other acts of defiance.

In 1960 the ANC was banned and Barayi was one of thousands arrested under state of emergency provisions. He was held for five months and on his release the police continued to harass him. He decided to leave the Eastern Cape, and sought shelter with his brother who worked on a gold mine in Brakpan, on the East Rand. His plans to cross the border into Lesotho and join Umkhonto we Sizwe failed to materialise after his contact was arrested.

In December 1960 Barayi obtained employment as a time clerk at a gold mine in Brakpan. He remained there until 1973 when he found a job at Blyvooruitzicht gold mine near the Western Transvaal town of Carletonville. At the time Rand Mines was trying to introduce communication channels for the workforce, and Barayi was elected to chair the mine's liaison committee. Barayi recalls that he 'tried to raise political issues such as racial discrimination and underpayment,' and when his term of office expired management refused to allow him to stand for election again.

In 1981 he met Cyril Ramaphosa and became one of the first miners to join NUM. 'By then I was not a card-carrying member of the ANC,' he recalls, 'but I remained a very big supporter.' He was elected as an NUM shaft steward at Blyvooruitzicht and the following year was elected NUM vice-president, the position he held at the time of Cosatu's launch. In this capacity Barayi played an active part in building the union and redefining its relationship within Cusa.[3]

Chris Dlamini was the former president of Fosatu. Born in 1944, he grew up in the townships of Benoni and Springs on the East Rand although he completed his last three years of formal education in Natal. His studies were cut short when he was expelled from school in 1963, but his Standard Eight certificate helped him obtain his first job in 1964 as a store 'boy' at Sanbra Engineering. In 1973, while working at Denham Brass, again as a store 'boy', he joined Calvin Nkabinde's Engineering and Allied Workers Union. The union 'didn't do much,' he recalls. But it gave Dlamini his first taste of unionism. That year the workers downed tools because of unhappiness over their Christmas bonus. They were pleasantly surprised when management responded by giving them each an extra R3.

The following year Dlamini went to work at Rank Xerox, this time as a store 'man' – 'perhaps because it was an American company.' He sat on the company's liaison committee but found it 'useless' and no substitute for a union.

Dlamini's first serious union involvement began in 1977 when he went to work at the Springs plant of Kellogg, a US multinational food company. Kelloggs' workers had started joining SFAWU and Dlamini helped organise the factory. In 1979 he became a shop steward after the company agreed to sign a preliminary recognition agreement – one of the first in the entire country. But many workers were not happy with the union's leadership, and Dlamini was part of a membership coup which ousted general secretary 'Skakes' Sikhakhane and took the union into the newly-launched Fosatu. In 1979 Dlamini was elected president of SFAWU, and in 1982 was voted in as Fosatu president. To help him fulfil his duties the union negotiated for him to become a full-time shop steward from 1984.

At the time of his election as Cosatu vice-president Dlamini was well known for his union work, his community involvement and his political sympathies for the ANC. Unions in the food sector were alone in having made real progress, even before Cosatu's launch, towards merging into one super-union. Kellogg workers were known as innovators. They pioneered the sleep-in strike and, later, the 'work-in' – the continuation of production with management locked out. Their worker choir – the K-Team – was one of the first of its type. Kelloggs workers, and Dlamini in particular, played a major role in developing and encouraging the formation of local structures within Fosatu.*

Dlamini was one of the unionists who argued for the linking of union struggles with those of students, youth and the community as a whole, and was active in propelling Fosatu towards greater community and political involvement. In 1984 he helped launch the East Rand People's Organisation (Erapo), a community-based political formation, and was involved in organising the two-day Transvaal stayaway of November 1984. The success of this action led to his arrest on charges of 'economic sabotage'.

Politically, Dlamini regarded himself as an ANC follower since the late 1950s when he attended ANC classes in the township. During the 1960s and early 1970s his sympathies were not translated into action, but the 1976 uprisings had a profound effect on him when he saw workers and the community as a whole doing little to assist the students in their struggle against Bantu Education. In 1977 he joined the Springs branch of Azapo, a black consciousness political organisation. Within two years he had broken with Azapo 'because it did nothing over busfare hikes,' and moved towards a closer alignment with the non-racial Congress tradition. During the 1980s – he will not reveal exactly when – Dlamini joined the underground SACP.[4]

Makhulu Ledwaba, at age 28, was a shop steward at Metro Cash & Carry and had been national president of Ccawusa for little more than a year. Born in 1957 in Zebedelia in the Northern Transvaal, the second eldest of six children, his father was a railway worker while his mother worked at home. He was brought up in Alexandra township but forced removals soon saw his family resettled in Diepkloof, Soweto. A Standard Eight pupil at Madibane High School when the 1976 uprisings began in Soweto, he was involved 'not as a leader but at the middle level.' This experience influenced him deeply. It was also his last year at school as he had to find a job to help support the family.

For a few years he worked making candles as part of a self-help co-operative, helping organise for the Soweto Civic Association in his spare time. In 1981 he obtained a job as a filing clerk at Metro, a large chain store. Racism was rife within the company. Within a year he was

---

* Contrary to widespread belief, the development of local structures began in Natal, even before Fosatu's launch. The Tuacc unions – NUTW, Mawu and CWIU in particular – established locals in both Pietermaritzburg and Pinetown as early as 1977.

involved in a 'skirmish' when he assaulted a white worker who had been racially abusive, and was lucky to avoid dismissal. His father, a member of Sarhwu in the 1950s, advised him to find a workers' organisation. But, Ledwaba recalls, he did not understand what his father was talking about. Instead he approached the civic for help. Civic leader Dr Ntatho Motlana referred him to Ccawusa.

Ledwaba remembers that the union taught him that 'only a collective can have power and the ability to eliminate the power imbalance.' He took reading material from the union office and 109 joining forms, one for each of the African employees at Metro head office. Within a day he had recruited 107. Union officials suggested that it was imperative to organise not only the company's head office but also its 148 outlets countrywide. Every weekend Ledwaba and another worker would travel by train to all corners of the country. Within three months they had helped organise most of the Metro operations.

By early 1983 Ledwaba was vice-chair of Ccawusa's Johannesburg branch, and in July 1984 was elected national president. His meteoric rise was in part due to his energy and charisma. But this also meant he was less experienced than most of Cosatu's other national leaders.

Ledwaba's political outlook differed from the other office bearers. He was not a member of any organisation but strongly sympathised with the black consciousness movement and the PAC. However, his perspectives began changing in the second half of 1985 and shifted significantly during 1986 and 1987. The behaviour of many of the Cusa and Azactu unionists at the Ipelegeng unity talks upset him, and he also began to realise that 'many white comrades were as committed as us to the struggle.'[5]

Maxwell Sibuso Xulu, born in 1948 into a working-class family in Pinetown's Clermont township, was elected Cosatu's national treasurer. Xulu left school on completion of his Standard Eight and in the early 1960s began working at one of the giant Frame group textile factories in the area. He recalls earning R3,95 per week as the operator of a spinning machine. In 1970 Smith Industries in Pinetown employed him as a labourer.

Soon after his arrival workers downed tools for two hours, in one of the rare incidents of industrial action during the 1970-71 period. 'When the MD arrived people were scared,' he recalls. 'However we managed to get a wage increase. All the neighbouring factories rejoiced at what we had done.' In 1973 Xulu's factory joined in the strike wave – 'the Natal fever' – sweeping the region. 'A couple of us were sitting in the canteen and decided we simply would not return to work.' Other workers joined in. 'We knew we wanted more money but we didn't know what we were doing.' After the strike, management, like many employers, in-troduced a liaison committee and made Xulu head of it.

In early 1974 a friend told him about the unions being formed in Durban. 'He made a lot of promises. It sounded like an exaggeration to me.' Nevertheless Xulu attended a number of meetings at Bolton Hall but was not active despite his growing disillusionment with the toothless liaison committee. In early 1976 he met Mawu unionist Alpheus Mtheth-wa and discussed unionisation of the factory. Soon after this the government cracked down on the union movement and Mthethwa was one of many unionists banned for five years. 'The clampdown scared us,' recalls Xulu. However by 1977 he was again meeting with Mawu officials and he finally agreed to recruit workers into the union.

This organising drive faced a major setback in 1979 when manage-ment dismissed half the workers in every department and replaced them with female Indian workers. It took a year to organise these new workers into the union, and in 1982 the company finally agreed to recognise the union.

In the meantime Xulu was gaining prominence within Mawu. In 1978 he was elected to both its branch and national executives. By 1981 he was chairperson of Mawu's increasingly powerful Natal branch and also active within Fosatu. He soon became Mawu's vice-president and in 1984 was elected union president, the position he held at the time of Cosatu's launch.

Xulu was not active in party politics. As a child he remembers Chief Luthuli holding an ANC meeting in his township, where his aunt was secretary of the local branch. 'But politics was not for children in those days.' In the early 1970s he was sympathetic to Inkatha's revival – 'the uniform reminded me of the early days when our parents were in the ANC' – but he never became active. The murder of Ngoye university students by an Inkatha-linked impi changed his views dramatically, espe-cially after a younger cousin gave him an eye-witness account of this incident.

Xulu's political thinking developed largely through the union move-ment. He believes 'in socialism and the emancipation of the working people. Some people call me a workerist. I believe that if we change the colour of the government but keep the same policies then there will be no difference for ordinary people.'[6]

Jay Naidoo, the youngest of seven children, was born in Greenwood Park, Durban in 1954. His father was a court interpreter and his mother a housewife. In 1959 the family was forced to move when the Group Areas Act forced Indian families out of the area.

His political awareness started at an early age. 'I was always very resentful of anything white,' he recalls. His older siblings were involved with the black consciousness movement and would bring home their African friends. Naidoo recalls being taken to hear Steve Biko and other black consciousness leaders speak while still at school. 'I was very impressed by their militancy and fearlessness.'

After matriculating in 1972 Naidoo spent some time travelling and doing odd jobs before registering as a science student at the University of Durban-Westville in 1975, where he became involved in student politics. In the wake of the 1976 student uprisings he left campus and 'spent a lot of time just reading,' including works by Lenin, Mao Zedong and, he confesses, Stalin. He returned to university in 1977 and helped form a branch of the South African Students Organisation (Saso). By that time Saso was moving from a strictly black consciousness perspective to 'a more class-based analysis.' Saso activists decided to 'mobilise the masses' and Naidoo worked in the Malakazi squatter camp. In 1977 he again left university.

The Saso experience was crucial for many students, including Naidoo. At Malakazi students simply deserted the project at examination time and then left on vacation. 'I realised that students could never be a vanguard in the struggle.' Naidoo's reading of Lenin's *What is to be Done?* convinced him that it was not good enough to demonstrate. 'By the time you were ready to work seriously the police already knew you and arrested you. I began to accept that the crunch point was to organise the working class.'

After a short spell as a teacher Naidoo approached Fosatu's regional office in Durban in 1979 and offered his services. He was asked to assist in reviving the Sweet Workers Union by organising Indian workers at Beacon Sweets. The attempt failed. A 'very harsh management' victimised workers who even spoke to him. 'We should have organised Indian and African workers together. It was clear I needed more experience so I got a job as a shift worker at SA Fabrics in Clairwood.' He joined the NUTW and helped another union member, 'Prof' Sineke, to organise the factory. After six months Naidoo left the factory, exhausted by his brief encounter with shift work.

He was then sent to work in Pietermaritzburg and focused on winning control of the conservative Leather Workers Union. In 1981 a clash occurred within Fosatu's SFAWU following an attempt by Inkatha supporters (Willie Manthe and Norman Middleton) to take control of the union. The issue threatened to split Fosatu in the Natal region. A regional congress eventually ruled that Manthe had been wrong in sending reports to KwaZulu officials in Ulundi, and supported his expulsion.

Manthe and Middleton then formed a breakaway union. Naidoo was asked to rescue the situation and he began working for SFAWU. In 1982, after having re-organised most of the union's Pietermaritzburg factories, he began organising in the Durban area. Membership grew rapidly. Later that year SFAWU's national executive appointed Naidoo general secretary of the union. He soon proved to be more aligned to the Congress tradition than most Fosatu leaders, and exercised little influence outside SFAWU structures. Naidoo remained general secretary of the union until Cosatu's launch in 1985.[7]

Sydney Mufamadi was the youngest of the new Cosatu team. Born in Alexandra township in 1959, he grew up and went to school in Venda in the far Northern Transvaal. There he became active in the Zoutpansberg Students Organisation. The full impact of the 1976 Soweto uprising only reached the remote rural areas of the Northern Transvaal during 1977. In that year he was expelled from school with only a Standard Eight certificate.

He was already, he now acknowledges, a member of the ANC underground. Despite this he became a founder member of Azapo in 1978, and moved to Johannesburg soon after where he found work first as a shelf packer at OK Bazaars, then as an unqualified teacher before becoming a messenger for a firm of attorneys. He joined the General and Allied Workers Union while working for the legal firm, and in 1981 Gawu asked him to leave his job and assist the union. He did this, working as an irregularly-paid 'volunteer' organiser.

At Gawu's 1982 conference Mufamadi was elected general secretary. In that capacity he participated in the launch of the United Democratic Front in 1983 and was elected to its Transvaal regional executive as publicity secretary. At the time of Cosatu's launch Mufamadi was still Gawu's general secretary and a leading figure in the UDF bloc of unions. He was also a member of the SACP, having joined in the early 1980s. His ANC and SACP membership were unknown to delegates at the launching congress – not surprisingly since both organisations were illegal – although his sympathies were apparent to many.[8]

'Let us go with it to freedom'

The second day of the congress included a worker rally at Kings Park stadium in Durban. Attendance was disappointing, with only 10 000 workers gathering for the event. Insufficient work had gone into the planning for the rally. But the crowd was enthusiastic as the newly-elected office bearers were introduced and spoke. Barayi's speech stood out. Speaking in Xhosa, and with the wit and sharp tongue for which he would become well-known in worker circles, Barayi launched an attack on all homeland leaders, including KwaZulu's Buthelezi. Labelling them 'puppets', he called for the release of the people's 'real leader', Nelson Mandela.

Barayi also called on the government to scrap the pass laws and warned that unless they did so within six months Cosatu would call on the people to burn their passes. His language was hard hitting and well received by the crowd. But unfortunately his comments did not reflect issues agreed upon at the launching congress, although his militant tone probably reflected the spirit of the launch.

The launching congress was an enormous success. The new structures provided a framework within which differences could be aired and policies developed. Cosatu was launched with an unambiguous political stamp. Although the details remained to be finalised it was clear that the federation intended to adopt a militant political profile. Most importantly, hundreds of worker delegates were jubilant about the launch. It gave them hope. It was their achievement. This enthusiasm was infectious and, in the weeks which followed, these delegates reported back to workers throughout the country.

The songs sung at the congress were soon heard wherever workers gathered. One was particularly memorable. Composed by Ccawusa members it assumed, for a time, the status of the 'official' Cosatu song. Based on a church tune, it had an unusual tempo, a haunting melody, and was accompanied by a distinctive dance at the end of each refrain: *iCosatu sonyuka nayo/masingen' enkululekweni* ran the refrain – 'Cosatu is rising up/let us go with it to freedom.'

Notes

1. Ramaphosa's speech is reproduced in full in *South African Labour Bulletin*, 11(3), January 1986.
2. Minutes of launching congress of the Congress of South African Trade Unions, Durban, 29 November-1 December 1985, annexure 'C'.
3. Author interview with Elijah Barayi, Johannesburg, 17 April 1991.
4. Author interview with Chris Dlamini, Johannesburg, 9 January 1991.
5. Author interview with Makhulu Ledwaba, Johannesburg, 9 January 1991.
6. Author interview with Maxwell Xulu, Johannesburg, 2 March 1991.
7. Author interview with Jay Naidoo, Johannesburg, 24 October 1990.
8. Author interview with Sydney Mufamadi, Johannesburg, October 1990.

Part Two

1986 – The
First Year

4

Responses to Cosatu

'A big dog
with small teeth'

*I*NKATHA took particular exception to the comments by newly-elected president Barayi at the Kings Park rally. Gatsha Buthelezi – chief minister of Kwazulu and Inkatha president – immediately accused Cosatu of being an 'ANC front' and having 'declared war' on Inkatha. The more temperate Oscar Dhlomo, secretary general of Inkatha, commented that 'we feel trade unions have to do with the rights of workers... If any particular trade union abandons this prime responsibility in favour of playing a party political role' then Inkatha reserved its right 'to mobilise the full strength of Inkatha's workers to find alternative means of negotiating.'[1]

The support for foreign pressure and disinvestment shown at Cosatu's inaugural congress did nothing to ease Buthelezi's disquiet. Neither did Barayi's statement that Cosatu would work for the nationalisation of the mines. Buthelezi immediately announced that Inkatha intended mobilising its members into an alternative trade union, 'to counter insults and denigration' from Cosatu. 'We will not stand by...when the African National Congress mission-in-exile and the United Democratic Front move in to usurp the function of those trade unions...'[2]

Inkatha began working to launch its own union body – the United Workers Union of South Africa (Uwusa). On 19 January 1986 management transported a number of workers to a meeting in Empangeni. There, an interim committee consisting of Simon Conco – a businessman and prominent Inkatha member – and a number of individual worker leaders, was established. The committee included Johannes Mthiyane, a former Pwawu president, Fosatu regional chairperson and a supervisor at Zululand Sawmills, and MP Gumede, a senior Pwawu shop steward working at Mondi Board Mills. The meeting launched a serious and well-funded onslaught on Cosatu, particularly in Natal.

Enormous pressure was placed on other shop stewards, particularly those previously from Fosatu affiliates, to join in the anti-Cosatu initiative. A case in point concerned Jeffrey Vilane, a senior Mawu shop steward working at the giant Alusaf plant in Richards Bay. Vilane was a particularly influential worker leader in the area. He was also, importantly, a traditional praise poet of repute, and closely linked to Inkatha. During early 1986 Inkatha supporters repeatedly threatened Vilane and ordered him to resign from Cosatu. He refused. On the evening of 23 April his house and car were set alight. When he ran outside he was shot and wounded in the right arm. Other unionists in the area were similarly threatened. Most remained loyal to Cosatu.

It was not simply Barayi's speech which provoked these attacks. Nor were his utterances solely responsible for the decision to launch Uwusa. Hostility between Inkatha and the unions, and Fosatu in particular, had been growing over the years, although this was not always public. Tensions had arisen when both Fosatu and Inkatha representatives sat on a committee dealing with the Empangeni bus boycott. Inkatha pressure had also forced Mawu to call off a consumer boycott in Howick aimed at supporting dismissed BTR Sarmcol workers. As early as 1983, in discussions with the United States' union organisation, the AFL-CIO, Buthelezi had indicated that he sought closer ties with the unions, and that the unions should 'establish the possibilities for Inkatha's presence in their decision-making bodies.'[3]

Unions were suspicious of an Inkatha takeover attempt. Buthelezi, on the other hand, was wary of the growth of a mass union movement outside his control or direct influence. From the outset Inkatha intended to oppose the new union federation, and an Inkatha central committee meeting held shortly *before* the launch of Cosatu reserved the right to form Inkatha trade unions.[4]

Nevertheless, Barayi's criticisms of Buthelezi were a serious political error. They gave the impression that Cosatu's major aim was to oppose Buthelezi and the homeland system. His speech ignored the lesson learned by Natal unionists over the years: winning workers in the region to progressive positions was achieved by hard organisational work and not by attacks on Buthelezi. It gave Buthelezi greater opportunities amongst his own constituency to press for the establishment of a rival union. The fierce Inkatha counter-attack should have been anticipated. Instead, as one Cosatu observer has noted, it 'caught the unions in the region flat-footed.'[5] Open conflict between Cosatu and Inkatha was inevitable but the time, the place, and the style of the showdown could have been on terms more favourable to Cosatu. As it transpired, Cosatu's whole Natal region was placed on the defensive within a week of its formation.

Alec Erwin, a prominent Natal unionist, has recalled that workers were very critical of Barayi's speech. They liked his militant tone and his threat to burn passes, but objected to his attack on Buthelezi and his promise 'to bury Botha and Gatsha.' 'There was real anger and Barayi was called to a regional meeting to explain himself,' recalls Erwin. 'The unions had always related to Inkatha very cautiously and were slowly winning the battle.' There had been internal opposition to Inkatha entering the labour arena for some time, and Barayi's comment tilted the balance within Inkatha and 'gave Buthelezi the opening he wanted to launch Uwusa.' Without it 'we would have swept the board more effectively. There wouldn't have been an Uwusa,' is Erwin's strong conclusion. 'The Natal violence was different. That was inevitable.'[6]

Some within Cosatu argued that the uncompromising spirit of Barayi's speech set a militant tone for the federation. Delegates from all around the country returned to their regions with a fighting spirit. It is true that the launch of Cosatu unleashed enormous enthusiasm, but on balance Barayi's attack on Buthelezi was damaging.

Employers and the state respond

The government was equally hostile to the formation of Cosatu. Within days of the launch an SABC radio commentary, which usually reflected government thinking, argued that Cosatu

> with its declared aim of standing in for the ANC is, under the guise of a trade union movement, intent on furthering the aims of a banned organisation, namely to make the country ungovernable. The question is whether it should be allowed to do so.[7]

The question was rhetorical. With Buthelezi's 'ANC front' label and the existence of a state of emergency, it amounted to an invitation to the state and its allies to attack Cosatu.

Naidoo denied these allegations, stating that Cosatu was a workers' front, not a surrogate for the then-banned ANC:

> Our policy directions reflect the aspirations of our members and are taken in democratic structures where the majority are shop stewards from the factory floor. But our commitment to bury apartheid...has given us much in common with many organisations opposed to apartheid. Undoubtedly the most important of these is the ANC...[8]

Publicly, employer responses were more muted than those of Inkatha and the government. The bigger capitalists felt sufficiently confident of their own strength. Anglo American's Gavin Relly said he was not daunted by Cosatu. Relly, recently back from a much-publicised meeting with the ANC, was clearly untroubled by Cosatu's strong stand in favour of socialism and nationalisation. 'The trade union movement will realise,' he said patronisingly, 'if it hasn't already, that free enterprise is its best guarantor of independence and survival.'[9] However, on the ground, in large companies as well as small, employer responses were not as benign. Workers were confronted over their unions' relationship to Cosatu, and union recognition was in many cases linked to disaffiliation from Cosatu. In Natal particularly, but also in parts of the Transvaal, employers made their preference for an Inkatha-linked federation clear.

At one Mawu-organised plant workers were told they would not be retrenched if they left Mawu and joined Uwusa.[10] Similar reports were heard in union offices throughout the country. Cosatu's statements had 'put the fear of God into employers,' said one prominent industrialist. This had caused, he conceded, 'a bad reaction' from both employers and Inkatha.[11]

Other employers, while hostile to Cosatu, were scared of the prospects of a disruptive inter-union war erupting on the shop floor. Labour observers such as Professor Nic Wiehahn, architect of the new labour dispensation, noted that 'trade unions and politics are moving closer but there is no cause for alarm. We must just be able to handle it.' Cosatu, said Wiehahn, was 'a big dog with small teeth.'[12]

Naidoo meets the ANC

Not surprisingly, the launch of Cosatu was welcomed by the democratic movement. 'Through Cosatu workers will take their rightful place in the liberation movement to free our people from oppression and exploitation,' the UDF declared in a widely-distributed pamphlet. 'Let us join Cosatu in our millions.' Sactu also welcomed the launch saying it did not 'see any antagonism between Sactu and the new federation,' adding that

'A strong trade union movement will satisfy demands for higher wages, better working conditions, and ultimately achieving complete emancipation.'[13]

The ANC, broadcasting on Radio Freedom, called on Cosatu to become deeply involved in the activities of the UDF. It also appealed to Cusa and Azactu to join forces with Cosatu, 'or face irrelevancy.'[14] In its January 1986 New Year's message the ANC hailed the launch of Cosatu as a 'victory' which the democratic movement must 'defend at all costs,' and called on those democratic trade unions still 'outside the fold of Cosatu' to 'reconsider their positions...'[15]

A visit to Zimbabwe by Jay Naidoo led to further attacks on Cosatu. Naidoo had travelled to Harare immediately after the launching congress to speak at a World Council of Churches conference. This decision was approved by Cosatu's newly-elected office bearers, and aimed at obtaining international publicity for the new federation. ANC and Sactu representatives at the conference approached Naidoo for informal talks and welcomed the formation of Cosatu. Asked later by a Harare journalist if he had met the ANC delegates at the conference, Naidoo replied in the affirmative. This was seized upon by Inkatha and the state as evidence that Cosatu was an ANC front. It was a strange conclusion. In the preceding months many delegations had visited the ANC in Lusaka, beginning with leading businessmen Gavin Relly, Tony Bloom and others. Subsequently, a National African Chamber of Commerce (Nafcoc) delegation, which included delegates from the Inkatha-affiliated Inyanda, also met the ANC.

It was not surprising that Cosatu's enemies used the meeting to attack the federation. But the consternation it caused within Cosatu's ranks was greater cause for concern. A number of union leaders were unhappy that they had not been consulted, and first learned about the meeting in the press. Others spoke of 'a disregard for democratic practice' and charged that Naidoo was linking Cosatu with the ANC without any mandate from the federation to do so. Naidoo had issued a press statement on the meeting with the ANC and Sactu 'without discussion within Cosatu.' This was similar, charged the critics, to Barayi's announcement of 'a major campaign against the pass laws at the inaugural mass rally notwithstanding the fact that this had never been discussed at the Congress.' It was hinted that this showed the 'takeover of the trade union movement by populism.'[16]

Others within Cosatu supported the meeting, believing it reflected a necessary alliance with the ANC. Cosatu's leaders were correctly judging the mood of the membership, they argued. It was incorrect to bow down to the ANC-bashing lobby simply because that was legally easier. Cosatu had far more in common with the ANC than most other organisations. It should state its sympathies openly while rejecting allegations that it was an ANC puppet. Both critics and supporters had in common the mistaken belief that the meeting was a pre-arranged one between Naidoo and the ANC. Later, at the first CEC meeting, held in February, Naidoo's explanation of the chance and informal nature of the encounter was accepted. In reality the matter was a storm in a teacup. But at the time it highlighted the narrow consensus upon which Cosatu had been founded.

Cusa, Azactu and Tucsa

Cosatu's formation strongly influenced those unions which had withdrawn from the launch at the Ipelegeng unity talks of July 1985. In the month before the launch of Cosatu, Cusa and Azactu met to discuss a possible merger. Their main objection to joining the new federation involved the principle of non-racialism. Long-standing political differences between the black consciousness and 'charterist' traditions lay behind this. In a further meeting only days before the launch, Cusa and Azactu 'acknowledged' the formation of Cosatu. They also decided on their own programme of action, calling for a national strike if the state of emergency was not lifted by the end of December.[17] The significance of this call lay not in its failure to materialise, but in the fact that it was a joint Cusa and Azactu response. Thrown together by their isolation and shared suspicion of Cosatu's political direction, the two groupings were beginning a process which would result in their amalgamation within a year.

For the conservative Tucsa federation the formation of Cosatu turned the already-growing tide of resignations into a flood. Affiliates were leaving, recorded one set of minutes, on the grounds that the organisation was 'doing "nothing" for its members, and (its) "irrelevance" in the fight against apartheid.'[18] In desperation, Tucsa leaders met Inkatha in early 1986 to discuss co-operation against Cosatu. But Inkatha's leadership was reluctant to be identified too closely with a discredited and skeletal Tucsa.

The launching of Cosatu sparked off a realignment of forces within the labour movement. Its very existence seemed to cause fear, even panic, amongst its opponents. Ordinary workers were generally euphoric over Cosatu's formation, with the launch igniting hidden reserves of anger, organisation and militancy. Across the country there was an upsurge in the number of workers wanting to join the union movement. Invariably they did not look for a particular affiliate but asked for 'Cosatu'.

The power of the whole federation was far greater than the sum of its affiliate parts, but many labour observers were slow to realise this. Andrew Levy and Associates, well-known management consultants, predicted a slackening in strike action during 1986 following the record number of strikes in 1985. Many observers agreed with Levy's assessment. Events were to prove them very wrong.

Notes

1. Quoted in Yunus Carrim, 'Working-Class Politics to the Fore', *Work In Progress*, 40, February 1986, 10.
2. Quoted in *Business Day*, 09.01.86.
3. Mangosuthu G Buthelezi, 'Aide Memoire for discussion with Mr Irving Brown of AFL-CIO', *South African Labour Bulletin*, 9(4), February 1984, 80-81.
4. *Sunday Star*, 08.12.85.
5. Anon, 'Winning Away Inkatha's Base', *Work In Progress*, 45, November/December 1986, 30.
6. Author interview with Alec Erwin, Johannesburg, 24 January 1991.
7. *Business Day*, 06.12.85.
8. Speech delivered to the Canadian Labour Conference, Toronto, April 1986.
9. *Star*, 14.12.85.
10. Pippa Green, 'Northern Natal: meeting Uwusa's challenge', *South African Labour Bulletin*, 12(1), November/December 1986, 84.
11. *Financial Mail*, 04.04.86.
12. *Star*, 26.02.86.
13. 'Interview: South African Congress of Trade Unions', *South African Labour Bulletin*, 11(2), October-December 1985, 43.
14. *Business Day*, 11.12.85.
15. 'New Year Message from the African National Congress', Lusaka, January 1986.
16. Discussion paper from within NUTW, March 1986.
17. *Star*, 06.11.85; 27.11.85.
18. Minutes of a meeting of the Tucsa NEC held on 3-4 July 1986.

5

A growing tide of struggle

Strike while the
iron is hot

A MASSIVE strike wave accompanied Cosatu's birth, with one
industrial relations consultancy recording 185 000 'man-days' lost
due to industrial action during January 1986 alone. By the end of
March, this had risen to 550 000, more than the 450 000 days lost during
the whole of 1984.[1] Three-quarters of these strikes were ascribed to
Cosatu affiliates.[2]

According to official government calculations, 1985 had seen the
highest number of strikes in at least ten years. By early 1986 it was
apparent that strikes over the next 12 months would exceed even these
record figures.[*]

Cosatu was accused of fanning the political flames. Unless it stopped
its 'tough talk and irrational demands, we're going to have severe problems,' claimed *Finance Week*, an influential business magazine.[3]
Cosatu's very formation inspired workers and gave them confidence in

---

** Even these figures underestimate the scope of industrial action, since they
cover only strikes recorded in the press. In addition, they include industrial
actions in a limited sense, and specifically exclude the mass stayaways of this
period.*

their power, and the strike wave was accompanied by a massive growth in union membership.

The first ten weeks of 1986 saw over 100 000 miners on strike.[4] These actions were often 'political' or linked to events in neighbouring townships. They frequently involved new and more confident tactics, such as sit-ins and go-slows, and involved intense conflict with security forces, including 'homeland' security. And they were largely, but not entirely, over non-wage issues.

Impala Platinum's unhappy New Year

On New Year's Day 1986, 30 000 workers downed tools at four Impala Platinum mines in Bophuthatswana, which together produced over 30% of the world's platinum.[5] The miners' complaints included low wages; enforced overtime on public holidays without extra pay; and management's refusal to provide facilities to NUM. The strikers also demanded that white workers should travel in the same lift-cage as blacks, and that black workers – housed in single-sex hostels – should have access to married quarters in the same way white miners did. Management of these Gencor-owned mines had been notified of the demands well before the strike but had taken no action. 'Our unity started during our room discussions,' explained one worker.

> To communicate with the authorities, each room elected a monitor and each compound elected a senior monitor. The senior monitors formed a liaison committee which took our grievances to management. After days of negotiations between the liaison committee and management, it was clear that the committees were only able to make suggestions on improvements in compound conditions. They had no real base to negotiate on wages.
>
> When we realised that management always promised to look into our demands and when we saw that last year's increases were the lowest in years, we agreed not to work from New Year's Day.[6]

On 6 January, after six days of strike action, Impala dismissed 23 000 strikers. At the time this was the largest-ever mass dismissal of workers in South Africa. 'Employee representatives were not prepared to get down to solid discussions,' claimed Impala's Gary Maude. 'They left us no choice but to dismiss them.'[7]

The company later admitted to 'communication problems.' It had refused to talk to NUM about the strike, claiming that Bophuthatswana 'homeland' labour legislation prevented this. The homeland's Minister of Manpower, Rowan Cronje, was on record saying that labour law in the territory was specifically designed to prevent legal strikes in strategic industries like mining.[8] The law did indeed prohibit South African-based unions from operating in nominally-independent Bophuthatswana. But this had not stopped Impala from recognising and negotiating with Arrie Paulus' whites-only Mine Workers Union (MWU), which was registered in, and operated from, South Africa.[*]

The dismissals were a massive operation. Bophuthatswana police, in riot gear and equipped with teargas, combed the compounds. They searched rooms for weapons and frisked workers leaving the area. Police with dogs and shields marched through the compounds in a show of force. An armoured vehicle, with gunholes in the back, cruised up and down. Miners, carrying their few possessions in tatty suitcases and parcels, were loaded onto hundreds of buses brought in to transport them home. Workers were sombre, but unbowed by the dismissals. 'We were fired,' said one, 'but we know that our demands were genuine.'

'Management does not have sympathy for people,' said another worker after his dismissal. 'They don't listen to what we have to say. They regard us as animals. That is why they can do this.' The alternative to negotiating, according to one manager, was 'to get rid of the whole labour force and replace them. There is... massive unemployment in the country and that encourages us to take this kind of action.'[9]

Cosatu strongly condemned the mass dismissal. 'The Gencor group is clearly hiding behind Bophuthatswana's apartheid laws,' said assistant general secretary Sydney Mufamadi. Cosatu called on its affiliates, especially those with members in Gencor, to give solidarity support to the dismissed miners. NUM's annual congress, held in mid-February, labelled Gencor an enemy company. 'We will launch a national and international campaign against Gencor,' announced NUM general secretary Ramaphosa, 'including possible action to prevent the shipping and movement of Gencor coal abroad.'

The dismissals were even condemned by a leading business weekly, the *Financial Mail*. 'Gencor', it commented in an editorial,

is fast gaining the reputation of being SA's most hardline and implacable industrial relations operator – and for good reason... The dismissals also provide Cosatu with ammunition for its first major campaign.

The rationale behind the 'homelands' policy has always been, according to the National Party government, to allow each ethnic group the right to self-determination and self-management. It was therefore ironic that Cronje, who was neither black, nor Tswana, nor even South African, was Bophutatswana's labour minister, and responsible for drafting the law prohibiting the involvement of 'outsiders'. Cronje was a refugee from majority rule in Zimbabwe and had been a member of Ian Smith's Rhodesian cabinet.

Cosatu's campaign ended up mainly as a war of words. The federation was unable to muster the organisational strength to initiate blacking action,* restrictions on platinum exports, or solidarity strikes in other Gencor firms. This was partly because Cosatu did not yet have a deeply-rooted internal unity. But more importantly, it still had to develop its own structures before any effective campaigns could be launched. Nevertheless, the war of words did increase public and worker awareness about Gencor, and forced unions to plan more carefully before organising Gencor plants. In the longer term it was probably the trigger which forced Gencor to reassess its industrial relations policies, and become more accommodating towards progressive trade unions.

Other mine strikes

Collieries in the Witbank/Middelburg area also saw a rash of strikes in early 1986. Political unrest in the Eastern Transvaal was growing, and many of the strikes had a political flavour. A thousand workers at Anglo American's Bank Colliery downed tools, demanding the release of a colleague arrested for allegedly preventing customers from entering a nearby shop which was, at the time, boycotted by workers. In late February and early March, Rand Mines' Wolwekrans Colliery was hit by three strikes as workers protested against the hostel manager carrying a gun. On 16 February workers in a number of Witbank mining compounds joined in a stayaway with local township residents in protest at the detention of over 800 township residents. Its impact was felt as far afield as Pretoria, where workers at four Pick 'n Pay supermarket outlets organised by Rawu downed tools in protest against Pretoria staff being used to relieve staff shortages in Witbank.[10]

Other mine strikes centered around union recognition and wages. In early February, more than 1 500 workers embarked on a two-day strike at Consolidated Modderfontein. The strike followed the victimisation and dismissal of two NUM shaft stewards. The mine was not a member of the Chamber of Mines, and management – unwilling to allow unionisation of the workforce – responded to the strike by dismissing a further 72 workers. In the Namaqualand region of the Northern Cape, a well-organised 'rolling strike' over paid leave for the Easter weekend took place between 12 and 15 March. Some 1 300 workers at De Beers' Dreyers Pan mine started with a one-day go-slow. When they returned to normal work, another 1 000 miners at Kleinsee continued the action. They were in turn followed by 1 500 workers at Koingnaas mine. Eventually

---

* *'Blacking' is a form of solidarity action whereby union members refuse to deliver supplies to, or accept products from, a strike-hit company.*

management agreed that workers could take paid leave over Easter, but would lose one day's pay at the end of their contracts.

The Namaqualand action highlighted the growing sophistication in the tactics adopted by mineworkers. In areas where NUM was solidly organised, industrial action became more disciplined and imaginative. At Blyvooruitzicht in Carletonville, workers took action over a production bonus introduced to some shafts and not others. Normal strike practice on the mines involved refusal to go underground. But in this strike, workers went underground and then simply sat down and refused to work. At the end of the shift they returned to the surface, to be replaced by workers on the next shift who continued the action.

The underground strike at Blyvooruitzicht lasted two days. On the third day management refused to allow any further workers to go down on shift. In response the 1 200 workers underground at the time resolved not to return to the surface. They would remain underground, they announced, and transform the sit-in strike into a sleep-in. While 7 000 workers were 'locked-out' above ground, their colleagues remained underground without food, emerging only 36 hours later.

'Sit-ins are part and parcel of a new phase in the resistance of mineworkers,' commented NUM's Marcel Golding. While Blyvooruitzicht workers slept underground, 2 000 Mawu members at Haggie-Rand were also engaged – as we shall see – in a sit-in at their plant on the East Rand. The sit-in at Haggie-Rand resulted in victory. Blyvooruitzicht workers were not as lucky, and their industrial action was crushed after much bloodshed. When mine security attempted to arrest 'intimidators', workers responded angrily by stoning them. Mine security and South African police opened fire killing four miners. Another two miners died, allegedly at the hands of striking workers. Fifty-four miners and one NUM organiser were arrested and charged with a variety of offences including murder, public violence, striking and attending unlawful gatherings.

Repression and bloodshed

The mine companies maintain heavily-armed private security forces, and have no hesitation in calling police and army units to assist them. Repression and bloodshed are, as a result, common during mine strikes. The hostel system exacerbates this situation. These vast single-sex complexes, housing thousands of miners crowded in dormitory-style rooms, are structured along barracks or prison lines, and allow for easy surveillance and control of workers by employers.

The mine strikes of early 1986 saw many miners killed. They also showed miners fighting back. At Randfontein Estates a meeting of 250 miners on 19 January was dispersed by security forces, apparently because it was an 'illegal gathering.' Fifteen workers were hospitalised as a result of injuries sustained when the meeting was broken up. The following day violence erupted when police attempted to disperse a larger gathering which management had 'banned'. Approximately ten miners and two white policemen were killed. As a result over 500 workers were dismissed, and 112 workers arrested and charged, some for murder.

On 19 February, two miners were killed during clashes with police at Venterspost mine. This prompted a strike the next day by 10 000 miners. At about the same time, four senior black workers – 'team leaders' – were killed at Vaal Reefs mine, and four others seriously injured when they were attacked by other workers in their rooms. Workers claimed that the team leaders had plotted with management to kill or harm union representatives returning from the NUM congress. Management called this allegation 'nonsense.' When police detained about ten workers, 15 000 miners on three Vaal Reefs shafts went on strike demanding their release. At one stage the strike threatened to involve all 40 000 workers at this giant mine. The strike ended only after NUM recommended that strikers return to work, and the detained workers were brought to court. Six workers were later convicted, three of whom were sentenced to death.

One miner died and 18 were injured in mid-January, when 3 000 striking Foskor and Phalaborwa Mining Corporation (PMC) workers clashed with Lebowa police. The strike revolved around a long-standing dispute over the dismissal of 389 workers who had protested the detention of NUM's general secretary Cyril Ramaphosa by Lebowa authorities. In ongoing conflict, management dismissed another 1 500 workers.

The strike brought the union into direct conflict with 'homeland' structures, as had occurred at Impala. The clashes between workers and police took place in the local township of Namakgale. Like most miners, these workers had direct links with the local township and were not, as is sometimes believed, isolated from the surrounding communities. Indeed, the Foskor strike can be linked to the high level of militancy amongst township-based workers developing throughout the Eastern and Northern Transvaal at the time.

'Siyalala la'

The manufacturing sector was also hard hit by strikes. Mawu's dispute against 70 firms declared in early 1986 was significant. The union wanted employers to agree that negotiations at industry level, should be supplemented by plant-level, in-house agreements. A minimum increase,

Mawu argued, should be negotiated with the employer organisation, Seifsa, at the industrial council. Companies which could afford to pay more should then negotiate an increase over and above the industry minimum. This was a long-standing point of conflict between Mawu and the employers, with Seifsa ensuring that none of its members agreed to supplementary plant-level bargaining. During early 1986 Mawu organised a number of well-planned, legal strikes over the issue.

The question of appropriate bargaining forums affected many industries, and highlighted the extent to which even the bargaining table was a point of disagreement between organised labour and capital. This issue is returned to in a later chapter.

While Seifsa insisted on centralised bargaining only, the Barlow Rand group stood at the other end of the spectrum. Its general policy involved agreement to plant-level bargaining, but refusal of anything more centralised. At Nampak Paper it insisted that wage negotiations for each of its three paper mills take place separately. In February its Bellville paper mill, near Cape Town, saw a lengthy wage strike. While management held a lavish party with 300 guests to celebrate the installation of a new R33-million machine, workers gathered outside the gates to protest. They were dissatisfied with management's wage offer. 'How much money are they spending on this party?' asked a union official. 'But they can't give us 50 cents an hour.' Members of Nampak management were unable to comment. They were 'all at the party,' said the company receptionist.

One of the most significant strategies adopted by workers was the 'siyalala', or sleep-in, strike. SFAWU members at Kellogg on the East Rand had used this as far back as 1982, but 'siyalala' strikes began to spread in 1985. During the Durban bakery strike of July 1985, SFAWU members slept on the factory premises for a week. Later that year the strategy was used by Mawu members at Bosch in Brits, and by Pwawu members in a protracted two-and-a-half week sleep-in at Printpak.

The sleep-in tactic arose in response to a number of factors. Mass dismissals of striking workers were frequent, whether the strikes were legal or not. In addition, striking workers, gathered outside the factory gates, faced police harassment and assaults, and were often accused of intimidation. Finally, factory struggles were becoming longer and more bitter. Control of the premises, of production, and of entry of replacement labour was crucial for both workers and employers.

Workers had, and still have in 1991, no right to picket during strikes. The state of emergency gave the police extensive powers to detain and harass participants at any gatherings, a power which they used freely. While repression forced the unions to develop the sleep-in tactic, they also sought to turn adversity into advantage. The sleep-in strike could build better links between the factory and the community. It could allow for intensive education programmes amongst the membership. And it was a full-time strike and not a nine-to-five one, with all the advantages and disadvantages this entailed.

The Printpak strike received substantial publicity and took place in the month before Cosatu's launch. 'The tactic of sitting-in was consciously decided on,' explained Pwawu's Transvaal branch secretary Sipho Kubheka. 'Workers had learnt from the bakeries strike in Durban and the Brits one. They felt it would give them more control over the situation than an ordinary strike, although it needs more thorough organisation.'[11]

Printpak workers first took control of the changerooms. These were rapidly divided into areas for sleeping, washing and recreation. A group of workers, responsible for publicity, listed their demands on posters made out of old cardboard. Others, working in shifts, patrolled the factory premises and perimeter. Every worker was part of a sub-committee with defined responsibilities. Some dealt with the vital question of food supplies or handled negotiations with management. Others maintained discipline, ensured that no alcohol came onto the premises, and issued passes for entry and exit from the plant. An education committee arranged discussions during the evenings. Workers from neighbouring factories kept a watch for the police and donated food parcels to the strikers. Management found it virtually impossible to bring scab labour onto the premises.

Two lengthy sleep-in strikes proved crucial. They both took place during March 1986. The first involved 2 100 workers at two Haggie-Rand metal plants on the East Rand. For 18 days the workers occupied their factories in support of the demand for both industry-wide and company-level bargaining. Mawu had prepared for the action well in advance. Shop stewards and women workers had visited workers' families and tried to explain the issues to them. The families were invited to join in planning for the sleep-in strike. Priorities were the collection of food and money, and donations were received from metal factories in the area, as well as township residents. By the fourth day of the sleep-in, contributions of R150 per day were arriving.

Workers' families brought them food daily, which was handed over the fence to strikers inside. Significantly, black office workers and security staff also stopped work in support of the union. Two weeks into the strike management dismissed the entire workforce. This hardened the resolve of the strikers, and they refused to leave the premises. Eventually the company reversed its dismissal decision and agreed to negotiate on bargaining forums with Mawu.

The strike held a number of lessons for Mawu. These included the importance of better preparation, particularly with families and township groups; the need for the union to 'keep constant contact with workers' involved in the sleep-in and provide an education programme; the need to 'ensure democratic procedures' with support groups and families who may have 'no trade union background'; and the importance of maintaining 'links between the workers sitting-in and their families at home.' In the Haggie-Rand case, 'weekend visits on a shift basis were arranged.'[12]

Haggie-Rand management did not call in the police during the factory occupation. Workers at Pan-African Shopfitters/GB Engineering in nearby Germiston were not so lucky. Over 200 workers, jointly organised by Pwawu and Mawu, began a sit-in on 6 March as part of their battle against retrenchments. The sleep-in was organised in a similar fashion to the one at Haggie-Rand, and when management obtained an eviction order from the supreme court, the strikers decided to defy it. On 19 March police entered the factory and attacked workers with teargas and sjamboks. Many were injured, some seriously cut, when they were driven through plate glass windows. Those present were then detained by police and subsequently charged with trespass and contempt of court.

Sit-in strikes proliferated and spread throughout the country as the year proceeded.[*] They were an appropriate strike form, particularly under state of emergency conditions. Employers soon began planning counter-measures. They often sought and obtained court orders against workers sitting-in, and police reinforced these with violent evictions.

Scabs were recruited more systematically, often through companies created specifically for this purpose. Scab labour increasingly took on the flavour of vigilante movements or 'professional' scabbing, and was consequently less open to pressure from strikers occupying the premises. In many instances sleep-in and sit-in strikes were regulated after negotiations. Workers undertook to keep away from production areas, and union members sometimes left the premises after working hours in return for management's agreement to allow them daily access to the factory.

Growing membership

Unorganised workers flocked to join Cosatu in the first months after its launch. Many came looking for Cosatu, rather than the appropriate

---

* Some saw parallels between the sleep-in strikes and factory occupation movements in other countries. This is misleading. Factory occupations generally attempted to continue production, but under worker control. By contrast the sleep-ins were primarily a type of strike action, aimed at ensuring a more effective and intense strike, particularly in conditions of state repression.

affiliate. After being told that Cosatu was simply an umbrella body, they would be referred to a union. Mawu claimed that its membership increased by more than 30% during the first six months of 1986. Ccawusa also grew strongly in the same period, and claimed to have gained an additional 25 000 members. Substantial growth also occurred in the transport, chemical, food and paper sectors.

The December 1985 launch assumed 450 000 paid-up members. By March, Cosatu leadership claimed a paid-up membership of 600 000, and in mid-1986 the figure given was 650 000. There were two reasons for this startling growth rate, apart from the influx of unorganised workers enthused by Cosatu's formation.

Firstly, NUM's estimated membership figures at the time of the launch were too low. The miners' union came into Cosatu on the basis of 100 000 paid-up members, based on calculations made in early 1985. It clearly had a higher effective membership, as the strike wave of early 1986 showed. The union was in a phase of very rapid growth, and NUM's February 1986 congress reported a paid-up membership of 227 586.

Secondly, significant numbers of organised workers from other unions and federations crossed over to Cosatu. Many came from Cusa, particularly its food affiliate, FBWU. Almost all the Coca-Cola bottling plants joined Cosatu, and the entire Pretoria branch of FBWU joined FCWU. In Phalaborwa, significant numbers of Sacwu members crossed over to CWIU, while former Fosatu unions in the Eastern Cape grew strongly. Many workers, previously cautious about the political direction of Fosatu and its affiliates, now saw these unions in a more progressive light.

Cosatu's rapid growth came as a surprise to many local and international observers who had expected its political involvement to be a liability. But the bold and high-profile politics which accompanied Cosatu's launch did not detract from the federation's impact.

Apart from Natal, which must be analysed separately, Cosatu's politics attracted membership to its affiliates in almost every sector and region. Intense political involvement did, sometimes, lead to neglect of factory issues, or, more often, to a decline in the standard of union 'service'. But this was neither an inevitable result of Cosatu's political involvements, nor did it occur in all affiliates and regions. Declining standards of service were usually attributable to other factors, and Cosatu's politics generally boosted its membership and status amongst the working classes.

The political context

The political turmoil and mass uprisings which took place both before and after the launch of Cosatu played an important part in shaping Cosatu and influenced its direction during its first six months of existence.[13]

A new phase of resistance to apartheid began in 1984. In September an explosion of mass anger and unrest erupted in the townships of the Vaal Triangle. Residents marched in opposition to rent hikes, and there were physical attacks on community councillors responsible for these increases. Some were killed.

The previous year had seen the launch of the UDF and the strengthening of civic, student and other mass structures. The previous month had witnessed the successful boycott of the new tricameral constitution by anti-apartheid forces.

The uprisings soon spread around the country, particularly to the rest of the Transvaal and the Cape. The state responded with increased repression. In October 1984 it moved a force of 7 000 into Sebokeng township, including large numbers of SADF troops. They blocked entrances to the townships, conducted house-to-house searches, and detained hundreds of township residents. This was a pattern which would be followed repeatedly in the following months and years, leading to a popular demand for 'Troops out of the townships.'

Problems of rent increases, road blocks, detentions and disruptions of schooling touched almost every worker and parent. The trade unions were also directly affected. For example, a work stayaway might be called in the community. On returning to work, employees and their unions would have to defend themselves against disciplinary action and dismissals. The unions had also started calling for, and receiving, community support. Almost 400 SFAWU-organised Simba workers won reinstatement in November 1984 after a community-based consumer boycott. Union members and community activists, particularly in the Eastern Cape and the PWV area, started questioning the unions' stand on the crisis sweeping the country, and Cosas, a powerful student organisation, called for worker support of community struggles.

A joint union committee, including Fosatu, Cusa, UDF-unions and others, was established in the PWV area and decided on stayaway action in support of student demands. 'We have a plain duty', said Fosatu's Chris Dlamini, 'to support the democratic demands of the students. Workers pay for education and therefore want a say over it.'[14]

On 5 and 6 November 1984, approximately 800 000 workers in the PWV area stayed away from work. It was an historic occasion, marking a significant improvement in the relationship between unions and community organisations. The action showed the power of organised workers and forged close links, through action, between workplace and community demands. It encouraged workers to look beyond the next wage increase to the wider problems facing society. For unions within the powerful Fosatu bloc, the stayaway was a turning point in a process of internal political struggle and change. It played no small part in Fosatu's 1985 decision to re-open the union unity talks to unions from the UDF and black consciousness blocs.

A similar stayaway call was made in the Eastern Cape during March 1985. The established unions in the area, unlike their PWV counterparts, declined to support it. The stayaway nevertheless took place with strong mass support, further souring union-community relations in that area, particularly between the UDF and Fosatu. Its consequences were felt well after Cosatu's launch as ongoing conflicts plagued the Eastern Cape region. This incident also revealed that links between community organisations and unions were not without problems and ambiguities. Unions frequently misunderstood the organisational imperatives and dynamics of community organisation, and vice versa.

During 1985 mass mobilisation continued to grow. Its aim was to establish 'people's power' in the townships. This involved building organs of peoples power such as street committees, student councils and area committees. It also involved community isolation of collaborators, community councillors and policemen. Progressive organisations attempted to make the townships 'ungovernable' for the apartheid regime. The prestige and influence of the still-illegal ANC grew dramatically, and its banners and slogans were visible at meetings throughout the country. The SACP's profile also grew. Funerals for victims of the security forces turned into mass rallies to strengthen and continue resistance. The number of attacks by the ANC's armed wing, Umkhonto we Sizwe, increased dramatically. In less-structured actions, petrol bomb attacks were widespread, with those perceived as collaborators being attacked and their properties burned. Many were killed in gruesome circumstances, sometimes by the 'necklace' method, later condemned by both the ANC and UDF. Township councillors resigned in large numbers.

Many methods of mobilisation were employed. Consumer boycotts against white traders in town were common. So too were regional or local work stayaways. School boycotts were widespread, and in many respects the youth became the spearhead of the uprisings. Naturally, there were abuses. There were many instances of misuse of 'people's courts', and overzealous enforcement of consumer boycotts and stayaways. In turn, the period saw the beginnings of substantial vigilante attacks, as well as assassinations of political activists by state-linked hit squads.

More than 300 township residents were killed between January and July 1985, over half of them in security force actions. On 21 March, the anniversary of the 1960 Sharpeville massacre, police opened fire on peaceful marchers in Langa township, Uitenhage. Twenty were killed. Unions in the area participated in the subsequent protest stayaway. In the Transvaal a well-known Fosatu leader, Andries Raditsela, died in May 1985 shortly after being detained by police. Workers responded with work stoppages and community organisations actively participated in the subsequent mass funeral.

On 21 July, the government declared a partial state of emergency, covering mainly the Eastern Cape and the PWV area. Funerals were restricted. The following month Cosas was declared a banned organisation. By the end of October 1985 over 5 300 people had been detained under emergency legislation. The heaviest repression was directed against UDF-affiliated activists. Most unionists did not, at this stage, suffer lengthy detention. Where they did, it was often related to their community activities.

The state of emergency failed to curb the uprising, although it partly dampened it. In early August 1985, unrest exploded in Natal, sparked off by the assassination of Victoria Mxenge, a well-known UDF official. In the space of two weeks, some 70 died. Unrest also grew in the Western Cape, starting with grievances over education. Police attempted to stop student gatherings and protests. In late August a march to Pollsmoor Prison to call for Nelson Mandela's release was broken up by police, triggering an uprising in both African and coloured townships throughout the region. More than 30 people died at the hands of the security forces. The state responded by closing schools, detaining UDF leaders, and extending emergency rule to the region.

This was the political backdrop to Cosatu's launch. The federation was born into a state of emergency. It was a product not only of worker organisation, but also of a climate of uprising and even insurrection. Following Cosatu's launch, at least 12 regional stayaways took place in the period November 1985 to February 1986. These actions affected main centres as well as small towns and previously isolated areas. Cosatu members participated in most, if not all, of these stayaways. Often, however, Cosatu as an organisation played little part in the calling, planning or preparations of the actions.

The detention without trial of Moses Mayekiso, at the time Mawu's general secretary, gives some insight into the direct impact of the emergency on Cosatu. Mayekiso was detained on 21 February 1986 under the emergency regulations. Mawu immediately began campaigning for his release, and called for international support. On 5 March, thousands of metalworkers in Natal and the Transvaal protested the detention. Lunch-hour demonstrations were held in some factories. In others, more protracted actions occurred. Brits, Rosslyn, Pretoria, the Witwatersrand, Durban, Pinetown and Pietermaritzburg were the areas most affected by this action. CWIU workers, on strike at Dunlop, added Mayekiso's release to their list of demands. Management responded that the company could not interfere in police matters

Mayekiso was released on 7 March, the day the government lifted the state of emergency. Almost 8 000 had been detained under emergency laws, and 4 152 others under other security legislation during the nine months of emergency rule. At least 853 people had been killed in nationwide political violence. Despite this, the emergency had failed to suppress resistance.

For three months Cosatu operated without a state of emergency. The police and army remained in place, as did the government's extensive armoury of security legislation and repressive force. Nevertheless, there was a slight easing in repression. The government used this period to study the lessons of its failed emergency. Three months later, on 12 June, it imposed a new and significantly harsher state of emergency throughout the country. It would become apparent that it had only withdrawn the first emergency to prepare better for the second.

Notes

1. *Sunday Times*, 20.04.86.
2. Andrew Levy and Associates, *Industrial Action Monitor*, June 1986, 13.
3. *Finance Week*, 27.03.86.
4. See Phillip van Niekerk and Jean Leger, 'Conflict in the Mining Industry', *Work In Progress*, April 1986, for a summary of major mine strikes during early 1986.
5. *Star*, 07.01.86.
6. *Star*, 08.01.86.
7. *Business Day*, 07.01.86; *Citizen*, 07.01.86.
8. *Financial Mail*, 10.01.86.
9. *Weekly Mail*, 10.01.86.
10. *Business Day*, 21.02.86.
11. Estelle Randall, 'Factory Occupations and Sit-ins', *South African Labour Bulletin*, 11(3), January 1986, 27.
12. 'Sit-ins Continue', *South African Labour Bulletin*, 11(5), April/May 1986.
13. Figures used in the following account are drawn largely from *Political Conflict in South Africa; Data Trends 1984-1988*, Indicator Project South Africa, Durban, December 1988.
14. Internal Fosatu document in author's possession.

6

Adopting a political policy

Workerists and populists?

COSATU'S launching congress did not adopt or discuss political policy. This was referred to the central executive committee (CEC), Cosatu's supreme decision-making body between congresses. The CEC met for the first time at Ipelegeng Centre in Soweto from 7-9 February 1986. It was a crucial meeting. Tensions had increased following Naidoo's Harare trip and the sharp attacks from Inkatha, and the excitement and camaraderie between delegates to the CEC was tempered by the seriousness of the decisions which had to be made.

The CEC had four political proposals to consider. A motion from Sarhwu called for Cosatu 'to promote working-class leadership in the struggle' and committed the federation to work jointly with 'other demo-cratic forces.' A Mawu proposal called for all Cosatu's structures to discuss 'the demands and aims of workers in the struggle.' These discus-sions should 'include other organisations of the working class, especially the students and unemployed workers.'

A third motion, proposed jointly by CTMWA, NUTW and CWIU, called for 'consultation and co-operation' between Cosatu and all organisations 'in which workers are to be found and through which struggles affecting workers are being democratically conducted.' This proposal stressed independence and non-affiliation 'to any political tendency or organisation.'

Another draft resolution, proposed jointly by FCWU and SFAWU, asserted the 'independent political interests' of the working class and stressed the need for workers to 'participate in organisations and campaigns that struggle against oppression and economic exploitation.' It argued that 'disciplined alliances with progressive community and political organisations' should be formed, and that Cosatu and these organisations should jointly formulate a political programme including demands for 'freedom of political organisations; the release of political prisoners and detainees; the unbanning of organisations; the vote for all in a united SA etc.'

The CEC appointed a sub-committee to finalise a composite resolution taking account of the four proposals. The compromise it presented to the CEC was debated and amended, and the policy resolution finally adopted reflected a compromise over the significant political differences within the federation.

The resolution noted that the political and economic crisis in the country had resulted in unemployment, starvation and degradation, as well as violent repression. This 'repression, hardship and suffering' affected workers not only at their workplaces, but 'in every other aspect of their lives and within the communities where they live.' Cosatu and the working class should thus play a major role in the political sphere, and 'not hesitate to take political action.' The resolution also asserted the independence of Cosatu, and spoke of the 'independent political interests, position, action and leadership of the working class in the wider political struggle.'

This much was uncontroversial. But the political resolution was essentially a compromise, satisfying everybody and no-one at the same time. It consisted largely of generalities, gave the federation very little practical direction for political action and was open to differing interpretations.

The resolution expressed overwhelming agreement on two points: Cosatu would be politically active; and Cosatu would work in alliance with other organisations. But it revealed disagreement over *who* Cosatu should ally with and *how* such alliances should work. The attitude of the federation to the ANC and UDF remained vague. Although unaffiliated, the majority within Cosatu were clearly sympathetic to the Congress camp. The resolution did not unambiguously state this.

There was broad agreement that political action should take place in alliance with other forces and organisations. But the actual wording of this clause reflected the tensions within Cosatu. It was agreed that alliances would be formed with 'progressive' organisations – a term commonly, but not exclusively, used at the time to refer to groups with a pro-ANC/UDF outlook. This was tempered by the proviso that Cosatu would only enter 'disciplined' alliances with such organisations if their interests were 'compatible with the interests of the workers' and their 'organisational practices furthered the interests of the working class.'

This proviso indicated an attempt, albeit indirect, to introduce the precondition that any potential allies should share the goal of socialism. It also reflected, again indirectly, the fears of many that a large number of community organisations and UDF affiliates operated undemocratically. Unlike the unions, which generally had clear organisational structures, community groups were often composed mainly of activists who frequently took decisions without a mandate from any clearly-defined membership or constituency.

The clause resolving that Cosatu would participate in all campaigns of 'progressive organisations' was also qualified. These campaigns should be against 'oppression and economic exploitation (and) in the interests of the working class and a democratic society.'

The political resolution stated that Cosatu would not affiliate to any political organisation 'at the present time', although the question of individual union affiliation to the UDF was deliberately left vague. Despite reservations from some, the unity talks had agreed that no union would be asked to disaffiliate from UDF as a condition of joining Cosatu.

The resolution was deliberately vague in its definition of political goals. 'The struggle' was for a 'non-racial and democratic society' as well as being against 'economic exploitation'. This formulation was uncontentious, but avoided exploring the connection between these two goals. Emphasis on the national-democratic nature of the struggle implied the broadest possible anti-apartheid alliances. Emphasis on the anti-capitalist dimension assumed the centrality of a class-based alliance of working people. But what the resolution avoided was the practical relationship between the struggle for democracy and the struggle for socialism.

In addition, the resolution was unclear about the actual alliances envisaged. Those within Cosatu who saw the need for the closest links with UDF affiliates laid stress on the resolution's call to ally with 'progressive' organisations. Those who envisaged a more distanced relationship emphasised the provision that all alliances should be 'disciplined' and tightly structured. As neither 'progressive' nor 'disciplined' were defined, it was possible for the resolution to be interpreted in a variety of ways.

This lack of clarity did not prevent Cosatu from meeting other organisations or developing alliances. But it did make consistent relations
with others difficult, and each meeting with a potential ally became contested terrain.

Meeting the UDF and ANC

The February CEC agreed to a meeting with the UDF, although some
members wanted to limit it to a simple exchange of views. Cosatu's
ten-person executive committee (Exco) met UDF representatives on
18 February in the first of many meetings and consultations between the
two organisations.

The CEC had also called for a Cosatu delegation to meet with an
ANC/Sactu delegation for 'an open exchange of views.' This took place
outside of South Africa on 5-6 March 1986, the anniversary of Sactu's
launch. The ANC and Sactu delegations included senior officials such as
Oliver Tambo, John Nkadimeng, Chris Hani, Stephen Dlamini, Joe
Slovo, Thabo Mbeki and Mac Maharaj. Cosatu was represented by Exco
members Naidoo, Mufamadi, Ledwaba, Dube and Phike, and Ramaphosa and Motlatsi from NUM. Barayi, Dlamini and Ntombela could not
attend as the state had refused to issue them with travel documents.

The meeting was extremely warm, with both Cosatu and the ANC
finding much common ground in their political perspectives. Talks
covered South Africa's future economic system, the role of the working
class in the struggle for national liberation, the release of Nelson Mandela, and potential negotiations between the ANC and government.[1] The
ANC delegation stated that it had no economic blueprints and called on
organised workers to help conceive the economic future. The ANC also
noted that it did not foresee that any future negotiations with government
would involve it alone. Internal representatives of mass organisations,
including Cosatu, would have to be part of any negotiating team. The
contents of this meeting were widely reported within Cosatu. This was
done verbally, as there was a reluctance – for legal reasons – to place too
many details in writing.

In a separate meeting with Sactu the two delegations agreed 'that it is
not in our interest to be used against each other. Some mischievous elements abroad' were trying to do this. This meeting culminated in the
issuing of a joint communique. Lasting solutions to South Africa's social,
economic and political crisis, it read, 'can only emerge from the national
liberation movement, headed by the ANC and the entire democratic
forces of our country of which Cosatu is an important and integral part.'
The solution to this crisis lay in 'a system of majority rule in a united,
democratic and non-racial South Africa... It is inconceivable that such a

system can be separated from economic emancipation.' Cosatu had the task 'of engaging the workers in the general democratic struggle, both as an independent organisation and as an essential component of the democratic forces of our country.'[2]

Workerism and populism

In its first few years the dominant political position within Cosatu explicitly recognised the existence of classes and the need for strong, independent organisations of the working class. Unions and 'the party' (implicitly, the SACP) were seen as the most important of these. However, racial oppression was identified as the dominant contradiction within society. This made it imperative for Cosatu to stress popular political demands such as majority rule and a unitary, democratic state. At the same time, the federation aimed to inject a class content into these demands. The future was conceived as non-racial, democratic and socialist. Multi-class alliances, under working-class leadership, were seen not as an obstacle but a requirement for advancing to socialism. In practice, for example, this involved emphasising those clauses of the Freedom Charter which went furthest in proposing the radical transformation of society.

In March 1986 Jay Naidoo explained Cosatu's political policy in a speech delivered at the University of Natal, Pietermaritzburg:

> We see it as our duty to make sure that freedom does not merely change the skin colour of our oppressors. We are not fighting for a freedom which sees the bulk of the workers continuing to suffer as they do today. We therefore see it as our duty to promote working-class politics. A politics where workers' interests are paramount in the struggle. At the same time we recognise that no struggle has ever involved one social force acting alone...
>
> Our experience has taught us firstly, to avoid isolating ourselves as workers and defining our friends and allies too narrowly, ie the danger of workerism; and secondly, to avoid subsuming ourselves in an incoherent mass mood or desire for an ill-defined 'freedom', ie the danger of populism; and thirdly to choose our allies on the basis of what we know...and not on the basis of abstracted principles...ie the danger of impractical but nice-sounding theories.[3]

Naidoo's views, which reflected the dominant position within Cosatu, attempted to steer a middle course between the extremes of both 'populist' and 'workerist' perspectives. Others were less subtle in their approaches. Debates on political policy raged within Cosatu, particularly during its first three years. Talk of 'ama-workerist' and 'ama-populist' became daily fare in union structures and Cosatu locals.

All sectors of the South African liberation movement accept that there is some link between capitalism and white domination, and that both race and class dynamics exist in society. The majority of the population experience both racial oppression and class exploitation. However, the relationship between these two elements and its implications for political struggle are hotly contested.

'Populists' tend to argue that racial oppression is the central contradiction within society. Class differences, while often acknowledged, are devalued and held to be of lesser importance, and 'the struggle' is seen as being against apartheid oppression in all its forms. This requires the unification of all classes and sectors oppressed by the regime. Class differences and class issues are downplayed in the interests of the broadest anti-apartheid unity. A variant of populism suggests that the working class should fight for a socialist future, but only once apartheid has been eliminated.

'Workerists', by contrast, tend to see racism and apartheid as a mask concealing capitalist exploitation. Racism is simply a tool of the ruling class used to enhance the division and exploitation of the working class. Politically, workerists tend to counterpose the national-democratic struggle and the class struggle. The working class alone, on an anti-racist and socialist programme, can effect real change. Co-operation with other classes is likely to compromise working-class objectives. While class alliances are not ruled out in principle, workerists tend to underestimate them or view them with suspicion.[4]

Two key variants of workerism are found, in a variety of mixtures, within South African trade unions. The one is represented by 'revolutionary socialists' who see trade unions as a stepping stone to the establishment of a revolutionary Marxist party. They reject the SACP as a vehicle for this, believing that it has been absorbed by and subordinated to nationalism.[*]

The other involves 'economism', which tends to limit working-class struggle to the workplace; or 'syndicalism', which sees workplace struggles as the most important aspect of working-class political activity.

---

* *The revolutionary socialists are themselves divided between those who look to the creation of a vanguard Marxist party – the 'partyites'; those who seek to infiltrate unions covertly and create a 'tendency' within the ANC – the 'entryists', often represented by members of the the Marxist Workers' Tendency (MWT); and those who seek to bring together socialist factions within all mass structures, especially the trade unions – the 'embryonic partyites', today represented largely by the Workers Organisation for Socialist Action (Wosa). To elaborate further than this simplified description is beyond the scope of this book.*

In practice, 'economistic' and 'syndicalist' strands result in political abstentionism and a stress on trade union work. Trade unions are seen as the most important, and sometimes the only, instrument of working-class struggle.

Within Cosatu, neither workerist nor populist views were usually held in the pure forms expressed above. Positions adopted were not static, and developed and changed over time. Those associated with economism and syndicalism, for example, often encouraged their members to be involved, as individuals, in community organisations and even bodies like the UDF. And it is important to note that neither populists nor workerists described themselves such. While at lower leadership levels workers might occasionally have called themselves one or the other with pride, they were generally terms of abuse used against an opposing faction.

Three important discussion papers on these issues circulated within Cosatu circles at the time of the launch and during the first six months of its existence.[5] These papers, associated with SFAWU, NUTW and Mawu respectively, reveal the way in which debate unfolded in practice. Unfortunately, no equivalent paper was produced by the UDF bloc of unions. However, SFAWU's views were close to, although not identical with, the UDF outlook.

A SFAWU perspective

The first of these influential documents, drafted by SFAWU shortly before Cosatu's launch, aimed to influence the political policy of the new federation. At the time of its drafting, Jay Naidoo was SFAWU's general secretary.

It was the youth who were 'at the vanguard' of the mass struggles of 1984 and 1985, noted the SFAWU paper:

> The dynamic and pace of these struggles and the structures through which they are fought have developed independently of the organised trade union movement. They are taking place in parallel to those struggles being waged by the unions though there have been points of convergence , ...

such as the Transvaal November 1984 stayaway. To ignore the events in the townships would commit organised workers to 'irrelevance'. It did not make sense for organised workers to enter community and political struggles as individuals, argued SFAWU:

We have to enter the political struggle in an organised way so that on the one hand our organisational and historical role is not jeopardised and on the other hand that the interests of the workers are advanced... It is therefore imperative that workers seek alliances with other classes and organisations...on terms that do not subordinate the interests of the working class.

SFAWU noted that trade unions had two main limitations. Structurally they did 'not have the political cohesion of a political party' since they were built around the 'economic interests of the workers and a shopfloor dynamic.' And unions 'do not represent the entire working class... only a small percentage.' Nevertheless, SFAWU argued, 'in the South African context (where) all classes face national oppression...there is a need for the organised workers to lead the struggle.'

In practice, the paper suggested, the locals or shop stewards councils were the key component. They should begin 'in (a) real and constructive manner to link up with locally-based progressive organisations.'

A response from NUTW

In March 1986, individuals from within NUTW produced a discussion paper responding to the SFAWU position and addressing some of the early developments within Cosatu.

The NUTW paper argued that 1984 and 1985 had seen a severe crisis for apartheid. 'The politics of populism and nationalism' had sprung to the fore, and the 'destabilisation' of township life had directly affected 'the capacity of trade unions to provide any leadership and direction to the course of events.' How, the paper asked, did one relate 'working-class politics to the present circumstances where populist politics is both a reality and a very understandable one at that?'

NUTW criticised the SFAWU paper for suggesting that Cosatu should 'enter the limelight on all "crisis committees" and "action committees"... Populist politics is not "governable" through intervention', argued NUTW. In the populist tradition, 'leaders are leaders because they act as leaders, not because they are elected as leaders.' Such a leadership could be undisciplined and act without control. Joining with populist leaders, 'far from widening the terrain of class politics' would instead

neutralise workers as a class in their 'communities'... Despite the rhetoric about socialism...the practice and statements of such leadership compromises the political and organisational practices of the working class.

In their haste SFAWU's leaders forgot 'that we must start from grass-roots and organise first... By associating with individuals who justify their right to lead by the cause they represent rather than the people they have organised' there was a risk of causing serious division among workers. Joining with 'unstructured organisations' could drag unions into 'each and every adventurous action that is initiated' without the capacity to assess actions. 'The new alliance will not recognise when confrontationist practices are exhausting our unions rather than the state.'

NUTW conceded the need for 'workers to organise beyond the factory gates.' However, such action should be guided by three fundamental principles. Firstly, it should be based on 'working-class ideology' as opposed to 'other groupings, be they populist, liberal or "black nationalist."' Secondly, action should be based on the 'extension and development of existing working-class organs', in particular the shop steward councils. These should be the basis 'for the development of systematic activities in working class communities.' Unions could co-operate with community organisations provided these were 'supportive of any programme on which we are working.' Thirdly, alternative action should be based on independence, on 'our right and ability to act on our own... Of necessity, these actions have had to confront the politics of populism and have, in some cases, had to counterpose an alternative politics to it.'

The paper also criticised Barayi and Naidoo – Cosatu president and general secretary respectively – for acting without mandates. It hinted that the decision to bring the UDF-affiliated unions into the unity talks was a 'blunder'. A rearguard action needed to be fought to prevent a 'takeover of the trade union movement by populism.' The merger process was the key to this. 'Whilst populist elements will of course not disappear in the process of these mergers, the belief that they will redirect such merged unions fundamentally' was 'unnecessarily alarmist'.

The NUTW paper represented one extreme of the Cosatu spectrum. Its position was informed by a political perspective hostile to 'nationalist' politics and based on a politics of pure 'class'. Throughout the position paper, 'community' appears in inverted commas, suggesting the author/s denial of its very existence – presumably as a non-class concept.

The strongest criticism of the NUTW argument was that its proposed approach never resulted in actual community organisation. In practice NUTW's position was one of political abstentionism.

A view from Mawu

A further discussion paper entitled 'Trade Unions and Political Direction' emerged from Mawu circles. The position it advanced was essentially the one adopted by Mawu at its mid-1986 congress, and involved both similarities to and differences from the NUTW perspective.

The Mawu paper spoke of a government rejected by the majority and whose reform efforts had been unsuccessful. The economic problems of the country were serious, and repression had been only partly successful. Although the government and employers had no long-term solutions to the country's problems, the state was not about to collapse. It could, however, be forced to make concessions. Negotiations between the government and opposition forces would, at some point, ensue, but it was unlikely that these would lead to a socialist South Africa.

From this viewpoint, the paper then posed a key question: 'What kind of alliances should we make with political groupings who are going to end up involved in negotiations with the government?'

For Mawu 'there can surely be no question...that workers in the trade unions (the organised working class) must be part of the national liberation struggle.' But, at the same time 'we must start building for socialism...now... (W)e must establish the independence of Cosatu within the national liberation struggle.'

'Building for socialism,' argued Mawu, involved mainly the building up of 'democratic trade unions and democratic community organisations' which 'can then be our vehicles to socialism.' These organisations should be based on 'proper socialist principles like democracy, working-class leadership, mass participation and worker control.'

Trade union independence could accommodate unity with other organisations, but this should be 'unity...built out of action and not on the basis of big press conferences and vague promises.' This unity 'should be in order to carry out campaigns to win rights for the working class and thereby for other oppressed groups as well.' The Mawu position did not favour unity with any organisation. It stressed that unions 'should be clear that the groups we are campaigning with accept that socialism is the goal which must be achieved under the leadership of the working class.'

The Mawu paper also criticised some actions of Cosatu's leadership. There had been no mandate for many of their public utterances. In particular 'they should have got a very clear mandate to meet the ANC' and should have discussed the meeting within Cosatu before issuing a joint statement. The communique which was issued 'should not have agreed to Cosatu struggling under the leadership of the ANC.' Rather, Cosatu leadership 'should have made it clear that Cosatu...would struggle together with other progressive organisations, but independently, under its own leadership.'

The Mawu paper felt that while these mistakes were 'by themselves' not very great, they had created other problems. For example, there was a belief that 'there was no room for the other workers who did not fully support the ANC.' 'Strong personal attacks' on Chief Buthelezi had also 'created many problems for unionists.' In addition some unions now believed that 'it was not necessary to get full and proper mandates on all issues from workers.'

Many of these criticisms were undoubtedly valid. In particular, the attacks on Buthelezi had been ill-considered. Nevertheless, Mawu's perspectives did not enjoy majority support within Cosatu.

Understanding the differences

Cosatu's first 18 months saw deep differences emerge between affiliates. Tensions often paralysed the federation's ability to enter into effective alliances, act politically, and launch Cosatu's own structures. Labelling of opponents became the order of the day, with the tags attached to different unions or individuals frequently determining whether their positions were supported or opposed. Unions tended to vote in blocs, regardless of the merits of the issue.

Cosatu's leadership were well aware of this problem. A widely-circulated discussion paper drawn up by Cosatu's Exco in August 1986 noted that debates often occurred in the abstract, and in isolation from actual conditions. 'We do not share ideas, learn from each other or build...democratic and comradely debate... This also leads to a tendency of political mistrust.' Unity in action by the membership would ensure 'that a cohesive political approach can emerge for the federation.'[6]

Many observers attempted to explain these differences in terms of 'workerism' and 'populism'. While these labels provide some insight into the political debate within Cosatu, and indicate real theoretical and strategic differences which existed at the time, they are also extremely limited. In reality, positions within Cosatu involved a continuum, rather than being rigidly divided from each other. Many political strands existed and these were woven together in a variety of combinations. Regional experiences often influenced the blend, and the 'workerist/populist' labelling does not capture this complexity.

It would be more accurate to see political differences in Cosatu revolving around three practical questions: the relationship to the ANC; the attitude towards socialism; and how broad, both ideologically and in terms of class, alliances should be.

More importantly, the differences within Cosatu were not only political. Unions did not see eye-to-eye on many fundamental organisational questions. The issue of mandates, democratic processes and, especially, commitment to dissolution of the general unions and establishment of one union in each industry were key areas of disagreement.

These organisational differences were related to, but by no means the same as, the political disagreements. The fact that Cosatu's affiliates differed in both political perspectives and organisational approach cannot be explained by 'workerist' and 'populist' labels. Rather, the identification of three different political/organisational blocs within the federation is a more fruitful way of understanding these differences, at least during Cosatu's first two years of existence.

Differing political/organisational tendencies

The three political/organisational blocs were not totally rigid, neither were there absolute barriers between them. In practice they conflicted and co-operated according to circumstances. Developments within various affiliates also often saw movement closer to, or further away from, a particular bloc.

Firstly, there was the *'UDF' bloc*. Some 19 unions representing 106 761 members came from a UDF background. These were mostly general unions, such as Saawu, Gawu and a group of unions falling under the NFW banner. This bloc also included a number of smaller industrial unions such as Sarhwu, Mwusa and Rawu (CT).

The leadership of the UDF unions were politically confident. The political upsurge (and even semi-insurrection) then sweeping the country aided them, in that it was occurring largely under the UDF banner. This often led the UDF bloc of unions to assume, not entirely unreasonably, that they reflected the political views and aspirations of the ordinary members of other unions.

Within Cosatu these unions comprised 23% of the total membership. However, on the CEC, where each union had representation, they occupied 49% of the voting delegate seats. Politically strong, they were, in trade union terms, generally weak. Saawu was numerically the strongest union within the UDF camp, with Gawu following close behind. This group of unions was politically united both by previous loyalties and a common outlook. However, on many practical issues – such as mergers and the dissolution of general unions – they were less unified.

The second bloc, occupying the *'centre'*, involved a significant grouping of unions sympathetic to a UDF/ANC outlook. They included NUM and FCWU, as well as a number of former Fosatu unions such as SFAWU, Pwawu and TGWU. These unions had often been launched with more narrow economic trade union perspectives, and were not internally homogeneous. They contained within them a variety of political views, with the UDF/ANC position dominant. Despite the common perspectives which they and the UDF unions held, the two groupings were not comfortable with each other, differing on questions of style of organisation and union work.

This 'centre' group of unions emphasised the importance of strong grassroots organisation and representative democracy. While they shared common political ground with the first bloc, they were often suspicious of the UDF group's rhetorical and sloganeering style of politics. The UDF unions, in turn, frequently viewed this bloc as lukewarm in their support for the ANC, and accused them of making a fetish of 'mandates' and 'democracy'. The 'centre' bloc represented 168 907 paid-up members – 37% of Cosatu's total. But it occupied only 19% of the voting delegate seats at CEC level.

The third group involved a group of unions strongly located in the early Fosatu tradition. They constituted an *'independent worker' bloc*, and included Mawu, Naawu, CWIU and NUTW. Organisationally they placed great stress on democratic grassroots-based structures and shared much in common with the 'centre' bloc. Politically they were often, but not always, hostile or cautious towards the ANC/UDF tradition, and tended to be suspicious of community organisations as well as nationalist politics. Their politics envisaged an alternative working-class organisation in both factory and community, separate from the traditions of the UDF, SACP and ANC. Their practice, particularly in the case of NUTW, often amounted to political abstentionism. GWU, a non-Fosatu union, fell largely, but not always comfortably, into this camp. As with the other blocs, the 'independent worker' group were not internally homogeneous, and contained individuals sympathetic to the 'centre' camp. This bloc represented 121 068 paid-up members – 26% of Cosatu's total. They controlled 23% of the CEC seats.

In addition there were a number of other unions, such as Ccawusa, CTMWA and the Tin Workers Union, which did not fit comfortably into any of the three blocs mentioned above. Their leadership included people from a broad variety of political perspectives. In the case of Ccawusa this ranged from the a-political, through UDF/ANC sympathisers, to those holding a black consciousness or Africanist perspective. Despite these differences, Ccawusa had gained respect as a militant grassroots union.

By contrast CTMWA was not organisationally strong. Politically it included many individuals from the small Unity Movement (NEUM) tradition as well those with growing sympathies towards the mainstream non-racial democratic tradition.

In practice the 'UDF' and 'centre' blocs tended to vote together on political issues. On organisational questions, such as mergers, the 'centre' and 'independent worker' blocs tended to ally. Politically, the 'centre' and 'UDF' blocs constituted a majority. They believed that Cosatu should be clearly and unambiguously aligned with the ANC. While in their view unions could not themselves act as a political party, they could reflect their membership's support for the leading political role of the ANC. They also believed it was essential to alter public perceptions of the union movement, which was often seen as ambiguous and even hostile towards the ANC.

These two blocs accepted that the struggle was fundamentally for national liberation, and hence national democratic in character. But they were not hostile, particularly not the 'centre' bloc, to questions of socialism. However, they resisted the idea – implied in the Mawu position – of entering alliances only with working-class allies, or based exclusively on socialist programmes. As a result, they encouraged participation of the broadest possible range of classes within the anti-apartheid alliance. This, they believed, was the most important requirement to intensify pressure on the Botha regime.

This 'centre'/'UDF' position was not without contradictions. In practice it sometimes sacrificed trade union independence to its support for an alliance with the UDF and ANC. There was undeniably a real 'populism' in some unions where rhetorical allegiance to concepts such as 'working-class leadership' was not always matched in practice. In addition a narrow loyalty to the UDF often left this group unable to discuss alliances with anti-apartheid groups not seen as 'progressive'. One example of this occurred in April 1986, when Cosatu refused to meet Azapo, a black consciousness organisation.[7] The alliances envisaged by these two blocs, while broad in class terms, were narrow in ideological scope and confined to those in or close to the Congress camp.

In part, the 'centre'/'UDF' approach was a response to the 'independent worker' bloc's hostility to Cosatu's political orientation. This made political policy difficult to implement, and when Cosatu met political and community organisations it frequently did so without a united voice.

Political differences were deep but not, in themselves, unhealthy. Outside observers generally ignored the fact that what held the unions in Cosatu together was far more important than the political differences between them. At no stage, even when differences became extremely divisive, did any affiliate seriously think of withdrawing from Cosatu. The achievement of one 'super-federation' after four difficult years of talks, was too important to throw away.

Electing an executive

Cosatu's first CEC meeting dealt with a number of issues besides political policy. Constitutionally, it was required to elect four members to the executive committee (Exco), who would join the six office bearers elected at congress. The intention of this was not only that additional members would strengthen the executive. Balance was also important, and Cosatu's constitution specified that 'no more than three members of (Exco) shall be from one region, and no more than two members shall be from any one affiliated union.'

Daniel Dube, the Eastern Cape-based president of Mawu; John Ernstzen, the Cape Town-based general secretary of CTMWA; and Lizzie Phike, a Western Cape organiser for FCWU, were elected unopposed. Phike was a union stalwart, having been active in Sactu. She was also the only woman elected to the executive. The fourth Exco vacancy was decided by secret ballot and Jerry Ntombela, TGWU president from Northern Natal, was elected ahead of Matthews Oliphant, previously of the NFW.

An invitation for Cosatu to meet the Commonwealth Eminent Person's Group (EPG) then about to visit South Africa created heated debate at this CEC meeting. Many delegates opposed the meeting, arguing that total isolation of the regime was required. Engaging the government in talks, as the EPG intended to do, did little more than give PW Botha credibility. The EPG mission, argued many CEC delegates, was a plot by the 'imperialist Thatcher-dominated' Commonwealth to open the way for the easing of sanctions and a Zimbabwe-style political settlement. Despite this resistance, Exco tacitly gave approval to meet the EPG.

The EPG debate exposed Cosatu's inexperience in international politics. So too did the meeting itself, where some members of the Cosatu delegation implied that the EPG had been the idea of British Prime Minister Margaret Thatcher. Australia's Malcolm Fraser and Nigeria's General Obasanjo took offence and demanded an apology. Cosatu's delegation was in a militant mood and not about to apologise to anyone. Only some diplomatic footwork cooled the air.

As it transpired, the EPG initiative to broker a negotiated settlement came to nought. It was sabotaged when South African security forces launched raids into three neighbouring Commonwealth countries – Botswana, Zambia and Zimbabwe.

The EPG meeting was Cosatu's first involvement in international diplomacy, making the federation a recognised actor in political discussions both locally and abroad. From then onwards it became standard procedure for international visitors to South Africa to canvass Cosatu's views.

Cosatu's secretariat was working out of a small room in NUM's Lekton House offices. Without money and staff they relied heavily on NUM resources. The first CEC agreed that a head office could be found in Johannesburg and a large building was rented on the corner of Jeppe and End Streets. Dubbed 'Cosatu House', it included office accommodation and large meeting halls. Most major affiliates moved in and by mid-1986 Cosatu House was an important focus of union activity. As Jay Naidoo recalls it, 'we decided we needed to develop a centre and build an identity for Cosatu.'[8]

International policy

The CEC also addressed the issue of Cosatu's relationship to the international trade union movement, which was divided into three bodies combining most, but by no means all, of the major national centres around the world. There was the World Federation of Trade Unions (WFTU) based in Eastern Europe and the Soviet Union, which included many unions ideologically allied to the socialist bloc countries. There was the ICFTU which, as the Cold War deepened in 1948, had split from the WFTU. The ICFTU included most of the national centres of Western Europe and North America, and had for decades been noted for its extreme anti-communism. Finally there was the very much smaller World Confederation of Labour (WCL), which was linked historically to the Christian-Democratic unions of Western Europe and Latin America.

Cosatu resolved not to affiliate to any of these bodies. However, money was needed for the federation to establish itself, and affiliation fees would clearly be insufficient. The Cosatu secretariat was using money borrowed from NUM, and this was inadequate to meet the demands being placed on it. The CEC agreed that 'direct funding for Cosatu's budget' should be sought from the national trade union centres of Scandinavia, Holland and Canada. In a break from previous practice in South Africa, Cosatu decided to approach the national centres directly. At the time, it was common for foreign unions wishing to assist their South African counterparts to do so through the ICFTU.

Cosatu, it was decided, would not accept money from the ICFTU. The decision to go a step further and attempt to bypass the ICFTU on funding matters was based on the experiences of many unionists. The ICFTU, it was widely felt, had played a divisive role both historically and in the recent past of the South African trade union movement. NUM reported that an ICFTU functionary had approached them and advised against their participation in the launch of Cosatu. There was a strong feeling that many Cusa unions had withdrawn from the unity talks after similar approaches. Others claimed the ICFTU was promoting unions as an alternative to the ANC in an attempt to build a third force between the liberation movement and the government.

Cosatu's decision was not greeted kindly abroad. A federation delegation, sent to Europe in March, reported to the CEC that the ICFTU 'told us that they respect our non-alignment policy,' but 'expressed their disgust at being labelled "an imperialist front" by some individuals or unions affiliated to Cosatu. They felt that we have "misconceptions" about the ICFTU... After a heated debate,' the report continued, 'on what Cosatu saw as unnecessary interventions by foreign forces in our struggle,' the Cosatu delegation requested the ICFTU to leave the national trade union centres to decide whether to fund Cosatu directly or not. 'In fact discussion was quite cordial,' recalls Naidoo, 'but we agreed to disagree.'[9]

The delegation then proceeded to meet with union federations in Scandinavia, the Netherlands, the United Kingdom and Canada. 'That was tough,' recalls Naidoo, who was part of the delegation. 'We were attacked by the inclement weather and criticised by their national centres. It was the time when Olaf Palme was killed. We went to the memorial service with only canvas shoes and nearly froze to death.' Unions in the countries visited had many preconceptions about Cosatu. 'They thought we were just political.' They all expressed their concern at Cosatu's attitude towards the ICFTU: 'They were affiliates and felt we were attacking their family,' says Naidoo. The national trade union centres had no problem with bilateral links with Cosatu, although they stressed that financial support had always gone through the co-ordinating committees of the ICFTU.[10]

The Cosatu delegation responded by frankly stating their unhappiness with the ICFTU. 'The ICFTU as a centre has not contributed to the process of unifying South African workers,' they argued. 'The activities of certain functionaries within the ICFTU have stigmatised it.'[11] The delegation also convinced the Dutch and Scandinavian unionists that Cosatu was committed to building strong trade unions, and before the trip was over the delegation felt that Cosatu's strongest links were likely to be with unions in those countries. 'They were prepared to work with us on a bilateral basis,' recalls Naidoo. 'They were forthright and open in their criticisms and also in hearing us out. This laid the basis for a good relationship.'[12]

Ultimately these union federations agreed to provide direct financial support for Cosatu. In one sense, the argument was academic. Cosatu's financial donors co-ordinated their support, and they did so under the auspices of the ICFTU. Cosatu's relations, however, were with the national centres concerned and not the ICFTU. Politically, this was the important point. It signified Cosatu's attitude towards manipulation by 'cold war' imperatives, and declared Cosatu's intention to operate a policy of 'active non-alignment'.

While Cosatu's links with European unions received most attention, the federation was also committed to ties with unions in the developing world. Two early initiatives saw Exco members Mufamadi and Dube travelling to May Day celebrations in the Philippines and Nigeria respectively.

For all the fuss it caused externally, the CEC adopted Cosatu's international policy unanimously and with little debate. All three political/organisational blocs were in broad agreement. But when it came to domestic political and organisational questions the differences, as we shall see, ran deep.

Notes

1. Internal Cosatu document, 'Report on the trip undertaken by Cosatu's executive committee members abroad between the period of 5th March to 13th March 1986'.
2. Joint ANC-Sactu-Cosatu communique of 7 March 1986, reproduced in *South African Labour Bulletin*, 11(5), April/May 1986.
3. Jay Naidoo, 'The Significance of Cosatu', speech delivered at the University of Natal, Pietermaritzburg, 19 March 1986. Reproduced in *South African Labour Bulletin*, 11(5), April/May 1986.
4. Much of the above discussion draws on Devan Pillay, 'Trade Unions and Alliance Politics in Cape Town, 1979-1985', unpublished D.Phil thesis, Department of Sociology, University of Essex, September 1989.
5. 'Discussion paper' from within NUTW, March 1986; 'Draft 2: Trade unions and political direction', from within Mawu; and SFAWU, 'Discussion paper - draft'. A more detailed analysis of these unpublished papers is available in Karl von Holdt, 'Trade Unions, Community Organisations and Politics: a local case study on the East Rand, 1980-1986', unpublished BA (Hons) dissertation, Department of Sociology, University of Witwatersrand, Johannesburg, October 1987.
6. 'Establishing priorities on the way forward', discussion paper prepared for a Cosatu CEC meeting held on 15-16 August 1986.
7. Minutes of a Cosatu CEC meeting held on 15-16 August 1986.
8. Author interview with Jay Naidoo, Johannesburg, January 1991.
9. Written communication with author, February 1991.
10. Author interview with Jay Naidoo, Johannesburg, February 1991.
11. Internal Cosatu document, 'Report on the trip undertaken by Cosatu's executive committee members abroad between the period of 5th March to 13th March 1986'.
12. Author interview with Jay Naidoo, Johannesburg, February 1991.

7

Merger problems and May Day victories

Workers unite

PROBLEMS during the merger talks stemmed from political differences as well as the ambitious policy resolution adopted. The launching congress had resolved to merge all affiliates into national industrial unions within six months, and adopted the slogan 'One Industry, One Union'. This implied that all general unions would be dissolved and their members incorporated into appropriate industrial unions. Industrial unions were also expected to merge where necessary.

The aim of the merger programme was to form ten broadly-based national industrial unions in the following sectors:
● food and drink
● textiles, clothing and leather
● paper, wood and printing
● mining and electrical energy
● metal and motor
● chemical and petroleum
● commercial and catering
● transport (including railways), cleaning and security
● local government and public administration (including education, health and posts and telecommunications)
● domestic service.

In addition, construction and agriculture – where Cosatu's organisational presence was weak – were identified as targets for the establishment of national affiliates.

The proposal was unique in trade union terms. Foreign unionists tended to laugh at the notion of a 'forced march' approach to creating unified industrial unions. In their experience similar developments, when they occurred at all, took place over decades. Yet for Cosatu, this was one of the most important resolutions for implementation.

The unity talks had agreed that a tightly-knit federation was needed. The looser structures of Tucsa, or even Cusa, were seen as ineffective in building a disciplined union movement. Large industrial unions would be able to rationalise their operations and undertake activities inconceivable for a smaller union. NUM, for example, was already in a position to conduct research, introduce sophisticated education programmes for shaft stewards, and form a skilled health and safety department at its head office.

Broadly-based national unions would also be able to develop the muscle needed to challenge the handful of powerful conglomerates dominating the South African economy.

The constitutional structures of Cosatu were premised on the existence of a small number of large industrial unions. Before mergers took effect CEC meetings consisted of up to 100 people. In addition to being unwieldy, the CEC at this time combined delegates from large experienced national unions with delegates from small, local or regionally-based unions. It could be time-consuming, unrewarding and frustrating to discuss, for example, the Natal situation in a national meeting where most delegates had no membership or structures in that province. The merger resolution was therefore critical to the future of the federation, and at the first CEC meeting held in February a major union in each sector was appointed to convene that sector's merger talks.[1]

By the end of the six-month deadline, very little progress had been made, other than a merger in the food sector. Ongoing political and organisational tensions caused delays, and the resistance by some to mergers was often given a political veneer. Hostility to a merger would sometimes be presented as hostility to a political position.

Fawu and TGWU mergers

It was no accident that only the merger of unions in the food industry took place on schedule. Fawu, launched at the beginning of June 1986, brought together 60 000 organised workers in 340 factories. It was headed by experienced and talented worker leadership. Chris Dlamini, Cosatu's vice-president, was elected Fawu president with Peter Malepe as vice-president and Mordecai Mabaso as treasurer. Jan Theron was elected Fawu general secretary, and a senior shop steward from Beech-nut in Isando, Mike Madlala, was asked to leave his factory to become assistant general secretary.

The main components which merged to create Fawu were two large industrial unions, FCWU and SFAWU. Both were organised nationally. Both came from the same political/organisational 'centre' bloc, in that they combined strong sympathy for the ANC with a shopfloor organisational approach.

A third union involved in the merger, Rawu (CT), was a UDF affiliate with factories in Bloemfontein and the Western Cape. Strictly speaking, it fell within the UDF bloc, but its organisational methods made the union extremely close, in practice, to the 'centre' bloc. All these factors, together with a history of co-operation between SFAWU and FCWU which pre-dated Cosatu, made it inevitable that unions in the food sector would merge first.

The general unions had few members in the food industry, and these they handed over to Fawu. There was, however, an exception. While Saawu took part in the merger congress, it later refused to recognise Fawu or integrate its food membership into the new union. Only some time later, under extreme pressure from both Cosatu and Sactu, did it do so.

'We are compelled by reality to (take) on the whole food sector,' said Fawu's Jan Theron. He pointed out that Cusa's food affiliate, FBWU, had also been approached to join the merger, but had 'declined to re-spond' to the approach. He did note, though, that many 'members of FBWU have themselves, without any attempt to recruit them, approached us to become part of the new union.'[2] Indeed, in the following months large numbers of FBWU members – and in the case of Pretoria even whole branches of the union – crossed over to Fawu.

Another merger which occurred within the six-month deadline was that between TGWU, formerly a Fosatu union, and the largely Cape-based GWU. But this was not, strictly speaking, part of Cosatu's merger programme, as it included the total membership of both unions, some of whom would eventually be transferred to other industrial unions. Retaining the name TGWU, the two unions amalgamated at a congress held in Pietermaritzburg during May.

The merger brought together 26 000 workers, largely in transport and on the docks, but also across a variety of other sectors such as municipal, metal and construction. Jerry Ntombela, a member of the Cosatu executive and a worker from Richards Bay, was elected president, and Jane Barrett general secretary.

Merger talks progress slowly

'We are very satisfied with the progress that has been made, in spite of all the scepticism,' commented Jay Naidoo in June. 'We are optimistic that the vast majority of mergers will have been achieved by the end of the year.[3] While his optimism was to prove excessive, there were indeed signs of progress.

Ummawosa had agreed to transfer its members in the mining sector to NUM. Nismawu handed its small membership in Northern Natal to Mawu. The Pretoria-based Rawu had similarly decided to transfer its workers in the retail sector to Ccawusa. A number of the general unions, when approached by workers wanting to join, would refer them to an appropriate industrial union. The two larger general unions, Saawu and Gawu, had agreed in principle to facilitate mergers by dividing themselves into industrial sectors, although in the case of Saawu this was with some reluctance.

The momentum of mergers also involved unions outside of Cosatu's ranks. Talks aimed at establishing a giant metal union – held under the banner of the South African Council of the International Metalworkers Federation (IMF) – involved not only Mawu and Naawu, but also the more conservative Motor Industries Combined Workers Union (Micwu). The Cosatu-affiliated Sadwa was similarly involved in unity talks with regionally-based domestic worker organisations. This resulted in the launch of the SA Domestic Workers Union at the end of November 1986. Sadwu's conference, held at the University of the Western Cape, brought together representatives of a claimed 50 000 domestic workers. The union would 'stand up against exploitation, under the umbrella of Cosatu' said Sadwu's first president, Violet Motlhasedi. General secretary Florrie de Villiers stressed that there were more than a million domestics still to be organised.[4]

A number of unions indicated a desire to affiliate to Cosatu. The Western Cape-based, 1 500-strong Plastic and Allied Workers Union (Pawu) applied to join in May. Similar interest was shown by a number of other unions, including the 20 000-strong Tucsa-affiliated National Union of Furniture and Allied Workers (Nufaw), and unions in the forestry and clothing sectors.

Cosatu's CEC decided, in response to these applications, that all new affiliations should take place through the appropriate industrial union. This was aimed at strengthening the impact of the merger policy. Despite strong interest from a number of unions, Cosatu was cautious about seeking out new affiliates during its first year. There was a widespread feeling that unity of the founding affiliates was the first aim. New affiliates might simply complicate the merger process. Pawu quickly

ONE COUNTRY
ONE FEDERATION

Above: Cosatu launching congress – December 1985

Left: Delegates congratulate Florrie de Villiers (centre), first general secretary of the South African Domestic Workers Union – November 1986

Above left: Dismissed Sarmcol strikers meet in local church hall

*Above right: Platform for striking OK Bazaars
workers at Cosatu House – January 1987*

Left: White scab outside Johannesburg station during 1987 railway strike

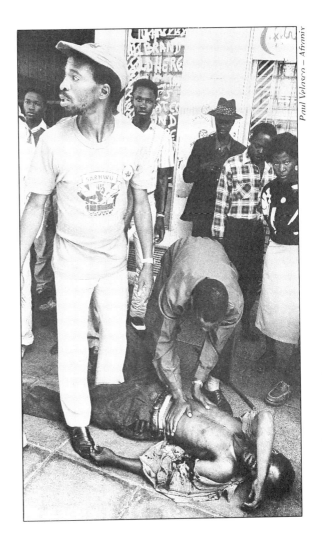

Paul Velasco – Afrapix

Above left: The siege of Cosatu House – 1987

Above right: Aftermath of police attack on
railway workers' march – November 1989

Left: Cosatu's national leaders, re-elected to office at the
second congress – 1987
Left to right are Jay Naidoo, Chris Dlamini, Sydney Mufamadi,
Elijah Barayi, Max Xulu (absent – Makhulu Ledwaba)

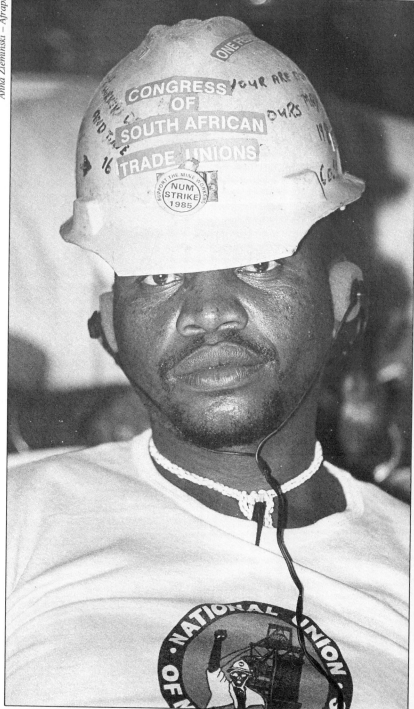

Cyril Ramaphosa –
NUM general secretary

Elijah Barayi at
Cosatu's second
congress – 1987

Anna Zieminski – Afrapix

Right: Chris Dlamini – 1987

Below: Jay Naidoo at Cosatu's third congress – July 1989

Cedric Nunn – Afrapix

integrated with CWIU and by September was effectively its Cape Town branch. On the other hand unions less committed to joining Cosatu, but under pressure from their membership, were not actively followed up. The affiliates failed to exercise sufficient influence on such unions, while Cosatu itself could probably have had a greater impact if these openings had been actively pursued.

Division in the textile union

In addition to mergers, Cosatu also had to deal with splits. The most significant of these involved the textile union, NUTW, where a split occurred during the federation's first year. NUTW, a former Fosatu union, had its stronghold in Natal, being Cosatu's largest affiliate in the Southern Natal region. The union's political perspectives have been outlined in the previous chapter. Dominant was a feeling of unhappiness over Cosatu's political direction.

The problems began with a leadership struggle. A group within NUTW, strongly supportive of the UDF tradition, convinced its national executive to elect Isaac Ndlovu as acting general secretary. However, through a combination of court actions and the fact that they were organisationally far stronger, the previously-dominant faction managed to reverse this decision. General secretary John Copelyn, and Elias Banda, were prominent within this faction.

Cosatu was informed of the rift. At the launch of its Southern Natal region, Ndlovu's supporters reportedly argued that 'it will be difficult for Cosatu to fight against Inkatha because within Cosatu there are comrades who are criticising Cosatu office bearers and show themselves to be anti-Cosatu.' At leadership level within the region, there was a lot of support for the Ndlovu faction and hostility towards the established bloc in NUTW. This related both to historical differences which had existed in Fosatu, as well as the political positions held by NUTW leadership. At the following REC meeting in Southern Natal, the majority of delegates went as far as suggesting that 'four comrades from NUTW should be dismissed from Cosatu ie Comrades Sineke, Gwala, Banda, and Copelyn.' While the REC had no powers to effect this, it clearly indicated the depth of feeling involved.[5]

Cosatu's second CEC meeting, sitting on 12-13 April 1986, asked both sides to present their case. Ndlovu's group, whose support-base consisted mainly of factories in Hammarsdale and Pinetown, alleged that NUTW was bureaucratically controlled and anti-Cosatu in its approach. They particularly resented what they saw as Copelyn's control of NUTW. In turn Ndlovu's group was accused of acting undemocratically, and trying to take over NUTW without majority support. The CEC established a commission in an attempt to heal the rift. It failed. In time the rift became a split and the Ndlovu faction launched the Textile and Allied Workers Union (Tawu) in opposition to NUTW.

At the CEC meeting of 16-17 August 1986, another commission was appointed with a simple mandate: 'attempt to settle the dispute.' The CEC itself appointed two people to the commission, and each of the parties was asked to nominate an additional person from the ranks of the CEC. The four commissioners, all from Natal, were Alec Erwin, Themba Nxumalo, Msokoli Qotole and Maxwell Xulu. The commissioners met with both parties amidst allegations and counter-allegations. The situation was so tense that threats and even violence reportedly took place. The commission proposed a compromise solution which NUTW accepted reluctantly, and Tawu rejected.

Although the commission failed to heal the split, its report – which was accepted by Cosatu – made crucial recommendations. Tawu was declared not to be an affiliate of Cosatu. It was also agreed that 'no member or official of any splinter union can make use of any facility of Cosatu or any of its affiliates.' The report was accepted even though a clear majority of CEC members were politically sympathetic to Tawu. Even within the Natal region, a significant number – probably the majority – of officials and leading union activists also sympathised with Tawu's political position. The CEC decision to back NUTW highlighted the fact that differences within the CEC were not purely political. Tawu was rejected despite the sympathy and support it had, and the CEC expressed total rejection of splinter unions 'as a way of resolving differences inside any affiliate.'[6]

The commission recommended that Cosatu 'must firmly establish the policy of one union in one industry so as to prevent splinter unions both now and in the future.' In addition 'our priority must be to unify Cosatu, especially in the Southern Natal Region,' where conflicts with Inkatha made unity even more imperative. The commission called for Cosatu to 'take a firm and absolute stand against violence as a means of dealing with disputes within our unions.' Violence was 'politically destructive' and rapidly 'becomes chaotic gang warfare.' The commission also noted that the growth of unions

> makes it inevitable that different political currents will emerge. Minority positions that emerge within structures will have to be accepted. Attempts at completely uniform political views and control will encourage splits and not prevent them.

Structures should be respected 'absolutely.'[7] These conclusions, amongst the most important ever reached by the federation, were not always absorbed in practice by many of the affiliates in later years.

The problems of merger

Failure to meet the six-month deadline led to Cosatu's leadership increasing its determination to push the merger process. Despite this, progress had still been extremely slow by the end of 1986. Almost all convening unions reported the total breakdown of talks in their sector. Politically there were differences within Cosatu. On 'purely' political issues the centre bloc and the UDF bloc of unions tended to ally. But on the merger issue, the centre bloc tended to join forces with the independent worker bloc. Both agreed that the mergers should proceed on the basis of majoritarian principles, ie the policies of merged unions would be decided by the majority of delegates at a merger congress, and regardless of differing political positions. The UDF bloc of unions was often resistant to this. They were generally smaller unions and undoubtedly felt they would be swamped politically.

Some individual unionists from all blocs feared losing positions and influence, although this was never openly expressed. Certain unions with a relatively small membership had relatively large numbers of officials, and the larger unions were often resistant to accommodating large numbers of officials in any merger process.

Another problem was the belief that larger unions simply wanted to swallow smaller ones. For genuine merger to take place, it was said by some, all unions in the sector should dissolve and a totally new union formed. While the argument was strong, the practical implications were usually problematic. Should NUM, for example, dissolve along with the minuscule SA Mine Workers Union (Samwu) so that a new union with a new name and new policies could be formed? Nevertheless, Cosatu's leadership tried to be sensitive to this problem, and in discussions usually spoke about 'integration' rather than 'absorption' or 'handing over' of membership.

The definition of an 'industry' also proved problematic. The launching congress had clearly defined the different sectors, but had also given the CEC some flexibility by empowering it to 'evaluate the viability of the sectors.' In the face of a number of applications, the CEC preferred not to make exceptions. Requests for a separate cleaning and security sector were rejected, as was the suggestion to separate 'commercial' from 'catering'. In both cases, the unions directly involved did not agreed on the request. By contrast, all unions concerned agreed that local government (ie municipal) workers should be organised separately from hospital and health workers, and this was ratified by the CEC.

Demarcation disputes even occurred between larger unions. The most notable involved NUM and Mawu (later Numsa) over the question of electricity workers. Both had members at the state-owned Eskom. Eventually it was agreed that as the power stations were mostly closely linked to the coal mines, both structurally and geographically, Eskom workers would be located within NUM.[*]

By far the biggest problem in the merger talks involved the issue of paid-up membership. The conflict was largely between those unions which kept national records and strict financial accounts and those with decentralised structures. The latter would frequently collect union subscriptions at their local offices, using these monies directly to pay salaries, rents and accounts. The lack of adequate financial procedures made calculation of paid-up membership extremely difficult.

It was only when the CEC decided that merged unions alone would be allowed to attend Cosatu's second national congress that unity talks in most sectors began in earnest. But it was well into 1987 before this happened.

Establishing Cosatu's structures

Differences within Cosatu severely hampered the launch of some of the regional structures. Cosatu's founding congress had empowered the CEC to establish ten regions. Because of the low level of organisation in the Northern Cape, the CEC later decided to combine the Kimberley portion of that region with the OFS, and the Namaqualand portion with the Western Cape.

Cosatu's constitution provided for regional congresses, the supreme regional structure, to be held every three months. Unions would be represented according to their paid-up membership in that region, on the basis of one delegate for every 250 members. A smaller regional executive committee (REC), made up of two delegates per affiliate, would meet monthly. Larger affiliates, with over 8 000 members in the region, would be entitled to four REC delegates. A majority of delegates to all regional structures had to be workers, rather than full-time union officials.

Setting up nine regions was no easy task. Each region had its own union and political traditions, and unions dominant nationally were not

---

[*] *Decisions are easier to make than to implement. To date, Numsa has still not transferred its Eskom membership to NUM. However, the two unions now work closely with each other.*

always dominant in a particular region. In addition, a particular union's political outlook in a region might be different from its national perspective. There was thus a complex tapestry of differences and unity at regional and national level, and over political and organisational matters.

The two Natal regions were established fairly easily. Both needed to be formed rapidly to deal with the threat from Inkatha. Both areas were dominated by former Fosatu unions, accustomed to working with each other. Nevertheless, these regions elected office bearers supportive of Cosatu's broad 'national-democratic' political position. The Northern Transvaal and Western Cape regions were also established relatively easily.

Delays in other regions were often due to factors outside of Cosatu's control. In the Highveld region, unions established a co-ordinating committee on 11 May 1986 to plan an immediate launch. Its work was disrupted by the state of emergency declared in June, and it was banned from holding meetings in any of five local areas. Eventually the co-ordinating committee decided to hold the launching regional congress (RC) in an area unaffected by the ban, Volksrust. Again police stopped the meeting. 'All comrades from Secunda travelling by bus were taken to the police station', it was reported to the CEC. There, 'their particulars were taken and they were escorted out of the town as far as Standerton.'[8] The region was eventually launched on 24 August in Embalenhle township, near Secunda.

The biggest problems were experienced in forming the Witwatersrand and Eastern Cape regions. The Wits region was launched on 22 and 23 March 1986 at a congress held in Katlehong, but could not reach agreement over the election of a regional secretary. There were two candidates for the post – Bangilizwe Solo and Moses Mayekiso. Mayekiso was nominated in absentia, a practice which many delegates refused to accept. Behind the differences was a complex line-up of the various political/organisational blocs. Solo, the favoured candidate of the UDF/centre alliance, came from NUTW, whose small Transvaal region had a different political complexion to that at national level.

At a second meeting, held on 4 May, attempts to resolve the problem led to further conflict. Mawu withdrew Mayekiso's name, proposing instead Tony Kgobe – widely labelled a 'workerist' – for regional secretary. A Sarhwu delegate called Kgobe 'politically unacceptable,' a comment declared out of order by the meeting's chairperson. Six unions – Gawu, Saawu, SFAWU, Sadwa, Sastawu and Sarhwu – stated they would not vote, and left the meeting, although they later returned. Another four unions – CWIU, NUTW, Pwawu and TGWU – indicated that they would abstain in any vote, out of concern for unity. The chair eventually ruled that voting should proceed and Tony Kgobe was elected regional secretary. Solo received no votes, since all his supporters had either refused to vote or abstained.

The situation was untenable. The six unions which had walked out were joined in their stand by Mwusa, Nupawo and Abwu. This meant that nine affiliates refused to recognise the regional secretary. Other unions, while recognising Kgobe, gave him less than full co-operation. The region was effectively paralysed. The regional chairperson, NUM's Paul Nkuna, himself accused by the nine unions of not being 'impartial' and of 'undemocratic' practices, reported on the problem to a CEC meeting held in August.[9] 'To say that the CEC would solve' the problem, he suggested,

> would be failing to understand the deep-rooted rationale behind it... We need to critically understand what is meant by tactical and/or strategic unity. We need to identify our primary enemy. We need a clinical analysis of the terms 'workerist' and 'populist'. One of the most important tasks of our region is to unite the different tendencies among the workers... There is still hope that even if we have not reached full agreement on all our principles we can work together and have unity (in) action. The question is how do we intend achieving this? Is it through constitutional democratic practices, or are we going to build our unity on deals?... Presently we are presenting a hollow unity to the outside world.

The matter was eventually resolved after the CEC urged, and then supervised, fresh elections in late November 1986. All previously-elected office bearers, including Kgobe, were returned to office.

The dispute in the Wits region highlighted a number of points. Firstly, unions perceived their political differences as being very deep. Secondly, the line-up of unions reflected regional dynamics in addition to the overall political/organisational blocs outlined in the previous chapter. Thirdly, the desire of all factions to 'control' the region politically appeared to override the need to keep Cosatu united. Fourthly, the issues of respect for structures and tolerance of differing views appeared identical in essence to those identified in the NUTW/Tawu split. Finally, the dispute revealed that gaining control of a structure through narrow voting majorities, rather than through developed consensus, paralysed that structure. Any victories won were pyrrhic.

Conflict in the Eastern Cape

The conflicts around the launch of the Eastern Cape region reflected similar problems. They centered on a protracted dispute around the paid-up membership and therefore the voting strength of each affiliate in the region. The REC continued to meet and perform certain essential regional tasks while the dispute continued. However, the Cosatu executive was eventually forced to intervene.

The dispute was essentially over control of the region. Saawu and its sister union, Satawu, failed to provide satisfactory proof of paid-up membership, claiming that a fire in their union offices had destroyed their records. Membership claims made by Macwusa and Gwusa were also challenged. Other unions felt that they were claiming high membership while paying affiliation fees to Cosatu on the basis of significantly lower figures. A compromise proposed by the REC was rejected by delegates to the regional congress, and the launch postponed for two months. Tempers were heated. According to the meeting's chairperson, CWIU's Thembinkosi Mkalipi, 'chairs were in the air and knives were out.' He was concerned about 'the disregard for the constitution and the disregard for democracy.' Saawu's Penrose Ntlonti claimed the dissatisfaction was over Mkalipi's chairing and bias.[10]

More disastrous was the fate of the mass rally which had been arranged for the next day, Sunday 18 May. Some 20 000 workers gathered jubilantly at Port Elizabeth's Dan Qeqe stadium to celebrate the launch of Cosatu in the region. The crowd gave a tumultuous welcome to the delegates from the abortive two-day regional congress. Cosatu's second vice-president, Makhulu Ledwaba, was obliged to inform the crowd that the launch had failed because of inter-union differences.* He criticised the local unionists in front of the crowd, accusing them of lacking direction. 'I want all the workers from different establishments and industries to come together and give direction to their delegates,' he said.[11]

Despite Ledwaba's dressing down, the regional conflict continued for months. Differences in the Eastern Cape ran deep. The UDF tradition in the area was particularly strong, while leadership of the non-UDF unions was exceptionally suspicious of the community leadership. Matters had come to a head shortly before the launch of Cosatu, when the majority of unions had opposed a stayaway call made by the UDF. Despite their opposition it had been almost a hundred percent effective.[12]

The region was only launched after heavy-handed intervention from Cosatu's Exco. By then Exco had concluded that Saawu was being disruptive. 'It was unacceptable,' stated Exco, 'that even when Saawu head office and Cosatu head office had sorted out the issue of Saawu's representation on the Eastern Province regional congress that Saawu...had chosen to reject this.' The region, Exco continued, 'will be launched' and 'any affiliate that does not accept (the final report on paid-up membership) will not be allowed to participate in the inaugural regional

---

* This was the second time the regional launch had failed. The first had been thwarted by a magisterial banning order in January.

congress.'[13] The region was finally launched in February 1987. Detained Macwusa official Dennis Neer was elected regional secretary, with Naawu's Les Kettledas appointed by the region to act in his place.

Early attempts to celebrate May Day

The first day of May is widely recognised as International Labour Day, and 1986 was its hundredth anniversary. May Day was first commemorated in South Africa in 1904, and over the years it had been a day of working-class celebration, mobilisation and struggle. In 1926, a Bill was introduced into parliament proposing the first Monday in May as a public holiday. After workers protested that 1 May was the symbol of international worker solidarity, the government of the time withdrew the Bill. In 1928, thousands of African workers participated in May Day celebrations, and during the 1930s and 1940s both the Communist Party and Cnetu helped popularise the day. A number of industrial council agreements included it as a paid holiday.

In 1950, in response to government intentions to ban the Communist Party, progressive organisations called for a national stayaway on 1 May. Despite heavy repression and many deaths, the call – the first ever for a national stayaway – received wide support. During the 1950s Sactu battled to keep the tradition of May Day alive in the face of government clampdowns. By 1961 a law had been passed excluding May Day as a paid holiday from all industrial council agreements.

Attempts to celebrate May Day were only revived in the 1980s. Even these small commemorative meetings met harsh state repression. A number of unions, and Fosatu affiliates in particular, began including the demand for May Day as a paid holiday in their negotiations with employers, but met with little success. From 1983 to 1985 they stubbornly kept it on the negotiating table hoping that, even where the demand was not won, the day itself would once more become popularised in workers' minds. By the time Cosatu was launched almost all its affiliates had experience in fighting for May Day although hardly any workers had won the demand. It was apparent that its achievement would require something far more dramatic than shopfloor struggle, for employers generally argued that public holidays were decided by government and thus beyond the realm of industrial negotiations.

At its founding congress Cosatu resolved that the federation should fight for 1 May to be a paid holiday and that it would 'initiate and organise celebrations...every year.' Workers also demanded 16 June – the anniversary of the start of the 1976 uprisings – as a paid holiday. In addition, some workers called for 21 March, the anniversary of the 1960 Sharpeville massacre, as a paid holiday.

Public holidays were contentious in South Africa. The symbols of both resistance and oppression were at stake. Workers wanted to celebrate days which were meaningful to them, and which commemorated political struggle. Instead, formal public holidays, apart from purely secular or religious ones, tended to commemorate days of importance to the Afrikaner nationalist movement. Four holidays in particular were offensive to the majority of the population. These were Republic Day, commemorating the establishment of a whites-only republic; Kruger Day, celebrating the birthday, no less, of a 19th century Boer president; Founders Day, which commemorated the first arrival of white settlers at the Cape in 1652 and the 'founding' of South Africa; and the Day of the Covenant, which recalled a sacred covenant allegedly made between God and the Afrikaner nation following the defeat of the Zulu army at the 'Battle of Blood River'. Cosatu declared that 'workers have no interest in racist political public holidays,'and should be 'prepared to sacrifice' these days if necessary.[*]

This was the year – 1986 – for Cosatu to prove its seriousness regarding public holidays. The launch of the federation required some concrete demonstration of strength; the political situation throughout the country was militant; and enthusiasm for Cosatu had been expressed in dramatic membership growth. In addition, Inkatha intended to launch its union wing, the United Workers Union of South Africa (Uwusa), on 1 May, with Simon Conco announcing that the anti-socialist Uwusa wanted to take on the socialists 'on their day'.[14]

May Day approaches

As May Day approached, the moderate union federation Tucsa was, as usual, out of step with the popular mood. Its president, Robbie Botha, claimed that most Tucsa unions preferred 2 January to May Day as a public holiday. Tucsa 'deplored the efforts of various factions attempting to turn May 1 into a political issue and the threatened violence to and intimidating of workers to observe this day.'[15] It called on its members not to take May Day off. By contrast, Cosatu's smaller rivals, Cusa and Azactu, urged workers to observe May Day. Cusa called for joint May Day meetings to be held with all federations. Cosatu, still angry over Cusa's last-minute withdrawal from the unity talks, and wanting to see Cusa prove itself, declined the offer.

---

[*] 16 December, the Day of the Covenant, was less contentious as a public holiday than the others. It often marked the beginning of the December shutdown period in much of the manufacturing sector, and was also the anniversary of the launch of the armed struggle in 1961.

The stand taken by the National Education Crisis Committee (NECC) was particularly important. At its March conference in Durban, attended by delegates from all corners of the country, it called on all students and youth to stand behind Cosatu's May Day call. The NECC decision effectively meant that the UDF's affiliates backed the May Day demand. As the day drew nearer many usually conservative or non-aligned organisations, came out in support of a May Day stayaway. HH Dlamlenze, secretary general of the African Teachers Association (Atasa), said his 54 000 member organisation had 'decided to throw (its) full weight behind the call for a complete workers' stayaway on May 1' in accordance with the spirit of the NECC resolutions. 'We therefore call on all black teachers to stay away from school on that day.'[16] Even the chairman of the African Chamber of Commerce (Nafcoc), Sam Motsuenyane, agreed that 'if black communities countrywide decide to observe May Day our members will follow suit.'[17]

On the union front, worker pressure was forcing a softening in management attitudes. Responding to demands at the metal industry wage negotiations, Seifsa declared that it would approach government to have May Day declared a national holiday in future. As the magnitude of impending stayaway action became clear, many employers, including the Federated Chamber of Industries (FCI) and Seifsa, adopted the relatively lenient policy of 'no work, no pay', instead of their customary threats of dismissal or disciplinary action.

The Chamber of Mines, however, still tried to resist the inevitable. Wanting to keep the weapon of mass dismissals in its armoury, it attempt to use the courts to this end. The previous year, 1985, the Chamber had rejected NUM's demand for a paid holiday on 1 May. NUM had accordingly declared a legal dispute, but had not pursued it. In early 1986 NUM revived the dispute and declared its intention to join the May Day strike. Only days before 1 May, the Chamber tried to interdict NUM from doing this, arguing in court that the union's demand for May Day was an old one which had expired. NUM had always, argued the Chamber, treated the demand as a low priority one. Surprisingly, the presiding judge found in favour of NUM. Although a considerable time had elapsed, he declared, the right to stage a legal strike, once obtained, could not 'go stale.'*

'We will be going out on May 1,' proclaimed NUM in response to the judgement, 'and in conjunction with the Congress of SA Trade Unions will be celebrating May Day. The Chamber of Mines is, in our

---

* The Chamber took the case on appeal, and a few months later the Appeal Court reversed the decision of the Supreme Court. But by then it was too late to affect the stayaway.

view, lagging behind the rest of industry in recognising that May Day is a day of celebration for labour.'[18] Legality in this proposed action was crucial for NUM. Mineowners had long shown a propensity to dismiss strikers, but would think twice before dismissing workers on a one-day legal strike!

Cosatu's CEC resolved to arrange rallies in all major centres, and called on all workers to attend. The CEC stressed that Cosatu was not calling for a stayaway – largely because such a call was illegal – but for workers to attend the rallies instead of going to work.

The CEC resolved to mobilise Cosatu's 'membership and the broad community' around a list of demands. Within the CEC this caused debate – not over principles, but over the tactics of campaigns. Some delegates wanted a limited number of demands, arguing that these would be memorable and easy to popularise. A long list of demands would be easily forgotten by both members and 'the enemy'. May Day needed a focus. Another grouping within the CEC felt that all the demands were equally important. Limiting them would show a limited perspective, they felt. In the end the latter group prevailed, and a long list of demands was agreed upon. These included May Day as a paid holiday; a 40-hour week and a living wage; social security and living pensions; full maternity benefits for working women; the right to strike; the right for students to form SRCs and 'an alternative system of people's education'; an end to pass laws and influx control; affordable rents; the unbanning of all banned organisations; and the release of all political prisoners.[19]

A statement was issued, and widely distributed, in the name of Cosatu's president. 'This is the one hundredth anniversary of May Day,' Barayi declared.

In SA itself we know that the discovery of gold in 1886 brought slavery to our people... We made South Africa rich. We built the roads, the cars, the clothes we wear... But in South Africa millions of workers and their families live in poverty, hunger and starvation...while a minority live in wealth so great that they are amongst the richest in the world... As Cosatu we must challenge this domination... We want our freedom from apartheid and the cheap labour system... We must build shop stewards, shaft stewards, street and area committees everywhere. This is the basis of our people taking power... Let us make this one hundredth May Day the biggest and most successful in our history.

'Two years ago,' lamented the *Star*, May Day 'was a low-priority item...but not an issue which kept employers awake.'[20] *Business Day* called union claims that over one million workers would participate, 'ambitious'.[21] But as 1 May dawned it soon became apparent that even this was a massive underestimate.

Millions stay away

The Labour Monitoring Group (LMG) estimated that a minimum of 1,5-million workers took part in the stayaway. The figure is almost certainly considerably higher. According to the director of the National Productivity Institute, the estimated loss to the economy was R150-million. But even this does not convey the magnitude of the day. Both figures exclude active participation by students, scholars, shopkeepers, self-employed people, the informal sector, the unemployed, and housewives. Many a hawker did not go to town, many a shopkeeper shut up shop, and many a taxi driver did not drive.*

Support for the stayaway was uneven. While over half the African workers remained at home in the Western Cape, for example, an insignificant number of coloured workers participated. Cape Town was organisationally one of Cosatu's weak spots. Africans, constituting almost half the black population, held less than 20% of the jobs. At the time, coloured workers, particularly in the crucial garment industry, were still under the influence of conservative Tucsa unionists.

In the country's industrial heartland, the PWV area, the stayaway was supported by some 79% of manufacturing workers, 87% of commercial workers, and 38% of public sector workers. The lower level of support in the last grouping reflected weaker unionisation. Public sector workers often lived in separate municipal compounds, and were also more frequently threatened by right-wing 'employers', the city councils being generally pro-government or extreme right wing.

Workers outside the urban centres also participated in the action. In the Steelpoort area of the Transvaal, large numbers of farmworkers joined a stayaway for the first time ever. On the mines an estimated 209 000 miners took a holiday. Throughout Natal some 60% of workers stayed away. Well-organised sectors such as chemicals and metals, saw worker participation in larger firms reach as high as 97%. An unusually large number of Indian workers in Natal also participated in the call.

The Eastern Cape saw the country's highest level of participation, with UDF activists playing a large part in organising the action. LMG's

---

* The LMG survey of the May Day stayaway was its first attempt to conduct such a study on a national basis. LMG has been criticised by Cosatu for being too conservative in its subsequent stayaway estimates and for relying exclusively on information gleaned from management. Management consultants, in turn, have accused it of a 'pro-union bias'. LMG sees its reliance on management statistics as a self-proclaimed limitation. In subsequent surveys it moved towards estimating the percentage participation in stayaways rather than actual numbers. LMG's work is in many ways indispensable and generally reliable. However, its 1986 May Day survey findings need to be re-examined.

survey revealed that in Port Elizabeth factories questioned only three out of 13 340 African workers reported for duty! In Uitenhage an estimated 99,8% of African workers stayed away. Participation by coloured workers was lower, ranging from 45% in Port Elizabeth to 79% in Uitenhage. This reflected the strength of union organisation in each area.

In the larger Eastern Cape towns, the stayaway was total amongst African workers. Towns affected included Grahamstown, Queenstown, Cradock, Graaff-Reinet, Somerset East, Fort Beaufort, Humansdorp, Port Alfred, Stutterheim and King Williams Town. Aliwal North, alone amongst towns with more than 10 000 people, saw no action taken. Coloured workers participated in the stayaway to differing degrees, with their support in Cookhouse and Port Alfred being total.

May Day 1986 was the first national stayaway called since the early 1960s. At the time, it was probably the largest ever stayaway in the country's history. While there was a relationship between union organisation and the level of support for the stayaway, this differed from area to area. The action was only partly organised, with Cosatu and the UDF being particularly important in the effort. But is also captured the mood of resistance amongst the mass of the population, and in many respects was the culmination of a spate of local and regional stayaways which had occurred since 1985.

Rallying the people

Cosatu organised rallies at a number of venues throughout the country on May Day. Those that materialised were attended by roughly 100 000 people in total. Many of the rallies were, however, banned. These included ones planned for Port Elizabeth, Uitenhage, East London, Empangeni, Ladysmith and Pretoria. In Empangeni's eSikhawini township the rally, due to be held in the local stadium, was banned by the Inkatha-controlled township council. One of the councillors, MP Gumede, who was also active in trying to launch Uwusa, said he believed the council had banned Cosatu meetings 'because there have been so many criticisms against the Chief Minister (Buthelezi) and Inkatha.'

Cosatu's members in the area decided to go ahead with the meeting despite the ban. 'They do not see why they should be the only workers barred from holding a meeting to commemorate May Day,' explained Jerry Ntombela, a prominent Cosatu leader in the area. About 3 000 workers attended the rally at the stadium. Surprisingly, the meeting went off without problems despite the increased presence of both KwaZulu and South African police.[22]

Not all participants in the rallies were so fortunate. The Western Cape region of Cosatu reported that it had arranged seven rallies to be addressed by shop stewards and students. All but two were attacked and disrupted by the police.[23] Similar experiences were reported from rallies held around the country.

The main rally for the day was held at Orlando Stadium, Soweto. Many participants were harassed on their way to the stadium, and army and police 'hippo' vehicles with heavily-armed security force members stood at the entrance. Many, fearful of conflict, refused to pass them and returned home. Finally about 20 000 people gathered in the stadium, rather less than had been hoped for. Soweto was expected to provide a larger turnout. The mood was both jubilant and tense. Unidentified people distributed thousands of SACP pamphlets, although many of these leaflets were later burned in an attempt to alleviate the teargas lobbed into the stadium by police. An informer, seized by youths outside the stadium, was brought inside where some wanted to 'necklace' him. Only swift action by Cosatu marshalls saved him from this grisly fate.

Barayi, the main speaker at the rally, delivered a scathing attack on Inkatha, Buthelezi and the formation of Uwusa. Well known for his oratory, he jokingly referred to Buthelezi as *uMntwana uphind' uphume* and labelled him a 'tribalist'. He called the launch of Uwusa an attempt to divide the workers. President Botha should also know, he said, that workers would eventually get May Day as a paid holiday, whether he liked it or not. Another speaker at the rally was Winnie Mandela who was enthusiastically welcomed when she arrived.

May Day 1986 was not without casualties. There were a number of deaths, some the result of police shootings, and at least one person was shot and killed by an Inkatha supporter at Durban's Berea station while returning from Cosatu's rally. At Bophelong, in the Vaal, residents at the May Day rally were teargassed and detained by police, who also killed a youth, prompting residents to stay away again on 2 May. In Port Alfred, events around May Day, as well as the rape of a woman, prompted a week-long stayaway led by the UDF-organised women of the town.

The year May Day was won

The press publicly conceded that the unions had won the right to May Day, and many employers grudgingly agreed. 'If there was ever any doubt about workers' May Day wishes, it was removed yesterday,' noted the *Star*. 'An undeclared holiday is disruptive, bedevils industrial relations, creates anomalies, undermines the authority of the law, makes a mockery of statutory holidays.'[24] 'South Africa's black workers', noted the conservative *Sunday Times*, 'have for all times unilaterally declared May 1 a public holiday. Government acceptance of this week's holiday by public fiat would not only be wise but gracious.'[25]

Later in May, Premier Foods became the first major employer to declare both 1 May and 16 June as paid holidays for employees of all races. Many companies followed suit and backed down during negotiations over the next year. However, a majority of employers preferred to take their lead from government on this issue.

The government was unwilling to concede Cosatu's demands, which it had labelled both communist and subversive. Having labelled 1 May a communist day with Marxist links, it had painted itself into a corner. In 1987 the state declared that the first Friday of every May would be known in future as Workers Day. The unions rejected this and stuck to their 1 May demand. However, conflict was avoided during 1987 since 1 May happened to coincide with the first Friday in May that year. The following year, 1988, saw 1 May fall on a Sunday. Many organised workers decided to celebrate 1 May and to also take off the first Friday, 6 May. What the government had sown, it should reap, they argued. For 1989 the government declared that, in future, Workers Day would be the first Monday in May! Conveniently, this happened to coincide with 1 May 1989. Only in early 1990 did the government finally announce that 1 May would in future be Workers Day. It had taken four years to acknowledge what the majority of the people had proclaimed in 1986!

May Day 1986 was undoubtedly a major success. It highlighted Cosatu's strength, and showed the power of a stayaway organised by both unions and community organisations. It indicated that a stayaway need not be an exclusively passive response, and that rallies could be organised as well. It won the right not only to May Day but a reassessment of the whole public holiday system. It imprinted May Day as a day of celebration and not a day of 'unrest'. It showed the power of a stayaway organised in advance, which coincided with the mood of the masses.

However, May Day 1986 was a victory tempered by certain weaknesses. Such was the pressure of events that Cosatu's CEC never assessed the action – the largest in the country's history! While some regions undertook assessments, these tended to be rather parochial. Wits region, at its REC of 25 May, noted that many workers could not get to the Orlando rally because the stayaway had also included transport workers. Those from outside Soweto had been stuck without transport. The answer, it was felt, was to hold more local rallies in future.[26] A more general weakness noted was that while so many had been mobilised to stay away, only 100 000 had attended the rallies. In later years this weakness became more apparent. Having won the day, the union movement appeared to lack the ability to use it to rally its forces. May Day started to run the risk of being simply another day off.

On balance May Day 1986 was an overwhelming victory for the union movement, and Cosatu in particular. But the same day also saw the launch of Inkatha's Uwusa. This was a direct challenge to Cosatu and for a time, at least in Natal, seemed to threaten the federation's very future.

Notes

1. Minutes of a Cosatu central executive committee meeting held at Ipelegeng Centre, Soweto from 7-9 February 1986.
2. *Star*, 04.06.86.
3. *Financial Mail*, 06.06.86.
4. *Business Day*, 02.12.86.
5. Southern Natal Regional Report to Cosatu's second central executive committee meeting, held in Soweto on 12-13 April 1986.
6. The report of the general secretary to the second national congress of Cosatu held at the University of Witwatersrand, Johannesburg, 15-17 July 1987; and report of the 'Cosatu commission appointed by the CEC...to attempt to settle a dispute in NUTW', 17 September 1986.
7. Report of the 'Cosatu commission...to attempt to settle a dispute in NUTW', 6-7.
8. Report of Highveld co-ordinating committee to a meeting of the central executive committee of Cosatu, held at Wilgespruit, 15-16 August 1986.
9. 'Memorandum from nine unions to Cosatu Exco re: Wits Regional Congress elections'; see also Wits regional report to CEC of 16-17 August 1986.
10. *Weekly Mail*, 23.05.86.
11. *Weekly Mail*, 23.05.86.
12. 'Trade Unions and the March Stay-aways', *South African Labour Bulletin*, 11(1), September 1985.
13. Minutes of a meeting of Cosatu's Exco, 17 January 1987.
14. *Weekly Mail*, 25.04.86.
15. *Star*, 30.04.86.
16. *City Press*, 27.04.86.
17. *City Press*, 27.04.86.
18. *Star*, 29.04.86.
19. The full CEC resolution and list of demands is contained in *South African Labour Bulletin*, 11(5), April-May 1986.
20. *Star*, 30.04.86.
21. *Business Day*, 18.04.86.
22. See Pippa Green, 'May Day Courage in Northern Natal', *South African Labour Bulletin*, 11(6), June/July 1986, for further details.
23. Regional report of the Western Cape to a Cosatu central executive meeting held at Wilgespruit, 15-16 August 1986.
24. *Star*, 02.05.86.
25. *Sunday Times*, 04.05.86.
26. Minutes of Cosatu's Wits regional executive committee meeting held in Germiston, 25 May 1986.

8

Uwusa and the emergency clampdown

Iron fists

*U*WUSA was launched at a rally held at Kings Park Stadium in Durban. Over 60 000 attended, although most were probably not workers. Inkatha had organised buses and trains for the rally, and in many rural areas chiefs asked local people to contribute towards transport, and attend the rally. Not all transport was easy for Inkatha to arrange. Pietermaritzburg busdrivers, organised by TGWU, refused to drive buses to the Uwusa launch. Nevertheless the attendance was impressive, and the stadium packed to capacity.

Cosatu's launching rally, held in the same stadium five months earlier, had attracted only 10 000 workers, while Cosatu's own May Day rally in Durban, held at the same time as the Uwusa launch, again attracted only 10 000. Cosatu, responding to the substantial attendance at the Uwusa launch, said it was not playing a numbers game. This was an inadequate reply, for the ability of Inkatha to mobilise large numbers was a significant pointer to its power.

Uwusa adopted the slogan of 'Jobs not Hunger.' A pamphlet circulated before the rally asked workers whether 'you want your factories to close?... If you want to keep your job join the new giant labour union at King's Park on May 1.'[1] Those who attended saw the rally open with a mock funeral, as coffins were carried into the stadium marked 'Barayi' and 'Cosatu'. This was an early indication that Cosatu, rather than employers, was to be Uwusa's main target of attack. Indeed, sharing the stage at the rally were a number of employers.[2]

Prior to the launch, it had been announced that several unions already supported Uwusa. These were introduced at the rally: the African Domestic Workers Union, the National Union of Brick and Allied Workers, and the Black Staff Association of SA Transport Services.[3] This was an unimpressive start. The domestic union was previously unrecorded. The brick union was well-known as a 'sweetheart' body started by a Corobrik personnel officer. The Black Staff Association was a creation of Sats management, formed with the aim of blocking the unionisation of black railway workers.[*]

Notably absent from the list of unions supporting Uwusa was the National Sugar Refining and Allied Industries Employees Union (NSRAIEU), a general union despite its name, and the only union affiliated to Inkatha. NSRAIEU, commonly known as 'Nsibande's union' after its general secretary, was hostile to the formation of Uwusa, as this implied its de-recognition as Inkatha's labour wing. Uwusa was equally reluctant to be associated with NSRAIEU because, according to Conco, it had tarnished its image 'by misappropriating money...and hanging... (its) dirty linen out for all the public to see.'[4]

According to Chief Buthelezi, the main speaker at Uwusa's launch, claims by Cosatu's 'pals' that Uwusa was a 'capitalist union' were:

> a lot of balderdash... Unless blacks are given entry into the free enterprise system it can have no future in a liberated South Africa. Despite the handicaps it has, I know of no other economic system devised by man which can create as many jobs as it can.

Responding to allegations that Uwusa was opposed to strikes, Buthelezi said he accepted the strike weapon. Nevertheless, 'there was no reason today why workers should go on strike before they have exhausted all the channels that are now available for negotiations.' Workers should 'guard against being used by people who want to carry out their own political programmes.' Finally, Buthelezi stated, he had 'no intention of interfering in Uwusa's affairs now that they are standing on their feet.'[5]

Before the Uwusa launch

After Cosatu's launch it was apparent there would be conflict with Inkatha, and Cosatu immediately began extensive preparations amongst its

---

[*] *Sats withdrew recognition of the Black Staff Association in Natal during the massive Sarhwu railway strike of 1989-90.*

Natal membership. Some 500 shop stewards from throughout Natal attended a meeting on 26 January 1986, where Cosatu leaders warned that 'the damage that Inkatha and its allies in big business could do to the trade union movement should not be underestimated... A war of words or, even worse, more serious physical attacks will not benefit anyone.'[6]

The meeting resulted in an important policy statement which was distributed throughout Cosatu in both English and Zulu. 'It is our considered view', the pamphlet stated, 'that the strategy for achieving liberation through the "Homelands" has very counter-productive costs.' It noted, however, 'that if political differences between Cosatu and any other organisation exist then we do not see this as a "state of war"', as Buthelezi apparently did. Regarding allegations that Cosatu was 'an ANC front', the pamphlet noted that 'this shows very little understanding of the democracy of workers' organisation... All decisions are based on mandates we receive from our membership.'

On its opposition to 'free enterprise', Cosatu noted that in KwaZulu's industrial areas of Peters, Isithebe and elsewhere,

> wages of R20 per week are paid... Free enterprise was built on the dispossession of the land from the majority by a minority ... (and on) the denial of political rights to the majority... Does Inkatha want us to support a system that has resulted in the enslavement and poverty of our people?

Regarding disinvestment, Cosatu's leadership asked why – with the clampdown, hundreds killed and jailed, and the world campaigning for the isolation of the apartheid regime – 'an organisation (should) deliberately campaign against disinvestment... Is it not better to remain silent?... We are opposed to a policy of investment at any price.'[7]

Within a week, Buthelezi had issued a public reply to the pamphlet. Implying that its authors were 'political idiots and surrogates of the External Mission of ANC,' he launched an aggressive and personalised attack. Barayi was labelled as 'a Ciskeian who did nothing to prevent Ciskei from going "independent"... He now comes to Natal with a bunch of people who come from areas like the Ciskei to tell us about opposition to the homelands policy...'

Buthelezi went on to argue that 'when we use words like the "state of war", we are using realistic language in view of violent confrontations' caused by Cosatu's policy of denigrating Inkatha.

> The imposition of a socialist future on South Africa after liberation, the rejection of the free enterprise system, the support for disinvestment and sanctions are clearly espoused by all those who are surrogates of the External Mission of ANC... We take strong exception to Inkatha members in the trade unions being carried willy-nilly on Mr Elijah

Barayi's back for handing over to Sactu and automatically to the External
Mission of ANC.

The statement also took 'strong exception' to Cosatu's suggestions
that Inkatha had been involved in violence against Cosatu members. 'We
are unaware of any violence against members of Cosatu,' it said.[8]

Attacks on Cosatu

Shortly after Uwusa's launch, Cosatu issued a detailed dossier of affidavits listing alleged Inkatha-related attacks on its members and officials.
According to this dossier, the house of a prominent official in Northern
Natal, Matthews Oliphant, was petrol-bombed on 26 January. In Ma-
dadeni and Newcastle, Cosatu officials reported the invasion of offices,
petrol-bombing of houses, abductions and arrests of officials, as well as
death threats from KwaZulu police. In Pietermaritzburg, an Inkatha
councillor abducted the son of a prominent Mawu official, John Makatini, at gunpoint. The young Makatini was forced into the boot of a car
and questioned about his father and Cosatu. In Durban the house of Cosatu's regional secretary, Thami Mohlomi, was attacked during April.
Three petrol bombs were thrown at it, and shots fired through the front
door and windows. Members of the Inkatha Youth Brigade and KwaZulu
police were alleged to be responsible. Cosatu's dossier listed many more
incidents similar to these.[9]

A state of war also developed at factory level. During May, workers
at a Ladysmith furniture factory were due to vote in a ballot between
Pwawu and Uwusa. Days before the ballot the anti-Cosatu manager of
the factory employed large numbers of temporary workers recruited and
brought to the factory by local Inkatha officials. Management insisted
that these workers should also vote. On voting day the same Inkatha
officials returned with an impi of almost 100 armed Inkatha warriors,
who chanted outside the gate awaiting the result of the ballot. Police
refused to disperse them. Given the presence of the temporary workers
and the threat of death to Pwawu supporters, it was surprising that
Pwawu lost the ballot by only five votes.[10]

At Durban's Clover Dairies, two workers recruiting for Uwusa were
threatened by Cosatu members. Some 1 000 Fawu members went on
strike demanding the dismissal of the two Uwusa members. At Jabula
Foods, in Springs, Fawu won a ballot against Uwusa, but this was accompanied by clashes between Fawu and Uwusa members. Fawu's chief
shop steward was killed in the incident.[11]

Similar clashes occurred throughout 1986 in a variety of factories,
often with bloody consequences. The most serious of these was at

Hlobane coal mine in Northern Natal. On 6 June, conflict at Hlobane resulted in 11 deaths, over 100 injuries, and the dismissal of 800 workers. The clash took place over a strike at the mine, and involved attacks by what NUM called 'Inkatha thugs' brought in by the busload from outside. 'We believe', said NUM, that 'mine security permitted non-mine workers to enter No 3 shaft with the aim of attacking the workers and breaking the strike.'[12]

In a speech made at the nearby Zululand Anthracite Colliery a few days earlier, the Zulu king, Goodwill Zwelethini, had attacked Barayi and NUM. According to one account,

> he accused some mineworkers of making 'a habit' of insulting Buthelezi and warned 'other blacks who come to work here' that while they were welcome 'they must behave themselves and respect black leadership of this region'.

Uwusa's weaknesses

Uwusa was able to draw on Inkatha's might, but rarely posed a serious threat to Cosatu's organised factories. Very few organised plants left to join Uwusa. Of those which did, most eventually returned to Cosatu. Nevertheless, Uwusa was a continual thorn in Cosatu's side, particularly in Natal and parts of the Transvaal. Its ongoing attacks compelled Cosatu to devote time and scarce resources to strengthening its structures in those areas. Affiliates were forced to maintain a relatively high standard of factory 'servicing'. This was, in itself, positive. But it was demanding work, particularly in the face of widespread management favouritism towards Uwusa.

Ultimately Uwusa's formation was a major political error by Buthelezi. While it placed Cosatu on the defensive to some extent, it alienated Buthelezi totally and irreversibly from the organised labour movement. Uwusa's leadership was inexperienced and inappropriate. Its general secretary, Simon Conco, was a businessman; its president, Petrus Ndlovu worked in the personnel department of a sugar conglomerate; its vice-president, Pepsi Msomi, was township superintendent in Tembisa; and Uwusa's treasurer, Peter Davidson, was a Durban-based entrepreneur.[14] Even Conco's subsequent replacement, GST Hadebe, was himself a corporate industrial relations officer.*

The much-vaunted worker leader who called for the formation of Uwusa, MP Gumede, was not elected onto the executive. He was apparently as unpopular within Inkatha as he had been previously within Pwawu and Fosatu. Many knew him by his nickname, S'cefe, meaning 'an irritation'.

Uwusa's major weakness lay in its reason for existence, which seemed to be little more than opposition to Cosatu. The gains it did make were usually achieved when Cosatu was particularly vulnerable. For example, during 1987 it signed a recognition agreement on behalf of more than 900 'scabs' taken on by BTR Sarmcol following the dismissal of Mawu's entire membership at the plant.* At the level of effective unionism, Uwusa was unable to deliver the goods to its members, and there is no record of any strike action by the union.

Uwusa's initial intention of transforming itself into a federation of industrial unions has never been realised. Its claim, made in June 1986, to be negotiating closer links with five trade unions representing more than 200 000 members never materialised.

Conco's statement made after Uwusa's launch, to the effect that its battle with Cosatu would 'be won or lost on the Witwatersrand,' proved accurate. Uwusa never managed to win significant support in that region. Two days after Uwusa's launch it claimed a membership of 85 000. By September 1987 it claimed 150 000 paid-up and 50 000 signed-up members. However, outside observers believed that by mid-1988 its paid-up membership was less than 50 000.[15]

A new state of emergency

One minute after midnight on 12 June 1986, armed men carrying machineguns and shotguns broke into the house where Jay Naidoo was living. A new state of emergency had been declared.

The group at Naidoo's home claimed to be police, although they refused to show identification and were not wearing uniforms. After asking all the residents to identify themselves, and after searching the house, they left. Fortunately, Naidoo was not at home. Thousands of other unionists and political activists were not so lucky.

Those not caught in the first net of arrests quickly went 'into hiding'. They developed irregular movements, sometimes changed appearance, avoided places usually frequented, and rarely slept at home. Union leaders steered clear of their offices and meetings with management.

For unions, the 1985/86 emergency was tame compared to the one declared on 12 June 1986. The second emergency was better planned, more-harshly implemented, and gave virtually a free rein to the army and police. In contrast to the first emergency, it was applied to every region of the country. Emergency rule reflected the total dominance of the security forces within the state. In time, it also revealed their total

---

* Two years later the scabs were approaching Cosatu. Uwusa was an ineffective union, they claimed, and they wanted to leave it and join Numsa!

inability to provide any solutions, other than naked terror and repression, to the crisis facing the country.

Many unionists were detained by the police. Some, but not all, had also been active in community organisations in their areas. Six weeks into of the emergency, the Labour Monitoring Group had recorded the detention of 2 700 unionists, of whom 81% were from Cosatu.[16]

LMG figures included only known detentions, and were an underestimation. Many detainees were released within two weeks, either because they were ordinary workers 'uninvolved' in 'politics', or because the jails were overcrowded. Those who remained in detention tended to be leadership figures. By the end of July LMG reported that some 320 'elected trade union leaders and officials' were among the thousands known to be in detention. Numbers alone were reported. It was illegal to name detainees, except those acknowledged by the police, and it was illegal to refer to police conduct.[17]

Trying to regroup

Detentions were not the only problem the unions faced. From the first day of the emergency, offices were raided, members intimidated, and the smooth running of the unions disrupted. Most unionists realised that a mass union movement could not be run from hiding. But common sense indicated the need to lie low until the situation had clarified. Cosatu leaders still outside jail immediately tried to regroup the federation's forces, and Frank Meintjies helped maintain contact between leaders. Employed by Cosatu as its information officer, he began duties on 12 June, the day the emergency was declared. Because he came from Natal, he was not well known to the Johannesburg police. He was, therefore, relatively free to move between union leaders. He recalls that on arriving in Johannesburg he had no idea where Cosatu's offices were. When he eventually located Cosatu House, Cosatu's newly-rented headquarters, he found the building

> barricaded by the SADF... During the next week the SADF came in on a day-to-day basis. They were presumably waiting for Jay (Naidoo) and Sydney (Mufamadi) to turn up.
>
> I seemed to have space to do things and move around. The leadership of the different unions often used me to communicate. I would relay the messages, decisions and the tasks which needed to be done. I was the liaison person and the one who organised clandestine venues and gathered information and money from the office to bring to Jay and Sydney. At one meeting, with all unions present, it was agreed to call a special CEC meeting.[18]

It was clear the federation would have to rely on its shopfloor organisation if it was to survive. It had been stressed for years that the unions were not the offices but the workers themselves. The first priority, therefore, was to keep union structures going. A pamphlet distributed nationally on 19 June called on all to 'ensure that factory general meetings, (shop steward) councils, RCs and REC meetings continue to be held.' The document listed eight demands to be put to major employer organisations. These included demands that detained workers should be paid in full and their jobs held open; that telephone, telex and other facilities should be granted to affiliates at the workplaces; and that shop stewards should be granted paid time off, where necessary, to attend to union business outside company premises. If the demands were not met a CEC meeting, scheduled for 1 July, would 'approve any further steps to be taken.'

Workers showed that they were prepared to defend their unions and their leaders. Despite the repression, mass action continued. On 16 June, the anniversary of the 1976 uprising, a nationwide stayaway – at least as big as the earlier May Day action – took place. While this showed a capacity to resist state terror, its significance as a direct act of resistance to the emergency should not be overestimated. Community organisations and unions had been planning the 16 June action for some time, and in many respects the stayaway was the result of an organisational momentum which began before the emergency was declared.

Workers resist detentions

By contrast, workers in some factories, mines and shops directly challenged the state of emergency. Militant Ccawusa members on the Witwatersrand took the lead, and received some support in other parts of the country. Workers at almost 100 shops downed tools demanding the release of detained union leaders and officials. The stoppages lasted up to two weeks. A Pick 'n Pay hypermarket, a Frasers warehouse and 12 of its stores, 37 Checkers stores, 11 CNA outlets, 23 OK Bazaars stores, a Woolworths warehouse and 13 of its stores were affected.[19] So too were the EMI and Gallo record companies.

After police detained five key members of NUM's regional executive, almost 2 000 miners at four of De Beers' Kimberley diamond mines stopped work. Police often responded to such protests by attempting to detain participating workers.

Around this time, Barayi, NUM's vice-president as well as Cosatu's president, was detained. NUM launched a national consumer boycott of bars, liquor outlets, and concession stores on the country's mines as a response to the detention. In early July, 5 000 miners at Free State

Geduld went on a go-slow in protest at detentions, while at Gencor's Matla coal mine, workers staged underground sit-ins. Miners at Grootvlei, Marievale and Kriel also took action. In addition protest strikes affected a number of pharmaceutical and chemical plants, organised by CWIU as well as Cusa's powerful chemical affiliate, Sacwu. Workers in other factories – including food, construction and metal plants – also took action in protest against detentions, but in many cases these protests went unreported.

These strikes caused concern amongst employers. Management complained of their contact with unionists being limited to 'ticky-box' public-phone calls.

Premier's Tony Bloom said in late June that 'we are now faced with attempting to run our factories and enterprises by dealing with the mob because the leaders are in custody.' One reporter noted that 'something akin to bedlam initially emerged in some factories but details cannot be disclosed as many incidents concern police action.'[20] A *Business Day* editorial in early July commented that the state was helping 'revolutionaries to legitimise violence on the grounds that lawful political activity is made pointless by government suppression.' Union leaders, it continued, 'should be immune to measures designed to deal with threats to security.'[21] The *Star* commented that 'the heavy hand of the state' was disrupting 'employer-worker relationships carefully nurtured for years.'[22]

However, most employers were silent in the face of the emergency clampdown, and many openly supported it. 'There is a view held, I suppose by the majority of business,' said JCI and Anglo American's Gordon Waddell, 'that the state of emergency was necessary and desirable to restore law and order.' The FCI's John van Zyl argued that 'while the emergency could create a period of relative calm in the country, the question was what one did with the time.' If the emergency had not been introduced, according to Donald Masson, past president of the Afrikaanse Handelsinstituut (AHI), 'the economy would have been finished. There was no way we could have continued to do business while people were burning down schools and murdering one another.'[23]

Detentions were not the only problem facing unionists. The police banned a number of organisations, including Cosatu and its affiliates, from holding indoor gatherings. Outdoor gatherings were already prohibited! 'The government has seriously disrupted our normal operations as labour unions,' said a Cosatu press statement issued in late June. Negotiations, affecting more than a million workers in the metal, mining and food sectors had been disrupted. The unions had been 'seriously disadvantaged' by detentions and 'the forcing into hiding of key leadership.' Nevertheless, said the statement, affiliates had decided 'that officials will begin returning to main offices' which for the past few weeks had been run largely by administrative staff and ordinary workers.

The confidence to return was enhanced by the strike action. Management rushed to meet the government hoping to secure the release of union detainees, and thus end the strikes. But the police refused to budge. The commissioner of police, General Johan Coetzee, claimed that no unionists were detained purely for trade union activities. Certain unions, he said, had 'entered the political arena with full knowledge of the possible repercussions.' With bizarre logic, Coetzee declared that trade union leaders and members would not be detained unless they were prolonging the state of emergency by their activities.[24]

Workers had undoubtedly responded to the emergency powerfully, but action could have been more widespread. The secretariat report to Cosatu's 1987 congress noted that generally 'we were ill-prepared for the crackdown and were thus unable to initiate strong shopfloor responses to the state of emergency.' In many factories, workers were awaiting guidance on action from their leadership. The leadership, however, was often in disarray.

Worker action and management fear that it would spread did lead to police backing off the unions to some degree. Mawu's national congress continued unhindered in early July, although security precautions were taken and some delegates were unable to attend. A number of unionists, including Barayi, were released from detention. The police withdrew their ban on indoor union meetings, claiming that the ban had been imposed in error. According to a police statement issued by the state-run Bureau for Information, the only source on 'unrest' which the media could quote legally, 'economic stability, which is dependent on sound labour relations, is vitally important in all spheres of the community.' Accordingly, 'no employee is or will be detained for bona fide trade union activities.' In one sense this was meaningless, given the police's narrow view of 'bona fide' unionism. Nevertheless, the mere issuing of such a statement at that time indicated a degree of retreat in the face of demands from workers and from employers paralysed by strikes. By midAugust the pressure on union leaders had eased slightly, and it became apparent that police chiefs had withdrawn instructions to detain certain senior unionists, including Naidoo. Although many remained in detention, others were able to operate openly. It was a significant victory.

The emergency experience

The emergency was experienced differently in various parts of the country. In the Eastern Cape, there was hardly a factory which did not have workers detained, often for periods of up to three years. Many were ordinary union members who had been active in township street or area committees. In Northern Natal, every organiser and many key shop stewards in the region were detained. The Empangeni offices, Cosatu's regional centre, were left with a single administrator to run them. Politically, this was Cosatu's weakest region. Its organisers, almost without exception, did not participate in activities outside of simple unionism. As regional secretary Oliphant stated, 'there is no UDF or Azapo in this area that we could be associated with.' The area had experienced little, if any unrest. And yet officials were held for months, paralysing Cosatu activities.[*]

The Northern Natal detentions came in two waves. Firstly, six key officials and workers – Ntombela, Vilane, Mchunu, Mkhonza, Mkhwanazi and Oliphant, were detained immediately the emergency was declared. Then, on 15 June, police entered a Cosatu regional executive meeting and detained everyone present. It was months before they were released. Oliphant's conclusion was inescapable: 'The state must have been helping Uwusa to organise.'[25]

In a number of areas police showed no hesitation in detaining an entire striking workforce. Over a hundred striking Katlehong municipal police were detained under emergency regulations during October. Some 1 200 dismissed municipal workers, organised by Cusa's Sabmawu, were also held briefly in a mass detention. In Johannesburg, 950 Nels Dairy workers were detained for over two weeks after protesting against the detention of two unionists. On their release they discovered that management had dismissed them all.

When some detainees were released, they were placed under severe restriction orders. Cosatu president Barayi was held for only two weeks, but on release was prohibited from leaving the town of Carletonville without permission. This effectively prevented him from carrying out most of his constitutional duties as Cosatu president.

Unions put a great deal of energy into fighting for detainee rights. Job security and salary payment during detention were the priorities. Cosatu aimed to prevent management from taking advantage of the detentions to dismiss workers. Unions also aimed to ensure that detainees would not have to worry about financial problems while imprisoned, and that their families would be looked after. Unions generally managed to win job security for detainees, but payment during detention was more difficult. When achieved it was usually only after substantial pressure, including the declaration of disputes and the threat

* *Recruitment and political education continued in prison. Northern Natal detainees held lengthy discussions with detained students. One, Nkosinathi Nhleko, joined the union movement on his release. In late 1989 he was elected general secretary of TGWU.*

of strikes. Most employers took the attitude that detainees were absent from work 'without permission'!

Cosatu holds a special CEC

The CEC met in special session on 1 July, with observers from local structures in addition to the usual delegates attending. Cosatu had openly stated that a meeting would be held, although it decided to keep the venue secret. Delegates were told to gather at a variety of places, and from there were taken to the meeting. The eventual venue was the first floor of the plush Johannesburg Sun hotel. It was felt that a meeting in a busy city hotel would be less noticeable than elsewhere, and a massive police raid on a hotel housing international guests would also not be undertaken lightly. In the event, the CEC meeting proceeded unhindered, and police were not in evidence. Either they did not know the venue, or had decided to allow the CEC to take place without disruption.

It was a strange gathering. Ordinary Cosatu activists kept a careful watch for signs of police activity in the vicinity. Some monitored street corners. Others kept an eye on the hotel lobby. The CEC delegates came in unusual attire. Most wore suits and ties and carried briefcases. Some had rapidly-grown beards and moustaches or now wore spectacles to help alter their appearance. Yet other delegates arrived wearing overalls. None wore the T-shirts with fighting slogans which, until a few weeks previously, had been standard unionist garb. A few of the most sought-after delegates decided it would be wisest not to come to the meeting at all, and sent others in their place.

The CEC laid down two sets of demands. Firstly, there were demands of a general nature. These called for an end 'to all harassment, victimisation and intimidation of shop stewards, officials and workers'; the release of all union leaders; an end to repression and 'a movement to a democratic resolution of our country's problems.' A second set of demands was directed at employers. These were essentially the same as those contained in the 19 June pamphlet, and aimed to give ordinary worker leaders the facilities and time-off necessary to help the unions continue functioning. They also aimed at winning job security on full pay for all detained union members.

The CEC also decided that a satisfactory response to its demands should be forthcoming by 10 July. If not, a call would be made for a national 'Day of Action' to take place on 14 July. It was a hotly-debated decision. The majority of delegates were angry and wanted to take defiant stayaway action. They argued that workers were awaiting direction from Cosatu. The emergency affected community organisations as well as unions. A stayaway, it was argued, was the appropriate action. The people had shown their muscle during stayaways on both May Day and 16 June that year, and this could be repeated. A strong argument was made for more than one day of action.

A minority of CEC delegates felt that factory-based action, such as a national stoppage, should take place. They felt Cosatu was not strong enough to call a stayaway, and were hesitant about calling another action, fearing having to deal with subsequent dismissals. The most vociferous calls for action, they argued, often came from unions least able to deliver participation from their membership.

This debate reflected all the tensions existing within the federation, and the decision eventually reached was a compromise. It called for a Day of Action, but limited the call to one day.

It was left to the various Cosatu regions to decide on the appropriate form of action. Northern Natal was exempted. All its leadership was in detention and mobilisation was impossible. However, the understanding of most in the CEC was that a call for a stayaway had been made. It was being referred to as a 'Day of Action' both for legal protection – calling for stayaways being unlawful – and to accommodate any region which decided on some other form of protest. The call was reported to Cosatu's ranks following the CEC. However, it was only on Thursday 10 July that it was publicly announced that action would take place the following Monday. In making the call for a Day of Action, Cosatu noted

> the intensification of the government's campaign against all forms of democratic opposition. Our leaders are detained, scores are in hiding, many offices are closed and our statements are censored. The industrial relations system which workers have painstakingly established over the years is being systematically assaulted.

The response to the 14 July stayaway call was disappointing, with the action being effective only in Kwandebele. There were pockets of support in townships known for their strong organisation, such as Alexandra in Johannesburg and Duncan Village in East London. In Port Elizabeth large numbers stayed away but their action appeared to be linked to simultaneous student demands in the area. In Kwandebele, similarly, action was connected to the ongoing insurrection in the homeland and was no indication of Cosatu's strength. The industrial workforce there was, in any case, small. In the normally strong Uitenhage, no protest action took place. On the Witwatersrand, an average absenteeism of only 13% amongst African workers was reported. In Cosatu-organised plants this rose to 24%. In the retail sector, however, only 11% of Cosatu members – possibly exhausted by their earlier militant actions – stayed away. Southern Natal had decided to take workplace action, but a negligible number of factories held protest actions. In the Western Cape, the region had decided the previous Friday to call off the stayaway. Clearly, the Day of Action was a failure.

Cosatu's Kempton Park local complained to the Witwatersrand REC about 'the short notice the shop stewards councils were given' which 'resulted in the National Day of Action not being effective.' The local warned the CEC, through the REC, 'not to make such blunders in the future.'[26]

The Western Cape region explained its decision in a report to the August 1986 CEC. Unions in the region had differences and were unable to unite in action. Complaints were also made that 'workers heard about a stayaway call when the decision was already taken. Further, insufficient time has been given to carry out decisions... Only one affiliate was actively working in the factories to carry through the national call.' Even this affiliate decided 'to call off the mobilisation in the light of the lack of support from the rest of the Cosatu affiliates in the region.' The local branch of at least one affiliate had decided not to support the call.[27]

Assessing the 14 July action

The failure of the 14 July action held a number of crucial lessons for Cosatu. To be successful, stayaway action requires the support of both community and worker organisation. It cannot be called by a union alone. The decision to call a stayaway had been taken emotionally and with insufficient analysis. Cosatu itself noted this in its 1987 report:

> In order to meet the challenges before us we have to develop appropriate responses based on a clear reading of the mood of our members, and our responses must relate to the capacity of our organisational structures to carry out such decisions.

In addition, not enough time was allowed to mobilise workers for action. Mobilisation could hardly be taken for granted, particularly with offices closed and operations disrupted. The CEC failed to read the signs. Many regions had not even been able to meet prior to the CEC to give mandates to their delegates. Finally, a number of key unions did not support the CEC decision and took no steps to implement it. The CEC would discover that decisions of such magnitude required a high degree of consensus, and not simply a majority vote.

Both Cusa and Azactu failed to support the call. Instead they put their faith in further talks with employers. While this probably had little practical impact on the call, it certainly did not increase its chances of success.

What had happened to the UDF and its affiliates in the action? Why had they not supported the call? Quite simply, their structures were not in place and had been devastated by the emergency. The mass detentions had left UDF largely leaderless and in disarray. For at least the first year of the emergency Cosatu found itself having to carry the flag of the mass democratic movement.

The failure of 14 July was a significant setback for Cosatu. The spontaneous strikes of mid-June had kept space open to operate, despite the state of emergency. The 14 July stayaway failed to widen that space. While the authorities backed off action against Cosatu to a limited extent, a more successful national stayaway would probably have widened its scope for operation further.

Resisting ongoing repression

As the state of emergency continued to bite, the ambit of state repression widened. Police interfered increasingly in simple industrial disputes. Cosatu and its affiliates frequently had their meetings restricted or banned. The detention of strike leaders, even during legal strikes, became a common practice. This, and the denial of the right to picket, led to an increase in strike violence as workers became desperate in their attempts to stop scabbing.

Emergency regulations, later challenged in court by the unions, prohibited the wearing of union T-shirts in the Northern Free State. In Northern Natal, wearing of any Cosatu garment was prohibited. While this was not explicitly restricted in other areas, experience showed that it was a certain invitation to police harassment and even detention. Repression against Cosatu was intense and ongoing. This was especially true in the rural areas.

Many landlords were prevailed upon to evict Cosatu and its affiliates from their offices. They often did so through fear of losing their property. Cosatu offices began to fall victim to arson attacks, and during August 1986 the East London offices were burned down. Police were consistently unable to find the perpetrators of these sorts of acts.

Police frequently seized Cosatu's newspapers and media, either from offices or while in transit from printers. Offices were often raided, while workers were chased out of perfectly legitimate union meetings. On many occasions property was seized, including documents, T-shirts and even telex machines. Pilfering by individual policemen was also reported. Detentions continued. Many Cosatu unionists were held for long periods without being brought to court. By July 1987, over a year into the emergency, at least 60 unionists remained in detention. Those held for lengthy periods included Amos Masondo, Dennis Neer, Noel

Williams and Enoch Godongwane. Some were only released in mid-1989 following the well-publicised detainee hunger strikes. Other detainees, most notably Moses Mayekiso, were charged with treason and denied bail. His protracted trial removed him from union work until his acquittal in late April 1989.

Campaigns for the release of detainees were ongoing but uneven. Mawu, and later Numsa, campaigned tirelessly for the release of Mayekiso. Despite action by membership in the factories and significant international protests, they failed to secure his release. Pwawu was more fortunate, successfully winning the release of its Transvaal secretary, Sipho Kubheka, who had been detained on 12 June during the first hours of the emergency. Pwawu embarked on a programme of mass action to secure his release, calling meetings to mobilise union members, releasing statements to the press and issuing pamphlets and stickers. Its campaign slogan was 'Release Sipho Kubheka and all detainees.' Shop stewards approached employers and called on them to intervene with the government. A handful of employers wrote letters to the Minister of Law and Order, although most responded that detentions were none of their business. The less co-operative employers then faced organised protests in their factories. Those employers who contacted the state were informed that no-one was detained for 'bona fide' union activities. Almost all of them accepted this explanation without question.

Pwawu was compelled to move onto the next phase of its campaign. In October it informed key employers in the sector that it intended to embark on an indefinite strike if Kubheka was not released. The strike would begin within three weeks, Pwawu stated. It again asked employers to intervene with the state. By now employers had little doubt of the seriousness of the union's intentions. A number of major employers, it transpired, had direct channels of communication with senior police officers responsible for the detention of unionists. These channels were established, it appears, following the strikes in the retail industry just after the emergency was declared. Pwawu meanwhile continued to hold mass meetings and factory demonstrations while it prepared for more sustained action. A few days before the planned action Kubheka was released. A well-planned and organised campaign had clearly borne fruit.

Not all such campaigns were successful. They did, however, make detention an ongoing political and international liability for the regime, and helped make some detainees – like Mayekiso – major public figures. Others, such as Amos Masondo, a leading Transvaal unionist and UDF activist, spent almost three years in jail, with very little effective campaigning undertaken on his behalf. In his absence he was elected as Cosatu's Witwatersrand regional education officer.

By mid-1987 the secretariat could report that Cosatu had 'developed the capacity to continue (its) work in these repressive conditions.' The state of emergency became simply a hurdle to be overcome, another obstacle to organising the workers. For Cosatu it reaffirmed the need to remain strong at factory level, and not to centre unions around offices. Unionists also developed a heightened sense of security.

More importantly, this period witnessed a growing spirit of defiance and disobedience. Increasingly, workers saw the deluge of emergency restrictions as a challenge. They became something to be sidestepped or disobeyed. When, in 1988, Cosatu was banned from any 'political' activities, its membership took it for granted that this edict should be defied. At times the federation simply ignored the cautious advice of its lawyers. At other times, affiliates took on themselves, officially, the campaigns from which the federation was banned. Minutes of meetings often became more limited, as sensitive issues were agreed upon but left unrecorded.

For Cosatu the real achievement of this period lay not in the tactics it adopted, but in its survival of the 1986 emergency. This it could do because of the underlying strength of its shopfloor structures.

Notes

1. *Financial Mail*, 04.04.86.
2. *IR Data*, 5(9), July 1986.
3. *Indicator SA*, 4(1), Winter 1986.
4. Interview with Simon Conco, *Indicator SA*, 4(1), Winter 1986.
5. *Star*, 05.05.86.
6. Cosatu paper presented to a meeting of Natal shop stewards, 26 January 1986.
7. 'Cosatu policies', policy statement compiled by Cosatu leadership and distributed as a pamphlet in early 1986.
8. MG Buthelezi, 'Comments on Cosatu's statement on its position in Natal', Ulundi, 8 February 1986.
9. 'Incidents involving attacks on or threats to union and union-related people by Inkatha in Northern Natal, Pietermaritzburg and Durban', report issued by Cosatu, 1986.
10. Author interview with Moses Ndlovu, Ppwawu organiser, 27 February 1991.
11. *New Nation*, 31.07.86; *Indicator SA*, 4(1), Winter 1986.
12. PG Maré, '"Mixed, Capitalist and Free": The Aims of the "Natal Option"', in (ed) G Moss and I Obery, *South African Review Four*, Johannesburg, 1987, 520; *Citizen*, 09.06.86; *Star*, 09.06.86; and *Sowetan*, 11.06.86.
13. Maré, '"Mixed, Capitalist and Free"', 520.
14. *Indicator SA*, 4(1), Winter 1986.

15. *Indicator SA*, 5(3), Autumn/Winter 1988; *Indicator SA* 4(1), Winter 1986; *Star*, 08.06.86.
16. *Citizen*, 25.07.86.
17. LMG, 'June 16th stayaway', *South African Labour Bulletin*, 11(7), August 1986.
18. Author interview with Frank Meintjies, Johannesburg, March 1990.
19. *Business Day*, 24.06.86.
20. *Business Day*, 01.07.86.
21. *Business Day*, 04.07.86.
22. *Star*, 04.07.86.
23. *Weekly Mail*, 27.06.86; *Star*, 13.06.86.
24. *City Press*, 29.06.86.
25. Pippa Green, 'Northern Natal: Meeting Uwusa's Challenge', *South African Labour Bulletin, 12(1), November/December 1986.*
26. Letter circulated to a meeting of Cosatu's CEC held in August 1986.
27. Western Cape regional report to a Cosatu CEC meeting held in August 1986.

9

Safe havens?

DESPITE the emergency Cosatu continued to grow and consolidate its organisation. In October the South African Railways and Harbour Workers Union (Sarhwu), first launched in 1936 but defunct since the early 1960s, was relaunched. Delegates to its inaugural congress, held in secret in the Grahamstown area, elected Justice Langa as union president, and Ntai Sello as general secretary.

Sarhwu's claim to be *the* organisation of railway workers was not unchallenged. The sweetheart Black Staff Association had more members, at least on paper. Two other organisations, the National Union of Railwayworkers (NUR) and the African Railway and Harbour Workers Union (Arahwu) also claimed worker support, but in the following months their weakness was revealed. Sarhwu itself was small and untested. However, it grew rapidly and, as we shall see, received a baptism of fire.[1]

A number of unions applied to affiliate to Cosatu. The 6 000-member Hotel and Restaurant Workers Union (Harwu) was accepted as an affiliate. It had a significant presence in the major hotel chains, and was admitted into Cosatu on the clear understanding that it would merge with other unions in the commercial sector, in line with the 'One Industry, One Union' programme.

During the second half of 1986 Cosatu was preoccupied with resisting the state of emergency and forging internal unity. Additional threats from Manpower Minister Pietie du Plessis went almost unnoticed. In September he publicly warned that the government would act against unions involved in dubious political activities. He accused 'certain trade unions' of encouraging the intimidation of workers, stayaway actions, boycotts and unlawful strikes. He also announced that he would soon introduce draft legislation to amend the labour law. Du Plessis made the proposed amendments sound innocuous. Only later would Cosatu realise that they were not.

The Kinross disaster

On 16 September a fire broke out during an uncontrolled welding operation at the Kinross goldmine. No fire extinguishers were available, and the flames ignited a 600 meter stretch of polyurethane coating deep underground. The fumes spread rapidly through the web of tunnels and literally suffocated the occupants. One survivor recalled that, as miners collapsed around him, he felt he could take no more. 'Our legs turned to jelly. I had to walk in the darkness and thick smoke holding the walls. I could feel my chest burning so bad I couldn't breath.'[2] Nearly 180 miners lost their lives at Kinross in the worst accident ever to occur on a South African gold mine.

Gencor, the mine's holding company, compounded the tragedy by their actions following the disaster. While the accident had occurred at 9-30 am, management delayed announcing it until after 5 pm that day. At that stage, Gencor reported that there had been 13 deaths, although the scale of the disaster was already apparent. When reporters rushed to the mine they were refused entry and faced an unco-operative management. Mine security officials informed journalists that police would be called if they persisted in their attempts to interview miners. A spokesperson for the mine hospital housing the injured miners said that access to patients was being denied to 'avoid conflicting reports'.[3]

NUM was permitted to interview injured miners and inspect the accident site. But a few days later Gencor refused to allow the union to bring in a team of international experts. 'We are horrified at their behaviour,' said union general secretary Ramaphosa. He accused Gencor of 'hiding the information and getting rid of the evidence' prior to the official enquiry.

Ironically, the day before the accident the Chamber of Mines boasted that fatalities and reportable injuries had reached an all-time low in the industry. 'We have now achieved one of our major goals – to bring the gold mine rate below the psychologically important level of one (fatality) per thousand,' announced Colin Fenton, chairman of the mine safety division. Reportable injuries – those leading to loss of a limb or more than two weeks off work – had fallen to an annual 18,81 per 1 000 miners.[4]

The Kinross disaster highlighted the dangers of secretive and management-controlled safety procedures. It also showed that a strong union movement is one of the best checks against unilateral and inadequate safety practices.

The full extent of the Kinross disaster was uncovered only because NUM existed, and was strong. Apart from safety matters, many racist procedures taken for granted by the mineowners were exposed and challenged. Shortly after the disaster the names and personal details of the white miners were released by the company. The black miners who had died, the world was informed, were: 'Sotho 45, Shangaan (Mozambican) 21, Pondo 20, Hlubi (Transkei) 6, Swazi 8, Venda 1, Xhosa 29, Tswana 14, Malawi 15, Pedi 1.' These men would remain nameless, purportedly because their next-of-kin had not yet been informed of their deaths. It had become common that the names of black miners killed in accidents were not published – they were simply statistics. The anger generated by the Kinross accident and the pressure from NUM was such that management did, eventually, release a list of names.

Mining, especially deep-level mining, is inherently dangerous. Death, it is chillingly said, is part of the process. The Kinross accident, however, arose from synthetic substances and human error. Polyurethane, used as a sealant underground, was known to be a hazardous substance, and had been banned by mining authorities in a number of countries. In addition, an uncontrolled welding operation had been allowed to take place. When this ignited the polyurethane, no fire extinguishers were on hand to control the blaze.

'The NUM', said Cyril Ramaphosa, 'has consistently condemned the safety standards practised in South Africa. Calls to radically improve safety standards have met with only a lukewarm response and boastful safety claims. Between 1973 and 1984, more than 8 500 miners were killed on the mines.'[5] Ramaphosa's figures excluded the hundreds of thousands of miners whose lives had been cut short or ruined by accidents and occupational disease. 'Black miners', added a Cosatu statement, 'were paying with their lives for the wealth and profits in which they did not share.'[*]

---

[*] *An official government inquiry into the Kinross case lasted a mere three hours. It decided that no one, not even the company, was to blame for the accident. In a separate case in the magistrate's court, the welder responsible for starting the inferno was fined R100 for breaking safety regulations.*

The 1 October protest

The Kinross accident angered black miners deeply. Their two biggest grievances had long been wages and safety. Kinross highlighted the cheapness of their lives in the eyes of the mineowners. Industrial workers might rally around the slogan 'organise or starve', but for miners the NUM slogan 'organise or die' was more appropriate. Reflecting this anger, NUM called for a workstoppage on all Chamber-affiliated mines for 1 October. Cosatu supported the call, asking members to hold one-hour commemoration services on that day. Black traders in a number of townships decided to close their shops from 1 pm. The Chamber of Mines was opposed to a whole day stoppage, but had to take account of widespread public indignation. It called for five minutes' silence on all mines.

The response to NUM's call was overwhelming and pointed to the union's increasing ability to mobilise miners. NUM announced that 325 000 miners had responded to the call, 300 000 of these on Chamber mines. The Chamber estimated that 250 000 workers stayed away, while the independent LMG estimated that 300 000 miners participated. Mines in the Anglo American and Gencor groups were most affected. Participation at Rand Mines and Goldfields operations, where NUM's level of organisation was weaker, was minimal.

Significant numbers of industrial workers also supported the call. At many organised factories, particularly in the PWV, Port Elizabeth and Natal areas, memorial services were held. They generally lasted between one and two hours.[6] Cosatu estimated that as many as 275 000 non-mineworkers backed the NUM call.

The call united miners and industrial workers in action over a workplace issue for the first time. It demonstrated the concern of workers over their health and safety, and popularised the slogan 'safety before profits' among workers nationally. Safety, and accidents particularly, became legitimate targets for public scrutiny. The secrecy of Kinross management after the accident created widespread anger, even in the commercial press, and there were growing demands from workers for safer conditions in mining and industry.

Health and safety

The emergent unions had dealt with health and safety problems since the early 1980s. In February 1986 GWU became the first union to sign a health and safety agreement following negotiations with Turnall, an asbestos cement manufacturer.[7] Other unions developed campaigns around a range of safety problems. As early as 1982 NUTW launched a campaign against byssinosis, a chronic respiratory disease amongst workers exposed to dust in flax, cotton and hemp mills. During the campaign against Brown Lung (another name for byssinosis), the union surveyed 5 000 workers. Shop stewards participated in planning the campaign, educating members, and ensuring that workers arrived for the lung-function testing. NUTW shop stewards followed this up by demanding improved conditions such as better ventilation and effective respirators, as well as adequate compensation for byssinosis sufferers.

The Brown Lung campaign was generally successful. Its major shortcoming, according to one observer, was 'its failure to define a role for workers at the shopfloor level.'[8] The campaign was run by Neil White, a union-appointed doctor. But when he left the union, NUTW's health and safety activities rapidly declined.

Over the years, and particularly after Cosatu's launch, a number of similar campaigns were conducted. Many tried, with varying degrees of success, to ensure that workers were involved in ongoing monitoring of health and safety. Fawu campaigned against noise and dust in the milling industry, particularly after a grain dust explosion at Jabula Foods in Springs during October 1986 resulted in the death of four workers. Mawu tried to deal with the dangers and physical accidents affecting foundry workers, while Pwawu confronted problems with poisonous chemicals and dangerous equipment in the sawmilling and forestry sectors. TGWU investigated the problems of poor suspension and badly-designed seats. However, many of these campaigns were at best sporadic.

By the late 1980s there were signs of progress. Ccawusa, later to become Saccawu, ran an active negotiating campaign demanding paid maternity and paternity leave. Other affiliates imitated their demands. As a result, many companies now provide maternity leave to pregnant women, although the extent of this, and the amount of paid leave, remain inadequate.

Problems associated with shift work were also raised by many of Cosatu's unions. Studies have shown that shift work disturbs regular human body rhythms, and is associated with stress, and digestive, sexual and sleeping problems. It also disrupts shift workers' participation in normal community and family life. No reliable information exists about the exact extent of shift work in South Africa, other than broad consensus that it is widespread and increasing.[9] Until the early 1980s black workers were rarely compensated for shift work, and existing shift allowances were generally meagre. In more recent years, particularly since the formation of Cosatu, shift allowances have increased and become more widespread.

Black shift workers, however, face additional problems. Many live in crowded rooms which they share with other workers in company or mine hostels. Others live in cramped and noisy township houses. The quality of day-time sleep in such circumstances is extremely poor, exacerbating the health problems of shift workers.

The state of emergency also took its toll, affecting shift workers in a particular way. Many townships were subject to effective curfews, and workers walking to work for the night shift complained of harassment and even assault by security forces.

Cosatu's ability to challenge the Kinross disaster, and the range of health and safety problems affiliates were increasingly able to take up, were signs of growing union sophistication. Raising health and safety involved a new frontier, and was an indication that union organisation had moved well beyond the 'recognition and wages' phase. Unions had the organisational strength, could draw on the necessary technical expertise, and had developed the capacity to make all workplace issues terrains of struggle.

'Safety must be our daily song'

The mining industry undoubtedly faces the most serious health and safety problems within South Africa. 'Safety must be our daily song,' said NUM president James Motlatsi in September 1986.

In 1974 Motlatsi found himself in hospital with a broken skull after a rockburst at Western Deep Levels. It was not an unusual experience. A NUM study concluded that 'a mineworker who spends 20 years working underground risks one chance in 30 of being killed and a 50% chance of being permanently disabled.' Since 1900, accidents have claimed the lives of over 68 000 miners. A further one million workers have been permanently disabled. Deep-level mining, with extreme rock pressure, intense heat, and unusually hard rock, contains inherent dangers. But the 'annual carnage', says NUM, can only be addressed when an appropriate working environment has been established on the mines.[10]

NUM has frequently blamed poor training procedures and inadequate monitoring by government-appointed mine inspectors for mine accidents. Apart from these accidents, miners also face occupational diseases related to high noise and dust levels.

Job reservation, in which only whites could become certified miners, compounded the problem. It was abolished only in 1987, although qualified miners remain overwhelmingly white. This meant that white miners were legally responsible for making dangerous conditions safe. In practice, however, white miners rarely came to the rockface, the place of maximum danger. They left this task to the black team leaders who had neither the safety training nor the authority to tell workers to leave an unsafe area. Team leaders attempting to complain of unsafe conditions to white miners, were often met with abuse and threats of punishment. And although white miners often did not face danger themselves, they were paid large production bonuses. 'Chasing production' frequently, therefore, came before safety.

For mineworkers, health and safety ranks equally with their demands for a living wage. Two campaigns form the basis of NUM's work. Its campaign against accidents has focused on the need for safety committees and the right to refuse unsafe work. NUM's second major campaign, for proper compensation, has challenged inadequate compensation and the policy whereby white workers receive up to ten times more in compensation than black workers. The union has an established health and safety department and employs regional safety organisers. It has safety stewards and safety committees in the workplace in addition to its shaft steward structures.

As a federation, Cosatu has achieved very little in the field of health and safety. The gains made have generally involved affiliates operating alone, or with the assistance of service organisations. The days where management could fob off worker complaints about their lungs by telling them to drink milk are receding. But management's approach to the issue has not substantially changed, with health and safety still, most commonly, seen as an aspect of 'loss control' management. 'Safety is only profitable', according to NUM's May Hermanus, 'when the direct and indirect costs associated with accidents *exceed* the final cost of eliminating the cause of accidents and ill-health.'[11]

Cosatu's second national congress resolved that a national health and safety conference should be called 'where workers from affiliates can share experiences and plan united action on health and safety.' However, this conference has never been held because, according to education secretary Khetsi Lehoko, 'with the exception of NUM, health and safety was never on the agenda.' Many unions also felt that a conference was not the appropriate way to launch the issue within the union movement.

Nor has health been seriously addressed as a social problem. With unequal health care for black and white, the rapid privatisation of health by the state, and the growing numbers of workers compelled by circumstances to join costly medical aid schemes, it is clear that health is a serious issue affecting the entire working class. While Cosatu is committed to demanding 'a free national health care system', little has been done to mobilise around this demand. In the face of repression and low wages many basic demands have been regarded as luxuries and moved lower down Cosatu's agenda.

Disinvestment and international pressure

Union approaches to disinvestment revealed growing sophistication and capacity, but also highlighted a number of union weaknesses. Throughout 1985 and 1986, the international campaign for sanctions and disinvestment gained momentum. In the United States in particular, companies faced intense pressure to withdraw from South Africa. Cosatu's launching congress supported 'all forms of international pressure on the South African government – including disinvestment or the threat of disinvestment.' It also called for international pressure to increase 'if this government remains intransigent.'

But what would happen when a company disinvested? What would become of the jobs, the machinery, the factory? Cosatu's initial approach did not explore these questions. It acknowledged that there would be hardship for workers, but this was considered a price worth paying to achieve liberation. No-one in the unions believed, however, that disinvestment should involve the removal of physical assets of companies from South Africa. The launching resolution spoke vaguely of a commitment 'to ensure that the social wealth of South Africa remains the property of the people of South Africa for the benefit of all.' But Cosatu, as a federation, had not thought through all the trade union implications clearly. Its acceptance of disinvestment was primarily part of its support for the general campaign to isolate the South African regime.

As pressures grew during 1986, Cosatu leadership was forced to explore the issues more deeply. Affiliates in sectors with significant foreign investment were most directly affected. At the beginning of October Alec Erwin, then Cosatu's education secretary, claimed that 'we have reached the point of sanctions because the truth of the matter is that we are governed by an intransigent minority regime. No people would freely vote sanctions upon themselves.' Cosatu rejected, he continued,

> the automatic assumption that profits and jobs should suffer equally from sanctions... It is our intention to resist every potential job loss. It is time for profits to bear the brunt of apartheid rather than enjoy its fruits.[12]

Within weeks this approach was adopted in challenging the disinvestment decision of General Motors.

Roger and us

On 15 October, press reports based on an interview in Detroit with Roger Smith, general manager of General Motors, claimed that the multinational was on the verge of quitting South Africa. The company's

Port Elizabeth-based workforce was not informed of his plans. When both the shop stewards and the unions involved, Naawu and Macwusa, approached South African management, they denied disinvestment plans, and insisted that Smith had been misquoted.[13] On 20 October, without any further meetings with the unions, the local GMSA announced it would be selling its assets to a group of South African executives.

The workers, mistrustful of management and used to retrenchments as a way of life at GMSA, demanded severance pay from the departing company; the right to elect two worker representatives to the board of directors of the new company; and that pension monies be refunded and placed in a provident fund jointly administered by company and union. GMSA dismissed these demands, publicly accusing the union of asking for 'conscience money'. GMSA argued that under the new owners matters would continue as before. However, they refused to reveal who the new owners were. The situation was ironic: in the US, the company was responding to disinvestment pressure and arguing that it was pulling out of South Africa. In South Africa, it was arguing that everything would remain unchanged!

On 29 October, workers downed tools and embarked on a sit-in strike. Despite meetings between the company and the union, no solution was reached. On 5 November, management summoned police and army units, which entered the plant to evict the workers. Faced by superior force the workers decided to leave peacefully. In the days that followed the company dismissed striking workers, while others returned to work in the face of management threats. The strikers were defeated.

Some observers saw in the strike worker opposition to disinvestment, but this was incorrect. Cosatu, supporting the GM workers, argued that the workers' demands were 'not a statement against disinvestment.' Rather, workers were insistent that companies should negotiate with them about their future. GM, according to the affected unions, 'now wants to pull out at no cost to itself, and make no provision for the future of workers, only of management.'

The disinvestment problem

The unions had clearly decided both to support disinvestment as part of international pressure, and fight any of its negative implications for workers. For the unions, the battles over withdrawal were often simply struggles against retrenchment, albeit in more complex forms. Many companies were not withdrawing, merely changing the form of their involvement. Direct investment was being replaced by an indirect form of involvement whereby multinational control and profits were still assured through licensing agreements, royalties and control of technology transfers. Cosatu, at its second congress, termed this 'corporate camouflage'. Others called it 'warehousing', whereby a caretaker management was installed, making it easier for a company to maintain its market share and return to South Africa when circumstances permitted.

Cosatu emphasised negotiated withdrawals and supported demands made of disinvesting companies by Mawu, Naawu and Micwu. These called for unions and workers to be given timeous notice of withdrawal, with full details of their plans and adequate information. On withdrawal certain minimum conditions should be guaranteed: no retrenchments or redundancies; severance pay; no employee benefits to be prejudiced; and negotiations with the representative unions on any issues affecting workers, including those arising from the withdrawal or sale of the company.

The GMSA experience was instrumental in forcing Cosatu to refine its position on disinvestment and sanctions. The second congress noted that selective sanctions were often ineffective and called for 'comprehensive and mandatory sanctions.' It agreed that 'where disinvestment takes place companies must give Cosatu notice of their intention to pull out...so that bona fide negotiations can take place.'

The general feeling of congress on these issues was well-expressed by Dusty Ngwane, a senior shop steward of CWIU, which sponsored the congress resolution:

> We support any kind of pressure for change in South Africa. So if sanctions will help hasten change, we would be in favour. But sanctions are not being applied totally, and partial sanctions are not effective. As for disinvestment, our stand does not mean that we don't want companies to go. They can go whenever they like, but if they do, they must do it on our terms.

Other disinvestment struggles

In the years which followed, other unions took up the disinvestment issue. Numsa and CWIU, in particular, were in the forefront of struggles for negotiated disinvestment. During 1988 and 1989 CWIU declared a number of disputes with multinational companies, demanding that they negotiate with the union in the event of planned disinvestment. The CWIU campaign achieved a number of successes.

Numsa concentrated, rather, on ensuring that the departing companies made adequate provision for the workforce. At Mono Pumps, for example, the union secured a R200 000 severance payout, and a R200 000 worker-controlled trust fund. At Samcor Numsa tried a more complex programme, but got egg on its face. Samcor, formerly Ford Motors SA, decided to disinvest from South Africa, agreeing to sell 76%

of the company to Anglo American. The remaining 24% was earmarked for a worker-controlled trust. Numsa had agreed to this. The deal would enable workers to nominate representatives to the board of directors. In addition, community trusts would be established in Pretoria and Port Elizabeth, where the company's plants were located. These would be run by community and worker representatives. Each would start with a R6-million contribution from the company, and receive the proceeds of the dividends from the 24% shareholding.

Numsa concluded the agreement with the company in November 1987. Fred Sauls of Numsa's automotive department commented that 'this is the first time a disinvestment arrangement has given any real content to Cosatu policy on the issue – namely that while disinvestment is desirable, the wealth must remain the property of the people of South Africa for the benefit of all.' Many, even in the US, saw it as a 'progressive' disinvestment.

These arrangements caused immense conflict amongst the workforce, leading to a strike directed against both the company and the union. A group of workers managed to win majority support for rejection of the deal. 'We do not want to be mini-capitalists,' one worker is reported to have said. 'We are plain workers, not businessmen.' Some argued that Ford was using the trust fund to avoid full disinvestment from South Africa. The majority of workers were won to the argument that the 24% shareholding should be sold and the proceeds divided up. This, they were told, could lead to each worker receiving R40 000. The strike seriously embarrassed Numsa, and clearly showed both the limits and the possibilities involved in trying to negotiate disinvestment.

Cusa and Azactu amalgamate

Neither Cusa nor Azactu had participated in the union unity talks after the July 1985 Ipelegeng meeting, and hence had stayed outside of Cosatu. The first weekend of October 1986 saw the merger of these two union federations at a conference in Broederstroom.

The merger brought together 12 unions from Cusa, and 11 from Azactu. The new federation was initially called Cusa/Azactu, since agreement on a new name could not be reached. Six months later, however, the new federation agreed to call itself Nactu – the National Council of Trade Unions.* Its elected leadership was dominated by

---

* The problem for the federation revolved around whether to use 'South Africa' or 'Azania' – the favoured designation of black consciousness and Africanist adherents – in its name. The name finally agreed upon avoided the problem altogether.

individuals from Cusa, reflecting the greater union experience within that federation. Piroshaw Camay was elected general secretary, with Mahlomola Skhosana and Pandelani Nefolovhodwe as his assistants. James Mndaweni, former president of Cusa, was elected president of the merged federation. The new federation claimed to represent between 248 000 and 420 126 members. Both figures were an exaggeration of the new federation's membership strength, as later struggles within Nactu revealed.[14]

Officially, Nactu was politically non-aligned. Unofficially, it propagated an uneasy mixture of black consciousness and Africanism. A few relatively a-political unions within its ranks stood on the sidelines. Its founding principles involved 'worker control based on anti-racism/non-racism'; black working-class leadership; political non-affiliation; financial accountability within unions; and independent internal actions by unions within federation policy.[15]

Nactu differed in a number of respects from Cosatu. It envisaged a looser federation with a high degree of autonomy for affiliates. More significantly, it differed over 'black working-class leadership,' an issue which had taken the form of 'non-racialism' vs 'anti-racism' at the Ipelegeng unity talks. Many observers found these differences between the two groupings difficult to understand. After all, Cosatu's policy of 'non-racialism' was clearly opposed to racism; it was 'anti-racist'. And Cusa/Azactu was at pains to point out that its black leadership policy should not be interpreted as 'crass anti-white racism'.

In an interview with the *Weekly Mail* Nefolovhodwe, who came from the black consciousness tradition, argued that leadership in the liberation struggle should come from the black working class,

> as the most oppressed class. People who do not belong to the black working class – including black intellectuals – but who wish to participate in its fight for a new South Africa have to 'commit class suicide' and identify completely with black workers. Whether they are black intellectuals or white sympathisers, 'they have to dance to the tune of the black working class.' They have to understand black working class thinking viscerally as well as cerebrally.
>
> 'If whites want to participate in the struggle, they must do so on the factory floor. If they are then elected to leadership positions in the unions by fellow workers, they can do so without violating the principle of black leadership.'[16]

A slightly different emphasis was given by Mndaweni, whose sympathies lay with the Africanist tradition. Non-racialism was impractical in the new federation, explained Mndaweni, because of 'the reality in our country.' Cosatu, he felt, did not have working-class leadership. 'Other people who are not workers come in as intellectuals in leadership positions.'

However, the debate was only formally around these questions. The fundamental, but unspoken, issue was that Cosatu, although politically non-aligned, was overwhelmingly sympathetic to the ANC and the 'Congress tradition'. The majority of the leadership in Cusa and Azactu were not.

Cosatu was extremely disappointed at the launch of Cusa/Azactu. Many unions, particularly amongst Cusa's affiliates, could have been accommodated easily within Cosatu. Cosatu had been too confident of simply winning over Cusa membership on the shop floor – which to some extent it had done. Cosatu had relaxed once the jewel in the Cusa crown, NUM, decided to join the new federation at Ipelegeng in 1985. As a result not enough effort was spent encouraging Cusa's more powerful affiliates in the chemical, transport, food, and construction sectors to join the unity drive.

Cosatu, correctly, did not anticipate that its differences with Cusa/Azactu would lead to violent conflict, as happened in the case of Uwusa. Political differences were less sharp, and Cusa/Azactu was simply not an organisational match for most Cosatu unions. For example, its mining affiliate, Bamcwu, claimed a membership of 75 000. This made it, technically, the country's second largest union. Evidence to support this claim was scarce, and by mid-1988 even Nactu had revised Bamcwu's paid-up membership to less than 4 000![17]

In the first six months of 1986, Bamcwu was involved in only one recorded strike with 2 000 man-days lost. By contrast NUM members were involved in strikes in which over 210 000 days were lost. Overall, Cosatu members 'were responsible for 22 times more industrial action in the first seven months of (1986) than unions in the newly merged Azactu/Cusa federation.'[18]

The birth of Cusa/Azactu was met with a great deal of ill-feeling from Cosatu, which felt that it had kept its doors open to all unions. Cosatu believed that forming a new federation was divisive, and against the generally-agreed principle of 'One Country, One Federation.' For a time it refused to work with Nactu. Only later would co-operation begin around the Labour Relations Act and other matters, although even this was not without problems.

The unlamented death of Tucsa

Cosatu proved to be the final nail in the coffin of the Trade Union Council of South Africa (Tucsa), which in December 1986 formally dissolved itself at a special conference. South Africa's emergent unions of the

1980s were widely considered to be the world's fastest-growing labour movement. Tucsa, by contrast, undoubtedly showed the quickest propensity to shrink. At the end of 1983 it had 57 affiliated unions with a combined membership of over half-a-million. Three years later it was dead.

Tucsa was formed in the 1950s and was extremely hostile to both Sactu and the ANC. Tucsa had responded weakly as the apartheid state introduced racial segregation into the union movement during the 1950s and 1960s. Verbally it opposed racial segregation but in practice accommodated apartheid by admitting and expelling African unions from its ranks according to the vagaries of the moment. Its affiliates were widely seen as bureaucratic and conservative 'sweetheart' unions. They were often labelled 'benefit' unions because of their focus on administering a range of membership 'benefits' rather than fighting for improvements alongside their members.

Tucsa appeared to grow rapidly in the wake of the Wiehahn labour reforms – from 252 000 members in 1979 to 508 000 by 1983 – but this was largely illusory. Many of its affiliates had grown simply by extending closed-shop agreements to cover African workers. Where African workers had previously been excluded from membership of these unions, they were now forced to be members. Employers, anxious to avoid the emergent unions, often collaborated in this recruitment programme.[*]

Under pressure from the emergent unions, affiliates started leaving Tucsa in growing numbers from late 1983. Two reasons were most often given for this. Firstly, Tucsa seemed unable to offer any concrete services or support to its affiliates. Despite high affiliation fees, Tucsa gave no help in training its affiliates to counter the sophisticated shop-floor challenge they were then facing. Secondly, Tucsa was white-dominated and politically conservative. For example, as late as 1986, it felt 16 June

---

[*] *Internationally, the closed-shop system has long been a worker weapon aimed at preventing the employment of non-union labour and addressing the problem of 'free riders'. In South Africa, it has historically protected white workers from competition and frequently acted to reinforce job reservation. The closed-shop has also been a mechanism to bolster conservative, sweetheart unions. In recent years, however, Cosatu has reconsidered its earlier opposition to closed-shop policies, largely because the 'emergent' unions have emerged and become the dominant unions.*

Renewed interest in the closed shop has been accompanied by discussion over the inclusion of safety mechanisms. These range from the regular balloting of members in every plant over their attitude to the closed-shop to the introduction of closed-shops only with the support of substantial, rather than simple, majorities of workers. Cosatu's affiliates are keen to avoid the 'forced membership' system which characterised so many Tucsa unions.

should not be a public holiday. Following the 1 May stayaway, it announced its support for a Labour Day – but not on 1 May!

Many of the unions which disaffiliated from Tucsa included membership amongst semi-skilled workers. These unions remained unaffiliated after leaving Tucsa although, in time, a number moved closer to Cosatu. This was first apparent when Micwu participated in the launching of the giant metal union, Numsa, during 1987. Later, ex-Tucsa unions in the textile and clothing sectors entered Cosatu.

By the time Tucsa dissolved, its affiliated membership was 120 000. Its last year of existence had resembled a farce. Its leadership was unable to grapple with either Cosatu's formation or the mass uprising sweeping the country. Tucsa tried to solve its leadership problems by appointing a former Transvaal Chamber of Industries' executive as its general secretary, but he resigned before the appointment was ratified. Tucsa also attempted to enter an alliance with Uwusa. It met with Inkatha's leadership, including Buthelezi and his entire cabinet, to discuss this. Uwusa, wisely, declined the offer.[19] In desperation, Tucsa decided to offer positions on its executive to the general secretary or president of any union that would affiliate. It also employed a public relations company to improve its image. This company's subsequent report amounted to an eloquent obituary.

'Nobody likes to be tied to a loser,' stated the report, 'and Tucsa has taken on the smell of a body that is dying.' It was 'perceived to have become Establishment, fossilised, distant from the workplace... Within Tucsa races are polarised... They can only agree if they do not discuss political issues.' In addition Tucsa was seen as 'pro-management, pro-industrial councils, pro-free enterprise – all against the stream of thinking in the majority of the workforce.' It also eschewed the use of strike action.[20]

There was nothing left but to dissolve. Tucsa's remaining stalwarts were bitter. Steve Scheepers, a former president, blamed intimidation and financial crisis for the collapse. 'Some of our shop stewards were attacking the (newer) unions and were getting murdered... absolutely murdered.' The new unions were also taking them to the industrial court. 'Monies...that we built up over the years must now go on litigation with these bloody radicals.'[21] At its dissolution conference, Tucsa's president, Robbie Botha, said the federation had 'never failed anyone or anything... (It) was let down, or failed, or even sabotaged on all sides.' With few restraints on them, argued Botha, unregistered unions were 'tailor-made for exploitation by ideological and political extremists... The day of the ultimate evil has dawned...'[22]

Tucsa drew on, and in turn reinforced, deeply conservative traditions among sections of the working class. While it was a bearer of the white labour and craft union tradition, its approach also had resonance amongst layers of the coloured and Indian workforce, many of whom were employed in skilled positions.

Tucsa's tradition of benefit unionism has continued until the present. Indeed, the death of Tucsa did not lead to the death of 'Tucsa-ism'. Tucsa represented real traditions amongst the working class, and Cosatu was unable to present itself as a home, at least initially, for many of these workers.

Towards a new year

Repression against Cosatu continued as 1986 drew to a close. Two incidents deserve particular mention, although they were by no means the only ones. In mid-November, police attacked Mawu's annual general meeting held in Durban, using shotguns, teargas and sjamboks on workers leaving the gathering. One worker, Simon Mchunu, was killed and others were seriously injured.[23] Mawu called for national action on 1 December in response to the killing, but there was only limited support for the call outside its own ranks.

The growing activities of death squads and vigilantes were even more ominous. On 5 December, leaders of striking Sarmcol workers were abducted from Mpophomeni township in the Natal midlands. They were brutally murdered and their bodies left at the roadside. Those killed included Phineas Sibiya, chairperson of the shop stewards committee; Simon Ngubane, a leader of the Sarmcol workers' cultural co-operative; and Florence Mnikathi, active in the Sarmcol workers' health committee. Their deaths were reportedly linked to the invasion of the township that night by a number of Inkatha supporters.[24]

A subsequent inquest directly implicated a number of Inkatha officials and the security forces in the abductions and killings in this strongly pro-Cosatu township.

'Your smiling and simple faces/meant sleepless nights/to bosses, rulers and their puppets,' wrote well-known Cosatu poet Mi Hlatshwayo. 'Your smiling and simple faces/gave hope to Sarmcol workers' struggle/to our liberation struggle.'[25]

At the beginning of 1987 Cosatu's leadership issued a New Year's message in an attempt to summarise the progress and problems facing the new federation on its first anniversary. The message is worth quoting at length for its assessment of 1986, its vision of the future, and its style of presentation

'The possibilities before us,' it noted, 'are greater than ever before. But so are the dangers. On every side we are being attacked. The bosses, their government and their allies...want to stop us from advancing by any means necessary.' The solution proposed to this was 'maximum unity and clarity to defend ourselves and move forward in our struggle.' In particular,

> we need to learn from our mistakes and setbacks since Cosatu was formed... This year we have to overcome our problems,...we have to overcome our divisions.
>
> In Cosatu we have to make sure that all our structures...are consolidated and working properly... Still we do not have ONE INDUSTRY, ONE UNION. This situation cannot be allowed to continue... We have to organise especially the millions of unemployed, farm, railway, construction and government workers into our ranks. We can never hope to do this if we have not built strong and powerful industrial unions. Workers – make sure that your union is coming together to form one big union in your industry!

Local shop steward councils, 'the pillars on which Cosatu stands,' should also be strengthened. If one did not exist in a particular area, 'then you – the organised workers in that area – must make sure that one is formed.' Differences were causing problems.

> The bosses and the government...saw how we built June 16th and May Day into the biggest national general strikes ever with millions taking action and they were scared. Then they saw how we failed to build July 14th and December 1st and they grew more confident...

'Differences', read the message, 'we will always have.' Indeed, they were 'necessary' to ensure healthy debate. But, the statement warned, 'once we have decided (on an issue)' then all should be 'loyal to that decision and we (should) do our best to carry it out in a disciplined and comradely way.'

'The struggle for a living wage will be Cosatu's main campaign this year, (and will) aim to strike at the heart of the bosses profit system.' It was important to build united mass action, and 'draw behind us the support and solidarity of the millions of workers, youth and progressive democratic organisations outside our ranks.' This would be resisted by the bosses and the state who would 'try and create vigilante gangs, especially from the unemployed, to divide and intimidate us.' The key was 'to organise millions of unemployed under our federation,' as well as 'to organise our own defence to protect ourselves and our struggle against any attack.'

It was important to build community organisation. 'Cosatu workers are at the front of the struggle to build street committees in the townships.' This should continue, said the statement. It was also important to 'do everything we can to build close links with the students and youth and their organisations.'

The message called for the participation of women and argued that their demands should be strengthened 'a thousand times over... If our liberation does not succeed in creating free people, equal to each other in every way, then we would not have succeeded.'

Finally, the leadership appealed to all workers to join Cosatu, 'the home for every worker in South Africa – employed and unemployed... Tucsa has broken up, ...the bosses are desperately trying to promote Uwusa.' These 'divisive efforts are doomed to failure if we are united... There should now be no obstacle for all democratic unions to come together with us and form ONE FEDERATION in ONE COUNTRY.'

'Comrade workers', the statement concluded, 'the future is in your hands. The struggle depends on you and you alone.'[26]

The message was a self-critical, yet optimistic assessment. It looked forward to an active year and to progress for the federation. Outside observers were less impressed. Management consultants Andrew Levy and Associates commented in their annual report that Cosatu had failed to 'maintain the forward momentum of the previous seven years.' It ascribed this to 'low growth levels, divisive and mediocre leadership and political disagreements, coupled with high levels of industrial action which were often poorly conducted... 1986', it continued, 'will probably be regarded as the year in which the first wave of Black unionisation ran out of steam.'[27] The new year would show, contrary to Levy's expectations, that there was still plenty of 'steam' in the workers movement.

Notes

1. See Pippa Green, 'Sats workers on track', *South African Labour Bulletin*, 12(1), November/December 1986.
2. *Business Day*, 18.09.86.
3. *Business Day, 18.09.86; Weekly Mail*, 19.09.86.
4. *Star*, 16.09.86; *Financial Mail*, 26.09.86.
5. *Star*, 17.09.86.
6. See LMG report, 'Kinross day of mourning', *South African Labour Bulletin*, 12(1), November/December 1986.
7. 'Health and Safety Agreement at Turnall a first in South Africa', *South African Labour Bulletin* 11(7), August 1986.
8. Ian Macun, 'The NUTW and the Brown Lung Campaign', *Critical Health*, 30, June 1990.
9. Taffy Adler, 'The Extent of Shiftwork', *South African Labour Bulletin*, 12(8), October 1987.

10. May Hermanus, 'Occupational Health and Safety. A NUM Perspective', unpublished, June 1990.
11. Hermanus, 'Occupational Health and Safety', 4.
12. *Sunday Tribune*, 05.10.86.
13. Much of the detail below relies on Glenn Adler, 'The strike at General Motors', *South African Labour Bulletin*, 12(1), November/December 1986.
14. See *Weekly Mail*, 12.08.88, reporting on membership figures presented to Nactu's second congress.
15. *City Press*, 12.10.86.
16. *Weekly Mail*, 19.09.86.
17. *Finance Week*, 26.05.88.
18. *Weekly Mail*, 09.10.86, drawing on a survey by Andrew Levy and Associates.
19. See minutes of a national executive committee meeting of Tucsa, Johannesburg, 3 July 1986.
20. 'Tucsa and the Future'. Report on workshops at TWS, quoted in minutes of special national executive committee meeting of Tucsa, Braamfontein, 20 October 1986.
21. *Sunday Times*, 19.10.86.
22. *Star*, 02.12.86.
23. Mawu communique, 'Shootings at Mawu AGM', *South African Labour Bulletin*, 12(2), January/February 1987.
24. Shamim Marie, 'Sarmcol killings', *South African Labour Bulletin*, 12(2), January/February 1987.
25. Mi Hlatshwayo, 'To you comrades', *South African Labour Bulletin*, 12(2), January/February 1987.
26. '1987 - The year of consolidation and decisive action', New Year's message by Cosatu leadership, January 1987.
27. Andrew Levy and Associates, *Annual Report, 1986- 87*, December 1986, 2-3.

Part Three

1987 –Year of Fire

10

The changing pattern of strikes

'An injury to one...'

EARLY 1987 saw two major strikes – at a large chainstore and on the railways. They held important lessons for the unions involved, and also heralded a period of intense struggle for the entire labour movement. Despite massive repression, 1987 was a year in which workers showed a capacity to launch protracted industrial action. In the process Cosatu came under severe attack and many workers lost their lives.

Everything not OK

The first of the strikes took place at OK Bazaars. Indirectly owned by Anglo American, OK had a reputation for bad labour practices. Since early 1985 the company had been trying to reduce its staff complement by some 2 000 workers. In the face of union resistance to retrenchment, management attempted 'back-door retrenchment'. Workers claimed that many employees had been dismissed for petty offences, and this resentment was intensified by anger over low wages. For example general assistants, the lowest-paid workers, received R232 per month – far lower than wages paid at other retail chain stores. Part of the blame for this lay with the union itself, which in September 1984 had signed an inadequate wage agreement. From mid-1986 newer leadership within Ccawusa tried to re-negotiate the wage contract, but OK Bazaars refused to budge.

Ccawusa duly declared a dispute, and laboriously followed the requirements of the Labour Relations Act. A conciliation board meeting between the parties deadlocked on 3 December 1986 when OK management rejected Ccawusa's demand for an across-the-board wage increase of R160, and a minimum wage of R450 per month. The union began preparations for a legal strike, and workers at 137 organised stores voted overwhelmingly in favour of industrial action. On 18 December the strike began, and involved over 10 000 OK workers out of a total workforce of 23 000.

Ccawusa had aimed for maximum impact by launching the strike days before Christmas. Perhaps unrealistically, it had expected a relatively quick settlement. 'The timing was good from the point of view of high sales,' recalled Ccawusa's Jay Naidoo.[*] 'But at that time of the year there are also many casuals available – school students etc – and progressive organisations are on leave. We certainly dented sales but OK shops continued to operate.'

OK Bazaars was also aided by police action, although management generally denied summoning the police. Detentions and arrests began within days of the strike commencing. Shop stewards were detained under state of emergency regulations, and in Natal over 220 striking workers at the Empangeni, Margate and Pinetown stores were arrested en masse. In all, over 1 000 workers were detained during the course of the strike, most being released only after bail of R1 000 each had been posted. The arrests proved a burden to the union, which was forced to send a delegation abroad to seek financial assistance.

Despite the dangers, the union encouraged striking workers to remain on the premises. There they picketed, and sang and danced in the surrounding streets. Management responded by obtaining court interdicts preventing workers from entering or being near OK premises. OK used selective mass dismissals in an attempt to break the strike. Over 500 workers were dismissed for a variety of reasons ranging from 'intimidation' to breaching of a code of strike conduct which management had issued unilaterally during the strike.

Detentions, arrests, mass dismissals and the total absence of strike pay failed to dent workers' unity. Seven weeks into the strike, a prominent Ccawusa official commented that workers were increasingly seeing the dispute as 'a war of attrition'. So bitter was the dispute that some workers were said to feel that 'if we cannot get a settlement we will

---

[*] *Ccawusa's Jay Naidoo is unrelated to his namesake, Cosatu's general secretary.*

fight to the death... (E)ven if we are defeated as a trade union, if we can also destroy our enemy in the process we will have won in political terms.'

Once it became clear that the strike would not be settled over the Christmas period, workers realised that they would have to gain wider sympathy and support for their action. This was soon forthcoming, not only from Cosatu but also from Cusa/Azactu and political organisations outside of UDF ranks. Cosatu called a meeting of shop stewards from Anglo American companies, which owned the OK Bazaars through the SA Breweries group. On 8 February, 300 shop stewards from all Anglo companies and from every region and affected affiliate met at Cosatu House in Johannesburg. The meeting was spirited and discussed ways to support the OK strikers. Following the meeting, varying degrees of pressure were used at Anglo plants. Some workers held demonstrations, while others decided on blacking action and refused to make deliveries to OK Bazaars. A few plants even embarked on short stoppages. Fawu was particularly active. At one OK store in Johannesburg boxes of food arrived literally covered with black spray paint, and Fawu members often refused to make deliveries to OK stores. Many employers inter-dicted Fawu in an attempt to force union members to undertake these deliveries. The Anglo shop steward council was successful, recalls one Ccawusa organiser, because 'it went through the mainline structures, through the national office bearers, and not through a Cosatu sub-committee.'

Public sympathy for the strikers was substantial. Black customers shopped elsewhere, despite the fact that no boycott was formally called. Ccawusa estimated that 60% of black customers, a significant share of the company's clientele, were effectively 'boycotting' OK. Stores also came under attack. On 9 January a bomb exploded at OK's central Johannesburg store, the site of its head office. It was presumably the work of Umkhonto we Sizwe, the ANC's armed wing. No-one was hurt. Publicly the company put on a brave face and organised a 'bomb blast' sale to clear damaged goods and, more importantly, to attract customers back.[*] However management was shaken by the attack, as the implica-tions of non-settlement became apparent.

As the strike continued, both management and workers became in-creasingly bitter. The costs of the strike, both financially and in terms of public image, became increasingly high for OK management, and Anglo American was also concerned that it might spread beyond OK Bazaars.

---

* The sale did attract customers, who were offered goods at 'two for the price of one.' But, at the height of the sale, a bomb threat was received by telephone. Customers fled the store without paying, taking vast quantities of goods with them.

The strike had assumed a political significance well beyond the shop-floor.

Eventually, OK management backed down. A mediated settlement was reached and 77 days after the strike commenced workers returned to the shopfloor. The settlement involved a wage increase of R100 across-the-board; a minimum wage of R400 per month; improvements in staff discounts; and the return of all goods repossessed by the company during the strike. In addition, 364 of the 510 dismissed workers were reinstated. Both parties agreed to refer the position of the remainder to arbitration. Significantly, the settlement extended to OK workers in the 'homelands' and women workers on maternity leave.

The strike did reveal certain weaknesses in the union, such as its inability to draw in substantial support from Indian, coloured and even white workers. However, it was a major victory for Ccawusa, and for years to come, OK employees would be among the most militant and politicised in the retail trade. OK's labour relations style liberalised slightly following the strike. Satisfactory settlements made in subsequent months, including with Pick 'n Pay, showed that other retail giants had also learnt from the strike.[1]

The dismissal of Andrew Nedzamba

The public sector, by contrast, was slower to learn. During October 1986 a South African Transport Services (Sats) driver, Andrew Nedzamba, returned to the railways depot at City Deep from his round of deliveries. In his pocket was R40,40 – collected for delivering a container to Springs. It was Friday afternoon and the cashier's offices were already closed for the weekend. As a result Nedzamba could neither deposit the forty rands, nor collect his own weekly pay packet. He paid over the money first thing Monday morning, was given a receipt, and his explanation for paying in late accepted. Five months later, on 11 March 1987, Nedzamba was summoned to the office. 'I was given an envelope containing two letters,' he said, 'one suspending me from work, and the other dismissing me.'[2] Those letters began a chain of events which led to one of the largest strikes the country had seen, leaving over ten dead, many imprisoned, four workers sentenced to death, a massive and sustained attack on Cosatu, and a fundamental rethinking of the position of workers in the public sector.

Most of Nedzamba's colleagues at City Deep were members of Sarhwu. At the time the union was still small and relatively weak, having been officially relaunched only a few months previously, in October 1986. Sarhwu was beginning to flex its muscles, particularly at certain depots on the Witwatersrand. In November 1986 there had been a number of food strikes in the railway hostels and workers were forming hostel committees under Sarhwu's guidance.

Black workers at City Deep downed tools in protest against Nedzamba's dismissal. Management's response, in contrast to its summary dismissal of GWU's railway members in 1982, was to talk to worker representatives. However, instead of simply reinstating Nedzamba, Sats announced it had decided to demote him to a labourer instead of firing him. Workers rejected this. Sats later suggested that they could reinstate Nedzamba on condition that he paid an R80 fine. Workers again rejected this. For what offence was he being fined, they asked? Sats' feeble attempts at dispute resolution were soon overtaken by events. Depot by depot workers downed tools in support of City Deep.

It was the first big railway strike by black workers in South Africa's history, and the issues involved went far beyond the dismissal of Nedzamba. Sats, a state-owned corporation, had long been an essential pillar of apartheid's white labour policy, providing secure and even sheltered employment to large numbers of poorer whites. At the time of the strike a majority of its 206 000 employees were white. Patronage and simple vote-catching towards white railway employees contrasted with a system of blatant discrimination against black workers. Racial abuse was common and low wages prevalent. Most black workers earned little over R300 monthly and, as migrant workers, were housed in poor conditions in large single-sex compounds.

Nedzamba's dismissal highlighted the fact that black workers, unlike their white counterparts, were never regarded as permanent employees. Job security, or the lack of it, was a burning issue. Black workers like Nedzamba were subject to a punitive disciplinary code which applied only to them. It allowed no representation and was used daily for minor offences. Black railway workers lacked the same level of job security of their unionised counterparts in the manufacturing sector. In addition, they were not covered by the provisions of general labour law. Instead, their conditions were governed by a special law, the 1983 Conditions of Employment (Sats) Act, which empowered the Minister of Transport to decide which unions to recognise.

At the time of the strike, management recognised 11 unions – all of them in-house. Most were structured along apartheid lines. African workers generally belonged to the Black Trade Union (Blatu), a puppet body established by management in the early 1980s which workers were 'encouraged' to join. Blatu was Sats's answer to the independent union movement, and a direct response to attempts to organise railway workers. At the time of the strike Blatu claimed a national membership of 61 000 out of 95 000 African workers.[3] On paper, most of the striking Sarhwu members were also members of Blatu.

Throughout the strike Sats refused to speak to Sarhwu. It claimed that Blatu represented the strikers, despite all indications to the contrary. This was, in part, a desperate attempt to maintain the in-house union system, and was also influenced by management hostility to Cosatu. Documentaries were shown on prime-time television purporting to prove that Sarhwu was part of Cosatu, which was affiliated to the ANC, which was controlled by the Communist Party, which was run from Moscow. It was never made clear how Andrew Nedzamba's unfair dismissal fitted into the plot. Sats placed newspaper advertisements accusing 'instigators' of causing the strike. Sarhwu responded by charging that Sats had refused to acknowledge that workers had genuine grievances.

Cosatu, concerned at the growing intensity of the conflict, offered to mediate. 'How could management even consider (this),' responded Sats 'when the cause of the strike can be traced to Sarhwu, a Cosatu affiliate.'[4] 'It would be naive,' said Sats spokesperson Jannie van Zyl, 'for Sats to negotiate with a union, which...seeks to overthrow the status quo not only of Sats but also other industries of our economy.'[5]

On the few occasions when Sats dealt directly with striking workers, it insisted it was speaking not to Sarhwu but to employees. This was partly an attempt to divide Sarhwu from non-Sarhwu strikers. It was also simple self-deception, and reflected the inability of Sats management to face realities. The policy was extremely short sighted. Sarhwu officials were jointly planning strategy with the workers' negotiating team. In refusing to allow Sarhwu officials to be present, Sats was making resolution of the dispute more difficult for itself. It sustained this myth long after the strike, and only after an even more bitter and violent strike during late 1989 and early 1990 did Sats finally recognise Sarhwu.

The 1987 strike occurred in the run-up to a white general election. Faced with an electoral challenge from the extreme-right Conservative Party, the government believed a conciliatory policy towards black strikers would lose it white votes. This, and the ultra-conservatism of Sats – itself a result of the railways' position as a bastion of apartheid – explains the general intransigence of Sats management during the strike.

The strike spreads

The striking workers at City Deep were soon joined by colleagues from neighbouring Kaserne depot. A week into the strike, 5 500 workers were out, and Sats admitted to a backlog of 1 800 goods containers at these two crucial depots.[6] City Deep alone, according to Sats regional manager Abraham Spies le Roux, was losing earnings of half-a-million rands a day.

Then the strike began spreading to depots throughout the country. Two weeks into the strike 16 000 workers had downed tools.[7]

As the strike grew, Sarhwu expanded its committee to reinforce the City Deep worker negotiating team. A crucial meeting of over 450 delegates from 12 depots was held on 25 March, which revised workers' demands. While Nedzamba's reinstatement was still an issue, more general demands were added. These included a commitment from Sats to eliminate racism; no disciplinary action against strikers; and payment for the period on strike. The strikers also wanted Sats to negotiate a disciplinary procedure once the strike was over, as well as 'a more democratic and efficient structure through which workers could approach management.' The demands were revised, Sarhwu announced, 'in a spirit of reconciliation and compromise.'[8] Significantly, Sarhwu did not directly demand recognition, although that was clearly the underlying issue. Sarhwu wanted a settlement, and attempted to keep the complicating factor of recognition out of negotiations. But it also wanted certain key demands addressed. This conciliatory approach eventually evaporated after it was met by an increasingly intransigent Sats response.

After its first feeble attempts at negotiations failed, Sats attempted to break the strike and destroy Sarhwu through a combination of repression, scab labour, and threats to the striking workers. Hundreds of railway workers were arrested. By the second week of April, at least 21 were held under emergency regulations. In Ogies, in the Eastern Transvaal, 300 Sarhwu members were detained while on their way to the union's offices. Police claimed they constituted an 'illegal gathering'. Since all gatherings were illegal at the time, police could simply decide in which cases to apply the law. One striker, who in 1991 was still on death row, recalled catching a train home during the early days of the strike.

I noticed a lot of police on the platforms... Before the train could leave...teargas was being sprayed into the coaches... When the train arrived at Mayfair (station, a fellow passenger) was shot by a (white) person on the platform wearing private clothes.

Attempts by strikers to speak to non-strikers were met with teargas and assaults by police.

Sats brought in scab labour. Its regular white workforce worked large amounts of overtime, at overtime rates. Unemployed whites and schoolchildren were also utilised. Management hired 750 white youths to clean the station at Kempton Park. Drivers were employed to keep container transport running.

Sats also attempted to evict strikers from their hostel accommodation. The hostels, despite being grim places, brought the workers together. As on the mines, they became strongholds of the strikers and the union, and were essential for discipline, organisation and unity. Early in the strike Sats gave notice that it intended to evict 400 strikers from a hostel in Kokstad, Natal. While this eviction did not materialise, others did.

Throughout the first six weeks of the strike, the threat of dismissal was Sats' major weapon against strikers. Other threats were contained in a variety of letters and ultimatums to workers. City Deep strikers were warned that 'those responsible for the strike...might be held legally responsible for the financial losses and damage suffered by Sats.' They were also informed that 'arrangements are being made to appoint whites on a permanent basis... These employees (ie the casuals) will not be transferred elsewhere once the strike has been called off.'[9]

Repression, scab labour and threats failed to break the strike. With management clearly unwilling to negotiate a settlement, workers decided to intensify their action. 'The only course left open to us at this point,' Sarhwu announced in mid-April, 'is to find different ways of putting pressure to management in order to force them back to the negotiating table with a more responsible attitude.'

The stakes are raised

The union's policy was to extend the strike nationwide. By the fourth week of April over 20 000 workers were involved. While the strike remained concentrated in the Southern Transvaal, it included workers as far afield as Louis Trichardt in the Northern Transvaal, Bloemfontein in the Free State, and Kokstad in Natal. Most black train commuters in affected communities refused to pay for tickets and rode free. This led to massive revenue losses. Many strikers went beyond Sarhwu policy and, aided by members of the public, decided that even more pressure was needed. In Soweto, trains were set alight on 14 and 15 April. This caught the imagination of militant youth in particular, and by 18 April, at least 50 train coaches had been torched. After a number of bomb blasts, presumably the work of Umkhonto we Sizwe soldiers, occurred on railway premises, troops were brought in to guard premises and property.

On 18 April Sats management issued an ultimatum. Unless strikers returned to work by Monday 20 April they would be dismissed. The ultimatum was later extended, with a stipulation that those not working on 22 April would be considered fired.

The union leadership was unsure how to respond. The strike was becoming an all-or-nothing battle, and many officials and leaders of both Sarhwu and Cosatu felt that a tactical retreat was needed. An orderly return to work would allow the union to live to fight another day. During the strike Sarhwu's membership had increased by thousands, and it was argued that this needed organisational consolidation.[*] If the workforce was dismissed, union organisation would be left shattered, and the union would have to be rebuilt from outside the workplace.

However, workers rejected these suggestions. One official recalled that 'workers were furious with me when I suggested that they return to work. I was asked if I (as an official) knew exactly what the conditions were like in Sats.' Workers felt that a return to work would mean defeat, and that Sats would never agree to their demands except under pressure. Their views prevailed – an important indication of Cosatu's policy of worker control. But as it transpired, the events of 22 April made anything other than a barefisted fight impossible.

Strikers refused to return to work on that day and announced that their action was still on. Sats responded that the strike was over since all striking workers had been dismissed. A large number of strikers gathered, as usual, at various meeting places. Trouble began when police confronted a group of striking workers at Cosatu's Germiston offices. Police forced their way into a meeting and began assaulting the workers with rifles and sjamboks. Workers scattered in panic. Many broke through plateglass windows, cutting themselves badly. Police then opened fire, killing three strikers.

Others made their way to Sarhwu's head office in Cosatu House, Johannesburg, some ten kilometers away. They reported the shootings to thousands of strikers assembled in the main hall on the ground floor, and workers immediately decided to send a delegation to Germiston to assist. The delegation rushed to the nearby Doornfontein station to catch a train to Germiston. As they approached the station they came face to face with police. Accounts differ over what happened next. Police claim the workers refused an order to disperse and they were forced to fire teargas. The workers claim the police attacked them. In any event, police again opened fire and another three workers were killed. Other injured workers, trailing blood from their wounds, returned to Cosatu House.

The siege of Cosatu House

Within hours, 200 heavily-armed police entered Cosatu House, after first sealing off Jeppe Street, which fronted the building and is a major artery

---

Sarhwu's membership in its Southern Transvaal region alone, grew from 9 000 to 22 000, with the majority joining during the strike itself. Commonly, a particular depot would join the strike, and then all go to the union offices to sign up. This imposed its own dynamic on the union. There was little time for the longer-term union aims, or its structures and policies, to be explained properly. After the strike the inability to consolidate this membership remained one of Sarhwu's greatest weaknesses.

---

into Johannesburg's city centre. They prevented anyone from entering or leaving the building, and forced their way into a meeting of striking workers. Police then went through the building floor by floor, union by union, until they reached the uppermost tenth floor which housed Cosatu's head office. Police herded everyone in the building into various rooms. There they were held for hours at gunpoint, spreadeagled and facing the wall – an image captured by Eric Miller in his well-known photograph of the scene. Miller was shooting pictures from a high-rise building one street away when police inside Cosatu House noticed him, and radioed to their colleagues outside to arrest him. Fortunately they did not get his film.

As police went through every office they destroyed property, union records and equipment. Papers were thrown out of windows, expensive machinery was vandalised or rendered unusable, food and coffee were laced with unknown substances, money was stolen and locked cupboards and safes forced open. Cosatu's Jay Naidoo claimed later that 'the damage caused was wanton and malicious.' Eyewitnesses reported numerous assaults. 'I saw a badly injured and handcuffed man pushed down the stairs of Cosatu House,' reported *Weekly Mail* journalist Sefako Nyaka.

> After hitting the bottom of the stairs head first with a dull thud, he lay still. A young policeman moved up to him and hit him once on the ribs with a rubber pick-handle. The man didn't stir. He was dragged on the ground to a police truck before being thrown in head first. The...man was one of several people I saw sustaining serious injuries.[10]

Over 400 people were detained. Police claimed that they had detained 'trained terrorists' but later withdrew this allegation.

On the same day Sats decided to proceed with evictions of workers from their workplaces. Days after the mass dismissals, mass arrests began. Over 400 Sarhwu members and officials were detained, including its president, Justice Langa; Transvaal regional secretary, Johannes Ngcobo; and education officer Mike Roussos. General secretary Sello was already in detention, having been arrested before the strike began. The union's Kroonstad offices were closed down, while arsonists destroyed the East London offices.

The killings, arrests and the siege failed to break the strike; if anything the repression made workers more determined to fight. It also showed other unions, and the public generally, the harshness of the repression Sarhwu faced. The workers, now dismissed, resolved to fight on, adamant that their demands should be met. Three elements were crucial if there was to be any possibility of victory: maintenance of unity amongst the strikers; disruption of Sats' operations; and prevention or limitation of scab labour. The last was the most difficult. Attempts to speak to scabs were invariably met with further repression and arrests for 'intimidation', while peaceful picketing was inconceivable, particularly under state of emergency conditions.

Scabs are killed

On 28 April a group of strikers accosted five scabs and took them to a hall in Cosatu House. They were beaten, and many strikers present felt they should be killed. Some of the strikers took the scabs to open land south of the city centre, near the Kaserne depot. There, four of the scabs were killed and their bodies burned by the then-notorious 'necklace' method. The fifth man escaped death by running away. The bodies were discovered in the early hours of 29 April.[11]

That afternoon a massive police cordon was thrown around Cosatu House. Armoured vehicles and trucks surrounded the building. Police placed the swastika of the extreme-right wing Afrikaner Weerstandse Beweging (AWB) on the bonnet of at least one of their vehicles.

Scores of heavily-armed policemen forced their way into the building, which no-one was allowed to enter or leave, and focused on the ground floor hall containing the railway workers. They surrounded it, adopting combat positions. Others took up positions on the roof of the neighbouring building. Their weapons were aimed at the entrance to the hall and at those trying to watch the scene from the upper floors of Cosatu House.

Railway workers initially refused to leave their meeting hall. Tension was high, many arguing that the police should be fought. Police were also uncompromising, threatening to force their way into the hall, a move which would undoubtedly have resulted in heavy casualties. Union leaders eventually persuaded workers to leave peacefully.

During this second siege police acted with greater discipline. But the fact that they were heavily armed, and undoubtedly prepared to shoot, made this episode more intense and frightening. Police claimed to be looking for the killers of the four scabs. Every one of the many thousands of people present in the building was slowly led out at gunpoint. They had to pass, one by one, in front of a video camera and informers wearing balaclavas. The informers pointed out certain individuals, and 11 were arrested, including a 12 year-old child.[*]

Eighteen people were subsequently tried for the murders. Eight were found guilty of direct involvement in the murders, and received a range of sentences. Four – Patrick Molefe, George Maungedzo, Wilson Matshili and Takalani Mamphaga – were sentenced to death and dispatched to death row.

Both Cosatu and Sarhwu denied responsibility for, and condemned, the killings. The first they heard of the murders was after the raid on Cosatu House. Nevertheless, it was a dark chapter in Cosatu's history. Police made maximum effort, with the help of state-owned television, to imply that the killings took place in Cosatu House, with Cosatu's approval. In a speech to workers, a month later, Jay Naidoo declared that: 'as unionists we know that violence is not the way in which to build a trade union... What the SABC forgets,' continued Naidoo, 'but what we cannot forget is that the police and Sats continually used violent and forceful means to smash...organisation and discipline. Who is therefore responsible for the violence that has occurred?'[12]

Towards a settlement

Even the second siege did not break the strike, although it was a personally intimidating experience for every striker present. A week later, on 7 May, Cosatu House was destroyed in a right-wing bomb attack. Many unions lost their head offices in the process. Sarhwu suffered a further blow. It lost both its head office and Transvaal regional office. The strikers only managed to continue meeting after Cusa/Azactu made its first floor Lekton House premises available briefly. Thereafter, temporary offices were found at Tudor Mansions in downtown Johannesburg.

During May, Sats issued eviction notices to 9 000 hostel dwellers. It also prevented food trucks, organised by Sarhwu, from entering the hostels. Sarhwu had meanwhile launched a legal challenge to the April mass dismissals. It had a strong case, Sats having dismissed workers in terms of a dubious set of regulations. Sats was also having trouble with its scabs. Many of the white scabs were proving unreliable and ill-prepared for hard and consistent work. Few black scabs were available, not only out of solidarity with the strikers but also, undoubtedly, through fear of the consequences. In the community at large, attacks on train coaches and Sats' property continued and commuters still refused to pay for transport. Other Cosatu unions began to take solidarity action. At a number of factories workers refused to unload railway trucks. While Sats was not crippled, certain depots and services were severely affected.

By late May, both Sarhwu and Sats were looking for a settlement. Sats still refused to have any dealings with the union, and maintained the fiction that lawyers, briefed by Sarhwu, represented only individual dismissed employees. A settlement was reached on 5 June. The strikers were vindicated. Sats agreed that all dismissed workers, including Andrew Nedzamba, would be re-employed without loss of benefits. No worker would be victimised for striking, and detained workers would be re-employed on their release from jail. Black workers would, in future, have the right to elect their own representatives. Sats would spend R10-million upgrading hostel facilities at Kaserne and Delmore. Finally, black workers would be entitled to permanent status after two years' service, a right long enjoyed by white workers.

It was undoubtedly a victory. In public advertisements after the strike, Cosatu claimed that only its persistence:

> forced Sats to re-open talks and abandon their notion that the strike was 'resolved' with the dismissal of 16 000 striking workers... Public sector management should realise...that it is folly to impose toothless liaison committees (appointed by management) on workers... Sats should transform to fit in with the established labour relations system. It should cease to force Blatu down the throats of workers.[13]

Sarhwu worked tirelessly to inform all dismissed workers of the settlement and to ensure that all reported for work within the agreed time. When workers returned, they did so with confidence. Sats' recognition of worker representatives meant, in practice, recognising Sarhwu's shop stewards. The settlement had addressed the broader issues facing railway workers. However the union was in no doubt that it still faced a long struggle. It had to consolidate its new, but battle-hardened, 22 000-strong Transvaal membership. It had to win the release of detainees and, later, defend those charged with murder. It still faced a hostile Sats management. Even after the settlement, Minister of Transport Eli Louw insisted that the settlement had nothing to do with Sarhwu. Sats, he stated, had settled with its employees. Blatu was still recognised as the representative of black railway workers. This was an attitude that would cause, in later years, an even bigger and more violent strike on the railways.

Many, even within Cosatu, were surprised when Sats agreed to settle. Its option was to prolong the dispute and wear out the workers. As a state-owned enterprise it could accommodate almost unlimited losses, and call on extensive police and army support to crush and disperse the strikers. Why then did Sats settle?

It was apparent to all that the strikers were determined to fight to the bitter end. For Sats, this implied long-term bitterness and problems with black commuters, as well as extensive and ongoing destruction of railway properties. Almost 23 000 dismissed railway workers would not simply disappear. There was also a real possibility that the courts would reinstate the dismissed strikers. 'They knew we had a strong case,' one organiser commented at the time. 'As the date for the court hearing came closer, management showed more and more a willingness to discuss a settlement.'

International factors played a part in Sats decision to settle. The sanctions campaign, then at its height, would have been reinforced if no settlement had been reached. Links between Cosatu and both the British National Union of Railwayworkers (NUR) and the International Transport Federation (ITF) were strong, and cutting transport links, including international container services, was a very real threat at the time.

Finally, Sats management was internally divided between hardliners and reformers. The former, together with the police, saw Sarhwu as something to be crushed, and as a threat to the apartheid status quo on the railways. Bart Grové, director-general of Sats, saw the strike as part of a revolutionary strategy against South Africa, and wanted it destroyed. The reformers, including deputy general manager Anton Moolman, felt Sats had to move with the times and should negotiate a settlement. As violence failed to crush the strike, the reformers apparently gained the upper hand within Sats management.

Violence and strikes

The railways strike brought the issue of strike violence to the fore. South Africa's labour history contained previous incidents where strikers had killed scabs. But, with a few exceptions on the goldmines, this had not usually occurred in union-organised disputes. In the months and years which followed the Sats strike, violence against scabs increased, as did violence against strikers. Assaults, attacks on homes and, most seriously, the killing of both scabs and strikers occurred. Scabs died in strikes involving NUM and the Chamber of Mines (1987), Numsa and Seifsa (1988), Ppwawu and Afcol (1988), and Fawu and SA Breweries (1989), to name only a few. In the particularly violent and bitter dispute between Sarhwu and Sats in late 1989, over 30 people, both strikers and scabs, died.

The death of scabs during the 1987 Sats strike was preceded by intense state repression against the strikers. It is not hard to see why a desperate workforce, denied other channels, should resort to killing scabs.

The killings undoubtedly made it more difficult for Sats to employ scab labour, and thereby break the strike. The killing of scabs was a rational and, to some extent, inevitable response from the strikers. This is not to say it was correct, morally or organisationally. But it was, overwhelmingly, the action of rational people for whom the victory of the strikers was a matter of life or death.

A complete analysis of strike-related violence has not been conducted, but a number of studies have revealed certain trends. Firstly, there was a significant increase in incidents following the declaration of the 1986 state of emergency. With the banning of organisations and the emergency clampdown, unions increasingly took up political issues. Township violence spilled onto the factory floor. One shop steward has explained that repression and detentions 'forced workers to assume the leadership role on the shop floor...putting a strain on inexperienced leadership.' Repression also closed off channels of communication.

Secondly, and relatedly, strike violence tends to be most intense in those sectors with the most repressive labour policies – mines, the railways, and sectors structured around substantial hostel-based labour. Thirdly, strike violence is more likely in protracted strikes – trials of strength – especially where the threat of dismissal exists, or where workers experience real hunger. Finally, violence is intensified, and takes on an ethnic dimension, when management replaces strikers with those of another ethnic group.

South African workers, as mentioned previously, have no legal right to picket. The Sats workers could only picket at their peril, risking arrest on 'intimidation' charges. Such arrests have occurred even when attempts to speak to non-strikers have taken place in the community and in a peaceful and non-threatening manner.

Strike violence has been used as a powerful propaganda weapon against Cosatu. The killings of Sats strikers by police was glossed over by the media, particularly radio and television. But the killing of the four scabs formed the basis of a major campaign to discredit Cosatu. This campaign was directly responsible for creating the climate in which Cosatu House was blown up in early May 1987.

Protracted industrial disputes, with management focusing on the employment of replacement labour, with strikers and their unions repressed, and with no legal right to picket, are a recipe for violent conflicts between strikers and scabs. On occasion management has even encouraged vigilante movements among scabs, and this has provided a way to attack strikers physically without direct police intervention. The pervasive culture of violence which now exists in South Africa only reinforces these trends.

It is ironic, but hardly surprising, that violence by strikers is rarely directed against property, employers or the state, but rather against scabs. The union movement has consistently dissociated itself from the killing of scabs, stressing that its weapons are organisation and persuasion. Violence, while it may result in short-term gains for the unions, is counterproductive. Violence by strikers leads to a culture of violence and 'short-cuts' in struggles. It is always directed at individual scabs, themselves usually poor, hungry and desperate for jobs. Scabs have often previously been union members.

In discussions within Cosatu during 1988 there was agreement that:

violence was counter-productive and gave employers a chance to justify strong-arm tactics to undermine the solidarity of strikers and the strength of their union... If the violence is not contained, at the end of the day other workers will have been used to divide and weaken us.[14]

Experience has shown that once a pattern of violence develops, there is a tendency for it to be used more frequently and more easily. A culture of violence is extremely destructive, running counter to the fundamental union principles of organisation, discipline and persuasion. Cosatu has, consequently, stressed the right of workers to hold peaceful pickets during strikes.

Unions have tried to develop the notion of strike rules, both as a guide to their members and as something to be agreed between management and union. During the 1987 mine strike NUM's proposed strike rules proposed a ban on liquor; no forcing of people to strike, or join the union; workers to remain on mine premises; and a prohibition on scabs. In 1988 Numsa circulated similar rules which stressed 'orderly discipline'; that workers should remain 'in the premises of the company' and not move onto the street; that workers should take instructions only from shop stewards; and that there should be 'no intimidation or violence.'[15]

But the rules suffered from two major problems. Firstly, employers did not agree to them. In particular they often wanted strikers off the premises so they could attempt to resume production using scab labour. This meant workers standing outside the gates, where they were vulnerable to arrest and assault. Secondly, the rules could only work if, in Naidoo's words, there was 'common agreement on the notion that the state must stay uninvolved.'

In trying to find solutions to the problem of violence in strike situations, Cosatu has stressed that responsibility lies with the unjust political and industrial relations system. A resolution adopted at Cosatu's 1989 congress noted that

> management severely provokes workers by repression of union organisation and industrial action, refusal to negotiate, the payment of slave wages, dismissal of striking workers and employment of scabs, evictions of workers from hostels and houses, use of spies and use of police, and false charges of intimidation.

Trends in early 1987

The OK Bazaars and Sats strikes were not the only ones of early 1987, although they were the most dramatic. Other lengthy strikes involved Pwawu and Anglo's Mondi Board Mills, and state postal workers.

Like Sats, the post office also had a recognised in-house union, the Post and Telecommunications Workers Association (Potwa). But Potwa, unlike Blatu, had been taken over by progressive forces. Militant postal workers, led by president Vusi Khumalo, succeeded during 1986 in changing Potwa from within, and the union became the vehicle for postal workers to air their grievances. In April 1987 a transport problem involving workers at Power Park led to a strike. This quickly spread until it involved 8 000 postal workers on the Witwatersrand and, later, in the Border region. The strike, which took place at the same time as the railway strike, lasted nearly five weeks. Since Potwa was recognised, negotiations were held between it and the state-owned post office. Management was also more committed to negotiating a settlement than their Sats counterparts.

Two factors assisted Potwa in forcing a settlement. Many of its members were performing relatively skilled work. And management was not as hostile to Potwa, given that it was not affiliated to Cosatu. At the same time, Potwa was able to use Cosatu facilities, and obtain its advice and assistance during the strike.

While the railway and post office strikes took place concurrently, this was not planned. It simply reflected the depth of anger of public sector workers. As with the railway workers, many Potwa grievances related to disciplinary procedures and racial discrimination between black and white post office employees. However, while police became involved in the strike – in fact they precipitated the action by locking workers out of their workplace – they did not resort to the level of repression Sarhwu faced.

The success of the postal strike played a major role in boosting Potwa, and drawing it closer to Cosatu. Potwa delegates attended Cosatu's July 1987 congress as observers, and in October 1988 the union formally affiliated. The April strike was followed by two national postal strikes during July and August 1987. The second lasted almost a month and involved 21 000 workers countrywide. While each strike had its specific causes, all arose from the same problems: racial discrimination, the lack of parity between black and white in wages and work status, and the absence of meaningful negotiation structures in the post office.

The OK Bazaars, railways, post office and other strikes in early 1987 showed a number of trends. They tended to last longer, and be more intense, than had previously been the case. They revealed employers determined to stand firm, but not always succeeding, and a workforce equally committed to victory, even at high cost to itself. Consequently, many of the struggles became protracted 'trials of strength' between management and labour. This was a pattern repeated in the massive mineworkers' strike some months later.

The strikes indicated that public sector workers were beginning to stand up for their trade union and economic rights. In time, electricity workers, health workers, education workers, teachers and even policemen and prison warders would echo these demands.

The strikes also demonstrated that the state of emergency, despite its intensity, had failed to crush the spirit of workers. It had damaged but not broken union structures, organisation and discipline. In the Sats strike it was only after unprecedented repression that the union lost a degree of control over the striking workers. Even then, Sarhwu was handicapped by its own inexperience and the fact that most of the strikers joined the union only during the strike.

The state was determined to break Cosatu and its affiliates in early 1987. The emergency declared in June 1986 had succeeded in disrupting most UDF structures, and in curbing the power of the 'young comrades'. The military and security establishment, the power behind the presidential throne, apparently decided that it was now time to crush the union movement. Major employers, by and large, had a more sophisticated approach to the unions. They did not want the unions destroyed because, unlike the security establishment, they knew this would be impossible. But they did want the power of the union movement to be severely curbed. Employers wanted the unions tamed. The security forces wanted them destroyed. From the standpoint of the ordinary unionist in the branches, this was a distinction too subtle to be noticed, and for most Cosatu unionists it became difficult to distinguish between employer and state attitudes. Attacks seemed to come from both sides.

Notes

1. This account relies largely on 'Strike at OK Bazaars', *South African Labour Bulletin*, 12(2), January/February 1987; and an interview with Jay Naidoo in *South African Labour Bulletin*, 12(2), January/February 1987; as well as a number of interviews conducted by the author.
2. *Weekly Mail*, 27.03.87. See also Sarhwu, *The History of the City Deep Dispute*, 1987.
3. *IIR Information Sheet*, April 1987, 2.
4. *IIR Information Sheet*, April 1987, 3.
5. Jabu Matiko, 'Sats: "No" to Sarhwu', *South African Labour Bulletin*, 12(4), 4.
6. *Weekly Mail*, 20.03.87.
7. *Weekly Mail*, 27.03.87.
8. *IIR Information Sheet*, April 1987, 2.
9. *IIR Information Sheet*, April 1987, 3.

10. *Weekly Mail*, 24.04.87.
11. Lauren Segal and Graeme Simpson, 'Off the Rails: violence in the railway strike of 1987', paper presented to the Association of Sociologists in South Africa (ASSA) annual conference held at Stellenbosch University, July 1990.
12. Jay Naidoo, speech at the launch of Numsa, 22 May 1987.
13. See, for example, *Weekly Mail*, 12.06.87.
14. Jay Naidoo, quoted in *Weekly Mail*, 20.01.89.
15. 'Strike rules', reprinted in *South African Labour Bulletin*, 14(3), August 1989, 39.

11

The bombing of Cosatu House

Clampdown!

*T*HE tension was palpable as May 1987 approached. Thousands of striking workers thronged the streets, particularly on the Witwatersrand. The killing of striking railway workers had angered unionists and black communities throughout the country. In addition the government was in the middle of an election campaign.

May Day, which fell that year on a Friday, passed off with few incidents. In an effort to avoid clashes, but still determined not to accede to popular demands, the government declared the first Friday in May a public holiday. This automatically covered commercial and, ironically, state workers, but excluded workers in industry and the mines, where paid holidays were determined by other legislation. Nevertheless, few employers objected when workers in those sectors stayed away. May Day had, after all, effectively been won as a workers' holiday the previous year.

The general election scheduled for 6 May was a major challenge to the unions and the entire democratic movement. As usual, the whites-only electorate was going to the polls to decide the future of black South Africa. Voters were asked to support PW Botha's reform moves, as well as his security action aimed at crushing 'communist subversion'.

The ruling National Party regarded the ultra-right Conservative Party as its major electoral challenge, and consequently ran a particularly conservative campaign. A central pillar of government strategy aimed to show the white electorate the strong stand taken against the trade union movement. Propaganda poured forth daily accusing Cosatu of murder, being communist puppets, and acting as agents of the ANC. Cosatu, said Minister of Police Vlok, was involved in 'the polarisation, politicisation, organisation and mobilisation of the worker to plan for a so-called living wage campaign.'[1]

Cosatu's Living Wage campaign (LWC), due to be launched on May Day, was declared a communist plot, and its launching rallies banned. In justifying the banning of Cosatu's Durban May Day rallies police argued that discussion of the campaign would not be in the interests of public safety.

> Furthermore, such discussion or advertising will in the opinion of the SA Police promote the objects and aims of unlawful organisations such as the ANC and the SACP because it will initiate an attack on the free market system. The police are also of the opinion that the LWC is based upon a philosophy, ideology or scheme which is developed from or which is relative to the doctrines and philosophies of Marx, Engels and Trotsky because it envisages common ownership.[2]

The May stayaway call

Cosatu and the democratic movement decided to make their presence felt on election day, and agreed with the UDF and NECC to support a call for a two-day stayaway on 5 and 6 May. 'The action', said Cosatu, 'should send signals to white voters and their government that attacks on Cosatu would lead to resistance and a deterioration in industrial relations.'

Within Cosatu there was debate on the stayaway call. A minority felt that a more cautious approach was needed. Cosatu should retreat, consolidate and live to fight another day, rather than counter-attack and risk annihilation. This view was generally supported by the independent worker bloc. However, the argument which prevailed called for intensification of pressure on the state. Only by standing up and fighting would repression be resisted. If Cosatu simply retreated, state attacks would continue and even increase. Resistance, it was argued, involved drawing on wide layers of support among youth and in the black community, and not only on organised workers. This view was supported by both the centre and the UDF blocs.

The argument was strong and, with hindsight, undoubtedly correct. The state and employers would have interpreted absence of resistance and protest as weakness, rather than moderation. At the time, however, the matter was not clear-cut. There seemed a genuine possibility that the state might totally destroy the union movement. In addition, little had been gained by repeated stayaway actions. While the masses had been mobilised, organisational advances had been few.

Debates over the tactics of mass action were ongoing within Cosatu, with arguments about whether community-based or factory-based action was most appropriate. Unresolved political differences within Cosatu lay behind these debates, and there were also genuine fears that Cosatu was being called on to substitute for a UDF weakened by intense repression. Circumstances were indeed forcing Cosatu to become the centre of mass resistance. This inevitably caused tensions. Cosatu structures were geared to consultation with members and the taking of union decisions. However, repression often made consultation difficult and forced the federation to take far-reaching political decisions. The state itself compelled Cosatu to become more politically active than its founding affiliates had ever intended.

This should not be misunderstood. Cosatu, like any union in South Africa, had to be politically active. However, under conditions of extreme repression, it was difficult to maintain a balance between political and economic/trade union tasks. Cosatu's affiliates, of necessity, tried to maintain that balance. But the federation structures found themselves obliged to allocate an overwhelming amount of time, energy and resources to political tasks. Cosatu was also compelled to adopt detailed political positions, when more general support for the liberation struggle might, at times, have been more appropriate. The state accused Cosatu of being a front for the ANC. This was untrue. Yet, ironically, state repression brought Cosatu and the ANC even closer together.

Massive state propaganda was unleashed to prevent a stayaway. Whites were assured that it would be safe for them to vote. Heavily-armed police were deployed in white residential areas and around polling stations. Employers threatened action against black workers intending to stay away. Troops distributed pamphlets in many townships. 'The security forces greet you. Your enemies are our enemies,' they announced in the newspeak of the government's Bureau for Information. The government had achieved peaceful reform, the pamphlets argued. 'This has been the result of peaceful negotiations between the elected leaders of the many groups in South Africa – not of senseless violence.' In response to the stayaway call, the pamphlet argued that 'the man who wants to ride a bus must be able to do so. The man who wants to go to work must be able to do so.'

At least 2,5-million people responded to the stayaway call. This included over 1,5-million workers and about one million students. The township themselves were generally quiet as people stayed at home.

While there were reports of isolated clashes with the police, it was impossible for the state to blame the response on intimidation. The stayaway intensified on 6 May, election day. As usual it was most strongly supported in the Eastern Cape where almost 100% absenteeism was recorded. Strong support for the call was registered in Natal with 60% of African workers absent on 5 May, rising to 70% the following day. Support for the call in the Transvaal was slightly below the levels of the big 1986 stayaway actions. There was also significant mineworker action, previously uncommon in 'political' stayaways. NUM estimated that 100 000 miners took part, although the figure was probably lower. It was, at that time, the largest stayaway action ever undertaken. While similar in scale to that of May Day 1986, it had lasted for two full days.[3]

Leadership of the democratic movement was elated at the response. It 'underscores the significance of our campaign for a national united action and the centrality of the UDF, Cosatu and the entire democratic movement in any attempt at resolving the problems of South Africa,' said UDF's publicity secretary, Murphy Morobe, then operating 'underground'. Cosatu warned that further government action against the federation could be expected. The stayaway:

> clearly demonstrated the opposition of the vast majority of South Africa's people to the mad, repressive course this government is bent on... PW Botha has called this election to get a clear mandate to continue with his policy of repressing democratic organisations. Any further attempt to undermine and attack Cosatu or its leadership will lead to renewed resistance and the rapid destruction of the labour relations machinery.[4]

The unions did not have to wait long for the next blow. Before the ink on their press release was dry, Cosatu's headquarters were bombed.

The bombing of Cosatu House

During the early hours of 7 May two massive blasts rocked Cosatu House. This was clearly the work of professionals, who entered the building from the rear, climbing a high wall and cutting through a heavy metal security fence. They placed two large bombs at the base of the main supporting columns of the 11-storey building. The damage caused was extensive. The building was declared unsafe by the Johannesburg City Council, and entry to the premises prohibited.

The blast was a serious blow. Cosatu, NUM, Pwawu, TGWU, Sarhwu and Mawu lost their head offices. The regional, branch and local offices of many affiliates were also destroyed, and the major meeting halls on the ground floor, located directly above the bombs, were totally devastated. The immediate victims were the railway strikers, deprived of a meeting venue in the middle of their strike. But the most important loss was of a political and trade union centre. Cosatu House had acted as a point of integration for various Cosatu affiliates.

The blast forced affiliates to disperse and find accommodation elsewhere. This was not easy. Landlords, intimidated by the blast or warned off by police, frequently refused to let premises to the unions. Many were informed that insurance cover on buildings would be withdrawn if they rented space to unions. Others were threatened with Group Areas Act charges. Blacks were not legally entitled to rent premises in 'white' city centres. In a number of cases, although with some notable exceptions, churches assisted Cosatu affiliates with temporary premises.

The state's anti-Cosatu propaganda created a climate which made the attack almost inevitable. To this extent an attack should have been foreseen. Technically, better security standards might have foiled attackers. Security around the building was admittedly inadequate. Cosatu's CEC had briefly discussed the matter in September 1986, but little had been done to implement the subsequent recommendations. Organisationally, however, a high level of security was difficult to implement. Cosatu was a mass organisation, its premises used daily by thousands of people. In practice it was impossible to install a shield against attackers without severely limiting general access to the building.

The real mistake, Cosatu subsequently assessed, was to have put too many eggs into one basket, and over-centralised its operations. In addition, Cosatu House was too isolated, being on the extreme east end of the city centre. A more central location, surrounded by a range of business premises, might have been more secure.

The perpetrators of the blast were never caught. The South African police have been singularly unsuccessful in capturing those responsible for assassinations and attacks on individuals and property associated with the democratic movement. A Cosatu press statement dated 9 May noted that the blast 'followed closely on constant raids and propaganda attacks on Cosatu.' During the 22 April raid police told Cosatu members 'that the building would either be burnt or bombed "to the ground." At the time,' continued the press release, 'we thought these statements were part of the usual "sick humour" that we have to put up with in operations of this nature. Now that the building has been hit, it makes us wonder.'

Shortly before the Cosatu House blast, government attacks had intensified. Law and Order Minister Adriaan Vlok warned that the security forces would act against unionists whose activities are 'not in the interests of the country.'

'Government is trying to create the impression,' responded Cosatu's vice-president Chris Dlamini, 'that the unions are in the forefront of the revolution, and that Cosatu is an ANC front, to scare employers and others from dealing with us.'

The bomb blast at Cosatu House was not the only attack on union premises during this period. On the same day the East London offices, housing nine affiliates, were burnt and seriously damaged, and the Mawu and Ccawusa offices in Germiston were broken into. The Pietersburg office was closed down after men 'believed to be police ordered everyone out and locked the offices.' On 5 May NUM offices at Vryheid's Coronation mine were attacked by Uwusa supporters and a NUM organiser was killed.

Sarhwu's Kroonstad offices were 'smashed up' during May, and other premises – including the Tudor Mansions offices in Johannesburg, the Nelspruit offices and the East London offices (again) – were burnt and bombed. Police seized 55 000 copies of *Cosatu News* and 90 000 pamphlets dealing with the Living Wage campaign in raids on offices throughout the country. That issue of the newspaper was also banned. In the months and years which followed, Cosatu and its affiliates' offices were repeatedly bombed, burnt and raided.

At the beginning of June 1987, a number of Cosatu unions housed at Tudor Mansions – including Gawu and Saawu – were served with eviction orders. These offices had been petrol-bombed twice in the previous 18 months. This, and the bombing of Cosatu House, were believed to have resulted in the eviction orders. At other places, including Piet Retief, police and landlords conspired to ensure that unions were totally unable to obtain premises. Police have never managed to identify or arrest the perpetrators of any of these attacks.

'Hands Off Cosatu'

Attacks on the federation continued. The SABC, a major source of information for most South Africans, embarked on a sustained propaganda drive. Items dealing with Cosatu were presented on television against a backdrop of Cosatu House, on whose walls the graffiti 'Torture House' and 'enter for torture' had been painted. News reports implied that Cosatu itself had been responsible for the explosion at Cosatu House! Lengthy documentaries were shown claiming to reveal Cosatu as a puppet of the ANC, itself controlled by communists and Russian agents. The essence of the message was that Cosatu was engaged in criminal activities and part of a revolutionary onslaught against South Africa. This meant, it was implied, that all means were justified in crushing it.[5] 'If fighting democratically for a living wage, decent working conditions and just labour relations are a crime,' said Cosatu in an official statement, 'then the mass of workers in this country are engaged in criminal activity all the time.'

A major business leader, FCI's John van Zyl, warned on 18 May that government was ready to introduce legislation aimed at curbing labour's power. Intimidation and violence by workers was causing growing concern, he said. Some elements of management were losing patience, and were considering a harder line in dealing with labour. Van Zyl called for a reduction in confrontation on all sides. Other employers were more concerned about the implications of a clampdown. John Wilson, chairman of multinational petrol giant Shell SA, argued that state attempts to crush Cosatu would adversely affect industrial relations and fuel growing polarisation between capital and labour.

A researcher from Stellenbosch University's business school believed that Cosatu had overestimated the instability of the South African government. Nevertheless he cautioned government to think carefully before acting. 'By clamping down you may win the battle but lose the war.'[6] A majority of employers supported a state clampdown, with a minority favouring a more co-optive approach. 'It's far more advisable to lock trade unions into the negotiating process than to lock them in jail,' was the view of one liberal politician.[7]

This was the climate in which Cosatu decided to launch a 'Hands Off Cosatu' campaign. Publicity was directed towards employers, the democratic movement and the international community, and an open letter to employers was placed in all major publications during the third week of May. 'Cosatu is the largest trade union federation, yet up to a few weeks ago it was a non-organisation to the SABC,' the letter read. Suddenly, it noted, Cosatu was being attacked and its position and policies distorted. 'Cosatu's clear condemnation of the (railway strike) murders and its numerous attempts to settle the Sats dispute are brushed aside.' Employers had influence, Cosatu argued. 'Are you sincerely and concertedly using this power and influence to secure and protect freedom of speech and association?'

In being refused permission to hold May Day rallies, and Living Wage Campaign meetings, Cosatu felt it had been 'accused, tried and condemned by shadowy Security Police Officers.' Cosatu asked:

> Do you wish to remain silent and watch Cosatu convicted in a SABC kangaroo court?... Human liberty can only be secured if each person fights for it when it is threatened. We have a choice and so do you.

In a speech at Wits University on 26 May, Jay Naidoo called on students and the democratic movement to support the 'Hands Off Cosatu' campaign:

We have demanded, as you have, the right to: speak freely without intimidation; meet freely without harassment; organise freely without victimisation; and campaign for our stake in a future, unitary non-racial South Africa. We are involved in politics... We do not apologise for this and we believe opposition is our democratic right.[8]

Law and Order Minister Adriaan Vlok responded in parliament to Cosatu's claims. The police did not interfere in 'bona fide union activities,' he said, 'in fact we encourage them.' Cosatu was, however, responsible for 'thousands' of blacks losing their jobs, and this made people angry with the federation. Vlok went on to quote from court evidence to 'prove' Cosatu's links to the ANC and the Communist Party. The government's opponents 'want us to allow Cosatu to get...Marxist goals, socialism and the final goal of communism.' The police would not allow anyone, Vlok continued, 'to hide behind the cloak of the labour movement.'[9]

Repression on the ground

During this period the state withdrew passports from many union leaders, thereby restricting their international travel. But the most significant attack, from an organisational point of view, was the effective banning of the Living Wage campaign. 'If demanding a living wage is a "communist plot",' read one Cosatu statement, 'then millions of workers and unemployed in South Africa are communists.'[10]

Many employers began refusing to recognise or deal with Cosatu unions. Taking their line from the state, they adopted a tougher approach. Unions frequently had to battle for rights which had been long-established and which were normally extended to newly-organised plants without much argument. Direct police involvement in industrial disputes also became standard practice.

Events in Queenstown during June 1987 were typical of a pattern affecting small towns in particular. Cosatu had recently launched its Eastern Cape region, and was aiming to hold public launches in a variety of towns and establish local structures. Thembinkosi Mkalipi, a CWIU member and regional vice-chair, travelled to Queenstown on 20 June 1987, accompanied by Hamilton Mlunguzi, the regional treasurer, and Les Kettledas, acting regional secretary. Regional secretary Dennis Neer was unable to participate, having been in detention since June 1986.

Outside the local Saawu offices the three were confronted by men driving an unmarked minibus. They searched the unionists, and found a Cosatu T-shirt in Mkalipi's bag. The three were then hauled off to the local police station. 'Let's go,' the policeman in charge is reported to have said, 'we want to torture you.'

At the police station Mkalipi was photographed in his T-shirt, which the police then decided to confiscate. The unionists argued that there was nothing illegal about a Cosatu T-shirt. The police meanwhile were holding sjamboks and canes which, according to the unionists, they seemed eager to use. The police then warned the three to leave town immediately. On their way out of town the unionists went into a shop to buy a cool-drink. The police entered the shop, removed them and escorted them out of Queenstown. Police later admitted to escorting them out of town, but denied 'this talk of sjamboks and canes.'

The extensive publicity given to this harrassment led to the police backing-off to some extent, recalls Mkalipi. Co-ordinating activities began again and the Queenstown local was finally launched in September 1988.[11]

Events in Queenstown were typical of everyday repression, which involved not only detentions and deaths, but restrictions on organising, on bread-and-butter unionism. Accounts of workers being harassed simply for wearing union T-shirts were commonplace. Frequently police action occurred without reference to even the draconian emergency regulations, let alone any other legal provisions. Police took it upon themselves to break up meetings, assault unionists, and force workers to tear off their T-shirts. Smaller towns, as well as the newer urban centres, often bore the brunt of this sort of police action.

Notes

1. *Weekly Mail*, 30.04.87.
2. *Weekly Mail*, 30.04.87.
3. Labour Monitoring Group, '5-6 May Stayaway', *South African Labour Bulletin*, 12(5), July 1987; *Weekly Mail*, 08.05.87.
4. *Weekly Mail*, 08.05.87.
5. See, for example, 'Hands Off Cosatu' documentation in author's possession; SABC editorial comment, 12 May 1987; and Cosatu's response on 13 May 1987, in author's possession.
6. *Finance Week*, 14.05.87.
7. Pieter Schoeman of the Progressive Federal Party, *Star*, 22.05.87.
8. Jay Naidoo, speech delivered at the University of Witwatersrand, 26 May 1987.
9. *Financial Mail*, 29.05.87.
10. Cosatu advertisement, 'Message to all Democrats', *Weekly Mail*, 29.05.87.
11. Jobi Matlou, telephonic interview with Thembinkosi Mkalipi, 1990.

12

Merger developments

'One industry, one union'

ALMOST everyone within Cosatu agreed on the necessity and urgency of mergers. But in practice, the merger programme caused arguments and resentment. Cosatu's leadership was accused of moving too fast. Some claimed it was too dictatorial, others that it was not being firm enough. Pressure was placed on unions in every sector to make concrete progress in their merger talks. Smaller unions were urged to transfer and integrate membership into larger, more established unions. Larger unions were asked to be accommodating in employing officials from smaller unions. General unions were informed that they would be regarded as defunct after the second Cosatu congress. Saawu faced particular pressure in this regard, as the majority within its ranks were suspicious of the merger process and opposed to dissolving the union.

By early 1987, progress was still limited. There had been significant movement only in the food sector, among domestic workers and, to a lesser extent, in the transport sector.

On 13 January 1987 a meeting was held in Johannesburg to analyse the slow progress of the merger process. All but one of Cosatu's national office bearers were present. So too were a number of Cosatu's regional secretaries, and representatives of most of the unions responsible for convening merger talks.

This gathering laid down merger guidelines for each sector, and established general principles to govern the process.

Three general principles were established:

● 'no individual should become an obstacle to the unity of the workers';

● 'any affiliate not prepared to accept and carry out the guidelines will be considered as expelled';

● only merged industrial unions would have 'the right to participate in the national congress in July.' This implied that general unions such as Gawu and Saawu could not attend the second congress.

The national office bearers and Exco were mandated 'to monitor and take all necessary steps to carry out these recommendations and guidelines.'

While these principles established a general approach, guidelines were also set out, giving specific directions to each sector. Recognition of Fawu as a merged union in the food sector was reaffirmed. Saawu was instructed to hand over its membership in the food sector to Fawu by the end of April 1987, or face immediate expulsion from Cosatu. In the paper sector, Pwawu was instructed to hold a merger congress to be attended by Nupawo: general unions with membership in the sector were instructed to transfer their membership. In mining, Ummawosa had agreed to transfer its membership to NUM by April. The meeting felt that the South African Mine Workers Union (Samwu) was defunct, and hence not relevant to any merger proceedings.

Mawu was instructed to include Ummawosa and Macwusa in the planned launch of a new metal union. General unions were asked to transfer membership after the launch. Those unions with a presence in the chemical sector were asked to transfer membership to CWIU before the end of April. In the commercial sector, Harwu and Ccawusa were to discuss the position of hotel workers before the next Cosatu CEC. Rawu had already decided to transfer membership to Ccawusa, while the convening unions expressed the opinion that CDWU had no paid-up membership, and should not be included in merger talks.

All unions in the transport sector were asked to transfer membership to TGWU. Cosatu's founding policy had spoken of one transport sector, encompassing both private and public sector transport. The national office bearers were asked to arrange a meeting between TGWU and Sarhwu 'to discuss the position of railway workers and formation of one union...possibly with a federal structure.' In the municipal sector, CTMWA was asked to convene a launching congress before the May CEC. All unions with membership in the construction industry were instructed to transfer their membership to the Construction and Allied Workers Union (Cawu), a new union about to be launched under Cosatu's umbrella.[1]

The principles and guidelines were heavy handed and firm, amounting to a clear message from the larger to the smaller unions: merge or leave Cosatu. They were ratified both at an Exco meeting and at the CEC meeting of 19-20 February 1987. But the CEC softened the principles slightly. Unions failing to comply would not be summarily expelled, although they would face disciplinary action. In practice this simply wrapped the iron fist in a velvet glove.

The easier mergers

With the exception of the commercial sector, real progress was made before Cosatu's second national congress. On 31 January 1987 Cawu was launched. It brought together 30 000 building and construction workers, previously members of Saawu, TGWU, Gawu, Mawu, Gwusa, the Brick, Clay and Allied Workers Union (Bcawu), and a Port Elizabeth-based non-affiliate, the National General Workers Union (NGWU). Cawu's inaugural congress elected Desmond Mahasha as general secretary. David Ngcobo, a shop steward from Grinaker and a former Mawu executive member, was elected president.[2]

In the chemical industry, CWIU was recognised by Cosatu. Its merger programme was relatively easy and involved the integration of a handful of chemical workers, including two or three Saawu-organised factories around Pretoria. The main union challenge to CWIU came from outside Cosatu, in the form of the Nactu-affiliated Sacwu. CWIU's June 1987 congress re-elected Rod Crompton as general secretary, and a laboratory employee at Liquid Air in Germiston, Calvin Makgaleng, as president.

On the same weekend public sector workers met in Soweto to launch the National Education, Health and Allied Workers Union (Nehawu). Over 9 000 paid-up members, mostly non-professional workers in hospitals and at educational institutions, were involved. They had previously been members of Saawu, Gawu and the Health and Allied Workers Unions (Hawu). Nehawu was intended to be Cosatu's public sector union, but because of its relatively small membership a health and education focus was recognised as an interim step. Bheki Mkhize, a worker at the University of the Witwatersrand was elected Nehawu's first president. Yure Mdyogolo, formerly of Saawu, was elected general secretary. He was to die tragically in an accident in November 1988.

On 9-10 January 1987, the National Unemployed Workers Coordinating Committee (NUWCC) was established after a number of different groupings agreed to merge into one organisation. These included the Transvaal-based UWCC; the Western Cape's Unemployed Workers Movement; the Unemployed Workers Union of East London; and groups of retrenched workers from Port Elizabeth. While NUWCC was not formally affiliated to Cosatu, it was a recognised structure participating at all levels. It aimed to fight for the right to better unemployment insurance benefits, and negotiate for jobs.[3]

A giant metal union launched

On 23-24 May the National Union of Metalworkers of South Africa (Numsa) was launched. With 130 000 paid-up members it was truly a giant and, in terms of numbers, NUM's only serious rival within Cosatu. The merger involved six Cosatu affiliates – Mawu, Naawu, Macwusa, Gawu, Ummawosa and TGWU – all of which had members in the metal, engineering and automobile sectors. Earlier, Nismawu members in Northern Natal had been incorporated into Mawu.

The merger also involved a non-Cosatu affiliate, the 35 000 strong Motor Industries Combined Workers Union (Micwu). A Tucsa affiliate until the early 1980s, Micwu had been brought into the unity process as a result of union co-operation – particularly with Mawu – at the annual metal industry wage negotiations. This emphasised that the backbone of Numsa was Mawu's 70 000-strong membership.

The unity process managed to overcome historical divisions. Numsa incorporated Ummawosa members, who in mid-1984 had split from Mawu in a bitter conflict. It also included the former Fosatu-affiliated Naawu as well as its rival, the UDF-affiliated Macwusa. The only blemish at the launching congress was Saawu's exclusion from participation. Some delegates argued that Saawu should be admitted to the hall in the interests of building worker unity. However, a majority stressed that Saawu had failed to meet three deadlines to supply membership details and credentials for the metal sector. Saawu, the majority felt, was welcome to bring its organised metal workers into the new union at any stage after the launch of Numsa.

In an act of solidarity and defiance, the congress elected Moses Mayekiso, still in prison, as its general secretary. It was almost two years before he could take up the post, and then only after 33 months in detention and his acquittal on charges of high treason. Daniel Dube, formerly of Naawu, and a worker at a Uitenhage-based multinational, was elected president. David Madupela, a former Mawu executive member, was elected first vice-president, while Micwu's Percy Thomas assumed the position of second vice-president.

In Mayekiso's absence, three departmental secretaries – Bernie Fanaroff, Fred Sauls and Des East – were instructed to perform his duties.[4]

Textile, paper and municipal mergers

In the textile sector NUTW convened a congress, as instructed by Cosatu, during June 1987. One other Cosatu union, the South African
Textile and Allied Workers Union (Satawu), had membership in this sector. An industrial union which had developed out of Saawu, Satawu was
concerned that it would be politically and organisationally dominated by
the numerically far-stronger NUTW, and refused to attend the congress.
Its mother body, Saawu, was largely hostile to Cosatu's merger programme. Cosatu withdrew recognition of Satawu as an affiliate, and it
was instructed to transfer its membership to NUTW. Satawu's membership, concentrated in the East London area, did eventually return to
Cosatu. But this was only after further mergers in the sector between
NUTW and unions which had previously belonged to Tucsa.

Cosatu accepted that mergers in three other sectors could not be
achieved before its second congress. In the paper and printing sector a
merger between Nupawo and Pwawu was planned for September. Pockets of membership from Saawu and Gawu were also involved. Workers
from this sector were allowed to attend Cosatu's congress as one combined delegation under the banner of Pwawu. When the merger did take
place, the 23 000 strong Paper, Printing, Wood and Allied Workers
Union (Ppwawu) was formed with Jeremy Baskin as general secretary
and Malachia Ndou as president. Similarly, municipal workers were
allowed to attend the second congress as a single 'municipal sector' delegation, representing 17 000 members. Three months later, in October
1987, the South African Municipal Workers Union (Samwu) was launched with John Ernstzen, formerly of CTMWA, as general secretary, and
Petrus Mashishi, a worker with the Johannesburg municipality, as
president.

A more unusual exception was made in the case of Sarhwu. According to Cosatu policy, it should have merged with TGWU to form one
union in the transport sector. However, Sarhwu had only just emerged
from its bruising conflict with Sats, and argued that it had not had time
even to think of mergers. Cosatu accepted this and allowed TGWU and
Sarhwu to attend the congress as separate unions.[*] TGWU willingly

* At the time of writing, four years later, there was still no merger between
Cosatu's private and public sector transport unions. An uneasy relationship
between Sarhwu and TGWU leadership was partly to blame. The two unions
have since decided to merge during the second half of 1991.

accepted the arrangement. The merger process in the transport sector had been problematic enough as it was.

Difficulties in the transport sector

The merger convened by TGWU was bound to involve controversy. Cosatu's merger policy defined transport, cleaning services and security workers as part of one industrial sector. A number of small Cosatu affiliates, such as the Amalgamated Cleaners Union of South Africa (Acusa) – formerly Abwu – and CSAWU, had membership concentrated in the cleaning services. They argued, and found some support in Cosatu, for the view that the cleaning and security sectors should be separated from the broader transport sector. The interests and problems of these workers, they claimed, were different. If organised together with transport workers they would be neglected. There was also little, if any, connection between the sectors.

At the CEC a majority of Cosatu unions supported TGWU in opposing this separation. TGWU argued that cleaning and security, unlike transport, were not strategic areas. Workers in sectors like this should not be organised separately, isolated from a stable industrial base. Even the achievement of stop-order facilities would be difficult with the multitude of employers and no history of previous industrial bargaining. Lack of financial security would limit the capacity of a union to stabilise and organise properly. In addition, argued TGWU, even though they were still weak in cleaning and security, they were far stronger in that sector than the other unions.

Cosatu's policy envisaged broadly-based national industrial unions each encompassing a variety of related sectors. The alternative was to create a large number of narrowly-defined industrial unions, such as Nactu's Laundry, Drycleaning and Dyeing Workers Union or its Brushes and Cleaners Workers Union. All Cosatu's affiliates, at least after the mergers, had a broad range of sub-sectors within their scope.

The Cosatu position was accepted reluctantly by a number of the unions involved in the transport, cleaning and security sectors. This did not make for an easy merger congress. The first day of the congress was attended only by delegates from TGWU, CSAWU, some regions of Saawu, and the non-Cosatu Zakheni Transport Workers Union. Delegates from Gawu, Acusa and Sastawu arrived a day late, and found the congress in progress. A heated argument about the agenda ensued. When the time eventually came to decide on a name for the new union, angry TGWU delegates (a majority) adopted an inflexible position and insisted on retaining the name TGWU. There were walkouts in protest. Within Cosatu some argued that a merger congress had not taken place. But in the months following, those who had walked out were integrated into TGWU.

The merger congress enabled TGWU to focus on unionism in the transport, cleaning and security sectors, and marked the final chapter in the handing of 10 000 TGWU members working in sectors such as municipalities and construction to other unions. The congress elected Vivian Zungu as first president of the merged union and Jane Barrett as general secretary. Both were former office bearers of the old TGWU.

Why did Cosatu leadership push so impatiently for the mergers to take place? All within Cosatu knew of the differences which existed. These had manifested themselves within affiliates, within regions and at the CEC.

However, a majority believed that a multiplicity of unions created fertile ground for destructive differences to grow. It allowed cliques and individuals to play an unusually important role in making or blocking decisions. And the mergers were going to be difficult however slowly they were effected. During 1986, when Cosatu had not been aggressive in promoting mergers, there had been very little progress. A firm approach was needed. There would be unhappiness over a 'forced march' approach to mergers. But there would also be unhappiness if political in-fighting was allowed to continue. Merged unions could at least lay the basis for overcoming deeper political differences.

The Ccawusa disaster[5]

Problems in the TGWU merger were relatively easy to overcome in comparison to those in the retail and catering area. Three Cosatu affiliates were involved – Ccawusa, Harwu and Rawu. Two non-Cosatu affiliates, the Liquor and Catering Trades Employees Union, of the Cape and Natal respectively, were indirectly involved in the merger process, having taken part in parallel talks aimed at uniting with Harwu.

During the first six months of 1987 merger talks were tense. Ccawusa, the convening union and overwhelmingly larger than both Harwu and Rawu, rejected Harwu's proposal that catering workers be organised separately from retail workers. In line with Cosatu policy, the CEC had backed Ccawusa and rejected any idea of creating two sectors. At the same time political and organisational tensions within Ccawusa were growing. A number of branches around the country accused Johannesburg – Ccawusa's oldest, largest and strongest branch – of dominating the union. These problems had previously surfaced within Ccawusa's NEC, but had not been resolved.

From 12-14 June 1987 Ccawusa held its own national congress, largely to prepare for a second, merger congress. Over 300 delegates representing 66 000 members attended. The congress was divided on many issues, with a substantial minority position supported by about 40% of delegates. The minority grouping was unhappy. 'We felt like a rubber stamp at the congress,' one delegate complained. 'They wouldn't listen to our viewpoint at all, they would simply force a vote.'[6] As a result, delegates from four branches abstained from voting on a number of major resolutions, particularly those concerning political policy and the upcoming merger. At a certain point in the congress, recalls one leading figure from the minority group, 'we decided that we would not participate in the resolutions. We closed our files and stayed silent. We thought that in two weeks there could be a merger congress and the tables would be turned.'

Despite this non-participation the congress adopted two key resolutions. To avoid 'serious divisions' it was resolved to adopt neither the Freedom Charter nor the Azanian Manifesto.[*] 'The demands of the Freedom Charter though important are limited,' said the resolution adopted. The alternative was to develop 'a socialist programme of action.'

The second contentious resolution concerned merger. Ccawusa resolved to 'go to the merger congress as one union with one mandate.' This meant 'that the Ccawusa name, logo, office bearers, national officials and constitution should be adopted for the new union... Saawu and Gawu,' the resolution continued, 'should not attend the congress and must simply hand over their membership.' The two liquor and catering

---

The Freedom Charter was orginally adopted by thousands of delegates gathered at the Congress of the People held in Kliptown in 1955. The document itself was drawn up after volunteers throughout the country had asked ordinary people, from all walks of life, what sort of South Africa they wanted. The process of collecting demands from the people was spearheaded by the Congress alliance, a coalition of the ANC and its four main allies – the Indian Congresses originally formed at the turn of the century by Mahatma Gandhi, the Coloured People's Congress, the white Congress of Democrats, and the trade union federation, Sactu. The document finally adopted amounted to a set of basic democratic demands. It envisaged a non-racial, democratic South Africa where racial hatred would be banished. 'South Africa belongs to all who live in it, black and white,' its preamble proclaimed, and 'no government can justly claim authority unless it is based on the will of the people.' Remaining clauses of the Freedom Charter envisaged social, economic and political justice.

The Azanian Manifesto was adopted at the June 1983 founding conference of the National Forum, a body describing itself as a loose forum of 'anti-collaborationist' individuals and organisations from the black consciousness and related traditions. The manifesto demanded the immediate establishment of 'a democratic, anti-racist worker republic of Azania' and saw the 'black working class inspired by revolutionary consciousness' as the 'driving force' of the struggle.

unions 'should be invited to attend as observers.' The reasons given for this were that Ccawusa was 'much older and more established,' and 'a household name with a good reputation.' Ccawusa was also 'vastly larger' than Harwu with its 10 700 members and Rawu with 5 400 members. This wording tended to confirm allegations of inflexibility. Even before the merger congress Harwu claimed that Ccawusa 'was not interested in merging but wants to absorb the two smaller unions and retain the name.'[7] The resolution adopted at Ccawusa's own national congress did little to allay these fears.

The 'merger' congress

Problems began even before the Ccawusa merger congress opened at the University of the Witwatersrand on the weekend of 27-28 June. The credentials committee was unable to agree on the paid-up membership, and hence the number of delegates, of the participating unions. Harwu challenged the membership figure of 40 000 claimed by Ccawusa's Johannesburg branch, alleging that it had at most, 22 000 paid-up members. Four hundred delegates from Ccawusa, Harwu and Rawu waited idly while the credentials committee tried to resolve the problem.

Control of the new retail union was at stake. Politically, Harwu and Rawu were closer to the minority grouping within Ccawusa. An alliance between them could have lead to control of the union by people holding a 'national-democratic', pro-Freedom Charter political position. The majority faction within Ccawusa, politically close to the 'independent worker' position, was aware of this possibility. For this reason they had tried to force all Ccawusa delegates to support the merger resolution adopted at Ccawusa's own congress two weeks earlier. However the minority grouping did not feel bound by political and merger resolutions which they believed were imposed upon them.

The challenge to the membership figures of the Johannesburg branch was critical. Somewhere between the figures of 22 000 and 40 000 paid-up members stood control of the new union. Both groupings claimed to have a majority. But any majorities were narrow indeed. Essentially, the retail sector was split right down the middle.

There are two versions of what happened next. One grouping maintains that as no agreement on credentials was reached, the chair closed the congress late on Sunday afternoon. The other group insists that the closure of the meeting was reversed by a resolution from the floor. In any event, delegates continued to meet, in the presence of people such as Ccawusa general secretary Vivian Mtwa and Cosatu's Sydney Mufamadi, but in the absence of most delegates from the Johannesburg branch.

Delegates from Cape Town and Klerksdorp had left earlier because of transport problems.

The remaining delegates, representing Harwu, Rawu and the Natal, Eastern Province, Orange-Vaal and Pretoria branches of Ccawusa, decided to launch a new merged union. They resolved to retain the name Ccawusa, for the time being, and adopt the Freedom Charter as the basis of political policy. Makhulu Ledwaba (president of the old Ccawusa, and Cosatu's second vice-president) was elected president; Herbert Mkhize first vice-president (the position he had held in the old Ccawusa); Chris Mohlatsi of Harwu second vice-president; and Dinah Nhlapo treasurer (the position she had held in the old Ccawusa). Papi Kganare was elected general secretary, and other officials were elected to national positions. One of these, Jeremy Daphne, withdrew days later on the grounds that the merger meeting was undemocratic.

Will the real Ccawusa please stand up?

A Cosatu statement hailed the merger congress.

> The merger of Ccawusa, Harwu and Rawu into a giant Ccawusa is a great step forward for Cosatu's One Union One Industry policy. Cosatu salutes Ccawusa and calls on all members to respect the democratic decisions of the majority and build Ccawusa into the organised fighting voice of every shop and hotel worker in the country.[8]

The Johannesburg branch, covering workers throughout the Witwatersrand and Eastern Transvaal, responded with their own press release.

> The meeting was of course unconstitutional, totally undemocratic without a mandate and divisive. As such all decisions are null and void. We cannot go along with this meeting, its decisions and do not recognise the merger and new office-bearers. At a time when we face massive state repression and attacks by the bosses these moves are reactionary and cannot be supported by any progressive force.[9]

According to one report presented to Cosatu's CEC,

> Four branches of Ccawusa representing a minority within Ccawusa and not keeping to the Ccawusa mandate cannot under any circumstances represent the whole of Ccawusa and merge with two other unions... In effect this group...have split from Ccawusa.[10]

A small part of the Johannesburg branch supported the merged Cca-wusa. The majority, including key officials such as former general secretary Vivian Mtwa, did not. The Cape Town branch soon declared its loyalty to the Johannesburg branch, although there were differences even within their own branch. As the split deepened observers began labelling the two groupings as the 'Mtwa faction' and the 'Kganare faction', after their respective general secretaries.[*]

The problem for the Mtwa faction was that it became unclear who its office bearers were. Apart from Mtwa himself, the other three former office bearers – Ledwaba, Mkhize and Nhlapo – had accepted positions in the new Ccawusa, although Ledwaba's loyalties would later become unclear. The problem for the Kganare faction, on the other hand, was that it could not command the loyalty of over half the members of the pre-'merger congress' Ccawusa. This amounted to thousands of well-organised and militant members. In addition, the Kganare faction had no control over most of the union finances. Most contributions continued to be sent to the old Ccawusa head office, in practice the Johannesburg branch, on behalf of many nationally-organised shops.

The Kganare faction decided to appeal directly to the workers in the Johannesburg branch. 'We want YOU to decide what must be done... YOU must decide whether the democratic decision of the *majority* of workers in your union is reactionary.' A legitimate merger congress had taken place, the pamphlet argued, despite attempts at disruption by 'some of the Jo'burg branch delegates.' Delegates from that branch were informed that the congress was continuing 'but most *refused to come back*.' Proceedings continued, and Vivian Mtwa and Jeremy Daphne were even present and accepted nominations for positions, the Kganare faction's pamphlet argued.

> Why is it that there are some comrades who will not accept worker control and worker democracy? There will always be differences. This is not in itself a bad thing – if we work according to the method of worker democracy... Comrade Vivian Mtwa is a general secretary without office bearers. His national office bearers recognise the new Ccawusa and believe the merger is a progressive move... JOIN THE PROGRESSIVE FORCES; WORKERS TAKE CONTROL NOW!

---

[*] *I have accepted these terms to make the reader's task easier, but am aware that they are inadequate. The division in the union was not between two individuals, Mtwa and Kganare. In time, the Mtwa group tended to call itself the 'socialist' Ccawusa, and label its opponents the 'charterists' or 'populists'. The Kganare group, however, while supporting the non-socialist Freedom Charter, also saw itself as socialist. Its members tended to label themselves 'pro-Cosatu Ccawusa', and their opponents as 'anti-Cosatu'. The Mtwa faction rejected this label.*

Few workers crossed permanently from the Mtwa to the Kganare faction as a result of the pamphlet. Likewise, there were few defections in the opposite direction. For many workers the dispute was one between leadership. Ordinary members tended to remain loyal to the union as they knew it – through the shop stewards, organisers and union offices closest to them. In the absence of deep dissatisfaction with these people or the functioning of their local office, the appeals of rival factions to 'higher' political principles usually fell on deaf ears.

Two weeks after Ccawusa's controversial 'merger' congress, Cosatu's second national congress was held in Johannesburg. Thousands of worker delegates from all affiliates heard both factions claiming to be the genuine Ccawusa. It was an issue which threatened to disrupt the congress itself. Cosatu vice-president Chris Dlamini, with the support of the house, ruled that both factions would be allowed to speak on all issues at the congress. Neither, however, would be entitled to vote or propose and second resolutions. The dispute within Ccawusa, Dlamini ruled, would be referred to the CEC for resolution.

This was a practical solution aimed at allowing the congress to proceed. Nevertheless, during the political policy debate, the congress was told that 'the real Ccawusa' had either adopted or not adopted the Freedom Charter, according to the loyalties of the Ccawusa speaker concerned. The open hostility between the two factions left all delegates aware of the depth of division within Ccawusa.

The CEC recognises one Ccawusa faction

Cosatu's second congress instructed the CEC to try to heal the rift within Ccawusa. The CEC was briefed by both sides at its meeting held from 7-9 August 1987, and decided that a special congress of the union be held 'to reconcile the two wings' of Ccawusa. In the interim both wings would be represented on Cosatu national structures, but with non-voting status. A six-person commission was also established – two nominated directly by the CEC, plus a further two CEC members chosen by each of the Ccawusa factions. Sydney Mufamadi, Lungelo Mbalane, Rod

---

* *Immediately after the 'merger' congress the Kganare faction managed to win significant layers of support within the Johannesburg branch. But they largely failed to maintain this in the face of strong pressure from the Mtwa faction's well-organised local structures and ineffective organising by Kganare's Johannesburg branch officials. The Kganare faction also managed to win significant support within both the Klerksdorp and Pietersburg branches. In turn the Mtwa faction gained pockets of support within the Natal and the Vaal branches and, later, in Pretoria. But on balance defections between the factions were few.*

Crompton, John Copelyn, Chris Dlamini and Jane Barrett were given the unenviable task of trying to resolve the problem.

Both the Kganare and Mtwa factions of Ccawusa were trying to consolidate their support, organisationally and financially. Both groups met supporters, giving their version of the dispute and rallying support. Both sides believed they could 'win'. Most unionists within Cosatu believed it was a 'no-win' situation. Not surprisingly, the CEC commission failed in its task. 'Neither party wanted to settle,' recalls Jane Barrett. 'Both had a winner-take-all approach. In retrospect it was clear that attempts to mediate would not work. Both sides only accepted the commission because they wanted to stay in Cosatu.'

At the November CEC the commission reported that it saw little hope of the two factions re-uniting. After lengthy discussions the CEC decided that as the commission had been unable to resolve the problem, it should be disbanded. The CEC then resolved to recognise 'the Ccawusa which merged on the 27th and 28th June 1987', ie the Kganare Ccawusa. It also resolved to convene a congress 'together with the recognised Ccawusa to deal with all outstanding issues.' It was envisaged that the 'disaffected group', ie the Mtwa Ccawusa, would attend this congress and 'raise its problems.'

Recognition of the Kganare Ccawusa meant, said the CEC, that only it would be allowed to participate in Cosatu structures. The CEC also decided to send the president and general secretary of Cosatu to explain the decision at a rally of Ccawusa's Johannesburg branch, being held at the nearby Jabulani Amphitheatre on that day. On arrival at the rally, Jay Naidoo and Elijah Barayi were refused entry into the stadium by a prominent member of the Mtwa faction. The CEC condemned 'the disaffected group's refusal to comply with the CEC decision,' feeling it confirmed 'the group's anti-Cosatu stance.'

The CEC decision was firm and decisive. It put an end to squabbling, already affecting a number of regions and locals, over which faction was the 'real Ccawusa', and expressed the clear sympathy which the majority of the CEC felt for the politics of the Kganare faction. The decision was taken in a climate where it appeared that the two factions could not be reconciled. The majority believed it was therefore better to accept the inevitable. A clean, clear split was preferable to ongoing and debilitating battles. This did little to help resolve the dispute. Conflict continued, both factions battling for loyalty and support.

The conflict also affected negotiations within the industry. Ccawusa, which negotiated with major companies at national level, often found itself confronting management as a divided force.

Although both factions generally came together to maintain a united negotiating team, differences inevitably emerged. Within the joint negotiating teams there was often a struggle over who would co-ordinate, who would correspond with management and who would send information to the branches. Workers from different factions would often give different mandates to their negotiators, or propose differing strategies. It was an unsatisfactory situation. 'Mostly we avoided fighting but there was no agreement to work together,' recalls one Kganare faction official. 'It severely reduced our capacity to pull off united strikes.'

Exploring differences in Ccawusa

The dispute within Ccawusa was fundamentally over control of the union. There had been hostility to the Johannesburg branch's perceived domination of the union, overlaid by substantial political differences. Control of Ccawusa, including political control, was at stake. What political position should Ccawusa adopt? With which political forces should it align? What should be the political content of the union's education programmes? Who should be its education officer? These were some of the questions posed. Issues of procedure and democracy were associated with this. How could sub-sectors within the union, such as hotel workers, be accommodated? What did mandates and union democracy mean?

Within Cosatu, the Ccawusa division raised the question of how differences should be handled. A paper circulated within CWIU argued that 'there is nothing unprincipled about promoting a political position within a trade union or any other mass-based organisation. What is crucial is the manner in which it is done and the method employed.' It was 'politically wrong of the one grouping to bureaucratically try and force a union which had hardly merged to adopt the Freedom Charter... The basis was never yet laid...through discussions by rank and file' of either faction. 'Hence the workers strongest weapon, its unity, was sacrificed for the formal, paper adoption of the Freedom Charter.'*

Undoubtedly the same could be said for the other faction. The Mtwa group presented their call for a 'socialist programme of action' as 'non-sectarian' and a unifying programme. In terms of practical politics it was, however, undoubtedly an alternative programme. As one Kganare faction spokesperson put it:

> Non-sectarianism as a slogan sounds good in language, but in political practice it is operated to divide and to attack the mainstream mass democratic movement, to attack Cosatu, and to attack the alliances that Cosatu was beginning to build in embryonic form.[11]

* The Kganare faction has argued that it was never its intention to force through adoption of the Freedom Charter, claiming that the Charter was only adopted after the Johannesburg branch had left the controversial 'merger' congress.

Attempts to adopt major and controversial policies by narrow majorities are clearly counter-productive. Trade unions, as mass organisations, need to accept policies which take most of their members along with them. Patience is as much a requirement of political as organisational work. At the same time, delaying adoption of policies on key issues until near unanimity is reached can condemn a union or a federation to irrelevance. It can result in political abstentionism, or leave trade unions trailing behind political developments outside the labour movement. Alternatively, it can create a politics of the lowest common denominator, with policies so general and uncontroversial that they are useless. In the context of 1987, where so many were looking to Cosatu for direction, conflict was probably inevitable. The need to give direction necessitated the adoption of bold and unambiguous policies, clearly aligned with a particular political current.

The Ccawusa division also raised questions of tolerance of political differences, political pluralism, and respect for majority decisions. The Mtwa faction placed great emphasis on the fact that the Kganare faction had broken with the majority decision of Ccawusa's own congress, held prior to the 'merger'. That congress, they argued, had bound all Ccawusa's representatives to vote as a bloc in the merger congress with Harwu and Rawu. The alternate view, argued their opponents, was that 'all participating delegates are simply delegates and are not representing any particular union. This view is particularly disturbing, and shows no understanding of how the democratic process works.'[12]

This is a difficult position to sustain. Mandates are not always inflexible, particularly in a merger congress where it is often necessary to have flexibility. Congresses cannot be adjourned repeatedly while delegates return to the general membership to change or reconfirm an earlier decision. The Kganare argument that a mandate is a direction, an approach, 'an instruction to delegates to conduct themselves in a particular manner,' is persuasive.* More importantly, worker delegates attending a

---

* An example might illustrate this. A retail worker from East London is delegated by shopworkers in that area to express their support for the Freedom Charter. At a Ccawusa conference she must express that view. If this is a minority view within the union, then the Freedom Charter clearly cannot become policy for the union. But, coming to the next congress – whether a merger or Cosatu gathering – the issue might emerge again. How best can this worker now perform her delegate duties? By reaffirming that the workers who sent her support the Freedom Charter, or by stating that her union as a whole does not? The argument that she must again express support for the Freedom Charter is strong. Block voting discourages democracy in the long run, particularly on issues which do not affect a particular union but are of interest to the working class as a whole. This is a question still unresolved within Cosatu.

congress must surely bring to that congress the views of the workers they know, the workers who have sent them – their 'base'. After all, are the delegates representing the union or the workers who elected them as delegates?The Ccawusa conflict affected the unity process involving the Natal and Cape-based liquor unions, which were understandably alarmed at developments. However, by November 1987 the Cape Liquor union had decided to join Ccawusa's Kganare faction, and effectively became its Cape Town branch. The Natal Liquor union withdrew from the unity talks and later affiliated to Nactu.

In time Cosatu withdrew its decision to recognise only the one Ccawusa faction. It is a story to which we will return later.

Notes

1. Minutes of a meeting of convening unions to prepare guidelines for mergers, held in Cosatu House, Johannesburg, 13 January 1987.
2. *Financial Mail*, 30.01.87; *Business Day*, 05.02.87; Coletane Markham, 'Cosatu construction workers unite', *South African Labour Bulletin*, 12(2), January/February 1987.
3. 'Organising the unemployed', *South African Labour Bulletin*, 12(2), January/February 1987.
4. 'Numsa Launch', *South African Labour Bulletin*, 12(5), July 1987; Ingrid Obery, 'The new metal union. A new road to socialism', *Work In Progress*, 48, July 1987.
5. This account of the Ccawusa problems relies heavily on interviews and discussions with participants from all factions, and an extensive collection of papers and leaflets in the author's possession.
6. Quoted in Coletane Markham, 'Ccawusa settlement the beginning', *South African Labour Bulletin*, 13(2), February 1988, 92-3.
7. *Weekly Mail*, 19.06.87.
8. 'Divisions Mar Ccawusa Merger', *South African Labour Bulletin*, 12(5), July 1987, 23.
9. 'Divisions Mar Ccawusa Merger', *South African Labour Bulletin*, 12(5), July 1987, 23.
10. Report dated 6 August 1987 on the commercial and catering sector from Ccawusa (Mtwa faction), presented to the Cosatu CEC.
11. Quoted in Coletane Markham, 'Ccawusa Settlement the Beginning', *South African Labour Bulletin*, 13(2), February 1988, 88.
12. 'Comment' by Ccawusa (Mtwa) to Cosatu commission, unpublished, 19 August 1987, 2.

13

Charting the road ahead

*O*VER 1 400 delegates gathered at the Flower Hall on the West Campus of Wits University for Cosatu's second national congress, held from 14-18 July 1987. It was organised far more professionally than the inaugural congress. Delegates were provided with briefcases containing all relevant reports and resolutions to be considered. Registration was computerised to facilitate accommodation and ensure that constitutional provisions, such as majority worker representation, were fulfilled.

Politically and organisationally, unity did not run deep. At Cosatu's inaugural congress enthusiasm had overwhelmed any potential problems. Eighteen months later the pressures were beginning to show. Many unions attending had merged only months, even weeks, before, and had not yet developed their own internal unity and style of operation. Other unions, not yet merged, were attending and having to vote as if they had one delegation, while the delegation from Ccawusa arrived effectively split into two camps (see table of attendance).

Unions/sectors and delegations at second national congress

Affiliate	Delegates Entitled	Delegates Present (Workers)	Delegates Present (Officials)	Paid-up Membership
NUM	524	484	40	261 901
Numsa	262	187	54	130 796
Fawu	131	117	12	65 278
Ccawusa	112	91	21	56 000
Sarhwu	69	58	11	34 411
NUTW	61	50	10	30 538
CWIU	60	49	11	29 859
Cawu	53	35	18	26 291
Paper sector	47	39	8	23 310
TGWU	37	24	13	18 281
Municipal sector	34	29	2	16 967
Sadwu	19	14	5	9 402
Nehawu	19	14	5	9 197

NUWCC   20 observers present – membership unclear
Potwa   9 out of 10 observers present – not yet an affiliate

Political pressures also played their part. Delegates to the congress were gathering one year into a harsh state of emergency. Cosatu had shown an ability to survive the repression, but many other components of the mass democratic movement were not so fortunate. In most townships UDF and other political structures were either not functioning or extremely weak. Not only Cosatu members, but the entire democratic movement, the state and the international community were looking to see what leadership Cosatu would provide.

The congress opened with a speech by Elijah Barayi, Cosatu president. 'Our place is in the frontline of struggle, and to the frontline we must go!' was his rallying call. 'We make no apologies', said Barayi,

about connecting issues on the shopfloor and issues facing workers in society as a whole. Politics, and especially the lack of even the most basic democratic rights for the majority of our people is a *bread and butter* issue for the working class... The fact that many of our major affiliates have endorsed the *Freedom Charter* as a *guide* in our struggle for *democracy* and *socialism* seriously places the question of a *political programme* to guide our action on the agenda. Our congress must confront this question fully.

Guest speakers from other components of the mass democratic movement also addressed the gathering, including UDF's Murphy

Morobe, South African Youth Congress president Peter Mokaba, and Frank Chikane of the South African Council of Churches (SACC). Messages of support were read out, with delegates responding most enthusiastically to those from the ANC, Sactu and SACP. A pamphlet, produced by the ANC underground, circulated widely.

All these inputs made reference to the political situation and the debate then sweeping Cosatu. Should Cosatu adopt the Freedom Charter, and commit itself to a policy more openly and unambiguously aligned to the 'Congress tradition' of the ANC? Did Cosatu need its political policy to be clarified and made more specific? Should a workers' charter be adopted? These were the major questions raised for discussion.

NUM adopts the Freedom Charter

NUM had started this political debate at its fifth national congress held in February 1987. It was a militant gathering. Delegates honoured Nelson Mandela, elected the previous year as NUM's honorary president, and declared 1987 as 'The Year Mineworkers Take Control'. The other major slogan at the congress asserted that 'Socialism means Freedom'.

After five hours of discussion delegates unanimously adopted a carefully-worded political policy noting their aspirations for 'a democratic socialist society controlled by the working class.' Apartheid and capitalism were 'two inseparable evils that must be smashed.' This required workers to join hands with other progressive organisations. However, the resolution continued, there was confusion 'as many organisations claim to be progressive.' There therefore needed to be a clear definition of what constituted a 'progressive organisation'. The mineworkers resolved to adopt the Freedom Charter 'as a guiding document.'

The working class, argued NUM, should play a leading role 'in the struggle for a non-racial and democratic South Africa.' Progressive organisations should be judged by four criteria:

● 'a proven record of mass mobilisation and action in our struggle';
● principles and policies 'compatible with those of the working class';
● 'a mass-based constituency' to which it was answerable; and
● whether it was 'a democratic organisation'.

Read in conjunction with NUM's adoption of the Freedom Charter, it was apparent that the union envisaged alliances with mass-based organisations sharing a similar political perspective. It was a subtle formulation, arguing for working-class leadership within a national democratic, rather than a socialist, struggle.

'The Freedom Charter', declared NUM's Cyril Ramaphosa, 'contains the minimum demands that have been put forward by the oppressed people in this country... It does not lay down a socialist programme and at the same time it is not pro-capitalist.' NUM felt that Cosatu's existing political policy was too vague in that it spoke of alliances with 'progressive organisations' without clarifying which organisations were envisaged. 'We found', said Ramaphosa, 'that organisations that did not have a constituency,... that did not account to any constituency,... that did not have a proven record of mass mobilisation were jumping on the bandwagon.' In addition, NUM felt Cosatu should declare its political alignment with the ANC and UDF.

Ramaphosa argued that politically the Freedom Charter 'focuses on the national oppression that we are fighting against.' The demands in the Freedom Charter 'are the immediate demands: apartheid has to go.' This was 'by no means a negation of the struggle for an exploitation-free society... Ultimately there has to be a system where there would not be any exploitation by anybody – a socialist system.' While national consciousness and socialist consciousness were complementary, 'of necessity the end of national oppression has to be achieved first.'

'Commitment for an exploitation-free society is there,' commented Ramaphosa, but 'it would be incorrect at this stage to actually say we want this kind of socialism...when it is an issue which needs to be canvassed on a much wider scale.' Socialist thinking should develop in time, 'as we proceed.' But this did not mean 'that there is a gap between attaining national liberation and socialism.'[1]

Few disagreed that Cosatu's political policy required clarification. Its ability to relate to other organisations was being paralysed by ongoing political disputes within the federation. Cosatu had been called upon to guide anti-apartheid forces during a period of repression, yet its ability to do this was limited by lack of political direction within its own ranks. NUM's call to Cosatu was to assume the role being thrust upon it and rally all mass-based forces sympathetic to the ANC around it. But not all unions agreed with NUM's approach.

Debating the Charter

In the months preceding Cosatu's second national congress a variety of positions in the political debate emerged. Numsa's inaugural congress adopted two resolutions, differently flavoured, even if not diametrically opposed, to the NUM position. Numsa had agreed, partly as a concession to a strong minority within its own ranks, to adopt the Freedom Charter. But it did so with qualifications. The Charter was simply a set of 'minimum political demands' which could only be realised

through the practical leadership of the industrial working class in the struggle for the establishment of a socialist society, where workers' control of government and industry will be enforced in the practice of a liberated South Africa.

In a separate political policy resolution, Numsa stressed the primary importance of the struggle for socialism in which the Freedom Charter was simply 'a good foundation stone on which to start building our working-class programme.' The working class could only make 'correct alliances', and 'lead these alliances if it has a clear programme and aims.' Discussions should take place within the union and Cosatu to develop such a programme.

The differences between the Numsa and NUM positions were, in practice, significant. For Numsa, socialism was the primary and immediate objective. Socialism, it implied, would bring democracy in its wake. Alliances should be built, but potential allies should be committed to both an anti-apartheid and an anti-capitalist position. By contrast, NUM called for the broadest possible alliance around democratic and anti-apartheid demands such as those expressed in the Freedom Charter. For NUM, the immediate objective was a non-racial democratic state. Potential allies should not be required to be anti-capitalist, only anti-racist. While a socialist future was envisaged, moving towards this was through working-class participation in the national-democratic struggle, thereby earning a position of leadership.

Numsa, in turn, was not in principle opposed to participation in the anti-apartheid struggle. But if the working class participated without its own clearly-defined programme it would be overwhelmed by other class forces. Hence Numsa's qualified adoption of the Freedom Charter.

The question of political policy had been raised at a Fawu NEC meeting, and referred back to regions for discussion. At a subsequent national executive committee meeting in mid-1987, Fawu adopted the Freedom Charter without qualification, thereby aligning itself broadly with the NUM position.

By contrast the NUTW congress in early July opposed adoption of the Freedom Charter. 'If we want one union for our industry,' said general secretary Elias Banda, 'we had better be sure we run it in such a way as to make everybody comfortable to be a member.' At the time NUTW was involved in talks with two large non-Cosatu unions in its sector – the Textile Workers Industrial Union (TWIU) and the Garment Workers Union of South Africa (Gwusa). Banda was concerned that

if we want to adopt a programme of one organisation or another then, clearly, we will wind up with one union for each political tendency within the liberation movement. Such divisions can only weaken the working class.[2]

Within Cosatu, the NUTW position was relatively isolated. The union had argued previously for Cosatu not to become involved in the Natal conflict or take sides against Inkatha, and its leadership envisaged a relatively abstentionist trade union federation as far as politics was concerned.

Ccawusa, as we have seen, was divided. The first Ccawusa Congress, from 12-14 June, noted that the Freedom Charter was 'limited' and declined, in the interests of unity, to adopt either the Charter, or the black consciousness Azanian Manifesto. By contrast, the contested 'merger' congress adopted the Freedom Charter, revealing a perspective similar to that of NUM.

At CWIU's June congress, delegates debated political policy for an entire day. While consensus was reached on principles such as 'non-racialism' and 'working-class leadership', there was no agreement on the Freedom Charter. One group wanted the union to adopt the Freedom Charter, while another believed a 'workers' charter/working-class programme' was preferable. 'In the interests of unity,' the post-congress statement declared, 'neither position was adopted and the issues were referred back to the rank and file membership.' CWIU's president, Calvin Makgaleng, has recalled that the union was never opposed to the Freedom Charter, as its critics have alleged. Rather, it wanted more time to discuss the matter thoroughly.[3]

Both Nehawu and Sarhwu – overwhelmingly linked to the Congress tradition – adopted the Freedom Charter at their founding congresses.[4] Pwawu decided to support adoption of the Freedom Charter at its NEC held before the Cosatu congress, while Cawu formally adopted the Charter only at its 1988 congress. However key individuals within its ranks were strong ANC supporters and expressed support for the Charter during Cosatu's second congress.[5]

During the Cosatu congress TGWU argued for adoption of the Charter as a set of minimum demands in an attempt to bridge the gap between NUM and Numsa. The union suggested that discussions to develop a working-class understanding of the Charter, and to explore the relationship between socialism and democracy, should be pursued after the congress. TGWU went on to adopt the Freedom Charter at its 1988 congress.

The political policy debate

Cosatu's affiliates had debated political policy widely by the time of the second congress. Contributions to the debate were also made by certain guest speakers, and in a number of messages of support read at the beginning of the congress. Sactu, while welcoming the widespread discussion of socialist ideas, expressed the view that 'this should not be elevated and adopted as a policy of Cosatu. Your interests should be in strengthening Cosatu and fight for the interests of all workers.' The SACP stressed that the struggle was for a united, democratic and non-racial South Africa. Nevertheless, it added,

> through its organised strength our working class must ensure that liberation will not merely bring a new flag and a new anthem but that it will also begin to lay the foundations for a return to the people of our country's wealth and riches, both beneath and above the soil.

Nactu, the rival union federation, tried to appeal to delegates through an advertisement placed in the press, calling for Cosatu to join it in 'developing a worker manifesto.'[6]

The most direct intervention came from Peter Mokaba, delivering a speech as newly-elected president of the South African Youth Congress (Sayco).[*] 'The idea of socialism', he said, 'has correctly occupied the minds of the workers and the youth and the majority of our people.' The political debate, said Mokaba is not

> between those for socialism and those against... Those who stand for the adoption of the Freedom Charter are also those who are committed to the socialist transformation of the South African society... The argument (between those calling for the Freedom Charter and those calling for a workers' charter) is about nothing else but the South African route and methods to reach socialism... No socialism can be created in South Africa by ignoring the plight of the colonially oppressed black communities... The Freedom Charter remains the only programme that correctly represents the transitional post-apartheid society.

Naidoo and other Cosatu leaders, anxious to avoid possible divisions, tried to play down the extent of differences on the issue. The NUM and Numsa resolutions were not contradictory, declared Naidoo prior to the congress. Both

> emphasise different aspects of the workers' struggle against apartheid and capitalism for national liberation and socialism... Both unions see the

---

* *Mokaba's speech was controversial. A number of delegates objected to his polemical denunciation of certain left-wing marxist groupings and individuals as 'political hobos'. Others believed a detailed intervention was inappropriate from a guest speaker. Mokaba himself declared that 'because we, together with the rest of our people, including the workers, cherish a society free of national oppression and economic exploitation, we feel we have a right to add our word to the debates taking place in Cosatu.'*

Charter as laying the basis, or being the minimum programme, for the struggle for socialism... The struggle for socialism is already unfolding within the struggle for national liberation.

However, said Naidoo, there was undoubtedly a need to develop 'more concrete guidelines' regarding alliances.[7]

It was clear that the political policy debate would not be easy. Cosatu's congress had became the forum for debates about the direction of the entire mass democratic movement. It needed to send a clear message, both to workers and the oppressed community generally, about who Cosatu would be marching with on the road ahead. Differences were deep on this question, involving fundamentally different attitudes towards the liberation struggle. Even as delegates entered the hall, the singing prefigured the contest of political positions. *'Socialism ke thebe'* ('socialism is our shield') competed in volume with *'iFreedom Charter, iyo bakala ngayo'* ('the Freedom Charter is what everyone is calling for.')

Gwede Mantashe, a prominent member of the NUM from the Witbank region, motivated the NUM proposal, which was similar to the resolution adopted by NUM at its own congress. It called for the adoption of the Freedom Charter as 'a guiding document', for 'disciplined alliances' with 'democratic and progressive organisations', and defined these. Significantly, and differently from NUM's own congress resolution, allies were required to be not only 'democratic' but also 'non-racial'. NUM's intention was that Cosatu's allies should be largely drawn from the non-racial, Congress tradition. NUM also called for the establishment of 'permanent structures at local, regional and national levels' with other sectors of the democratic movement, to 'promote the leading role of the working class in a united front alliance'.

'We cannot divorce the struggle for national liberation from the struggle against capitalist exploitation,' said NUM's Mantashe. 'We cannot have our struggle demarcated into a workers struggle and a community struggle.'

Numsa proposed two resolutions as counter-motions to the NUM resolution. In practice they were dealt with as one. Numsa called for adoption of the Freedom Charter as a document 'containing the minimum political demands that reflect the vision which the majority of workers have of a free, democratic and non-discriminatory South Africa.' But, argued Numsa, a working-class political programme, also needed to be developed. This workers' charter, as some called it, aimed at developing a programme for 'true socialism and democracy.' This, implicitly, would go beyond the limited democratic vision of the Freedom Charter to an alternative socialist vision.

This was the underlying debate. Numsa's second resolution made its position more apparent. The struggles against 'apartheid oppression' and 'capitalist exploitation' were 'inseparable'. Alliances 'with the natural allies of the workers, ie the youth, women, students and the unemployed' should be forged and led by 'organised industrial workers.' Alliances should be guided by the principle of 'March Separately and Strike Together.' Cosatu should forge a 'united front alliance' with any organisation committed to 'a non-racial, democratic and socialist South Africa.' Any organisation entering the alliance should have 'a clear programme', 'mass support', and 'a proven record'. It should also recognise worker leadership, and have 'a single national mass-based constituency to which it is answerable', as well as 'clearly defined structures locally, regionally and nationally.'

By any standards this was a tall order. To restrict alliances to national organisations supporting socialism would leave only the newly-launched Sayco as a possible ally. Sayco itself, as reflected in Peter Mokaba's speech to the congress, did not favour such a restricted alliance. Delegates to the congress soon criticised Numsa's narrow conception of alliances. 'The Freedom Charter', said a speaker from the Kganare faction of Ccawusa, 'is a programme which can unite all sections in our society.' David Thathe, a Fawu delegate, asked what Numsa meant by leadership of the 'organised industrial workers'. Did this suggest that farmworkers and miners were excluded? Did it imply that the trade unions should lead the political struggle?

'There is no contradiction between the struggle for socialism and the Freedom Charter,' declared Nehawu's Khisa Dlamini. 'We have no need for another programme. The Freedom Charter is the programme of the national-democratic struggle... The working class does not only liberate itself,' he continued. 'We must go all out to the petty bourgeoisie, to the professionals, to the intellectuals and play our hegemonic role. NUM's resolution calls for that.'

Numsa's position was also criticised by delegates from Pwawu, Sadwu, Sarhwu, TGWU and Cawu, all of whom supported the NUM resolution. The Numsa proposal was seen as counterposing a socialist programme to the national-democratic vision of the Freedom Charter.[*]

The Numsa resolutions were also criticised for being inconsistent, which they undoubtedly were. They reflected a compromise between three broad positions within the union. A dominant viewpoint saw the

---

[*] Numsa's idea of workers drafting a charter of demands was, in itself, a creative one. Indeed, at its third national congress in 1989, Cosatu supported this. But at the second congress it emerged as an alternative to the Freedom Charter. This alone, given the support which the Freedom Charter enjoyed amongst delegates virtually guaranteed that Numsa's resolution would be defeated.

existing mass democratic movement as weak and ineffective. The solution involved the building of mass movements in all sectors, in much the same way as the unions had been built – factory by factory, and with the gradual growth of a shop steward movement. This would lead to both a different organisational style from the bulk of the UDF, as well as a democratic and socialist perspective. The road forward, in this view, was the building of a mass, socialist movement.

But this dominant view had to accommodate two other viewpoints within Numsa. Firstly, there were a significant number of supporters of the Freedom Charter and the national-democratic perspective within the union. Indeed, during the political debate at congress one Numsa speaker, Nonyukela, reluctantly announced that a large minority of Numsa delegates favoured the NUM political resolution. These delegates also felt that Numsa's views on community and other mass organisation were utopian and out of touch with the realities of different sectors. Secondly, there were a number of supporters of a left-wing marxist, sometimes trotskyist, perspective. These were accommodated in the resolutions by the incorporation of phrases such as 'united front alliance' and 'march separately, strike together', both key slogans from this perspective. Their influence could also be seen in formulations revealing both a vanguardist approach to politics and a view of a new South Africa ruled by worker-controlled 'soviets' along the lines of the 1917 Russian revolution.

The debate on the congress floor revealed that Numsa had pockets of support for its resolution and a large number of sympathisers, but was largely politically isolated. A number of unions wanted to oppose the NUM resolution but were unable to support Numsa's position. NUTW indicated that it could go along with Numsa's idea of a worker programme. But 'for the interests of unity and worker control,' declared Amon Ntuli, NUTW's president, 'and to avoid division amongst our members, we cannot adopt the Freedom Charter.' Within CWIU there was clear sympathy for the Numsa position. But on the issue of the Freedom Charter, CWIU stated that it had no position at that stage. The situation in the municipal sector was similar. The Mtwa faction of Ccawusa more obviously supported the Numsa position, but opposed adoption of the Freedom Charter. However, neither faction of Ccawusa could propose or second resolutions unless both agreed on these.

The Numsa resolution, therefore, had sympathisers but no seconder. By adopting the Freedom Charter, Numsa isolated itself from those who felt Cosatu should not adopt any programme, as well as from those opposed to the Freedom Charter. Without a seconder Numsa's resolutions fell away, and the NUM political policy resolution was seconded and adopted. The majority view within Cosatu had clearly prevailed, but it was a victory which left many within Numsa, CWIU, Ccawusa and NUTW unhappy and believing they had been bullied into submission. The mood of the congress thereafter was deeply divided.

Unity and division

Political policy debate dominated the congress, but other important decisions were also taken. Cosatu resolved to support Namibian workers by directly aiding their mine, metal and food unions, and helping to revive the Swapo-aligned National Union of Namibian Workers (NUNW). This was the first occasion on which Cosatu gave, rather than received, international worker solidarity. There was also heated debate on the merits of affiliating to the Organisation of African Trade Union Unity (OATUU). A decision was postponed after it became clear that opposition to affiliation was based less on antagonism to OATUU than insufficient knowledge of its activities.

Cosatu reiterated its support for comprehensive and mandatory economic sanctions, and suggested areas of action to be considered by the international community. There was speculation, both before and after Cosatu's congress, that the union movement was deeply divided on the issue of sanctions. An alleged Cosatu report – in fact a survey commissioned, but never endorsed by Cosatu – was quoted in support of this contention. This had outlined the difficulties and hardships which sanctions could be expected to cause the workers' movement. However, differences on sanctions took place within a framework of overwhelming support for international pressure on the apartheid regime, including mandatory sanctions.

The sanctions debate within Cosatu focused on the lack of co-ordination of internal and external pressures for sanctions, and on the possibilities of sanctions not merely punishing the oppressor but also empowering the oppressed.

The second congress made one significant change to Cosatu's constitution. By a vote of 863 to 219, with a number of abstentions, congress adopted an NUTW proposal to change the composition of Cosatu's executive committee (Exco). No longer would Exco consist of the six elected office bearers and four additional members chosen by the CEC. In future the office bearers would be joined by two delegates from each affiliated union. The congress ended with all six office bearers returned to office unopposed.

For all its problems the second congress did reflect some of Cosatu's achievements. The achievement of merged industrial unions within 19 months was significant. Some argued that many of the tensions, such as those within Ccawusa, were as much a result of over-hasty mergers as political differences. There is much truth in this. However, tensions were building up before the mergers. Conditions did not allow for Cosatu to develop a political policy in a relaxed and leisurely way. Nor could it continue as a federation with a totally disparate collection of unions. Mergers were essential to build both organisational coherence and political direction. Without mergers Cosatu would have continued to flounder, enjoying growth without direction. The merger process, while causing tensions in the short term, was essential for medium-term unity and development.

Membership criteria were more strictly tested by the credentials committee of the second congress than had been the case at the inaugural congress. Nevertheless, in the space of 19 months Cosatu's paid-up membership had grown by over 58%. As Elijah Barayi said in his address to the second congress:

> From our launch in 1985, with delegates from 33 trade unions representing 450 000 paid-up members, we today enter our second congress with delegates from 12 recognised industrial unions/sectors representing about 712 000 paid-up members with up to 1 000 000 members if we include our signed-up membership.

Delegates left the congress with Cosatu deeply divided. The newly-merged affiliates, however, were internally united, even if sometimes shakily so.

The second congress developed Cosatu's political policies. It made them less ambiguous, but did little to build a climate of greater unity. The effects of this disunity would be felt for at least the following 12 months. However, in the immediate aftermath of the congress another issue gripped the imagination of the workers. It was the Great Miners' Strike, the largest industrial dispute in the history of the country.

Notes

1. Interview with Cyril Ramaphosa, *South African Labour Bulletin*, 12(3), May/June 1987.
2. *Star*, 08.07.87.
3. Author interview with Calvin Makgaleng, CWIU president, Germiston, 10 April 1990.
4. Jobi Matlou interviews with Katherine Mavi, Sarhwu official, and Sisa Njikelana, Nehawu general secretary, Johannesburg, 1990.
5. H Matlou interview with Desmond Mahasha, Cawu acting general secretary, Johannesburg, 1990.
6. *Sowetan*, 16.07.87.
7. 'Jay Naidoo on Cosatu', *South African Labour Bulletin*, 12(5), July 1987.

14

The 1987 miners' strike

'Twenty-one days that shook the Chamber'

*T*HE 'Great Miners' Strike', as it became known, was the largest strike in South African history. At its height, 340 000 miners were involved, and almost five million working shifts were lost. NUM dubbed the action '21 days that shook the Chamber', but it was also a strike with major repercussions for the union and Cosatu as a whole.[1]

It was perhaps inevitable that 1987 would be the year of showdown between NUM and the Chamber of Mines. NUM was growing rapidly. By 1985 it had 100 000 paid-up members, growing to 227 586 members by the end of 1986. By June 1987 the union claimed 262 000 paid-up members, but signed-up membership was considerably greater. NUM could legitimately claim to be the fastest-growing union in the world.

NUM expanded within a climate of mass politicisation, drawing workers influenced by the 1985/6 insurrectionary climate into its ranks. It also attracted members with previous political experience – Lesotho Congress Party activists and ANC supporters from the Transkei region.

During 1986 alone NUM reported that mineworkers participated in 113 strikes involving 'well over 250 000 workers.' This was in addition to significant mineworker participation in three stayaways that year

(1 May, 16 June and the Kinross disaster protest). NUM membership
was beginning to push back the boundaries of management control on
the mines. The compound system in particular, with its associated structures of indunas, isibondas and security forces, was coming under attack.

'Mineworkers take control'

NUM held an annual congress in February 1987. The congress slogan –
'The Year Mineworkers Take Control' – reflected the mood of membership, and attempted to channel militancy and enthusiasm into a challenge
to the pervasive control structures on the mines. Delegates also resolved
to dismantle the migrant labour system and take control of the hostels.
Workers left the congress to put the slogan and this decision into effect.

In the Witbank region and on the Kimberley diamond mines workers
demonstrated their rejection of the hostel system by unilaterally moving
their families into the single-sex compounds. At Anglo American's Fred-
dies gold mine, 8 000 workers were locked out in April after refusing to
do 'demeaning' tasks for white workers – in this case carrying their bags.
A manager at JCI's Randfontein mine felt that sections of the workforce
were 'breaking down the supervisory structure at the mine' and 'breaking down existing disciplinary procedures and channels of
communication.' Favoured targets, he said, included 'indunas, tribal representatives, team leaders and others employed in supervisory roles.' A
senior Anglo industrial relations executive spoke of 'disruptions...to a
point where supervision comes to a grinding halt... The local guys at
mine level were having real problems.'[2]

By the time of the 1987 mid-year wage negotiations the scene was
set for a showdown between NUM and the Chamber of Mines. NUM
and its members were determined to win a decent wage increase. Mineowners, and particularly Anglo, were in turn determined to stop NUM
before it became too strong. 'We were not the darling of the industry
they anticipated when we were launched,' explained one union official.
NUM 'had to be stopped dead in its tracks, before it grew too big.'

From mid-1986, recalls Anglo's Bobby Godsell, 'there was a pattern
of wildcat strikes, go-slows, half-shifts, sit-ins. All of this became prevalent. When the 1987 strike happened it was as much a battle for physical
control of the workplace as it was about wages.'

Wage negotiations deadlock

NUM undoubtedly had a strong case for vastly improved wages. Its congress report had noted that:

In 1987, the South African gold mining industry enters its second century. In spite of gold being the highest foreign exchange earner for the country the workers who dig this wealth are still lowest paid workers apart from agricultural workers.

Miners in most other countries, by contrast, earned higher wages than manufacturing workers. In early 1987 the lowest monthly wages, according to NUM, were R200 on gold mines, and R194 on coal mines. While most miners earned more, their wages were still low: in 1986 the average black mineworker earned a mere R427 per month.[3] During that year mine industry profits reached a new record of R8,3-million.[4]

NUM had experienced problems during previous wage negotiations, which its 1987 congress described as 'long and drawn out'. The Chamber had refused to be reasonable. 'Only when preparations for a national strike were underway' had the Chamber 'capitulated and tabled a more reasonable offer.' More importantly, the report suggested that NUM had been wrong to accept split offers in the past, which involved different settlements with different mining houses. NUM resolved that in 1987 it would fight for a decent wage increase for all miners and would not accept split offers from employers.

Negotiations began in May 1987, and soon deadlocked. NUM, following established legal procedures, applied for the establishment of a conciliation board. Two meetings of this board failed to achieve an agreement. By this stage NUM was demanding a 30% increase, while the Chamber was offering 17-23% for goldmines and 15-23% for coalmines. In previous years the parties had usually reached last-minute agreements at this stage of negotiations. However, this time employers were determined not to give ground. 'We left no stone unturned', said Anglo's Godsell, 'to indicate to the NUM that this year was different. We were going to stand together.'[5]

NUM proposed mediation or arbitration to settle the dispute. The Chamber rejected both, feeling that its final offer was reasonable. To make further concessions, as invariably happened during mediation, would seem like capitulation and only encourage NUM's membership. For NUM the dispute was over wages and the Chamber's ability to afford a decent increase, For the Chamber, and especially Anglo, it was about regaining control of the mines. This was the real obstacle to settlement, and with the Chamber's rejection of mediation, strike action became inevitable.

At the beginning of July NUM members voted in a strike ballot. This was intended both to legalise any strike action, and demonstrate to the Chamber the depth of support for a living wage. The results of the ballot were overwhelming: with 210 000 workers at 27 gold mines and 18 coal mines participating, 95% voted in favour of strike action.

NUM's NEC met to discuss strike preparations, and announced rules of conduct for the strike. Branch committees were directed to initiate the formation of strike committees, and arrangements for the strike were left in the hands of the regions. As a result, plans were implemented unevenly. On 3 August NUM announced that a legal industry-wide strike would begin the following Sunday evening, 9 August.

After seeing the results of the ballot employers began to tighten control. According to Marcel Golding, 'they restricted meetings and denied facilities... Roadblocks began to be erected, and workers' movements were monitored more closely.'

Anglo established its strike monitoring headquarters at its Main Street head office. NUM crammed its operations into an open-plan office at Darragh House in Wanderers Street. These offices were a recent and temporary arrangement, as NUM's head office had been destroyed three months earlier in the bombing of Cosatu House. An atmosphere of organised chaos prevailed. Hundreds of messages of support were pinned to the walls. Young Sayco members maintained a watchful eye outside the offices and around the building.

Tensions mounted as the strike approached. Anglo's Peter Gush announced that workers would lose wages and have to pay for food and accommodation during the strike. JCI mines searched workers entering the hostels and confiscated all union pamphlets. The union's Kimberley offices were gutted by fire only days before the strike. In response to the growing clampdown NUM asked the Chamber for guarantees that neither mine security nor the police would interfere with strikers. It offered to negotiate a code of conduct with the Chamber, a set of strike rules. The Chamber refused on both counts.

The strike begins

On 9 August 75 000 miners did not report for night duty.[6] They were joined by dayshift workers the following morning, increasing the number of strikers to 300 000. Mines in the Anglo group were particularly hard hit. At Western Deep Levels workers took control of hostel kitchens, to guarantee food supplies. At Gencor's Bracken operation, mine security forced workers underground. At St Helena, six strike committee members were arrested. Workers from a number of JCI mines began leaving for home. Fake pamphlets appeared, particularly in the Klerksdorp region, announcing that the strike had been called off. Miners at Rand Mines' Harmony gold mine staged an underground sit-in after being forced to return to work, while at Anglo's President Steyn mine and Anglovaal's Lorraine mine, security officials shot at workers.

Despite repression the strike grew during its first two days. At its height 340 000 miners on 44 gold and coal mines were out.[7] This was greater than NUM's official membership, and far more than its membership directly affected by the dispute. 'It grew because word spread,' according to Marcel Golding, NUM's assistant general secretary. 'Where there were mines not organised and recognised, they also heard about the strike and joined in.' But the union was uneasy about some mines joining the strike. Where the union had only pockets of support, where it was unrecognised and not party to the dispute, or where workers had not balloted, NUM called on strikers to return to work. 'We were sticklers for the law,' recalls Golding, 'to avoid mass dismissals.'

After two days, participation in the strike dropped to its original level of approximately 300 000 miners, and remained fairly constant at this level for the first two weeks of the strike. The extent of participation surprised not only the mineowners but also the union. Once NUM members had passed the two-day mark the union was entering uncharted territory. 'We had never been beyond two days,' recalls one NUM official. 'Once it went beyond a week, we realised we had the capacity to keep it going.' The Chamber, which had anticipated a short strike, was the most surprised. But it was determined to sit out any strike, whatever the losses to its members and the economy.

Two days into the strike police raided NUM's Klerksdorp offices and detained the entire regional leadership as well as 78 regional strike committee members. Elsewhere, a total of 177 NUM members were arrested. At Anglo's Vaal Reefs heavily-armed security personnel patrolled from room to room. At Gencor's Bracken mine, management threatened to cut off water and food supplies to over 4 000 workers. At the Ergo refinery, where workers were on a separate sympathy sleep-in strike, Anglo threatened eviction of all striking workers from the premises. The following day, 13 August, the supreme court gave Anglo the go-ahead to evict. Anglovaal, which did not recognise NUM, threatened to dismiss striking workers at its Lorraine mine. On NUM's advice, and because their strike was not legal, 2 000 Lorraine workers met management's ultimatum and returned to work.

As the strike progressed into the first week the battles became more intense. Much of the conflict revolved around control of the hostels and the supply of food. Sixty workers were injured and an almost equal number arrested after police mine security fired rubber bullets and teargas at a group of 700 singing workers at Anglo's vast Western Deep Levels mine. Management at Vaal Reefs cut off electricity to the hostel kitchens. On 15 August police and mine security invaded the hostels at two Gencor coalmines in the Witbank region – Matla and Optimum. They fired both rubber bullets and live ammunition. The Chamber meanwhile alleged that NUM supporters were involved in widespread intimidation of non-union members.

By the second week Anglo threatened that if the strike continued it would close certain marginal mines such as Landau Colliery and a shaft at Western Holdings. The Chamber declared that while it was prepared to meet NUM it would not improve its wage offer. The only concessions it would discuss involved the establishment of a provident fund and improvements to the death benefits scheme.

Throughout the second week attacks on striking workers continued. At Gencor's Bracken mine, workers were teargassed in their rooms and forced underground. There they staged a sit-in strike, only for teargas to be used again, this time underground. On 18 August Anglo and NUM met to discuss strike violence. The union proposed that mine security be demobilised and removed from the hostels. Anglo countered with a suggestion that all hostels should function 'normally' under management control. Not surprisingly, the two parties could not agree. Control of the hostels was the key to power during the strike.

While this meeting was in progress reports were received that police had injured 15 workers at Anglo's President Steyn mine. NUM walked out of the talks in protest. 'Anglo treated the strike like a war,' recalls Howie Gabriels, a NUM official centrally involved in the strike.

Financial donations to NUM from outside the country were held up by the Reserve Bank, apparently on instructions from the government. In mining towns there were reports of commercial banks, and the mining industry's own TEBA banks, preventing striking miners from withdrawing their money. In many cases, telephones were cut to prevent contact between striking miners and the NUM offices.

NUM's level of organisation in the various mining houses was uneven, and support for the strike was strongest within the Anglo group – the largest of the mining houses – and weakest within Goldfields.

Participation in 1987 strike by mining house[8]

Mining House	Number of strikers
Anglo American	196 272
Gencor	79 242
Rand Mines	36 215
JCI	26 207
Lonrho	1 300
Others	2 200
Total	341 436

Support was also uneven from one region to another, and from mine to mine. While support in the OFS and Witbank was strong, with most mines participating, mines in the Witwatersrand responded weakly or not at all.

Participation in 1987 strike by NUM region[9]

Region	Number of strikers
OFS	146 933
Carletonville	34 514
Westonaria	26 207
Witwatersrand	9 366
Secunda	30 698
Klerksdorp	70 374
Witbank	23 344
Total	341 436

Blyvooruitzicht mine, in the Carletonville region, was expected to come out but did not. This was a particular disappointment for the union as it was the workplace of NUM vice-president and Cosatu leader Elijah Barayi. NUM's Carletonville regional structures were particularly weak. The union had lost a significant leadership layer at Blyvooruitzicht the previous year following a militant, but ultimately unsuccessful, underground sit-in strike.

The Witbank experience

NUM's Witbank region had organised majority support at 14 of the 15 coal mines affiliated to the Chamber. All 14 responded to the strike call. This included all three of the affected Rand Mines operations, and one of the two Goldfields mines in the area. At Matla colliery, a particularly militant mine, workers began the strike four days earlier and stopped a day later than other miners.

NUM had membership at a number of non-Chamber mines in the area, many of which joined the strike after declaring their own legal disputes. They were organised to come out during the main strike 'for impact', recalls one member of the strike committee, Gwede Mantashe. 'The problem with collieries is that if some are striking and some working, they can transfer that coal to the power stations.'

'In preparing for the 1987 strike,' explained Mantashe, 'we made sure that report-backs were held in every mine and that the decision to strike was taken by the workers.' Black university students from

Medunsa and Wits assisted shaft stewards in holding the ballot. 'That ballot actually boosted our membership, because nobody is allowed to vote if he is not a member. Workers were joining the union and proceeding straight to go and vote for a strike. It was 99,9% who voted for a strike.'

Management knew the strike would be well supported. 'We were so strong in the collieries that in 1985, 1986 and 1987 there were actions in the Witbank region almost every week, in one mine or the other,' explained Mantashe. In the months before the strike 'there were quite a number of actions, including the campaign to scrap the migrant labour system, when workers just took women into the hostels,' recalls Mantashe. 'Even before the strike, signals were sent through that Anglo was no longer prepared to be more liberal. In March Derek Wiggell told us that Anglo is no longer prepared to be the walloping boys of the NUM.'

To ensure discipline and reduce disruption strike committees were formed in all the mines. They were, according to Mantashe,

> sort of marshalls. They set up roadblocks 24 hours a day at the entrances to the hostel. Everyone who was entering a mine had to go through roadblocks that were set up by the workers themselves. We thought management would set up vigilantes to attack workers. So we were making sure workers were on guard. As a result on the few mines where workers had confrontations with mine security, workers were fully aware that mine security were coming.

As a result, confrontations in the Witbank area were generally not serious. One exception was Matla colliery, owned by Trans Natal (Gencor). There, mine security went to the hostel claiming that it was protecting people wanting to work. 'Comrades made a mistake,' according to Mantashe. 'They assembled in the centre of the hostel, in an area which workers call James Motlatsi Park.' The key leadership was at a regional meeting, otherwise 'we would have told them to remain in their blocks. They were more vulnerable all in one place.' The security people came and opened fire with birdshot and tearsmoke. 'There were no serious casualties apart from one comrade shot in the testicles.'

An injury to one...

Two days before the strike began NUM briefed Cosatu's CEC and outlined its strike plans. The CEC agreed that the first of an ongoing set of solidarity meetings would take place on 11 August. Plans were made for the dissemination of daily information bulletins within the federation, and it was agreed that affiliates could pressurise employers to influence the Chamber. Although NUM was not requesting immediate and direct solidarity action, it was asking affiliates to prepare for this.

The mines are vulnerable to pressure from workers in other sectors of the economy. Mining is, literally, the backbone of the South African economy. Industries such as engineering and timber are directly linked to mining, and most mining houses have industrial arms which control the major parts of the manufacturing sector. In 1987 it was estimated that Anglo alone controlled some 57% of the shares on the Johannesburg Stock Exchange.

Cosatu distributed information to its affiliates and members throughout the strike. But while industrial workers were aware of and sympathetic towards the strike, no solidarity action of note took place. Work in Anglo's and Gencor's industrial arms continued as normal. Metal workers under Numsa had planned to take their own strike action simultaneously with the miners. However their plans were thrown into disarray when government declared their strike illegal. Workers in many factories approached their managements and expressed support for the miners, but little in the way of solidarity or blacking action occurred.

As late as 17 August, as the strike entered its second week, meetings of Cosatu's solidarity committee were still discussing the need for a national living wage conference to be held within two weeks. This would consider, among other matters, 'NUM strike/solidarity'.[10]

Cosatu called an extended CEC meeting of over 100 people in response to NUM's obvious need for urgent support. It sat on 22 August in the hall of Johannesburg's Central Methodist Church. In addition to the normal CEC delegates from affiliates and regions, a representative from every Cosatu local was present. The meeting resolved to take action and called for workers to pressurise their employers. But it was too little, too late. Within days NUM faced mass dismissals. It could not confidently expect solidarity action from other Cosatu affiliates, and was forced to strike alone, fight alone, and settle alone.

Within Cosatu, there were criticisms of the way in which NUM had conducted the strike. Information had not been adequate; NUM had not sent out speakers to rally support; preparations had begun too late. The issue, it was said, had not been discussed at Cosatu's second congress in July, although the results of the strike ballot were already known. These criticisms, while valid, avoided the real problem – Cosatu's inability to take effective inter-union solidarity action at shopfloor level. The NUM strike highlighted, yet again, this weakness. 'During the 1987 strike everything was normal in the other unions,' commented one NUM official. 'That is a lesson of the strike, not for NUM, but for the whole federation. It is a problem that has not been addressed up to now.'

Mass dismissals

As the strike entered its third week the miners held firm despite massive repression. A few workers trickled back to work while others belatedly joined the action. But, on balance, 300 000 miners appeared unbudgeable. On 25 August, 400 workers at Anglo's Johannesburg head office stopped work in sympathy with the striking miners. NUM claimed that 345 000 miners were still on strike. The Chamber estimated the figure to be 230 000.

There had been dismissal threats from the first days of the strike, mainly in mines where the strike was illegal. But the major challenge to NUM came at the start of the third week when Anglo American began locking out workers at Springfield colliery, Vaal Reefs, Western Holdings and Saaiplaas, amongst others. By Monday 24 August, 22 000 Anglo miners faced an ultimatum to return to work or be dismissed.

On Wednesday 26 August the Chamber made a final offer to NUM. It would not improve its wage offer, and only discuss side issues such as death benefits. NUM rejected this. Hundreds of its members demonstrated outside Chamber headquarters.

Immediately after talks broke down Anglo started dismissing workers. NUM learnt that many of its members were being bussed out and deported. 'This was often without our knowledge, without proper steps being taken as in normal dismissals,' recalls a NUM official.

Repression accompanied dismissal threats. On 26 August, after NUM had rejected the Chamber's offer, Anglo mine security – assisted by mine security from Goldfields – attempted to regain control of the hostel at Western Deep Levels. Armoured 'hippo' vehicles entered the compound and surrounded the singing workforce. Workers refused to move. 'At 6-30 pm the shooting started' recalls one worker. 'It lasted 15 minutes. I found one worker who was shot in the face. I was in room 13 with injured workers. As I wanted to take them to the medical station, mine security came towards me and forced me back into the room.'

Following the shootings workers were forced underground. 'No. 3 shaft was forced down first. Management did not even wait for people to find their working clothes. Even if you were barefoot you had to go down.' More than 3 000 workers then staged an underground sit-in. The following day, 27 August, Anglo dismissed more than 10 000 workers from the mine. Most were bussed back to the 'homelands'. It soon became clear that Anglo intended to dismiss every striking worker, if that was what was needed to break the union's power.

The union was surprised by the mass dismissals. 'I didn't expect it to be undertaken as a course of action,' explains Marcel Golding. 'We were expecting the harsh action less from Anglo than any other group,' said another official. NUM believed that a legal strike offered workers protection against dismissal, a belief backed up by the result of its recent court case against Gencor's Marievale. NUM had been careful to make sure that its strike was a legal one, and had even called on members striking illegally to return to work. Anglo ignored this and dismissed workers striking legally.

Anglo American's Godsell has linked the dismissal decision to two factors. Firstly, management was receiving reports that the stopes and stope faces were closing. 'We were losing hydraulic props and areas were becoming dangerous and unmineable.' The strike was leading to permanent damage to deep-level mines in particular. Secondly, management was 'devastated' when on Wednesday 26 August NUM rejected its offer of the previous night. 'We didn't know what else to do... There was no counter-proposal... The strike just carried on.' According to Godsell, 'of the 50 000 people (dismissed) you won't find more than a couple of thousand dismissals before Wednesday night.'

Settlement

The dismissals were the turning point in the strike. By the evening of 26 August thousands of miners had been fired. Was NUM heading for an historic and shattering defeat similar to the one suffered in 1946? On that occasion the defeat had been so severe that it took 35 years before mine unionism resurfaced.

NUM leaders recall that they began 'discussing the issue, whether this was another 1946 or not. We could prevent another 1946 by turning back. Also, unlike 1946 this was an organised strike led by the union.' Discussions took place during the early hours of the morning. Present were Ramaphosa, Motlatsi, Golding, Howie Gabriels and Lebogang Hlalele. Other office bearers were not available, being at their respective mines. 'We agreed we could not prosecute the strike with no members, that is, from home.' The core committee at NUM head office then contacted the union's regional strike committees, encamped in union offices around the country. They discussed the issue and by 4 am all had telephoned back and agreed that NUM should take the necessary steps to meet Anglo and call off the strike. 'It was decided to initiate a meeting with Anglo to clarify their position, whether it was their intention to dismiss all workers.' Before dawn, NUM contacted Anglo's 'Kallie' van der Kolf to arrange a meeting which occurred later that morning at the Carlton Hotel. Anglo stated that 'the *quid pro quo* for stopping the dismissals was that we would recommend to our members the acceptance of the offer' rejected the previous day.

NUM decided to recommend acceptance of the Chamber's offer to its members. The leadership of the regions took this back to the members. 'We said', recalls one regional leader, 'that it seems as if Anglo American is determined to dismiss everybody. If that is the case, then the union will be destroyed, since Anglo is the strongest mining house in our union.'

Despite the agreement reached at the Carlton Hotel, 4 400 workers at President Steyn mine were dismissed. Anglo argued that this decision had been taken by mine management before the agreement was reached. On Friday 28 August NUM announced that it had accepted the Chamber's offer. The strike was over. On the evening of 30 August, 21 days after it all began, NUM's members returned to work.

It was an orderly retreat by NUM. The settlement was a slight improvement on the Chamber's pre-strike final offer. The package relating to death benefits and holiday leave added another 1,7% onto the employers wage bill. However, casualties were heavy. Eleven workers had been killed, 600 injured, and over 500 arrested. Over 50 000 miners were dismissed by Anglo, Gencor, JCI and Goldfields, including the union's president, James Motlatsi. The strike cost the miners approximately R5,5-million in lost wages per day. The employers refused to reveal their losses but Cosatu and NUM estimated that these amounted to some R250-million.[*] Production output, particularly at deep-level mines, only recovered well into the fourth quarter of 1987.[11]

The Chamber goes on the offensive

Although the strike was over, employers continued their offensive.[12] Anonymous propaganda pamphlets attacking NUM started appearing on the mines. Many were headed 'SA Trade Union Monthly Titbits', and workers returning from underground found them throughout the hostels. Its appearance within the hostels suggested management involvement. 'Titbits' was a well-known anti-union pamphlet and its origins are explored in a later chapter. An edition after the strike accused NUM leadership of theft. 'The union controlled by the ANC and Cosatu tried to overthrow the workers' source of bread and butter,' proclaimed one. 'They failed!!! Even the ANC agreed – they lost. You, the workers, you shout "AMANDLA" for what? You pay your subs, for what? You go to NUM meetings, for what?'

A NUM study produced after the strike revealed management's efforts to roll back the union within the Anglo group. Prior to the strike

---

* By contrast, settlement of the miners' wage demands would have added R34-million to that year's wage bill.

NUM was recognised at all 13 Anglo gold mines. Either during or short-ly after the strike management withdrew recognition at five of the mines. This, according to the report, led to effective prevention of shaft stewards from representing workers; intense victimisation of members and shaft stewards; threats of physical violence and dismissal; refusal to allow union members to hold meetings; and removal of union office facilities. In addition, following the strike, management actively encouraged workers to resign their NUM membership.

> Mine managements at the Anglo American gold and coal mines have attempted to reassert their control and to reclaim their position of power... In almost every arena, the abuses of supervisory power are again manifesting themselves... Every branch reported an increase in dismissals since the strike.

'They have gone back to the old system of calling people kaffirs,' one miner is reported to have said. The report also revealed a marked tightening of mine security, compound admission rules, and room searches.

Workers at one mine reported that 'if you are four or five workers walking in or outside the hostel, they say you are holding a meeting and you are arrested by mine security. You are then questioned about what you were discussing when walking as a group.'

Where meetings were allowed, they continued under massive restrictions. On Anglo gold mines, 'only 31% of branches have been able to hold monthly meetings whereas before the strike 92% of branches held meetings at least monthly.' At almost all mines the union had to name the intended speakers at union general meetings in advance. Outside speakers were generally refused permission to address meetings, including senior officials like Ramaphosa and Motlatsi. At most mines workers were refused permission to sing at meetings. On occasion workers were refused permission to speak from the floor, on the grounds that they had not been listed by the union as intended speakers. At most Anglo mines, management insisted on their right to video and tape-record NUM meetings.

Similar patterns emerged on the coal mines. However they were not as severe because NUM was more strongly organised there.

Intimidation against NUM took place not only in the hostels. At mine recruiting offices in the rural areas workers were warned against joining NUM, and dismissed workers blacklisted.

Clearly management was able to inflict heavy blows on the union after the strike. According to the union, strike action on the mines during 1988 'declined significantly'. Participation by miners in the June 1988 three-day stayaway against the amendment to the Labour Relations Act was 'limited and very uneven', according to Ramaphosa's report to the 1989 NUM congress. This was 'largely a result of membership and leadership losses experienced during 1987 and the intimidation by mine security forces, the army and the SAP.'

Mass dismissals were NUM's major problem, In addition, a number of key union leaders, particularly those from Lesotho, had been deported from South Africa following the strike. Many dismissed members were clearly unhappy and blamed the union or accused it of not doing enough.

The fight for reinstatement was long and hard. At the 1989 congress, NUM leadership reported that of the 42 000 workers dismissed by Anglo, 23 000 were reinstated soon after. The union challenged the legal validity of dismissals of the remaining 19 000. This resulted in a settlement in which Anglo offered re-employment to 10 000 of the workers and a compensation package to all 19 000 totalling R60-million. The dismissal of 2 500 Western Deep Levels workers on the grounds of 'misconduct' was referred to an arbitrator who ruled that the dismissals were fair.

JCI management agreed to reinstate the 7 000 workers it dismissed during the strike. But the deadline set for return to work was extremely short, and many workers were unable to return from the rural areas in time. NUM failed to win the reinstatement of 312 dismissed Gencor workers, and only a handful of the 100 dismissed Goldfields workers got their jobs back. According to NUM, 'up to 10 000 workers permanently lost their jobs after the strike.' It also noted that 'many workers who were re-employed demonstrated their undying commitment and loyalty to the union by rejoining the union once re-employed.'

Victory or defeat?

In the aftermath of the strike Ramaphosa optimistically called it a 'dress rehearsal' for 1988. Some within NUM categorised it as 'a combination of setback and victory'. Shortly after the strike, NUM saw the position as 'a tactical retreat and a stalemate'. Others have termed it a defeat for NUM. In its 1989 annual report NUM labelled this as 'a very simplistic assessment of a very complex process', and preferred to term the strike a 'setback'.

The strike revealed a high level of support for NUM. The number of miners on strike and the length of the strike were unprecedented in South Africa's history. The strike also proved to be 'a school of struggle', argued NUM's 1989 report. It brought together miners from different areas 'irrespective of language, religion and cultural persuasion.' Even the Chamber, said NUM, conceded that the strike had demonstrated the union's 'muscle, organisational capacity, determination and skill.'

The very fact of pulling off so large a strike was 'a major victory,' argues Gabriels. 'It revealed the depth of our organisation. We surprised ourselves at the organisational capacity we had, despite the deaths, killings, lack of facilities and adequate records.' But the strike was also a defeat, according to Gabriels. 'We didn't get our wage increase and there were mass dismissals of 50 000.'

Anglo's Bobby Godsell labelled the strike a 'setback for NUM' but a 'costly victory for management... In the short term it was a victory for management. But in the longer term both sides were losers.'

Clearly NUM underestimated the power of its opponents, and had not anticipated the level of repression and violence which the mine-owners unleashed. 'We had misjudged the power of capital,' recalled one union official. Confronting the whole mining industry involved more than simply taking on the sum of the different mines. NUM had challenged the country's key industry, and massive corporations were prepared 'to defend their interests at all costs.'

'We learnt that there is nothing like a liberal employer,' recalled another NUM leader. 'We were expecting the harsh action less from Anglo than from Gencor and others. But it came the other way around.'

The strike also carried specific lessons for NUM. More pre-strike preparation was needed, and too much of the actual planning was left in the hands of the regions. Weaknesses in certain regions were only detected once the strike was underway. Active central co-ordination was needed from an earlier stage. Where worker leadership was strong, the strike was forceful. Where it was weak, it was vulnerable once contact was lost between a mine and the union's regional or head office.

The weak support received from workers in some mining houses, particularly Goldfields, was a problem. A key issue in the strike involved NUM's rejection of lower, split offers – a favoured tactic of Goldfields. Without strong strike action in such mining houses, the union's leverage was significantly reduced.

Solidarity action from other Cosatu unions needed more preparation than expected. Jay Naidoo admitted after the strike that 'there was a real weakness on our side in mobilising support for the miners.' Anglo and Gencor, in particular, would have been vulnerable to effective solidarity action. But the physical distance of most mines from the major industrial areas meant that solidarity action could not be taken for granted. NUM also needed to make more preparations in the rural areas. The problem of replacement labour was underestimated. 'We should have had a more effective network of contacts in the rural areas to stop scabs from coming to the cities,' commented NUM's Marcel Golding afterwards.

NUM did not achieve the wage increases it intended. However, the union was not destroyed, nor did it lose its capacity to organise. It took over two years to rebuild membership levels to those existing before the strike. But the strike also built a tougher and more experienced union. 'Even regions reluctant to take actions, understand issues better than they used to,' claims Gwede Mantashe. 'The level of consciousness has heightened.'

The miners' strike marked a turning point for Cosatu as a whole. The federation's membership had proved its militancy in all sectors, and affiliate structures had proved their ability to withstand heavy repression. But political tensions within Cosatu remained serious. The failure to provide meaningful support to the miners reflected a deeper problem within the federation, revealing an organisational inability to make blacking action and sympathy strikes a reality. In part this reflected deep currents of political mistrust between and even within affiliates. Cosatu was still largely a collection of its parts, rather than a united whole.

The setback faced by NUM was a setback for the whole federation. The following 12 months were to be some of the darkest for Cosatu, and a year in which it almost fell apart.

Notes

1. This account relies heavily on NUM reports, internal Cosatu documents, the author's interviews with a number of NUM officials and workers including Marcel Golding, Gwede Mantashe, Howie Gabriels and James Motlatsi, and an author interview with Bobby Godsell and Don Ncube, both directors of Anglo American specialising in industrial relations.
2. Bettina von Lieres, 'The 1987 NUM Strike', unpublished BA (hons) dissertation, Department of Political Studies, University of Witwatersrand, March 1988, 37.
3. Statistics provided by NUM economist Martin Nicol, May 1991.
4. Chamber of Mines Newsletter, January/February 1987.
5. Quoted in Von Lieres, 'The 1987 NUM Strike', 32.
6. NUM documents in author's possession.
7. NUM, Report to sixth national congress, 1989, 15.
8. Calculated from NUM documentation in author's possession.
9. Calculated from NUM documentation in author's possession.
10. Minutes of National Living Wage/NUM Strike Solidarity meeting held at NUM offices, Darragh House, Johannesburg, 17 August 1987.
11. Coletane Markham and Monyaola Mothibeli, 'The 1987 Mineworkers Strike', *South African Labour Bulletin*, 13(1), November 1987.
12. The following relies heavily on the report of NUM Media and Research Department, 'Collective Bargaining at Anglo American Mines – a model for reform or repression?', Johannesburg, 9 December 1988.

Part Four

Defence and
Consolidation

15

Structures and campaigns

Back to basics

WITH the massive strike wave of the first three-quarters of 1987 subsiding and the second congress over, attention turned to building Cosatu's structures, campaigns and internal political unity. Political differences within the federation were healthy, argued Cosatu's leadership, and should be accommodated and debated rather than becoming sources of division. In an attempt to enhance unity, the office bearers initiated discussion around a proposed code of conduct to guide leadership at all levels of the federation.

Cosatu never officially adopted the code. Its importance lay in the debate over its principles, rather than any formal adoption as policy. The code was an attempt to establish practices which could contain differences within Cosatu. It encouraged democracy and openness but also recognised the limitations of these in the context of political repression.

The code attempted to explore two areas – 'how comrades need to work in their organisations' and 'how comrades need to behave'. It emphasised the need for democratic centralism. Discussions and debates should be democratic and take place through 'a mandated body' or recognised structure. All present had 'a right to be heard' and 'a right to differ'. But 'once matters have been debated, decisions need to be taken', and majority decisions were then binding on all concerned. 'The right to differ', it was argued, 'then transforms itself into the duty of implementing the decision.' The code also argued strongly against 'cliquism' and 'factionalism', and attacked habits of intolerance. Members of factions

> owe their loyalty first to their own faction and secondly to the organisation... Cliques or factions succeed in causing a lot of confusion and division. They automatically oppose whatever non-clique members propose, without considering the merits of the proposal...
>
> The basis of comradely discussions is mutual respect, equality among comrades; honesty and frankness in discussions; the willingness to grant a point made by another comrade; the readiness to withdraw uncalled for remarks and to apologise sincerely and with humility; the willingness to return the courtesy of a comrade who has had the courtesy to hear another comrade; self-criticism etc.

The code stressed the need for discipline. 'Every organisation needs to exercise control over the actions of its members by means of rules, norms, etc.' But 'some comrades' equated disciplinary action with 'excessive punishment, the use of force and humiliation.' This was wrong. 'The most important part of discipline...is re-education.' Suspension or expulsion from the organisation were appropriate only if this failed. 'To summarise: persuasion, reprimand, suspension, expulsion in that order.'

'Senior comrades' were not exempt. 'On the contrary, senior members committing errors must be seen in a more serious light than junior members.'

Finally the code recognised that 'no-one is perfect. None is only a saint or only a satan. For each comrade possess(es) good and bad qualities. The point however is to use the finer political qualities as stepping stones to smooth out the rough edges.'

A major seminar in early December 1987 brought together 110 delegates from Cosatu's local and regional structures countrywide. The gathering played an important role in ensuring that the code of conduct was widely debated within Cosatu. Delegates were all leaders of Cosatu structures at grassroots level, where many of the broader political differences manifested themselves. Often organisational and even personality differences would be wrapped in the cloak of differing political positions. Local leadership had to be able to deal with differences creatively. Education was a crucial component in this.

Culture and education

Cosatu's education programme was largely ineffective during its first two years. The first CEC meeting, held in February 1986, had appointed Alec Erwin as education secretary. He was an obvious choice – a highly-experienced unionist with particular expertise in the educational field. But Erwin was not unanimously welcomed. A minority, mainly from the UDF bloc, were suspicious of his Fosatu background and believed he was politically close to the 'independent worker' bloc. Some affiliates denied Erwin full co-operation, and as a result he was hampered in his duties.

Erwin's approach to union education was expressed in a speech delivered to the NUM education conference of November 1986, in which he called for an education programme to be developed around the acceptance of three important points.

> Firstly, education cannot and must not be separated from organisation. Only through this link will education be used to solve the problems that people face. Secondly, education can take place anywhere, at any time and involves people of all ages. We must break the idea that education takes place in schools and is for our children. Any meeting, any strike, any wage negotiation and any lunch break can be used as places where education takes place. Thirdly, always respect the knowledge people already have. Do not make the mistake of believing that in education the teacher has the knowledge and the pupil is blank.

Erwin was the right education secretary at the wrong time. While he could be relied on for imaginative and inventive thinking, political differences and problems in the education structures limited the effective implementation of educational programmes. The national education committee (Nedcom) and regional and local education committees (Redcoms and Ledcoms respectively) did not function well. It was difficult to expect, for example, a region's educational structures to work when its constitutional structures (RECs and RCs) were not operating properly. As a result the education department concentrated on producing publications and resources for affiliates and regions to use. Cosatu education courses only commenced properly during 1987 and their success differed from region to region, in direct relation to the strength of Cosatu's structures.

Cosatu's second congress noted these weaknesses and resolved to hold an education conference every two years to establish educational needs and priorities, as well as elect an education secretary and education office bearers who would head Cosatu's Nedcom.

Nearly 150 union delegates attended the first education conference at Nasrec, Johannesburg, during October 1987. In addition delegates from regions, as well as relevant Cosatu departments such as media, culture, printing and information also attended. Delegates broke into commissions to explore education structures and courses, and make detailed recommendations to the CEC. The conference also examined a number of areas which Cosatu traditionally lumped together with education.

These included Cosatu's cultural unit, sport, the development of Cosatu media, and, oddly enough, the organisation of women.

Finally, the conference elected education office bearers. Khetsi Lehoko – previously in Cosatu's media department, and prior to that a worker at Plate Glass – was elected education secretary. Chris Seoposengwe, a NUM member, was elected education chairperson, with Numsa's Esion Mashego as his deputy and Fawu's Pule Thate as education treasurer.

The conference was 'the first opportunity for workers to come together to define a programme of education... It was an attempt to democratise education in content and organisation,' said Lehoko later. It 'advanced a fundamental principle of involving those who are to be "taught" in determining what they want to learn.'

'Education in Cosatu', Jay Naidoo said in his opening speech to the conference, is 'fundamentally different from bourgeois education.' Cosatu rejected the idea 'of educators lecturing workers.' Rather, it was committed to bringing worker leaders together, 'and extracting maximum value from the collective experience and understanding of the working class.'

This approach had considerable support within the democratic movement generally. Union education programmes were developing not only to meet union needs but also as an alternative and a supplement to the system of Bantu Education.

Most union members had been educated in schools which delivered inferior education to black students, both in resources and course content. Cosatu supported the call for the scrapping of Bantu Education. It played a role in the 1986 conference of the National Education Crisis Committee (NECC), and after the June 1986 clampdown continued to stress the need to rebuild NECC structures. There was broad consensus that Bantu Education should be replaced by 'people's education' which should be democratic and liberatory in content, and democratically controlled by elected committees.

Even after Cosatu's education conference many of the problems of the first two years continued. Cosatu conducted very few seminars and courses during the remainder of 1987 and the whole of 1988. What training did take place was unevenly spread between regions. The education department was still feeling the effects of political differences within the federation. Education secretary Khetsi Lehoko was also overburdened with other Cosatu duties, and had to undertake a number of international trips since he was one of the only elected leaders with a passport!

Massive membership growth during Cosatu's first two years was accompanied by a growth in the number of shop stewards and union officials, most of whom needed training. Within Cosatu there was general acceptance that affiliates would train shop stewards while the federation conducted more general training. A number of affiliates ran their own training programmes. However, some affiliates – mainly the larger ones – provided both shop steward and more comprehensive training, while others undertook almost no training whatsoever.

Workers were hungry for knowledge, but this was not always easy to deliver. Unionists worked under pressure, in a climate of crisis, repression and struggle. Educational work, by contrast, required time and an environment conducive to learning. These were rarely available and stopgap methods had to be developed. The 'cross-nighter', or overnight seminar, was frequently used by both regions and affiliates. Workers would arrive from work and spend the whole night in discussions before leaving the seminar venue in the morning. Enthusiasm to learn overcame the problems of exhaustion, although it was not an optimal arrangement.

There was growing evidence of affiliates taking their educational tasks more seriously. Before mid-1987 very few had full-time education officers. After the mergers affiliates increasingly employed education officers who began developing affiliate education programmes. Progress was slow. Only by 1989, were there signs of significant progress in Cosatu's internal educational programmes.

Cosatu made great strides in the field of culture, and by 1989 over 300 cultural groups existed within the federation. Workers wrote and performed plays describing working-class life or struggles in their factories. No major strike was complete without being accompanied by a dramatic version of the conflict. A number of these plays, particularly in Natal, were put on for the general public, including the well-known Sarmcol workers' play which even performed to audiences in Europe.

Other workers recited poetry, often before large and enthusiastic audiences. Worker poets commonly adapted the oral traditions of 'praise poetry' to modern circumstances and struggles. Many developed large followings, particularly in their home regions, and reached audiences of thousands at a time. Alfred Qabula and Mi Hlatshwayo were two of the better-known worker poets, and in 1987 Hlatshwayo was appointed Cosatu's national cultural co-ordinator. By 1989, 15 Cosatu locals – of which the Johannesburg local was the most notable – had developed their own cultural groups which performed at rallies and meetings.

The cultural groups were inspired by, but developed largely without direct assistance from, Cosatu. Encouragement was limited to events such as the cultural festivals which accompanied both the second and third Cosatu congresses, or cultural days which some affiliates arranged at the same time as their national meetings.

Worker culture has emerged as a voice of the working class. Frank Meintjies and Mi Hlatshwayo have stressed that while working-class

culture forms part of a 'broader progressive culture', it 'emphasizes that
the struggle against apartheid is unfolding in a class context.' The very
act of building this culture has high-lighted this. Lacking resources and
venues, and having to rehearse after working long hours, has meant that
every cultural work is 'an act of sacrifice as much as an act of creation
and imagination.' Importantly, worker culture has been notable not only
for its content but also for its form. Meintjies and Hlatshwayo have
pointed to a number of stylistic features which have emerged. The widespread use of African languages, and the fact that productions are usually
the result of collective work, are examples of styles which go to the root
of popular expression and reinforce the 'anti-hierarchical position' of the
unions. Important too has been the revival of the oral tradition, the
chanting style of the imbongi, and the use of 'the isicathamiya music and
dance forms which have developed out of the experience of migrant
workers.'[1]

Building structures

The main task of the federation following the second congress was to
build and strengthen Cosatu structures. The merger process, and the
adoption of a more coherent political policy, made this task easier. However, the political tensions which remained after the congress hampered
it. In any event, it was one thing to establish regional and local structures
but quite another to breathe life into them, to make them vibrant and
powerful.

At the end of 1987 the national office bearers undertook an assessment of Cosatu which they presented to the first Exco meeting of 1988.
It was open, extremely critical and concentrated on weaknesses rather
than self-praise. Cosatu, according to this assessment, could only be
strengthened by 'openly acknowledging our weaknesses and strengths
and then carefully reassessing our strategies and tactics.' Of Cosatu's
nine regions only the Highveld and Western Cape regions, according to
the office bearers, were functioning actively:

> The majority of our regions are paralysed by the lack of discipline and
> initiative by (regional) office bearers as well as the consistent
> non-attendance by affiliates and the weakness of sub-committees such as
> Redcom and the Living Wage Committee.

A large part of the problem, it was felt, lay with the quality of leadership. 'Leaders elected on purely political considerations may not, in all
fairness, contribute to building all aspects of Cosatu.' Instead, 'the most
capable, disciplined and hardworking comrades' with 'a history of

consistent organisational work' should be put forward for election. However, Cosatu affiliates were understandably reluctant to release their most experienced officials to stand for election to regional positions.

Local structures, 'the pillars on which Cosatu stands', were also weak. In many areas locals had not yet been set up. The office bearers urged affiliates to assist the development of locals by giving their support and providing resources. Dealing with political tensions was a key element: affiliates should 'accept and accommodate the tensions that could develop between locals and union structures. This is what maintains the militancy and vibrancy of Cosatu and generates the leadership which makes the workers movement insurmountable on the ground.'

Not only were structures weak, concluded the office bearers, the federation's three organisational initiatives were also inadequate. While the NUWCC had made some progress, there was not enough participation by affiliates, locals and regions in organising the unemployed. There had been little progress in the organisation of farmworkers, a crucial project for Cosatu because it 'begins to bridge the gap between rural and urban workers.' The responsibility for organising farmworkers had been given to Fawu. Yet 'no cohesive national strategy' had been developed 'on the ground'. Fawu needed to be more accountable to Cosatu regarding progress in this sector. In the building and construction sector, Cawu still existed as a project of the federation rather than as an autonomous union. It had 'not proceeded satisfactorily', said the office bearers, and 'many problems plague the organisation.'

The struggle for a living wage

Alongside the weaknesses in structures and organisational initiatives, it is important to look into the effectiveness of Cosatu's campaigns, the most important of which was the Living Wage Campaign (LWC).

Cosatu's call for a 'living wage' captured the imagination of the working class. 'It has inspired a new confidence and assertiveness' amongst workers, commented Cosatu's information officer, Frank Meintjies. 'The strike barometer soared to record levels as workers became more determined to share in the wealth they produced,' said Meintjies, and the major wage strikes at the OK Bazaars and on the mines were merely the tip of an iceberg. During 1987, according to official figures, almost six million working days were lost through strike action (excluding stayaways). One management consultant spoke of this being a ninefold increase on the previous year,[2] and there was general agreement that the campaign succeeded in pushing wages up.

The LWC took a long time to get underway. Cosatu's inaugural congress of 1985 resolved to set and then campaign for a legislated minimum wage which would be linked to inflation. Cosatu would campaign for companies to open their books 'so that workers can see exactly how the wealth they have produced is being wasted and misused by the employers' profit system.' It was also agreed to press for the abolition of general sales tax (GST) on essential items, and for worker control of pension, unemployment insurance fund (UIF) and other deductions.

Cosatu's CEC never did set a minimum wage. Nevertheless, the 1985 resolution laid the basis for the LWC. The idea of a living wage campaign was not new. The Freedom Charter had called for 'a 40-hour working week, a national minimum wage, paid annual leave and sick leave', as well as 'maternity leave on full pay for all working mothers.' This had inspired the successful 'Pound-a-Day' campaign during the 1950s, which mobilised workers behind Sactu. In 1980 Saawu called for a minimum wage of R50 per week, linked to inflation, and a minimum of R80 per month for domestic workers. In 1981 Fosatu launched a campaign calling for a minimum wage of R2 per hour.

It was only in March 1987 that Cosatu's CEC took steps to initiate the LWC, agreeing to launch the campaign at a series of mass rallies on May Day. These plans were aborted when the state banned all the rallies, alleging that the LWC was part of a communist plot.*

Cosatu's second congress adopted a further resolution on the LWC, which endorsed the direction provided by the CEC, and resolved to build a campaign 'around a set of national demands'. These included a living wage (although no figure was set); a 40-hour working week; 21 March, 1 May and 16 June as paid public holidays; job security; six months paid maternity leave; an end to hostels and the provision of decent housing near places of work; and the right to decent education and training.

The 1987 resolution expressed the view that a living wage was a social concept going beyond a monetary figure. It shifted the focus from setting a minimum wage to developing a broad notion of one. Some regions and affiliates wanted a national minimum figure to be agreed upon. But, the secretariat reported to the second congress, the CEC had decided against this 'as conditions in various sectors differed so vastly.'

---

*This attitude continued to inform the state's approach to the LWC for years to come. In November 1987, Police Commissioner General Hennie de Witt accused Cosatu of attempting to paralyse the economy together with the Communist Party. The objective, he said, addressing a meeting of the Motor Industry Employers' Federation, was to turn the country into a socialist state. Politically motivated strikes and Cosatu's LWC were an important part of this plan. 'The assault on the country's labour front is fiercer than in any other sphere. The communist needs the worker for his revolution.' Cosatu responded by 'rejecting this criminalisation' of the LWC, and insisting that 'the working class has every right to call for a greater share in the wealth produced.'

A realistic figure would, in practice, be less than actual minimum wages in higher-paying sectors such as pharmaceuticals, beverages and the automobile assembly. And it would appear unobtainable in some of the lowest-paying sectors, such as agriculture and domestic work, as well as in the rural areas generally. It was therefore, argued some, better for each sector to determine its own target figure. Trying to define a national minimum wage figure would, in itself, cause division, and would be used against workers in higher paying sectors. By establishing a minimum figure, the LWC would limit its focus to wages alone, and encourage a narrow economism amongst workers.

The counter-argument, although unsuccessful, was strong. A clearcut figure, like Sactu's 'Pound-a-Day' or Fosatu's 'R2-an-Hour' calls, would provide a concrete minimum target. It would mobilise the majority of Cosatu's members, and draw in the unorganised. Better-paid sectors could support it as a national minimum while themselves attempting to better the figure. In practice, the lack of a concrete amount would work against the low-wage sectors. Without some common figure, it was argued, each union would effectively be running its own LWC. The non-wage demands, such as a 40-hour week and decent housing, were an insufficient basis for a Cosatu LWC. Whether to set a minimum wage figure continues as a debate within Cosatu, and we will return to it in the penultimate chapter.

Many employers asked what a living wage meant in concrete terms. They were provided with a range of figures, differing from union to union, and from sector to sector. Employers invariably accused workers of aiming too high, of setting unrealistic targets. Cosatu hit back at this approach. 'It is hypocritical', said Meintjies, 'for those who themselves enjoy a living wage to cry foul when other human beings demand the same for themselves.' No employer had come out in support of the notion of a living wage. None had even endorsed 'the need to strive towards the ideal of a living wage,' said Meintjies.

During wage negotiations, major employers relied heavily on company-funded research undertaken by the Bureau for Market Research (BMR) and the University of Port Elizabeth (UPE). They conducted regular and detailed surveys based on standard 'shopping lists' of items deemed essential. BMR derived the concept of the Minimum Living Level (MLL), as well as the slightly more generous Supplemented Living Level (SLL) from these surveys. UPE derived the broadly comparable concepts of Household Subsistence Level (HSL) and Household Effective Level (HEL) respectively. Both systems have been extensively criticised by the union movement and by a number of academics, particularly for the range of essential items they exclude from their calculations. By August 1989 the various monthly figures for a five-person family were R423 (HSL), R521 (MLL), R635 (HEL), and R691 (SLL). The unions regarded these not as a living wage but rather as the amount needed to keep a family of five from literally starving.

The Labour Research Service (LRS), a union-linked service organisation, attempted its own calculations and found that in mid-1989, a living wage was R1 140 per month. The average labourer's monthly wage contained in union settlements during the last six months of 1989 was R667, and only a handful of automobile, and multinational food and chemical companies were paying minimum wages above the LRS estimate.

The failure to build the LWC

The August 1987 CEC agreed to use a NUM strike solidarity meeting as a 'springboard' to rebuild the living wage campaign. With the NUM strike then underway, this approach would emphasise not only the wage but also the solidarity aspect of the LWC. But as the NUM strike turned into a setback, so the springboard lost its bounce.

During early October 1987 a special CEC seminar assessed the Living Wage Campaign in detail. The LWC had, it was felt, emerged as Cosatu's most important campaign and one which had taken root strongly amongst Cosatu members. It had encouraged the membership to be more militant and determined on the factory floor, but had failed to develop solidarity action between different affiliates. Failure to build structures and national co-ordination was identified as the fundamental weakness of the LWC. The CEC seminar suggested a number of solutions. These ranged from establishing living wage committees in every region and local and giving a more active role in the campaign to regional secretaries, to arranging 'crash courses for union organisers on basic union skills.'[3]

Delegates agreed to formalise the proposals at the next CEC. However, the November CEC failed to discuss the LWC. It had too many other matters to deal with including the Natal violence, Inkatha attacks, widespread detentions, proposed amendments to the labour law, and the report into the split within Ccawusa.

The following CEC, held from 12-14 February, was faced with similar problems and managed only a cursory discussion of the campaign. Ten days later Cosatu was heavily restricted. The federation was forced to expend its energies in warding off this attack and organising a special congress scheduled for May 1988 in response to the state-imposed restrictions on its activities. Again, the casualty was the Living Wage Campaign.

Preoccupation with mergers stunted the LWC during Cosatu's first 18 months. Then repression and preoccupation with the Labour Bill made it ineffective until at least Cosatu's third congress in mid-1989. The LWC had three broad organisational aims. With the first of these, that of building effective co-ordinating structures, it failed totally during the first four years.

With the second aim, that of developing broad unifying demands, its successes were limited and partial. Cosatu undoubtedly determined the national agenda on issues such as public holidays. It also succeeded in popularising demands for maternity leave and decent housing. However, demands such as a 40-hour working week and an end to tax deductions under apartheid resulted in little, if any, success. These were precisely the demands which could only be won through well-organised and disciplined national campaigns.

With its third aim, that of building unity in action, the LWC has been largely unsuccessful. It is still rare to see, for example, effective blacking action in South African trade union circles. Unionised workers, fearing dismissal for insubordination from their own employer, still make deliveries of raw materials to factories affected by strike action. Similarly, it is rare for unionised workers to refuse supplies from anti-union or low-paying companies. When solidarity actions do take place, this is usually on the initiative of the union concerned rather than a result of Cosatu's structures.

Despite these failures, the LWC registered substantial gains at the subjective level. The idea of a 'living wage' spread rapidly and became, according to Meintjies, 'rooted in the hearts and minds of millions of organised as well as unorganised workers.' This ensured that employers felt the effects of the LWC in negotiations throughout the country.

Patterns of wage increases

Cosatu's LWC was 'an important force in determining the high levels of settlement recorded' during 1987, commented one leading industrial relations consultancy. 'Black union members have been the only group in the economy to have successfully kept up with inflation.'[4] A 1988 survey by the union-linked Labour Research Service (LRS) came to similar conclusions. While the inflation rate for 1988 was 13%, the average union settlements for the first and second half of the year had been 23% and 20% respectively. The drop shown during the second half of the year, argued LRS, was partly the result of NUM, weakened by the outcome of the miners' strike, concluding many settlements with a 16,5% increase.[5] Again, in 1989, LRS noted union-negotiated increases of

22,5% during the first six months, and 19,7% during the last six months (see table). *

The union movement's wage strategy has generally embraced a number of aims. Firstly, to ensure that all union members, even the highest paid, receive increases not less than the rate of inflation; secondly, to work towards a living wage by ensuring that most members win increases in real terms, ie increases higher than inflation; thirdly, to increase the minimum starting wage to a meaningful level; fourthly, to expand the bargaining frontiers by demanding basic rights to things such as shift allowances, maternity benefits, and paternity leave; and fifthly, to flatten the wage curve – the ratio between the wages of the highest and lowest paid employees – by reducing wage differentials. The last of these aims has often proved the most difficult. It directly challenges the system of white privilege. Many employers have managed to evade this demand by refusing access to financial information and by giving

Union-negotiated wage increases: (1987 - 1990)[6]

Percentage increase

	2nd half/87	1st half/88	2nd half/88	1st half/89	2nd half/89	1st half/90	2nd half/90
Inflation	15,6	13,3	12,4	14,2	15,1	14,4	14,2
Labourers' increases	20,6	22,9	20,6	22,5	19,7	20,9	21,9

Source: LRS Feb '91

* The LRS survey can be criticised for exaggerating the union movement's achievement, since it is based on an analysis of the wage increases achieved for labourers. Cosatu unions have, generally speaking, attempted to raise the minimum wages paid in each industry. This has often resulted in higher wage increases, at least in percentage terms, being won for lower-paid workers. The LRS surveys can also be accused of underestimating union achievements by ignoring improvements in non-wage items, such as annual leave. Despite these limitations, they remain the most authoritative guide to the union movement's economic achievements.

management a range of non-monetary perks. The pattern throughout the 1980s is similar. Strongly-unionised workers managed to increase their share of the economic cake. This was, and remains, the most persuasive argument for workers to join a strong Cosatu union.

Unfortunately, the other side of this achievement has been the growing gap between unionised and non-unionised sectors. Some of the lowest-paid workers, such as farmworkers and domestics, have found their conditions relatively worsened. Differentials have also grown within many sectors, and within many unions. Numsa, which organises a number of related sectors, is a typical example. In early 1990, the minimum wage in its automobile manufacturing plants was over R5 per hour. The minimum in the engineering sector was R3,56 while in the motor sector it was as low as R1,76. Similar differentials exist in TGWU, for example, between its low-paid cleaning and security sector, and its higher-paid drivers, as well as in Fawu with its sugar plantation workers, and its members employed at major breweries and Coke bottling plants. Differentials also frequently exist on non-wage items such as the existence of pension or provident funds, company housing and medical aid schemes. This economic dualism between workers in different sectors contains dangers both for unions and the economy generally.

During early 1988 the then state president, PW Botha, announced plans to introduce a general wage freeze. Wages in the public sector would be frozen; in the private sector, where government had no direct control over wages, Botha called for wage restraint. His announcement was presented as a programme to counter inflation. It was also a recognition of the government's financial crisis. During 1987 and 1988 spending on the military was rocketing as the army became bogged down in the Angolan war. At the same time state revenue was declining, in part due to the widespread township rent boycotts.

The unions rejected Botha's call for wage restraint. If there was a need for cuts in government expenditure, argued Numsa, then expenditure on apartheid – the tricameral system, the duplication of homeland services, and especially, the security forces – should be the target. Cosatu asked why wages should be frozen, and not prices? When, in April, PW Botha threatened to extend the wage freeze to the private sector, Cosatu was alarmed. Employers must decide, said the official Cosatu response,

> whether they will be browbeaten or use their clout to oppose the wage freeze. For it is they who will have to deal with consequences on the shopfloor. Employers must realise that if a wage freeze were implemented, the exercise of labour relations could easily become meaningless.

'Bothanomics', as it was dubbed, failed. In practice, only public sector workers – where unionisation of black workers was weak and most white unions were submissive – found their wages frozen.

The freeze became a major stimulus to the organisation of the public sector. Without strong unions, workers realised, they would continue to be on the receiving end of the government's economic policies. In the years which followed the wage freeze, unionisation spread. Even professional and semi-professional employees, such as nurses, teachers and hospital workers, started joining unions in substantial numbers. Black workers in local government, previously poorly organised, also flocked to join the union movement. Their presence in Cosatu would be felt increasingly from 1990 onwards.

Bargaining forums

Many of the problems of the LWC can be traced to the lack of centralised bargaining in South African industrial relations. The union movement, which re-emerged during the 1970s and early 1980s, faced extreme hostility from employers and the state. Union success required solid organisation, plant by plant. This was essential, not only to build effective power, but also as a guarantee of survival. If organisation could be sufficiently strong at the grassroots, repression would be unable to crush the union movement. These early foundations explain the tenacity of the union movement over the years, but ran counter to the existing industrial relations system.

By the early 1970s three different systems of determining wages and working conditions had been established.

Firstly, and in the majority of cases, the employer simply decided on increases. This happened even in major industries such as mining where, until 1982, the Chamber of Mines unilaterally decided on black mineworkers' wages.

Secondly, the government-run Wage Board determined wages for a range of sectors and job categories. These were decided on after representations from 'interested' parties, in practice usually only employers. On the few occasions when the unions made representations, this had little effect. Wages were, without exception, set at very low levels by the Wage Board.

Thirdly, there was an industrial council system which covered a number of sectors, establishing minimum wages as well as actual increases. In a few industries, such as metal and printing, industrial councils operated on a national basis. In most others, regional industrial councils existed.

Of these three, only the industrial councils could be called a bargaining system. However, by the 1970s their shortcomings were legion. A majority of industrial councils had become stagnant and bureaucratic and spent most of their time administering a variety of benefit funds. In theory industrial councils reached agreements after negotiations between the union and employer parties to the council. In practice the balance of power was overwhelmingly in the employers' favour. Almost all the unions involved were weak and ineffective, and had a cosy relationship with the employers. They were invariably white-controlled, although some had coloured and Indian members. Being weak, and unable to satisfy their own members, they would often cynically conclude agreements by accepting better increases for the skilled (white) workers at the expense of low-paid black workers who were not their members.

Not surprisingly, black workers resented the industrial councils. When they complained about wage increases, they were told these had been determined by the industrial council and approved by the government (all IC agreements being approved and made legally enforceable by publication in the government gazette).

Many employers refused to negotiate with emergent black unions, even after the new labour dispensation was introduced in 1979. Unions were told that they should join and negotiate at the industrial councils. Plant-level bargaining, which the unions wanted because it paralleled their organisational approach, was invariably rejected by management.

Kate Jowell, a former member of the National Manpower Commission (NMC), has argued that until the early 1980s employers and the state were the main supporters of the industrial council system. Centralised bargaining was, for them, a 'useful method of minimising wage competition between companies', and could also 'neutralise unions, by weakening their plant base and causing them to focus more on maintaining benefit funds...than on grassroots organising.'[7]

Unions had adopted similar arguments to reject participation in industrial councils. But during 1982 and 1983 voices were increasingly heard, mainly in Fosatu-affiliated unions such as NUTW, Mawu and Naawu, calling for a reappraisal. They began to argue that unions should not focus on plant-level bargaining and centralised bargaining should not be rejected along with the industrial council system. As unions grew, it would become increasingly difficult to negotiate effectively at plant level. Hundreds of different agreements at different plants would not lead to the construction of a united union movement. Nor would it result in more uniform conditions of employment.

As the unions grew in strength plant-level bargaining turned into its opposite. Where once it was the means for building power, now it became a dispersal of power and reflected union difficulties in concentrating their forces. Moving towards centralised industrial bargaining did not involve discarding plant-based strength, it was argued. On the contrary, strong factory organisation and supplementary plant-based bargaining should be retained, as they were essential to make centralised bargaining effective.

Unfortunately for the unions many employers, using similar arguments, had concluded that centralised bargaining with strong unions could endanger their interests.

By mid-1987, almost all Cosatu affiliates were committed in principle to centralised bargaining and participation in industrial councils. But the road to centralised bargaining has been far from smooth. In a number of cases, established unions used their legal right to veto the entry of Cosatu affiliates onto industrial councils. Actwusa successfully challenged its exclusion from the leather industrial council in 1989. Ppwawu was not so fortunate when, in the same year, the industrial court rejected its appeal to be admitted to the furniture industrial council.

The attempt by certain employers to undermine centralised bargaining was even more dangerous for the unions. Barlow Rand, a conglomerate responsible for some 10% of the country's gross domestic product, was a major culprit. It argued that its decentralised management style demanded that all dealings with unions be decentralised. For example its arm in the timber merchandising industry, Federated-Blaikie, insisted on reaching separate recognition agreements and holding separate wage negotiations at each of its outlets. All of these operations were small, some employing as few as ten or 15 workers, and the company had scores of outlets throughout the country. Management's approach often appeared cynical. Union negotiators at these decentralised plants found themselves negotiating, not with local management, but an industrial relations manager from the company's regional or national offices.

Barlow Rand had once been a major proponent of centralised bargaining. During the 1970s and early 1980s, when emerging unions were weak, it frequently refused to recognise plant-based unions. 'We would like to see negotiations at industry or national level between the employer organisations and multi-racial unions,' said the chairman of its board in 1977. As late as 1980 the company was arguing that it 'would ideally like to deal with registered unions in an industrial council structure.'

As the unions grew stronger, and particularly after the launch of Cosatu, Barlows changed its tune, arguing that 'industrial relations should be managed at plant level.'[8]

NUM, alone amongst Cosatu affiliates, has always been involved in centralised bargaining. Its annual negotiations with the Chamber of Mines formed the centre of its negotiating programme. Union support for centralised bargaining was matched by the major employers who had an interest in retaining a strong and centralised Chamber of Mines.[*]

Numsa's centralised bargaining strategy has managed to overcome a variety of obstacles erected by both employers and the state. Mawu (now merged into Numsa) joined the National Industrial Council for the Iron, Steel, Engineering and Metallurgical Industry in 1983. In the years which followed, its participation was undermined as employers continued to sign unsatisfactory agreements with the established unions, despite Mawu opposition. As late as July 1987 an agreement reached in the face of Numsa objections was gazetted by the government. At the time Numsa was the largest union on the industrial council. The gazetting of the agreement behind Numsa's back effectively outlawed its dispute and planned legal strike over wages.

The following year, and only after a three-week strike, Numsa for the first time became party to an agreement reached at the industrial council. The strike convinced Seifsa that employers had to deal with Numsa on the basis that it was the largest union in the council. This time the government refused to gazette the agreement for almost 12 months, finally publishing it seven days before it was due to expire, in June 1989. The government objected to the fact that metal employers had agreed to grant 1 May and 16 June as public holidays, and that wage increases would be backdated to 1 July. It excused the delay by claiming that the industrial council was insufficiently representative, despite the fact that Numsa's membership made it more representative of employees than ever before.

Numsa's perseverance has, however, paid off. Its membership has grown dramatically since 1987, in large part because of its sophisticated national bargaining strategies. After a series of national meetings, Numsa members participate in drafting the demands as well as deciding strategy and possible strike action. By 1989, general secretary Moses Mayekiso could report to the union's congress that Numsa was now the majority union in the council and had succeeded in developing it into a powerful weapon of struggle.

Numsa's strategies forced many of the older, established unions on the council to 'adapt or die'. These unions faced pressure from their members to back Numsa's more militant approach. Where they refused, many of their members left to join Numsa. Where they agreed, Numsa's bargaining leverage has been strengthened.

Numsa's experience in the industrial council has been accompanied by a similar drive in the other sectors which it organises. In its auto

---

[*] *NUM also negotiates in many other forums, particularly for workers on mines not affiliated to the Chamber or operations mining minerals other than gold and coal.*

manufacturing sector, union members staged work stoppages and demonstrations in an attempt to establish a centralised bargaining forum with the National Association of Automobile Manufacturers of SA (Naamsa). In 1989, following major stoppages, most car manufacturers acceded to this demand and the National Bargaining Forum for the auto industry was established. Numsa had already achieved success in the tyre manufacturing sector, managing to have the Eastern Cape industrial council agreement extended nationally to cover all plants except Dunlop.

One observer has correctly noted that 'where militant unions have entered industrial councils, or succeeded in establishing them, they have been able to tilt the balance of power in their favour.'[9] The Numsa experience is the most obvious example of this. But clothing workers, as we will see, also achieved impressive results, particularly in 1988 and 1989.

Different employer strategies

In mid-1988 Jan Hiemstra, a Barlow Rand labour specialist, predicted the demise of the industrial council system. It had survived 'the first post-Wiehahn decade', he said. 'I don't think it will see out the second decade.'[10] At the time his conclusions carried much weight. Attempts by his company, amongst others, to destroy centralised bargaining had met with some success, and were supported by a government equally determined to curb a strong national union movement.

From the mid-1980s onwards, employers and the state sought to avoid centralised bargaining, or reduce its impact, through collapsing industrial councils. In these cases, employers usually withdrew from the council, as in the printing industry, the hotel industry in the PWV area, and the less-successful attempts to undermine the metal industrial council.

The hand of Barlow Rand has invariably been visible in such moves. Barlow's subsidiaries in the metal industry withdrew from the industrial council and tried unsuccessfully to prevent the 1988 agreement being extended to its employees. Another Barlows subsidiary, Nampak, was the largest member of the SA Printing and Allied Industries Federation (Sapaif). When, in 1989, Ppwawu applied to join the printing industrial council (Nicprint), Nampak was instrumental in getting Sapaif to withdraw. This resulted in the dissolution of Nicprint, the oldest and most established industrial council in the country. A confidential employer document warned that once Ppwawu gained entrance to Nicprint, 'they will be able to force the employers to continue negotiating at national level.'

In a number of industries, including the grain milling and dairy sectors, employer organisations have de-registered. The effect has been to limit the unions' ability to push for centralised bargaining, since industrial councils require participation by both registered unions and registered employer bodies. In addition, it is legally impossible for a union to declare a centralised dispute with an unregistered employer organisation.

A further employer tactic has involved objections to the gazetting of agreements, and particularly extension of minimum wage provisions to employers not party to the industrial council. This has gone hand in hand with government refusal to gazette agreements, or at least portions it objected to – such as 1 May being a paid holiday.

Not all employers agreed with the Barlow's approach. Many favoured the restructuring of industrial councils and the development of a system with clearly-defined boundaries of centralised and plant-level bargaining. These employers felt that the trend towards centralised bargaining was irresistible, and therefore something to be agreed upon and structured.

By 1990 it was far from obvious that centralised bargaining had reached the end of the road. Jan Hiemstra's funeral oration had been premature. Cosatu regarded centralised bargaining as so important that it formed, as we shall see, one of the four core demands of its revived Living Wage Campaign. But before this could happen Cosatu had to fight off a challenge to its very existence – a new labour law.

Notes

1. Frank Meintjies and Mi Hlatshwayo, 'Comment', *Staffrider* 8(3/4), 1989.
2. Andrew Levy and Associates, *Annual report on labour relations in South Africa, 1987-88*, Johannesburg, 1988.
3. *Cosatu information bulletin*, October 1987.
4. Andrew Levy and Associates, *Annual report, 1987-1988*, 41.
5. LRS, 'Wage review of settlements in the second half of 1988', Cape Town, January 1989.
6. LRS statistics supplied to author.
7. Kate Jowell, 'Basement Bargains versus Central Deals – will industrial councils survive the 1990s?', *Indicator SA*, 7(1), Summer 1989.
8. Ebrahim Patel, 'The case for centralised bargaining', *South African Labour Bulletin*, 15(4), November 1990.
9. Marcus Toerien, 'The struggle for industrial councils', *South African Labour Bulletin*, 14(4), October 1989, 81.
10. Quoted in Jowell, 'Basement Bargains versus Central Deals', 82.

16

Restrictions and the new labour law

Acts of aggression

DRAFT changes to South Africa's basic labour law, the Labour Relations Act (LRA), were first published in September 1987. These proposals were far-reaching and had three dimensions. Firstly, they restricted the right to strike. Secondly, they attempted to reverse many of the union movement's concrete gains on issues such as job security. Thirdly, they aimed to cow the union movement into submission through the threat of punitive damages for strike action taken against employers.

The initiative to change existing labour law came from employers. This was confirmed by the architect of the 1979 LRA, Professor Nic Wiehahn.

> It was a direct result of pressure from the employers. Employers felt that strikes were costing them a lot of money and they wanted to be able to claim damages... They asserted a lot of pressure to have the law changed.[1]

Bokkie Botha, at the time speaking for the FCI, admitted that 'there are some employers who are concerned that wildcat strikes and that sort of thing are getting out of hand.' They 'would like to see the power of unions drastically curtailed.' Some employers 'feel that they've suffered, that some of their rights have been restricted... There is in fact a harder approach developing.'[2]

In a talk delivered in April 1988, NUM general secretary Cyril Ramaphosa confirmed that unionists had been surprised to find something 'strangely familiar' in the proposed amendments.

> They had almost all been demanded by various managements during recognition agreement negotiations: an end to sympathy strikes, no-strike clauses for the duration of an agreement, unions to be responsible for management losses during industrial action... It is clear that though the bill comes from the state, capital's opinion was extensively canvassed before compilation. It is then no surprise that business has greeted the bill, on the whole, with deafening silence. There can be no doubt that capital, as a whole, supports the bill.

Employer attitudes blended easily with those of the government and, in particular, the security forces. At a press briefing held in November 1987 the head of the security police, Lt-General Van der Merwe, claimed that 'legal radical organisations' such as UDF and Cosatu posed a far greater threat to security than the banned ANC or PAC. Police would pay 'close attention' to Cosatu, he warned. He was later supported by Law and Order Minister Adriaan Vlok, who said the security forces would continue to 'take out or remove revolutionary elements from society'[*] in order to establish security and normality.[3]

The enthusiasm of the security establishment for action against Cosatu was matched by unashamedly one-sided statements from the Minister of Manpower, Pietie du Plessis. 'Changes in labour legislation', he was reported as saying in mid-November, 'would bring irresponsible and militant unions to heel... It will be the most effective disciplinary action instituted against trade unions since Wiehahn.' The awarding of damages would have a disciplinary effect on the unions. It would 'hang like a sword over their heads,' said Du Plessis.[4]

This convergence in views of employers, the security forces and the normally more 'liberal' Department of Manpower was significant. The 1979 changes in the labour field were one of the few areas where the government could, with some justification, claim to have introduced genuine reforms. From the mid-1980s the government's overall 'reform' programme had been increasingly replaced by naked repression. The new labour bill, said one observer, was 'consistent with the overall shift

---

* Vlok's words were particularly ominous. In the argot of the security forces, 'take out' generally means 'kill', 'eliminate' or 'assassinate'. Vlok, at the time Minister of Law and Order under PW Botha, retains the position under FW de Klerk.

in state strategy from a policy of co-optive reform...to the policy of out-right repression.'[5] Employers apparently felt that there was no reason why they should be forced to accommodate unions, and strong unions at that, when in other spheres the ruling class could rely on repression.

During 1987 Cosatu members were the only workers to win wage increases above the rate of inflation, despite the effective banning of the Living Wage Campaign. All other groups of workers, both unionised and non-unionised, saw their real wages drop. A massive increase in strike action was associated with these Cosatu members' increases. According to one management consultant, Andrew Levy and Associates, a million hours of lost production was recorded in 1986, rising to a record nine million hours in 1987. The major strikes of 1987 – on the railways and mines, and at OK Bazaars – undoubtedly caused a hardening in management attitudes. So too did the repeated stayaway actions Cosatu called in response to state action. In addition, many employers were impressed that a mid-1987 legislative decree had managed to prevent a Numsa-led strike in the metal industry.

The state at the same time faced a deepening fiscal crisis. Its solution included a call for wage restraint. Growing mobilisation by state sector workers, including those in the post office and on the railways, threatened to block any wage freeze policy unless Cosatu's power could be curbed. The 1986 and 1987 experience showed that security action alone would not suffice. Cosatu's resilience came from its popularity amongst workers which, in turn, came from its ability to deliver the goods to its membership. Limitation of union power required not only repression but also legal restriction of union rights at the point of production. This meant Cosatu's ability to achieve economic gains would have to be rolled back.

Proposed changes to the LRA

The new labour law and Cosatu's struggle against it formed a major element of the federation's work over the next few years. Key proposals of the draft law, also known as the Labour Relations Amendment Bill (LRAB), placed severe restrictions on the right to strike. Sympathy strikes, 'on-off' intermittent strikes, as well as boycott actions were all to be outlawed.

The proposed changes allowed employers to claim damages from unions engaged in illegal industrial action. The onus would be on the union (defined as officials, office bearers and shop stewards) to prove its non-involvement. This would be difficult. A strike where shop stewards did not participate was unthinkable. Yet their participation could be taken as proof of their involvement in, or at least sanctioning of, the industrial action. Given that most strikes in South Africa take place illegally, the proposed changes would allow employers to claim damages with ease. The law went further. Strikes – even legal ones – labelled 'unfair' by the courts could result in damages claims.

The threat of damages, and the limitations on the right to strike, were to be reinforced by other provisions. The steps to be followed prior to a legal strike would be made more complicated, more time-consuming, and more bureaucratic. Workers attempting to follow legal procedures would find their path obstructed by a minefield of technicalities waiting to be challenged by company lawyers.

Finally, the powers of the industrial court would be reduced. A schedule of 'unfair labour practices' would, it was proposed, be included in the LRA. This was an attempt to reverse gains made by the progressive union movement during the previous few years. Retrenchments, for example, could be undertaken without consultation with the unions and without employers taking steps to avoid job loss. Employers would be able to retrench according to 'reasonable criteria' such as the 'ability, capacity, productivity and conduct' of the employee. This amounted to a license to weed out unwanted workers through retrenchment. It was an attempt to reverse the status quo, which required employers to retrench according to objective criteria such as 'last-in, first-out' (Lifo).

A number of other provisions also revealed the intentions behind the proposal. It would become an 'unfair labour practice' for a union to prevent an employer from bargaining with any other union. An outside observer might see nothing more than acceptance of trade union pluralism and tolerance in such a provision. But in context it was an attempt to protect minority and racist unions. For years the emergent non-racial union movement had struggled for employer recognition. Every possible obstacle was placed in its path, including the requirement that unions should first have the support of the majority of employees in a particular factory or company – the famous 50% plus one formula. The emerging unions accepted the challenge and the principle of majoritarianism became part of the South African labour scene. The story of the emergent labour movement in the 1970s and early 1980s is largely about how it achieved majority support despite the odds. The proposed changes to the LRA aimed to reverse the majoritarian principle now that the majority was black and pro-Cosatu.

For some time, the government had been suggesting that changes to the LRA were on the way. Cosatu was initially slow to respond. Other problems, such as mergers and the clampdown, absorbed its attention. It finally awoke to the enormity of the threat when the government published proposed amendments to the LRA in September 1987.

Exco, meeting on 10 October 1987, saw the proposals as 'a clear attack on Cosatu'. It referred the problem to the next meeting of the CEC, a larger and more representative body, and agreed to draft a pamphlet explaining the amendments and 'building a campaign to resist these attacks.' When the CEC met five weeks later it considered the proposals in detail, and resolved that shop stewards should request their managements to sign a standard letter to the Minister of Manpower. This would state Cosatu's objections to the amendments. Cosatu would also, it was agreed, 'mount a campaign (at home and abroad), to prevent this bill from being passed,' and meet national employer bodies to explain its position.

The letter campaign had limited success. Most major employer bodies initially welcomed the new bill. As Cosatu's campaign grew, employers avoided direct responses. The bill, some argued, had both positive and negative aspects. Others refused to reply and referred the unions to larger employer federations such as FCI and Assocom. But the letter campaign did begin the process of mobilising shop stewards and workers.

A willingness to fight

As workers began to understand the seriousness of the threat, they decided to stop the bill at all costs. Three unions – CWIU, Ppwawu and Numsa – took the lead. Thousands of stickers condemning the bill started appearing in Ppwawu-organised factories. Ppwawu members began demonstrating against the bill during their lunch-breaks. Numsa launched a pamphlet campaign informing its members of the dangers of the bill and calling on them to organise protest meetings. In early February 1988, 200 CWIU shop stewards in the Transvaal condemned the bill and prepared for action.

Cosatu's next CEC meeting, held in mid-February, endorsed a programme of weekly factory demonstrations. Further action would be decided on at a CEC meeting scheduled for March, once employer response to the letter campaign and government reaction to Cosatu's objections had been assessed. The CEC agreed that the LRAB should be completely rejected. Its few positive features were totally overshadowed by negative ones. Besides, Cosatu argued, it was wrong for labour legislation to be introduced without the support of the trade union movement. Employers had access to the vote and legislative power while most Cosatu members had no vote. In the circumstances, Cosatu would oppose the adoption of undemocratic labour legislation.

Cosatu's total rejection of the bill was 'not a wise tactic', commented FCI's Bokkie Botha. 'Do they honestly think it can be rejected at this stage?... It's not going to be scrapped. That's clear.'[6] Within Cosatu a few argued that expectations of stopping the bill were unrealistic. But even these pragmatists came to see the depth of worker opposition to the bill, and their determination to resist. 'People are clear about what the bill will do, what it will take away from us,' said one chemical worker. 'People remember what used to happen to us and is no longer happening. You never used to be able to refuse overtime, for example... We have a resolution which says that we will stop at nothing to protect our union.' It was a view spreading rapidly amongst the rank and file of Cosatu.

By March, the Tuesday lunchtime demonstrations were becoming widespread. In a number of areas, workers organised industrial area committees. In Industria, west of Johannesburg, for example, the industrial area committee organised joint demonstrations of all workers in the area, not only those belonging to Cosatu affiliates. Workers would stream into the streets at lunchtime, carrying placards and singing. Their slogans and banners attacked the labour bill and took up a variety of political issues. 'Workers unite against the labour bill', 'Save the Sharpeville Six', and 'Away with the bill – forward to socialism' were typical of the handmade placards. As the workers marched down the streets of their industrial area, they would be joined by others from different workplaces, including the single factory in the area organised by a Nactu affiliate.

These demonstrations were not always easy. On 29 March police with dogs broke up the march. Many workers were injured, while 21 from the Ppwawu-organised Steele Bros and the Fawu-organised United Tobacco were arrested. Most of the demonstrators escaped arrest by retreating into the factories. They were pursued and attacked by overzealous police. Workers defended themselves using staple-guns and other industrial equipment. Scared of potential damage to property, management prevailed on police to withdraw from the premises. The following week Industria workers were again demonstrating against the labour bill.

With the right to protest restricted, Cosatu members in many areas took to spreading the message on trains and buses. In these moving meetings workers could be politicised and told of the dangers of the LRAB. The effect was powerful and the state's ability to prevent these gatherings severely limited. Few police would be brave or foolhardy enough to attempt arrests in a crowded, moving third-class train carriage. Meetings could be adjourned each time the train pulled into a police-guarded station, only to resume again on departure. Organising on the trains became a common worker response to repressive laws and restrictions on meetings. This tactic served the labour bill campaign well.

Nactu's membership was involved in many of the meetings on the trains and the industrial area demonstrations. However Nactu leadership was, by March 1988, still pessimistic about the chances of a successful campaign against the bill. According to Piroshaw Camay and Pandelani Nefolovhodwe, Nactu believed that neither business nor government would reject a bill so obviously favouring their interests. Nactu's strategy, therefore, concentrated on amending existing recognition agreements to protect its relationship with management, and protect its structures from the anti-union provisions of the bill. Nactu also refused to make representations to the parliamentary sub-committee then considering the bill. To do so would mean 'co-operating with state structures.'[7]

Cosatu differed with Nactu. While its programme of demonstrations and mass education continued, it resolved also to make representations to the parliamentary sub-committee. It need not have bothered. Of Cosatu's 27 objections to the bill, 20 were rejected, four were partially agreed to, and three accepted by the sub-committee. All its major objections were rejected. The bill sent to parliament by the sub-committee was, in essence, the same as that rejected by Cosatu in October 1987. Those changes that had been made were welcomed by most employer bodies. Revisions were in accordance with management representations, acknowledged Seifsa. The bill was an advance, not an assault on trade unionism, claimed Assocom. 'It was balanced and would curb irresponsible behaviour that could harm both employers and workers.'[8]

The bill was even supported by the inappropriately-named Labour Party, a coloured political organisation occupying the separate coloured chamber of PW Botha's tricameral parliament. Technically the Labour Party had the power to block so contentious a bill, at least temporarily. Instead, Archie Poole, the Labour Party's Belhar MP, called it 'one of South Africa's best pieces of legislation.' Les Abraham, his colleague, said that 'only those who planned to use trade unions for purposes other than improving work conditions would be opposed to it.'[9]

Cosatu's strategy to oppose the bill included international pressure and discussion with employer bodies. The CEC meeting held in February 1988 decided to lodge a formal complaint with the International Labour Organisation (ILO) and call for international arbitration. The proposed labour law, Cosatu argued, was in breach of international standards and conventions. The ILO, a tripartite organisation of employers, governments and unions, was a respected international agency of the United Nations. It had the right to adjudicate such a dispute, but only if the government of the country concerned agreed to ILO jurisdiction. Cosatu had few illusions that the South African government would agree to this. But it wanted to internationalise the issue, and expose management claims that the proposed amendments were in line with international, and in particular 'Western', labour legislation. The ILO eventually accepted the complaint but the South African government used delaying tactics and effectively rejected ILO adjudication.

Meanwhile major employer organisations were facing pressure from workers to oppose the bill. Most had openly supported it. Only a few bodies, such as the American Chamber of Commerce (Amcham) and its West German counterpart, opposed the bill. Amcham declared that while it agreed with some aspects of the bill, it was unnecessary to make further changes to the labour law. Their opposition was largely pragmatic. At the time many multinationals were facing intense pressure from the international sanctions lobby to disinvest from South Africa totally, and the 1979 labour law was one of the few instances of reform they could use to justify continued investment.

On 15 February, the major employer bodies met under the auspices of Saccola, the South African Consultative Committee on Labour Affairs.* Participants in the meeting included Assocom, FCI, Seifsa, the Chamber of Mines, AHI, the Building Industries Federation of South Africa (Bifsa), Automobile Manufacturers Association, Motor Industries Federation, and the SA Federation of Civil Engineering Contractors. The Saccola meeting focused on two issues: how employers should respond to the Cosatu call for them to oppose the bill; and whether to meet with the unions to see if common ground on the bill could be found. FCI and Seifsa had already publicly expressed a willingness to meet Cosatu, while Assocom had said such a meeting would be 'premature'.

Employer organisations and Cosatu eventually met for the first time on 2 March 1988. A large Cosatu delegation, numbering some 25, met about 15 employer representatives. Most, but not all, Saccola members were present. The venue was the main boardroom of the Anglo American Corporation. Staring down from the walls were oil paintings of the Oppenheimer clan and other captains of industry. The room exuded an air of power and established wealth. On the vast boardroom table were antique silver containers, with cigarettes and Cuban cigars! Tea was served by black men wearing colonial-style white coats and white gloves and whispering 'viva comrades' as they passed the union delegation their cups. It was a bizarre setting for the first-ever meeting between the captains of industry and the commissars of labour. The meeting was largely unproductive. The Cosatu delegates called on the employers to reject the labour bill. The employers refused.

* Saccola was originally formed in 1919. For many years it had acted as the representative of South African employers at the ILO. Its expulsion from the ILO in 1983 resulted in it becoming less active. With the dispute over the labour bill, Saccola took on an increasingly high profile, and co-ordinated employer negotiations with the union movement.

Cosatu restricted and UDF banned

While the campaign against the labour bill was gathering momentum, the state decided to strike again. On Wednesday 24 February 1988 the government effectively banned 17 organisations. This included the UDF, Cosatu's closest ally, and many of its major affiliates. The state also promulgated far-reaching restrictions against Cosatu, in effect declaring its 'political' activities illegal.

Organisations banned included the influential SA Youth Congress (Sayco); Sansco, an organisation of black students in tertiary education; the National Education Crisis Committee (NECC); and the Detainees Parents' Support Committee (DPSC), a grouping looking after the welfare of the many thousands of detainees. Also banned were organisations such as the End Conscription Campaign (ECC), and the black consciousness Azanian Peoples Organisation (Azapo). Most of these organisations had worked closely with Cosatu, and shared a common political perspective. Together with Cosatu, they constituted major components of the mass democratic movement, and their banning was something Cosatu would find impossible to ignore.

Cosatu, unlike the other organisations, was not banned outright. This was, ironically, one of the first indications that behind the strong-arm tactics lay a floundering government unable to respond creatively to pressure. The government was not strong enough to ban Cosatu outright, or, put another way, it realised that Cosatu was too strong to be destroyed by edict alone. Nevertheless, the restrictions on Cosatu – promulgated in terms of the virtually unlimited powers of the state of emergency – were far-reaching. Cosatu noted in response that

> the state is attempting to restrict Cosatu to what they see as legitimate trade union functions. We reject this because there is no democracy in South Africa, and Cosatu and other organisations are part of the extra-parliamentary opposition that are legitimately putting forward the demands and interests of our members both on the shopfloor and in the broader society.

Cosatu reasserted its right to be politically involved. 'The restrictions on Cosatu and the banning of UDF must not succeed,' said one young worker, herself a shop steward at a chemical factory in Germiston. 'The UDF is also workers. If they are pointing fingers at UDF they are also pointing fingers at us. If they touch UDF they also touch us.'

'By banning UDF, Sayco and other organisations', commented a furniture worker, 'it is the same as banning us, because we work hand in hand with these organisations... Restrictions will not stop people. We are going to operate, we are going to discuss, we are going to preach wherever we are.' These defiant attitudes were widespread. Increasingly, leadership and ordinary workers were not cowed by repressive measures. The virtually-unanimous consensus within Cosatu was to defy the restrictions.

This was reflected in Cosatu's carefully-worded official response. In listing what it was banned from doing, it restated all the federation's political concerns. The restrictions, Cosatu noted, would prevent it from calling for the unbanning of banned organisations; calling for the release of detainees; calling for the release of comrades in prison, such as Moses Mayekiso and his co-defendants; calling for the commuting of the death sentence, including impending executions of three NUM members and one Ccawusa member; opposing local authorities or boycotting municipal elections; commemorating days of mourning such as 16 June or Sharpeville Day; helping to develop democratic structures in the community in opposition to state structures; and supporting disinvestment and international sanctions.

A special CEC meeting was called to discuss the restrictions, and met on 24 February. It was resolved, but not minuted, that Cosatu would ignore the restrictions placed upon it. The federation would not act foolishly, but it would also not feel constrained in what it would discuss or campaign for. It was also agreed that individual affiliates would take over certain key campaigns on behalf of the federation. Thus Numsa would run the campaign for the release of Moses Mayekiso and his co-defendants, the Alex Five.

Most importantly it was agreed that the attacks on Cosatu were so severe that they justified the calling of a special national congress to discuss the restrictions and bannings, as well as the new labour bill. Cosatu would invite representatives of 'the community' to attend the special congress and participate in the discussions. This was, in effect, an invitation to the UDF and its banned affiliates. The CEC warned that if the state made any attempt to ban the special congress it would call on its members to embark on three days of 'national protest'. Some CEC delegates were clearly unhappy at the decision to be so defiant, apparently feeling it was unwise to provoke the state. However, their views were not expressed clearly. The spirit of defiance ran deep and they were reluctant to risk being labelled as fainthearted.

The federation's energies were immediately thrown into preparations for the congress. Cosatu's allies, UDF affiliates in particular, were consulted. Debate was initiated on how to advance the struggle and defend against state attack. There was consensus that the congress should make a broad political assessment of the situation, not simply respond to restrictions and the proposed labour law.

Cosatu was at the crossroads. It faced attack in both the political and trade union spheres. Deep political differences within the federation, expressed at the second national congress, had not been healed. The mass strike wave of 1987 had receded significantly during the first months of 1988. All sections of the ruling class, even previously 'liberal' businessmen, seemed to be rallying around the government and its repressive policies.

Taken together with the new labour bill, the restrictions made Cosatu determined to fight back. This was the opposite effect intended by the state. When a man faces execution, remarked Samuel Johnson two centuries ago, it concentrates the mind wonderfully. In the face of impending doom, differences were put aside. Cosatu's affiliates rallied to its defence. A shop steward addressing a CWIU local meeting in Germiston expressed the situation graphically:

> When the government introduced the state of emergency it did not explain the emergency thoroughly. Now, with the labour bill and the restrictions it is trying to explain thoroughly to the workers what the state of emergency is.

State actions

The restrictions also sent a message to the security forces, and repressive actions against the unions intensified during March. Smear pamphlets began to appear widely. On 23 March pamphlets condemning Cosatu militancy, and calling for acceptance of the new labour bill, were issued in Numsa's name and widely distributed on the East Rand.

During 1988 and 1989 fake pamphlets appeared in large numbers. They were clearly the work of a well-funded propaganda unit, with access to basic information from within the union movement. On occasions the same pamphlet would appear simultaneously in different parts of the country, itself an indication of the extent of the operation. The producers of these pamphlets have never been publicly exposed. However, a similar case of fake pamphlets against the End Conscription Campaign was revealed as the work of military intelligence.

The fake union pamphlets were of four kinds. There were those purporting to be the views of ordinary workers opposed to strikes, Cosatu militancy, or attacking the leadership of a particular union. These were often produced in a rough style, using typewritten or handwritten stencils, presumably to give them an air of authenticity. 'It is clear to us', stated one distributed in Cape Town, 'that the Labour Bill will protect us against Cosatu and the unions not to misuse us workers.'

Then there were pamphlets issued in the name of political organisations or factions, aimed at causing friction within trade union and broader liberation circles. Cosatu's leadership was stealing money, claimed one pamphlet allegedly issued by the 'Internal Wing of the Marxist Workers Tendency of the ANC'. The working class should 'unite and fight these Charterists and Populist elements in our ranks... They are enemies of the working class, let us get rid of them at the first possible occasion.'

'We want to be free from oppression and exploitation – especially Charterist exploitation,' proclaimed another, issued by the non-existent 'Cosatu Workerists Committee of SA (Natal Region)'.

Thirdly, there were those designed to look like Cosatu publications, but containing disinformation. A typical example was a fake copy of *Cosatu News* which, amongst other things, called on workers to counter the 'lies and propaganda' contained in fake pamphlets. 'Don't give any information about Cosatu to any worker who is not a union official,' was one solution offered.

Fourthly, there were publications aimed at causing suspicion within the unions. The most common of these was *Trade Union Titbits*, a gossip sheet which cleverly used half-truths to sow mistrust and suspicion. It relied heavily on access to information available only by tapping the union movement's telephone and telex lines.

These publications were clearly the work of one or another section of the police or military, and hence financed by taxpayers' money. Their impact was, however, limited. Workers grew to mistrust publications distributed anonymously and found lying in large numbers at bus stops in industrial areas. Cosatu and its affiliates warned membership not to accept any pamphlets received anonymously. All official Cosatu publications would be distributed through union structures such as the shop stewards or branch and regional offices.

During 1990 there was a decline in the number of these fake pamphlets. By 1991, however, *Titbits* was back on the streets.

All around the country security police raided union offices, confiscating posters and stickers – including those opposing the new labour bill. Press regulations required that the newspapers obtain comment from the police before publishing reports on these raids. Standard police response was that they 'cannot comment on routine police duties (such as visiting of premises, confiscation of property, etc), and consequently we are not prepared to make inquiries in this regard.'[10]

The three incidents described below were not unusual, but revealed something of the nature of repression at that time. On 20 March 1988 Cosatu's Highveld regional secretary, 'JJ' Mabena, and ten other Cosatu members were returning from a union meeting. They were stopped on the road, accused of robbery and assault and taken to Hendrina police station. There they were arrested and spent three nights in jail before Cosatu's lawyers managed to get them out on bail. 'We cannot understand why Cosatu should consider this worthy of mention,' was the police response to inquiries. 'After all, nobody is above the law and assault/robbery are criminal offences.' The police response appeared reasonable. But all who knew Mabena realised the charges were without foundation. The case was nothing more than wrongful arrest and legalised harassment. Indeed, Mabena and his colleagues were all acquitted and later won a civil claim for damages against the police.[11]

Police raided a meeting of Cosatu's Grahamstown shop stewards council on 16 March. All present, that is the entire worker leadership in this small Eastern Cape town, were simply detained in a police armoured car. Most were released in the middle of the night but four shop stewards from Fawu, Numsa, TGWU and Nehawu remained in detention. The incident can only have been intended to dissuade workers from attending local meetings.

Another example of harassment showed the problems of organising in the rural areas. Lawrence Mooi was a Ppwawu official organising forestry and sawmill workers. One Sunday he went out into the forests around Barberton in the Eastern Transvaal. He was wearing a pair of orange trousers and a torn yellow jersey. His meeting with the workers continued later than usual, and it was already dark by the time he departed. As he left the workers' hostel he noticed a troop carrier and two police vans cruising slowly down the road. He ducked out of sight and only continued once the vehicles had passed. A young boy approached him. 'The soldiers are looking for you,' he was told. 'They are looking for someone in an orange trouser and a yellow v-neck. They say you are a member of the ANC.' Mooi pleaded with a middle-aged woman for help. She eventually gave him a pair of old trousers but refused to take his orange ones. Luckily for Mooi there was no water-borne sewerage in the township, and Sunday was the day when all the buckets had been put out for collection. His orange trousers soon found their way into a sewage bucket, and it was only then that Mooi could catch a bus home. The price of failure would have been high, particularly in the Eastern Transvaal. Arrests and assaults were frequently reported by union organisers and workers. Union offices in the area were destroyed in arson attacks on more than one occasion, and police were known to hunt for organisers as soon as they heard reports of them recruiting in a rural area.[12]

Despite – or perhaps because of – intensifying repression, worker response to Sharpeville Day was far more militant than expected. Despite minimal preparations by the unions, and no calls for action, significant numbers of workers stayed away from work on 21 March.

The stayaway strengthened the hand of those calling on Cosatu to advance to greater levels of resistance. But it did little to convince those who argued that mass action without proper organisation or direction would condemn the union movement to defeat.

Assessing strengths and weaknesses

Throughout Cosatu there was debate over the appropriate response to the labour bill and restrictions. 'We must defend and advance at the same time,' was the view of one Germiston CWIU shop steward. 'If you only defend you get pushed into a corner and you won't be able to move out.'

Traditionally, the most common weapon used was the stayaway. But within union ranks there was long-standing dissatisfaction with this strategy. The major criticism was that it was too passive. 'Staying at home and doing nothing – people just sitting in the townships drinking beer, or watching TV. They are not gaining anything from that,' was the view of one shop steward committee in Johannesburg. 'There is no action involved,' they continued. 'Then after the stayaway we go back to work and nothing has changed. The state is used to the stayaway.' The solution proposed by these workers was for everyone to go to work, but not commence production. Instead, workers would demonstrate in the streets in every industrial area, and students and youth would conduct similar demonstrations in the townships. The argument was that this would involve everybody. 'People would really be taking part in the struggle.' This involved extending the militancy of the Industria workers countrywide, and developing similar programmes for non-workers in the townships.

It was an imaginative plan but one which over-estimated the organisational strength of Cosatu in most areas. In addition, general strikes in South Africa have historically taken the form of stayaways.

Another criticism of the stayaway strategy was that it was too easy to enforce. Ideally a stayaway should be the culmination of mass political activity explaining the aims and purpose of the action. However, the temptation to take short-cuts, especially in the face of repression, was often difficult to resist. In some cases stayaways occurred largely through the blockading of transport routes from the townships. In other cases people were instructed, rather than persuaded, to stay at home. This, naturally, created tensions within townships, and provided fertile terrain for state encouragement of divisions.

'We need to think creatively and innovatively about different responses,' argued one unionist. He conceded that other forms of industrial action could create difficulties 'for incorporating and involving non-trade union organisations. But I believe there are a range of ways of incorporating such organisations in joint campaigns without always relying on a stayaway.'

Proponents of the stayaway strategy recognised many of its weaknesses. Nevertheless, they felt it was a form of action which could express a broad community response. 'Recent national stayaways', commented the UDF-oriented journal *Phambili*,

> have actively drawn in wider and wider layers of the community, extending well beyond the unionised workforce. Millions of non-unionised workers, unemployed, students, and the middle strata (traders, taxi drivers, professionals, church ministers etc) have mobilised in support of the stayaway actions.[13]

'Other forms of industrial action are okay for organised workers,' argued another unionist, 'but what about other sectors and unorganised workers – should they just go to work as usual?' This acknowledged that organised workers were a minority of the working population. And the failure of Cosatu's 14 July action, called in 1986 in response to the state of emergency, had left many wary of narrowly union-based calls.

At core, this debate reflected different perceptions of the strength and weaknesses of the union movement and the democratic movement as a whole. Cosatu's national leadership insisted that decisions should be based on accurate and honest assessments of the strengths and weaknesses of all sectors of the democratic movement. To this end it circulated a discussion paper to all structures of the federation. The paper was revised after discussion and, in its final form, constituted the major input at Cosatu's special congress in May.

As the congress drew nearer, debates intensified. Was the union movement advancing or retreating? Was it wise to confront the state? It soon became clear that the special congress would be a make-or-break affair.

Notes

1. Interview with Professor Nic Wiehahn, *South African Labour Bulletin*, 14(5), November 1989, 59-60.
2. Interview with Bokkie Botha, 'You cannot operate in an unrest situation...', *South African Labour Bulletin*, 13(3), March/April 1988. In this interview, Botha was not necessarily expressing his own views, but reflecting what most businessmen were thinking at the time.
3. Quoted in Karl von Holdt, 'The battle against the Bill', *South African Labour Bulletin*, 13(2), February 1988, 7.
4. *Business Day*, 15.09.87 and 16.11.87; *Star*, 12.08.87 and 17.12.87.

5. Karl von Holdt, 'The battle against the Bill', 7.
6. Interview with Bokkie Botha, 'You cannot operate in an unrest situation...', 27.
7. 'Nactu fights the Bill with recognition agreements', *South African Labour Bulletin*, 13(3), March/April 1988, 22-3.
8. *Business Day*, 20.05.88.
9. *Weekly Mail*, 23.05.88.
10. *Financial Mail*, 07.04.88.
11. Author interview, 'JJ' Mabena, Johannesburg, 31 January 1991.
12. *Weekly Mail*, 30.03.88.
13. *Phambili*, special supplement, October 1988, 20.

17
Cosatu's special congress

'A barometer and a compass'

T HE special 1988 Cosatu congress was called to consider the banning and restrictions of organisations and develop a response to the new labour bill. Delegates to the congress were expected to analyse the overall situation, and assess the strengths and weaknesses of the democratic movement. All affiliates would then report on steps taken to resist the labour bill and the political clampdown.

The special congress undoubtedly marked a turning point for Cosatu. The questions the federation faced were central to its development and existence: how should it respond to the attacks on the unions and the whole democratic movement? Did it have the muscle to match its defiant words? Could it sustain factory-floor organisation while simultaneously devoting so much energy to political questions? Could it overcome its own political differences which marred the second congress?

There were also differences over tactical questions within Cosatu. The federation needed to decide whether the tactics of survivalism and retreat were more appropriate than those of advance and challenge. Mistaken approaches at this time could result in the destruction of Cosatu itself.

A range of factors – both internal to Cosatu and beyond its structures – had to be considered. The state had implemented a policy of intense repression against the democratic movement, while hardline employers were increasingly allied with the government. Organisationally the democratic movement was severely weakened. And there were political weaknesses and differences within Cosatu, combined with a growing rank-and-file militancy and preparedness to act.

The congress had to assess and analyse the overall situation. It had to develop a strategic response, not only for Cosatu, but for the entire democratic movement. Apart from the 1 324 union delegates present, some 120 delegates from UDF affiliates, sports organisations and churches attended the congress and were granted full speaking rights.

The congress was underway by mid-morning of Saturday 14 May. The venue, as with the second congress, was the Flower Hall of the University of the Witwatersrand. The police, to the surprise of many, did not ban the meeting. They did, however, monitor it closely and contingents of police were posted around the perimeter of the venue.

'Comrades', said Barayi in his opening address, 'we are dealing with a regime whose main preoccupation at the moment is to find a way out of the crisis it is in. All its actions – be it repression or even so-called reform – are calculated to perpetuate its infamous rule over us.'

The regime had lost direction, said Barayi. Its repressive activities were a sign of fundamental weakness. While 'the regime's erstwhile supporters' were losing confidence, the people had the possibility of victory. 'The mood of the people must at once act as a barometer and a compass.' By retreating Cosatu would 'be giving the enemy the space he so desperately needs.' The biggest weakness of the state, added the secretariat report, 'remains that it hopes to win the support of the people by attacking them.' Most delegates expressed similar views. 'There is no government. We are governed by security councils, soldiers and martial law,' argued one speaker from Numsa. Many insisted that the democratic movement was still strong. 'The people's will to resist is unquestionable,' said a delegate from NUM.

A number of delegates also noted the emergence of divisions 'in the camp of the oppressor.' For some, this necessitated intensified resistance. For others, it meant trying to pull disaffected elements towards the democratic movement. Yet others emphasised Cosatu's own weaknesses. Organisation was not strong enough, stressed a CWIU delegate. A speaker from 'the community', (in fact from the UDF), stressed that organisation was built through struggle. 'If we are not going to act against PW Botha, we cannot build organisation.' The speaker acknowledged the state's militarily strength. 'But we are campaigning on the political terrain, where the state is weak. The state's weakness on this terrain is our strength.'

There was broad consensus that the survival of the democratic movement required decisive action. Retreat would simply invite further attacks by the state. The democratic movement was not dead. The 21 March stayaway, organised without union participation, was a small indication of that. And yet organisation, in terms of structures and discipline, had been badly damaged. Weaknesses in the democratic movement, recorded the official congress minutes, include 'division, weak or non-functioning structures and a lack of self-sufficiency.' The movement remained strong although the organisation was weak.

Even Actwusa, the only dissenting union, argued for caution rather than retreat. 'To retreat now', commented Cosatu's vice-president Chris Dlamini after the congress, 'is not going to mean that the Department of Manpower will withdraw the bill, or that the Minister will lift the restrictions. In fact retreat will make it worse.'[1] However, consensus on the need for action did not involve unity over the form action should take.

Broad front or united front?

Three resolutions were placed before the congress. A joint Numsa/CWIU resolution called for a tightly structured broad front. This would include 'all working-class organisations' as well as 'organisations of the oppressed and exploited masses...working actively and unreservedly for the immediate end of apartheid.'

An alternate resolution, tabled by NUM, called for a united front to be formed bringing together Cosatu and 'tried and tested mass-based organisations' with compatible political programmes. These would come together in a conference to work out a programme of action which would 'unify the broadest possible section of the South African population.' A third resolution, proposed by TGWU, called for Cosatu to convene a conference against repression. This would include all anti-apartheid organisations, including those centred around liberal whites.

The TGWU resolution was essentially a short-term proposal envisaging a unifying conference rather than a structured front. The other two resolutions proposed the building of longer-term alliances. Numsa (and CWIU) suggested an ideologically broader front, but narrower in class terms. For example Nactu, the rival union federation, would be included because it was a working-class organisation. Numsa also envisaged the inclusion of both UDF and Azapo in a broad front, although this was not made clear at the congress. The crucial issue for Numsa was to bring together organisations of the oppressed and exploited, regardless of ideology. But this did not extend to Uwusa which, argued Numsa delegates, was a creation of Inkatha and not workers.

The NUM resolution proposed a united front incorporating all those opposed to apartheid. This would be a multi-class alliance including liberal white organisations such as the Black Sash and Five Freedoms Forum. At the core of this front, and its leading force, would be the major organisations subscribing to the Freedom Charter – in practice, Cosatu and major UDF affiliates. Cosatu's Chris Dlamini later explained that NUM opposed Numsa's proposal because it feared that it would not lead to any joint action. 'If you look at the history of some organisations, and the struggles waged by them, you find there is no significant struggle that has been waged. Action was never taken by them.' This was a widespread perception. Organisations like Nactu, Azapo and others in the Africanist and black consciousness traditions were seen as ineffective and unable to take action. The mass uprisings and mass mobilisation of 1984 to 1988 were seen, with some justification, as being largely the work of the ANC, Cosatu, UDF and their allies.

The debate over the relative merits of the 'broad front' and the 'united front' resolutions was heated.[*]

---

[*] *Much of the heat of the debate related to long-standing differences in analysing the South African revolution between, on the one hand the ANC and SACP, and on the other hand, a range of left-wing non-SACP socialists. The theoretical analyses of both groupings had often hardened into dogma. The differences were rarely made explicit at the congress. Nevertheless they simmered just below the surface of the debate, and resulted in many of the contributions being rigid and inflexible.*

The SACP was accused by its left-wing critics of adhering to a 'two-stage' theory of revolution. This implied, said the critics, that socialism was not its primary goal. Entry into alliances with 'bourgeois' elements would lead to betrayal of the socialist and working-class character of the revolution. These critics saw in every suggestion of meetings or co-operation with, for example, the Democratic Party, the Black Sash or Five Freedoms Forum, proof of a SACP policy of class collaboration and betrayal.

The SACP (and to a large extent the ANC) accused their critics of 'ulta-leftism'. Socialism would never be achieved, they argued, by isolating the working class. The best guarantee for socialism would be working class leadership within the national-democratic struggle. There was no short-cut to socialism. Racism, national oppression and an undemocratic state were the main issue and the primary grievance of the mass of the people. The South African revolution was national-democratic in character. This implied, they argued, joining forces with all anti-apartheid elements, whether or not these supported a socialist vision of the future.

In more recent years, the dogmatism of both outlooks has declined significantly.

It was, in many respects, a re-run of the political policy debate at Cosatu's 1987 second congress. But there were three crucial differences.

Firstly, state and employer attacks had become so intense that a compromise had to be found.

Secondly, the differences were more practical, and therefore more capable of practical solutions.

Thirdly, there were substantial areas of common ground between the contending positions. NUM conceded that it had no in-principle objection to working with black consciousness and other non-Congress organisations. Numsa and its supporters had to admit that many of its proposed allies, such as Azapo and UDF, were themselves multi-class organisations. The real problem for Numsa appeared to be the liberal bourgeoisie, which it believed would hijack any united front.

In the end a compromise resolution was brokered by TGWU, Ppwawu and Ccawusa. Cosatu's CEC, together with its allies 'as defined in the political policy resolution' would set up a joint committee to look into developing 'a programme of action and organisation against repression.' It would then call a conference of 'a broad range of anti-apartheid organisations' to 'further deliberate on the above issues.' The compromise resolution acknowledged that Cosatu and its allies – the UDF, Sayco and others in the non-racial democratic tradition – would form the organising core of an anti-apartheid conference. Since Cosatu and its allies shared the same strategic perspectives, they should plan such a conference jointly.

The resolution also accommodated Numsa's belief that any conference should incorporate anti-apartheid forces outside of the Freedom Charter tradition. There was an implicit recognition that Cosatu would have to develop closer relations with Nactu in particular.

The compromise resolution was accepted by all delegates. It still left open the question of exactly who would, and who would not, be invited to the proposed anti-apartheid conference. This would be a source of debate in the months to come. Nevertheless, Numsa's argument for an ideologically broader conference was accepted. The resolution also laid the groundwork for closer co-operation with Nactu, particularly in the fight against the new labour law.

The drop in membership

At the conference, it emerged that the total paid-up membership of affiliates had dropped three percent in the ten months since Cosatu's second congress in July 1987 (see table).

Cosatu's membership by union, 1987-1988.

Union	July 1987	May 1988
Actwusa	30 538	68 507
Cawu	26 291	18 176
Ccawusa	56 000	42 221
CWIU	29 859	32 739
Fawu	65 278	65 803
Nehawu	9 197	5 876
NUM	261 901	207 941
Numsa	130 796	156 519
Ppwawu	23 310	25 046
Samwu	16 967	14 892
Sadwu	9 402	8 700
Sarhwu	34 411	23 685
TGWU	18 281	21 046
Total	712 231	691 151

This decrease was cause for concern. However, for a number of unions the drop in membership can be traced to a stricter application of the rules by the credentials committee rather than a significant decline in strength. The figures of Sarhwu, Samwu, Nehawu and Cawu declined most noticeably because of this. The decline in membership of Ccawusa related directly to the split within that union. The 1987 figures embraced the combined membership of both wings of Ccawusa, while the 1988 figures referred to the Kganare wing of Ccawusa, at the time the only faction recognised by Cosatu. NUM's loss of some 54 000 members was directly related to the mass dismissals of miners, primarily by Anglo American, during the 1987 mine strike.

In the case of TGWU, Ppwawu and CWIU, the figures reflected a continuation of steady growth underway since the mid-1980s. Numsa's growth was more dramatic, largely the result of 'take-off' of this new 'super-union', as well as an effective and well-organised wage campaign in the metal industry. In the textile sector membership had more than doubled. Following the 1987 congress, NUTW had merged with two non-Cosatu unions in the industry, and had launched Actwusa. The growth of membership in the sector was, almost entirely, the result of this process. The figures did reveal, at the very least, a slowdown in Cosatu's rate of growth. They also showed that NUM had not recovered from its 1987 setback, and the rapidly-growing metal union was challenging NUM's position as Cosatu's largest affiliate.

Cosatu's rapid growth during 1986 and 1987 had been largely the result of it being well placed to ride the wave of popular insurrection and worker militancy. Henceforth, Cosatu and its affiliates would not grow automatically. Planning, coherent policies and growth strategies would become increasingly important.

Peaceful national protest

The special congress resolved to reject the restrictions placed on Cosatu and other organisations, and reaffirmed Cosatu's 'commitment to carrying out our policies and resolutions to the full.' The wording was cautious, but the message clear. Nearly every delegate stressed the need to defy illegitimate restrictions. The spirit of defiance was gaining ground both among activists and ordinary people countrywide.

The delegates debated at length over how to express their opposition to the attacks. There was wide consensus that a call for a stayaway should be made. Only Actwusa delegates, arguing that it was 'unrealistic', indicated their opposition to any stayaway call. Other union delegations differed over whether a two-day or three-day stayaway was appropriate, and whether or not to coincide the call with 16 June. Some voices of concern were raised that Cosatu's actions needed to go beyond stayaway calls. While not opposing a stayaway, these speakers stressed, they felt there was a need to avoid one-off actions and develop ongoing fighting tactics.

With time running out, the chair decided to put the matter to the vote. The majority voted to call for three days of action on 6, 7 and 8 June 1988. In an attempt to sidestep the restrictions on Cosatu, the resolution made no mention of the word 'stayaway'. Rather, it was resolved 'to put aside three days' to enable 'all freedom-loving people' to get together and discuss ways of opposing the bannings and restrictions and demonstrate 'our rejection of the results of 40 years of Nationalist rule.' Cosatu later publicised the call as a three-day 'national peaceful protest', and insisted – for its legal protection – that it would be up to each 'community' to decide on the form action should take.

However, all union and 'community' delegates to the special congress understood the decision clearly. They left the congress and returned to all corners of the country to spread the call for a three-day stayaway. They also took home another decision. Workers should intensify their weekly factory floor protests against the labour bill, and take steps to ensure that recognition agreements between unions and employers superseded the proposed amendments to the law.

The call for a three-day stayaway was greeted with shock, even by observers sympathetic to Cosatu. Cosatu was being too ambitious, it was suggested. It had set itself 'a formidable task', argued a *Weekly Mail* columnist, adding that no successful stayaway of that length had ever been called in South Africa. Almost all affiliates began to work hard to make the event a success, helped by youth and community activists. 'We used to have one-day stayaways,' explained one active unionist.

> Before November 1984 people were very sceptical about a two-day stayaway. But theory has to be tried and tested. The November stayaway was successful. Now we are talking about a three-day protest. To see whether it will be successful it must be tested in the field. Because of the repression the language is different. It is a protest, not a stayaway.

The message was spread mostly by word of mouth. One of the few pamphlets distributed, presumably issued anonymously by UDF, proclaimed :

> Azikwelwa! Stay Away! The Boers have banned our organisation, the United Democratic Front (UDF)... They have restricted our mighty federation, Cosatu, and now they want to use the labour bill to crush our trade unions... At this very moment, they are planning to impose a third year of the hated state of emergency.

Another pamphlet warned employers:

> To the bosses we say: You are making a serious mistake by siding with the Boers on these issues. You are wasting your time attacking Cosatu... By threatening Cosatu, you are challenging the entire oppressed community to treat you as the enemy.

In the aftermath of the special congress, weekly protests on the factory floor increased. One union local alone reported that it had drawn 9 000 workers from 33 factories into weekly protests.[2] Stickers and posters proliferated as the stayaway call gathered momentum.

In the week after Cosatu's congress a gathering of Nactu shop stewards resolved to call for a five-day stayaway, from 6 to 10 June, in protest against the labour bill. Following a meeting with Cosatu, Nactu agreed to back the three-day call. It was a first, tentative and cautious meeting between the leadership of the two federations.

Chief Buthelezi and his Inkatha movement opposed the call for action.[*] So too did police and employers. On 24 May over 100 police surrounded a meeting of Cosatu's Port Elizabeth local. After photographing and taking details from all shop stewards and organisers present, a senior security policeman addressed the meeting. No

---

* This opposition was indicative of the deep rift between Inkatha and the broad democratic movement, which has long charged that Inkatha never called for or supported action against the state. (continued on page 285)

discussions on the special congress decisions were permissible, he announced. Delegates could discuss trade union affairs, but nothing else. On 25 May, scores of police raided Cosatu's Germiston offices in the World Centre Building. The five-hour raid was aimed at Cosatu's Witwatersrand regional office as well as the offices of seven affiliates. Two days later, on 27 May, police sealed off and prevented access to a hall in Pretoria. The hall had been booked for a union training session, but police thought a meeting linked to the special congress would be held.

Days before the stayaway was due to begin, employers launched their own offensive. A number of employers obtained legal interdicts preventing unions from calling for stayaway action. Such calls were illegal, they argued. Employers and the state threatened dire action against workers who stayed away from work. Employers said they intended to discipline absent workers, who could face dismissal. These threats were widely publicised on television and radio, and in the press. They were reinforced by government spokesmen who announced that workers would have only themselves to blame if they lost their jobs.

On the evening of 2 June, Saccola representatives invited Cosatu's leadership to meet them. It was the first formal meeting between the two organisations. The employers asked Cosatu to call off its plans and consider alternative methods of protesting the LRAB. Cosatu, anxious to avoid prosecution, stressed that it had not prescribed what form the 'national peaceful protest' should take, and could thus not call off the action. Instead it challenged employers to avoid calling in security forces, and not victimise workers nor engage in mass dismissals. The employers rejected this challenge. In retrospect the meeting seems to have been aimed at discrediting Cosatu's leadership. Employers could now argue that they had tried, unsuccessfully, to make Cosatu see reason. Workers should not blame employers for harsh actions if they stayed away. As Cosatu delegates departed, they found the press and television waiting outside the meeting room.

Cosatu's Jay Naidoo termed the meeting a 'publicity stunt'. The morning after the meeting, adverts placed by Saccola appeared in newspapers countrywide. Cosatu's allegations that the LRAB was 'repressive and directed at attacking trade unions' was without foundation, the

---

(continued from page 284) Inkatha has often justified its opposition to these sorts of actions by stating that its leaders were not consulted before the call was made. Yet Inkatha has never launched or proposed its own mass actions against the state. This lends weight to the view in the mass democratic movement that Inkatha's primary role appears to be to oppose the ANC, Cosatu, UDF and other ANC-oriented organisations. Even verbally, the democratic movement has found Inkatha and Buthelezi's vitriol against the mass democratic movement is more vicious than that directed against the apartheid regime.

advert declared. 'The revised version of the bill', Saccola falsely claimed, 'deals with most of the objections raised by Cosatu.' That evening Saccola's Bobby Godsell appeared in a lengthy interview on TV2, the state's Nguni-language TV channel. The unions did not have grounds for calling the protest, he argued. In a separate statement published on Saturday 4 June, the Chamber of Mines alleged that Cosatu

> was either unwilling or unable to back up its allegations that the bill was a repressive measure aimed at curbing trade union activity. This, coupled with Cosatu's refusal to call off the protest, suggests that its campaign against the bill is politically inspired.

Cosatu was simply using the bill 'as a rallying point to polarise the workforce and employers, to destabilise workplace relations and to engineer a confrontation with the state.'[3] This was a revealing comment, ignoring that the protest was as much against the restrictions as against the bill. It implied, as the government did, that union involvement in politics was illegitimate: as if one could oppose government laws and bannings without entering the realm of politics! The Chamber of Mines clearly assumed the protest was not the result of genuine grievances, but rather the work of agitators. It also implied that Cosatu, rather than the government, had engineered the impending confrontation with the state.

Internationally, Cosatu received considerable support for its protest call. Messages streamed in from trade unions worldwide. Many promised to exert pressure against employer retaliation. 'Every success in combatting the gross violations of workers' rights', said the Dutch union federation FNV in a typical message. A communication from the United Nations Special Committee Against Apartheid condemned management tactics which revealed 'that certain corporations – despite their occasional pronouncements against apartheid – remain collaborators with the regime.' A strong message of support came from the newly re-emerged Namibian trade unions. 'We stand united with our sisters and brothers in Cosatu; the workers of Southern Africa form one working class, united by the same interests.'

As 6 June approached all eyes were on Cosatu.

Notes

1. See *South African Labour Bulletin*, 13(4/5), June/July 1988, 20-53, which focuses on the special congress.
2. David Niddrie, 'It's testing time for Cosatu', *Work In Progress*, 54, June/July 1988.
3. *Star,* 04.06.88.

18

The June stayaway and beyond

Unity in action

*T*HE entire democratic movement nervously awaited the dawn of 6 June. It was not disappointed. Between two-and-a-half and three million people stayed away from work on that day. Support in some areas dropped on the second and third day – partly due to massive radio and television propaganda threatening workers with dismissal. While estimates of the numbers involved were approximations only, the action was indisputably the first national stayaway to last three days.[*]

Support for the stayaway was strongest on the Witwatersrand and in Natal. The Eastern Cape and Border also saw major actions, as did Pretoria. In the Western Cape support was limited. But workers in organised factories in rural areas such as the Eastern Transvaal stayed home. Statistics on participation in smaller towns were never gathered. Some participated, for the first time, in stayaway action. In others, for example Grahamstown, most workers decided that they were not strong enough to stay away. But they did organise lunchtime demonstrations calling for the labour bill to be scrapped, and restrictions on Cosatu to be lifted.

---

* There had been calls by the ANC and Sactu, in 1958 and in 1961, for three-day work boycotts. Similar calls were made by the Soweto Students Representative Council during 1976. However, none of these were very successful. The 1958 action, for example, was called off on the first day.

287

According to the Labour Monitoring Group, an average of between 70% and 80% of African workers in the manufacturing sector of the PWV region – South Africa's industrial heartland – participated in the action. However, support for the stayaway in the commercial, transport and public sectors in that region was substantially smaller, and overall participation by non-African workers was low.

LMG also found surprisingly high support for the action in Natal – again between 70% and 80%. This included significant participation by Indian workers, particularly in the clothing and textile industry, which was largely due to the support of the non-Cosatu Garment and Allied Workers Union (Gawu). Gawu was the result of a takeover of previously-conservative unions by workers and officials close to Cosatu thinking. However, in the Western Cape, Gawu failed to bring out its substantial membership. Most of the factories which participated in that region were strongly unionised and had an overwhelmingly African, rather than coloured, workforce.

The low level of participation by mineworkers was the major disappointment of the stayaway. The Chamber of Mines reported that 9 000 workers had stayed away on 6 June, and that participation had dropped further on the remaining two days. NUM claimed that 35 000 workers, including those employed on non-Chamber mines, had stayed away on Tuesday 7 June. Both figures indicated an extremely low level of support for the action. NUM had clearly not recovered from the 1987 strike.

Cosatu leadership was surprised at the high level of support for the stayaway. But it was employers and the state who were truly astonished. The action, said a *Weekly Mail* columnist, had 'dumbfounded' government and business leaders 'who before the protest appeared convinced the labour movement did not have the capacity to mount such an action.' Assocom reported that the action had resulted in losses of approximately R500-million.[1]

Mid-way through the protest Manpower Minister Du Plessis announced that his door was open to Cosatu and that he would consider suspending some of the clauses in the labour bill. This was an unusual comment from a National Party government minister, where the tradition had usually been to become more intransigent in the face of protest, or ignore it altogether.

Assessing the action

Cosatu's leadership was generally satisfied with the strength of the protest, which was assessed during Exco meetings held in June and at a CEC meeting held from 8-10 July. Non-participation of coloured workers in Port Elizabeth, and the poor support for the protest in the Western

Cape, were debated. NUM argued that support for the action on the gold mines was 'not as low as had been indicated.' NUM's participation, or lack of it, was 'also related to the weakness of Cosatu structures' in the Western Transvaal and OFS regions.

In many factories the mood was muted after the stayaway. 'A few factories are very militant and are talking about a week of protest action,' said one union official. 'But the majority are very cautious.' This mood of caution did not indicate defeat. 'An action like this takes a huge amount of energy. It seems that people need to pause and gather their strength before taking another step.' The overall effect in the metal industry was severe. Numsa, which had been threatening industrial action around the mid-year wage negotiations, was unable to contemplate such a move. It was impossible to launch another major action so soon after the stayaway.

Phambili, an underground publication linked to the banned UDF, argued that the stayaway was a 'successful demonstration of power by the democratic movement' and showed 'the high morale and unity of the masses.' The action had also deepened divisions in the ruling bloc, argued *Phambili*, and undermined the state's strategy of repression as the road to reform. It forced 'the state and capital to pay a price they could ill-afford.' But *Phambili* also noted weaknesses in the action. There was 'inadequate strategising between Cosatu and community organisations.' This enabled the media to narrow the focus of the action to the labour bill rather than the equally-important restriction and banning of organisations. 'As a result the political impact was not as powerful as it could have been.' The participation by coloured and Indian communities was 'on the whole, inadequate.' This required 'a creative approach' which accommodated the particular conditions and problems in these communities. Lack of propaganda such as pamphlets and graffiti was also identified as a weakness.

The stayaway revealed, argued the *Phambili* article, that 'our actual strength is far from our potential strength.' The democratic movement should always be sure to

> understand the mood of the masses... The militancy and political awareness of the people must not be confused with a preparedness to back any action, no matter how rash or ill-considered... We should be careful not to be overconfident and embark on campaigns which do not correspond to the mood of the people. We should remember that the pace of a column is not determined by the fittest and fastest soldier but by the slowest and weakest.[2]

The stayaway was not without casualties. While the magnitude of the action undoubtedly curbed aggressive employer responses, many still took a hard line. Thousands of workers were given final written warnings, many without standard disciplinary hearings. Workers whose previous records already contained final warnings were summarily dismissed. The unions attempted, with some success, to fight all these dismissals. Certain employers dismissed their entire black workforce for participating in the action. Nactu affiliates reported 1 600 members dismissed in this way, while Cosatu reported that seven companies had dismissed their entire workforce, resulting in almost 2 000 lost jobs. The brunt of these dismissals was borne by Ppwawu members in the Eastern Transvaal. Forestry and sawmill companies, incensed at the worker protest, fired almost a thousand workers.

A number of employers illegally locked out workers for the rest of the week, thus extending the stayaway to five days. Others cancelled recognition agreements and union check-off facilities, or refused union officials access to their members. Cosatu resolved to monitor all such actions and ensure that affiliates took adequate steps to reverse these attacks. This monitoring continued for a number of months, and was the first time Cosatu had been so active in following-up the consequences of a stayaway.

In the longer run the stayaway laid the basis for a deeper unity with Cosatu's allies, as well as a broader unity embracing Nactu and others. The special congress resolution calling for an anti-apartheid conference had opened the way for broader unity, commented Jay Naidoo shortly after the stayaway.

> But the protest action actually initiated this process by pulling in a diverse range of groupings. This illustrates the point that was made at the congress, that unity is forged in action, not around conference tables. The protest therefore laid the groundwork for the (anti-apartheid) conference.

As a result of the stayaway, Saccola asked Cosatu to reopen talks on the labour bill. Cosatu agreed, and decided to consult Nactu about the planned meetings.

A 'bitter experience'

On 9 June, the day after the stayaway ended, Saccola, the Director General of Manpower and Cosatu's lawyers met. They agreed that promulgation of the bill would be postponed until 1 September to 'allow a process of negotiation to take place that would impact on the bill.' A timetable was agreed whereby the parties would submit representations.

By 7 July, and according to schedule, Cosatu submitted its detailed objections to the bill to Saccola. These were endorsed by Nactu and the two federations agreed to join forces for the negotiations with Saccola.

Saccola's response was expected by 12 July but Cosatu only received it on 1 August 1988. This was a breach of the earlier agreement reached with the Department of Manpower. On 5 August Saccola met the Department of Manpower to explain the delay. Cosatu was then informed that an understanding had been reached, namely 'that Cosatu, Nactu and Saccola would jointly decide which clauses should not be promulgated.'[3] Cosatu accepted these delays in good faith. But time was running out. Only three weeks remained before the bill was due to become law.

On 11 August Cosatu, Nactu and Saccola met at Cosatu's head office and agreed on six 'offensive clauses' which should be suspended to allow time for further negotiations. These went to the heart of union objections to the bill, and dealt with consumer boycotts, solidarity strikes and intermittent (on-off) strikes being regarded as 'unfair labour practices'; special provisions allowing racially-based minority unions to register; a number of technical clauses making the declaration of disputes more complex and time-consuming; and, importantly, the clause allowing employers to sue unions for damages. The employers agreed that promulgation of these clauses should be delayed to allow time for further negotiations. Saccola's ranks were not entirely united, and the Chamber of Mines opposed any delay in promulgation of the damages clause.

The parties immediately communicated the details of their agreement to the Department of Manpower and agreed to meet the Department the following Monday to discuss the specifics of non-promulgation. However, to Cosatu's amazement, on 12 August a notice appeared in the government gazette announcing that from 1 September the new labour bill – to be known as the Labour Relations Amendment Act (LRAA) – would become law in its entirety. No clauses would be suspended.

It was a bitter experience for Cosatu. 'The Botha government's action sabotaged the negotiated agreement', said the September edition of *Cosatu News*.

Cosatu called on employers to honour their agreement with the unions. Saccola should ask employers to waive their right to the six 'offensive clauses'. Saccola refused. Cosatu members then approached individual employers asking them to undertake not to use the six clauses against the unions. Encouraged by Saccola's refusal, management attitudes hardened. Some employers told the unions to negotiate with Saccola. Others, including major industrial conglomerates, claimed to know nothing about Saccola's negotiations with the unions or any agreements made. Yet others asked for unions to suspend support for stayaway action or sanctions before they would consider suspending the six clauses. By November only two companies nationwide, both multinationals, had agreed in principle to give up certain rights which the LRAA granted them.

Saccola wanted talks to continue. But both Cosatu and Nactu felt betrayed and believed that neither government nor Saccola could be trusted. On 1 September the labour bill became law. It was a dark day for the union movement, the end of a chapter, and the end of the first phase of the campaign.

With the new labour law in place unionists discussed how best to adapt. Many favoured redrafting recognition agreements, effectively 'opting out' of the statutory industrial relations system. This unrealistic notion was a popular solution offered by labour lawyers, similar to the proposal made by Nactu in March 1988. 'Contracting out' was time consuming and likely to benefit only well-organised factories or employees of multinational corporations. It would increase the growing dualism between unionised and non-unionised workers.

Others proposed a programme of defiance. The law was simply another obstacle, 'just one of the many laws we are fighting... Management will have to negotiate with faceless people,' argued one Numsa organiser. Management would summon the union to deal with an illegal strike, he predicted. To avoid damages claims the union would deny all knowledge of the strike. 'It will make things very difficult for management. Maybe workers will just make a placard and stick their demands on the wall.' This threat to return to the 'faceless' days of the pre-Wiehahn era would, as we shall see, materialise later.

The anti-LRA campaign had failed in its primary objective, to stop promulgation of the new labour law. An assessment of Cosatu's campaign must, however, look beyond that failure. The campaign succeeded in placing the LRA on the agenda. It virtually guaranteed that there would be no further amendments to labour law without the approval of the union movement. It also succeeded in popularising the issue amongst the mass of working people. It did this in a way which heightened awareness of the undemocratic nature of lawmaking in South Africa, and improved understanding of labour law among ordinary workers. Even those who did not grasp the amendments in detail understood key elements (such as the damages clause), and what this meant for the union movement.

The campaign threw into question the whole of existing labour law, not simply the amendments. This was a major setback for the state. Industrial relations was one of the few areas where government reforms and state structures had previously enjoyed some legitimacy. The campaign forced workers to address not only the proposed changes, but also longstanding omissions. Why, many began to ask, did the labour law exclude farmworkers, domestic workers and state employees? Why did the labour movement have no say over the appointment of judges to the industrial court, the final arbitrator of labour disputes? Why did the LRA not guarantee the right to strike? The campaign increased ordinary workers' disrespect for labour law. Many workers became determined to defy interdicts and other rulings of both the industrial and supreme courts.

The anti-LRA campaign succeeded in strengthening Cosatu's alliance with the broader democratic movement. Both locally and internationally, it came to the defence of Cosatu. This had the important side-effect of legitimising Cosatu's defiance of the restrictions imposed on it in February.

The campaign against both the LRA and the restrictions strengthened Cosatu's own internal coherence. It involved concrete issues which could unite all affiliates. Ironically, measures aimed at curbing and weakening Cosatu provided one of the spurs to the growing internal unity within Cosatu's ranks.

However, the anti-LRA campaign revealed a number of organisational weaknesses. Not all unions put in equal effort with the result that worker actions, such as workplace demonstrations, were not always as strong as they could have been. The stayaway was organisationally exhausting, and it was difficult to continue demonstrations after the June action. Too much effort had been put into one major action (the stayaway) and not enough into an ongoing programme of action.

In addition, the campaign was directed almost entirely against employers. There was insufficient focus on the government which, after all, had finally pushed through promulgation of the new labour law. While Cosatu understood the need to combine talks with Saccola and pressure on employers, it did not have a similar strategy regarding the state. Even once talks on the proposed labour law materialised from June onwards, Cosatu refused to meet the Minister of Manpower directly. Exco overruled the office bearers' recommendation that Cosatu should meet the Minister, preferring instead to send Cosatu's lawyers to joint meetings with Saccola and the state.

At times during phase one of the anti-LRA campaign, negotiations became a substitute for mass action. 'From the outset', commented Cosatu's Frank Meintjies, 'employers saw the talks as an alternative to further industrial action in protest against the LRA.' It was wrong, agreed an extended Exco meeting in August 1988, 'for us to suspend our on-the-ground activities and rely almost entirely on the talks with Saccola.'

Geoff Schreiner, a Numsa official deeply involved in the campaign, has commented that following the June stayaway, 'discussions proceeded with Saccola in a way which weakened activity on the ground.' As a result, according to Schreiner, a number of lessons were learnt. Firstly, there was a real risk of central negotiations becoming too distant from the rank-and-file. Secondly, 'negotiations should be linked to ongoing mass action and should not be a substitute for action.' Thirdly, 'negotiations should never involve compromises unacceptable to the masses.' This implied that negotiating teams, on both sides, should be 'properly representative.'[4]

These hard-learned lessons, as we shall see, informed phase two of the anti-LRA campaign.

The anti-apartheid conference

Cosatu and its allies still had to implement the other decision of the special congress – to call a broad-based anti-apartheid conference (AAC). At the CEC meeting held from 8-10 July it was unanimously agreed that approximately 520 delegates should be invited to the conference. Numsa's proposal that organisations be invited according to sectors was approved, and the CEC recommended that the union sector should send 200 delegates, political organisations 108 delegates, student and youth structures 60, religious organisations 35, and so on.

Twelve sectors were identified, and allocations were made by analysing the known, active organisations in each sector. The widest possible ideological spectrum was included. It was agreed to invite Nactu, Cosatu, National Forum, New Unity Movement, Black Sash, Five Freedoms Forum (FFF) and UDF affiliates, among others.

The CEC proposed that the conference theme should be 'Unity and organisation against oppression – one person one vote.' The special congress had called for the AAC to be convened and arranged jointly by Cosatu and its allies (the UDF). Cosatu's Exco was empowered, therefore, to take the proposals to a joint meeting with the UDF's national executive which, although banned, continued to function as the co-ordinator of UDF affiliates.

Cosatu's Exco met the UDF's NEC on 5 August 1988. Cosatu's proposals on who should be invited were, by and large, accepted. A number of organisations were excluded as they were understood to be defunct. The joint meeting agreed to invite organisations aligned to both Africanist and black consciousness perspectives. It was also decided that rural organisations should be invited, including opposition parties operating within various homelands – the Seoposengwe Party from Bophuthatswana, the Transkei Democratic Party, and Enos Mabuza's Inyandza

movement. These organisations, although functioning within the homeland system, were politically close to the Congress tradition.

The joint Exco/NEC meeting established a small working committee
to approach organisations and begin practical arrangements. When details were reported to an extended Cosatu Exco meeting on 18 August,
some delegates expressed dissatisfaction. But the meeting felt that issues
previously agreed could not be reopened. Nevertheless CWIU wanted it
recorded that 'they were not happy with the list of organisations that are
going to attend the conference.' They also recommended that a person
from Nactu should be asked to become one of the members of the secretariat. Dissent also began emerging from vocal minorities within a
number of affiliates and regions. A replay of the arguments over 'broad
front' and 'united front' threatened.

Opposition to the AAC came in two forms. There were those opposed to the arrangements. In particular they wanted other political
tendencies to be more involved in the planning of the conference, and a
more-thorough process of consultation. Others opposed the AAC in principle. Cosatu's 'populists', this small but vociferous grouping argued,
were promoting class collaboration and 'a negotiated settlement strategy', rather than 'a policy of class struggle.'[5] It became increasingly
obvious that Cosatu would have difficulty in making the AAC constructive if the federation had no internal agreement over what it wanted to
gain from the conference.

With the AAC scheduled for late September it was essential to resolve differences rapidly. A special extended CEC meeting was called for
8 September.[*] Nactu, it was reported, had agreed to the list of organisations invited. And each of the 12 teachers' organisations had been invited
to send one delegate each.

Thembinkosi Mkalipi reported that there were objections to the AAC
in the Eastern Cape. Some of the organisations invited were 'unacceptable because of the collaborative roles they play within
government-created structures.' These included homeland opposition parties and the National Democratic Movement (NDM), a white
parliamentary party championing links with the extra-parliamentary
movement. Further, it had been agreed that only national organisations
would be invited, but this had not been adhered to. In addition, the increase in the number of conference delegates meant that 'the input of the
labour sector would be diluted.' The conference would be 'a propaganda

---

* 'Extended' simply meant that the CEC included representatives of Cosatu
locals, who could participate in debate, but who, constitutionally, had no voting
rights. Extended CEC meetings had taken place on a number of occasions,
particularly when a major issue was being debated, and when Cosatu's office
bearers or Exco saw a need for a larger and more representative forum.

stunt', it was said. The fear was expressed that the AAC would end with nothing more than a press statement. It would focus, said some critics, on the short-term problem of opposing the forthcoming municipal elections, rather than on the longer-term goal of building a broad anti-apartheid front.

Defending the broad front

'The idea of the AAC', explained Jay Naidoo, 'was not the sole property of Cosatu,' which could not simply decide to withdraw invitations or reverse previous decisions. Cosatu's allies had agreed to the proposed date and theme. They had also agreed to the proposal about sectors and that 'ideology' should not be a criterion for invitation. Naidoo was supported by the delegate from NUM. Exco, he argued, had been given a flexible mandate for its meeting with Cosatu's allies. The organisations which the Eastern Cape objected to had been included in the original CEC recommendation sent to the UDF. Ordinary Cosatu shop stewards, claimed one organiser, were becoming confused:

> They are used to a very strict alliance with the UDF. Now they see the taxi drivers, Nafcoc, the ZCC and the NDM being invited, and they do not trust these organisations. Nonetheless, this is very positive because it is opening up the debate and clarifying the issues. Why do we enter alliances? What are our tactics and strategies? What is the difference between short-term and long-term goals?

Other unionists felt the goals were clear. Cosatu frequently approached taxi owners and asked them to support stayaways, commented one unionist.

> We must build that relationship and win them over to our side. It is the same with Nafcoc – for example, they give money to pay for community funerals. We want to build that into an ongoing relationship on the basis of the leadership of the working class. Now more than ever we need to have all forces part of the front.

Eventually the September CEC decided to endorse the arrangements made, despite Numsa and CWIU's formal objections to the inclusion of certain organisations. Sydney Mufamadi attempted to deal with these objections. 'It seems inconceivable to some', argued Mufamadi,

> that having taken a principled stand against the bantustan system, we can invite opposition parties from the bantustans... We hate the bantustans for reasons which are obvious. However, we cannot wish bantustans away.

We have to tackle them as part of our objective reality... Most of the activities of our people in the bantustans have not taken place under the auspices of the mass democratic movement. To sit back and wait for the day when all the people in the bantustans will shout the slogans we are already shouting within Cosatu will amount to a dereliction of leadership duties... If we are to broaden our moral and political influence...(then the bantustans are) a terrain we have to contest.

Liberal whites should also be approached, Mufamadi argued. 'Part of our responsibility is to dislodge them from the trenches of the enemy.' Such whites were unlikely to become 'as militant as the millions of oppressed.' But the positions they took continued to 'constrain the regime.' Another unionist, writing in response to critics of the AAC, argued that 'we have to provide direction and powerful strategies.' Working-class leadership would be achieved 'by demonstrating leadership in practice, rather than demanding a simple majority' of union seats. The real questions which Cosatu should be asking about the AAC were: 'Do we have meaningful direction to give the broad democratic movement? Do we have strategies to suggest? Do we have a unifying plan of action?'

The AAC was scheduled to be held at the University of Cape Town on 24 and 25 September. Delegations travelled there from all corners of the country. At the last minute a number of organisations announced they would not be attending, including Nactu, Azapo and others from the black consciousness camp, as well as the New Unity Movement. The final nail in the AAC coffin came when, with most delegates already en route to Cape Town, the police banned the conference. The banning, ironically, lent weight to the argument that a broad front against an oppressive regime was needed.

At the time the failure of the AAC was very demoralising. There had been insufficient preparation of organisations and even Cosatu's own grassroots for such a large event. Nevertheless, despite appearances, political unity was developing. There was growing agreement on the need for a strategy which reached out to a broad range of allies. Abstract arguments based on 'principles' and political jargon became less acceptable. Delegates to Cosatu structures were increasingly forced to provide concrete arguments against working with organisations they objected to. Those who argued that simply talking to or meeting with an organisation was treacherous, were themselves becoming increasingly isolated.[*]

---

[*] *One of the last instances of this extreme attitude emerged at a Witwatersrand regional congress in late 1988. Delegates were informed that the Progressive Federal Party (PFP), a white parliamentary political party with liberal policies, had asked to meet Cosatu representatives. This did not involve a major policy decision by the PFP, whose East Rand regional committee had simply suggested an exchange of views with Cosatu's Wits region.* (continued on page 298)

Three political/organisational blocs within Cosatu were identified earlier: the UDF bloc, the centre bloc, and the independent worker bloc. By late 1988 this arrangement was shifting. The merger process had reduced the UDF bloc in size. Within Cawu, Nehawu and Sarhwu its perspectives still remained dominant, but the UDF bloc was a spent force. Indeed, it was no longer even an accurate term, since none of the unions mentioned were UDF affiliates.

The independent worker bloc was also breaking up as a coherent group. 'Pragmatists' were beginning to share common ground with the centre bloc and adopting a more practical approach to alliances. The 'fundamentalists' remained opposed to all talk of broad fronts and continued to promote the notion of pure 'red trade unionism'. An increasingly strong 'centre' was developing in Cosatu. It had grown in size and influence and incorporated most of the political perspectives of the UDF bloc.

These trends and this change in the balance of forces were becoming increasingly clear by the time of Cosatu's third congress, held in mid-1989.

(continued from page 297) *The congress accepted the invitation. White politics, the majority of delegates argued, was becoming increasingly fractious, and there were growing divisions within the ruling bloc. Any attempts by whites to reach out to the extra-parliamentary forces should be encouraged. Cosatu would have an opportunity both to explain its policies, and challenge PFP members over certain of its policies, such as its support for military conscription. Cosatu could lose nothing by a meeting.*

A minority at the regional congress was, however, outraged. 'Instead of rebuilding organs of working-class power, such as street and boycott committees', a unionist from this camp argued, 'we opted for organising liberals and big capitalists... The PFP has clearly aligned itself with the enemy.' It had endorsed the second state of emergency and continued to participate in parliament. No alliances could be entered into with Zac de Beer, the party's national leader. He was, the minority argued, a director of Anglo American, the company which had crushed the 1987 miners strike.

'The PFP is the political expression of the liberal capitalists. We can only widen the divisions within the ruling bloc and the racist parliament by intensifying the political and economic struggle against the regime and not by meeting the PFP.'

This type of argument was, however, losing ground within Cosatu. No alliance with the PFP had been proposed. No-one had proposed that a meeting with the PFP would be a substitute for building organisation. The majority within Cosatu was losing patience with repeated accusations of being 'sell-outs', and with the minority's repeated conflation of 'talks' with 'negotiations'.

Notes

1. *Weekly Mail*, 10.06.88.
2. 'Historical significance of three days of national protest', *Phambili*, special supplement, October 1988.
3. This account relies heavily on Frank Meintjies, 'Talks with Saccola: a bitter experience', *South African Labour Bulletin*, 13(7), November 1988.
4. Geoff Schreiner, 'On strengthening the anti-LRA campaign', *South African Labour Bulletin*, 14(7), March 1990.
5. See, for example, Solomon Mlambo, 'Popular front or united front?', *South African Labour Bulletin*, 13(8), February 1989.

19

New sectors join Cosatu

Expanding unity

*T*HE banning of the September anti-apartheid conference was a setback for Cosatu. The state feared that the AAC would unite anti-apartheid forces, and in particular that it would result in an organised boycott of the forthcoming municipal elections. In the event, the state's fears were unfounded. Indeed, for Cosatu, the banning may have been a blessing in disguise. The federation and its allies had made insufficient preparations to ensure a successful conference. Within Nactu there were differences over whether to attend, and there was not unanimity, even within Cosatu, over the invitation list.

Late 1988 and early 1989 involved a period of consolidation and growing unity for Cosatu. In this chapter some of the events of that period are touched upon: the boycott of the October municipal elections; the growth of organisation in the homelands; the increase in union membership in the public sector and clothing industry; the teachers' unity talks; and the differences which emerged within Sarhwu and Nactu.

October municipal elections

The government spent R5-million to convince black people to vote in local council elections scheduled for 26 October. 'You can make it happen' was the slogan, and millions did – by boycotting the elections! On average, less than 10% of eligible voters in the African communities voted. In the coloured and Indian communities the poll was only slightly higher.

Grievances against black local authorities had been at the root of the 1984-5 uprisings. Established by the government as self-financing bodies, these councils had to provide services to the black townships. In an attempt to do so they increased rents and imposed a variety of levies on impoverished communities. Many councillors had a reputation for corruption, particularly in the allocation of housing and trading licenses.

A high percentage poll, the government argued, would be a vindication of its plans for 'peaceful development'. Even after the election results were announced, Minister of Constitutional Planning Chris Heunis proclaimed them 'a victory for those who want an extension of democracy,' and blamed the low polls on apathy and ignorance.

The government made every effort to achieve a high percentage poll. It allowed ten days of 'prior voting', with voters not subject to public scrutiny. On election day voting could be done without identification, allowing individuals to vote a number of times or vote in the name of others. In addition, claimed the Human Rights Commission, there was 'extensive coercion and corrupt election practices.' In Witbank, for example,

> residents report that the police have been visiting shebeens and arresting people, saying they should be voting, not drinking. They also report that residents are being loaded on trucks at gunpoint and taken to the polls.[1]

Cosatu encouraged its members not to vote in the election, despite the February restrictions and state of emergency regulations which made such calls illegal. Significantly, many church leaders openly defied restrictions and advocated a boycott of the elections, joining community organisations in their call for a national day of peaceful protest on 26 October.* This was widely interpreted as a stayaway call, but while Cosatu supported the boycott, it proposed no stayaway action.

No work stayaway materialised, but the election boycott was a major victory for the entire democratic movement. It revealed that the

---

*On 31 August 1988, Khotso House, the headquarters of the South African Council of Churches (SACC) was destroyed by a powerful bomb blast. On 12 October, barely two weeks before the election, the offices of the Southern African Catholic Bishops Conference were devastated in a fire. Some have suggested that there was a direct link between these attacks and the churches' boycott call. As had happened at the time of the Cosatu House explosion, the police issued statements implying that the attacks had been perpetrated by the ANC's armed wing!

government was unable, despite repression, to gain the political support of the oppressed, and that the mass mood of defiance ran deep. The municipal elections proved to be a turning point. Defiance became more widespread, and from then onwards it became clear that the 'total strategy' policy of PW Botha and his generals was doomed.

A four-day stayaway in Venda during August 1988 was a further indication of the changing climate. Venda, an 'independent' homeland run by a corrupt and repressive tribal leadership, had been largely isolated from the waves of mass resistance which swept the country throughout the 1980s. Its small working class laboured under appalling conditions in forests and at sawmills, and in the factories of the industrial area around Thohoyandou. Many earned less than the legal minimum wage of R110 per month. The few trade unions which attempted to organise in the area were driven out by the Venda security police.

The stayaway was called over the issue of ritual murders. At least 15 had taken place that year alone, and there were persistent allegations that the killers were being protected by senior members of the government. 'AA' Tshivase, the cabinet minister responsible for the Departments of Justice, Prisons, and Law and Order, was accused of being directly involved.

The response to the stayaway call was overwhelming as students stayed out of class, teachers did not teach, and workers refused to work. Even civil servants and police heeded the call.

Tshivase was forced to resign, and the success of the stayaway boosted mass organisation in the area. By the end of 1988 a number of new demands had emerged, including the legalisation of trade unions, improvements in education, the release of all detainees and an end to harassment by security forces.[2]

There were signs of turbulence in many of the homelands. KwaNdebele had been in a state of insurrection for most of 1986 and 1987 with mass resistance to the attempted imposition of 'independence' on the territory. In early 1988 a military coup in Transkei replaced the Matanzima dynasty with a young soldier, Bantu Holomisa, who promised less corruption and repression. A similar coup attempt in Bophuthatswana was crushed after South African troops rushed to the rescue of Lucas Mangope, a long-time friend of Pretoria.

Public sector problems and strategies

Most Cosatu affiliates experienced steady growth throughout late 1988 and early 1989. Numsa's increase in size was most impressive as it began to reap the fruits of the 1987 merger and a well-organised wage campaign. Fawu and Ppwawu also experienced significant growth, while workers in the municipal and health sectors were steadily joining Samwu and Nehawu respectively.

The October 1988 CEC accepted Potwa as a Cosatu affiliate. The union had been working closely with Cosatu since the 1987 postal workers strike and its affiliation boosted Cosatu's membership by over 16 000. Potwa's acceptance was little more than a formality although, strictly speaking, it violated the definitions of Cosatu's 'one industry, one union' policy, there being no provision for a separate post office union.

At the time of Cosatu's launch, workers from mining and industry formed the backbone of the union movement. Those public sector workers within Cosatu were usually employed at manufacturing plants such as Sasol or Iscor. These were run largely like industrial companies and organised by affiliates in the chemical and metal sectors. The heart of the public sector – the railways and transport services, the postal service, electricity and water facilities, health and education services, prison departments and the vast administrative bureaucracy – were either absent, or grossly under-represented at Cosatu's launch. These workers were simply not organised.

The launching congress accepted that municipal and local authority workers would constitute a separate sector, given that approximately 300 000 municipal workers needed to be organised. Sats employees, it was agreed, would form part of a merged transport union. For the remainder, the launching congress decided that one union for public sector employees should be formed once organisation was strong enough. When Nehawu was launched in 1987 Cosatu recognised it as a health and education union, but this was seen as an interim measure in the establishment of one public sector union.

By late 1988 Cosatu's public sector unions were meeting together. A public sector co-ordinating committee (PSCC) was established, bringing together representatives from Potwa, Nehawu, Sarhwu and Samwu. There were two different views on how to structure this committee. One proposed the establishment of a joint forum which could take binding decisions on common issues. The other involved the building of a single union with internal sections structured to match the divisions within the public sector.

The challenges to the public sector unions were great, apart from the primary one of increasing membership. The state had embarked on a privatisation drive, which implied both job losses and fragmentation of the affected workforces. Strategies had to be developed to deal with the enormous numbers of white workers in the public sector who were often under the influence of right-wing or ineffective unions, and constituted the majority of the workforce in some industries.

The establishment of the PSCC was the first step in developing unity and reassessing Cosatu's approach to the public sector as a whole.

Gawu and Actwusa

The garment and textile sector was another promising area of growth. In November 1987 the Amalgamated Clothing and Textile Workers Union (Actwusa) was launched. It brought together the Cosatu-affiliated NUTW as well as two former Tucsa affiliates, the Textile Workers Industrial Union (TWIU) and the National Union of Garment Workers (NUGW). Satawu, a Cosatu affiliate linked to Saawu, did not take part in the merger. Neither did two other former Tucsa affiliates, the Western Province Garment Workers Union (WPGWU), and the Natal-based Garment Workers Industrial Union (GWIU), although both had been invited to participate.

A month after Actwusa's launch these two unions came together to form the Garment and Allied Workers Union (Gawu). Satawu, no longer recognised as a Cosatu affiliate, integrated its membership into Gawu. By early 1988, therefore, Actwusa and Gawu between them dominated the clothing and textile industry.

The situation was politically complex. At the time Actwusa found itself on the political fringes of Cosatu. It tended towards political abstentionism and had been the only union at the 1988 special congress to oppose stayaway action called to protest the new labour law. Gawu, ironically, was developing open sympathies for the politics of Cosatu's mainstream. Indeed, the union invited Cosatu's Jay Naidoo to be the keynote speaker at its launch. Actwusa objected to this, arguing that it would give credibility to Gawu and imply Cosatu's acceptance that Gawu had not participated in the launch of Actwusa.

Actwusa delegates to the November 1987 CEC argued that the unions which would form Gawu had a long history of collaboration. These unions, Actwusa said, had a cosy relationship with employers, were not prepared to use strike action, and were dominated by a bureaucratic style. Their weekly union newspaper reflected this. It was dominated by social announcements and pictures of beauty contests of garment workers held at every factory. Actwusa's arguments were not without substance, but the CEC was not persuaded. The majority felt that progressive and militant individuals had gained the upper hand within both GWIU (Natal) and WPGWU, and the CEC agreed that Jay Naidoo should address the Gawu launch as this could only increase Cosatu's influence on the new union.

Gawu brought together 112 000 workers, making it the third largest union in the country after NUM and Numsa. Women made up 86% of its membership. In his speech to the congress, Naidoo explained the policies of Cosatu to the assembled delegates. 'Every worker in Cosatu', he added, 'looks forward to the day when you will merge with our affiliate (the 70 000-strong Actwusa) to form the biggest clothing and textile union that Africa has ever seen.'

Gawu's general secretary, Desmond Sampson, blamed the lack of unity with Actwusa on 'unrealistic deadlines' and 'illogical pressures'. The congress nevertheless committed itself to the principle of 'one union, one industry', and to a process of mergers to achieve this. The Gawu congress also resolved 'to request observer status on Cosatu forums for a period of six months whereafter formal affiliation be applied for.'

'We will commit ourselves today', said Gawu's first president Ismail Muckdoom, 'to new forms of organising and mobilising of workers in our industry. Gone are the days when we go cap in hand to the bosses. Now we shall demand and struggle for our rightful share of the wealth we produce.'[3]

During its first 12 months, Gawu certainly fulfilled the expectations it had raised. Through mass mobilisation and extensive restructuring, control of the union was returned to workers. Shop stewards committees and local shop stewards councils were built, where none had existed before. The union conducted training courses to equip these shop stewards with basic skills. It transformed the union's newspapers into militant and informative publications. It built workers confidence by adopting an aggressive approach to management. 'No issue was too small to raise with management,' according to one Gawu publication. 'Every issue was a learning experience for the hundreds of newly-elected shop stewards.'

Most importantly, Gawu built its Living Wage Campaign. Wages in the garment industry were very low. By 1988, qualified machinists (some 60% of the workforce) earned around R94 per week in the Western Cape, Natal and the Transvaal. In the Boland and the Eastern Cape, conditions were even worse, with machinists earning approximately R77 a week. Even these were not the lowest wages paid. Earnings for the lower grades were as little as R43 per week in the Eastern Cape – R190 per month. This after 60 years of trade unionism in the Tucsa tradition!

A strike at the giant Rex Trueform factory in Cape Town during March 1988 proved to be a turning point. Almost 3 000 workers downed tools demanding an interim cost-of-living increase. They were strongly supported by Gawu's other members in the Western Cape. A union account of the strike recalled that thousand of rands in relief money poured in from garment and textile workers who could ill afford it. Sporadic strikes, work stoppages and other forms of industrial action occurred every day in different factories. The demands were the same and the cry went up all over the Western Cape: 'Support Rex workers! A victory for Rex is a victory for all Gawu members!'

After almost four weeks of strike action employers backed down and offered 55 000 Western Cape clothing workers an interim increase of R14 across-the-board. The workers accepted. Similar increases were achieved by the union in Natal and the Eastern Cape.[4]

Another sign of the changes within the union could be seen when garment workers supported stayaway calls. The three-day June action against the new labour law was strongly supported in Natal where 90% absenteeism was recorded. This was particularly significant in that it involved many Indian women workers, traditionally one of the most quiescent sections of the working class.

Gawu's application for observer status, pending affiliation to Cosatu, was tabled at the CEC meeting of 12-14 February 1988. The CEC decided to meet Gawu for discussions over 'the future of the unions in the industry and the steps towards unity of workers in this sector.' In the meantime Gawu would be allowed to participate in Cosatu's local structures, and have observer status on the CEC 'on the basis of an extended Actwusa delegation', and under the Actwusa banner.

Cosatu was reluctant to admit a second affiliate in the same sector, particularly after the traumatic merger processes which most affiliates had experienced the previous year. There was a strong feeling that new unions should enter Cosatu by merging with an existing affiliate, in this case Actwusa. At the same time, however, Cosatu could not be seen to discourage a union as large as Gawu from joining its ranks. CEC delegates also had to take into account that tensions remained between the leadership of Actwusa and Gawu.

Throughout 1988 there were major shopfloor battles between Actwusa and Gawu, particularly where both had members in the same plant. These differences became extremely heated and the possibilities of unity receded as 1988 progressed. Cosatu's national office bearers worked hard to retrieve unity prospects, and the 14-16 October CEC endorsed their proposal to call a meeting of the executives of both unions. 'Much persuasion preceded this meeting,' recalls Jay Naidoo. 'It was remarkable that workers on both sides recognised the enormous advantages of unity and were able to persuade leadership to abandon their parochial union interests.'[5]

In December 1988 Actwusa's national executive and Gawu's central executive committees met at Durban's Island Hotel, where problems between the two unions were thrashed out. The unity process was back on track and it was apparent that Cosatu's membership in the clothing and textile sector would soon more than double.

The Gawu experience held major lessons for Cosatu as a whole. It was possible to reform and rejuvenate conservative and established unions from within, particularly in the case of unions representing semi-skilled workers. Reforming an established union called for a different approach to organisation. The union had first to be reformed at the top, by persuading existing leadership of the need for a new direction and by bringing in new blood. Only then could an appeal be made to workers, unleashing their energies in a process of democratic renewal. Great care had to be taken not to alienate existing union officials unnecessarily. Most of these would willingly join the reform process if given proper understanding of the need to change, although many would find it hard to give up their bureaucratic and desk-bound style.

The Gawu experience made Cosatu affiliates considerably more flexible in their approaches to conservative unions. In particular, a deeper understanding of the organisation of coloured and Indian workers – long a weak point in Cosatu's membership – developed. From 1988 onwards there was increasing co-operation with unions and organisations previously regarded as untouchable. These ranged from staff associations in the post office and railways, to organisations of teachers.

The teachers' unity talks

Teachers' organisations had long reflected the chaotic state of education in South Africa. By 1988 there were 250 000 teachers in the country, half of whom were members of a teachers' organisation. School education was administered by 17 different ethnic education departments, and 27 teachers' organisations existed. The majority of teachers in black schools were poorly qualified and poorly paid, and the authorities showed little hesitation in dismissing, suspending or transferring troublesome teachers.

The crisis in education in South Africa is too well-known to need recounting here. It is sufficient to note that education is ethnically divided, and that education of black schoolchildren is vastly inferior to their white counterparts in respect of standards, teacher/pupil ratios, facilities and per capita expenditure. The education of black children, and Bantu Education in particular, was inferior by deliberate government design, not simply as a result of circumstances. Over the years, educational grievances have sparked off major resistance against the government and state structures. The uprisings of 1976, following the 16 June massacre in Soweto, are the most obvious but by no means the only examples.

The formation of one teachers' organisation was raised as an idea at the December 1985 consultative conference on the education crisis hosted by the Soweto Parents' Crisis Committee (SPCC). This gathering called for the formation of a united teachers' organisation within one month. The unrealistic nature of the resolution, and the state of emergency clampdown, allowed for little progress on this front. In 1987, Cosatu's education conference resolved to encourage the formation of a democratic teachers' union, and in the same year both the UDF and NECC made similar calls.

Teachers' organisations at the time were divided into three broad camps. Firstly, there was the Teachers' Federal Council (TFC), a statutory body representing teachers at white schools. A second group involved ten state-recognised teachers' associations representing black teachers. These were, in turn, members of federations structured along ethnic lines. The African Teachers' Association of South Africa (Atasa) had 65 000 members in African schools; the United Teachers' Association of South Africa (Utasa) represented 27 500 coloured teachers; and the Teachers' Association of South Africa (Tasa) represented 8 600 Indian members. Thirdly, the so-called 'progressive teachers' unions', denied state recognition, had a combined membership of 5 000. Often affiliated to the UDF, these groups organised teachers in opposition to the established unions. This camp included the National Education Union of South Africa (Neusa), the Western Cape Teachers' Union (Wectu), the East London Progressive Teachers' Union (Elptu), and a host of other organisations.

When teacher unity was first mooted, white teachers' organisations were not contemplated. And there were different views as to whether unity should unite 'progressive teachers' unions' into one organisation, or attempt to unite these with the established teachers' associations in black schools. There was no love lost between these two camps. Atasa, Utasa and Tasa were regarded as 'collaborators with apartheid education'. The progressive teachers unions were in turn seen as 'an insignificant fringe group of hotheads.'[6]

Neusa and Wectu wanted to affiliate to Cosatu. Jay Naidoo recalls advising them that this was not the correct approach, as Cosatu 'saw possibilities for all teachers' organisations to unite.'

Finally, the ANC took an initiative to advance the unity process and ensure that it was broadly based. All teachers' organisations, apart from the TFC, were invited to a unity seminar in Harare hosted by the All-Africa Teachers' Organisation (Aato) and the World Confederation of Organisations of the Teaching Profession (WCOTP). Cosatu, Sactu and

ANC representatives were also present at this meeting, which was held in April 1988.

The gathering exceeded all expectations, with delegates agreeing to a 15-point statement outlining policy and action. They decided to canvass support for 'one national teachers' organisation' which would be 'committed to a unitary, non-racial, democratic South Africa'. While ideology would not be 'a precondition for unity', the organisation would see itself as part of the 'national mass democratic movement'. The envisaged organisation would have two main aims. It would promote, in contrast to apartheid education, 'a free, non-racial, non-sexist, compulsory, democratic education in a single education system.' It would also 'protect and promote the rights of teachers as workers and professionals.' Finally, delegates agreed to request Cosatu to convene the unity talks.

Entrusting Cosatu with this sensitive task implied recognition of its political and organisational importance. It also reflected increasing emphasis on the trade union, rather than just the professional orientation of the envisaged teachers' body. Cosatu convened the first round of talks in August 1988, followed by further talks in November. Many delegates from the established unions were openly suspicious of Cosatu. They had expectations, inculcated by state propaganda, of meeting 'agitators' and 'terrorists'. But Cosatu's open and honest approach soon changed these perceptions. Support for the 15 unity principles was growing, and it was agreed to cement this on the ground by developing regional co-operation between the various teacher bodies. Backing for the unity process began developing amongst white teachers. By the December meeting, three TFC affiliates – those representing white English-speaking teachers – had indicated their desire to join the talks.

In December 1988 two of the participants, Wectu and the Democratic Teachers Union (Detu), were restricted by government proclamation.[*] When the teachers' unity talks reconvened in March 1989, the restrictions were condemned and labelled an attempt 'to disrupt the unity that was being forged.'

Elements within Atasa were unhappy with moves towards unity. In addition, tensions remained between the established black teachers' associations and their newer counterparts. Nevertheless, a year after the Harare talks the process was at least moving forward. We will return to the organisation of teachers in a later chapter.

At the time both Wectu and Detu were engaged in campaigns against the suspension of teachers. The restrictions meant that three of the participants in the talks were effectively banned, since Neusa had been restricted in February 1988. All three bodies continued to participate in the unity talks, in defiance of the law.

Conflict within Sarhwu

The late 1988 and early 1989 period was a time of consolidation and gradual progress for Cosatu. But the railway union, Sarhwu, was one notable exception to this. Its membership had grown enormously in the wake of the 1987 strike and after similar strikes in Natal and East London during the second half of 1988. Sats was beginning to back away from its refusal to recognise Sarhwu. The union gained 10 000 new members in the wake of the Natal strike, and Blatu – Sats' protégé 'union' – was effectively de-recognised in that province.

Sarhwu was, however, growing too fast and was unable to consolidate its membership or take full advantage of the gains it was making with Sats. Its leadership faced problems of inexperience. They also had to devote a great deal of time to legal matters. Following the 1987 strike, Sarhwu had to defend no less than 1 000 members in some 150 separate trials. On the ground it faced dissatisfaction. Progress was seen to be slow, and each of its regions seemed to be fighting Sats' highly-centralised national operation separately.

Matters came to a head at the union's national congress in October 1988, when delegates voted to replace all existing office bearers other than union president Justice Langa. Electioneering and caucusing for the position of general secretary was particularly bitter. One group wanted head office official Stan Nkosi elected, while another favoured Martin Sebakwane, an official from the Pretoria region. In the end, Sebakwane was elected general secretary and Nkosi assistant general secretary. According to Sebakwane, the conflict involved a mixture of personal differences, dissatisfaction with previous office bearers, and the head office's lack of a coherent national strategy.

Within days of the congress three senior head office officials, including Nkosi and education secretary Mike Roussos, announced their resignations and circulated a letter containing virulent denunciations of a number of the newly-elected office bearers. The union was thrown into crisis. The new office bearers needed the co-operation of head office staff to allow for a smooth transition. There was a crisis in East London where a major strike still required resolution. Finally, Sarhwu was about to enter into recognition negotiations with Sats. All of these required the skills and knowledge of existing staff.

An emergency national executive committee meeting called within weeks of the congress decided that two office bearers, Sebakwane and second vice-president Potgieter, would step down 'in the interests of unity'. Nkosi would act as general secretary while the two other head office officials who had resigned would resume their duties. It was a short-term solution which did little to ease tensions. And in reversing a decision of the union's supreme body, the NEC went against established union traditions of democracy and respect for structures.

The conflict was eventually settled when a special national congress was held over the last weekend of February 1989. Cosatu was asked to assist and the congress was presided over by Chris Dlamini and Sydney Mufamadi. During the congress workers asked both sides to present their cases, and the problems were then debated in detail. Delegates then unanimously decided that no new elections were needed since they had elected the office bearers at the previous congress.

The 1988 Nactu congress

Nactu's national congress, held at the Standard Bank Arena during August 1988, had important implications for Cosatu, although these only became apparent later. The congress, attended by some 200 delegates, revealed a significant drop in the federation's paid-up membership, with Nactu's 24 affiliates reported to represent 144 418 paid-up members compared to its 1986 estimates of between 248 000 and 420 000 members. The most dramatic decline involved the slashing of Bamcwu's recognised membership from its October 1986 total of 148 000 to 3 100.

Nactu office bearers claimed that the figures reflected at the congress were incorrect, and promised to produce accurate statistics early in 1989. They were certain that these would reveal membership of between 250 000 and 300 000. It appeared undeniable, however, that Nactu's membership had declined, and that earlier claims had been inflated.

Nactu's congress resolved to drop the principle of 'black working-class leadership' and replace it with 'African working-class leadership'. This reflected the increasing ascendance of Africanist perspectives within the organisation, as opposed to previously-dominant black consciousness views. While Nactu retained its official position of political non-alignment, its 1988 congress saw effective control fall into the hands of PAC sympathisers. Cunningham Ngcukana was elected first assistant general secretary, ousting BC diehard Pandelani Nefolovhodwe; and another PAC supporter, Patricia de Lille was elected vice-president. With James Mndaweni retaining the presidency, PAC supporters were clearly pre-eminent. Only general secretary Piroshaw Camay and second assistant general secretary Mahlomola Skhosana fell outside the Africanist camp. They were elected more on the strength of their experience as unionists than their political affiliations.

The Nactu congress committed itself to 'work towards one country one federation for the benefit of the working class.' Shortly before the congress, Mndaweni claimed that 'since Nactu was formed in October 1986 we have been making approaches towards Cosatu in trying to ensure that we take joint action on any matter that affected workers in this country. Our attempts have, however, not been successful.'

A few months earlier, in May, a Nactu delegation met the ANC in Harare. A joint communique concluded that 'it was imperative for the labour movement inside the country to strive toward unity with the eventual objective of a single labour federation.' At about this time the Organisation of African Trade Union Unity (Oatuu) offered to host unity talks between Cosatu and Nactu.

Nactu accepted the offer, but Cosatu's public response was restrained. While stressing Cosatu's commitment to the principles of 'one country, one federation', Jay Naidoo cautioned that any accord would have to deal with the differences which caused the unions in Nactu to leave the unity talks in 1985. To many outsiders, it appeared as if Nactu was the more flexible party on the issue of unity. The issue would be put to the test in early 1989.

The malady lingers on

By the end of 1988 it was clear that Cosatu was making progress despite the debilitating effects of repression on both affiliate and federation structures. Dealing with the effects of repression occupied some unions to such an extent that organisational tasks were neglected. This, in turn, created fertile ground for divisions and tensions.

The effects of repression were often devastating. Publicity was invariably given to larger incidents such as the killing of unionists or the 'disappearance' of union leaders. But the cumulative effect of endless incidents of 'minor' repression often went uncatalogued. Workers and officials frequently complained of being arrested, sometimes assaulted, simply for wearing union or 'struggle' T-shirts. To have 129 members arrested for holding a peaceful demonstration against the labour bill, as Fawu and Ppwawu did, demanded enormous resources of time and money to organise bail and legal representation.

Detention, even for a few days or hours, disrupted one's work and equilibrium. During February 1989 Ppwawu's general secretary Sipho Kubheka was twice detained at roadblocks while travelling between Cape Town and Johannesburg, because police felt the book he was reading was undesirable. The effect was the loss of two days' work and scheduled meetings, to say nothing of other union officials having to spend time finding out why and how and where Kubheka had disappeared. Detentions like these were common.

Arson and bomb attacks, or major raids on union offices, were publicised. Many smaller incidents went unreported. These often left unions without key documents. In November 1988, police raided and ransacked

Cosatu's Kimberley offices. On other occasions, organisers had their diaries seized, with the obvious result that appointments were not kept, and telephone contacts had to be carefully compiled again.

In October 1988 John Mkhize, an ordinary union member peacefully picketing outside the luxury Johannesburg Sun hotel, was shot dead. We can understand the tragedy of Mkhize's death. But what about the stress on his colleagues who still had to picket next day? What about the fear of other workers, and the anxieties of their families?

Again, we know that the Northern Transvaal regional congress in Mamelodi township on 29 November 1988 was surrounded by police and army contingents. All delegates were repeatedly searched. Police then remained in the hall and took videos of the entire proceedings. But it is impossible to know what worker delegates did *not* say in their congress because of the police presence, or what organisational efforts had to be made to ensure that attendance would be satisfactory at the next regional congress.

Cosatu's major achievement during 1988, said Jay Naidoo in a lengthy interview, was that 'we not only survived, but also achieved significant consolidation despite a massive onslaught from both the government and capital.'[7] There was a dramatic increase in membership. Affiliates also made major breakthroughs, he said – Ccawusa on maternity benefits; Sarhwu on recognition; Ppwawu on wages; NUM on achieving a provident fund; Numsa on racism in the workplace and the new labour law; and Gawu on wages and the LRA. 'Many of our regional and local structures', continued Naidoo, 'are now functioning in a more disciplined and consistent way.'

Cosatu 'consolidated its role as an important formation in the mass democratic movement,' and it was important, in Naidoo's view, to continue the initiative towards broad unity. 'Even after the anti-apartheid conference was banned,' said Sydney Mufamadi in a separate interview, 'the idea itself of coming together remains alive... We are beginning to see a much broader coalition of forces taking shape.'[8]

'Unity (between Cosatu and Nactu) can only bear fruit', said Naidoo, 'if it unites workers in action on the ground. This is why Cosatu has supported its affiliates who have sought to forge united action with unions outside Cosatu.' However, he cautioned, 'real unity in action on the ground can best be ensured through forming national industrial unions in each sector united into a single federation.' The first round of unity talks in the early 1980s had bred an awareness of the limitations of 'ad-hoc unity' and 'co-operation' for many Cosatu leaders. Nevertheless, said Naidoo, possibilities for unity in action with Nactu existed in joint opposition to the LRA. This issue is explored in the following chapter.

Notes

1. Human Rights Commission, 'A Free Choice?', memorandum on repression and the municipal elections, 25 October 1988.
2. Eddie Koch and Edwin Ritchken, 'General strike in Venda', *South African Labour Bulletin*, 13(7), November 1988.
3. Gawu(SA), *First anniversary booklet*, 1987, 4.
4. Gawu, 'Garment workers rush into action', *South African Labour Bulletin*, 13(7), November 1988.
5. Jay Naidoo, written communication with author, February 1991.
6. Ian Moll, 'Towards one South African teachers' union', *South African Labour Bulletin*, 14(1), April 1989.
7. *New Nation*, 01.12.88.
8. *New Nation*, 12.01.89.

Part Five

Advancing

20

The first workers summit

'Standing back'

T HE unions had put all their efforts into stopping the new labour law, but it was enacted with effect from 1 September 1988. They now waited to see how employers would utilise the new weapons in their armoury.

The first problems encountered were technical. It was virtually impossible for unions to obtain the new dispute declaration forms needed to apply for the appointment of a conciliation board. The Department of Manpower claimed not to have any itself. When forms were finally obtained, many unionists fell foul of the new, and more complex, bureaucratic procedures. Even labour lawyers made mistakes. 'The Act is mindboggling in its complexity', one exasperated lawyer was reported to have said. 'We have to find another way. We cannot live under a regime like this.' In some cases the Manpower Department prevented disputes from being heard by claiming, for example, that a union had not submitted financial statements or membership figures to Pretoria in previous years; or that the union's vice-president was not entitled to sign the relevant forms in the absence of the president.

Section 79 of the new law, allowing employers to sue for damages, was potentially the most dangerous clause for unions. Even the smallest damages claim had the potential to bankrupt any of Cosatu's affiliates. The value of one hour's lost production at a medium-sized manufacturing concern exceeded the assets of almost all affiliates. The damages provisions assumed that any union member involved in a strike was 'acting with due authority on behalf of the trade union.' The onus was on the union to prove otherwise.

Within months the first damages claims were reported. Ullman Brothers threatened a R2-million suit against TGWU; Fawu faced a R1,7-million claim from Kwela Meat Wholesalers; and Ccawusa faced a R500 000 demand from Pyramid Wholesalers despite the fact that its members were dismissed within an hour of embarking on a work stoppage. All three companies had employed the same labour consultant, a Mr Van Welbergen, who reportedly believed the new labour legislation was long overdue, and that 'rogue' unions should be dealt with ruthlessly.[1] Damages claims were also received from Spar, SA Breweries and Clover Dairies, amongst others.

Numsa's Witwatersrand region responded by developing a 'standing back' approach to protect itself from damages claims. During early 1989 the union refused to take responsibility for, or intervene in, wildcat strikes until the affected company waived its right to sue for damages. Without a written waiver, Numsa suggested that management deal with the workforce as a whole.

When 1 200 Haggie Rand workers downed tools in April 1989 the company went to the industrial court, and argued that by not playing a constructive role in settling the dispute the union and its shop stewards had committed an unfair labour practice. Hundreds of strikers then insisted that they be cited in any court case. After all, they argued, ordinary union members – not only shop stewards – were liable for damages. The company, facing a lengthy court case and protracted strike, then agreed to forgo its right to claim damages. Numsa stepped in and the strike was speedily resolved. Many other metal strikes were unnecessarily lengthened when employers refused to waive their right to sue.

The 'standing back' tactic showed employers that the new labour law would be more trouble than it was worth. Following the Numsa strikes, an editorial in *Business Day* called for Section 79 of the LRA to be scrapped as a 'striking failure'. 'Management cannot go on trying to deal with an amorphous mass.' Thereafter, damages claims became less frequent. Those already instituted were not pursued. Section 79(2) became, in effect, a dead letter. Two years after its introduction, no union had paid damages to an employer.

In the industrial court, however, there were signs of the LRA being used effectively against the unions. The court regularly granted urgent interdicts to employers, often on an *ex parte* basis without the union being given an opportunity to present its side of the story. The content of industrial court judgements became visibly more conservative, and a number of its orders effectively rendered legal strikes illegal. One example involved BTR Dunlop and Numsa, where the court ruled that Numsa's threat of legal strike action was an unfair use of economic power.

Earlier union gains in the industrial court began to be reversed. While the court had previously ruled against minority unions, they now compelled employers to recognise and deal with them. Bakers Bread in Durban had to recognise the Natal Baking Industrial Union (NBIU) despite an existing recognition agreement with Fawu. NBIU, a conservative ex-Tucsa union, had declined over the years as its members left to join Fawu. By the time of the court case it represented only 90 out of a workforce of 700.

But many employers were reluctant to confront the unions using the new law, since they were unsure of likely union responses. No company, it appeared, wanted to be the first to pursue a damages claim to its conclusion. Worker militancy did not diminish. If anything, determination to resist the new law increased. Workers often defied court interdicts obtained after 1 September. In many minds, the credibility of the industrial relations system was shattered. This was probably the highest price which the state and employers had to pay. Despite all conflicts the post-Wiehahn industrial relations system had enjoyed a high degree of credibility amongst unions and workers. With the new LRA, workers often blamed the new law for any adverse judgement in the industrial court, even if it had little direct connection with the legal amendments.

The second phase of Cosatu's anti-LRA campaign unfolded slowly. Some argued that new legislation now existed and that unions should concentrate on making the best of a bad law. The previous law had not been perfect, they argued, and yet the unions had managed to grow. Others argued for a policy of total defiance. Unions should de-register, refuse to appear in the industrial court, and generally make the labour relations system unworkable.

Many, however, realised that union refusal to go to court would not prevent the enforcement of negative judgements such as eviction orders or damages claims. Non-collaboration could also prevent unions from declaring disputes. The broad consensus, therefore, was to train union officials in the workings of the new law, and at the same time revive the anti-LRA campaign.

The first workers summit

A key question for Cosatu was how to broaden resistance to the LRA. The federation had intended to raise the issue at the broad Anti-Apartheid Conference scheduled for September, but this had been banned. By the time Cosatu's Exco met on 1 October 1988, it was clear that union talks with Saccola were faltering.

Sydney Mufamadi reported to the CEC on meetings held with Nactu to discuss 'possible future action'. Nactu, he said, had suggested convening a workers 'summit' with one representative per 1 000 paid-up members 'to discuss what should be done.' Exco agreed to refer the suggestion back to affiliates 'for thorough discussion'.

The next CEC, held in mid-October, approved the idea of a workers summit in principle. However, 'the size and composition of such meeting or conference, and which unions outside the two federations should be invited' was left open. The CEC proposed that the themes of the summit should be the LRA and 'the building of one federation in our country, and one union in each industry.' A small working committee, it was agreed, should meet with Nactu to discuss these points further.

The CEC decision was not reached easily. Many in Cosatu were suspicious of Nactu and saw the suggestion of a workers summit as an attempt to replace the banned Anti-Apartheid Conference. 'But through debate', recalled Chris Dlamini, 'it became clear to everyone that the idea of a summit was a genuine one.'

Cosatu and Nactu delegations met on 18 November, and agreed on the LRA theme for the summit. Nactu accepted the additional unity theme 'in principle'. It was also agreed that only worker delegates should attend, not union officials, and that a range of other, unaffiliated unions should be invited.

Many workers believed that divisions within and between unions were largely caused by officials, and this was a major reason for the exclusion of officials. A summit without officials, it was felt, would be more united. 'What happens in most structures', said Chris Dlamini in relation to the summit,

> is that officials speak and workers mainly respond around what officials are saying... The problem with officials is that they have personal grudges. They sit in offices, they phone one another, and they happen to clash. They use the grudges in meetings, and you find that people are diverted from what they were debating, and end up supporting their official against the official from another organisation.[*]

---

[*] *Dlamini's arguments are a commonly-heard expression of the need for worker control and arise, in part, from bad experiences with paid officials.*

An alternative view within the unions is that worker control is as much about control of worker leaders by ordinary members as it is control of union officials. Officials are a reality to be accommodated, not isolated. Involving them in decisions, rather than allowing them no constitutional recognition is, in this view, a better means of control. (continued on page 320)

Cosatu proposed that representation to the summit should not be proportional, but that both Nactu and Cosatu each send 250 delegates. This was agreed.

Arrangements continued and 4 and 5 March 1989 were agreed as the dates for the summit. Cosatu decided to postpone its first CEC meeting for 1989 until after the summit, to ensure that recommendations from the gathering could be rapidly acted upon. Cosatu also decided to invite shop stewards from Nactu and the independent unions to regional and local meetings to discuss the workers summit. Final arrangements were approved at Exco's meeting of 3 February, Cosatu's last scheduled national meeting before the summit. Exco was informed that Nactu had raised a problem with the theme of 'one country, one federation/one union, one industry', and had instead suggested that the second point on the agenda, after the LRA, should be 'co-operation at a regional and local level'. Exco discussed this and decided to recommend to Nactu that the second agenda item be simply called 'unity'.

This suggestion was taken to the joint Cosatu/Nactu working committee of 13 February where Nactu proposed calling the agenda item 'ironing out differences between Cosatu and Nactu'. Cosatu delegates replied that they found it difficult to accept that the summit should be limited to discussing differences. While not ignoring these, 'we must also discuss the process towards overcoming these differences and building unity.' Besides, argued Cosatu, what would the 200 delegates from the non-affiliated unions be expected to do while Cosatu and Nactu debated their differences? The minutes of the meeting record that the Nactu delegation, including general secretary Camay and second assistant general secretary Skhosana, accepted the Cosatu position 'in principle... They do not have anything to the contrary to put to us. But they need to confirm this understanding with their structures.' The minutes also made it clear that 'the summit must go ahead'.[2]

In an attempt to build support within Cosatu for closer ties with Nactu, 150 office bearers of Cosatu regions and locals attended a seminar on worker unity in early February. Participants agreed that Nactu and all independent unions should be invited to attend locals and industrial area committees 'as full participants'. Unity, between affiliates in the same industry and between the two federations, it was argued, should be built around common solidarity action. 'When building unity with others', commented one delegate to the seminar, 'we should not criticise them and praise ourselves.' The long-term aim should always be 'to

(continued from page 319) In practice Cosatu unions attempt to maintain a balance between these two views. The exact approach adopted by a union plays a major role in establishing its 'organisational culture'.

build unity and work towards one union per industry and one country one federation'.[3]

Nactu pulls out

On the afternoon of 20 February Cosatu was informed that Nactu's national council wanted a postponement of the summit to an unspecified future date. After consultations with its affiliates Cosatu announced on 22 February that the summit would proceed. It had been informed by Nactu, said a Cosatu statement, that a postponement was required because Nactu needed more time to formulate its position on unity. 'We cannot accept this. The apartheid state and its allies in big business will not wait for us to prepare our blueprints.' Cosatu was 'greatly disturbed that a certain section of the organised working class chooses to exclude itself from one of the most significant strides by workers to unify themselves.' The summit could not be postponed because of 'vague tactical considerations'. Nactu remained committed to the summit, responded its president James Mndaweni. But the issue of building unity was a serious one and Nactu members needed a full discussion on the issue.

The decision to continue with the summit was widely supported within Cosatu, with the only opposition coming from a section of Fawu in the Eastern Cape. In an extravagant public statement, it complained of a lack of consultation and the exclusion of union officials from proceedings, and labelled the summit a 'gimmick'. The 'so-called invitation' to Nactu unions was a 'sham' and the summit should be boycotted. The statement, however, had less to do with the summit than with tensions between Fawu's national office and its Eastern Cape leadership.[*]

On 28 February, 11 Nactu affiliates decided to break ranks. The unions, announced spokesperson Mbulelo Rakwena, planned to attend the summit. 'Our failure to rise to the expectations of our struggle will inevitably render us irrelevant to the historical struggle of our people,' said Rakwena in criticising the official Nactu position.[4] He insisted that the decision was in line with Nactu policy on striving for union unity, and that the rebel unions remained committed to Nactu. The 11 unions represented approximately one-third of Nactu's 150 000 paid-up members and, apart from the Food and Beverage Workers Union (FBWU), were mainly Nactu's smaller affiliates. They were all unions with predominantly black consciousness, rather than Africanist, leadership.

Nactu was not opposed to unity, responded assistant general secretary Cunningham Ngcukana. However, 'the question of unity is a political

---

[*] *In April 1989 Fawu's NEC decided to dismiss its Eastern Cape regional secretary, and expel the regional chairperson.*

issue in the variegated national political spectrum' and the decision to request a postponement had not been taken lightly. General secretary Piroshaw Camay was conspicuously silent, and later cited Nactu's attitude to the workers summit as one of his reasons for resigning from Nactu at the end of 1989. 'Despite the fact that congresses and national councils had taken decisions on building working-class unity', said Camay in an interview,

> we found that the representatives to a national council decided to ask for a postponement of the workers summit when they actually knew that arrangements had progressed beyond a cancellation of the summit... To pull out of conferences or summits at the last minute for some small short-term political gains does not benefit the unity of the working people nor does it benefit the unity of the liberation struggle as a whole.[5]

This was damning comment indeed and tended to confirm that Nactu's predominantly Africanist leadership were rethinking the advisability of closer relations with Cosatu.*

It was not clear, however, whether the Nactu 'rebels' felt very differently from the Africanists, or were merely opposed to the tactics of

---

* Africanism was the term used to describe the political philosophy of the banned Pan-Africanist Congress (PAC). In 1959, Robert Sobukwe led a breakaway from the ANC and launched the PAC. It was a time when independence had come to many African countries, when the 'winds of change' appeared irresistible, and when the pan-Africanist philosophies of Kwame Nkrumah were sweeping the continent. 'Africa for the Africans' was the PAC's cry. The PAC proposed uncompromising mass action to sweep white rule away, and accused the ANC of being dominated by whites and Indians, many of them communists. Following the Sharpeville massacre of 1960, both the ANC and the PAC were banned. In exile the PAC had little success. It was riven by internal conflict, corruption and a singularly unsuccessful military wing. Even the black consciousness movement, formed in the late 1960s and early 1970s, found it difficult to take the PAC seriously, although BC was ideologically much closer to the PAC than to the non-racial ANC tradition.

From the mid-1980s, however, there were signs of greater unity within PAC ranks and a determination to increase its strength in the country. Africanism experienced a limited revival, and a number of armed attacks were carried out by PAC members. Africanist organisations, particularly amongst the youth, began emerging, and PAC supporters rose in prominence within Nactu. Following the state clampdowns in 1986 and after, Nactu became one of the only significant internal and functioning organisations promoting the Africanist cause. This was particularly true after its 1988 congress.

Therein lies the root of Nactu's reassessment of its relationship with Cosatu. Within Nactu the Africanists could predominate. Within a united union movement they would be a relatively small segment.

withdrawing from the summit at the last minute. FBWU president Mlin-delwa Kwelemtini argued that 'unity in action' did not have to lead to 'one federation or one union. Those are just sentimental slogans... Let's respect each other as organisations,' continued Kwelemtini. 'Only at a later stage can we form one organisation.' He agreed that unity, in the form of one organisation, was possible, but only in the long term and only after liberation. 'Not now, not in five years, not in ten years... Only when we are as free as other countries can we have unity.'[6]

The summit continues

Some 700 worker delegates gathered at Wits University on 4 and 5 March 1989. The mood was excited, the summit without precedent. All 14 Cosatu affiliates sent delegates, as did the Cosatu-linked NUWCC. The Nactu affiliates attending, which represented 50 000 members, were the Food, Beverage Workers Union; Black Electronics and Electrical Workers Union; Brushes and Cleaners Workers Union; Banking Insurance, Finance and Assurance Workers Union; Black Domestic Workers Union; National Union of Public Service Workers; SA Laundry, Dry-cleaning and Dyeing Workers Union; Black Allied Mining and Construction Workers Union; Natal Liquor and Catering Trades Employees Union; and the Electrical and Allied Workers Trade Union. In addition, individuals from a number of other Nactu affiliates attended 'in their capacity as workers committed to action against the LRA.'

The 16 non-affiliated unions attending the summit represented far greater numbers of workers. Most notable were the 100 000-strong Garment and Allied Workers Union, the Orange-Vaal General Workers Union, and two unions catering for coloured and Indian postal workers.

Three keynote speakers – Barayi from Cosatu, Mlindelwa Kwelemtini on behalf of the Nactu unions, and OVGWU's Laurence Phatlhe on behalf of the 'independents' – addressed the summit. 'Differences will no doubt be aired', said Barayi 'but at the end of the day we must concentrate on the many things which unite us as workers.'

The proceedings were far from smooth. Suspicions ran deep and while most present tried to avoid conflict, it was not easy to build trust. For two days the delegates discussed the new labour law. Decisions finally taken were labelled 'recommendations' at the insistence of the Nactu delegates. Ironically, there was no time left to discuss the question of trade union unity.

The summit recommendations were practical and bold.[7] They noted the shortcomings of the LRA and that 'despite our protest action against the Bill on 6, 7 and 8 June 1988, employers trapped us shrewdly into fruitless negotiations and supported that the Bill be enacted.' The summit went on to recommend that, in the long term, workers should formulate an alternative LRA to cover all workers in the country.

In the short term, the summit recommended that unions find ways to avoid the industrial court, isolate employers who used the LRA against the unions, and revise recognition agreements 'to circumvent offensive clauses' of the LRA. In addition, it was recommended that Saccola and all employers and employer organisations should be presented with a list of six demands by 2 May: the right to strike and picket; no dismissals without proper hearings; no retrenchments without negotiations and fair selection procedures; recognition of majority unionism; the right to secondary industrial action such as sympathy strikes; and any other demands which the unions had previously listed in their negotiations with Saccola. This last clause was aimed at maintaining both the consistency and the legality of the union movement's negotiating position.

It was also agreed that the unions would mobilise for these demands by holding meetings and rallies, and link the anti-LRA campaign with the Living Wage Campaign and the campaign for a meaningful unemployment benefit. If employers did not make 'positive progress towards meeting the demands' within 30 days, a national dispute would be declared and workers balloted over what steps to take next. Finally, the summit recommended 'further protest actions' against the LRA, and suggested that future worker summits should be held.

The Cosatu CEC held on the weekend after the summit endorsed these recommendations. Affiliates began submitting their demands to employers and preparing for disputes. Cosatu was concerned to fight not only the amendments to the LRA but also the continued exclusion of public sector and agricultural workers from labour law. Demands were accordingly also forwarded to the relevant state departments in the public sector, the Commission for Administration, and the South African Agricultural Union (SAAU), the major representative of white farmers.

For Cosatu, the summit was a success in two respects. It revived the anti-LRA campaign on a broader basis than before and around a concrete programme of action. It also laid the basis for unity with unions outside Cosatu ranks, even though this issue was not discussed. 'Unity comes in different forms', commented Chris Dlamini after the summit.

> To some it means co-operation and demarcation, that we should talk to each other, not fight each other as trade unions. We have a different understanding of unity, and our understanding is that the final stage of unity is one country, one federation. That is our ultimate goal. But we are prepared to debate that, and let others come up with their understanding of unity, and on the basis of that we could arrive at a position where we agree.[8]

The summit was also welcomed by many of the independent unions. Gawu and OVGWU actively took up the anti-LRA campaign.

The official Nactu response to the summit was less enthusiastic. Cunningham Ngcukana remained insistent that 'there were no Nactu affiliates at the summit', only individuals. 'We leave it to our affiliates to take action against the individuals who attended in their name.' Nactu was not averse to action, said Ngcukana, and would still discuss the summit recommendations. However, Nactu had problems with these. It did not agree with asking employers 'to contract out of the LRA', as this would mean 'some workers will have to contract out of action against the LRA'.*

Nor did Nactu agree about 'drafting an LRA for the government' as this would 'give legitimacy to a government that is illegal in the eyes of the majority.' Nactu was also unhappy, said Ngcukana, about linking the anti-LRA campaign with the Living Wage Campaign. This stemmed, apparently, from reservations about the LWC itself. 'To campaign for a living wage also clouds the issue of the exploitation of workers by the ruling class. Workers are led to believe that there can be such a thing as a fair wage.'[9] Nevertheless, in time Nactu would join the anti-LRA campaign and accept the recommendations of the summit.

Phase two of the LRA campaign

Following the summit, meetings between Saccola and both Cosatu and Nactu resumed. At Saccola's invitation, representatives of the National Manpower Commission (NMC) also attended. But there was little progress apart from a statement that the NMC would 'urgently advise' the government to review Section 79(2) of the LRA – the damages clause.

Cosatu proposed that employer claims that the new law was in line with international standards should be put to the test. But the government

---

* This criticism was shared by many within Cosatu. By August 1989, only three companies had explicitly contracted out of the LRA amendments. These were all foreign companies – Pepsi, Kellogg and Mercedes Benz – subject to a range of pressures including those of the disinvestment lobby. There were examples, of specific clauses in the new LRA being by-passed in other companies. At Dorbyl, a giant engineering company, Numsa had gone as far as a strike ballot in its campaign for unfair dismissal cases to go before a private arbitrator rather than the industrial court. Dorbyl eventually agreed to the union's demands. But this constituted only a partial 'contracting out'. Bobby Marie, the union official concerned, stated at the time that 'this was not seen as a comprehensive strategy against the LRA. More than anything else the campaign aimed to strengthen our national shop steward structures in a company which refuses to bargain nationally.'

effectively refused to submit to the jurisdiction of the International Labour Organisation. Neither would Saccola agree to an independent arbitrator hearing the matter.

Some unions made progress in amending their recognition agreements to suit the changed circumstances. Others tried to develop relations with employers outside the official industrial relations system. In general, however, the unions made little headway in circumventing the new labour law.

The six demands made at the workers summit were submitted to individual employers, Saccola and various state departments. 'Employers were given until 30 June' to respond, according to the secretariat's report to Cosatu's third national congress. If progress in meeting the demands was not made 'we would then consider ourselves to be in dispute with them.'

A meeting between Saccola, Nactu and Cosatu was held on 26 June, but ended inconclusively. Employers refused to accede to the union movement's demands.

Cosatu's third national congress scheduled for July would be a forum for workers to decide on their next step. But before examining this, a painful detour to the lush, undulating, blood-stained region of Natal is necessary.

Notes

1. *Star*, 31.10.88; and *Sowetan*, 07.11.88.
2. Minutes of a meeting between Nactu and Cosatu, 13 February 1989.
3. *Cosatu News*, February 1989.
4. *Weekly Mail*, 03.03.89.
5. *New Nation*, 12.01.90.
6. Interview in *South African Labour Bulletin*, 14(1), April 1989, 17.
7. The text of the recommendations is reprinted in *South African Labour Bulletin*, 14(1), April 1989, 32-3.
8. Interview in *South African Labour Bulletin*, 14(1), April 1989, 15.
9. Interview in *South African Labour Bulletin*, 14(1), April 1989, 20-3.

21

Cosatu and the Natal conflict

The valleys of death

THOUSANDS have died in the violence which has swept Natal since the mid-1980s. Previous chapters have described the early conflict between Cosatu and Inkatha, and Inkatha's launch of the United Workers Union of South Africa (Uwusa) as a rival trade union movement. We have seen Uwusa's singular lack of union success despite widespread favouritism from employers and the repeated detention of Cosatu organisers. We have recounted how Inkatha-linked vigilantes were implicated in the abduction and killing of Sarmcol worker leaders in Mpophomeni township, and have also examined Inkatha's opposition to the stayaway of 6-8 June 1988 called in protest against the new labour law.

Details of the Natal conflict have been well-covered elsewhere and this chapter makes no claim to be comprehensive or authoritative. It focuses rather on the tensions between Inkatha and both the unions and broader democratic movement, the scale of violence, its effects on workers and the union movement, and attempts to negotiate peace in the region.

The 'homeland' policy has long been a cornerstone of the apartheid system. White people, regardless of whether they were of Afrikaner or English origin, or more recent immigrants from Eastern Europe or the Portuguese colonies, were defined as part of the white nation and thus privileged. By contrast black people did not exist as a nation. Rather, claimed apartheid theory, there were ten different black nations, each one 'developing separately' until it achieved 'nationhood' and independence in its own 'homeland'. Apartheid's architects claimed that the demand for majority rule was therefore meaningless, since South Africa was a country of minorities. Whites would rule over whites, claimed the theory, and each black 'nation' would rule itself.

All African people were expected to exercise political rights in their respective 'homelands'. Although a majority of the African population lived and worked in the 'white' cities they were seen as visitors, guests of the white 'nation'. While whites retained 87% of the land, including all the industrial centres, the key ports and most of the country's mines, the ten black 'nations' had 13% of the land and few of the country's natural resources. It was hardly surprising, therefore, that the entire democratic movement opposed the 'homeland' policy, seeing it as little more than 'divide and rule'.

Those homelands that became legally 'independent' in terms of this policy – Transkei, Bophuthatswana, Venda and Ciskei – literally had it thrust upon them by the white government, with the collaboration of certain chiefs and a puppet bureaucracy. None of the homelands was economically viable. They were, in effect, labour reserves for mining, agriculture and industry. All were fragmented – the KwaZulu homeland, for example, consisted of some 40 different pieces of land. The separateness of each 'nation' was also open to question. Ciskeians and Transkeians spoke the same language, Xhosa. This, in turn, was part of the Nguni group of languages encompassing Zulu, Swati and Ndebele, each of whose practitioners could communicate fairly comfortably with the others. A similar situation existed with the Sotho group of languages.

Buthelezi, Inkatha and the democratic movement

Why then, in the late 1960s and early 1970s, did the ANC encourage Mangosuthu Gatsha Buthelezi to participate and assume leadership within KwaZulu homeland structures? And why did it give him the go-ahead to form Inkatha yaKwaZulu, as it was then known, in 1975?

At the time the ANC had been effectively crushed within the country and was looking for opportunities to revive its organisation. It advised Buthelezi to participate in homeland structures and accept government appointments, but stressed that he should resist all pressure to accept independence. According to Mzala, a prominent ANC member:

the ANC believed Chief Buthelezi would use the legal opportunities provided by the bantustan programme to participate in the mass

mobilisation of the oppressed people (and focus) on the struggle for a
united and non-racial South Africa.[1]

Relations between the ANC and Inkatha cooled after the 1976 uprisings shifted the focus of national opposition from Natal to the Transvaal.
Thousands of young activists flocked to join the ANC. Most were totally
hostile to the homeland system and explicitly challenged Inkatha's participation in it. Many pointed to Inkatha as the reason why the Natal
region remained calm while unrest swept the remainder of the country.

By 1979 the two organisations had parted ways. ANC president
Oliver Tambo later admitted that:

> unfortunately, we failed to mobilise our own people to take on the task of
> resurrecting Inkatha as the kind of organisation that we wanted, owing to
> the understandable antipathy of many of our comrades towards what they
> considered as working within the bantustan system. The task of
> reconstituting Inkatha therefore fell on Gatsha Buthelezi himself who
> then built Inkatha as a personal power base far removed from the kind of
> organisation we had visualised.[2]

The trade union movement which re-emerged in the early 1970s also
had an ambiguous relationship with Buthelezi. Inkatha's councillor for
community affairs, Barney Dladla, played a role in the 1973 Natal
strikes and intervened repeatedly, invariably on the side of the striking
workers. Dladla served on Tuacc, the co-ordinating body for the emergent unions, and was widely seen as 'a champion of the workers' cause
in Natal.'

Bhekisisa Nxasana, a Sactu activist in Durban during the early
1970s, recalls that he and his comrades found Dladla 'very sympathetic.
We wanted to use him and the KwaZulu government as some kind of
protection. It worked until Dladla was axed.'[3] In a 1974 showdown with
Buthelezi, Dladla was removed from office. Many have argued that the
root cause of this conflict was Dladla's growing popularity. Dladla's
work increased Inkatha's working-class appeal, and as late as 1975 a
survey of Durban workers revealed that 87% saw Buthelezi as their
leader.

Despite Dladla's axing, the emerging unions continued to see Buthelezi as an important ally. They had few enough friends as it was, and
Buthelezi consistently called for legal recognition of unions. However,
his conception of unions was undoubtedly different from the early unionists. In 1974 he attacked the use of strikes, and his calls for unionisation
were accompanied by a strong desire to see them fall under Inkatha's
umbrella.

After the 1976 uprisings unions continued their relationship with Inkatha, particularly in Natal, but were determined to protect their independence and resist Inkatha control. As late as 1980 Buthelezi was a guest speaker when a number of Fosatu affiliates were launched in the Northern Natal region. But in the early 1980s there was an important, yet restrained, showdown when Fosatu decided to discipline certain union officials trying to pull the federation into the Inkatha camp.

Conflict between Inkatha and the rest of the democratic movement increased after 1980 and particularly after the launch of the UDF in 1983. Inkatha regarded the Natal region as its terrain and the Zulu people as its property. There were reports of attacks on communities and individuals either opposed to Inkatha or organising outside of its ambit. Numerous examples of this were documented in a 1985 report of the Institute for Black Research (IBR). In 1980 Inkatha supporters were reported to have acted with police in an attempt to break a school boycott in the region. In 1983 Inkatha supporters attacked students at the University of Zululand, killing five and leaving many others injured. The students had been critical of Buthelezi, not wanting him to speak on campus. The same year various communities resisting rent and transport increases as well as forced incorporation into the KwaZulu homeland found themselves in conflict with both the state and Inkatha. A key community leader, Msizi Dube, was assassinated. The following year Inkatha supporters attacked Hambanathi residents. According to the IBR report, 'bus-loads of Inkatha supporters and combi-loads of impis invaded the township, and armoured four-wheel drive vehicles equipped with flame-throwers set ten houses alight including that of Alfred Sithole who was murdered.'[4]

Inkatha's conflict with the broad anti-apartheid movement runs deep, with its critics charging, for example, that despite its control of the KwaZulu homeland, labour legislation in that area has been more restrictive than in the rest of South Africa. Similarly, when students tried to organise themselves into the UDF-affiliated Congress of South African Students (Cosas) they found the organisation outlawed by the KwaZulu authorities even before it was banned by the South African government.

Maré has commented that Inkatha

> has a remarkably consistent record of verbal and physical conflict with other groups opposing apartheid, while its relationship with the state and parliamentary politics, though verbally tense at times, has never broken down for very long.[5]

Buthelezi and his Inkatha movement are something of a paradox. They participate in the apartheid system and at the same time condemn it

– at least rhetorically. Buthelezi is not satisfied with leading the small and impoverished KwaZulu homeland and has successfully resisted Pretoria's independence plans. However, his actions have often brought him into sharp conflict with the rest of the democratic movement and this, his detractors allege, places him firmly in the camp of the apartheid regime. But it is simplistic to label Buthelezi a 'stooge', although the label sticks comfortably to most other homeland leaders.

Buthelezi has both a strong regional and ethnic chauvinism and aspirations to national leadership. Although Inkatha is today technically open to all, it is essentially a conservative Zulu ethnic movement. Buthelezi has frequently indulged in ethnic abuse against his opponents, labelling the ANC as 'Xhosa'; mobilising his supporters by continual reference to aspects of Zulu tradition; calling UDF patron and Anglican bishop Mcebisi Xundu 'a Xhosa priest and troublemaker'. And when Indian students called him a 'puppet on a string' he threatened the Indian community with revenge similar to 1949, when major Zulu-Indian ethnic violence occurred.[6]

Inkatha claims a membership of well over a million. Most observers have cast doubt on this and there is strong evidence of forced recruitment campaigns and that membership is 'advisable' in the KwaZulu area if one wants access to pensions, education and other services. Nevertheless Inkatha undoubtedly has substantial backing and is able to muster physical support when necessary. The tens of thousands crammed into Kings Park stadium to herald Uwusa's launch were a sign of this, even though many rural people were obliged to pay and attend the gathering. Another indication was its ability to muster an 'army' estimated at between 3 000 and 12 000 during the 1990 fighting in the Pietermaritzburg area.

The union movement in Natal, prior to the launch of Cosatu, went out of its way to avoid conflict with Inkatha. However Fosatu – the dominant union force at the time – repeatedly had to assert its independence in the face of Inkatha attempts to bring it within its orbit. As the unions grew to be a powerful force in the region, yet remained independent of Inkatha, it was inevitable that conflict would grow. Their very existence was a challenge to Inkatha's claim that it represented all Zulu people and controlled the region. In this sense the Natal violence was inevitable.

Violence erupts in Pietermaritzburg

The dispute at British multinational BTR-Sarmcol was a turning point. In May 1985 the company dismissed 900 striking workers from its plant at Howick near Pietermaritzburg. All were Mawu members. As a result, the workers and their union called a consumer boycott and a one-day work stayaway in the area for 18 July 1985. Buthelezi opposed both tactics and called on people to ignore the call. He declared that the strikers had no popular support and that continuation with the campaign in the face of his personal opposition constituted a deliberate challenge and an insult. Despite this the stayaway was a success with almost the entire black population in the area absent from work.[7]

In September 1985 the president of Inyanda, the Inkatha-linked African Chamber of Commerce, explained Inkatha's attitude:

> If Fosatu persists in its boycott call in Natal this will mean that it will be openly challenging the Chief Minister's influence. We warned them not to push us into a corner where Inyanda will combine with Inkatha in an open battle to see who is who between Fosatu and KwaZulu leadership.[8]

Fosatu called off the consumer boycott, largely in an effort to reduce tensions. Nevertheless questions remained. The boycott and stayaway call had not been directed against Inkatha but against BTR-Sarmcol. Why had Inkatha taken it as a challenge? According to John Jeffreys, a civil rights lawyer active in the Pietermaritzburg area,

> Inkatha portrayed itself as the sole political representative of the Zulus and was dependent on the practical realisation of this image in order to secure its position on the national political stage. Consequently, Inkatha felt threatened by the growth of a mass-based political organisation, independent of Inkatha and opposed to its policies, in the Zulu heartland.[9]

It was not surprising that Pietermaritzburg became the first focal point of intense and widespread conflict. It was an important industrial area (the second largest in the region) where support for Inkatha had never been very strong. Fosatu (and from December 1985 Cosatu) unions had a powerful presence. The UDF was also active in the area, working among the youth as well as attempting to establish civic organisations.

Inkatha supporters tried to reverse this trend, with little success. In 1985 members of the UDF-affiliated Imbali Civic Association were harassed and the chairperson's house fire-bombed. The same year senior Inkatha leaders led a march on the Federal Theological Seminary, accused it of harbouring UDF supporters and ordered it to close. In December 1986 senior Sarmcol worker leaders were abducted and killed by vigilantes following an Inkatha rally in Mpophomeni (Howick). Later that month township residents who switched off their lights and cut out all festivities in support of the UDF's 'Christmas against the emergency' call, saw their homes attacked by vigilantes. Despite these assaults support for Cosatu and the UDF grew. Cosatu's 5-6 May stayaway call of 1987, protesting the whites-only election, was well-observed in the area in spite of Buthelezi's opposition.

The turning point came when Inkatha allegedly embarked on a forced recruitment campaign during the August to November 1987 period. This was the immediate cause of the 'war' which broke out in Pietermaritzburg.

According to Jeffreys many community councillors, chiefs, indunas and school committee members

> responded to their crisis of legitimacy by trying to force people to join Inkatha... Initially they attempted to coerce people through threats and intimidation, but as these methods failed, they resorted to more severe methods, such as arson and murder. Thus they earned the name of 'warlords'. Their modus operandi was to target a specific area. Residents were called upon to join Inkatha. If a small proportion were reluctant to do so they would be attacked. If however, the community was opposed to Inkatha a wave of terror would be directed at them. The terror was indiscriminate.[10]

Sixty people were killed in the Pietermaritzburg area during September. In October another 83 died. Cosatu and its UDF allies then agreed that the Pietermaritzburg Chamber of Commerce (PCC) should host peace talks between Inkatha and themselves. Prior to the meeting Cosatu/UDF activists stressed that 'talks could only succeed if all the parties involved had the will to end the violence.' They also felt that peace could not be established for as long as the 'warlords' were 'free to continue with their killing sprees. The police had to act against the warlords.'[11]

Talking peace

The first meeting chaired by the PCC was held in late November 1987 and went surprisingly well. All parties endorsed the principles of freedom of association and expression and committed themselves to halting 'all forms of aggression' and 'forced recruitment'. All agreed on the need to establish a process to 'bring about an end to the violence in the Pietermaritzburg area.'[12] A joint UDF/Cosatu mass rally, held only after enormous public pressure forced the state to allow the democratic forces to report back, was held at Wadley Stadium on 6 December. It endorsed the direction of the peace talks and heard the leadership make a strong call for unity.

The optimism was short lived. In a December speech to Inkatha's central committee Chief Buthelezi argued that Cosatu and UDF were 'not worthy' of reconciliation and accused the alliance of trying to make Pietermaritzburg a 'no-go area' for him:

> I am now coming close to believing that the only reconciliation that there will ever be in this country is the reconciliation of the most powerful with those who pay homage to the most powerful. We are talking about a life and death struggle. We are talking about all-or-nothing victories. We are talking about the final triumph of good over evil.[13]

This attitude emerged clearly at the second PCC-hosted meeting in early December. Inkatha included three senior officials from outside the Pietermaritzburg area, declaring that peace talks should be handled at national rather than local level. Its delegates insisted that the talks could not continue unless both Cosatu and UDF repudiated the October edition of *Inqaba*, the journal of the self-proclaimed Marxist Workers Tendency of the ANC, which contained a vitriolic denunciation of Inkatha.* The Cosatu/UDF delegation pointed out that it had not seen the *Inqaba* article, that it did not come from any of its structures, that it had not been distributed in the area and that it did not reflect their views. It was well known that the Marxist Workers Tendency was a tiny Trotskyist grouping (a cousin of the British 'Militant' tendency) expelled from the ANC in 1985. Yet Inkatha refused to accept these comments and the second 'peace' meeting broke up.[14]

Cosatu attempted to revive the peace process and even proposed a national meeting of leaders. This time talks were sabotaged by state intervention. Between November and January 1988 over 700 people in the Pietermaritzburg area were detained and in February, as we have seen in an earlier chapter, both the UDF and Cosatu were restricted. This dealt the peace process a death blow and severely weakened UDF in the area. Key members of the UDF's negotiating team such as Martin Wittenberg and Skhumbuzo Ngwenya were among those detained. Cosatu, with its factory base, was more difficult to crush.

Inkatha was not affected by the clampdown and few, if any, of its supporters were detained. 'The police intend to face the future with

---

* *The Inqaba article, according to Musa Zondi of Inkatha, described Buthelezi as 'vigilante-in-chief' and labelled Uwusa the 'reactionary Inkatha gangster clique extended into the work places.' Inqaba called for 'a clear national strategy to defeat Inkatha, Uwusa and all vigilantes.' It criticised Cosatu's leadership for its 'softness and hesitation on Inkatha and Uwusa' and for dignifying Uwusa by calling it a 'tribally-based union' rather than 'a strike-breaking murder squad... In all battles it helps to call things by their real name... Venomous snakes do not become harmless worms because they are referred to as such.'*

moderates', said Law and Order Minister Vlok at the end of February. 'Radicals, who are trying to destroy South Africa, will not be tolerated. We will fight them. We have put our foot in that direction, and we will eventually win in the Pietermaritzburg area.'[15] Peter Gastrow of the Democratic Party noted 'a well-established pattern whereby the state intervenes each time it seems peace talks may get off the ground.'

Repression intensified in the months that followed, as did Inkatha-linked attacks. There were repeated claims of police support for Inkatha during attacks on UDF supporters. Activists tried to defend their communities from attack as best they could, but with so many leaders detained discipline and organisation often broke down. Cosatu attempted to use the legal procedures during this period although it had few illusions that the courts would actually be able to provide protection from attack. By December 1987 13 court interdicts had been granted against officials and members of Inkatha. The details of these cases paint a disturbing picture but are too lengthy to be recorded here. According to an August 1989 Cosatu dossier in which Inkatha was labelled 'the aggressor', union and UDF investigations together with court evidence had

> exposed the phenomenon of warlords: influential Inkatha people who are leaders of armed groups at the centre of the campaign of forced recruitment. They operate openly, expect total obedience to themselves and their organisation, and apparently have no fear of prosecution. If Inkatha or the police had taken immediate action against these ten warlords first identified some 20 months ago, about a thousand lives could have been saved...
>
> Cosatu lawyers have compiled detailed information of direct police involvement on the side of Inkatha. Cosatu has charged that policemen and Inkatha warlords have co-operated in the detention, shooting, interrogation and harassment of residents in the Pietermaritzburg area... Inkatha has defended the actions of its impis.[16]

A shift in white public and business support away from Inkatha was an important side-effect of the campaign of terror. The chief mediator during the PCC talks commented in February 1988 that he had seen the attitude of his colleagues

> change drastically from one of suspicion, hostility even, to one of a certain respect for the way the union (Cosatu) has conducted itself. Their discipline, their democratic procedure has had a very positive influence. The conflict in Pietermaritzburg has made a lot of businessmen sit up and question Inkatha's real commitment to negotiation.[17]

The string of court interdicts did little to restrain Inkatha, the warlords or the police. They did, however, open the way for a new peace initiative. An out-of-court settlement in September 1988 resulted in a Cosatu/Inkatha accord. Both parties, once again, rejected the use of violence and recognised freedom of association. They established a complaints adjudication board (CAB) chaired by a retired judge to hear accusations against any Cosatu or Inkatha member alleged to have breached the agreement.

The CAB agreement led to some tension between Cosatu and the then-banned UDF. Cosatu effectively dealt with this second peace initiative alone. It spoke to those few UDF leaders who were available but was unable to communicate properly with ordinary UDF members. Thami Mohlomi, Cosatu's Southern Natal regional secretary recalled that 'when the youth saw on TV and in the newspaper that Cosatu and Buthelezi had signed an agreement, they naturally felt that they had not been properly consulted.'[18] It took some time to repair the relationship.

Despite good intentions the CAB had little success. Inkatha members generally refused to participate in its proceedings. Nevertheless the CAB did hear two cases. In the first the judge found that there were compelling grounds to believe Chief Shayabantu Zondi was in breach of the accord. This he had done by prohibiting non-Inkatha meetings in his area and intimidating and threatening residents because they were members of non-Inkatha organisations.

The second case was brought against two Inkatha leaders, Gasela and 'Thu' Ngcobo. The Duma family alleged that these two men were harassing them and trying to kill their eldest son, Nicholas. The judge recommended strong disciplinary action against the two and advised that Inkatha deprive Gasela of office. Inkatha ignored this recommendation. Not long afterwards Nicholas Duma was murdered. As a result Cosatu suspended its participation in the CAB.[*]

Impact of the violence

It is hard to convey the magnitude of the violence and the extent to which it escalated. The sheer scale of death exceeds that of the Belfast or even Beirut conflicts. The figures are cold and clinical, yet shocking. In the Natal Midlands (the greater Pietermaritzburg area) political violence

---

[*] *Councillor 'Thu' Ngcobo was charged with his murder and released on R800 bail. What followed was indicative of the lack of popular faith in the law and the cycle of revenge killings which has developed. Witnesses to the murder of Nicholas Duma claimed to have seen Ngcobo commit it but were too scared to testify to this or even prepare affidavits. Ngcobo himself died after he was gunned down by unknown people outside a fast food outlet on 1 January 1990.*

resulted in a mere 12 deaths in 1985 and 13 the following year. There were 413 deaths in 1987; 691 in 1988; while 696 people were killed in 1989. In the first seven months of 1990 alone some 620 people were killed. This excludes the estimated 1 411 people killed in the Durban region from 1987 to mid-1990, not to mention those killed in other parts of the province.[19]

What did the conflict mean to ordinary people? An affidavit by the grandmother of Makhithiza, a young boy, provides some indication:

> At midday we saw the Inkatha people appearing at KwaMphumuza. We all went into the house because we were afraid. Two police vans then arrived with five white policemen and two black policemen in them. Both vans stopped near our home and all the white policemen got out... Three white policemen ran into my house and tried to get the three boys but they ran away. One white policeman shot my dog.
>
> The policeman chasing Makhithiza fired three shots... The third shot hit Makhithiza at the top of his back near his neck. He fell down. The policemen came up to him and beat him with their shotguns. They picked him up and dragged him to the van where they put him in the back. He was bleeding slightly from the wound. I asked them if I could take out the bullet, and said I would bring it the next day if he would be charged. The white policeman said no, he was arrested. Mr Agrippa Bhengu, a counsellor of the induna Mr Ntombela, was wearing a police uniform and carrying a gun, though he is not a policeman. He said 'we will kill him'. Then they drove away with him...
>
> In the morning a girl came to me, sent by Mr Mncwabe, to say the boy was outside the homestead of Mr Mncwabe, near the bus stop. I went to see him. He was lying on his back on the grass near the road. He was dead. There were many stab wounds in his chest and back and sides.[20]

As the conflict developed it took on a territorial dimension with some areas seen as UDF and others as Inkatha strongholds. Bus drivers, mainly TGWU members, frequently found themselves in the frontline as they drove through different areas. In Inkatha areas they were frequently attacked, stoned or shot at because of their Cosatu membership. Neither was their relationship with the UDF youth uncomplicated. One of the local bus companies was owned by the KwaZulu government and many young 'comrades' saw these buses, particularly those heading for Inkatha destinations, as fair game for attack. The difference, commented one driver philosophically, is 'between being caught in the crossfire and being the actual target.'[21] Many bus drivers have died in the process.

The violence was devastating for union structures. Workers complained of staying awake all night defending their homes from attack and then having to perform a full day's work. Attendance at Cosatu locals and other union meetings declined, particularly those held in the evenings. Workers wanted to travel straight home from work and avoid the added dangers of the dark. However union meetings at the workplace continued and indeed became a major source of communication.

A Cosatu report issued in early 1989 estimated that 3 000 homes had been destroyed in the Pietermaritzburg area alone and that over 30 000 people had become refugees. Some, particularly the youth, tried to escape to other areas but discovered that the violence was not limited to Pietermaritzburg. Indeed similar patterns of forced recruitment, attacks and counter-attacks occurred in most parts of Natal. For example Mpumalanga, mid-way between Pietermaritzburg and Durban, has experienced some of the most intense conflict with an estimated 2 000 lives lost in four years of conflict.[22] A member of KwaNdengezi Youth League related his experience after fleeing to Durban. 'We found comrades, refugees from Inkatha, from up and down the coast – KwaMakhuta, KwaMashu, Inanda and townships around Eshowe and Empangeni. The truth is that Pietermaritzburg is happening all over Natal.'

In November 1987 conflict erupted in Isithebe, Mandini, on the Natal North Coast. Fares for the kombi-taxi service rose sharply and residents and workers decided to walk to work. Vigilantes began attacking workers, forcing them to board taxis. In the days which followed a number of taxis were stoned and damaged. Inkatha accused Cosatu members of instigating the boycott and the violence. An attempt at local peace talks was disrupted, according to Cosatu regional secretary Matthews Oliphant, when senior Inkatha national leaders entered the meeting and announced there was 'no way they (Inkatha) can talk to the perpetrators of violence' and that Cosatu was lucky not to have 'been chucked out of KwaZulu.'[23]

During March 1989 Cosatu publicly accused the police and the state of encouraging vigilante violence. It submitted a detailed memorandum showing police reluctance to prosecute vigilantes, or their seemingly-deliberate incompetence when attempting to do so. This 'partisan policing' was a key reason why there could be no lasting peace in the area, argued Cosatu, and why an independent commission of enquiry into police activity and conduct was necessary.

The state announced that it would investigate whether, by releasing such information, Cosatu was breaking its restriction order banning it from political activities. Law and Order Minister Vlok suggested that the solution to violence lay in an iron fist approach towards Cosatu/UDF activists and structures. Chief Buthelezi demanded that Cosatu withdraw the document. And Pietermaritzburg police briefly detained Mandla Mthembu, an informant who assisted in compiling the dossier. During his detention Mthembu was 'seriously assaulted by means of fists, hooding, the helicopter, and being forced to eat salt.' Shortly afterwards Jabu Ndlovu, a Cosatu shop steward who had addressed the media on the role of the police in the violence, was murdered together with her husband and daughter in a vigilante attack.[24]

The 1989 peace initiative

Cosatu remained committed to peace despite the failure of the PCC and CAB peace initiatives. Local peace attempts had generally failed or been short lived. Cosatu as an organisation was suffering. Its major efforts were going into defence against vigilante attacks leaving little time to fight for normal union rights. Persistent attacks had damaged the federation and virtually crippled its UDF ally.

Cosatu's working group on Natal violence undertook a frank assessment of the situation. In a report to Cosatu's February 1989 CEC it noted that the level of organisation of the democratic forces was 'poor' and would 'not increase under the present conditions... Our supporters are undisciplined and a cycle of revenge killing is increasing.' The community was 'increasingly becoming alienated by this violence.' Each time Inkatha lost the upper hand 'the police step in to join the killing or detain activists, thus making the battle unwinnable.' The state was 'systematically fueling the violence so as to occupy us with its puppets and not be able to fight against the state itself.'

The report noted growing contradictions within Inkatha between ordinary supporters and 'the "Mafia" warlord element.' Organisation and political struggle could only take place effectively in a climate of peace or if the 'warlords' were isolated from the base of Inkatha supporters. It was in Cosatu's interests 'to obtain peace at all costs rather than allow the war to continue and have more people dying.' There were 'no magic formulas' for peace and the process would be a long one, requiring patience and a multi-faceted approach.

The approach suggested to the CEC was four-pronged. Ending the violence was a priority and should include direct talks with Inkatha. The co-ordination and functioning of structures, particularly in the community, needed strengthening. A mass campaign for peace should be launched reaching out to the grassroots, as well as to business interests and 'disillusioned Inkatha supporters'. Finally there was a need to 'improve the discipline of our supporters, especially youth' and to 'strengthen our ability to defend ourselves.'[25]

In early 1989 Cosatu and the banned UDF supported the calling of a peace conference bringing together the widest possible spectrum of people and organisations in the Natal region. This was rejected by Chief

Buthelezi who opposed the involvement of outsiders in what he saw as 'black-on-black' conflict. To prevent any possible peace process stalling, Cosatu and UDF agreed to a direct meeting with Inkatha leadership. Inkatha then insisted that the meeting take place in Ulundi, KwaZulu's capital and Buthelezi's stronghold. Cosatu and UDF rejected this and proposed a neutral venue. Only direct representations by the Anglican church broke the deadlock and it was agreed to hold 'five-a-side' talks in Durban. However Buthelezi declined to attend these himself and the Inkatha team was led by its more temperate general secretary Oscar Dhlomo.

Cosatu entered the five-a-side talks better prepared than in the past. It recognised the need to ensure that its constituency was well informed. With UDF structures in the community often extremely weak or non-existent it was important to take the people with it in any peace moves. Many ordinary combatants on the ground were sceptical of talking peace to Inkatha. As part of the information process a joint Cosatu/UDF newsletter, *Ubumbano*, was issued in the Natal region. Joint meetings and workshops were held around the region to prepare for the peace initiative.

The five-a-side meetings appeared to make progress when, during July 1989, a peace process was agreed upon. This involved a number of steps – an immediate end to hostile propaganda and vilification; a 'presidents' meeting' (of necessity outside the country) of ten delegates each from Inkatha, the ANC, Cosatu and UDF; a joint peace conference of Inkatha, Cosatu and UDF delegates from the areas affected by the violence; and, finally, joint rallies for peace in all areas. The agreement also envisaged joint peace committees, an effective enforcement structure, and measures to resettle the tens of thousands of Natal refugees.

As will be seen in the next chapter, Cosatu took immediate steps to improve the climate. At its third national congress at the end of July delegates ratified the peace agreement and made a conscious effort not to attack Inkatha in their singing or speeches. It was a hopeful moment. July 1989 saw the greatest possibility ever for a negotiated peace in Natal. The five-a-side agreement involved senior leadership of all organisations and was both comprehensive and well-considered. Unfortunately this chapter cannot end on that note.

Cosatu was led to understand that Inkatha's national conference had endorsed the agreement. However, in late July, Inkatha's central committee demanded – in breach of the agreement – that Inkatha send an equal number of delegates to the presidents' meeting as Cosatu, UDF and the ANC combined.

'We wish to clarify an important point,' responded Naidoo in a letter to Inkatha:

Cosatu and UDF are separate organisations. Each organisation must seek mandates and report back to their own structures. We co-operate closely, particularly in regard to the peace process in Natal... However, we remain separate organisations and we are not affiliated to each other... Each organisation needs to be represented separately at the proposed meeting.[26]

Nevertheless Cosatu and the UDF, anxious that the peace process should not flounder, suggested that each organisation send a minimum of ten delegates but that the maximum delegation size not be limited.

When Inkatha's central committee met in September it rejected this proposal. It also demanded that any talks be opened to additional groupings such as Uwusa and a hitherto unknown organisation – the Natal region of the PAC-in-exile! Inkatha raised further obstacles. It produced an anonymous document, allegedly written by Sactu and UDF supporters in Pietermaritzburg, calling for selective violence against Inkatha. Although Cosatu, Sactu and the UDF publicly distanced themselves from its contents, Buthelezi was not satisfied. Inkatha also demanded that the ANC apologise for remarks made by Thabo Mbeki at a Copenhagen press conference in June. Finally Inkatha effectively rejected the peace accord when it called for a moratorium on all talks 'until there is the prospect of success.'

'Once again', said UDF's Murphy Morobe and Cosatu's Naidoo in a joint statement, 'we see the same pattern of introducing external documents and demanding apologies and of introducing new demands which have the effect of sabotaging the peace process.'

Jeffreys has ascribed Inkatha's response to Chief Buthelezi's attempt to 'assert his equal status with UDF, Cosatu and the ANC in anticipation of future negotiations with De Klerk.'[27]

Dividing lines

An upsurge in violence throughout Natal followed the collapse of the 1989 peace initiative. Boundaries were redrawn as control of areas shifted from Inkatha to the UDF or vice versa. Pietermaritzburg, Mpumalanga, Durban and the Natal South Coast were severely affected. There was considerable violence outside the orbit of any organisation. Anti-Inkatha forces would often be labelled 'UDF' although they had little if any connection with that organisation. A cycle of violence became more apparent with killings followed by revenge counter-attacks.

In recent years much of the violence has become criminalised. On the one hand warlords have asserted their newly-found power for non-political ends, with patronage and extortion widespread. On the other hand youth has often used its power similarly, and there have been frequent reports of lootings and muggings. In addition, criminal elements have taken advantage of the fighting to wreak havoc and make their own demands on a battered and war-weary populace. Peace is now only partially dependent on talks and good intentions at leadership level, with its achievement at local level and an end to the endemic violence of the region as a whole more difficult.

Many, including Buthelezi, have referred to the conflict as 'black-on-black violence' or have seen it as tribal – an attack on the Zulu people. The conflict in Natal does have an ethnic dimension, particularly since Inkatha seeks to present itself as the voice of the Zulu people. Inkatha tends to portray any attack on it as an assault on the Zulu people, sometimes implying that Xhosa or Indian trouble-makers have been behind attacks on Inkatha. At grassroots level it has frequently stressed that Cosatu's president Barayi is Xhosa-speaking and that this explains why the organisation is anti-Zulu. However the depth and intensity of the Natal violence has largely laid such claims to rest. All parties to the conflict, at local and regional level, have been overwhelmingly Zulu-speaking.

To describe the Natal violence as 'black-on-black' is accurate only at the most superficial level. It ignores the role of the police and army. It avoids detailing what is being fought for, and what is being opposed. Ultimately it is a deeply racist explanation implying that innate and savage violent tendencies among black people have caused the conflict.

Any state committed to creating divisions, as the apartheid state is, will use existing tensions and then portray them as rifts amongst the people. There is clear evidence, particularly during the 1980s, that the state's counter-insurgency and anti-revolutionary strategies consciously orchestrated conflict between the democratic movement and non-state forces. Death squads and 'dirty tricks' units not only killed, but did so in a way which attempted to direct blame away from the apartheid state. The shooting of black people by white troops was politically and internationally unacceptable. By channelling conflict into fighting between different sections of the oppressed population the South African state has been able to present the violence as 'black-on-black' and itself as merely a peace-keeper.

The tragedy of the Natal situation goes well beyond this cynical manipulation of division and conflict. The violence no longer affects only the oppressed. It has begun tearing apart the entire fabric of society, affecting the comfort and security of the white population and employers. More ominously, as we shall see in a later chapter, during 1990 the violence spread to every corner of the country, bringing South Africa to the brink of uncontainable civil war.

Notes

1. Mzala, *Gatsha Buthelezi. Chief with a double agenda*, London, 1988, 23.
2. Quoted in Mzala, *Gatsha Buthelezi*, 124.
3. Author interview with Bhekisisa Nxasana, February 1991.
4. Shamim Meer, 'Community and unions in Natal', *South African Labour Bulletin*, 13(3), March/April 1988, 82-3.
5. Gerhard Maré, 'Inkatha: "By the grace of the Nationalist government?"', *South African Labour Bulletin*, 13(2), February 1988, 71.
6. Mzala, *Gatsha Buthelezi*, 231.
7. Matthew Kentridge, *An Unofficial War. Inside the Conflict in Pietermaritzburg*, Cape Town, 1990, 219-20.
8. *Sunday Tribune*, 01.11.87.
9. John Jeffreys, 'Rocky path to peace in Natal', *South African Labour Bulletin*, 14(5), November 1989, 62-3.
10. Jeffreys, 'Rocky path to peace', 63.
11. A collective of Pietermaritzburg activists, 'Negotiations and violence in Pietermaritzburg', strategy paper reprinted in *South African Labour Bulletin*, 13(2), February 1988, 56-7.
12. Minutes of 24 November 1987 peace meeting.
13. *Weekly Mail*, 11.12.87; and Cosatu dossier, 'The Natal violence: prospects for peace', August 1989, 5.
14. Musa Zondi, 'Inkatha/UDF peace talks', speech delivered on 9 December 1987.
15. *Natal Witness*, 27.02.88.
16. Cosatu dossier, 'The Natal violence'.
17. Interview with Paul van Uytrecht, general manager of Pietermaritzburg Chamber of Commerce, '*South African Labour Bulletin*, 13(2), February 1988, 42-3.
18. Interview with Thami Mohlomi and Willis Mchunu, *South African Labour Bulletin*, 14(2), June 1989, 71.
19. John Aitchison, 'Death and Revenge', *Daily Mail*, 14.08.90.
20. Affidavit quoted in *South African Labour Bulletin*, 13(2), February 1988, 23.
21. Kentridge, *An Unofficial War*, 36.
22. *Natal Witness*, 12.10.89.
23. Notes of a meeting between Cosatu and Inkatha representatives held in Isithebe on 11 November 1987, in author's possession.
24. Memorandum submitted to a press conference held by Cosatu/UDF in Pietermaritzburg, 29 March 1989; see also Cosatu, 'The role of the police in vigilante violence in the Pietermaritzburg area', March 1989; and a subsequent confidential Cosatu briefing document, 'The role of the police in relation to the violence in Pietermaritzburg', undated.
25. Working group, 'Report on Natal violence', presented to the Cosatu CEC, 6 February 1989.
26. Letter from Jay Naidoo to Oscar Dhlomo, 14 August 1989.
27. Jeffreys, 'Rocky path to peace', 69.

22

Cosatu's third national congress

Negotiating positions

NASREC, the venue for Cosatu's third national congress, is situated on the edge of Soweto. Delegates, staying in a number of Johannesburg's city-centre hotels, arrived there by the busload. The evening before the congress Cosatu arranged a social gathering in the ballroom of one of these hotels. It was a bizarre sight. Hundreds of informally-clad unionists danced and sang freedom songs. Other guests in the staid hotel ducked out of sight as the chandeliers rocked to the rhythm of toyi-toyi.

From the early hours of 12 July groups of singing workers marched into Nasrec's cavernous hall. Their singing was as much an attempt to keep warm as an expression of resistance. Delegates from the coast complained of the bitterly cold Johannesburg winter weather. The venue, an enormous hall with concrete floors and high ceilings, did little to help. Massive gas turbine heaters only emphasised that the venue was more suited as an aircraft hanger. It had been chosen only because no other suitable venue large enough was available. Cosatu had outgrown the Flower Hall at Wits University, where previous congresses were held.

Some 1 858 delegates attended, representing over 924 000 paid-up members. There were scores of observers present as well, including representatives from restricted community organisations and Nactu. A delegation from the National Union of Namibian Workers (NUNW) was given place of honour amongst the international guests. A number of unionists from abroad were, for the first time, invited to sit in on the entire congress proceedings, including the 'closed sessions'. This was a sign of self-confidence which had been lacking at earlier congresses.

The spirit of the congress was unusually defiant. Delegates' most popular songs lauded the ANC's military wing, Umkhonto we Sizwe. Flags of the banned Communist Party and ANC were in evidence. So too were hundreds of posters calling Nelson Mandela's release. SACP members covertly distributed their party's newspaper, *Umsebenzi*. All these were signs of defiance, reflecting a sense that the government was unable to contain the tide of resistance. Even the official congress slogan, 'Educate, Consolidate and Advance to Victory', emblazoned across a ten-metre high banner, reflected the faint whiff of freedom in the air.

The state's security forces were also busy. They were seen in and around hotels where delegates stayed, and kept a watchful eye on proceedings from outside the congress venue. On arrival at Nasrec delegates found the area strewn with fake pamphlets. Similar ones had been distributed in other parts of the country in the week before the congress. One, distributed around Port Elizabeth factories, contained streams of wild allegations. In one breath, it called for Cosatu's leaders to stop dabbling in politics, then demanded that the Freedom Charter should 'be expelled and replaced by a socialist workerist document.' There were clearly forces which wanted to perpetuate the political differences evident at the 1987 and 1988 congresses.

The credentials report revealed that membership was up in almost all affiliates (see attendance table). Although it was not yet an affiliate, special provision was made for Gawu's 211 delegates to attend. CWIU objected to this on constitutional grounds but received no seconder. Actwusa explained to the congress that it had finalised merger arrangements with Gawu, which would take place in September that year. The two unions asked to be seen as an Actwusa/Gawu delegation, and this was how they were labelled throughout the remainder of the congress. While CWIU's objection was technically correct, the congress decision to admit Gawu delegates was an acknowledgement of that union's size, and of the need to encourage the forthcoming merger. Significantly, no-one approached the issue from the perspective of which 'bloc' would be strengthened most by Gawu's presence.

Unlike the 1988 special congress, the Ccawusa delegation was made up of all its sections – by this stage there were three. The participation of all three sections as one delegation was a result of re-unification talks which were then underway. In order not to disrupt this process, the congress agreed that Ccawusa speakers could talk and vote as individual delegates, not as a bloc.

Union delegations

Union	Paid-up Members	Delegates Entitled	Worker Delegates Present	Officials Present
Actwusa	72 408	145	121	24
Cawu	21 000	42	26	16
Ccawusa	72 823	148	111	37
CWIU	35 151	71	56	15
Fawu	77 507	156	126	20
Gawu	105 500	211	168	19
Nehawu	14 295	29	21	8
NUM	212 000	424	372	21
Numsa	188 013	377	315	62
Potwa	16 842	34	29	5
Ppwawu	31 215	63	44	18
Sadwu	14 525	30	21	9
Samwu	23 638	48	39	9
Sarhwu	16 400	33	23	10
TGWU	23 182	47	38	9
NUWCC	-- ---	25 (observers)		
Total	924 499	1 858		

Negotiations

Three guest speakers had been invited to address the congress, and all explored the issue of negotiations with the regime. Harry Gwala, recently released Robben Island prisoner and a well-known ANC and SACP veteran, was unable attend the congress, but his speech was read out by Sydney Mufamadi.

'The workers of our land have no parliament of their own,' he said. 'You, their congress, are their parliament. You are called upon to give a bold and unwavering lead to the people of South Africa... The working class has built the most powerful force in the history of South Africa – Cosatu.' Gwala went on to warn against the dangers of 'so-called negotiations' and imperialist manoeuvres. 'Those who have negotiated from a weak position have only sacrificed their own birthright... Our path', concluded Gwala,

lies in the determined united action of the people, not to reform apartheid, not to fight for structural reforms like Kwa-Natal Indaba, but to destroy and bury apartheid so that on its ashes they may build a new non-racial democratic South Africa.

Valli Moosa, acting general secretary of the UDF, argued in his speech that the armed struggle, international isolation and mass struggles had forced the regime to acknowledge that it had to negotiate. 'FW de Klerk has realised that during his term of office he will be faced with one of two ways of losing power: either he enters into genuine negotiations with the ANC now, or he gets swept away by the rising tide of mass militance and action.' Genuine negotiations could only occur, continued Moosa, if 'the regime unilaterally creates a climate conducive to negotiations.' Neither could negotiations be genuine 'if they are held above the heads or behind the backs of the people.'

The third speaker, the SACC's eloquent general secretary Frank Chikane, also addressed the issue of negotiations. Popular resistance had driven the state 'to a point where it has no option but to talk about talks, to send its emissaries around the world projecting its willingness to change and its readiness to negotiate.' Referring to state repression and the situation in Natal, Chikane commented that the government 'expects the peoples' organisations to formulate positions on the question of negotiations, yet we ourselves are not allowed to talk about peace.' Every South African had a responsibility 'to create a climate that will force the government to stop its violence against the people once and for all.'

The issue of negotiations was a major topic at the congress. It was a discussion located in a contradictory set of circumstances. On the one hand the security forces were, if anything, becoming more repressive, and were facing an increasingly defiant mass movement. PW Botha remained state president despite having suffered a stroke in January. While effective power had already shifted to FW de Klerk, he was anxious not to upset Botha's 'securocrats', and there was little indication of impending shifts in state policy. On the other hand, the mass democratic movement was aware that negotiations were on the agenda. The ANC had indicated to Cosatu that it was facing pressure from the international community to enter into negotiations with the government. The ANC believed the government was facing similar pressures. Nelson Mandela, from his prison cell in Paarl, had also communicated similar messages to Cosatu leaders. He asked Cosatu to indicate under what conditions it would find negotiations with the regime acceptable. Even as delegates gathered at the congress venue there were press reports of Mandela meeting his captors and talking 'peace'.

While government talk of negotiations sounded like its previous pronouncements – negotiations without genuine leaders or banned organisations – there were indications that something more substantial was afoot. Cosatu and the democratic movement were suspicious. This sounded like something they had heard before. And yet...

Delegates to the congress were also following the Namibian independence process, then underway. It appeared to most observers that Namibia would reach independence without full territorial integrity (the major port of Walvis Bay was excluded); its public sector sold off; the racist security forces and civil service still intact; and after an election under conditions extremely unfavourable to Swapo. It was also apparent that whatever the advantages of this 'independence', Namibian workers, and the NUNW in particular, would not benefit greatly.

'Whilst the regime continues to force its infamous rule down our throats,' said Barayi in his presidential address to the congress, 'we continue to hear from some quarters that FW de Klerk needs to be given a chance because he is a new man with a new heart.' Many things needed to be changed by the government 'before a climate and framework for negotiations can be reached... The ball is in the regime's court and it will have to play it', said Barayi. 'We are not going to heed any bogus signals... We submit', he continued,

> that FW de Klerk is not a new man at all. The outcome of the forthcoming (September) elections will place him at the head of a regime whose rule is not based on the will of the people. His troops continue to emasculate the will of the people through brute force. He is attempting to win legitimacy and respectability which is denied him by the overwhelming majority of our people. Please do not sell him to us for any price. He is not a good buy.'

A similar theme was echoed in the secretariat report. There was no sign, said Naidoo, that Pretoria was serious. A climate of free political activity would have to be created, involving the release of political prisoners; unbanning organisations; an end to executions and political trials; the repeal of security legislation; withdrawal of troops from the townships and their confinement to barracks. Calling for a 'constituent assembly' Naidoo said that 'what has always been envisaged is that only a forum representative of our mandated representatives and exercising sovereign authority can draw up a constitution for a new South Africa.' The congress debate centred on a Numsa resolution entitled 'The process of political settlement.' Numsa's position had been developed at its own national congress held in mid-May. Moses Mayekiso, general secretary of the union, expressed the consensus within the union as follows:[*]

---

[*] *Mayekiso had been released from prison in April 1989, following his acquittal, together with four other activists from Alexandra township, on charges of treason. For most of Cosatu's existence, Mayekiso had been behind bars. Three weeks after his release, Numsa's congress reaffirmed his position as the union's general secretary.*

I believe that the solutions to our country's problems will finally come through negotiations. I don't believe that we will be able to get to Pretoria and oust Botha from those buildings. But I also don't believe that negotiations are near.

Until a range of minimum conditions was met, 'we don't think we should engage in any negotiations.' The important thing, said Mayekiso, was to 'build our organisations so as to have power and control. The political initiative towards negotiations, the concept of negotiations, must come from us.' In addition, it was important to prepare for the future by encouraging the working class 'to discuss their future aspirations so that when we get to that position we know the aspirations of all the sectors of society.' Mayekiso also stressed that a 'proper solution' required that 'all those organisations with a mass base have to be represented' at any negotiations.[1]

Numsa proposed to the Cosatu congress that 'any negotiated settlement' should be rejected, and even actively opposed, unless certain preconditions were met. Those listed were essentially the same as mentioned in the secretariat's report. NUM suggested a range of amendments to the Numsa proposal. These included calling on 'the frontline states, OAU and all international forums' to pressurise the regime into creating a climate conducive to negotiations. In addition, NUM proposed 'that no negotiations take place without the democratic participation of the people', a more diplomatic formulation than Numsa's opposition to 'secret negotiations'. NUM also proposed that 'only a sovereign body' – a constituent assembly – should have the power 'to develop a new constitution', and that the mass democratic movement (MDM) should develop a common position on 'the South African road to power through negotiation.'

NUM's amendments aimed at tightening the Numsa resolution, and at presenting a more positive attitude towards negotiations if the climate was right. NUM envisaged negotiations as a medium-term possibility. 'One cannot rule out negotiations', said NUM's president James Motlatsi before the congress. Numsa accepted NUM's amendments.

The debate on the congress floor revealed basic agreement on the issue. Fawu's Mandla Gxanyana said that Cosatu should 'bring workers forward as a class, not just as voting forces.' A speaker from CWIU felt it would be wrong 'to commit ourselves to negotiations at this stage.' Other speakers stressed that a negotiations strategy did not mean ending other aspects of struggle. The only serious objections came from a Ccawusa delegate who opposed negotiations on principle. 'Once you say you are for negotiations you fall into the trap of reformism,' he said. The only correct path was one which would 'smash the capitalist state and usher in a dictatorship of the proletariat.' His views, however, received very little support, and the resolution adopted was substantially in line with ANC thinking on negotiations. The Cosatu resolution was influential in the OAU's decision to adopt a similar document, the 'Harare Declaration', which was subsequently endorsed by the United Nations and the Non-Aligned Movement (NAM) during the latter half of 1989.

Greater internal unity

The second congress, and to some extent the special congress, had shown that Cosatu was divided into two main political camps, and at least three major political/organisational blocs. The third congress, by contrast, revealed a federation increasingly united. Differences remained, but it was no longer accurate to talk of political/organisational blocs. A multiplicity of dynamics was at play and unions chose to agree or differ in a far more flexible way than before. It was no longer easy to predict which way a union would vote or what approach it might take.

Mayekiso felt that there was now more 'political openness' and more 'respect for democracy... Before, if one believed the position was wrong he just fought and fought... NUM and Numsa were at loggerheads', continued Mayekiso. 'That was uncalled for. NUM would go there thinking we would get Numsa. Numsa would go there thinking we would get NUM. That antagonism was unnecessary.'[2]

Differences at the third congress were more over style and emphasis than deep conflicts. In the first place, the circumstances facing the labour movement required a more united approach to state and employer attacks. Secondly, there had been ideological shifts by many of the major participants. Numsa, for example, had greater sympathy for the view that its socialist aims could best be furthered within the context of a national-democratic struggle. A key policy document presented at Numsa's 1989 congress stated that 'the removal of the apartheid state will be a step towards the liberation of our people', and added that 'the working class must play a central role in the national-democratic struggle.' NUM and a number of other unions had also started stressing the importance of a transformative vision within the anti-apartheid struggle. 'Let's not say we are fighting apartheid and that's all,' said NUM's James Motlatsi. 'We must be able to make the kinds of changes that can benefit the people.' Finally, there was 'more political openness', and a greater concentration on finding points of agreement rather than difference. There was increased commitment to making decisions within structures and after open debate. The power of secret caucuses was declining.

The secretariat report to congress noted a dramatic improvement in the relationship between affiliates. 'We are learning to accommodate diverse views within Cosatu and deal with sensitive issues in a mature and comradely manner.' Since late 1988 there was also 'a more serious commitment to build the CEC and Exco as a vehicle of unity and as a forum of debate and discussion.'

This improved climate was demonstrated during the debate on the three major 'political' resolutions dealing with the anti-apartheid coalition, a workers' charter, and the building of the mass democratic movement.

Debating alliances again

Debate on the anti-apartheid coalition was, in essence, a replay of the 1988 special congress dispute over the broad front and the anti-apartheid conference. NUM proposed that the banned AAC be reconvened. This time, however, the unifying perspective of the conference should be made explicit, with the conference drawing in 'all forces and individuals opposed to apartheid.' All major organisations should be drawn in and involved from the beginning. Groups participating in the anti-apartheid coalition would 'retain their own autonomy and decision-making structures' but would be 'united by the perspectives arising out of the conference.'

'Nowadays the groups opposed to apartheid have never been so various and widespread,' said a NUM speaker motivating the resolution. 'The task is to effectively harness all those forces.' He listed four target groups for the AAC – 'a-political' forces in the black community which should be approached 'not only with the aim of drawing them into the MDM'; 'genuinely patriotic' forces with different perspectives, such as BC or Africanist groupings; whites opposed to apartheid who should not be pushed 'back to the laager of the enemy'; and even some people from the homelands who opposed fragmentation of the country.

Delegates argued their points articulately and passionately but, in contrast to the previous year's debate, were also flexible. Strong arguments were considered and accommodated by various speakers to the motion. Numsa raised objections to the NUM resolution on two key points. Firstly, it called for the convening committee to consist of 'Cosatu/Nactu and their allies' and not, as NUM proposed, 'Cosatu and UDF'. Secondly, Numsa agreed to invite all anti-apartheid organisations, but only if 'their class interests are not diametrically opposed to those of our members.' The Numsa motivation reflected a softening of its position. 'We do not have a problem', said a Numsa speaker, 'with the middle class, with the petty bourgeoisie, with the churchpeople, with the sportspeople, with the small businesses, with the professionals. We are opposed to representatives of the bosses' organisations' attending the

AAC. Numsa's objections appeared to focus on individuals like Anglo American's Gavin Relly and Zach de Beer, and organisations like the liberal Democratic Party.

During debate there was strong opposition to convening the AAC jointly with Nactu. Cosatu did not share a common outlook with Nactu, it was argued, and this would make co-convening difficult. The experience of the first workers summit had undoubtedly left an impression of Nactu as an unreliable partner. NUM explained that it envisaged a convening committee which included organisations such as Nactu, Azapo, and the churches, but that Cosatu/UDF should lead the committee. Numsa conceded this point, but repeated its other objection to the NUM resolution. Support came from a speaker in Ccawusa's Mtwa faction who felt that 'class enemies should not be invited into the AA coalition.'

NUM responded that 'a purist approach, on the basis of class interest, will not enhance our struggle in any way,' and was supported by speakers from Fawu, Cawu and Nehawu. An observer from UDF, Jeff Molapo, argued that 'the key problem facing us today is apartheid, and there are many forces opposed to apartheid, for different reasons.' Shared interests did not make these forces identical. It was necessary, he said, to form a 'tactical alliance' – one that was 'conditional', 'temporary' and 'limited'.

Numsa's John Gomomo asked how Zach de Beer could be included. Despite his anti-apartheid proclamations he was a director of Anglo American. His company exploited and dismissed workers, especially mineworkers. His party, the Democratic Party, was the voice of big business. Even former DP leader Van Zyl Slabbert represented interests hostile to workers, said Gomomo.

The turning point came with an eloquent contribution by NUM's Cyril Ramaphosa. NUM saw the necessity of tactical alliances, even with big capital, said Ramaphosa. The Natal peace initiatives were an example of this. Cosatu had worked with representatives of local employers 'for the sole objective of saving lives.' If 'some form of tactical alliance' was necessary 'in order to destroy the monster of apartheid' then, said Ramaphosa, 'we clearly don't see anything wrong in doing that.' It was a powerful argument given Numsa's deep involvement in the Natal initiatives.

In the end Ppwawu managed to broker a compromise. Numsa withdrew its objections, and NUM added a clause stating that 'at this stage we do not envisage inviting representatives of big companies and big business such as Anglo American Corporation, FCI, Saccola, etc.' The resolution was then approved unanimously, to applause from the assembled delegates. The movement in Numsa's position reflected not only flexibility and a desire to reach consensus. It also indicated an increasing acceptance that the broadest possible anti-apartheid alliances need not contradict a socialist perspective.

The workers charter

Debate on a workers charter also emphasised the common ground growing within Cosatu. At the 1987 congress advocates of a workers charter were, rightly or wrongly, seen as presenting it as an alternative to the Freedom Charter. At the third congress NUM, TGWU and Actwusa proposed resolutions on the question of a workers charter. The composite resolution finally tabled called for a workers charter to be drawn up, after thorough consultation and debate. This should 'articulate the basic rights of workers' and be 'guaranteed by the constitution of a people's government.' A campaign should be launched, culminating in a special congress to draft the charter.

The congress agreed to this proposal despite spirited opposition by Fawu and Ppwawu which feared that some unions were trying to replace the Freedom Charter. There were no 'hidden agendas' argued Gawu. There was simply a need to develop a common understanding of workers' rights and the entrenchment of these under a future government.

While the AAC resolution reflected the need to develop the broadest conceivable opposition to apartheid, the decision on a workers charter expressed the need to assert working-class demands within that struggle.

A related resolution, on rebuilding the mass democratic movement (MDM), generated a lot of heat. The congress eventually reaffirmed 'the strategic alliance of Cosatu and UDF', and called on union members to be active in strengthening and rebuilding structures at national, regional and local levels. It emphasised the need to build street committees and develop strong national organisations amongst youth, women, students and other 'sectors'.

Cosatu's relationship with the UDF was not exclusive of other organisations. But it was a special relationship centred around a shared 'strategic' perspective. 'A strategic alliance', said Naidoo after the congress,'is when the objectives and programmes of action of different organisations converge. As the core of the MDM, Cosatu and UDF affiliates have a strategic alliance.' Cosatu and UDF held similar views about the nature of their common enemy, the apartheid state, and about the means required to destroy racism. Both defined the immediate enemy as the system of racial oppression. Both recognised the central role of the ANC within the liberation movement. Both sympathised with, but could not openly support, the ANC's armed struggle. And both held similar views on the importance of mass action and international pressure in the liberation struggle.

Naturally, there were differences of emphasis between Cosatu and UDF. Cosatu tended to give equal emphasis to both mass action and disciplined, mass organisation. There was a widespread view within Cosatu that UDF affiliates, despite important exceptions, often gave undue weight to action at the expense of organisation. UDF activists, in turn, often felt Cosatu was obsessed by its structures and mandates, to the point of paralysing it from taking any action. These differences of emphasis would often emerge over major protest actions such as stayaways. A second difference between Cosatu and UDF related to longer-term political perspectives. Cosatu invariably proclaimed its belief in both democracy and socialism. UDF tended to restrict its proclamations to the need for a non-racial democracy, although this often extended to calls for economic democracy and social justice. An important exception was UDF's youth affiliate Sayco which had called for 'democracy and socialism' since its inception in 1987. UDF's outlook was, in part, a result of its composition as a broad multi-class front of organisations, as well as its belief, which it shared with Cosatu, that the struggle against apartheid and national oppression was the immediate objective.

Debating the role of women

Four resolutions touched directly on the position of women. They revealed both Cosatu's strong verbal commitment to the equality of women, and its difficulty in translating this commitment into practice. A resolution from CWIU proposed that all 'references to gender' in Cosatu's constitution should be replaced by 'non-sexist terms'. It was unacceptable, argued CWIU, for terms like 'chairman' or 'his duties' to be used since this implied that only men could hold these positions. The CWIU resolution was adopted without objection.

Another resolution, proposed by TGWU, pointed out that while women were entitled to hold any leadership position within Cosatu or its affiliates, very few actually did. There were also few women organisers, noted TGWU, 'even where a large proportion of the affiliate's membership is women.' TGWU proposed affirmative action. Cosatu should 'actively encourage the election of women shop stewards on the factory floor', and 'consciously' promote the election of women within federation and affiliate structures. In addition, Cosatu should deal with the 'practical barriers' faced by women. There should be childcare facilities at meetings, help with transport late at night to dangerous areas, and greater sharing of housework between men and women.

The most active opposition to the proposed resolution came from Fawu and Sarhwu. Affirmative action was unnecessary, argued Fawu. Women did not attend meetings or participate fully in organisation. Even within the congress hall few women were present, and even fewer were participating. Therefore, argued Fawu, it was premature to talk about women in leadership. Sarhwu was more blunt, arguing that women were 'not ready for leadership positions.'

Sadwu, a union composed almost entirely of women, supported the TGWU resolution but proposed that women should be 'educated and groomed to enable them to play a leadership role in their unions.' Gawu supported Sadwu, arguing that it was impossible to 'deal with a historical problem simply by electing women to leadership positions.'

Almost all other unions supported the resolution without amendments. Ppwawu pointed out that it was necessary not only to adopt, but also to implement the resolution. Numsa argued that women's issues were not taken seriously and were often not even placed on the agenda. The few women in leadership positions faced pressures to prove themselves in a way that men did not. Finally, the Numsa speaker argued against women receiving 'special grooming... Were men in leadership today given special training,' she asked? A Ccawusa speaker supported this view. Women did not need 'special attention'. They were 'ready for leadership positions.' A CWIU speaker argued that both men and women leaders needed education. She also made the telling point that unions had largely nominated women delegates to speak on this resolution, but they were rarely chosen to speak for their unions on other resolutions. After about an hour of debate the TGWU resolution became Cosatu policy, without amendments.

A further resolution, proposed by NUM, noted that 'in South Africa women suffer triple oppression.' Women are 'an indispensable social force for the realisation of democratic demands enshrined in the Freedom Charter.' It was necessary that they unite, not only in the existing 'regionally-based organisations', but in a national organisation. Thus, argued NUM, Cosatu should facilitate the revival of the Federation of South African Women (Fedsaw).[*] The resolution was adopted by the

---

* Fedsaw was formed in 1954 as a federation of women's organisations. It was closely aligned to the ANC and led by women such as Lillian Ngoyi, Ray Alexander, Elizabeth Mafekeng, Helen Joseph and Frances Baard. One of its earliest and most notable actions was the march by some 20 000 women to the Union Buildings in Pretoria on 9 August 1956, protesting the extension of the pass laws to African women. Since then, 9 August has become known as National Women's Day. Fedsaw became defunct during the early 1960s following the banning of the ANC and the repression of the Congress movement. The early 1980s saw the revival of women's organisations, many linked to the UDF. These included the Cape-based United Women's Congress (UWCO), the Natal Organisation of Women (NOW), and the Federation of Transvaal Women (Fedtraw). All were agreed on the principle of re-establishing Fedsaw as a national mass organisation of women.

congress after a Sadwu addition, calling on the women's sub-committee of Cosatu's Nedcom to monitor and co-ordinate the implementation of the resolution, was accepted.

The final resolution of direct concern to women was proposed by TGWU and entitled 'sexual conduct'. It was the last resolution scheduled for debate on the Friday night of the congress, and succeeded in awakening both lethargic delegates and deep-rooted prejudices. The TGWU resolution noted 'many incidents of sexual harassment of women comrades by male comrades.' Men often became involved in relationships with 'newly-recruited women members' and these were 'often characterised by an imbalance of power because of the greater political experience and organisational seniority of the male comrade.' When the relationship collapsed, the woman concerned would often drop out of the union or divisions would develop. This type of problem, argued the TGWU resolution, was one of the reasons for 'the lack of consistent participation by women comrades in our structures.' The resolution called for 'tighter sexual discipline' and that the issue should be focused on 'in discussing a code of conduct for our federation.'

The problem had arisen at Cosatu's 1987 congress, noted a TGWU speaker. Fawu had seen fit to formally complain about the harassment of Cosatu women delegates. Unions had long fought the issue when it involved management. Jobs in return for sexual favours was a common worker complaint, particularly against foremen and middle management. 'What became clear to us', commented TGWU's general secretary Jane Barrett after the congress,

> was that it is all very well discussing the issue as it manifests itself with management, but sexual exploitation was taking place right within our own union structures. This was particularly apparent in relation to young male organisers and newly recruited female members.

'These things are killing the struggle and women's involvement in the union,' commented CWIU's Elizabeth Thabethe. Her union was the only one to support the TGWU resolution unreservedly.

A variety of responses came from the remaining unions. Some speakers argued that there was no such thing as sexual exploitation. Women had a right to say 'no'. In any event, argued one speaker, women also harassed men. If such a resolution was adopted it would 'embarrass Cosatu'. These speakers voiced a deeply-rooted sexism and an inability to comprehend women's oppression. This, in turn, undoubtedly reflected the outlook of the majority of male workers in South Africa.

NUM proposed an alternative motion, which managed to avoid any reference to women, harassment or even sexism. The (male) NUM official who drafted the motion realised that it needed to be presented to the congress by one of NUM's women delegates. One by one the women he approached refused to motivate it. Eventually one woman agreed to present it. Workers were victims of the 'ideas, values and morals of the ruling class,' argued the NUM resolution. This corrupted them 'morally and ideologically'. The solution was to cultivate and educate workers about 'proletarian morality'. Workers should be 'encouraged to conduct themselves in a disciplined fashion befitting the noble cause they are fighting for.' Union leaders should take the lead and be 'paragons of the moral characteristics' of the noble cause. NUM's resolution was seconded by Sarhwu.

Ppwawu argued that, while it agreed with the points made by TGWU, these were part of a wider problem of lack of discipline amongst many unionists. They were not simply a 'women's issue' but also a 'union issue'. The problems of sexual harassment should form part of the ongoing discussions over a Cosatu code of conduct. Numsa seconded the Ppwawu position, and asked that the TGWU resolution be noted and referred back to affiliates for further discussion 'with a view to incorporating issues of sexual conduct into the Cosatu code of conduct.' Having received no unambiguous support, apart from CWIU, TGWU accepted the Ppwawu proposal 'with regret'.

'We do not view the responses as negative', said Barrett after the congress. 'It was no surprise that there was not overwhelming support', particularly from unions with a majority of male members 'who have never really had to face these issues. But the issue got debated, and that was positive.'

International policy

International policy was debated in some detail. The congress endorsed the support Cosatu was giving to the National Union of Namibian Workers (NUNW). NUNW had been repressed in Namibia during the 1970s, much as Sactu was in South Africa during the 1960s. Steps to revive worker organisation began in early 1986 on the initiative of Ben Ulenga, John Pandeni and a number of other Swapo members recently released from Robben Island. 'We looked at the way the NUNW started to organise in the late 1970s', recalled Ben Ulenga,

> and they did it more or less at the Swapo level. They went to the hostels and organised workers and this resulted in a situation where workers felt very strong when they were all together in the hostel. But they didn't do much in the workplace. So people felt that there was a need to start organising on the factory floor and organising industry-wide.

Committees were established in many workplaces. By September 1986 the Namibian Food and Allied Union (NUFAU) was launched, followed in November by the Mineworkers' Union of Namibia (MUN).

The struggle of the Namibian people, and of Swapo, was close to the heart of most black workers in South Africa – not surprisingly, given that the SADF was occupying Namibia much as it was occupying South African townships. But concrete links between workers of the two countries were historically weak, even though most Namibian workers were employed by South African-based multinationals. An unusual exception to this was TGWU's 1988 congress resolution that none of its members should transport weapons to Namibia.

Cosatu assisted NUNW to re-establish itself, while its key mining, metal and food unions were helped by NUM, Numsa and Fawu respectively. During April and June 1989, Cosatu delegations travelled to Namibia to discuss a concrete programme of solidarity and attend the NUNW's consolidation congress. Cosatu established, together with other sections of the MDM, a Namibia solidarity committee expressly aimed at helping Swapo win an election. During 1989 this committee produced a widely- distributed *Solidarity with Namibia* newspaper. A more substantial booklet, *Namibian Workers Organise*, was produced as a joint NUNW and Cosatu publication.

Barnabus Tjizu from the NUNW was the only international guest invited to address Cosatu's third congress. Following his speech, the congress decided to mobilise and educate people around the question of Namibia. It was also agreed to give 'material and moral support' to the Nambian people, and to Swapo and NUNW in particular. All Cosatu members were asked to donate R1 towards Swapo's election fund. But, like many Cosatu resolutions, the implementation fell short. Old clothes were collected for the thousands of returning Namibian refugees, and money was contributed by workers. But nothing approaching the goal of R1-million was reached.

Cosatu's international relations, more generally, were also debated at congress. A new resolution, proposed by Ppwawu, re-affirmed Cosatu's decision not to affiliate to any of the international confederations – the ICFTU, WFTU or WCL. It stressed the development of bilateral links with trade unions in other countries, East and West. Cosatu's affiliates were also urged to develop relations with the relevant ICFTU-aligned International Trade Secretariat (ITS) and the WFTU-linked Trade Union International (TUI). Cosatu, it was agreed, should also relate to unions in socialist countries 'openly and without excuses to the South African government or its apologists.' This was, in part, a challenge to prevailing state ideology which made contacts with the Soviet Union and Eastern Europe virtually illegal.

The resolution called for the strengthening of Cosatu's ties with major Third World unions in countries like Brazil, Philippines, South Korea and Turkey. These were often engaged in similar struggles to Cosatu, and had developed a militant, factory-based and highly-political style of unionism under conditions of harsh repression.

The resolution pointed out a number of weaknesses in Cosatu's international policy. The federation did not give adequate briefings to delegates travelling abroad. Cosatu did not co-ordinate the international work of affiliates, or monitor the South African-based activities of the various ITSs and TUIs. Little had been done to address 'the continuing funding of splinter unions by the ICFTU's South African Co-ordinating Committee', or monitor the flow of funds to the union movement as a whole. Part of the solution, argued Ppwawu, was for Cosatu's CEC to elect a full-time international secretary. The resolution was adopted by the congress in all its major aspects, except that the appointment of a full-time official was felt to be premature.

Despite Cosatu's high international profile, international work has always been low on the federation's agenda. International relations were a potential point of conflict within the federation, and an attempt was made to avoid differences on this issue.

In the aftermath of the Second World War the international union movement split into two major camps, the International Confederation of Free Trade Unions and the World Federation of Trade Unions. There was also the small World Council of Labour (WCL) which is irrelevant in the South African context. The major national union centres of Western Europe, North America and Japan made up the heart of the ICFTU while the WFTU was centred around trade unions in Eastern Europe and the Soviet Union. Both ICFTU and WFTU competed for affiliates in other countries, and in the process both made many destructive interventions, particularly in Africa.

Cold War divisions lay at the root of this competition. For most of the post-war period the ICFTU was fervently anti-communist in its outlook, while the WFTU was an equally dogmatic supporter of Soviet foreign policy. Each attempted to work, not only with the national centres but also with the industrial unions of different countries. The International Trade Secretariats operated broadly within the ICFTU orbit while the WFTU established Trade Union Internationals.

At its launch Cosatu found itself in a dilemma – it was not impressed by the ICFTU, while the WFTU offered little and relations with it were probably illegal. Cosatu's politics were broadly allied with the Congress tradition. This implied that Cosatu would develop cordial relations with the ANC's ally and WFTU affiliate Sactu, and reject all forms of anti-communism, since the SACP was a part of the liberation alliance. There was strong sympathy in Cosatu's ranks for the socialist countries because of their substantial moral and material support for the liberation movement. Messages from the Soviet Union or Cuba, for example, always received the warmest reception from the thousands of ordinary delegates at Cosatu congresses.

Many within Cosatu supported Sactu's continuing affiliation to the WFTU and shared its total hostility to the ICFTU. The ICFTU, in turn, was extremely hostile to Sactu and, by extension, to the ANC. Many Sactu functionaries in exile did little to ease these tensions and often published slanderous articles attacking the ICFTU as little more than a product of the American CIA. More ominously, there were indications that prior to Cosatu's launch ICFTU functionaries had approached Cusa unions and suggested that they withdraw from the new federation.

The WFTU had little to offer in trade union terms, and Cosatu had little effective contact with it. Multi-national companies operating within South Africa all came from the capitalist bloc. South Africa's major trading partners were the major 'Western' industrialised countries, workers in most of these countries belonged to unions affiliated to the ICFTU. If Volkswagen workers in Uitenhage wanted international support they would get it through contacts with the relevant ITS, not through the TUI. In addition it was legally and practically impossible for Cosatu to affiliate to the WFTU.

In the light of these factors, Cosatu's launching congress decided on a policy of active non-alignment. The federation would be active in the international arena but would not affiliate to the ICFTU, the WFTU or the WCL. It was largely a pragmatic policy aimed at avoiding conflict within Cosatu's ranks.

Most major affiliates began developing links with the relevant ITS in their sectors. These were seen in a different light to the ICFTU since many could offer concrete solidarity to their South African affiliates. Over the years these links have grown, with Cosatu affiliates playing an increasingly active role in the ITSs. By early 1991 only a few Cosatu unions remained unaffiliated to any ITS, and even these maintained close links with them. One exception was the International Union of Foodworkers (IUF). Fawu disaffiliated from it in 1989 partly for political reasons (the union was strongly sympathetic to the WFTU), and partly because of the IUF's particularly interventionist style. The IUF was accused of becoming embroiled in the internal politics of the Ccawusa split where its involvement was contrasted to the relatively neutral and cautious approach of the ITS in the commercial sector.

Cosatu not only developed links with trade unions around the world but also played a direct political role in the international arena. With South Africa at the centre of the world stage and with Cosatu being the largest internal anti-apartheid organisation, this role was largely thrust upon the federation. Its international work included lobbying governments, dealing with a regular stream of visiting politicians and even addressing the United Nations and other major international institutions. During the darkest years of the state of emergency Cosatu carried the flag of the mass democratic movement, not only internally but also internationally, often working closely with the banned ANC. Cosatu's international activity played a major part in intensifying the isolation of the apartheid regime, discrediting Inkatha's claims to be a force for peace, and broadening international support for the anti-apartheid movement.

Cosatu attempted to build links which could publicise state repression and the anti-apartheid struggle. This was an important part of the shield raised in its defence. International pressure helped ease the state's campaign against Cosatu and softened, even if it did not end, the blows. Cosatu worked closely with many of the international anti-apartheid movements, and used its union connections to develop new areas of anti-apartheid support. The Commonwealth Trades Union Conference (CTUC) was particularly helpful in publicising Cosatu's cause, as was the United Nations Committee against Apartheid. Both worked tirelessly to ensure that the world was informed of developments in South Africa.

The International Labour Organisation (ILO) was also a key forum for Cosatu and gave it access to a far wider range of people than the traditional anti-apartheid movements. As a tripartite structure, ILO forums included representatives of government, labour and employers from all countries around the world. The ILO's immense resources and its internationally-accepted conventions were also crucial ammunition in the long struggle against the LRA.

Much of the international support for Cosatu has been financial. Its strained relationship with the ICFTU forced the federation to search elsewhere for support. It managed to obtain this through bilateral links with a number of ICFTU-affiliated trade union centres in Western Europe. Since 1986 the trade unions of Sweden, Denmark, Norway, Finland and the Netherlands have given millions of rands to assist Cosatu and its affiliates. Other union centres, such as the major Italian federation CGIL, have assisted with specific projects, and the Canadian federation, the CLC, has provided extensive assistance for humanitarian and legal work related to the Natal violence.

Financial support has been a mixed blessing. Funding was vital in enabling Cosatu to defend itself as an organisation. Pamphlets and publicity could be produced, victims of repression assisted, detainees given legal representation, and key meetings such as the 1988 special congress called. None of these would have been possible without foreign funding.

Cosatu originally aimed not to divert limited resources from affiliates to the federation. Jay Naidoo has commented that, in retrospect, this was wrong. 'We should have insisted from the start that the federation was paid for by affiliates.' As a result, financial self-reliance was not stressed and the federation depended heavily on foreign funding. Without this financial support Cosatu would today be a smaller, more battered, but tougher organisation.

A related problem involved the excessive self-centredness of South African unionists. With apartheid at centre stage South African unionists were thrust into the spotlight. A narrow attitude developed whereby international solidarity was seen as a one-way obligation, something to take not give. The rare exceptions only confirmed the trend. NUM gave some assistance to Peruvian miners, and Ccawusa members at 3M went on strike in solidarity with their counterparts in the United States. But the only major example of international support given was Cosatu's involvement in Namibia. One result of this is that South African workers remain largely ignorant of international developments.

By 1990 Cosatu's approach to international solidarity was showing signs of change. Its hostility towards both the ICFTU and the American AFL-CIO lessened as it was realised that links could co-exist with differences. The federation also made tentative contacts with the WFTU although this frequently resulted in little more than the rude shattering of illusions about that organisation. Most importantly, Cosatu began increasing its involvement in Africa through its links with the Organisation of African Trade Union Unity (OATUU) and the Southern African Trade Union Co-ordinating Committee (Satucc).

Other congress resolutions

Financial self-sufficiency: A variety of other issues was dealt with by the third congress. There was a lengthy debate over a joint Fawu/CWIU proposal to raise affiliation fees paid by unions from 5 cents to 10 cents per member per month. Financial self-sufficiency and reduction of dependence on foreign funding was at stake in this discussion. During 1988 over 71% of Cosatu's income for day-to-day running costs came from foreign funding.[*]

---

[*] *These figures refer only to the federation and not its affiliates. The financial report presented to congress revealed that Cosatu received grants totalling almost R6,5-million during 1988 alone – primarily from the trade union federations of Sweden, Denmark, Norway, Finland and the Netherlands. A large proportion of the funding went to assist projects run by affiliates, such as the NUWCC, or to legal assistance and relief work arising from the Natal situation and the repression of the state of emergency.* (continued on page 363)

Opponents of the resolution suggested that since affiliates also received outside funding it would be ridiculous to make Cosatu more self-sufficient by making affiliates less so. Others argued that Cosatu should look to reducing its expenditure. Supporters of the motion claimed that some unions were not taking the matter seriously, and that Cosatu had not 'strictly adhered' to previous congress resolutions on the matter. In addition, government threats to restrict the inflow of funds to democratic organisations had to be viewed in a serious light.

This view found support in the secretariat report to congress. 'The huge amounts of money flowing into our country can have a debilitating effect on our discipline and the character of our struggle.' There was an attitude in some quarters that no work could be done without 'large budgets'. Very few affiliates had complied with previous resolutions calling for 'full disclosure of funding... We need to look to our constituencies to raise the finances necessary to defend our organisation and advance our struggle for liberation,' concluded the secretariat report.

The congress finally agreed to raise affiliation fees, but only with effect from July 1990. It also agreed that Cosatu should curtail its costs, that affiliates should pay for services such as printing, and that dependence on outside funding of Cosatu should be reduced by 10% per annum. Cosatu was also instructed to encourage self-sufficiency amongst affiliates.*

The death penalty and violence: The congress adopted a NUM resolution calling for the scrapping of the death penalty. The issue was of direct concern to Cosatu. Not only did South Africa have the highest execution rate in the world, but many were sentenced to death for direct-

---

(continued from page 362) *However even after excluding those 'special funding' elements, Cosatu still received R2,9-million towards its 1988 running costs. By contrast income from affiliation amounted to slightly less than R400 000. Income generated through sale of T-shirts, affiliate refunds of rentals paid by Cosatu and the like totalled R760 486. The most generous interpretation was that only R1,1-million out of a total income of over R4-million was locally generated – a mere 25%.*

---

* The situation within affiliates differs greatly. Some receive little or no funds other than membership subscriptions. At the other extreme are a few affiliates still highly dependent on funding. Most funding received by affiliates comes from the International Trade Secretariats. The most common practice is for unions to rely on membership dues to cover regular running expenses, and raise funding for special projects. These range from running a newspaper, to health and safety or education programmes. Many unions also rely on outside funding for major items of capital expenditure. In recent years most affiliates have attempted to increase their subscriptions to more realistic levels. Subs still differ greatly between affiliates, and by late 1990 these ranged from R2 to over R6 per month.

ly political offences. Death Row in Pretoria Prison was filled to capacity and included trade unionists and ANC soldiers.[*] Cosatu called for captured guerillas to be granted prisoner of war status. Some opposed the death penalty on principle, seeing it as cruel and inhuman punishment. Others opposed it in the South African context arguing that the apartheid system had turned many ordinary black people into 'criminals'. There was clear evidence that black accused were more likely to be sentenced to death than their white counterparts charged for similar offences.

A related resolution, proposed by Numsa, examined the increasing violence in the country. Apart from the 'reign of terror' in Natal there was growing vigilante violence in areas as diverse as Alexandra, Brits, Cape Town, Venda and KwaNdebele, as well as the 'bombing and burning' of union and other offices. These were all 'part of the strategy of reform and repression of the apartheid state.' Employers frequently used police and security forces, as well as vigilantes and detentions, against striking workers. Other management actions – unfair dismissal of strikers, employment of scabs, eviction of strikers from accommodation, and the use of spies and 'false charges of intimidation' – 'severely provoked' workers. The state and employers used 'the issue of violence between workers', usually between strikers and scabs, as an excuse 'to increase the repression of the trade unions.' But they ignored 'state and management violence.' The resolution called for Cosatu and all affiliates to work out 'common positions on the problems of state violence, vigilante violence, management violence, and violence between workers.'

The resolution was strongly supported. Arrests of striking workers were commonplace as a strategy to break up strikes. And with no right to picket, some union members resorted to violence in their efforts to deter scabs. Strike violence was virtually unknown prior to the state of emergency, and during the early years of the Wiehahn reforms. By 1989 it had become a regular feature of major strikes, despite being against union policy. Union officials were often faced with a sceptical workforce when they could suggest no legal or peaceful method to deter scab labour. NUM was particularly vocal in its support of the resolution. Mineworkers faced perhaps the most intense repression, particularly from the private armies – 'mine security' – which existed on every mine. The NUWCC also supported the resolution. The unemployed often found themselves at the cutting edge of violence between workers. Many

---

[*] By late 1990 trade unionists on death row included Lucky Nomganga of NUM and Wilson Matshili, Patrick Molefe, Takalani Mamphaga and George Maungedzo of Sarhwu. A number of other unionists from TGWU, Ccawusa and NUM were removed from death row after their sentences were reduced on appeal. The fate of these prisoners depends largely on the outcome of political negotiations on South Africa's future.

were being used not only as scabs but were also, said a NUWCC speaker, being 'recruited into SADF or used as vigilantes.'

Homelands: A resolution called on Cosatu to 'develop an overall strategy' for organising workers in the 'homelands'. The homelands were repressive and governed, said the resolution, 'by ruthless hirelings and puppets.' They were intended as 'havens from trade unionism' and were 'reservoirs of cheap labour'.

South Africa's ten homelands were creations of 'grand apartheid', aimed at dividing black South Africans along 'tribal lines'. They were all nominally independent or 'self-governing', ethnically-based territories. The labour laws of the Wiehahn era did not apply within their boundaries, and each had its own set of regulations. Some maintained the outdated provisions of the old Black Labour Relations Regulation Act, which effectively prohibited strikes and unions. Others, such as Bophuthatswana, prohibited 'foreign' unions – ie unions from South Africa! Union head offices were also required to be in Bophuthatswana, and all union officials had to be Bophuthatswanan citizens.

The lack of trade unions, and the almost total absence of any legislation governing minimum wages, health and safety or environmental protection, made these areas attractive propositions for industrialists. They were further encouraged to relocate to these so-called 'border areas' or 'development points' by the provision of infrastructure and generous financial incentives. Throughout the 1980s a significant number of factories relocated to these areas, particularly in industries such as clothing and furniture.

These regions were not rural backwaters. Most employed urbanised workers and were industrial areas like any other. Their workforces were simply unfortunate to be employed in places like Dimbaza near East London, Isithebe near Mandini, or GaRankuwa near Pretoria, therefore falling under the Ciskei, KwaZulu or Bophuthatswana regimes respectively. The organisation of these workers was vital for Cosatu. It was self-defeating to win higher wages at a Johannesburg plant, for example, when the GaRankuwa plant of the same company continued to pay starvation rates. This would simply result in firms relocating. It was also common for Cosatu to see organised city workers embark on industrial action, only to find their unorganised counterparts in the homelands being forced to work overtime to compensate for lost production. It was an illustration, if one was needed, of the most basic union slogan – 'united we stand, divided we fall.'

Natal violence: The previous chapter outlined the question of violence in Natal, and Cosatu's involvement in various peace attempts. The third congress endorsed the steps taken by Cosatu's leadership to secure peace in that region. The Natal problem was one of the major discussion points of the congress. It was a national concern, affecting all unions and with implications for the country's political future. The Cosatu leadership wanted to ensure that they had the widest possible support for their actions. Part of their proposed programme of peace included high-level meetings with Inkatha, despite massive popular resistance to meeting the organisation most delegates blamed for the carnage. Cosatu had shown its seriousness in trying to end the violence, commented the secretariat report to congress.

> Attempts such as setting up a joint working committee, establishing a complaints adjudication board in Pietermaritzburg, holding mass meetings to discuss the campaign for peace, consulting with the leadership of the African National Congress and even meeting with Inkatha

were all indications of this. The role of the police was 'highly questionable', continued the report, and they could not

> be entrusted with the task of restoring peace in Natal... Cosatu had proved on the basis of detailed research in Pietermaritzburg that the security forces license these third party vigilantes. For our enemies this is an effective and cheap way of controlling political opposition to the system.

AIDS: Another significant resolution concerned the spread of AIDS. The congress noted estimates that 40% of the population could be AIDS-infected by the year 2000. Poverty, 'the migrant labour system, forced removals and the state of emergency' contributed to the instability of families and communities and created conditions for the spread of AIDS. On the mines, for example, hundreds of thousands of men were accommodated in single-sex hostels, separated from their families for months on end. In addition, noted the resolution, employers were beginning 'to discriminate against workers who suffer from AIDS.' State and employer education and information programmes were often 'racist' and had caused 'suspicion' amongst workers and even 'a doubt that AIDS exists.' The congress resolved to launch 'our own' AIDS education programme, to campaign against the dismissal of workers with AIDS, and work to eliminate the conditions which help spread the disease.[*]

* In practice unions have undertaken little AIDS education work since the congress, with the important exceptions of TGWU and NUM. TGWU has actively promoted an AIDS awareness campaign, particularly among its many long-distance drivers, who spend lengthy periods away from home and traversing the countries of the Southern African region. On the mines, the Chamber policy is to test all black miners. Those found to have (continued on page 367)

Elections

The third congress was unusual in many respects. The standard of debate was higher, and there was greater consensus than ever before. Many union delegations arrived better prepared than at previous congresses. The Numsa delegation, all wearing the union's smart new tracksuits, was particularly impressive. Its delegates elected a panel of speakers, all workers, to present Numsa's views to the congress. Many other unions still relied excessively on officials to argue their union's standpoint.

For the first time ever, noted Chris Dlamini before closing the congress, not one resolution had to be put to the vote. He congratulated delegates for showing flexibility and willingness to compromise. Another sign of cohesion was that the congress completed its lengthy agenda. Previous congresses had ended with a large number of items being referred to the CEC. All that remained, before closing, was to elect national office bearers for the coming two years.

Here too nominations were unopposed, having been discussed between unions beforehand. Elijah Barayi was re-elected president, despite reservations voiced by some unions outside the congress hall.[*] Chris Dlamini was re-elected first vice-president, and Jay Naidoo and Sydney Mufamadi were re-elected general secretary and assistant general secretary respectively. Two new faces were brought onto the six-person team. Both, perhaps surprisingly considering the 'women leadership' resolution adopted only hours earlier, were men. John Gomomo, a senior shop steward at Volkswagen in Uitenhage and member of Numsa's executive, was elected second vice-president. He replaced Fred Gona who did not stand for election. Similarly, Ronald Mofokeng replaced Maxwell Xulu as national treasurer. Mofokeng, a senior CWIU shop steward at the Germiston plant of PG Glass, had joined the union movement in the 1970s. Support for his election was aided by CWIU's reputation as a union with

---

(continued from page 366) the AIDS virus face dismissal and repatriation back to the rural areas, in most cases to environments where they cannot expect any meaningful health care. NUM is campaigning for AIDS testing to be voluntary, for AIDS carriers not to be dismissed, and for medical care to be provided by the mines. NUM has also identified the migrant labour system as a fundamental contributor to the spread of AIDS, and has called for the negotiation of an appropriate housing policy as part of the dismantling of single-sex hostels.

---

* The main reservations were that he had not provided sufficient leadership to the federation, and that his workplace – Blyvooruitzicht mine – had a weak union presence. However, those unions unhappy with Barayi were unable to convince Chris Dlamini, the only obvious alternative, to stand for the position of president.

strict financial procedures, and the fact that Mofokeng was CWIU's national treasurer.

The national office bearers had been elected unopposed at Cosatu's launching congress. This was understandable since ordinary union delegates did not know each other well. They had relied on the leadership of the various unions, those who had attended the unity talks, to put together a balanced and suitable team.

At the second congress tensions were high, and it was important not to let this affect the elections. The national office bearers were needed as a unifying force. A leader elected in controversial circumstances would have found his (or her!) authority diminished. Hence, the collective sigh of relief when the existing national office bearers were returned to office unopposed.

With growing unity, the need for contested elections will grow. In these circumstances, unopposed elections will come to indicate not consensus, but lack of democracy.

Notes

1. *South African Labour Bulletin* 14(2), June 1989, 44-5.
2. *South African Labour Bulletin*, 14(2), June 1989, 48-9.

Above: James Motlatsi – NUM president

*Below: Moses Mayekiso welcomed by Numsa members
shortly after his release from prison – May 1989*

Anna Zieminski – Afrapix

Benny Gool – Afrapix

Above: Union leadership at the second workers summit – August 1989. From left to right are John Gomomo, unknown, Chris Dlamini, Elijah Barayi, James Mndaweni, Patricia de Lille, Piroshaw Camay, Lawrence Phatlhe, Philip Dlamini

Left: Domestic workers protest against the new labour law – 1988

Karen Hurt – Speak

Peter Auf der Heyde – Afrapix

Left: Women march against the labour law – April 1990. From left to right are Maggie Magubane, Joyce Khoali, Sister Bernard Ncube, Rahmat Omar, Refiloe Ndzuta

Bottom left: Cosatu leaders occupy the Manpower Department offices in protest against the labour law – June 1990. In the background is Potwa's Vusi Khumalo

Below: In Johannesburg, four public sector unions march against privatisation – 1989

Paul Grendon – Southlight

Above: The launch of Cosatu's Western Cape region – 1986

Right: A night-shift worker takes her place at the boardroom table

Lesley Lawson

Above: Cosatu's cultural day – 1987

*Below: Hoping to bury Cosatu –
Uwusa launch, Durban 1986*

The luxury Mercedes Benz specially produced for Nelson Mandela is unveiled by the workers who built it

23

Women and the union movement

Thirty-six percent

S HORTLY before he died in police custody Andries Raditsela – at the time chair of Fosatu's Transvaal region – was fond of telling the story about a training manager at his factory. The year was 1984 and the factory was Dunlop in Benoni on the East Rand. Many women workers at the factory had approached the shop stewards with the same complaint: their jobs depended on acceding to the sexual demands of one of the managers. It was a typical example of the 'jobs for sex' syndrome common in many factories.

The shop stewards discussed the issue. If they complained the manager concerned would simply deny it. Instead they decided to trap him. They waited until they saw a new woman employee summoned to the training office at lunchtime. When the shop stewards saw her enter the office for an 'interview' they checked and found the door locked. They rushed to the senior manager and demanded that he accompany them. Together they burst into the room and caught the training manager, literally with his pants down.

The manager was fired on the spot. The shop stewards' plan worked, commented Raditsela in a publicity leaflet. It was far better 'than allowing workers to assault him as they wished.'

Women in South Africa

The Dunlop incident was not an isolated case: sexual harassment has long been a complaint of women workers, who also have a range of other grievances. Most South African women maintain the home and do the cooking and cleaning. Their work usually goes unrecognised and unpaid. Housework is 'invisible', and regarded as a woman's 'natural lot'. Even women in paid employment are expected by their husbands, their families, and sometimes themselves, to return from work and assume their domestic duties. This is the tyranny of the double shift. Only wealthier women, most of them white, escape this fate by employing domestic servants to help with housework and childrearing.

'People don't think we can share the work in the house', commented union stalwart Lydia Kompe.

> They think there's a specific job for women and for men. But here in town there isn't anything for the men to do like there is in the rural areas. The men just come from work, take the paper, sit on the chair and relax. (But as a woman) you have to have a job, be in the union and run the home. If you're a young woman maybe there's also a baby to look after. Maybe in the mornings I take my child to a creche or an old woman. If my husband comes earlier he hasn't the ability to go and fetch the child and look after him while I'm still working. He expects me to come and fetch the baby, put it behind my back, get to the stove and cook for him. And we do it happily because we grew up that way, we saw our parents do it and we think it's the African law.[1]

Women do as much, if not more, of society's labour as men. But this is not always reflected in the recognised formal economy – the factories, shops, mines and farms. Official government statistics reveal that women constitute 36,4% of total employment in the formal economy.

The position differs greatly from sector to sector. Within the mining industry there is hardly a woman to be found. Mining is 'man's work'. Similarly there are few women in the metal, construction or transport industries. At the other extreme, women make up the majority of workers in the clothing, domestic work and service sectors. Women also constitute a substantial proportion of the workforce in farming, food processing, footwear and textiles, and in the low-paying factories situated in the homelands.

In general, women in all sectors perform the lowest-paying jobs. They are also more likely to be found in temporary employment than men. Statistics indicate that women's participation in the formal economy is slowly increasing. But while the percentage of African male workers performing 'unskilled and menial work' decreased over the last two decades, the opposite was true for African women: 'The increase in women menial workers ie cleaners, nursemaids and others not involved directly in production, was particularly marked – from 22% in 1965 to 54% in 1985.'[2]

The position of women in the economy is mirrored in other aspects of society. They are generally treated as inferior, in the black community no less than in the white. Cosatu women often say that they experience a triple oppression – as blacks, as workers, and as women. In the hierarchy of race, class and gender there is no doubt that black women are at the bottom of the pile.

Women in Cosatu

No comprehensive survey of the number of women who are members of Cosatu has been undertaken. The most that can be done is to combine informed guesswork with figures presented by affiliates to Cosatu's 1989 national women's seminar. These suggest that by 1990 women comprised approximately 36% of Cosatu's paid-up membership – the same proportion as participate in the formal economy.

Women comprise the majority of members in Sactwu, Ccawusa (now Saccawu), Sadwu and Nehawu, while in Fawu the numbers of men and women are roughly equal. Women also make up the majority of members within certain sub-sectors of other affiliates, such as cleaning workers within TGWU.

Women workers in South Africa – unlike many other countries – are no less keen to join unions than men. Indeed, experience reveals that women are often in the forefront of those joining unions. They also tend to be the most militant and dedicated members during industrial action. Individual women often provide the strong and charismatic leadership essential for the unionisation of a factory. However, while these women often remain powerful figures on the shopfloor they rarely become senior shop stewards or the chair of shop steward committees.

As seen in the previous chapter, Cosatu's third congress called for affirmative action to promote women's leadership. Action was certainly necessary. The fact that 36% of Cosatu's membership were women was nowhere reflected in the composition of its leadership. At the time of the congress all six of Cosatu's national office bearers were men. So were all nine regional secretaries and all 36 regional office bearers. Cosatu's national education office bearers, elected at the bi-annual education conference, were all men. Their duties included direct responsibility for developing women's organisation.

Only a handful of women could be found amongst the hundreds of local office bearers countrywide. None, as far as can be ascertained, chaired a Cosatu local. Two Cosatu national seminars in 1987 and 1989 bringing together two office bearers from every region and local were attended by a handful of women – not more than 10%.

The situation was not much better in the affiliates. By 1990 only one general secretary – Sadwu's Florrie de Villiers – was a woman. In earlier years, particularly during the early 1980s, major unions in the paper, food, metal, commercial and transport sectors had elected women as their general secretaries. Only one, TGWU's Jane Barrett, remained at the helm for most of Cosatu's first five years.

Looking at the national office bearers of Cosatu and its affiliates, the picture remains uninspiring, with women occupying less than 10% of all positions. If one excludes Sadwu the figure drops to a mere 5% (see table).

Women leaders in Cosatu affiliates, late 1990

Union	Number of national office bearers	Number of women	Positions held by women
Cosatu	6	None	None
Cawu	7	None	None
CWIU	4	None	None
Fawu	5	None	None
Nehawu	7	One	National treasurer
Numsa	4	None	None
NUM	5	None	None
Potwa	6	None	None
Ppwawu	5	None	None
Sadwu	4	All	President; vice-president; treasurer; general secretary
Samwu	4	None	None
Saccawu	6	None	None
Sactwu	8	Two	First vice-president; treasurer
Sarhwu	6	None	None
TGWU	6	One	National treasurer
Total	83	8	

Saccawu, two-thirds of whose members are women, is one of the few affiliates to have studied the participation of women in union structures. By 1990 only 10% of its national executive committee (NEC) members were women. In its branch executive structures throughout the country only 12% of delegates were women. In its local structures women comprised approximately 25% of local office bearers. The proportion rose on the shop floor. Some 35% of Saccawu's shop stewards were women. A far lower proportion were senior shop stewards, who were expected to attend other union meetings after working hours.[3]

By early 1991 Sactwu, with 70% female membership, had two women among its four regional chairpersons. However this figure is misleading and probably exceptional. Participation by women was far lower when looking at the regional structures as a whole. In the Western Cape 'a significant number', although not a majority, of delegates to the regional executive were women.[4]

Large numbers of women work for the union movement. However the division of labour based on gender is extreme, with the overwhelming majority of women employed in administrative positions. By late 1990 only one of Cosatu's regional secretaries, Luci Nyembe in the Western Cape, was a woman. All but one of Cosatu's regional administrators were women. So too were most of Cosatu's other administrative staff.

The situation in affiliates was broadly similar. Many still have women holding key branch secretary or regional secretary positions. But indications are that even this is diminishing. Numsa is a union with a more active women's forum than most Cosatu affiliates. Yet a mid-1990 survey revealed that all but two of the union's 110 administrative staff were women. And of Numsa's 150 non-administrative staff – the union's organisers, regional and branch secretaries, field workers and key head office staff – only four were women.[5]

Numsa, arguably, operates in an overwhelmingly male industry. Only 12% of its members are women. However a similar pattern emerges in Saccawu. Only 40 of the union's 168 full-time employees were women. Most were administrative staff. Only 8% of non-administrative staff were women.

These figures cannot be dismissed as irrelevant head-counting since they have important implications. During the OK Bazaars strike of 1986/7, for example, a significant number of striking women were assaulted by their unemployed husbands. Being on strike meant a drop in household income and real hunger for many families. These women would come to union strike meetings daily, recalls one organiser, with bruises and black eyes. And yet not once did they raise the problem in the meeting. A survey conducted after the strike revealed that they did not feel free to raise it. All the organisers they dealt with were men.[6]

Looking for reasons

The participation of women in Cosatu's leadership is, if anything, becoming less. The complexities of struggle have led to changes in the demands made on leadership and the type of leaders elected. There has been a tendency in recent years for better-educated and more skilled workers to be elected to leadership positions. Being literate and cosmopolitan has been a definite advantage to today's worker leaders. This affects women workers negatively in that they tend to be less educated and in less-skilled positions than their male counterparts.[*]

There has also been a redefinition of the jobs of union officials. In earlier years a union secretary was viewed as a lowly job. The incumbent was seen as 'only a secretary', often appointed by the executive and responsible for taking minutes and dealing with correspondence. Over the years the situation has changed. The position is now seen as a political one, and politics is seen as the domain of men. General secretaries, regional secretaries and branch secretaries are now elected officials holding real power. With the change in job definition has come a change in the likelihood of finding a woman elected as secretary.

Finally, in recent years the union movement has drawn heavily on the student and youth movements for recruitment of officials. These organisations – mainly Cosas, Sansco and Sayco – have been overwhelmingly male-dominated, and this has reinforced the union movement's own male-dominated tendencies.

Women have always had to overcome a number of hurdles to participate effectively in the union movement. They must overcome the hurdle of domestic responsibility – housework. It is virtually impossible to have a full-time job, be an effective union leader, and still have to do all the housework. 'To increase women's participation in unions means changing the relationship between men and women,' says Elizabeth Thabethe, an office bearer in CWIU's Transvaal branch. 'It needs men to share domestic duties with women, and we have a long way to go before this happens.'[7] Within Cosatu there is increasing verbal acceptance of shared housework. But those women in leadership positions still complain of no sharing in practice.

Almost without exception women centrally involved in union work are single, separated, divorced or widowed. It is a daunting thought that women must overcome so basic a social institution as marriage if they are to participate effectively in trade unions. Experience indicates that

---

* This is also affecting layers of existing male leadership. In the late 1970s and early 1980s a high proportion of union leadership came from the ranks of migrant hostel dwellers. In many respects they built the union movement. But it is unusual to find such people (often semi-literate, unskilled labourers) in senior leadership within Cosatu and its affiliates today. In 1986 and 1987 meetings of Cosatu's CEC were still conducted in a mixture of English, Zulu and Sotho. Today English is almost the only language heard at CEC meetings. Even at Cosatu's third congress most speakers addressed the meeting in English. Local languages are now only commonly heard at regional and local meetings.

women wanting to be active in the unions must either avoid marriage or ensure that their husbands accept their right to be actively involved in union work and agree to share responsibilities for housework and child-care.

Women also have to overcome the hurdle of language. This is direct-ly linked, as we have seen above, to the problem of literacy, education and the performance of less-skilled work. A related hurdle is that of as-sertiveness. Women are often afraid to participate and speak out on issues.

Finally, women aspiring to leadership must overcome the hurdle of prejudice. 'It is our tradition', says Thabethe, 'that a man is the head of the family. This means men don't accept women telling them what to do. This attitude is very tough to crack.' There is also a common perception of women as 'unreliable' union members. They are often accused of not attending meetings and being apathetic. But women are as likely to join unions as men, and their 'apathy' is often linked to childcare problems, housework and the dangers of transport home after dark.

The resolution on 'women leadership' adopted at Cosatu's 1989 con-gress recognised this problem. It called for the breaking down of 'all practical barriers to the full participation of women.' Providing 'childcare facilities at all meetings where it is needed', assisting with transport home in the evenings and 'spreading the idea that housework should be shared between men and women', were seen as crucial. But there has been little progress in implementing these clauses. Sactwu's recent at-tempts to provide transport to and from meetings at night and its encouragement of women to bring their children to Saturday morning meetings are a small but important beginning. It must be noted, however, that not one Cosatu national meeting or conference since the resolution was adopted has provided creche facilities.

Fighting for the rights of women

'Leadership' is not the only indicator of the position of women within the labour movement. We must also examine the gender-related issues being taken up by the unions before moving on to explore the organisa-tion of women.

The best-known campaign has been the fight for parental and child-care rights. The unions which re-emerged during the 1970s discovered that many women workers, on becoming pregnant, were simply losing their jobs. Initial union demands centred on job security and maternity rights, particularly the right to return to one's job. Ccawusa was in the forefront of this struggle, but faced strong resistance from employers.

The first major breakthrough came in 1983 when OK Bazaars agreed to allow one year's unpaid leave with re-employment guaranteed. A number of other companies, particularly in the retail sector, followed suit. The next step forward came when Ccawusa concluded an agreement with Metro Cash and Carry in 1985. This allowed mothers seven months' leave, during which time they would receive one-third of their normal pay. Social security, under the Unemployment Insurance Fund provisions, could add another 45% of salary for some of this period. The Metro agreement also included health and safety provisions as well as three days' paid leave for the father – the first time paternity leave had been won.

Ccawusa began to interview its membership and research the issue more thoroughly. What was needed, concluded the union, was adequate provision for the rights of parents (not only mothers), paid time off, and consideration of the health and safety needs of both parents and children. From the mid-1980s the union began moving away from the concept of maternity rights towards demands for parental rights and the equal involvement of both men and women in family life.

Other unions started to follow Ccawusa's lead. The demand for paid maternity leave with job security increasingly became a standard part of the bargaining agenda. In 1986 Mawu (now Numsa) fought for maternity provisions in the national agreement for the metal industry. This became the first industry-wide agreement and provided for six months' leave – although on less than full pay. One limitation to the agreement was that women could only obtain leave for a maximum of two pregnancies. By 1990 Sactwu's agreement for its 56 000 members in the Western Cape clothing industry provided for 75% pay for three months and 45% pay for a further three months of maternity leave.

The most advanced parental rights agreements have been those won by Ccawusa (now Saccawu) at Pick 'n Pay in 1988 and Game in 1990. The Pick 'n Pay agreement is particularly significant in that it covers some 18 000 workers, a majority of them women. It provides for 11 months' parental leave, nine of which are on approximately 75% of pay. The leave itself can be broken up and taken at any time until the child's fourth birthday. The agreement does not require parents to be legally married in order to benefit. Provision is also made for miscarriages and stillbirths as well as for breastfeeding.

The Pick 'n Pay agreement entitles fathers to eight days' paid leave when the baby is born and a further one day's leave per month for the first six months to take the child for check-ups at a clinic. This provision, indeed the whole concept of paternity leave, has been questioned by some. While admirable in its goals, it still needs research to ascertain whether most workers taking paternity leave are in fact assisting the mother and newborn child.

Not only maternity rights

Union struggles involving gender issues have not been confined to maternity rights. Other concerns include demands for adequate childcare and equal pay, as well as objections to strip-searching of women.

The campaign for the provision of adequate childcare has been an important focus of Cosatu women. In South Africa care of children is almost entirely a private affair with little state intervention. Childcare, and the lack of creches, are an ongoing problem for all but the wealthiest of working parents. Most leave their children with a poorly-paid and untrained childminder or another family member (usually a sister, grand-mother or an older child). The result is childminding rather than childcare and development.

To highlight the problem Cosatu organised a national childcare day on 20 September 1990. Workers were called upon to bring their children to work and at many factories they did so. Most employers refused admission of either parent or child to the premises. The campaign was a small but important beginning limited mainly by inadequate planning, participation and publicity.

Part of the problem involved insufficient consensus on the demands the unions should be making. Some unionists supported the call for workplace-based creches. These would allow parents, especially breast-feeding mothers, easy access to their children. They would also be non-racial, an important developmental consideration in South Africa. Others have argued that workplace-based creches are appropriate mainly for large workplaces and thus run the risk of benefitting only a layer of the working class. Too close a linkage between employment and child-care fails to accommodate children of the unemployed. This has been argued by those calling for employers to subsidise community-based childcare centres which would be open to all.

In March 1989 Gawu, the clothing union, reported to a Cosatu women's seminar that it was fighting against strip searching. This humil-iating practice, allegedly to prevent theft, involved stripping women workers naked as they left the factory. Gawu exposed the practice in its newsletter. The publicity was accompanied by work stoppages and march-outs past security guards waiting to search. These actions effec-tively abolished strip searching in the industry.

Numsa has spearheaded the campaign against wage inequalities with its slogan of 'equal pay for work of equal value'. In practice the issue has proved to be complex. The 1988 amendments to the labour law included a handful of enlightened changes, one of which was to proclaim 'unfair discrimination' on the grounds of sex illegal. But legislation does not remove discrimination.

Women do not usually perform exactly the same job as their male counterparts. This provides an opportunity for employers to grade them differently. Many employers have argued that equal pay simply means that minimum wages should be the same. They then pay male workers above these minimum rates. Many male workers share the attitude that they deserve more and tend not to regard women as breadwinners in their own right. Wage differentials between African men and African women are extreme – to say nothing of racial differentials. Women workers on the lowest unskilled Paterson grade – probably the most common job grading system in South Africa – earned an average of only 77% of the wage of their male counterparts.[8]

Fighting to implement the right of equal pay has sometimes proved counter-productive. A Cosatu publication noted employer threats to replace women workers with men if women pushed for full equality. It recounted a court case which NUTW won against SA Fabrics. A year later there were only two women left in the factory – both of them serving tea.[9] However there have been major victories achieved without negative consequences, and in a large number of plants union concentration on boosting the minimum wage has often been most beneficial to women workers. This has led to dramatic increases, for example CWIU's 136% increase for women workers at Sasol in 1986. Significant wage increases in the retail industry have also boosted the earning power of even the lowest-paid women workers.

In many industries the road to skilled work has been through training and the apprenticeship system. Over the decades this has been used as a means to prevent black workers from entry into skilled work. In recent years, however, black workers have increasingly entered apprenticeship, although not equally in all industries. But for black women the barriers remain extreme. Only 30 companies in the whole of South Africa employed women apprentices in 1988. Only in the hairdressing trade did women apprentices outnumber men.[10]

Numsa has been one of the few unions to take up this issue. Commitment to affirmative action forms part of its policy on vocational training and restructuring of the metal industry. A union publication recounted the difficulties experienced in raising the issue at a meeting of the Metal Industry Artisan Training Board. Numsa proposed that

> in addition to the criteria suggested, it should be specified that no training institution should be accredited if it did not have change rooms and toilets for women as well as men. The response from Seifsa (the

employers) and the white unions was hysterical laughter. One employer said: 'Do you want to close down training in the industry?' Numsa then suggested that centres without these facilities should be given a fixed time (eg three months) within which to build such facilities. Again hoots of laughter! 'Next you'll be wanting separate parking lots and separate lecture halls', said one employer. 'Ridiculous,' we replied.[11]

Looking beyond the factory

The factory floor was not the only focus for Cosatu women. The third congress resolved to help revive the Federation of South African Women (Fedsaw) as a national organisation. At the time only regional women's organisations existed, and many Cosatu women were active in these. Other Cosatu women, particularly in the Transvaal, complained that community-based women's organisations made little attempt to accommodate working-class women.

Co-operation between Cosatu women and their community counterparts was common, particularly in Natal. In 1989 Cosatu and the Natal Organisation of Women (NOW) worked together to organise women's protest marches in Caluza, Mpophomeni and Pietermaritzburg. They also organised two women-only stayaways in Ashdown and a massive picket along Pietermaritzburg's Edendale Highway to protest at police and army harassment of residents and the inability of security forces to prevent Inkatha attacks. Cosatu and NOW also mobilised jointly for National Women's Day, the 9 August anniversary of the women's march on Pretoria in the 1950s. In other regions Cosatu women regularly shared platforms with community-based women's organisations. And during the darkest years of repression from the mid-1980s onwards, Cosatu offices were often a relatively safe haven where women's organisations could meet.

But it has mainly been individual unionists who have contributed to the strengthening of community-based women's organisations. Cosatu's own women's structures have had little impact in the campaign to revive Fedsaw. Many felt that Cosatu women had to develop their own leadership skills, and that until they were strong and confident they could make only a small contribution to the community-based organisations. The focus within Cosatu has therefore been on building strong women's structures within both affiliates as well as Cosatu's regions and locals.

Organising Cosatu women

Building women's structures has been a controversial issue within the federation. Debate has focused on the principle of separate structures, and on how best to ensure that women's issues are raised both within Cosatu and at the negotiating table.

Cosatu's launching congress resolved to fight 'against all unequal and discriminatory treatment of women at work, in society and in the federation.' The congress agreed to establish 'a worker-controlled sub-committee within its education programme' to monitor the progress made in implementing the resolution. By the time of the second congress in 1987 it had to be conceded that almost nothing had been done.

Cosatu's first two years were marked by differences and political tensions, with union mergers and political unity priorities for the federation. There had been little success in establishing education structures, let alone a women's sub-committee of the education department.

A national education conference held in October 1987 examined this lack of progress and decided to call for a Cosatu women's conference. Convened in Johannesburg from 22-24 April 1988 it was attended by 159 delegates from all the affiliates as well as the NUWCC. Of these, 117 were workers while the remainder were union officials. Unions were informed that they were welcome to send both male and female delegates if they wished, and ten of the 159 delegates were men.

In his opening address Chris Seoposengwe, chairperson of Cosatu's national education committee (Nedcom), admitted that 'the women's issue' was not an easy one:

It involves criticising ourselves and the social attitudes and prejudices of our members as much as it involves building the liberation of women into our struggle to fundamentally transform this apartheid and exploitative society.

The resolution adopted at Cosatu's founding congress was only a beginning, continued Seoposengwe.

It was not the outcome of a process of debate and struggle. It was not the end of a long-standing trade union concern with women's issues. Rather we were setting ourselves a goal and a commitment that we should strive for. Today this resolution stands in judgement of us.

Seoposengwe's speech was a challenge to transform intentions into action. Unfortunately the conference was not a success. Many fine resolutions were adopted – on sexual harassment, childcare, women at work, cervical cancer, violence against women, AIDS, child abuse, and the need to organise women on the farms and in domestic service. But the conference was deeply divided and debates were heated.

Differences centred around the issue of women's forums. In May 1987 a Johannesburg women's forum was formed but this collapsed within a few months. There were also embryonic women's structures in other areas. Some unions, most notably NUM, argued strongly against establishing a national women's committee within Cosatu, considering it an attempt to build a separate power structure. Proponents of a national women's committee were accused of wanting to set up structures separate from and in the place of Fedsaw. Women should organise at the community level only, argued unionists supporting NUM's position.

Opponents of this view agreed on the need to join community-based women's organisations. However, they argued, this did not stop Cosatu forming its own women's structures. Working women needed to talk about problems affecting them in the workplace and in the community. Numsa was most vocal in expressing this view.

The women's conference ended by formally adopting resolutions to encourage 'individual women in Cosatu to join progressive women's structures in the community.' The conference also committed itself to building women's forums 'in all Cosatu locals'. Where co-ordination was needed, however, this would have to take place strictly under the auspices of the regional and national education committees.

The hostile spirit which prevailed in the conference had little to do with women's issues. Tensions were still high between unions within Cosatu, particularly around national political issues. In the aftermath of Cosatu's second congress in mid-1987 these differences tended to polarise around NUM and Numsa, the two largest affiliates. At times it appeared as if the substance of a debate was ignored: if NUM proposed something Numsa would automatically counter it, and vice versa. The women's conference was one of the last victims of such conflicts. It was held a month before Cosatu's special congress in 1988, where substantial progress was made in overcoming these differences.

Women's forums slowly gained momentum, although not without hostility and resistance from some affiliates, locals and regions. These structures, linked to Cosatu locals, were open to male unionists although few attended. A number of affiliates, notably Numsa, CWIU, TGWU and Ppwawu also established their own women's committees.

A world apart?

Separate women's structures are seen as a place where union issues can be brought to women, and women's issues brought to the union. They give women an opportunity to raise issues affecting them directly and ensure that these are attended to within the union's formal structures. The women's forums are also aimed at building confidence and leadership.

'Women will start to pick up when they are on their own,' explained Nehawu's Ntsiki Matakane. The confidence gained helps them raise issues in union general meetings. Other workers notice them and this can result in their election as shop stewards. 'Women have got a problem that has been there for a long time,' says Reginald Thanda, a TGWU shop steward from the Eastern Cape. 'It is an old problem created by our cultural traditions. Women have got valid ideas, but in the presence of men they cannot come out and speak. With other women around them they are more encouraged.'[12]

The forums are also seen as watchdogs ensuring that women's issues are attended to. 'Sometimes you feel that men comrades have no interest in women's issues', commented Ppwawu's Refiloe Ndzuta. 'We worry also that there are no women at negotiations and wonder how male comrades represent women's issues in negotiations'. Jane Barrett recalls the 1989 wage negotiations at Cargo Carriers. 'One of the male organisers was allocated to deal with our demand for maternity leave. He got his arguments confused and ended up motivating for compulsory pap smears!'

Many in the women's forums are keenly aware that they should not confine themselves to 'women's issues'. This carries its own risks of marginalisation. Women have taken up the Living Wage Campaign, and organised marches to protest the labour law. 'As women we are also affected by the LRA,' according to one participant.

> For instance we have a lot of women in the domestic and farm areas, and the law doesn't cover them. So we demand legislation to cover such people. It is also important that we motivate the women to come forward, to take up leadership, to be active in the union and the organisation as a whole.

More recently there has been a re-opening of the debate on separate women's structures, although the right to form women's forums is now rarely challenged. The women's forums have been a mixed success. While they have undoubtedly helped many women develop their confidence and leadership skills, some have argued that they tend to become limited to 'complaint sessions' and their purpose has often been unclear. In many cases they have simply removed active women from the union, or made them less active in other union structures.

Active union women now have to attend an additional union meeting – the women's forum. This causes problems since inadequate time and the 'double shift' are the most frequently cited reasons why women fail to take up leadership positions in the first place. Women's forums should be aimed at ordinary women members of the union, argues one Saccawu organiser. They help the rank and file more than those already in leadership.

Different solutions are needed for different problems. In unions like Sactwu, Saccawu, Nehawu or Fawu the struggle is for women to gain real control of their own unions. For these unions the slogan of 'worker control' can mean nothing less. In unions where women form a minority of the membership the struggle is for the right to be heard and for their problems and demands to be taken seriously.

Unions will have to confront the structural problems limiting the participation of women. It is not enough to be committed to equality, as Cosatu and most of its affiliates are. They will need to address the problems of women like Mathilda, an OK Bazaars shop steward, recounted in a booklet prepared for Saccawu.

'Once I became a shop steward' recalls Mathilda,

> I realised how much work there was to be done. There were many meetings to attend. I was committed to properly representing the workers from my department and reporting back to them.
>
> But it was not long before I realised that I would have to be superhuman to continue with this job for a long time. You see, I was working full time, I was a mother of two children and now I was also a shop steward.
>
> My husband did not help me in the house – it meant that I had to do all the work when I got home in the evenings, after my meetings. And if my sister was not there to help me with the children, it would have been impossible. After two years I began to realise that commitment alone was not enough. I needed my husband to support me in my new role.[13]

If unions are to take these issues seriously they will have to confront the whole structure of relations between men and women both at work and in society. They will have to explore affirmative action more thoroughly, and face a number of testing questions. Why can they not employ more women organisers? Why can they not reserve a reasonable proportion of seats on all executive committees for women? Why can they not restructure their meeting times to do more union work during working hours?

Unions will also have to explore their whole style of operating. What, for example, are the implications of expecting more women to stand for leadership but retaining an outlook where aggression and toughness are prized leadership qualities? These are some of the issues the union movement has only begun to explore.

Notes

1. Author interview, Johannesburg, December 1982.
2. Debbie Budlender, 'Women and the Economy', paper presented to a conference on *Women and Gender in Southern Africa*, University of Natal, Durban, February 1991.
3. Author interview with Fiona Dove, Saccawu official, Johannesburg, 10 December 1990.
4. Author interview with Ebrahim Patel, Saccawu official, Johannesburg, 22 January 1991.
5. Author's survey conducted during December 1990 with assistance from Gill Evill.
6. Author interview with Fiona Dove, Johannesburg, 10 December 1990.
7. Quoted in *South African Labour Bulletin*, 14(5), October 1989, 15.
8. Budlender, 'Women and the Economy'.
9. Cosatu, *Women and the Living Wage Campaign*, Johannesburg, no date, 3.
10. Budlender, 'Women and the Economy'.
11. Numsa, *Numsa Women Organise*, Johannesburg, 1989, 26.
12. Quoted in Tammy Shefer, 'The gender agenda', paper presented to a conference on *Women and gender in Southern Africa*, University of Natal, Durban, February 1991.
13. Lacom, Learn and Teach and Saccawu, *Sharing the Load*, Johannesburg, 1991, 55.

24

Multiple visions

*T*HE workers summit had decided to submit six demands to employers as part of the anti-LRA campaign. These called on employers to abide by international standards on dismissal and retrenchment, and to waive their right to use certain provisions of the new LRA. If the employers refused these demands workers would be balloted over the possibility of further action. A second workers' summit would then decide on the next step.

Cosatu's third congress discussed the anti-LRA campaign in some detail. In its report to the assembled delegates, the secretariat argued it was important to build on the first workers summit in creating a 'mass-based' campaign. Unfortunately, however, the letters of demand agreed upon at the workers summit in March had only been submitted to employers on 1 June.

The Cosatu congress, continued the report, had 'a historic duty to shape the struggle against the LRA into a potent weapon.' The success or failure of the anti-LRA campaign would be a test of Cosatu's political capabilities. 'If we are to play a major role in shaping the future', commented the report, 'we have to establish the role of organised workers under Cosatu and the working class as a whole as a decisive political factor to any solution to the present crisis.' The congress was asked to give Cosatu's delegation to the second workers summit 'a decisive mandate' to take the campaign forward. The secretariat reported that Cosatu, Nactu and the independent unions had met with Saccola on 26 June. Employers had refused to accede to the six demands drawn up at the first workers summit, and as a result employers and the unions were in dispute.

Debate on the congress floor revealed that unions had not prepared sufficiently for the next phase of the campaign. Not enough workers had been ballotted over whether or not to take action, noted a Numsa speaker. Congress accepted Numsa's proposal that ballotting should be extended from the original deadline of 24 July until 15 August, and that the second workers summit should be postponed until 18 August so that the ballot results could be considered. Ppwawu's view that Cosatu go to the second summit with a concrete set of proposals was also endorsed.

Ppwawu suggested 'a week of action' against the LRA from 1-6 September. Some delegates felt that this would pre-empt the summit's decisions. Others argued that it was crucial for Cosatu to go to the summit with clear ideas which could be debated and modified. Action should not be limited to one week, argued CWIU. The mistakes of the previous year, where Cosatu had been unable to sustain an ongoing programme of action, should be avoided. After much debate it was agreed to recommend 'sustained action' beginning on 1 September 1989 and 'linked to the white racist elections'.

The first day of September was the anniversary of the LRA's promulgation, while the general election was scheduled for 6 September. 'The two issues are related,' commented Jay Naidoo after the congress. 'It is, after all, this racist parliament that passed the LRA, and it is precisely because the vast majority of workers have no say in this parliament that an Act like this can be passed.'

Ballotting the workers

Nactu accepted the three-week postponement of the second summit and indicated that all its affiliates would be attending. It also agreed that unions needed more time to ballot their membership. The ballot aimed to mobilise the rank-and-file membership and test their views, with union members being asked whether they were prepared to take action in the dispute with employers over the LRA. 'On the basis of the response (to the ballot), as well as the progress of negotiations with bosses through Saccola and the state, we will decide on what action to take,' said Sydney Mufamadi shortly before the summit.

The ballot results, when they were finally announced at the workers summit, revealed a mixed picture. An overwhelming majority of workers who voted – 98% – supported action. Only 1% opposed action (see table). But less than half of Cosatu's membership was ballotted, although all unions which reported announced that they were still collecting results.

Ccawusa, Fawu, Potwa and Sadwu provided no ballot results to the summit, while Cawu's figures were clearly an estimate. The Gawu component in the clothing and textile sector had ballotted, but Actwusa members had not been canvassed at all.[*] In certain other sectors the percentage of membership voting was unacceptably low. Only Ppwawu, Sarhwu, TGWU and Numsa could report that they had ballotted over half their membership, only one unaffiliated union, OVGWU, had ballotted its members, and not one Nactu affiliate had done so.

Results of ballot against the LRA[1]

Union	Votes for action	Votes against	Spoilt
Ppwawu	23 328	497	232
Samwu	11 511	238	---
CWIU	13 553	413	140
Sarhwu	19 314	27	46
TGWU	18 796	361	58
Nehawu	3 338	---	---
NUM	78 213	783	122
Numsa	130 438	2 284	1 003
Cawu	14 000	---	---
Gawu	38 320	---	---
OVGWU	7 114	18	39
Total	357 925	4 621	1 640

A number of factors were involved in the poor Cosatu ballot.[**] Employers, particularly on the mines, prevented some workers from being

[*] Actwusa's attitude to the anti-LRA campaign had been a source of tension within Cosatu since the second congress. There was a widespread belief that Actwusa was more committed to 'contracting out' of the LRA than to the wider campaign against it. By the time of the second summit 25 000 Actwusa members were covered by agreements with employers which side-stepped the amendments to the LRA. Actwusa argued its actions were in line with the decisions of the first summit and that all its members, contracted out or not, would continue supporting the anti-LRA campaign. Its detractors argued that continued 'contracting out' contravened a subsequent Cosatu/Nactu agreement. 'Contracting out,' argued CWIU organiser Martin Jansen, 'addresses the problem in a very piecemeal manner, and undermines a sustained campaign by the whole labour movement.'

[**] The reasons for the poor ballot, insofar as they concern Nactu and the unaffiliated unions, are beyond the scope of this work.

ballotted. The results also showed that some unions were organisationally unprepared for the complex arrangements and co-ordination
involved in a national ballot. Other affiliates simply did not give high-
enough priority to the anti-LRA campaign.

Bobby Godsell, a senior Anglo executive, justified management's
lack of co-operation on the mines by labelling the ballot 'an exercise in
sham democracy.' Workers had not been educated in depth about the
LRA, he argued, and the term 'action' on the ballot paper was not
clarified.

> Essentially (the unions were) asking their membership for a blank
> cheque. If they want co-operation from employers the ballot must be
> mutually agreed upon – it must ask meaningful questions. Sound
> democratic practice is based on informed choice. This certainly isn't.[2]

The second workers summit

The ballot results formed part of the immediate backdrop as workers
gathered on 26 August for the second workers summit. So did continuing
employer and state refusal to accommodate union concerns over the
LRA. However, when the 750 worker delegates assembled at Shareworld, near Soweto, they faced a more immediate problem –
heavily-armed police!

Scores of police wearing riot-blue outfits and armed with R1 rifles,
gas grenades and sten guns had arrived at the summit venue in the early
hours of the morning. They were occupying the meeting hall and parking
area when the first union delegates arrived. Police informed union
leaders that the meeting had been restricted in terms of the state of emergency. It could continue, a police colonel said, on condition there were
no flags, banners or stickers; no speeches other than those dealing directly with the LRA; and no singing or talking after 5 pm. In addition, in a
move aimed at preventing the attendance of invited guests from 'the
community', only union members could attend. Union leaders asked if
this meant that police would also be leaving since they were not union
members. Police would attend the summit, replied the colonel in charge,
and would monitor proceedings with a video camera.

The colonel then asked Chris Dlamini to read out the restriction
order to the assembled workers. He refused. The police had drawn up
the order and they should read it out, he said. The colonel refused and
the summit opened with the restrictions unannounced. In the meantime
union leaders were trying to think of ways to avoid the restrictions. Delegates needed to discuss both the forthcoming parliamentary elections and
mass actions against the LRA, but this was illegal in terms of the

restrictions. Police video units were already installed in the hall, and not only would delegates risk arrest for speaking their minds, but police would have concrete evidence against them.

The union leadership came up with an imaginative plan. Delegates were asked to break into smaller groups. Each would meet separately and appoint a scribe to take notes. Other delegates would act as messengers, shuttling ideas and proposals back and forth between groups. It was an effective move. There were simply not enough video cameras to film every group and there were not sufficient police to monitor proceedings. This also made it impossible for police to hold any particular individual accountable for decisions taken.

Using these tactics the summit adopted a plan of action under the very noses of the police. There would be brief stoppages or demonstrations in all factories on 1 September, and a two-day stayaway on 5 and 6 September. This would be followed by a month-long consumer boycott of white-owned shops starting on 13 September. Finally, workers would ban overtime indefinitely, although this decision would be reviewed on a monthly basis. The union movement would continue talks with Saccola and other employer bodies as part of the link between ongoing mass action and negotiations.

The question of a stayaway was the major point of tension at the summit. Nactu proposed a week-long stayaway starting on 11 September, but Cosatu delegates rejected this unrealistically protracted action. Some Nactu delegates were also opposed to linking the anti-LRA action to the general elections which were, they argued, a non-issue.

The week-long action was ultimately rejected in favour of a two-day stayaway. Some Nactu representatives then objected to the proposed dates. The two-day stayaway should be split into two, they argued. Workers should stayaway on 6 September, in opposition to the LRA, and again on 12 September, in commemoration of the death of black consciousness leader Steve Biko, who died in police detention. Because of the restrictions, the matter could not be finalised on the open conference floor, and the decisions taken could legally not be publicly announced. The union movement had to rely on those present to take the message back to the shopfloor.

The September stayaway

A large number of demonstrations took place on 1 September. In the Western Cape thousands of workers marched in the industrial areas. In most regions, however, the response to the call was uneven. Actions differed between locals, regions and affiliates according to the level of mobilisation of the workers concerned.

Several days later confusion emerged over the question of the stayaway. The response was weaker on its first day, 5 September, than on the next. As usual there were differences from region to region. A survey conducted by the LMG revealed that in the PWV area 39% of black workers stayed away on the first day, rising to 72% the following day. On the first day, 'larger and better organised companies experienced high stayaways while smaller unorganised companies generally experienced low or negligible stayaways.' On the second day the situation was different.

The response in Western Cape was higher than usual with 25% absent on 5 September, rising to 41% on election day. Although this was 'lower than other urban areas', commented the LMG, 'it was considerably higher than the stayaway in June 1988.' In the Eastern Cape well over 80% of black workers supported the action on both days. The greater Durban area reported a strong response, with 68% of black workers absent on 5 September and 80% absent on the next day, including a large number of Indian workers.

The mines and rural areas were less responsive. Transvaal country towns recorded a 12% stayaway, while towns in the OFS saw only 10% absenteeism. In the Eastern Transvaal 19% of workers were estimated to have stayed away. On the mines, the Chamber of Mines estimated that only 30 000 workers, or 6% of employees, were absent on both days. NUM figures supplied to the LMG included miners who did not fall under the Chamber of Mines. The union estimated that 57 000 members at over 28 mines stayed away on the first day, rising to 100 000 members on the next, with support on collieries being stronger than on gold mines.[3] School students and community organisations also took action, particularly on election day.

Most employers adopted a 'no work, no pay' approach. About 160 workers, nationwide, were dismissed. In addition many companies, particularly those owned by Barlow Rand, locked their gates until the following Monday, 11 September. This illegal lockout was apparently aimed at punishing the workers and depriving them of pay for the remainder of the week. In fact it simply intensified Cosatu's growing animosity towards Barlow companies. In a number of other factories workers were given written warnings.

Overall the stayaway was successful although the PWV area showed major weaknesses. The area was particularly weak on the first day and worker responses in both the Eastern Cape and Natal were higher. Some observers argued that it was significant that Nactu supported stayaway action on 6 September, the day that absenteeism was greater. While the argument had some validity, particularly in the PWV area, it failed to explain the negligible response, even from Nactu members, to the call for another stayaway on 12 September. More probably, confusion over the stayaway call of 5 September resulted in a lower response. Doubts over the starting date of the action were widespread, largely because it had been impossible to summarise decisions at the end of the summit meeting. In the Kokstad-Matatiele area of Natal, workers were mistakenly informed by their delegates to the summit that the stayaway should start on 1 September. The stayaway in that area, commented the Southern Natal regional report to the CEC, 'went on quite effectively until 6 September.'

The consumer boycott and overtime ban

After the stayaway Cosatu's head office received reports from a number of regions that workers were not yet mobilised for further action. Cosatu immediately consulted both Nactu and the unaffiliated unions, and Exco agreed that the proposed consumer boycott should only commence on 22 September and last for two weeks, not one month as originally planned. Exco's last-minute postponement caused some confusion and was widely criticised. It had decided on a key issue without properly consulting the regions, it was argued. 'The workers summit is more representative than the Exco which reversed the decision,' commented the Wits region at the following CEC.

The Border area decided to go ahead with its original plans and implemented a highly-effective consumer boycott which started on 13 September. Both the Eastern and Western Cape decided not to proceed with a boycott, even on the 22 September. Western Cape later agreed to boycott from the 7 to 20 October. The Highveld region reported that support for the boycott was strong in Witbank and Bethal, but not in other Eastern Transvaal towns. Generally, the consumer boycotts were poorly observed and petered out within days. They depended heavily on local conditions. Cosatu received reports that township shopkeepers were overcharging, a major incentive for people to buy at cheaper prices from shops in town.

The ban on overtime agreed upon at the summit was postponed to coincide with the consumer boycott. It was a qualitatively different type of action to the other components of the anti-LRA campaign. Based in the factories, it could only be undertaken by unionised and well-organised workers. It could only be applied in factories where overtime was being worked, and this differed from industry to industry and from month to month. Although agreed upon by an entire workforce, it needed to be implemented by individual workers asked by their supervisors to perform overtime. In practice a whole factory generally does not work overtime. Rather, specific individuals or departments do so.

CWIU organiser Martin Jansen sees it as a problematic strategy, difficult to build unity around. 'It is "invisible" behind the factory gates, so it is difficult for workers to see each other united in action.' This makes it 'a fragmented form of action' between factories and even within factories, he argues.[4]

An overtime ban is, undoubtedly, a difficult national action to implement. But it can also be an extremely powerful weapon. Overtime work is largely unavoidable when it is aimed at overcoming an urgent production problem or dealing with the temporary or short-term requirements of a particular plant. However, in many South African plants overtime is a regular and permanent feature of the working week. In these plants the employer finds it more convenient to work with a smaller labour force working 'flexible' hours – in short, understaffing of the plant. Individual employees are not always opposed to this, since regular overtime can supplement meagre wages.

Cosatu's Living Wage Campaign had long called on workers to refuse overtime – without much success. The LWC call rested on two arguments. Firstly, workers should be able to earn a living wage without having to rely on overtime. They should receive a fair wage for a 40-hour week. Secondly, companies working regular overtime should rather increase their workforce and restructure production systems or shift arrangements. This could help reduce the level of unemployment in the country. This second argument was strongly supported by the NUWCC.

The overtime ban had definite, although limited effects. Cosatu was unable to monitor the action nationally. This was a major weakness of the campaign. Without detailed assessment it was difficult to judge the effectiveness of the action. The LMG looked at the impact of the campaign in unionised plants in the PWV area during the first four weeks of October, but did not monitor the construction and commercial sectors as it was clear 'that no overtime ban was being implemented by the workforces.'

By far the strongest response came from workers in Ppwawu, Numsa, CWIU and Fawu. However, only Ppwawu members' participation in the overtime campaign was consistently high, rising to 61% by the fourth week of the survey. Numsa and CWIU participation tended to drop after two weeks of action, while Fawu's participation only became high after a slow start. On average, the survey found, 36% of black workers observed the overtime ban. In practice this was highly significant, with serious effects on production.[5]

Numerous interdicts brought against the unions testified to the effectiveness of the overtime bans. Many companies went to court in an attempt to have the bans classified as 'illegal strikes'. Management was accustomed to its employees working overtime regularly and without dissension. The matter had long been contentious. The unions argued that overtime was, by its nature, voluntary. It involved hours of work in addition to those which constituted the regular working week. Workers were entirely within their rights, therefore, to refuse overtime work. Employers acknowledged that individual workers could refuse to work overtime on a particular occasion. An overtime ban was different as it was a form of collective action. Therefore, they argued, the overtime ban constituted 'industrial action', and illegal action at that, since it had been undertaken without following the procedures of the LRA.

These differences were far from academic. If refusal to work overtime was legal then management could take no action against participating workers. If, on the other hand, it constituted an 'illegal industrial action' then workers had little protection if management chose to discipline or dismiss them.

Different courts had given entirely different judgements on the issue. Fortunately for Cosatu, a test case came before the appellate division of the supreme court on the eve of the overtime ban. In a case brought by SA Breweries against Fawu, the court ruled that Fawu's members were entitled to refuse overtime work. The judgement gave impetus to the campaign.[*]

Employers did not only rely on court interdicts. Faced with an overtime ban many cancelled recognition agreements, while others withdrew stop-order facilities. CWIU achieved a small victory at the Dutch multinational Shell, which first threatened to interdict the union, but later agreed to introduce an additional shift, and thereby reduce the need for overtime.

The launch of Sactwu

The South African Clothing and Textile Workers Union (Sactwu), the product of a merger between Actwusa and the unaffiliated Gawu, was launched during 1989. The merger process, which created Cosatu's third-largest affiliate, was fraught with difficulties, as we have seen in an earlier chapter. Tensions came to a head around elections for the position of general secretary, when Lionel October of Gawu defeated Des Sampson. Sampson, also from Gawu, had the backing of most of the Actwusa delegates.

The launching congress elected John Copelyn as assistant general secretary, Amon Ntuli as president, Eleanor 'Bubbles' Beaumont as first

---

* This test case failed to settle the matter. Strictly speaking, the judge decided in favour of the SAB workers only because the requirement to work overtime was not written into their contracts.

vice-president, Bert Pitts as second vice-president, and Joel Ndongeni as treasurer. Because of the tensions surrounding the launch only simple resolutions were adopted – those establishing branches and regions, and affiliating to both Cosatu and the International Textile, Garment and Leather Workers Federation. Controversial and more-complex resolutions were referred to the union's national executive.

Differences between the two component unions were essentially political. Ebrahim Patel, an Actwusa official, has argued that some, mainly from Actwusa, feared that the union would lose its independent political line in the merger and 'become a transmission belt for the ANC.' Others, mainly from within Gawu, were scared to lose the union's hard-won pro-Freedom Charter direction.[6]

The merger brought together 180 000 workers, making Sactwu the only affiliate representing as many as 80% of workers in its industry. Approximately 10% of the workers in the sector remained totally unorganised, while another 10% were members of the National Union of Leather Workers. About 1 000 workers in Natal remained members of Tawu, a splinter union formed in 1986.

Perhaps the most significant aspect of the merger was that, for the first time, it brought large numbers of coloured and Indian workers into Cosatu's ranks. African workers made up a little over half of Sactwu's total membership. The merger also increased the number of women within Cosatu dramatically. The overwhelming majority of Gawu's membership were coloured and Indian women.

Since its launch Sactwu has faced the challenge of building a genuinely non-racial union, combining workers from a variety of ethnic groups. This was, and remains, a difficult task. The democratic union movement has always been strongly African in membership as well as in organisational style and culture. Meetings are usually conducted in one or other of the indigenous African languages – not calculated to welcome coloured and Indian workers who usually speak English or Afrikaans.

Sactwu has succeeded in creating a culture of union struggle among coloured workers, who hold senior positions within the union. This is particularly so in the Western Cape. Afrikaans freedom songs – often in the traditional 'klopse' style – are frequently heard at union meetings. 'This has stunned Zulu-speaking workers from Natal,' says one Sactwu unionist. 'These workers, who pride themselves on their singing, are now trying to learn the Afrikaans songs. By contrast Indian culture hasn't developed at all. Our Indian members have retreated.' They remain intensely loyal union members who are happy with the union. But Indian workers no longer generate the vast shop steward layer they once did within the industry.

How does one explain the different experiences in the aftermath of the merger? 'Perhaps it is coloured numbers in the Western Cape (where they are a majority),' explains Ebrahim Patel. 'Or perhaps it is because of greater coloured assertiveness' in contrast to the traditionally unassertive Indian women.'

South Africa's democratic movement has usually avoided tackling these questions head-on. Understandably, it has responded to apartheid's emphasis on differences and division by stressing the unity, common interests and shared nationhood of all South Africans. The discourse of those fighting apartheid has tended to avoid ethnic terms other than reference to 'white oppression'. However, ethnic differences are often present as undercurrents within the union movement. These generally take the form of occasional hostility towards whites active within the unions; or towards Indian and coloured workers who – in the complex pecking order of apartheid – are seen to be more privileged. Sometimes there is also hostility between African workers from different ethnic groups. Genuine non-racialism is undoubtedly a real phenomenon within the union movement. But it is also as much an aspiration and challenge as a reality.

Sactwu has not been the only union to tackle theses issues. Potwa has engaged in unity talks with two staff associations – the Postal Employees Association of South Africa, an organisation with over 5 000 coloured members; and the South African Post and Telecommunication Employees Association with over 1 000 Indian members. The Durban Integrated Municipal Employees Association, with over 5 000 predominantly Indian members, has also agreed to merge with Samwu.

While genuine unity is now being forged between African, Indian and coloured workers, the same cannot be said for white workers. Approximately 1 000 white workers have joined Cosatu. They have generally joined for that which affiliates can offer them in terms of job security, increased wages and so on. They join despite, not because of, Cosatu's political profile and non-racial perspective.

Consolidating education

Cosatu's second education conference was held in October 1989. In his report to the conference Khetsi Lehoko, the education secretary, acknowledged that affiliates had undertaken insufficient shop steward and organiser training in the previous two years. However, there had been some progress and Nedcom structures were working better, reported Lehoko. The education officers of the various affiliates also met regularly, and this served as a forum for the exchange of ideas. Nedcom had mandated the education officers to develop a uniform approach to basic shop stewards' education, training of educators, and instruction on basic Cosatu policies. A number of regional education officers had been appointed to work with the Redcoms and develop educational work in the regions.

However, reported Lehoko, there were a variety of problems with other aspects of the education department's work. Cosatu's programme of study tours was a mixed success. These tours, arranged in conjunction with the CTUC, the CLC and the ILO, enabled a number of worker leaders to visit trade union centres in both the Commonwealth countries and Eastern Europe. Many of the tours proved valuable, but Cosatu had difficulties in ensuring adequate preparation before these visits and in feeding the experience back into its structures.

A number of the department's tasks were not, strictly speaking, educational, and this, too, created difficulties. The department was responsible for overseeing the building of one national teachers' union. It was also charged with the development of women's forums within Cosatu, and overseeing research into key aspects of post-apartheid economic policy. These were all, arguably, organisational and policy matters with only limited connection to the task of education.

But, overall, one major weakness remained. Not enough education was being undertaken by the federation. The gap had also widened between those affiliates running active education programmes of their own, and affiliates with no education programmes to speak of.

While no survey has been done, it is probably true that the majority of shop stewards in Cosatu affiliates have received no training whatsoever. This leaves them ill-equipped to deal with employers, many of whom utilise sophisticated industrial relations consultants. Similarly, it is almost unheard of for any union organiser to be given training before commencing duties. New organisers and shop stewards are simply dropped into the deep end. The best that they can expect is informal on-the-job training or advice from more experienced colleagues. This 'sink-or-swim' approach to training has produced a degree of autonomy, innovation and resourcefulness among many organisers and shop stewards. But it has major limitations. Untrained unionists often handle problems with insufficient skill. On many occasions a court case could have been avoided or a strike averted by a more skillful negotiating team. There is no system for new organisers to learn from the mistakes of an older generation, and frequently a sense that each new organiser must reinvent the wheel.

With Cosatu growing rapidly and facing sustained attacks it was, perhaps, inevitable that unions would throw all their resources into issues of the moment. Understaffed and over-extended, it was hardly surprising that skilled education officers were asked to assist with organisational as well as political tasks. The second education conference resolved to improve the skill level of Cosatu and affiliate staff members, but it was only in 1990 that staff development and training began to receive the attention it deserved.

The conference ended with the re-election of the four education office bearers, Lehoko, Chris Seoposengwe, Pule Thate and Esion Mashego, for a second two-year term.

Healing the Ccawusa split

When we last examined the Ccawusa dispute the differences between the Mtwa and Kganare factions were deeper than ever. The CEC commission had failed to resolve these, and the November 1987 CEC had effectively recognised the Kganare faction as Cosatu's affiliate in the commercial sector.

In late 1987 and early 1988 the Mtwa faction applied to the supreme court for an interdict against the opposing faction. The Kganare group opposed the application. While the Kganare faction had achieved recognition from Cosatu, the Mtwa faction was determined to win legal recognition. The faction which achieved this would retain the name Ccawusa, the assets of the union, and existing legal agreements with employers. The situation was clouded further when Ccawusa's pre-merger president, Makhulu Ledwaba, withdrew from the conflict and accepted a scholarship to study in the United Kingdom. Ledwaba had been recognised as president by both factions of Ccawusa, and was also Cosatu's second vice-president.

During the course of the legal battles it was discovered that Ccawusa's 1986 constitution had never been officially registered. Legally, the effects of this were devastating. All factions had understood that both the pre-merger and merger congresses of 1987 had been held in terms of the 1986 constitution. However, legally, the previous 1981 constitution applied, and both 1987 congresses had been unconstitutional. It appeared as if the court would rule that neither faction constituted the legal Ccawusa! The dispute was threatening to become a comedy of errors, but one with serious implications.

Rather than let the case proceed, both factions agreed to an out-of-court settlement which recognised the old Ccawusa office bearers – Vivian Mtwa, Herbert Mkhize and Dinah Nhlapo, but not Makhulu Ledwaba. Both factions agreed to hold a re-unification conference before 15 May 1988, in terms of the 1981 constitution. Harwu and Rawu would revert to operating as separate structures. Each branch would hold a meeting of its general membership and elect eight delegates to the national conference. In terms of the out-of-court settlement, the

Independent Mediation Services of South Africa (Imssa) was given the unenviable task of presiding over the counting of votes.

The planned re-unification conference never took place. While a number of branch general meetings were held, others failed because the two factions in some areas were unable to agree on ground rules. The 1981 constitution was too shaky a vehicle to hold Ccawusa together. Neither faction wanted it. It made no allowance for branches of different sizes to have differing numbers of delegates. Both the small Cape Town branch and the large Johannesburg branch would bring eight delegates to conference. The out-of-court settlement also failed to recognise that Rawu members had been fully integrated into the Kganare Ccawusa, and that the integration of Harwu members was well under way.

Most importantly, the out-of-court settlement was not the product of real unity moves between the factions, and did not address the extreme hostility between them. Individual leaders recognised that there would have to be compromise. 'For the sake of unity' no contentious political motions should be taken at the re-unification conference, argued Kaizer Thibedi of the Mtwa grouping. 'Our attitude is that we don't want to vote. You don't build unity by votes,' was the view expressed by the Kganare faction's Jay Naidoo. But on the ground both groups' supporters retained a '50% plus 1' mentality. Each wanted to 'win', to control a re-unified Ccawusa. The out-of-court settlement laid the seed for re-unification, but the time was not yet ripe for its germination.

Tensions developed within both camps during 1988 and 1989. In the Mtwa grouping a division took place in the Johannesburg branch, resulting in a leading organiser, Oscar Malgas, and a number of PAC-aligned supporters joining the Nactu-affiliated Hotelica. Almost 2 000 workers, predominantly in catering, left the union as a result. There were also tensions within the Mtwa camp between Africanists, black consciousness supporters, and left-wing socialists. Differences in style of work – between a 'toned-down' and a more vocal 'militant' approach – also affected relations both within the Mtwa camp and between it and the Kganare faction.

The Kganare faction also had serious problems. Tensions had developed between its leadership and Harwu, which had not yet formally dissolved. Harwu had long wanted hotel and catering workers to be regarded as a separate sector. After the merger they continued to feel that their members were neglected, and pressed for 'sectoral rights' within the union. This was opposed by a majority of the Kganare faction who argued that Harwu officials wanted to avoid merging properly and retain an 'empire within Ccawusa.'

These conflicts, like those in the Mtwa faction, were underpinned by political tensions and overlaid by differences in style of work. Politically, there were differences between hardline Congress supporters and those closer to the politics of the left-wing socialists in the Mtwa camp. Alan Horwitz, a key figure within Harwu, was accused of 'individualism' and refusal to work within Ccawusa structures. His accusers, in turn, were labelled 'stalinists' and accused of political intolerance. Tensions were most extreme in Johannesburg and revolved around control of resources and assets. Harwu was expelled from the Johannesburg office. One Harwu official has alleged that the Kganare faction's operation in the area was run by 'incompetent, incapable and corrupt' individuals. 'They had no union skills and were just activists – township politics at its worst.' By February 1989 Harwu was effectively operating as a separate union. It was joined by the Cape Liquor union, although a number of members of both unions remained supporters of the Kganare faction.

The splits within Ccawusa were demoralising and debilitating for both membership and leadership. We have seen in an earlier chapter how both factions tried, immediately after the split, to win defectors from each other's camps. Over time, very few workers changed camps permanently. But between mid-1987 and December 1989, unionisation in the retail sector grew far more slowly than in Cosatu as a whole. Too much time and energy was devoted to dealing with the consequences of the split, leaving insufficient time to organise. In Checkers' Silverton branch, for example, each camp maintained its own shop stewards. A similar situation existed in a number of other shops.

While some shop stewards developed a clearer understanding of political differences between the factions, most Ccawusa members did not. They were simply loyal to their faction. Political positions were often oversimplified in the explanation of differences. Those who understood the differences often did so in a dogmatic and inflexible fashion. This, in turn, stimulated the differences which emerged within each camp.

Financially, the split was disastrous. Each faction had to ensure that its supporters' subscriptions were not 'grabbed' by the other. Both tried to obtain financial assistance from various sources. Outside funding from Fiet, the international trade secretariat (ITS) covering retail workers, dried up. It did not want to get involved in the split. Another ITS, the International Union of Foodworkers (IUF), continued to assist first the Kganare faction, and then only its Harwu component. This, in turn, became a further source of tension.

The major effect of the split was on wage negotiations. Both factions accepted that they should not destroy the national bargaining forums which existed between the union and major companies such as Pick 'n Pay or Checkers. But how were they to bargain jointly? 'Mostly we avoided fighting', recalled one official, 'but there was no agreement to work together.' Tensions existed within the joint negotiating teams over co-ordination of the team, who would correspond with management, and who would send information to the union's branches. Joint negotiations also culminated in separate report-backs where workers gave different mandates to their representatives. One group might accept a company's offer while the other wanted to declare a dispute.

'Workers became sick and tired of the split,' recalled one official from the Mtwa camp. In one extreme case, in mid-1989, Woolworths withdrew from negotiations with the union and implemented a unilateral wage increase after the two factions were unable to constitute an agreed union negotiating team. The Ellerines strike, in late 1987, was in the words of one official 'a fairly dismal affair'. While the situation differed from company to company, in general the split meant Ccawusa did not have the capacity to undertake united strikes. It is a tribute to the under-lying strength of the union that it managed to maintain wage increases above the inflation rate during this period.

The re-unification process

The re-unification process envisaged in the out-of-court settlement was endorsed by Cosatu at the CEC of 12-14 February 1988. 'We note with great interest and appreciation the steps being taken to amicably resolve the problems,' read the official resolution. Cosatu would recognise all office bearers elected at the envisaged branch general meetings and re-unification conference. However, until such time, the 'merged Ccawusa' – the Kganare faction – would remain 'the recognised Ccawusa in Co-satu structures' in line with the decision of the November 1987 CEC. This remained a source of grievance within the Mtwa faction for some time. Cosatu, it argued with some justification, was taking sides.

Despite the failure of the out-of-court settlement, leading figures from all sides were realising the need to re-unify by late 1988. 'We had concluded', said the Kganare faction's Jay Naidoo, 'that we could fight for as long as we liked but that neither side would make major dents into the layers of support each had.' The split was hurting all sides and it appeared as if the differences could be overcome. The Kganare Ccawusa held a 'national consultation' in December 1988 where it resolved to attempt to re-unify the union. The Mtwa Ccawusa was receptive to this, having reached similar conclusions.

During early 1989 the Cosatu office bearers mediated in a number of meetings between the factions. They then proposed establishment of a 'unity executive' – a joint committee of all factions including Cosatu representatives. It would attempt to iron out the problems and re-unify Ccawusa. Cosatu's office bearers managed to convince all factions to agree to this, and the result was drafted into a resolution presented to

Cosatu's third congress. The unity initiative was so finely balanced that debates on the congress floor could have upset the process. Chris Dlamini, chairing that session of congress, used his extensive skills to ensure that the motion was proposed, seconded and adopted within the space of 30 seconds. It was the fastest resolution ever adopted by Cosatu!

The resolution called for the CEC decision of November 1987 to be 'reviewed'. It established a 'unity executive' of six people from each of the three groupings – Harwu, Ccawusa (Mtwa) and Ccawusa (Kganare). The office bearers recognised in the out-of-court settlement would be included as well as four people from Cosatu. The Cosatu representatives would act 'in a mediating capacity and maintain neutrality.' The process would aim 'to create one unified, national union in the commercial and catering sector that is an affiliate of Cosatu' before 12 November 1989. The unity executive would operate on the basis of consensus. The August CEC appointed Cyril Ramaphosa, Sydney Mufamadi, Chris Dlamini and Numsa's Bernie Fanaroff to the unity executive. As Ramaphosa was not available, NUM's assistant general secretary Marcel Golding took his place on the committee.

The unity executive had to resolve a number of complex issues which reveal some of the prerequisites and difficulties involved in mergers. The Mtwa faction wanted to open the process to other unions in the sector, such as the Federal Council of Retail and Allied Workers (Fedcraw), the National Union of Distributive and Allied Workers (Nudaw) and the Natal Liquor and Catering Union. But it was eventually agreed that the first aim of re-unification was to heal divisions within Ccawusa.

It was further agreed that any potential legal problems should be avoided. Ccawusa would be the constitutional vehicle for the merger, on the basis of agreed amendments to its 1986 constitution. Other key issues included the procedures for establishing a system of nationalised union finances; international affiliation; and the name of the union. It was agreed to have fraternal relations with both Fiet and the IUF, but to affiliate to neither. Lengthy debates over the name of the union ended with agreement to call it the South African Commercial, Catering and Allied Workers Union (Saccawu).

Policy resolutions on a range of issues were agreed to, but no major decisions were taken on the question of political policy. The key issue of elections was resolved by a carefully-balanced agreement dividing key positions amongst leaders from the different groupings. It was also agreed that an independent membership audit would be done after the re-unification congress. This would give guidance on the number of officials from each grouping which the merged union could absorb. Agreement on all these questions involved structuring a complex, but fair, package. All groupings had to make compromises in the interests of unity. The agreement was only finalised on 8 November when all parties signed a bulky 42-page legal document.

On 11 November 350 delegates gathered and endorsed the agreement in a congress which lasted a brief three hours. It was jointly chaired by Fanaroff and Golding. Duma Nkosi, of the Kganare faction, was elected president, with first vice-president Miller Moela, and second vice-president Chris Mohlatsi, coming from the Mtwa and Harwu groupings respectively. Vivian Mtwa was elected general secretary and Papi Kganare assistant general secretary. Similar accommodations were made in appointments to Saccawu's organising and education units.

'We have to a large extent taken care of the difference causing the split in 1987,' commented Mtwa after the congress. 'As far as political policy goes, we will leave this to be debated in all structures,' culminating in a national congress to be held in mid-1990. While the November congress formally re-unified Ccawusa, much remained to be done to develop united structures.

The membership audit found that the former Mtwa faction had 39 000 paid-up members; the former Kganare group had 36 000; and the Harwu/Cape Liquor bloc had 9 000. This gave Saccawu an initial paid-up membership of 85 000. The figures revealed that no faction had made serious inroads into the support of another. If anything the Kganare group was probably larger than most observers had expected.

Re-unification was welcomed by many major employers. The Ccawusa split had led to 'uncertainty, low productivity and shopfloor unpleasantness,' commented a Metro Cash and Carry spokesperson. A Checkers director agreed. 'We would much prefer to deal with a strong and undivided union.'

Saccawu held its first congress from 13-15 July 1990 in Johannesburg. Some 390 delegates from 55 locals countrywide attended. The congress adopted resolutions stressing the need for political tolerance as well as 'the right of freedom of association and expression of all and the right to organise.'

Learning the lessons

The re-unification of Ccawusa was a major victory for Cosatu. It showed a capacity to mediate effectively between groupings holding diverse views and having different interests. The divisions within Ccawusa held lessons, not only for that union, but for the whole of Cosatu.

The new union which emerged was not simply a fragile pasting together of the pieces of Ccawusa. Saccawu was born with the realisation that differing political views had to be contained within the organisation. Political pluralism had to be accepted in a context where the union's internal unity was paramount. Saccawu would have to be politically involved, take political decisions and political actions. But these should emerge from open debate and be based on as broad a consensus as possible. The union could not simply be a vehicle for the political views of the ANC, left-wing socialists, or any other grouping.

Duma Nkosi, Saccawu's first president, has argued that the split forced all factions within the union to come to terms with the practical implications of political differences. It forced the leadership to be sensitive to pluralism, consensus and unity without resorting to an apolitical approach. 'First you build a trade union – a representative organisation,' argued Nkosi. 'Then you start tackling your political differences. If you do it the other way around you are turning everything upside down, including the union.'

The healing of the split has resulted in a stronger union with more worker control. There is less room for organisers to use their political views to avoid disciplinary action for incompetence or inefficiency.

It is not always possible to avoid divisions within unions. Even with the best intentions and the most sophisticated handling of differences and contradictions it is possible for divisions to occur. Avoiding splits – or healing them – requires dealing with the three aspects of any division: differences of interest; differences of outlook; and differences between personalities. The Ccawusa split showed Cosatu that it is possible to contain a diverse range of views within one union.

Notes

1. *South African Labour Bulletin*, 14(4), October 1989, 58.
2. Thanks to Lael Bethlehem for this quote from her interview with Bobby Godsell, July 1989.
3. LMG report reprinted in *South African Labour Bulletin* 14(4), October 1989, 92-99.
4. Martin Jansen, 'Weakness of the anti-LRA campaign', *South African Labour Bulletin*, 14(5), November 1989, 51-9.
5. LMG, 'Report on Overtime', *South African Labour Bulletin* 14(5), November 1989, 45-47.
6. Author interview with Ebrahim Patel, Johannesburg, 22 January 1991.

25

The road to February 2nd

Defiance!

ON 6 September 1989, while millions stayed at home in protest, the white electorate returned the National Party to power. FW de Klerk was installed as state president. Like his predecessor, PW Botha, he faced growing resistance from the ranks of the oppressed. However, De Klerk tried to adopt a more moderate face, announcing his preparedness to accept 'every political party's right to organise' provided they signalled 'in words and deeds' their commitment to peace.

He had little choice. The alternative was increasing the level of repression, the preferred option of the security forces. But this was having less and less effect, and repression alone was no longer viable.

Cosatu's two-day stayaway action had mobilised millions in opposition to the racist elections. Both before and after the election a spirit of defiance, organised by the mass democratic movement, swept the country.

Political detainees embarked on determined hunger strikes demanding their freedom. Many were released, some having spent years in jail without being charged or convicted. But the police and army remained determined to crush all signs of resistance and defiance.

Repression and the spirit of defiance

For the unions it was repression as usual. Officials – including Dennis Neer, Sipho Cele and Zwelinzima Vavi, the secretaries of Cosatu's Eastern Cape, Northern Natal and Western Transvaal regions respectively – were detained. Neer had already spent most of Cosatu's existence in prison. On 31 August Cosatu's head office was raided. Police spent the whole day searching it, having already spent three hours that morning going through Jay Naidoo's home in Yeoville.

Many other unionists were detained during September. They joined leading UDF figures such as Valli Moosa, Curnick Ndlovu and Titus Mafolo behind bars. In late September NUM's Cyril Ramaphosa condemned the detention of the union's publicity secretary. He also reported that NUM offices in Kimberley, Natal, Namaqualand, and Rustenburg had been raided. De Klerk's government, said Ramaphosa,

> while on the surface calling for talks with black leaders, is in fact conducting a secret war of attrition aimed at silencing and removing from the public arena mass democratic movement activists and spokesmen for the trade union movement.

'We are not making idle threats,' said Jay Naidoo, 'but we warn that Cosatu will not tolerate these invasions of our offices or actions against officials.' The regime was 'unable to contain the mood of defiance' and was 'seeking to make scapegoats of the leaders of our organisations', said Cosatu in an official response.

Despite repression unionists grew bolder and more defiant. Striking factory workers increasingly ignored court interdicts and eviction orders. Restrictions and bannings were not respected. Even ordinary workers saw them as simply further obstacles to be overcome, circumvented or ignored – products of an illegitimate government and unrepresentative courts.

Ppwawu's annual national congress from 15-17 September illustrated unionists' increasing defiance. The congress itself was an unremarkable gathering at which 200 delegates discussed the union's wage policies and examined the political situation. Unionists planned to conclude the congress with a general meeting of members at Shareworld, near Soweto. On arriving at the venue it was discovered that police had restricted the meeting under state of emergency regulations. Only shopfloor issues could be discussed, police said, and only union members could attend. To ensure compliance with the order police insisted on being present, heavily armed, within the hall. They also insisted on recording the meeting and placing vanloads of police in combat gear around the venue.

Ppwawu's leaders huddled together to discuss their response, and decided to continue with the meeting. Minor adjustments were made to the programme. No-one from the UDF spoke. What the police did not understand, explained a Ppwawu speaker in a lengthy substitute speech, was that it was impossible to restrict the meeting to union members and think the UDF had been kept out. Union members also belonged to UDF, he said. 'The UDF speaker could not speak because the order prevented him from calling for the release of political prisoners.' Loud applause from the assembled workers. 'The UDF speaker could not speak because the order prevented him from calling for the unbanning of the ANC.' Shouts of 'viva ANC' from the crowd. 'The UDF speaker could not speak because the order prevented him from calling for every person to have the vote.' The speech continued, punctuated by cheering and cries of 'bua' and 'amandla' from the crowd. The police in the hall grew agitated during the speech. They called in reinforcements and threatened to break up the meeting, but eventually backed off.

The meeting reflected the growing confidence of ordinary workers. Ppwawu received not one report of a member turning back from the meeting when finding the venue surrounded by police. Repressive measures were no longer succeeding. They were simply breeding defiance and disrespect for the law. If the government refused to lift the state of emergency then the people would. Organisations banned under the emergency publicly re-emerged and declared themselves unbanned. Individuals with restriction orders began defying them. Publications started quoting banned individuals and organisations.

All sections of the mass democratic movement had been discussing the need for defiance. Cosatu's third national congress resolved to mobilise a defiance campaign against 'all unjust and discriminatory laws' through disciplined and peaceful mass defiance of segregated facilities. On 26 July the MDM, with Cosatu and the UDF as its core, announced the launch of the National Defiance Campaign. The response was overwhelming, with the Defiance Campaign both encouraging and reflecting the popular mood.

In the Border region students marched on white schools demanding admission. In the Transvaal and the OFS black people demanded admission to whites-only hospitals. In remote towns and villages people marched demanding the end of apartheid.

Tens of thousands flocked to 'whites-only' beaches in Cape Town and Durban demanding that they be opened to all. They carried the banners of the ANC and other mass organisations. The Cape Town protesters faced strong resistance from police who used teargas, dogs, sjamboks and even police helicopters to disperse the demonstrators. But police action failed to crush resistance, if anything fuelling it.

Cosas, UDF, End Conscription Campaign (ECC) and other organisations began meeting openly although they were still banned. In factories and mines workers demanded the end of segregated toilets, canteens and residential areas. The battle was most intense on the mines where apartheid remained more entrenched than in industry. At its April congress NUM had resolved to fight 'repression and discrimination at the workplace and in the community'. The first action took place at Rustenburg when miners attempted to sit in parks reserved for whites. Mine security and police were brought in and many workers injured and assaulted. Nevertheless the campaign grew. Black miners began using whites-only changerooms, toilets and canteens. Many were assaulted by mine security or white workers. At Arnot Colliery in Witbank management locked the toilets and changerooms to prevent entry. At Rand Leases white workers going underground were forced to queue with black workers, rather than going to the front of the queue as was the custom. In Carletonville Elijah Barayi led a march against the town's whites-only parks.

A teacup in a storm

The defiance campaign revealed the depth of white workers' racism, sometimes with tragic effects. At JCI's Rustenburg Refinery, workers protested against racist practices such as black workers' being forced to use separate toilets without doors; only black workers being searched at the entrance to the mine; segregated changerooms and eating facilities; black workers not being allowed to sit on chairs reserved for whites; and the fact that there was not a single black supervisor. Jeffrey Njuza was one of the NUM members participating in the campaign. Management responded by bringing disciplinary charges against NUM members, including Njuza. He faced disciplinary action for sitting in a chair reserved for whites in the refinery canteen. Despite the charges Njuza continued to defy – this time he used a 'whites-only' teacup.

For some of the white employees at the mine this, apparently, was the final straw. On 2 September a white supervisor came into the purification plant where Njuza worked and shot him at point-blank range. Njuza died instantly, leaving behind a young wife expecting the couple's second child. Workers downed tools in protest and only returned to work later that week when management agreed to install metal detectors to prevent white employees bringing firearms to work. The supervisor, Ockert Vermeulen, was later found dead, having apparently committed suicide.

The following month another teacup episode came to a much happier conclusion. On that occasion the victim was Matthews Ntshiwa, a

Numsa member. Ntshiwa had scratched the words 'PW we want our land', 'Release N Mandela', 'Amandla Ngawethu' and 'Remember our Leaders', on the enamel of his metal mug. A supervisor saw the mug and reported him to the police.

Ntshiwa was arrested, held for four months as an awaiting trial prisoner, and then sentenced to three years imprisonment in terms of the Internal Security Act. The union helped arrange R3 000 bail for him pending an appeal. By this stage Ntshiwa had lost his job and, although he was a skilled diesel mechanic, he found it difficult to get another. 'Every potential employer turned me down after he had contacted my former employers.'

The irony is that Ntshiwa had never been politically active. His experience changed that. 'I felt bad about being charged with taking part in and promoting the activities of a banned organisation', he recalled, 'because I was not actively involved in any political organisation.' Since he was convicted for being involved, he reasoned, he might as well be. The experience transformed him into an active member of both Numsa and the UDF-affiliated Dobsonville Civic Association. Finally the appeal court set aside Ntshiwa's jail sentence.

The defiance campaign heightened the levels of militancy on the factory floor. Employers responded by clamping down. There was an increase in lockouts, mass dismissals and police involvement in factory disputes. After workers were locked out at the Fawu-organised Mama's Pies in Johannesburg, police arrived and opened fire on them. Nineteen were injured and many others arrested.

De Klerk responds to pressure

De Klerk's government moved immediately to defuse the defiance campaign, announcing its intention to repeal the Separate Amenities Act. In a few cases, such as the march on Durban's beaches, police were instructed not to enforce the law on segregated beaches nor use excessive force against the tens of thousands of protesters.

The democratic movement made full use of the space provided and organised marches in protest against the security laws. A massive display of strength took place in Cape Town on 13 September, followed two days later by marches in Johannesburg and Pretoria. In Cape Town 50 000 people led by Archbishop Tutu and Jay Naidoo marched on parliament. Many carried the flag of the banned ANC. 'Today we have witnessed the might of our people,' said Naidoo in a speech to the crowd. 'We are saying that our leaders Oliver Tambo and Joe Slovo are indeed the people who will be sitting in the parliament of the future.'

During the following six weeks massive crowds gathered and marched in many towns and cities. The largest took place in the Eastern Cape. In Uitenhage, for example, the idea of a march emerged at an MDM meeting involving Cosatu and community organisations in the area. The secretary of Cosatu's local shop stewards council was mandated to apply for permission to march, and workers in all factories received report-backs on planning. Wednesday 11 October was set for the action and workers resolved to absent themselves from work and join 80 000 people in the march to the police headquarters of this medium-sized industrial town.

The Uitenhage marchers demanded the establishment of a non-racial municipality; lifting the state of emergency; unbanning of the ANC, release of political prisoners and the return of exiles; the withdrawal of the security forces from the townships; the scrapping of all discriminatory legislation; one-person, one-vote in a unitary South Africa; and the scrapping of the Labour Relations Act. After handing their petitions to the police, the marchers gathered at the local stadium where they were addressed by Cosatu's second vice-president, John Gomomo.

The fact that marches like these were allowed indicated a difference between FW de Klerk and his predecessor, PW Botha. De Klerk had become convinced that old-style apartheid, based on the 'separate development' approach, was no longer viable. Internal and external pressures were forcing the regime into a corner. Extending the powers of security forces had proved unsuccessful. International pressure would only increase in response to sjamboks, teargas and helicopters being used against black people trying to swim in the sea. De Klerk attempted to manoeuvre his way out, making concessions to reduce the pressure. By contrast the 'securocrat' faction of the government still believed it could shoot its way out of trouble.

New opportunities were opening up for the entire democratic movement. In early October the government announced that in future it would recognise 1 May as Labour Day – hardly a concession since the union movement had managed, for some years, to make it a *de facto* public holiday. But it did indicate a greater realism in government circles. More significant was the decision to release all the Rivonia trialists, except Nelson Mandela himself. The October release of Walter Sisulu and other senior ANC leaders was an important turning point. These men, imprisoned for 27 years, were living symbols of the banned ANC.

Their release gave impetus to the MDM's 'ANC Lives, ANC Leads' campaign. Mass action was effectively unbanning the ANC, and De Klerk's government was recognising this reality. In a speech to an 80 000-strong crowd at FNB stadium near Soweto, Sisulu called for the defiance campaign to continue:

> We cannot wait for the government to make changes at its own pace...
> Our duty is to intensify the struggle, until we are able to get the regime to
> discuss the issue of normalisation of the situation in South Africa. At this
> stage we cannot relax on the basis of mere statements.

Sisulu also paid tribute to Cosatu 'for organising workers on a scale unequaled in the entire history of our struggle.' Cosatu's meteoric rise symbolised 'the centrality of the working class in our struggle.'

All was not easy however. People promoting the ANC continued to be arrested. Most applications to hold peaceful marches were turned down. Protest, it appeared, was to be regarded by the government as a privilege and not a right. Towns and cities outside the glare of international publicity were most caught in the contrast between the promise of reform and the continuing practice of repression.

The experience of Cosatu's Western Transvaal region, based around the towns of the Vaal Triangle, provided a typical example. Vereeniging, the centre of Cosatu's regional activities, was also the home town of FW de Klerk. Prior to the September elections the white local authorities had tried to stop the union campaign against the LRA. On 18 August a Vanderbijlpark magistrate refused Cosatu permission to hold a union rally in Sebokeng. The rally had been planned jointly by Cosatu, Nactu and the unaffiliated Orange-Vaal General Workers Union (OVGWU). Two days later the Vereeniging magistrate banned the three unions from meeting to discuss the LRA. Two further attempts to hold joint shop steward meetings the following week were both prohibited by the magistrate. On 1 September the police, clearly angered by continuing attempts to hold meetings, detained Cosatu's regional secretary as well as key officials of both Nactu and OVGWU. They were held for seven weeks, and no reasons were ever given for their incarceration.

Despite harassment, Cosatu tried to convene a regional congress on 3 September. This was restricted and police arrived at the venue to take photographs and full particulars from every delegate. Cosatu then attempted to convene a meeting of the smaller regional executive committee (REC) on 13 September. By this stage De Klerk was indicating his preparedness to be more open, but the REC meeting was banned outright. On 19 September police detained more unionists, holding some for up to five weeks. On 28 October permission to hold a peaceful march against the LRA was refused, although similar marches had been allowed in Johannesburg and Cape Town. To prevent workers simply defying the order Vereeniging police blocked all routes to Cosatu's offices, the intended starting point for the march. Workers waiting in the vicinity were arrested and charged for 'loitering'. On their release some were followed home and beaten.

These incidents took place against a backdrop of widespread 'informal repression'. Cosatu's regional officials claimed knowledge of 'countless' incidents such as assaults on the relatives of activists, police issuing death threats and claiming to be 'Wit Wolwe' – a shadowy far-right paramilitary organisation – and the smashing of windows and throwing of acid solutions at the homes of activists. A statement issued by Cosatu's Western Transvaal region challenged the sincerity of De Klerk's reform programme. The authorities in his home town were 'consciously creating obstacles in the path of a movement towards genuine democracy in South Africa.' The region announced that it was calling for one-hour peaceful protests in every factory on 15 November and planning further actions if the right to hold a peaceful march was again refused.

Mass mobilisation and the defiance campaign were only one aspect of widespread resistance. Cosatu's ongoing campaign against the LRA was another. The two-day stayaway in early September was directed as much against the LRA as against the whites-only elections. It was the first shot in a revived campaign planned, as we have seen in the previous chapter, to include consumer boycotts and a ban on overtime work.

The talks go on...and off

'Saccola is totally committed to negotiations with the unions on the subject of the LRA,' said Bobby Godsell shortly after the 5-6 September action. 'It does not need to be pressurised into talks by a stayaway.' On 22 September Saccola announced that it was suspending further talks with the unions. These could not continue with a consumer boycott and overtime ban aimed at employers. Such actions, said Saccola, were 'precipitous and unhelpful.'

Cosatu responded that it was not interested in talking for its own sake. The aim of talks was to solve the problem of the new labour law. Very little progress had been made and hence the workers summit had decided to intensify peaceful mass action, thereby indicating how serious the matter was.

In addition, argued Cosatu, negotiations were not an alternative to protest. 'We have not refused to negotiate with you when your LRA was passed,' said one unionist. 'We cannot put down our weapons while every day you use your LRA weapon against us.'

Despite Saccola's suspension of talks there were signs of movement in government ranks. Shortly after Cosatu's third congress, the Minister of Manpower had indicated that section 79 of the Act, the clause providing for damages claims against unions, would be reviewed. On 13 October the government's National Manpower Commission (NMC) invited proposals for an investigation into 'consolidation' of the LRA. Manpower Minister Eli Louw appointed a private advocate to examine union allegations that the industrial court was no longer 'fair', and also announced the appointment of a commission of parliamentarians and farmers to consider the question of trade union rights for farmworkers.[*]

These moves were not directly related to union talks with Saccola. They indicated, nevertheless, that the government felt the need to show some flexibility on the LRA issue. After all, the threat of damages had been one of the major government motivations in introducing the new law. Despite these glimmers of hope Cosatu felt it was essential to maintain a high level of mass mobilisation around the LRA issue.

De Klerk's limited approval of marches provided further opportunities for mobilisation which had to be utilised, and Cosatu's Exco agreed to mass marches against the LRA. These were scheduled to take place in all major centres on 14 October.[**] The political climate was highly volatile in the days before the marches. The government announced that it intended releasing Walter Sisulu and other Rivonia trialists, excluding Nelson Mandela, and celebration of these impending releases became a part of the anti-LRA marches.

Almost 150 000 people marched in 17 different centres around the country. Port Elizabeth's action, where over 80 000 participated, was the most impressive. Not only workers marched, but also students, youth, women, church people and the unemployed. Indeed the size of the marches demonstrated the strength of the democratic movement as a whole as much as it reflected Cosatu's power.

Police prevented a number of marches, including one in Vereeniging. In Secunda, 5 000 people marched despite the refusal of permission. Police accepted reality and reached a compromise with local union officials whereby marchers would follow a shorter route.

There was an impressive show of strength in some areas, but an extremely disappointing response elsewhere. In Johannesburg only 15 000 people marched, even though the march was led by Cosatu's national leadership. The march organisers had hoped for 100 000 to attend, which was a realistic expectation, given Cosatu's massive Witwatersrand membership of over 300 000. Many unionists blamed the poor attendance on competition from a major open air pop concert and a

---

* This last step was announced despite the fact that a 1982 NMC investigation had made a detailed study of the issue – the results of which were never released. The report was rumoured to have recommended the recognition of union rights for farmworkers. This finding, and the strength of the conservative white farmers lobby, apparently led to the report's suppression.
** Uitenhage was not included, having held its 80 000-strong march only days earlier.

double-header soccer match held on the same day. There were, however, deeper problems.

The low attendance reflected the weaknesses of Cosatu structures in this key region. Most affiliates, with the notable exception of the newly-launched Sactwu, did not mobilise members to attend. Within the factories, Cosatu affiliates often found their membership in the Witwatersrand area among the most militant and politicised in the country. However, federation structures were weak, perhaps because union members found adequate expression for their political and economic aspirations in their own affiliates.

In addition, activities of the Wits region were often conflated with programmes of the national office. All other regions of the country were expected to plan and execute action, with publicity, mobilisation and organisation the responsibility of the region. However the Wits region often relied excessively on the resources of head office, which in turn would rely on the regional organisation – to the detriment of both.

Progress on the LRA

Saccola's suspension of talks did not last long. On 18 and 19 October, employers agreed that the damages provisions of the LRA should revert to the pre-September 1988 position. There was also agreement on the application of international standards to dismissals and retrenchments.

In January 1990 proposed government amendments to the labour law were leaked to the union movement. These addressed some of the problems of the 1988 amendments, such as the damages clause but, commented the Centre for Applied Legal Studies (CALS), the state had only acted 'in areas where the changes were a problem for *both* employers and trade unions.' The unions' major difficulties, such as the exclusion of millions of workers from union rights and the serious limitations on the right to strike, were not addressed. In addition, commented CALS, there was no proper consultation over the changes. 'The state does not appear to have realised the necessity for entering into proper discussions with trade unions over the law.' As NUM's Marcel Golding, a member of Cosatu's working committee on the law, put it, 'Unilateral changes to the LRA, which do not take into account what Cosatu and the trade union movement as a whole say, will not bring industrial peace.'

The revival of the anti-LRA campaign was one of Cosatu's major achievements during 1989. It signalled to both the state and employers that the issue would not disappear, and that the unions were prepared to go to great lengths to succeed. The campaign also mobilised large sections of the working class and involved them in a range of mass actions.

Even while it did this, however, organisational weaknesses within the union movement were exposed: the failure to develop effective regional campaign structures; insufficient support from community and political organisations; and little effective participation in the campaign by almost all the independent unions and Nactu affiliates, as well as some Cosatu affiliates.

Talks with Saccola yielded frustratingly little, and there were calls within Cosatu for an end to 'the dogged pursuit of this strategy when clearly there are no gains.' But by late 1989 unions gained the impression that the state and employers were prepared to make limited concessions on the LRA issue. This was a process the unions wanted to encourage. The majority within Cosatu felt it was wrong to see negotiations as a sign of weakness. They were 'part of the struggle *against* employers, and not an alliance *with* them,' argued Numsa's Geoff Schreiner.

There were some successes in building unity between unions, which was an important aim of the anti-LRA campaign. Cosatu's relations with a number of the independent unions improved, and by 1990 some were seeking to affiliate to Cosatu despite attempts by certain of the independent unions to build themselves into a 'third force' bloc. In general, however, the independent unions proved weak allies.

Cosatu largely failed in its efforts to develop a closer working relationship with Nactu, although there were isolated instances of co-operation at local level. For a period Nactu members attended the Cosatu locals in some areas, such as Tembisa, or participated in activities of, for example, the industrial area committee in Industria, Johannesburg. In other areas, such as Standerton, joint meetings took place over key issues like the consumer boycott. In Natal meetings between the two took place, attended by five delegates from each federation. However, in most areas, meetings were sporadic and irregular.

There appeared to be a fear within Nactu that Cosatu was simply trying to swallow it. Others wanted to maintain Nactu as a power base linked to the non-Congress tendencies within the liberation movement. Many Nactu leaders also showed a definite lack of seriousness over union unity. The most damning criticism came from Nactu's own general secretary, Piroshaw Camay, speaking shortly after his resignation at the end of 1989. The workers' summit decision to hold joint meetings at regional and local level was crucial, he argued. Camay charged that Nactu officials were responsible for the failure of these to materialise. 'Cosatu is steadfast in its commitment to implementing these resolutions, whereas Nactu has vacillated in its decisions.'

Political tensions between Africanists and the BC tendency remained within Nactu, and as a result issues such as the LRA campaign became political footballs. Nactu continually revised its position on the LRA campaign, agreeing to participate in marches against the LRA, for example, only to withdraw at the last moment because the march organisers had applied for permission to march. This was extremely frustrating for Cosatu. Again, during early 1990 Nactu objected to meeting with the Minister of Manpower to discuss changing the LRA, although this tactic had been previously agreed upon. A parallel PAC objection to the ANC's preparedness to enter into talks with the De Klerk government was apparently involved in this decision.

By early February 1989 Cosatu's anti-LRA campaign committee noted that 'Nactu has not been participating regularly in the campaign. Despite repeated invitations to attend meetings and to participate in joint activities at regional and local level, this has not materialised.' The committee recommended that the door should be kept open for Nactu 'if it wishes to continue to participate' but that Cosatu 'should not be held back by their refusal to agree on matters.' Rather, it was felt, 'the emphasis should be on local and regional co-operation, where workers are located.'

The struggle intensifies

With the release of Walter Sisulu and other ANC leaders the process of change appeared unstoppable. The final months of 1989 and the first month of 1990 were busy, turbulent and exciting. The democratic movement organised its Conference for a Democratic Future (CDF) in an attempt to develop a common position on negotiations. Workers grew increasingly confident. A number of protracted strikes began, notably in the breweries and on the railways.

In areas like the Transkei unions emerged from the shadows of illegality. It had been the first homeland to gain 'independence', doing so in 1976 under the oppressive rule of the Matanzima brothers. Labour remained the region's chief export and there was little industrial development. However, during the 1980s a number of factories were attracted to the area by the promise of a cheap and docile labour force and the offer of substantial subsidies to employers relocating operations.

Corruption and repression were the order of the day. In late 1987 the Transkei was shaken by political infighting, and a young soldier, Bantu Holomisa, ousted the Matanzima clan. Holomisa came to power committed to fighting corruption. Ordinary workers were told they could bring their problems to the new government and minimum wages were increased. But Transkei workers saw few concrete gains. They remained without any effective labour law and had no rights to join unions or embark on legal industrial action. Holomisa had created space but only organisation could secure meaningful changes. The first attempts to organise came in early 1988. These were often inspired by NUM members, particularly those dismissed after the 1987 strike and deported to Transkei, and NUM was able to establish structures in over 20 Transkei districts.

During August 1988 there was a spate of worker action, particularly by nurses, civil servants and post office employees. The postal workers went on to form Trapowa, effectively the Transkei branch of Potwa. The strikes and attempts at organisation were heavily suppressed by police, whose connections to the Matanzimas remained strong. Many workers were arrested.

During early 1989 links with Cosatu affiliates improved and coordinating committees were set up. A May Day rally called by NUM revived worker spirits. More important was the 1 October speech delivered by Elijah Barayi at the re-burial of Chief Sabata Dalindyebo. Sabata, known as 'the comrade chief', had been a long-time opponent of the Matanzima clan and a supporter of the ANC. He had been driven into exile where he died.

Barayi's speech was particularly militant and addressed to a crowd of tens of thousands, including workers from all parts of the region. He challenged Transkei workers to wake up. Liberation would not be given to them. They would have to organise and get it. Within two weeks Transkei workers were on strike demanding a living wage and union recognition.

The strikes began in Butterworth in mid-October and rapidly spread to include most of the factories in the area. Thousands of Umtata workers then joined the action. Three days into the strike Holomisa invited each establishment on strike to send two representatives to meet him. Over 200 delegates told Holomisa that their grievances had been ignored. Nothing had been done about their wage demands and complaints about physical abuse. Workers returned to work on 20 October after employers, at Holomisa's urging, agreed to negotiate with elected worker committees.

Transkei workers knew that, by returning to work before their demands were fully met, they could be giving up what leverage they had. They therefore decided to sustain pressure by organising marches within days of resuming work. In Umtata over 15 000 workers joined a march organised by the Workers' Co-ordinating Committee. They demanded the legalisation of trade unions, dramatic changes to labour legislation and the lifting of the state of emergency. By January 1990 Cosatu affiliates were organising strongly in the Transkei despite resistance from both employers and sections of the Transkei military government.

Bitter struggles also developed in the major industrial centres in late 1989. Employers adopted a hard line against union demands, often in conjunction with police. In November police arrived at Pretoria's Boerstra Bakery while union representatives were in the middle of negotiations with management. The attack which followed, with certain managers allegedly taking part, led to the arrest of 200 workers, while another 204 sustained injuries. Many had broken limbs and hands.

The most protracted disputes were at the Fawu-organised SA Breweries (SAB) and among Sarhwu members on the railways. Breweries workers embarked on a nine-week long legal strike in pursuit of higher wages. They faced a sustained propaganda onslaught from the company which accused the union of being unreasonable in its demand for a 38% increase. Its workers were already amongst the country's highest paid, said SAB. The strike developed into a major showdown between the union and management. Fawu called on the black community to support it by boycotting beer, but this brought the union into conflict with many shebeen owners and members of the public. The SAB strike was also marked by high levels of violence, with at least 12 people losing their lives in strike-related violence.

From the start management decided to sit out the dispute. SAB had a virtual monopoly of beer production in the country, and its links with the Anglo American Corporation meant the company had the resources to sustain substantial short-term losses in revenue. The strike ended in a major setback for Fawu. Workers returned to work without forcing the company to adjust its final pre-strike offer.

An even longer strike took place on the railways, reaching resolution only in late January 1990. It was one of the bloodiest in South Africa's history. Thirty thousand railway workers joined the strike demanding wage increases, recognition of Sarhwu, and a halt to privatisation of the railways. The main support came from Sarhwu members in Southern Natal, Kimberley, Bloemfontein and in the railway hostels of Johannesburg and the East Rand. Workers in the Western Cape supported the action to a lesser extent. In Port Elizabeth and East London railway workers continued working throughout the strike, largely because of mass dismissals and Sarhwu's defeat in that area during the previous year.

Sats management refused to discuss wages with Sarhwu, arguing that the union was not yet registered. Following the 1988 Natal strike Sarhwu had agreed to register as a precondition for recognition. Sats argued that it could not negotiate with a union which failed to comply with previous agreements.

Sarhwu's failure to register was a result of two factors. Its members continued to oppose registration. Some asked why Sarhwu should register since railway workers were not covered by the LRA. Sarhwu was also still suffering the effects of its leadership struggle earlier that year. The union, while militant on the ground, was poorly organised in its offices and administration, and its systems and methods were not adequate to the tasks it needed to perform. It had difficulty maintaining detailed membership records, themselves a prerequisite for registration.

The strike soon became heated. Sarhwu members were renowned for their militancy, Sats for its conservatism and inflexibility. Attacks on railway property began. Scabs were accosted and some attacked. Sats decided to break the strike by dismissing workers and evicting them from their hostel accommodation. Some 23 000 workers were dismissed. More ominously, vigilante attacks on the strikers began. There were persistent reports of scabs using railway workshops to make weapons, and of white supervisors encouraging and helping plan attacks on strikers.

The most serious onslaught took place in Germiston on 9 January when a thousand heavily-armed non-strikers, wearing their Sats overalls, attacked 800 strikers arriving for a union meeting. In the ensuing bloodbath eight people were killed and 67 injured.

As violence escalated it became clear that dismissals would not solve the problem. Both Cosatu and the MDM urged the parties to negotiate a settlement, and agreement was finally reached on 27 January. Sats undertook to re-employ the dismissed workers, to grant Sarhwu interim recognition pending registration, and to include Sarhwu in its April 1990 wage negotiations.

The settlement was a setback for the union, showing it had been unprepared for major industrial action and inexperienced in negotiating strategies and tactics. Sarhwu would have to consolidate its structures, and improve its strategies if it was to make progress. The 13-week strike had been costly for both sides: R38,5-million was lost in destroyed coaches and railway property; R44-million worth of wages was forfeited; and at least 24 people lost their lives in strike-related violence.

Not all was violence and gloom as the new decade dawned. Saccawu, perhaps Cosatu's most innovative affiliate, decided to take a stand against Mike Gatting and his rebel cricket team. Gatting had been paid to bring a top-class team to South Africa in defiance of the international sports boycott. They had sneaked into the country to avoid international protests, but soon received a shock. In every centre where they played thousands demonstrated peacefully against the team.

At their first stop, the plush Sandton Sun, hotel workers held placards and refused to serve the team. 'No service for rebel tour' and 'Forward to democratic sport in a democratic South Africa' read some of the placards. 'I'm sure someone will serve us a beer somewhere,' was Gatting's reported response. Saccawu members, well organised in the country's major hotels, threatened to repeat their action at every venue where

Gatting and his men stayed. Management quickly negotiated an agreement with the union: workers would have the right to refuse to serve the cricketers, and would be allowed to demonstrate for up to 30 minutes on the team's arrival at any Southern Suns' hotel. The union agreed, in turn, that switchboard operators would not withdraw their labour.

The Conference for a Democratic Future was called by the Mass Democratic Movement in December. Over 3 000 delegates representing a broad range of organisations gathered on 9 December at the University of the Witwatersrand. The CDF was partly an attempt to revive the 1988 anti-apartheid conference which had failed when banned by the government. However the CDF organisers tried to avoid some of the problems which had beset the earlier effort. They not only invited representatives of Africanist, BC and other non-Congress political tendencies, but also tried to involve them in the planning of the conference.

CDF aimed to develop a broad consensus within the democratic movement. The most important issue was whether, and under what conditions, the democratic movement should negotiate with the government. The CDF succeeded on paper, but failed in practice. As a conference it was too large and unwieldy to allow meaningful participation. Most delegates, even if they agreed with the resolutions adopted, felt they had played little part in their formulation. The CDF failed to include all components of the liberation movement. The Africanists, including Nactu, withdrew at the last minute citing the proposed presence of 'bantustan leaders' such as General Holomisa.

Nactu's decision caused rumblings within its own ranks. As at the workers summit, unions dominated by non-Africanist leaders decided to attend the CDF in defiance of the Nactu decision. Those attending represented no more than 25% of Nactu's membership, said assistant general secretary Cunningham Ngcukana. They were guilty of 'blatant opportunism' and could face disciplinary action, he warned. Nactu's withdrawal was the final straw for its long-serving general secretary, Piroshaw Camay, who resigned his position. Nactu had sat on the convening committee of the CDF, said Camay later,

> (and) as such was aware of all decisions made by the convening committee. For some people to try to make short-term political gain out of issues like the workers summit and the CDF is in fact a negation of building working-class unity and the national liberation struggle.

The CDF decisions essentially endorsed the Harare declaration and the international position on negotiations of the Non-Aligned Movement, the OAU and the United Nations. These bodies called on the government to create a climate for negotiation by removing all obstacles to holding talks. The mood of the CDF was confident. Most delegates expected a gradual process towards negotiations with the regime. Few anticipated the dramatic announcements made by De Klerk at the opening of parliament on 2 February 1990.

February 2nd and beyond

A massive demonstration in Cape Town, outside the parliamentary buildings, was timed to coincide with the opening of parliament. The democratic movement expected De Klerk to announce reforms in his opening address. However, few were prepared for the far-reaching package he unveiled. De Klerk announced the unbanning of the ANC, SACP and PAC. The ANC and PAC had been banned for 30 years, while the SACP had been illegal for four decades. De Klerk also announced the freeing of some political prisoners; the partial lifting of the state of emergency; the suspension of the death penalty; and the government's intention to release Nelson Mandela unconditionally.

Cosatu termed De Klerk's announcements 'far reaching and courageous' but warned that they nevertheless 'fell short' of 'the fundamental steps needed to end political conflict' in the country. Only two of the eight preconditions for negotiations listed in the Harare declaration had been met. Cosatu called on De Klerk to release not only Nelson Mandela but all political prisoners. ANC president Oliver Tambo responded similarly. The SACP labelled De Klerk's moves as 'positive steps'. Calling on the democratic movement to take 'full advantage of the new political climate' it also warned of the need to 'remain vigilant and alert for provocations.'

Ordinary black people were jubilant. Thousands poured into the streets that day and in the days that followed. In every township and every suburb thousands marched, toyi-toyied and sang freedom songs under the green, black and gold banner of the ANC. Black policemen began giving the ANC salute. White policemen generally reacted with horror, some trying to stop the chanting and taunts being thrown their way while others remained aloof and disbelieving.

This spontaneous response reached into most factories, shops and mines. In many factories workers stopped work to celebrate. In the Eastern Cape stoppages ranged from one day to one week. Celebrations intensified when it was announced that Mandela would be released on 11 February. Hundreds of thousands gathered on the Parade in Cape Town to welcome him. The following day, 12 February, the jubilation continued as workers took over train coaches, and sang the songs and waved the banners of the ANC, SACP and Cosatu. In Johannesburg workers negotiated for time off to attend Mandela's homecoming rally at

FNB stadium. Over 120 000 crammed into the stadium – an unprecedented crowd for an unplanned and unadvertised rally held at mid-day during the middle of a week. Thousands more remained outside the stadium unable to gain entrance.

On the factory floor tensions were heightened by Mandela's release. White supervisors generally opposed De Klerk's reforms while black workers had gained in confidence and were uncompromisingly challenging management authority. The response to Mandela's release was particularly strong in the homeland areas. Strikes, marches and demonstrations rocked Ciskei, Venda, Gazankulu and Bophuthatswana. Workers' demands ranged from a living wage and union recognition to calls for the resignation of homeland leaders and the reincorporation of the areas into South Africa.

At the East London plant of Mercedes Benz Numsa members resolved to build a special bullet-proof luxury model as a gift for Mandela. Union power in the plant was such that management rapidly agreed. Mandela's car came off the production line with nine faults. 'In this company cars don't come off the line with less than 68 faults,' commented company chairman Christoph Köpke later. 'Normally it takes 14 days to build that car. Mandela's was built in four days! Only nine faults!'

The cost of the vehicle was covered by each employee working a few hours of unpaid overtime. It was a sign of the respect in which workers held Mandela. 'We look to comrade Mandela to initiate a process of political settlement which will incorporate the needs and aspirations of workers,' said Numsa's general secretary Moses Mayekiso, announcing the offer. Cynics noted that Mandela would be driving a luxury car and saw in it the premature emergence of a privileged 'wabenzi' class. Others saw in it a sign of workers' expectations and their vision of the future. After all, the workers had insisted that Mandela's car be painted not black, but red.

Part Six

Into the 1990s

26

Post-February 1990

Counting the minutes

THE second of February 1990 was clearly a turning point. Enormous possibilities opened up for the democratic movement, but enormous dangers too. There were turbulent developments in the homelands; the ANC took the first tentative steps towards negotiations; workers launched a major strike offensive; and violence claimed thousands of lives.

During May management at JCI's Lebowa Platinum mine reinstated 1 500 workers dismissed for demanding recognition of NUM. Known for its tough anti-union stance, JCI backed down only after pressure from Lebowa's homeland government, which in turn had been asked to intervene by the ANC and NUM.

Lebowa was not the only homeland government to feel the heat. In QwaQwa virtually the entire civil service downed tools for a month. A number of strikers were injured when police opened fire on 15 000 workers marching on the homeland's parliament. The strike ended when QwaQwa authorities agreed to allow workers to join Cosatu and request central government for money to increase wages. In the Ciskei homeland pressures were so intense that Lennox Sebe was ousted in a military coup within a month of Mandela's release. Widespread looting and burning of local factories followed. In one of his first pronouncements Ciskei's new ruler, Brigadier Gqozo, accepted that workers had the right to unionise. Unco-operative industrialists were warned that 'they can no longer phone a despotic head of state and arrange for uniformed louts to beat up their labour when it dares to disagree with management'. Despite these strong words Gqozo virulently opposed public sector workers' attempts to join Nehawu. The Venda government also fell to a military coup. Rulers in the remaining homelands faced similar pressures to grant union rights and align themselves with the ANC. Only the Bophuthatswana homeland authorities, aided by the SADF, remained relatively firm in the face of mounting pressure.

Cosatu held a number of meetings with first the ANC, and later the SACP. The three decided to formalise their strategic alliance. There were also two crucial meetings between the ANC and the government. These 'talks about talks' culminated in the Groote Schuur and Pretoria minutes, which attempted to clear the obstacles to serious constitutional negotiations. The De Klerk government made some moves forward, and the ANC agreed to suspend armed actions unilaterally. But by the close of 1990 most political prisoners remained behind bars and most exiles remained outside the country.

Cosatu intensified its mass campaigns, particularly the living wage and anti-LRA actions, and redoubled its organisational efforts. Formulating economic policy became a top priority in the energetic debate over the federation's vision of a post-apartheid South Africa. It was a key issue, given the vast disparities in wealth in South Africa and the failure of East bloc countries to offer a viable alternative to capitalism. The debates were not only theoretical – thousands of public service workers demonstrated against the state's privatisation drive.

Mass marches were a feature of the post-February period. Over 50 public marches took place in the ten weeks following Mandela's release, many involving tens of thousands of people. Land invasions by the homeless were given added impetus. Even thousands of domestic workers marched to demand basic rights. A strike wave swept the country in factories, shops and mines. As double-digit inflation eroded wages, strike levels approached those of 1987. Major strikes involved the public sector (health workers and civil servants in particular), a national action at Nampak, and the controversial Mercedes Benz strike. Even farmworkers took action, the most publicised strike being organised by the Nactu-affiliated National Union of Farmworkers at Zebedelia Citrus Estates in the Northern Transvaal.

Violence spreads

Natal continued to be a major battleground. Almost 200 000 people flocked to see Mandela at a rally in Durban. It was visible proof, if any

was still needed, that Zulu-speaking Natal was not simply Inkatha territory. Mandela's message of peace – his call to 'comrades' to 'throw their
weapons into the sea' – was less-well received, and there was extensive
popular pressure on the ANC to provide weapons for self-defence.

During March thousands of armed Inkatha supporters attacked black
residents in the Pietermaritzburg area; almost 100 people died in these
attacks. The democratic movement alleged police complicity, and on
9 April most Natal workers heeded a Cosatu stayaway call to protest
police action in the townships. In Pinetown absenteeism was as high as
90-95% while in Durban it ranged from 50-90%.[1]

Chief Buthelezi responded with a scathing attack on Cosatu which,
he said, was,

> looking forward to becoming a Cosatu government over a Cosatu-run
> South Africa. I predict that we will yet see the Cosatu dog bite the ANC
> master and shake it like some vicious brute turned master killer. God
> knows, if I had to say yes, let us go and clean that mess up there, (it)
> would be an awesome spectacle of absolute brute power sweeping all the
> muck out of the greater Pietermaritzburg area.[2]

Buthelezi's attack was 'unfortunate', said the normally-cautious
Natal Witness in an editorial. 'Only an extremely narrow understanding
of modern politics would exclude the power of organised labour.'

Buthelezi's statements were almost as provocative, continued the editorial, as his comments to Zulu chiefs the previous month that

> we should place ourselves on a war footing... But most hurtful is the
> appellation 'muck', which will be seen as a grave insult by many of the
> ordinary people who have lost their homes and loved ones in the latest
> demonstration of brute power.[3]

'Let our enemies know our organisation has survived the fiercest attacks by the apartheid state,' said Cosatu in a May Day message. 'We
will never be crushed by the violence of the police and the warlords in
Natal.' Unless de Klerk did something to end the 'reign of terror' being
conducted by Inkatha in Natal, warned Cosatu's Willis Mchunu in early
June, then action could be expected countrywide. Cosatu, he said,
wanted to see the disbanding of 'the armed wing of Inkatha', the Kwa-
Zulu police; the removal of Buthelezi as KwaZulu's Minister of Police;
the arrest and trial of Inkatha warlords; and the replacement of the army
by a 'non-partisan' force.

When no response to these demands was forthcoming Cosatu,
together with the ANC and UDF, called a national stayaway to protest
the violence and Inkatha attacks. The Natal violence was no longer a

regional problem and the entire country, it was argued, should show its concern. The call was widely supported, and three million people stayed away from work on 2 July in an action estimated by employers to have cost the economy R750-million. It was a powerful indication of support for the ANC-led alliance and severely dented Buthelezi's image.

However, in other respects, the action failed. Inkatha managed to present the stayaway demands to its followers as an attack on the Zulu people. Why did Cosatu and the ANC call for the disbanding of Kwa-Zulu police and not those of the other homelands, it asked. This was a further sign that the ANC was anti-Zulu and dominated by Xhosas, claimed Inkatha.

Violence spread to all parts of the country, particularly in the latter half of 1990. During August and September violence on the Witwaters-rand claimed the lives of over 1 000 people. Eyewitnesses regularly alleged police complicity with Inkatha impis. One senior Inkatha leader in the Transvaal was arrested with a carload of automatic weapons, but later released. There were strong indications of 'warlord' complicity in machine-gun attacks on train passengers in which scores died. These appeared to be little more than random terror attacks, but many other attacks took an ethnic form. Violence was particularly extreme between Zulu hostel-dwellers and other sections of the community. In many areas hostels and hostel-dwellers, widely seen as the bases of vigilante forces, were attacked. In other areas communities responded with narrowly anti-Zulu attacks.

The violence seriously affected the unions, whose activists were often in the forefront, digging trenches and organising community self-defence. Workers absented themselves from work to help defend their families. Few wanted to attend union or Cosatu local meetings. Unions such as Numsa, with large membership in township hostels, were hardest hit. At least five Numsa-organised factories saw clashes between Inkatha and non-Inkatha forces, and a planned strike at Usco Steel was aban-doned after 19 Numsa members were killed in an attack on the Sebokeng hostel.

The ethnic aspect of the conflict was something new for the unions. All Zulu workers, including Cosatu members, were forced out of the Sebokeng hostel following an Inkatha attack. In one Katlehong hostel all non-Zulu workers were driven out. Many hostel-dwellers simply left to sleep at their workplaces or in the veld. Numsa's Moses Mayekiso warned in late September of 'anarchy' if the problem was not brought under control. Uwusa members were a small minority in plants, he said, but were heavily armed. Many Zulu-speaking workers were physically threatened and told to leave Cosatu. This left Numsa members 'demor-alised and fearful'.[4]

Organisational and political developments

The horrific carnage was the central feature of the post-February period. There were also key organisational developments. Tens of thousands of civil servants went on strike in all parts of the country, as did prison warders and black policemen, many of them under the banner of the Police and Prisons Civil Rights Union (Popcru). Domestic workers marched in their thousands demanding recognition and basic rights. And in the homelands Cosatu not only organised but became deeply involved in negotiations to formulate basic labour laws for these areas.

One of the most significant developments was the launch in October of the South African Democratic Teachers Union (Sadtu) which brought together 100 000 teachers. Sadtu succeeded in uniting both the established ethnic teachers' associations and the more militant UDF-oriented teachers' organisations. The depth of its achievement was undermined slightly by the last-minute withdrawal of Tuata, which represented many African teachers in the Transvaal.

Sadtu's launching congress elected Randall van den Heever as general secretary and Shepherd Mdladlana as president. It resolved to keep its doors open to all teachers organisations and to debate affiliation to Cosatu at its 1991 congress.

One of the first major organisational initiatives amongst 'professional workers', Sadtu's formation succeeded in bringing together even the most conservative and sectional teachers' bodies into a new non-racial organisation, a historic achievement given the centrality of ethnic education in maintaining apartheid. Sadtu also established itself as a body with both professional and trade union aspirations, breaking the established mould where teachers were expected to have neither 'demands' nor 'rights'. Cosatu could claim credit for facilitating much of the unity process. It had helped iron out problems on the road to unity and made its resources available to the new body.

Political developments moved rapidly during 1990. Both the ANC and Cosatu embarked on a determined campaign to woo homeland leaders. This was done on the clear understanding that the ANC would not act as a shield for unpopular rulers. Cosatu's Northern Transvaal region focused its attention on Bophuthatswana's intransigent Lucas Mangope. It launched strikes and stayaway actions calling on him to unban the ANC and allow unions to operate freely. By late 1990 there were signs that this pressure was bearing fruit.

The SACP emerged from 40 years of illegality at a July mass rally attended by 40 000 people. The party had extensive worker support, and its public re-emergence was accompanied by the announcement that four senior Cosatu unionists – Chris Dlamini, Moses Mayekiso, John

Gomomo and Sydney Mufamadi – were members of the SACP's interim leadership group. It was one of the few communist parties in the world whose popularity was growing, an irony not lost on observers. The SACP's relaunch was accompanied by efforts to distance itself from its Stalinist past. The slogan of the rally was 'forward to democratic socialism' and leadership committed itself to building an open and democratic party.

The ANC ran into major problems attempting to establish itself as a mass party. Its membership drive was slower than anticipated, particularly after the wave of violence unleashed against it. It was also slow to establish its official structures and consolidate its organisational apparatus. The ANC undoubtedly retained mass support, particularly among workers, but had difficulty translating this popularity into strong organisation. This in turn led to complaints from membership dissatisfied with slow progress and insufficient consultation by the leadership. Tackling these problems became the main purpose of the ANC's December consultative conference.

The events from February to the end of 1990 are too recent to allow proper analysis or adequate historical description. The remainder of this chapter, therefore, concentrates on three areas of crucial importance to this period and Cosatu's role in the future. These are Cosatu's strategic alliance with the ANC and SACP; Cosatu's major campaign initiatives, particularly the anti-LRA and living wage actions; and Cosatu's vision of a post-apartheid South Africa, particularly future economic policy, privatisation and the call for a workers charter to guarantee basic worker rights.

Background to the tripartite alliance

Alliances are an established feature of South Africa's political history. During the 1950s the ANC, at the time open to Africans only, worked closely with bodies that operated in other communities such as the Natal and Transvaal Indian Congresses. Indeed, the drafting and adoption of the Freedom Charter was not simply the work of the ANC but of the Congress Alliance as a whole, including Sactu.

At the time the Communist Party (SACP), illegal since 1950, operated underground. It maintained no public profile, although individual communists remained well-known public figures, particularly within the trade union movement and component organisations of the Congress Alliance. When the ANC was banned in 1960, key leaders in the ANC and SACP decided to form Umkhonto we Sizwe (MK) and launch armed struggle.

During the long years of illegality the ANC supplanted the Congress Alliance, becoming non-racial in composition. It was seen not as a political party, but a national liberation movement, a home to all those fighting for a united, non-racial and democratic South Africa. Some within the ANC presented the organisation as an alliance of class forces committed to national liberation. Others spoke more concretely of an ANC-SACP-Sactu alliance. Its members fought together, were imprisoned together, survived together and died together, and this strengthened the alliance.

In time, the three organisations became virtually indistinguishable in outlook and approach. Some argued that the ANC was controlled by the SACP. Others argued the SACP was effectively defunct since its members were wholeheartedly involved in building the national liberation movement. Indeed, during the early years of Cosatu's existence, underground SACP members were often most opposed to Cosatu articulating socialist slogans, arguing that this was premature.

This historical background is essential to understand the relationship between the ANC and SACP. It is an alliance rooted in over 30 years of shared experiences, not an electoral pact between parties, entered into or broken at a moment's notice. A similar alliance was formed between Cosatu and the UDF, the two main legal organisations operating from the mid-1980s. This alliance was marked by the paradox of being both extremely strong and notoriously weak. Its weaknesses arose from the inability to develop strong alliance structures, or work together effectively in campaigns and planned action. Its strengths lay in the depth of shared perspectives and that the activities of each, generally speaking, strengthened the other. Both saw political developments in a similar light and shared the same broad outlook, largely that of the banned ANC. Both faced the repression of the apartheid state.

Shortly after 2 February 1990 it became common to hear of the ANC-SACP-Cosatu alliance. Before examining some of the debates surrounding the tripartite alliance, we must explore what happened to Sactu; how Cosatu decided to enter into the alliance; and the basis on which the alliance exists.

Sactu phased out

Since the mid-1950s Sactu had been part of the Congress Alliance. Although never banned, by 1965 it had effectively ceased to operate within the country. Most of its leading cadres were either in exile, with MK, or serving prison sentences. A handful of affiliates survived by moving into the conservative Tucsa camp. The rest collapsed, with the notable exception of the Food and Canning Workers Union, although even it became both organisationally weak and politically inactive. As a trade union federation Sactu died. As a collection of activists committed to rebuilding political unionism it remained an influential force both internationally and locally. It operated, in a sense, as the labour wing of the ANC. When Cosatu was launched it did so with Sactu's blessing, but it would be a mistake to claim, as some have done, that Cosatu was Sactu's creation.

Shortly after the unbanning of the ANC there were suggestions, largely from non-unionists within the democratic movement, that Cosatu would dissolve in favour of Sactu. In this view the labour movement was – or should have been – simply the instrument of the ANC. On 5 February Sactu president Stephen Dlamini announced in Lusaka that Sactu was likely to merge with Cosatu. As it was the longest-serving federation and the 'kingpin', any amalgamated body should bear Sactu's name, he said.[5]

A different view was presented by Sactu general secretary John Nkadimeng who announced that 'Sactu accepted Cosatu was the dominant trade union force in South Africa' and that Sactu would have no problem integrating into Cosatu structures. 'Cosatu, by building a large scale organisation and surviving, had done more than Sactu had been able to do,' said Nkadimeng.[6]

These different perspectives were debated within Sactu, and the view which prevailed was that Sactu should not attempt to re-emerge as a labour federation within the country. Parallel discussions within Cosatu revealed consensus that Sactu should be phased out, although there were differences over the question of timing.

On 19 March a joint meeting of Sactu's NEC and a large Cosatu delegation was held in Kafue, Zambia. The meeting acknowledged the historic 'vanguard role' played by Sactu. Both organisations agreed 'to the phasing out of Sactu with the objective of achieving the principle of one country, one federation.'

A facilitating committee of five delegates from each organisation was appointed to oversee this process. This would expedite 'the return of Sactu cadres' and facilitate their integration into Cosatu and its affiliates 'as far as it is possible.'[7] It was clearly understood that Sactu cadres were not guaranteed jobs, nor would they be parachuted into positions. They would be considered along with other applicants for vacancies. The joint meeting did not explore in detail the implications of these decisions for the future of the ANC-SACP-Sactu alliance, although it assumed Cosatu would become the third partner in any alliance. It was agreed that 'more debate should be held to give content to the alliance with the SACP and ANC'.

Principles governing the tripartite alliance

Cosatu held a number of meetings with the ANC inside the country. During the last weekend of March a Cosatu delegation met the SACP in Zimbabwe, and both organisations agreed they should assist 'to build a massive, above-board ANC.'

Debate at Cosatu's CEC meeting held in early May centred on the form the alliance should take, rather than whether there should be an alliance. The ANC was 'the overall leader of the national democratic movement' whose objective was 'to dismantle apartheid and to effect a national-democratic transformation.' There was 'a commonly held position', the office bearers noted, 'that in the coming period the historic alliance of the ANC, the SACP and the organised workers of our country will continue to function.' However, this alliance needed restructuring to meet 'the new situation'.

Delegates to the May CEC endorsed the alliance and proposed five points to be taken to a consultative meeting of the ANC, SACP and Cosatu scheduled for 9 May:

1. Each organisation is independent and will develop its own positions on various issues and campaigns.
2. The task of the alliance (is) to formulate a joint programme on agreed issues.
3. The alliance is a strategic alliance with a central objective of dismantling apartheid and building a non-racial, democratic and unitary South Africa.
4. This alliance must take on a structured form at national, regional and local level with mandated representatives from each organisation.
5. The alliance must work out how it relates to (a) range of organisations and different class forces outside it.

The alliance meeting on 9 May accepted these points and added four others, the most significant of which was the recognition of the ANC as 'the leader of the alliance'. The meeting also agreed to base the alliance 'on democratic principles and practices' with 'consultation and consensus' as 'the basis of decision making'. It was stressed that the alliance should not inherit past mistakes and that interlocking leadership in particular should be avoided. Finally it was decided that a three-person commission should examine details of the nature, structure and content of the alliance and look at the UDF's relationship to the alliance.

The 9 May meeting formally constituted the new tripartite alliance. By late 1990 few meetings of the alliance had been held and those that did take place involved only the highest leadership. This makes the alliance difficult to assess, for only when it is functioning at regional and local levels can it be judged as a living force. However, problems within the alliance have been experienced, and it has not been universally accepted within Cosatu ranks.

The alliance undoubtedly reflects the sentiments of the overwhelming majority of Cosatu's membership. The rank-and-file have deep sympathy for Nelson Mandela, for the ANC and, to a lesser extent, the SACP. An internal Cosatu document expressed this when it noted that the ANC was 'the primary vehicle for our people to achieve their political aspirations in South Africa.'[8]

The alliance has been criticised, particularly from the left. The Workers Organisation for Socialist Action (Wosa), which has pockets of support within Cosatu, argued that 'it is not possible to be genuinely independent when you give your support entirely to one political organisation.' However Wosa's position is ambiguous in that it does not suggest political non-alignment. Its chief concern, expressed in its newspaper *Vukani Basebenzi*, appears to be that an alliance 'with a multi-class organisation (the ANC)' will lead to 'the surrender of socialism as the goal of the struggle.' Entering the strategic alliance meant that Cosatu became 'the trade union wing of the ANC, bound to defend the decisions of the ANC and unable to defend working-class interests unless the ANC agrees.'[9]

Wosa's argument points to real dangers if union independence is not continually asserted. However, Wosa assumes that Cosatu's main purpose in the alliance will be to receive orders rather than contribute its perspectives. In practice Cosatu has proved to be nobody's pet poodle.

The question of independence was explored further at the first full meeting of the alliance national co-ordinating committee held on 15 November 1990. Alliance decisions, it was agreed, would have the status of recommendations to the three organisations and only be made on the basis of consensus. The allies would consult on major policy decisions and campaigns, although this would in no way prevent independent decision-making. If, for example, Cosatu wanted to call a general strike on a certain date it would consult both the ANC and the SACP. They would be entitled to refuse to support the action. If this happened it would still be possible, although perhaps inadvisable, for Cosatu to pursue its action.

The 15 November meeting explicitly noted that 'the allies should not be expected to agree on all policy matters.' Indeed Cosatu has used alliance meetings to raise criticisms of both policies and practices. Insufficient leadership consultation with ANC membership was raised at the November meeting. So too was the point that 'the talks about talks process is being used by the regime to separate the ANC from the masses.'[10]

The tripartite alliance is based on a shared objective and shared interests and it is unlikely to result in any party sacrificing its independence. It is true that during the long years of exile the ANC-SACP-Sactu alliance was not notable for the independence of its partners, and reached the point where the three organisations appeared virtually indistinguishable. Both Sactu and the SACP subsumed themselves to the task of building the ANC.

But this situation is unlikely to be repeated, especially since all partners have their own reasons for wanting a looser alliance. Cosatu has always jealously guarded its independence. The role of a union is to ensure that its members' views are transmitted upwards to those in authority – whether employers, the state or even a future government. To do the opposite is, for unions, a fatal error. The SACP, in the recent period, has shown itself concerned to develop a strongly-independent profile and existence as a working-class political party. Particularly following events in the Soviet Union and Eastern Europe, the party has accepted that it cannot, and should not, attempt to control mass organisations – the 'organs of civil society'. And the ANC is attempting to win the widest possible support from all layers of society including big business. It wants to retain strong working-class support, but is keen to avoid the suggestion that it is somehow in the grip of either the SACP or the trade union movement.

The tripartite alliance is both a continuation of and a break from the earlier ANC-SACP-Sactu alliance. Cosatu has not simply occupied Sactu's seat at the alliance table. Instead the alliance is being reconstituted and restructured in accordance with the needs of the post-February period.

'Too many hats?'

In previous years the ANC-SACP-Sactu alliance was often termed 'indestructible' and 'permanent', a formulation neither dialectical nor realistic. This response was, in large measure, an attempt to prevent the Cold War ideology of anti-communism from disrupting the alliance. In this it was successful. The ANC, while never communist, has also never succumbed to anti-communism.

The reconstituted alliance is neither indestructible nor permanent. It exists for as long as it is in the common interests of all parties. And Cosatu is well aware that its role is not merely, or even mainly, to provide electoral support to the ANC in a democratic election.

One of the alliance's challenges is to conduct its business in the public eye. It has been agreed that 'the alliance must at all times have a public existence', but it is not clear what this means in practice.[11] While the existence of the alliance is public knowledge, the independence of its partners is not. Many ordinary South Africans, black and white, undoubtedly see each partner as interchangeable. All alliance partners have long experience of the state using differences to sow mistrust and division. This has led to a public face of unity, with problems being raised behind closed doors. It is hard to see this continuing, and the alliance will therefore have to express differences publicly and ensure that both the public and membership do not interpret this as division. This necessitates the development of a culture of openness, criticism and political pluralism within the democratic movement and the alliance itself.

Another issue under debate involves leaders wearing more than one hat. Most Cosatu leaders are also members of the ANC, SACP, or both. The right of individuals to join the political party of choice is unquestioned. More debatable has been the wisdom of individuals holding leadership positions in more than one organisation. Jay Naidoo and Elijah Barayi were invited to serve on the ANC's interim leadership committee (ILC) to supplement the efforts of its NEC. These appointments have, however, been more symbolic than real. But more significantly, that many members of the ANC's regional executive committees are also leading figures in Cosatu. For example, Cosatu's Wits regional secretary Amos Masondo also sits on the ANC's PWV executive. A similar situation has occurred in the SACP. No less than three of Cosatu's six national office bearers are members of the SACP's interim leadership group (ILG). Many other leading unionists are involved at regional level. Cosatu's Southern Natal regional secretary Thami Mohlomi, for example, is also secretary of the SACP's regional committee in that area.

This situation is not without its problems. Cosatu has accepted that it is in the federation's interests to help build both the ANC and SACP into strong and democratic organisations, and certain experienced unionists have had to devote time and energy to these tasks. Invariably this entailed additional work for those concerned and, inevitably, a degree of neglect of their union duties. On this point there is broad consensus within Cosatu – there are risks of overloading any one individual, just as there are risks of union resources being abused.

More complex is the problem of building the alliance into a living force. How can the alliance take shape if, for example, one person is the leading figure of more than one partner in a particular region? Must that person arrange meetings with himself or herself, and then prepare separately for the meeting with two different teams? This dilemma saw Chris Dlamini withdraw from a meeting of the alliance after Cosatu's Exco objected that it was incorrect for him to represent the SACP in a meeting with Cosatu.

Sactwu and CWIU have argued most strongly for a separation of leadership. CWIU's Rod Crompton has opposed 'horizontal overlaps', whereby individuals hold leadership positions at equivalent levels in two or more organisations. Sactwu has focused on the issue of independence. 'How many independent organisations can (one individual) lead?' asks an internal Sactwu discussion paper. 'We say one.'

According to NUM's Cyril Ramaphosa, the union was flexible 'but would like our leaders to treat the union as the primary organisation and not to act to the detriment of miners.' By late 1990 a number of senior NUM officials held key positions in both the ANC and SACP.

Other unionists have argued that there is no problem holding elected positions in more than one organisation. If attending a meeting as a Cosatu representative, one presents Cosatu's views; and when one attends wearing an ANC or SACP hat then the views of that organisation are presented.

A strong case has been made for accepting interlocking leadership as a necessary interim measure. Cosatu unionists should actively help build and lead the political organisations, it is argued. They are able to bring a depth of experience and knowledge of mass work to organisations which for decades have operated underground. In the current phase, aimed at establishing a non-racial democratic government, the partners in the alliance are all moving in the same direction and none holds state power. Numsa's general secretary Moses Mayekiso – who also holds a senior position in the SACP, and is head of the influential Civic Association of the Southern Transvaal – has argued this strongly:

> We are still struggling for democracy, and the contribution of union leaders will be vital, especially as the political organisations have recently been unbanned. We can represent workers better with a foot in both camps. If unionists won't lead the ANC, who will? And who's going to lead the working class party (the SACP) if not workers?
>
> The policy in regard to the ANC is likely to be transitional. Once it takes over the government, union officials will not be able to serve in its leadership.

The 'two hats' issue is not yet resolved within Cosatu and will undoubtedly be a key debate at its next national congress. The consensus likely to emerge within Cosatu is that interlocking leadership between unions and the ANC and/or SACP will be allowed as an interim measure (although with 'interim' undefined), but subject to a set of guidelines or code of conduct.

There is unlikely to be sufficient support for the view that one cannot hold an elected position at the same level in more than one organisation – for example, preventing an elected national leader of Cosatu from holding a NEC post in either the SACP or the ANC. Similarly, Cosatu's elected regional leadership would not, on this argument, be able to hold elected office in regional structures of either ally. This last position, if adopted, raises as many questions as it answers. Would such a policy be workable if applied only to Cosatu leadership and not to leadership of affiliates? Is such a policy realistic at local level where Cosatu unionists play a particularly important role in building the ANC? The majority within Cosatu is likely to see this approach, similar to the Italian union movement's 'incompatibility principle', as premature. However in the long run it will be difficult to retain the independence of the union movement without it.

Cosatu's LRA campaign

In 1990 the union movement's protracted anti-LRA campaign bore fruit. Phase one – the 1988 attempt to stop promulgation of the new law – had failed. Widespread mass action during phase two had been highly effective and succeeded in making the new labour law more of a liability than an advantage for employers. Nevertheless repeated talks with Saccola yielded little. During early 1990 the situation began to shift as the post-February winds of change were felt in the corridors of the major corporations.

On 30 March the National Manpower Commission (NMC) published proposals for consolidating the LRA, including a recommendation that *all* workers should be covered by the law. At the same time talks with Saccola started to bear fruit with employers conceding that the 1988 amendments had been disastrous and that there was a need to re-think the labour law. These talks culminated on 11 May with the signing of the Cosatu-Nactu-Saccola accord. This endorsed basic labour rights for all workers and agreed to reverse the most offensive provisions of the 1988 amendments.

The unions were, however, deeply suspicious of agreements with Saccola. The accord itself would be meaningless unless passed into law, and the 1988 experience had shown the government to be contemptuous of such agreements. Saccola's credibility was also at stake. The unions and Saccola immediately dispatched a delegation to Cape Town to meet Eli Louw, the new Minister of Labour. He agreed to take 'reasonable steps' to see that the accord became law during the 1990 parliamentary session. Within days it was published in the government gazette for comment.

The government received a range of objections. Some were submitted by racist whites-only unions, others by various employers, many of whom were party to the Saccola talks. Minister Louw found himself in a corner. He appeared to be personally committed to respecting the accord but was opposed by a combination of free marketeers and conservatives in the cabinet, as well as senior bureaucrats in his own department. On 13 June Louw announced that the cabinet had decided consultations would continue and the Act would be amended only in 1991.

It was unclear whom the government still wished to consult. Cosatu and Nactu's position as the largest federations was generally recognised. Saccola spoke for 70% of private sector companies outside of agriculture, and employed approximately 60% of the country's workforce. 'One can only assume that the government's hesitancy has been prompted by a desire to pander to the right wing,' said a despairing Theo Heffer, a leading management consultant. 'It is only people on the Right who indicated that they want some aspects of the 1988 amendments to be retained.'[12]

To Cosatu the message was clear – pressure should be maintained. Workers throughout the country held demonstrations. Fifteen Cosatu leaders marched on, and occupied, the offices of the Department of Manpower in Johannesburg. 'We had no intention of staying there indefinitely although we gave that impression,' recalls Jay Naidoo. That evening the delegation met with the Johannesburg shop stewards council which had gathered outside the Manpower offices. Naidoo telephoned FW de Klerk and asked him to intervene. 'I said to him that the government had an opportunity for the first time to strike a deal with the trade union movement, yet they were busy throwing their chance away.' De Klerk promised to respond urgently.

The union leaders left the building the next morning, announced that they were expecting to meet De Klerk, and then marched back to the union movement's Rissik Street headquarters. It was a day of high drama in central Johannesburg. Thousands of striking OK Bazaars workers held their own demonstration march, as did hundreds of dismissed workers from Reckitt and Colman. In the middle of Rissik Street the Cosatu leaders stopped and held a mass meeting, explaining to the crowd the problems with the LRA and the delays in promulgating the accord.[13]

Even Saccola was angry at the delay. Chief Saccola negotiator Bobby Godsell jokingly complained that he had not been invited to join the sit-in. The logjam was broken at a meeting on 26 June between FW de Klerk and representatives of both Saccola and the union movement. 'It was eerie,' recalls one participant visiting the government's Union Buildings for the first time. 'We were in the portals of National Party history. There was pink marble, china cups and Afrikaner maids serving us tea.' Hardliners within the Department of Manpower argued that nothing could be done to implement the accord. Cosatu argued back – 'we had to make them understand negotiations' – and called for a working committee to report within 30 days. This view prevailed and the meeting agreed to set up a joint working party to explore ways of resolving the crisis.

Cosatu decided to use the joint working party to expand the scope of union demands. A new LRA should actively extend union rights to all workers, not simply acknowledge that right as the Cosatu-Nactu-Saccola accord had done. Cosatu's July CEC agreed on a programme of action which would include mass marches and mobilisation of members through regional shop stewards councils. If progress was not made, a national stayaway would be called for early October.

The pressure worked. Further negotiations culminated in a 12-hour meeting on 13 September, involving representatives of Cosatu, Nactu and Saccola, Eli Louw, key officials of his department and the NMC. The meeting thrashed out a 'minute' to be placed before union members, Saccola members and the cabinet for endorsement.

The LRA minute was an historic document. The state agreed that all workers should have basic rights including the right to join unions and bargain collectively. It agreed to ask the NMC to prepare a bill extending rights to farm and domestic workers before June 1991. The unions agreed to sit on a restructured NMC which would operate democratically and publicly. The Cosatu-Nactu-Saccola accord would be placed before parliament for ratification in February 1991. Finally, it was agreed that no future labour law would go before parliament before Saccola and the unions had considered it.

On 20 September the cabinet endorsed the LRA minute. Both Saccola and the unions did so shortly afterwards. Cosatu called off its stayaway action scheduled for 8 October and hailed the LRA minute as 'a major victory'. A report presented to Cosatu's October CEC stressed the need to continue the LRA campaign. It said a new phase had already begun, which revolved around two issues – extension of the scope of the LRA to include farmworkers, domestic workers and those in the homelands and public sector; and extension of the rights of workers, 'focusing in the first instance on the right to strike.'

Phase two of the LRA campaign succeeded in reversing the 1988 amendments and placing the need for a new LRA on the agenda. Phase three aimed to take this demand forward and, in the final months of 1990, there were signs of progress. The government's Commission for Administration effectively conceded civil servants the right to join unions and agreed to stop-order facilities for Nehawu's thousands of members in the state health sector. Sats (now called Transnet) conceded a range of union facilities to Sarhwu. Draft legislation proposing basic union rights for some, though not all, farmworkers was also aired.

These developments posed new challenges for Cosatu. The unions in these newly-accepted sectors were not strong, and rights won by the union movement as a whole threatened to exceed the level of organisation. Rights not rooted in organisation would mean fundamental weaknesses. The challenge was to use the opportunity to strengthen organisation.

Entering the NMC would involve, for the first time, playing a participatory role in the development of labour policies. It would also mean learning to cope with the rules of tripartism – union participation in official structures on an equal basis with employers and the state.

The living wage

In 1990 there were serious attempts to revive the Living Wage Campaign by re-establishing an LWC committee and debating the issue at two national campaign conferences. These meetings agreed the campaign would be built around four core demands – the right to a living wage; job security; centralised bargaining; and an end to privatisation.

One of the more controversial debates was over a national minimum wage. 'The living wage has been estimated at between R1 140 and R1 500. This is our goal', proclaimed one issue of Cosatu's *Campaign Bulletin*. 'But for many workers this goal is still very far away. Their wages are too low to reach the living wage in one jump – they need a stepping stone.' The LWC sub-committee recommended that Cosatu should fight for a national minimum wage of R700 per month. This wage 'should not be so high as to become confused with the living wage.' 'Even high-wage industries have low-wage companies,' argued a paper in support of the R700 figure. A national minimum wage would protect high-wage workers by 'setting a floor to wages throughout the industry.' Because it was a 'minimum' these workers could still 'continue their struggle for the higher "living wage"'. The R700 figure could be applied to all sectors except domestic work, where even this demand was not realistic or 'credible'.[14]

Most delegates to the September campaigns conference rejected this position, with only NUM and TGWU backing it wholeheartedly. Three unions (Ppwawu, Fawu and Sadwu) supported the idea but felt the figure of R700 was too low. Samwu and Saccawu favoured the establishment of legal minimum wages for each sector. Numsa argued that a R700 minimum was neither a useful mobilising tool, nor was it economically implementable. Any attempt implement it would be inflationary since capitalists would increase prices in response. It would also result in job losses. A national minimum wage was therefore, argued Numsa, only realistic in the context of a restructured economy.[15]

Strongest opposition to the concept came from Sactwu which argued that a non-negotiated national minimum would undermine the process of collective bargaining. It would also weaken claims of higher-paid workers and reduce job security. For Sactwu 'negotiations in industrial councils' should be encouraged as 'the prime way of regulating wages and conditions in every industry.' Statutory minimum wages should only apply in sectors where unions were unrepresentative.[16]

A different perspective was presented in an anonymous paper from the Western Cape, distributed within Cosatu and to the press. It accused the LWC sub-committee of 'capitulating to bourgeois intransigence by introducing the national minimum wage.' Cosatu should adjust its target figure on the basis of the strength of the working class. But the figure set should be realistic for workers, not employers. Talking of a minimum wage would simply confuse workers and divert attention from living wage demands. 'Would the LWC be suspended', the paper asked, 'while the labour movement focuses on the National Minimum Wage Campaign?'[17]

Centralised bargaining was another important issue of 1990. Cosatu focused on the Barlow Rand corporation and its apparent campaign to destroy centralised negotiations and replace them with plant-level bargaining. On 23 May workers at Barlows companies launched a range of protest actions demanding centralised bargaining. Eight Cosatu unions – Ppwawu, Numsa, Sactwu, CWIU, Fawu, NUM, Saccawu and Cawu – were involved, covering most of Barlow's 80 000 workers belonging to Cosatu unions. In late 1990 Ppwawu embarked on a protracted strike at Barlow's Nampak plants throughout the country in support of this demand. However, the action failed to force the company to concede.

The nine-week Mercedes Benz strike which started in mid-August at the company's East London plant was more controversial for Cosatu. The action, not supported by the whole workforce, saw strikers demanding an end to the National Bargaining Forum (NBF) and the resumption of plant-level negotiations! This was a setback for Numsa which had battled for years to win centralised bargaining in the auto industry. It also undermined Cosatu when a range of employers began to argue that union leadership, rather than membership, wanted centralised bargaining.

While centralised bargaining brought workers long-term benefits, better short-term wages could often be won by strongly-organised plants going it alone. In the face of concerted pressure the Mercedes strikers backed down and accepted the NBF. Numsa, in turn, accepted the need to improve organisation and education of membership at the plant.

Cosatu's campaign conferences also explored new frontiers in collective bargaining. The closed-shop concept was supported in principle despite vigorous opposition from both NUM and Ppwawu. Even so it was accepted that democratic guarantees must be built in to these agreements to prevent abuses. Many Cosatu unions knew how the closed-shop could be misused by union bureaucrats to stifle workers. Established unions in the Tucsa tradition had used it extensively against the emerging unions. Its increasing acceptance reflected the fact that most Cosatu affiliates had 'emerged' and were now the established unions in their sectors.

The concept of 'essential services', long a favourite of employers and the state, was also addressed. Cosatu has accepted that there can be limitations on the right to strike in essential services – but only once the right to strike was a basic legal principle. Only strikes which were life-threatening could be curbed. Even then whole sectors should not be defined as essential, as for example the canning sector is at present. Workers prevented from striking, Cosatu decided, should benefit from agreements reached with other workers in their sector, and should not be open to additional exploitation because of their restricted right to strike.

Looking towards the future

Debates such as these attempted to confront the future, elaborating what Cosatu was fighting for, not only what it opposed. After 2 February Cosatu put greater effort into developing post-apartheid perspectives. Two areas, the workers charter and economic policy, are of particular importance.

Launched at Cosatu's 1989 congress, the workers charter campaign aimed to draw up a charter of rights which could be incorporated in the constitution of a post-apartheid South Africa. The process was not seen as one restricted to Cosatu, and views were solicited from a variety of organisations. The ANC, in its 1989 constitutional guidelines, supported a charter 'protecting workers' trade union rights.' The SACP proposed a more far-reaching charter including state control of the key means of production and the right to a living wage. A number of unions compiled proposals.

Sactwu has been the most active affiliate in the workers charter campaign. Actwusa (now Sactwu) had previously drafted a charter to establish and entrench rights in three areas: union organisation, such as the right to strike and to picket; industrial democracy, including participation in management, closed-shop rights and the power to dismiss anti-worker managers; and union independence from both the state and political organisations. The charter drafted by Sactwu was practical, voicing short-term trade union goals, but it undoubtedly lacked vision. 'The rights we articulate', said Sactwu's Ebrahim Patel, 'are achievable in the transformation phase of a post-apartheid South Africa.'

On various occasions during July and August, tens of thousands of Sactwu members left their workplaces in Cape Town and Durban 30 minutes before their normal lunchbreak. In the streets they linked hands to form a massive human chain around the industrial areas. This innovative tactic aimed to popularise the workers charter campaign among Sactwu's membership. It also provided visual proof of the power and sheer numbers of organised workers. Other affiliates have used a Cosatu questionnaire to canvass membership views. 'Should trade unions have a right to differ with the state?', and 'How can we ensure that all workers have equal rights and equal opportunities?' were some of the questions asked.

Lack of clarity over what to do with the demands which are eventually drawn up has been a weakness of the campaign. Some in Cosatu have seen its sole purpose as being to entrench basic worker rights constitutionally. Others have argued that the charter should express a broader vision of the social, economic and union rights which workers want, and that many of the demands are inappropriate for a country's constitution. The unions, therefore, should rather ensure that a democratic government includes these rights in legislation. Yet others have envisaged including the workers charter as an annexure to a democratic constitution, placing it somewhere in the realm between constitution and legislation.

The far-reaching nature of the campaign emerged at Cosatu's workers charter conference held in November 1990, when 'Gender and the Constitution' was a topic covered. Delegates felt issues included in a constitution should incorporate state responsibility for childcare and creche facilities; marriage laws giving women 'equal rights before marriage, in marriage and in the dissolution of marriage'; the legalisation of abortion; non-sexist education; 'non-toleration of rape, battery, abuse and harassment'; and equal pay for work of equal value. The conference also examined the possibility of reserving a proportion of seats in 'key state structures' for women, and of establishing an equal opportunities commission.

Cosatu has devoted much energy to developing its economic perspectives. International developments have thrown the centrally-planned economy into disrepute, yet the union movement has been confronted by the market economy's failure to meet worker needs. This has been accompanied by a sometimes religious adherence to free market rhetoric by South Africa's ruling class, and a drive to privatise state assets.

For a number of years Cosatu has hosted a programme of detailed economic research. Its tentative conclusions have been presented in a number of papers by Alec Erwin, Numsa's national education officer and, unofficially, Cosatu's chief economist. Erwin, whose perspectives are broadly representative of Cosatu's economic thinking, has argued that economists must take developments in the Soviet Union and Eastern Europe into account. However a union programme must be based primarily on 'an analysis of apartheid capitalism as it exists in South Africa today', and aim to find 'the solution to the glaring and tragic social, political and economic problems that exist in our society.'

Present state policies would 'at best lead to 50/50 (or 30/70) type societies – 50% in reasonable wage employment and 50% not,' argues Erwin. 'No truly democratic government could tolerate such a persistence of inequality', particularly since it would retain racial dimensions. It was also questionable whether democracy could survive such inequality.

The solution, argues, Erwin is a democratically-planned socialist economy. The planned command economy of the Soviet variety is not the answer. Neither are the free-market or the social-democratic options.

> A free market economy cannot redress the structural problems exhibited in our economy, and the social-democratic solution is also a cul-de-sac because it places undue obligations on the state, far in excess of the fiscal resources any Southern African state, now or in the future, will be able to marshal.

A planned strategy is needed, for certain key sectors in particular, to begin the process of transformation away from a high-cost/low-wage economy. This planned restructuring of the post-apartheid economy will have to take place within a mixed economy. In a warning to some of Cosatu's less-flexible ideologues Erwin cautions that this position is adopted 'not as some expedient to hoodwink capital, or as a minimalist position to unify forces in the first stage as a stepping stone to the second.' In fact, argues Erwin, 'a future socialist economy in South Africa should be a mixed economy.'

Erwin's approach makes two key assumptions: that unrestricted market forces do not provide the basis for rational growth, and that the state must therefore provide a relatively rigid framework within which investment can occur; and that the elimination of market forces and concentration of investment decisions in the state will destroy intrinsic growth mechanisms such as competition. One consequence of the research into economic trends has been that individual affiliates, particularly Numsa and NUM, have started to explore the question of industrial restructuring.

Privatisation has been a pressing concern for unions. The state has embarked on a concerted attempt to sell off state-owned corporations and privatise aspects of the public sector. This included making the metal giant Iscor profitable and then selling it to private investors. Portions of the state transport sector and its electricity and telecommunications operations are also scheduled for privatisation. Other state services, such as health care, have been allowed to run down through neglect, under-financing and a state commitment to boosting private medicine.

In its 1990 May Day message Cosatu described the privatisation of public corporations as 'theft'. The ruling class was attempting to prevent a democratic government from having the resources to address poverty caused by decades of apartheid. Cosatu threatened to 're-nationalise without compensation all companies that have been privatised.'

These corporations were all 'built up by our taxes', argued a Cosatu anti-privatisation document. 'Here we see a government representing the minority selling off the assets belonging to the people.' Cosatu, and par-ticularly its public-sector affiliates, had another concern – privatisation would be accompanied by widespread retrenchment and redundancies.

Cosatu unions in the public sector have been especially active in fighting privatisation. On 17 February thousands of workers marched in Johannesburg, Pretoria, Bloemfontein, Durban and Port Elizabeth in pro-test against privatisation of the post office. Another march, directed against a number of employers in the public sector, stretched for three kilometers through Johannesburg on 10 March. At the end of that month there was a week of action, including a march by 17 000 people in Bloemfontein. In Johannesburg 15 000 people marched on the Johannes-burg Stock Exchange, an action which led to a drop in the value of Iscor shares and a statement by the Minister of Privatisation indicating a pre-paredness to delay the privatisation drive.

Cosatu's fifth birthday, on 1 December 1990, passed almost unno-ticed with so many other issues preoccupying the federation. It had been an eventful and challenging year. The government was starting to release prisoners, and exiles cautiously ventured home. For Cosatu this meant that many of its members and officials were returning. Alfred Ndlovu, TGWU's vice-president, was released from Robben Island, as were a number of other unionists, both workers and officials. Others, like former Northern Natal regional secretary Matthews Oliphant, returned from exile.

The year had been a turning point for Cosatu and the entire demo-cratic movement, marking both a beginning and an end. It was a time to pause and reflect on both the achievements and future direction of the union movement.

Notes

1. *Business Day*, 10.04.90.
2. *Star*, 18.04.90.
3. *Natal Witness*, 19.04.90.
4. *Weekly Mail*, 28.09.90.
5. *Star* 06.02.90.
6. *Business Day*, 20.02.90.
7. Cosatu report on Cosatu/Sactu NEC meeting held on 19 March 1990.
8. 'The alliance of ANC-SACP-Cosatu', included in July 1990 CEC documentation.
9. *Vukani Basebenzi*, 1, June 1990.
10. Minutes of tripartite alliance meeting, 15 November 1990.
11. 'The alliance of ANC-SACP-Cosatu', included in July 1990 CEC documentation.
12. Quoted in Robin Rafel, 'LRA – two wasted years', *Work In Progress*, 67, June 1990, 9.
13. Author interview with Jay Naidoo, Johannesburg, February 1991.
14. LRS, 'A national minimum wage – stepping stone to a living wage', produced for Cosatu and circulated to all unions in March 1990.
15. Martin Nicol (NUM), 'The Living Wage Committee and the affiliates', 18 September 1990.
16. See *Weekly Mail*, 14.09.90; and Sactwu, 'What are the alternatives to minimum wage laws?' 28 August 1990.
17. Anon, 'For a Living Wage or a National Minimum Wage?', September 1990.

27

Inheriting the past

REPRESSION runs like a thread through the union movement's history. Cosatu was born into a state of emergency and for most of its first four-and-half years it worked under emergency rule. Concerted attempts to destroy Cosatu failed, largely because of its organised shopfloor strength. Repression toughened the union movement, making it a battle-hardened opponent. For some unionists this inspired greater commitment and determination to defend the organisation.

In the process, however, many unionists lost their lives. Others were seriously injured, driven into exile, imprisoned or mentally scarred. Tens of thousands of workers lost their jobs. Many were deported to the rural areas or neighbouring states. Another casualty, at times, was internal union democracy. Decisions were often made hastily, with insufficient consultation – Cosatu's first priority was to live to fight another day.

Possibly the federation's greatest achievement was survival in the face of intense repression. But it was at great cost – organisationally and individually. This must form the backdrop, but not the justification, for any assessment of Cosatu's shortcomings.

Organisational achievements

Cosatu not only survived, it grew. Total paid-up membership increased from the slightly optimistic figure of 460 000 at the launch to almost 1,2-million workers by late 1990. This is more impressive when one realises that in Cosatu workers lose union membership when they are dismissed or retrenched, resign or retire. Only employed workers paying membership fees on a regular monthly basis are included in the membership audit.

Union organisation has spread to all corners of the country, and workers in the most remote regions have started demanding union rights. Cosatu has also facilitated the unionisation of new sectors including health workers and teachers – areas never before unionised.

A precondition of this growth, and another of Cosatu's major achievements, has been the merger campaign under the 'one industry, one union' banner. Today Cosatu has 14 affiliates, rather than the unwieldy 33 which participated in the December 1985 launch. The strict, and sometimes harsh, enforcement of merger policy created unions which were stronger numerically and organisationally, and better able to make rational use of their resources and personnel. Strong, nationally-organised industrial unions were the foundation for both a quantitative and qualitative growth in membership.

Centralised finances in the merged unions discouraged division and the formation of breakaway unions. The merged unions made policy on a centralised basis, dispensed funds to the regions from the centre, and were strongly national (rather than regional) in outlook. They coordinated negotiations with major national companies from their head offices, and combined decentralised organisation through a strong shopfloor with centralised policy-making by a strong national leadership.

This was the key to preventing splinter unionism, resisting repression, and increasing membership. Naturally, it had negative features. Legitimate local and regional grievances could be ignored and democratic processes could be weakened by heavy-handed national leadership. This did happen on occasion. Indeed, the strongly-centralised approach may prove inappropriate to a later phase of union development.

Cosatu's ability to fight for worker rights has been another major achievement. Workers join unions for a variety of reasons, the most important being a desire to improve their material conditions. This is not to promote the idea that there is somehow a 'bread-and-butter' unionism in contrast to political unionism. The two are integrally connected. However, without the ability to deliver economic improvements political unionism is meaningless.

Surveys reveal that only Cosatu members have seen a real increase in their wages over a number of years. In contrast, workers belonging to other federations or unions have received increases below the inflation rate, while non-unionised workers have experienced the biggest drop in living standards. These were compelling arguments for joining a Cosatu affiliate. Workers knew this from their own informal surveys – from information gleaned in discussions on trains and buses and in township backyards. As a result, Cosatu unions – unlike their predecessors of the 1970s and early 1980s – have had to do very little recruitment, largely dealing with groups of workers who approached the unions wanting to join.

Cosatu unions have not only improved wages. Job security, maternity rights, service allowances, shift allowances, decent annual leave, compassionate leave provisions and severance pay for retrenched workers have all become standard for large sections of the workforce. Workers know that it is no longer acceptable to be fired at the whim of a supervisor. The union movement introduced the 'rule of law' into the workplace and brought an end to arbitrary management decisions. Within many plants the unions made it impossible for management to rule by dictate. They rolled back the frontiers of arbitrary management action.

At a macro-level this was shown in the anti-LRA campaign. By the late 1980s employers and the state could no longer simply impose their will. They had to negotiate and win consent even for basic laws. Some observers have argued that the unions won industrial citizenship without winning political citizenship and that therein lies the root cause of instability in South Africa's industrial relations.

The unions have also been responsible for developing health and safety awareness in the workplace and for exploring and introducing more-appropriate retirement provisions for workers, such as provident funds. All these major achievements help explain workers' preparedness to defend their unions from attack.

In summary, Cosatu has been responsible for a real increase in the standard of living of its members and a significant shift in the share of wealth black workers receive. The federation and its affiliates have helped to reclaim the dignity and rights of ordinary workers on the factory floor.

Political achievements

Cosatu's political achievements and organisational work have always been interlinked. Its political strengths have enhanced the federation's ability to organise, while organisational strengths have enhanced political effectiveness.

The welding of internal political unity between the second Cosatu congress in 1987 and the third congress in 1989 was a crucial achievement. Broad, although not unanimous, acceptance of a single and coherent political perspective greatly enhanced the federation's effectiveness. Had this occurred earlier Cosatu might, arguably, have achieved much more.

Creating this unity involved overcoming both workerist and populist political tendencies, and development of a general acceptance of a national-democratic perspective of the liberation struggle combined with a transformative vision. The essence of 'the struggle' was to rid the country of apartheid, racial oppression and undemocratic minority rule. Freedom, however, did not simply mean handing over power to a new black, or even non- racial, elite. Social and economic inequalities had to be addressed and exploitation ended. This unified perspective envisaged genuine empowerment of the mass of the people. 'Freedom means socialism' was the slogan on one NUM banner. The way to achieve this was by encouraging active worker participation in the struggle for freedom.

A key element of political unity involved acknowledgement of the UDF as Cosatu's principal ally, and acceptance of the ANC as the leading organisation in the fight for national liberation.

It was principally Cosatu which kept the mass democratic movement's torch alive between mid-1986 and mid-1988. This does not underestimate the importance of formations such as Sayco or civic structures, nor imply that the UDF died during this period. Popular resistance continued but organisation was seriously crippled. Cosatu acted as a centre in assisting the mass democratic movement to regroup its forces, and the unions' organised strength was central to the failure of the state of emergency. The state was never able to enforce its February 1988 political ban on Cosatu, and the federation became a major political force acknowledged by both friend and foe.

This achievement was possible because of Cosatu's organised strength on the shopfloor, and worker response to the wave of detentions in mid-1986 was a sign of this. This strength protected much of Cosatu's top leadership from being detained, as it was simply too costly, politically and economically, for the state to do so. In addition, Cosatu's focus on building local shop steward councils was crucial. These were Cosatu's backbone. They assisted in organisational work and developed ordinary worker leadership. The locals confronted the political issues of the day, and developed resistance in practice. They were often the first line of defence against repression, giving workers practical leadership experience.

Cosatu played a major role in popularising the ANC and building support for the idea of socialism. The tripartite alliance of the ANC, SACP and Cosatu was rooted in broad working-class support for these organisations. Cosatu played no small role in developing and reflecting that consciousness.

It was no accident that, when the ANC and the SACP emerged from the shadows of illegality, Cosatu members and leaders were so prominently placed in the ranks of their interim structures. Not all had been underground operatives of these organisations. Many were included in recognition of their organisational experience and importance as worker leaders.

Some observers have mistakenly accused Cosatu of being a puppet in the hands of the ANC and SACP. In reality the process involved a dynamic two-way relationship. Cosatu's position on negotiations adopted at its 1989 congress was vital in the drafting of the Harare declaration. Cosatu's outlook was also influential in convincing the SACP to move away from the notion that socialism was something to be postponed to a later date.

Cosatu was highly influential outside the union movement. Frank Chikane, addressing delegates to Cosatu's third congress, called on them to guide the church on the key issues of the day. 'It is important that you formulate a vision of our future because we need to be guided by you,' he said. Cosatu had a deep influence on many church denominations, and boosted those within religious circles who argued for the church to side with the oppressed. Political formations and even homeland leaders courted the federation.

Cosatu's outlook and organisational approach made a deep impact on the entire democratic movement. This could be seen in the almost universal acknowledgement of the importance of 'worker leadership of the struggle'; in the growing talk of 'socialism'; in the widespread use of African languages; in the style and content of cultural work; and in the increasing presence of unionists and workers within non-union structures.

Four key principles became more widely accepted, in theory if not always in practice. Firstly, that mass organisation should be based on a culture of democracy, mandates, report-backs and leadership accountability. Secondly, that change in South Africa should not be simply a change in the colour of the ruling class. A new dispensation would have to include fundamental transformation of the social and economic conditions of the majority of the people. Thirdly, that strong organisation was essential to effectiveness. Elaborate theories and beautiful slogans were meaningless unless backed by solid organisation. Finally, that mass action was the key to transformation in South Africa. Other elements of the liberation struggle – armed struggle, international pressure and underground work – had limited impact unless based upon effective and well-organised mass action.

These principles were not the sole property of Cosatu. But its existence and successes were the strongest argument in their favour. The influence of the trade union movement can be seen by a careful study of the policies, programmes and actions of a wide range of organisations – and not only those within the Congress tradition.

Finally, the anti-LRA campaign must be included among Cosatu's major achievements. By late 1990 the state and employers had conceded that their 1988 amendments, the 'sword over the head of the unions', would have to be withdrawn. They had conceded that future labour legislation could not be imposed without Cosatu's co-operation. They had also agreed, at least in principle, to the extension of union rights to all workers.

These concessions were not easily won. They were the product of worker action involving the revival of a campaign which had been apparently defeated. The anti-LRA road was long and hard and tested Cosatu's ability to mobilise. There were two general strikes lasting a total of five days, and resistance to mass dismissals. The campaign involved hundreds of thousands of workers taking action against the bill on the shopfloor and in the streets. Without this mass action the campaign would never have been won.

Failures and weaknesses

Cosatu also had its fair share of failures, disasters and frustrations. Perhaps the greatest disappointment has been the failure to organise farmworkers. The CEC strategy handed responsibility for this project to Fawu. Fawu argued that it was easiest to begin by organising the farms which directly supplied unionised food-processing plants. As farmworkers had no legal right to unionise, employers refusing recognition would face blacking action in Fawu's factory strongholds. That was the theory.

The reality has been different. All the unions combined – whether from Cosatu, Nactu or independent – have not been able to organise even 1% of workers in the agricultural sector. Two non-Cosatu initiatives to organise farmworkers, one by a Nactu affiliate and another by the unaffiliated OVGWU, have been at least as successful as the Fawu project.

Slow progress in this sector has, in part, been due to internal problems within Fawu. More importantly, handing the project over to Fawu amounted to abdication of responsibility by Cosatu as a whole. The organisation of South Africa's 1,4-million farmworkers is a major task. The associated problems are inevitably exacerbated when handled as a sub-section of another union.

The Cosatu decision assumed that the organisation of farmworkers would best be achieved by the intensive organisational method rather than the extensive campaigning approach. This was a major error and showed an inability to learn from the experience of organising mine-workers. Before Cosatu's launch there were two major attempts to organise mineworkers – one when Fosatu asked its metal affiliate to establish a mineworkers project; the other when Cusa established the NUM and gave Cyril Ramaphosa the task.

Most observers expected the Fosatu-linked Mawu initiative to succeed, since Fosatu had a far better organisational record than Cusa. Mawu approached the task by slowly trying to organise one mine at a time. In contrast NUM approached workers across a number of mines, boldly adopting a high-profile approach. NUM's efforts unleashed a wave of enthusiasm and mass energy which rapidly mobilised workers across a broad front.

The organisation of farmworkers remains a priority for Cosatu. Its success will have a major bearing on both the miserable conditions of farmworkers and the way land is redistributed and utilised in post-apartheid South Africa.

Cosatu's attempts to organise the unemployed have been equally unsuccessful. Very little has been achieved despite the enormous resources poured into the task. The importance of organising the unemployed was acknowledged at Cosatu's inception. It was widely seen as the solution to the use of unemployed workers as scab labour or vigilante forces.

No accurate statistics exist, but the most reliable estimates put the number of unemployed at between four and eight million. This startling figure implies an unemployment rate of between 20% and 40% of the able-bodied population.

The National Unemployed Workers Co-ordinating Committee (NUWCC) – Cosatu's project to organise the unemployed – has been ineffective, and plagued by allegations of corruption and incompetence. NUWCC has had little success in organising marches of unemployed workers or effectively challenging the inadequate existing system of un-employment insurance (UIF). Organised workers have done little to ensure that their companies employ only members of NUWCC. Nor has there been effective linking of the demand for a 40-hour week and an end to excessive overtime with the real possibility of job creation for the unemployed.

The most successful attempts to work with the unemployed may well have been undertaken by community organisations and Sayco, as well as a number of Cosatu-linked local initiatives. These raise the question of whether the union form of organisation is the most effective way of mobilising and tackling the unemployment problem.[*]

Two other shortcomings have also had important organisational implications. Cosatu has lacked the capacity to strengthen its weaker affiliates. The result has been enormous imbalances in the power, experience and structures of the various Cosatu unions. While some – like NUM, Numsa and Sactwu – have highly developed structures, others like Cawu and Nehawu are relatively weak. Cosatu only began addressing this problem in early 1991.

These imbalances have contributed to a low level of development of solidarity action. There have been remarkable instances of support and sacrifice. Yet it is undeniable that the strongest solidarity received by striking workers invariably comes from other workers in the same affiliate and not from Cosatu members as a whole. It must be remembered that in South Africa striking workers receive no strike pay from the union and usually no other financial support. The most they can hope for, in a well-planned strike, is an occasional food parcel. Lengthy strikes are therefore a trial of strength in more ways than one.

A few examples illustrate the problem. Striking OK Bazaars workers were helped by solidarity pressure from workers in other Anglo American companies, pressure which Cosatu facilitated. But in the crucial 1987 mineworkers strike Cosatu was unable to arrange meaningful solidarity action, even though the major mining houses were also the primary owners of the unionised manufacturing sector. Again, Cosatu was unable to facilitate significant solidarity action in support of Nampak strikers in 1990. This was despite the fact that Nampak's holding company, Barlow Rand, had been targetted by the federation on account of its industrial relations policy, and that the strikers were challenging a key aspect of that policy, namely Nampak's refusal to agree to a meaningful collective bargaining forum.

Cosatu's history has included a number of mistaken political judgements. One in particular deserves mention – the special CEC's 14 July 1986 stayaway call in protest against the state of emergency. This decision was taken when emotions were running high and with insufficient analysis of the objective strengths and weaknesses of the democratic movement at the time. The CEC mistakenly assumed that it could call a stayaway without involving the rest of the democratic movement. It also assumed Cosatu's members would rally to the call, although many union offices were still closed and inadequate preparations had been made. The failure of the 14 July stayaway was a serious error. It gave security

---

[*] *The ineffectiveness of NUWCC was such that in 1991 Cosatu resolved to close the project.*

forces renewed confidence and weakened the federation's ability to resist the emergency. A successful national action against the emergency, called with less haste and more planning and preparation, might have significantly reduced the effect of repression on the union movement during the following three years.

Challenges of the 1990s

A range of new challenges – political, organisational and structural – have emerged as Cosatu enters the 1990s. The federation must re-define its political role now that organisations such as the ANC have been un-banned. Organisationally it needs to determine how best to inject more vibrancy into its worker-controlled structures, how to organise the unor-ganised, and how to re-organise the disorganised. The union movement must ensure that its structures are adequate to the demands of the time. Many of these challenges involve rethinking the democratic process. Is democratic centralism appropriate for a mass organisation in the current phase? Can 'delegate democracy' be balanced with elements of 'direct democracy'? Is it desirable to entrench affirmative action constitution-ally?

There is still the enormous task of organising the unorganised. Most Cosatu affiliates have not yet organised half the potential membership in their sector. Sactwu, which represents 80% of workers in the clothing, textile and leather sector, is the glaring exception. In some sectors, such as construction, organisation has barely scratched the surface. There are also sectors which are essentially unorganised, notably agriculture, where millions are employed. Finally there is the task of consolidating organi-sation in previously-isolated areas of the country, particularly the homelands, and securing basic legal rights for these workers.

One of the key organisational challenges of the 1990s concerns white collar workers and workers previously considered beyond unionisation. Thousands in this category have flocked to join Cosatu affiliates, but often find their needs are not catered for by unions whose structures, traditions and style have developed around the organisation of blue collar and semi-skilled workers. The result has been relatively ineffectual unionisation among office workers, bank employees and computer oper-ators. These jobs are no longer the preserve of white workers, and their importance is increasing with changes in the production process and the introduction of new technologies.

Workers performing professional tasks – nurses, teachers, academics, technicians and others – have also demanded unionisation. Many have strong professional pride and commitment to their work – they are in a 'career' rather than a 'job'. Yet they feel they are also workers with rights to decent working conditions. The established union movement, for that is what Cosatu has become, has been slow to respond. It is no solution to insist, as Cosatu has sometimes done, that they join the existing industrial union for their sector.

Civil servants and other state employees have also shown interest in unionisation. This sector employs increasing numbers of black people, although at present most work for separate ethnic administrations. Organising these workers is a challenge with major political implications for a future South Africa. In the law-enforcement sector prison warders, policemen and even black soldiers have demanded union rights. Cosatu needs to develop a meaningful strategy to cope with these demands.

Mergers – phase two

Phase two of the union merger process has barely started. There is enormous potential for a broad range of established unions and staff associations to be brought into the mainstream of trade unionism. A number of these, led by conservative leaders, have affiliated to Nactu in an attempt to avoid incorporation by a Cosatu affiliate. However, many workers – particularly coloured, Indian and white workers – are still isolated and remain within their existing unions out of habit. Others are held there by the threat of losing benefits should they resign. Still others feel unable to identify with Cosatu's tradition of militancy and political involvement.

It is essential that Cosatu projects itself as a home for these workers – not an easy task in practice. Many white workers openly praise Cosatu affiliates and are jealous of their ability to win meaningful wage increases and ensure job security. However they are, generally speaking, deeply hostile to Cosatu's political outlook. As a result, Cosatu's white worker membership can be numbered in the hundreds rather than the thousands. It is no accident that rightwingers have launched whites-only unions which base their appeal on promises to be 'the white Cosatu'. Whether the federation can find a formula to appeal to larger numbers of coloured, Indian, and even white workers without sacrificing the essence of its political outlook and organisational approach remains an open question.

Unity with Nactu unions is another aspect of the ongoing merger challenge. Much of the tension between Cosatu and Nactu is political, arising from differences between the Congress/ANC tradition and those in the Africanist or BC camps. With the unbanning of political organisations, the pressures on unions to substitute for these bodies should lessen. There is no reason why, in a freer political environment, differences should not be accommodated within one democratic union federation.

The alternative is to pursue the unattractive model of certain European countries with a number of federations – socialist, communist and christian – each indirectly linked to the major political parties.

Strengthening democracy

Cosatu has retained its essentially democratic nature, but in many respects internal union democracy is weaker today than ever before. There are signs that rank-and-file membership no longer participate effectively in determining macro-policy in their own unions or Cosatu. The growing movement towards centralised bargaining structures increases the risk of leadership isolation from ordinary membership. The protracted 1990 strike at Mercedes Benz – directed at Numsa's leadership as much as at the company itself, exemplifies this. The weakening of democratic processes was one consequence of the state of emergency. Unions and youth organisations sometimes took shortcuts. There were cases where stayaway action, for example, was achieved more by stopping transport or blockading roads than actively winning support.

The growing number and complexity of issues dealt with by the unions has also weakened democratic participation. It is one matter to involve membership in a demand for recognition and higher wages, but far more difficult to maintain mass participation when negotiating the intricacies of a provident fund. The latter requires shopfloor leadership which understands the details of negotiations, can report back the salient points to the workforce, and develop a mandate over critical issues. Cosatu has often been unable to do this with its major campaigns. Mobilisation of mass support in the anti-LRA campaign has been one of the few exceptions. Sactwu's mass participation in the workers charter campaign is another.

Increasing the mass base of Cosatu campaigns is essential for the re-invigoration of union democracy. The post-February situation created the space for unions to concentrate again on democratic participation as much as on the issues themselves. Part of the challenge involves ensuring that union structures are adequate to the tasks of representing, educating and informing membership, and meeting their needs. Cosatu's campaign conferences are an attempt to do this.

Strengthening democracy also demands examination of the poor participation of women in Cosatu and its affiliates. The issue at stake is not simply increasing the number of women in leadership but also ensuring that a post-apartheid society is non-sexist as well as non-racial. For the union movement this means exploring affirmative action more seriously, for example by including constitutional provisions requiring that at least one-third of all executive committee positions are held by women.

Union and Cosatu structures

The union movement has three major weaknesses in its internal organisational functioning – it lacks professionalism, has inadequate or non-existent training programmes, and its constitutional structures are not the most suitable to meeting the challenge of the 1990s. Naturally there are differences within and between affiliates. Cosatu and a number of affiliates have recently started addressing these weaknesses. But to a greater or lesser extent, they apply to all affiliates and to the federation.

The lack of professionalism reveals itself in many ways. It is unusual to find a union head office where all recognition or wage agreements signed can be found easily. It is rare to find a union general secretary who can authoritatively say whether Everyman Sithole is a union member, how many shop stewards the union has, or what proportion of its members have been granted 16 June as a paid holiday. The problem repeats itself at regional and branch levels. Information systems are inadequate or non-existent. Efficiency is rarely practiced, nor is it valued. At local level, organisers and officials are generally forced to rely on their own resources and inventiveness. Those unions which have tried to address these problems have often resorted to bureaucratic solutions, further disempowering both local officials and the general membership.

The almost total absence of staff training is also a major weakness unions must confront. Almost all union officials – organisers, educators and administrators – receive no training or induction before starting work. Many are unable to use a calculator effectively, yet are expected to negotiate complex wage agreements. On-the-job training is the most a union employee can expect and even this is likely to be little more than advice from an experienced organiser. This sometimes releases great qualities of inventiveness and initiative. More often than not, it leads to poor administrative and organising methods and weak negotiating skills.

Finally, existing constitutional structures need a fundamental rethink. Progressive South African unionism is based on British unionism, albeit a more democratic version. The South African model rests heavily on shop-steward structures in every plant, worker majorities on every union committee, NECs composed of delegates from branches or regions, and a strong general secretary. With the exception of the last feature, which is a more recent development, the outlines of this model were developed when the union movement revived in the 1970s.

The system of majoritarian hegemony, whereby the majority position is binding on the entire union, needs careful re-examination. It has frequently been justified in much the same way as the Leninist concept of democratic centralism – that positions are debated thoroughly but decisions reached are binding on and must be propagated by all.

Some variant of this system binds all democratic organisations. Debates cannot continue endlessly and majority decision-making must be respected. In Cosatu's earlier years, with extreme repression and when the federation often had to substitute for political organisations, majoritarian hegemony was necessary to ensure a high level of discipline and unity within the organisation. However the strong version of majoritarian hegemony is inappropriate in the current phase.

The problem is revealed most obviously in the prevailing system of layered democracy and bloc voting. South African unionism is based on layered, rather than direct, democracy. Workers typically elect shop stewards by general ballot at the workplace. Some of these shop stewards then sit on local or branch committees and elect branch leadership and decide branch policies. Branches in turn send delegates to the region... and so on up to national level.

In theory the system is highly democratic. In practice it is only effective if, as Cosatu insists, delegates go to higher meetings with a mandate and report back to their constituency after every meeting. Experience reveals that this process is inconsistent and inadequate. While shop stewards generally have a direct relationship with the membership, leaders at higher levels do not. The danger, of course, is that national leaders may end up representing only the regional leaders that elected them and not the membership as a whole. Equally, they may represent the views of union activists rather than the general membership. To deepen the democratic process, the tried and tested system of layered democracy must be supplemented with direct consultation of the membership on key issues. In some countries major policy decisions or the election of national leadership is done by direct ballotting of union membership.

A related corollary of majoritarian hegemony is bloc voting. This emerges most strongly at Cosatu's regional and national congresses. National congresses are exciting, vibrant events and delegates arrive bringing the outlook and mandates of the workers who sent them. They invariably meet beforehand as delegates from a particular region of that affiliate and attempt to develop a uniform position. At the congress itself they caucus with other delegates from their union and develop a common union position. This is presented to congress as, for example, the Numsa position. The result is bloc voting, in practice, if not in theory.

This inability to accommodate democratic pluralism can have negative effects, as seen in the debate at Cosatu's second congress on adoption of the Freedom Charter. Numsa's Eastern Cape delegates were unable to vote in favour of the political position expressed by NUM despite having a mandate to do so from their members in the region. With bloc voting, pluralism assumes a bureaucratic form and emerges as conflict between monolithic unions rather than differing views of worker delegates. Concentric circles of majoritarian hegemony, even if they reach down to every factory and local, will eventually result in no democracy at all.

The existing system is not undemocratic. Indeed, these structures have largely proved themselves in practice: resilient in the face of attack, and with the multiplicity of layers resistant to state disruption. They have also given ordinary workers real power to decide on bread-and-butter issues affecting them in their plants. But the system has not always empowered workers in regard to the larger social and political issues Cosatu has taken up.

Cosatu is generally accepted to be greater than the sum of its parts, although this is not reflected in the federation's structures. These are composed entirely of delegates from the various affiliates. Although Cosatu locals, and local leadership, may be crucial in promoting the federation, they have no formal representation in the higher structures, national or regional. Delegations at Cosatu's bi-annual national congress are made up entirely of delegates from affiliates. None come from Cosatu's own local or regional structures. This discourages working-class consciousness in favour of a more sectional affiliate consciousness.

There is a real possibility that Cosatu will soon be the major player in drafting a new industrial relations structure, and there is every reason to explore other models of unionism. The British model is one of the weaker systems internationally. Its unions are declining in numbers and influence, and its membership is often extremely conservative. Its public image is of a defensive, reactive and narrowly sectional union movement. Developing union structures which deepen democracy, give direct power to ordinary members, and maintain organisational vibrancy is one of the key challenges Cosatu faces.

Workers and officials

A key area requiring reassessment is the relationship between 'workers' and 'officials'. A central tenet within Cosatu and its affiliates is that workers control the organisation and officials are simply full-time functionaries. Unlike most union movements internationally, all elected leadership positions are held by union members who continue to retain their ordinary jobs.[*] The intention is to maintain ongoing links between leadership and ordinary union members.

---

[*] *There is one exception to this. Since 1989 NUM president James Motlatsi has been in the full-time employ of the union. This move was hotly debated within the union, and the decision finally taken was partly a pragmatic one. Motlatsi had been one of 50 000 workers dismissed during the 1987 mineworkers strike and the union congress did not want to lose him as president.*

The only exception to this system is the position of union secretary which is generally held by a full-time official. As we have seen, acknowledgment that this position is a powerful one developed during the Cosatu era – and has also coincided with the almost total disappearance of women from the position of union secretary.

In practice, however, worker leaders have found great difficulty combining a full day's work with the demanding tasks of union leadership. Some have managed to negotiate time off from their workplaces, while others have the status of full-time shop stewards, essentially free to come and go as they please. This solution gives a union president, for example, an opportunity to tackle union duties while retaining links with the shopfloor. However, it is not a solution for most union members, tending to restrict leadership positions to those working in large, well-organised plants where they are able to negotiate extensive time off.

The problem becomes worse as the tasks of leadership become more demanding and complex. Major union issues cannot be adequately tackled and grasped on a part-time basis. As a result, it is usually union officials who wield real power, with elected worker leaders and executive committees acting as a check on the abuse of that power. The union general secretary is more likely to be better known, and called upon to resolve a crisis within the union, than the president. Since the principle of worker leadership was originally intended to ensure hands-on leadership by workers, the system clearly no longer works effectively. While the principle is retained, officials wield more power than ever before, and effective worker leaders no longer spend much time at work.

The challenge to Cosatu involves retaining 'worker leadership', making it more meaningful, yet avoiding its pitfalls where, for example, a worker is elected union president and then effectively retains that position for life. The solution to the worker/official dilemma may require changes to the country's labour law to facilitate time-off and job security for elected worker leaders, enabling them to return to the factory on expiry of their term of office.

The political challenge

The political context has changed greatly, both internationally and locally. International attitudes towards the apartheid regime are softening, and the global balance of power has shifted with the collapse of communist Eastern Europe and the end of the Cold War. These changes have major implications for any socialist vision, and the possibilities for its realisation, which Cosatu may have. They also highlight the dangers of sacrificing union independence whereby unions become mere 'transmission belts' through which party interests are conveyed to workers.

Here, the country's future hangs in the balance with numerous forces battling to determine and influence the shape of a new South Africa. Since 2 February 1990, the ANC and De Klerk have stood at centre stage. De Klerk and his government are preparing to share, and perhaps even transfer, political power, while keeping white social and economic privilege secure. Enormous opportunities for organisation have opened up for the ANC, PAC and others. Racism, despite scrapped apartheid legislation, remains at the core of the system. Opposition forces, including Cosatu, still face the task of transforming the country into one where the needs and aspirations of the majority of working people are respected.

Cosatu's political role has been called into question since the unbanning of the ANC and SACP. Why, some have asked, should Cosatu remain politically active? This view fails to understand the relationship between the trade union movement and politics. Cosatu did not become politically active simply because the ANC was banned. Its outlook came from an understanding, which pre-dated the federation's formation, that the union movement could not achieve its union goals without fundamental social and political changes.

The unions found politics on the factory floor. How could they call for improved training and job advancement opportunities without challenging racism, job reservation and unequal education? How could they challenge the LRA without confronting the undemocratic process by which it had been drafted and passed into law? How could they call for a living wage without challenging the profits of major companies and the distribution of wealth within South African society? These questions remain valid despite the ANC's unbanning and the as yet unrealised prospects of democracy.

Organised industry and commerce has never avoided political involvement. Indeed, the racial structures of South African society are in large measure a product and expression of employer interests. Mineowners and industrialists have had privileged access to governments of the day. Their political involvement has hence been less public, less oppositional and less confrontational than that of the union movement, but no less real.

A democratic system does not restrict politics to political parties. It is a peculiarly South African concept, propagated over the years by the National Party, that politics is something which belongs in parliament. Politics affects the entire social fabric. The union movement, like all major social institutions, has political interests. Economic policies affect its membership. So too do the structures and constitution of society. The right to freedom of speech or assembly; whether international trade barriers are restrictive or open; whether a new constitution is drafted by a constituent assembly or behind closed doors; the structure of the industrial relations system; whether the health-care system is centred on public or private medicine: these are all political issues which impact on the union movement, its members, and the working class more generally.

The post-February political situation is not, therefore, an argument against Cosatu's continuing political involvement. However, it does mean the nature of the federation's political role must be reconsidered. Many joined or became active in Cosatu because it offered one of the few means for legal political expression. ANC and SACP underground activists were specifically assigned to the task of building a strong trade union movement. In the repressive climate Cosatu became an outlet for the political hopes of far more than its membership. It acted as a political centre. Youths and students looked to it for guidance; churches asked it for political direction; ambassadors, foreign visitors and political journalists canvassed its opinions – and not because of any particular interest in or support for trade unionism.

To a large extent Cosatu spoke for the entire democratic movement. It was seen as the voice of the ANC in a situation where the ANC could not openly speak.

The key difference in the post-apartheid period is that Cosatu no longer has to engage in political substitutionism. It no longer has to attempt to speak for the entire democratic movement. The ANC, SACP, PAC and others can now openly speak for themselves.

Cosatu's direct role is not on the political terrain of parliament, elections and lawmaking, although its policies will continue to have major effects on these. For the federation this will probably mean a shift in emphasis from 'Politics' to 'politics', with its political role in the 1990s one of process and direction. It is likely to act as a watchdog on the political dimensions of the state's social and economic policies. In the short term this will cause a crisis within Cosatu, for its leadership is accustomed to a high-profile political role.[*]

While it is Cosatu's right and duty to call for a constituent assembly as the most democratic means of drafting a new constitution, its role is not to stand for election to that assembly. In the interim, however, Cosatu is still likely to play a direct political role – partly because of its mobilising ability and partly because the present period is one in which the

---

[*] *In the immediate post-February period this crisis expressed itself in a number of ways. Ironically, with the democratic movement on the threshold of major victory, there has been a distinct drop in motivation amongst union officials and leaders. The ideological glue of 'the struggle' and commitment to defeating 'the enemy' – which for so long held the unions together – is rapidly coming unstuck. A re-definition of Cosatu's political role is necessary to solve this problem.*

foundations are being laid for the country's social and political system for decades to come.

A key element of Cosatu's political activities will undoubtedly be to ensure that the voice of organised labour is heard when the policies of a post-apartheid South Africa are drafted. Cosatu has already begun, and will undoubtedly continue, to draft policies on issues such as housing, medical care, social security, and training. It is also considering economic policy in some detail – particularly the relationship between the state and the private sector, between market and non-market forces, and the role of the union movement in restructuring the economy.

The post-February situation not only challenges Cosatu on the question of political substitutionism. It compels the federation to consider its attitude to the structures of society in a non-racial democratic South Africa. It will no longer be sufficient for the trade unions to be a force of opposition and resistance. They will have to be a force for reconstruction and change.

A new industrial relations system

A major task facing the federation is the active reshaping of the country's industrial relations system. Many sectors still have no agreed national bargaining forums. There is no forum for organised industry and organised labour as a whole to negotiate issues of national importance such as public holidays, economic restructuring, basic employment conditions and a national provident fund. These gaps are destructive and perpetuate conflict. However, talks with Saccola over the LRA problem may have provided a foundation for such a national forum, and a restructured NMC may also offer possibilities.

A major part of any new system will involve drafting an entirely new labour law. Apart from the need to extend union rights to all workers, a new law must include dispute resolution and arbitration procedures which are both faster and more fair than at present. It must also establish basic bargaining structures and reinforce principles such as worker control of the union movement.

The present industrial relations system grudgingly acknowledges the union movement. A new system must accept unions as a necessary social institution. This demands that both employers and unions accept a new set of 'rules', including an end to the culture of violence which has become a hallmark of industrial relations since the 1986 state of emergency, and the establishment of basic rights and powers in the workplace.

In presenting its perspectives on post-apartheid South Africa the union movement needs to be aware of the dangers of sectionalism. As the voice of organised labour, unions have an inherent tendency to be sectional. Already unions face allegations of representing only a labour aristocracy – privileged workers employed by the larger corporations, or urban, rather than rural, workers. Two aspects of sectionalism require particular vigilance, namely disputes involving members of the public and a tendency to represent the views of relatively better-off workers.

In the health sector strikes of 1990 a potential conflict of interest emerged between workers and the broader public. On the one hand health workers were striking for the right to join unions and earn a decent wage. On the other hand members of the public were concerned about their health and the virtual collapse of medical services for the duration of the strike. In situations like this the union movement will have to spend more time and energy justifying its actions to the general public, black and white. This in turn implies greater responsibility, more openness, improved publicity, and a conscious attempt to win public support during industrial action. This principally affects unions in the service sector, where workers deal directly with the general public, although it may also be relevant during protracted disputes in the manufacturing sector.

South Africa's economy already contains a dangerous dualism, with large, technologically sophisticated enterprises operating alongside sweatshops and informal sector production. It is easier for the union movement to organise, mobilise and represent workers employed by major corporations. However, unless Cosatu can show that it is interested as much in employment creation as a living wage, as much in public health-care as medical aid schemes for its members, its influence will decline in society. The views the federation propagates at the political and economic level must be successfully presented as the interests of the vast majority of people.

The union movement is used to being labelled a disruptive force, and blamed for inflation, unemployment and a variety of other ills. Union leaders are accustomed to being called 'communists', 'terrorists' and 'agitators'. In the past unions have dismissed these charges, secure in the belief that they represented the interests of the great majority of the population.

The unions can expect to be accused of disruption even in the post-apartheid era. The charges will be packaged differently: there will be less talk of 'communists' and more of 'sabotaging national reconstruction'. The unions will have to take these allegations seriously, especially since they will come from a popularly- elected government. Cosatu is attempting to face this challenge by developing a comprehensive programme for union involvement in social and economic reconstruction.

Pluralism

Combatting dogmatism and intolerance within its own ranks is another difficult task facing Cosatu. In part this problem has arisen because of political substitutionism, where Cosatu was seen, and saw itself, as a flag-bearer of the banned ANC. Most unions attempted to adhere to a clearly defined line, maintaining political clarity and coherence during a period of harsh state attack. But when there were no clear majorities to determine that line, as in the case of the Ccawusa split or during Cosatu's second congress, the results were deeply divisive. Unions acting as bearers of one political position is unsustainable in the current period. They are essentially mass organisations which accept all workers as members, regardless of political affiliation.

All key political organisations now accept, at least in theory, the need for political pluralism in a post-apartheid South Africa. This involves the right of a variety of political parties to exist, contest elections, and compete for support for their political perspectives within all major social institutions – including the trade union movement. When this becomes a reality it will be hard to justify linking the fortunes of the trade union movement too closely with one political line – as happened not only in the Soviet Union but with many of the social-democratic parties of Western Europe.

Two alternatives can accommodate this situation. The first envisages separate federations linked to different political parties or movements. These could co-operate on industrial issues as required. In practice the situation would not be vastly different to continuing with Cosatu, Nactu and Uwusa, allied to the ANC, PAC and Inkatha respectively. The other option is to have one federation for all workers, and one union in each sector. This would require a high level of tolerance for differing political views expressed within its ranks, with majority and minority factions competing for support from the membership as a whole.

Cosatu's founding slogan of 'One Country, One Federation' impels it towards the second option, although this has implications for the existing tripartite alliance between Cosatu, the ANC and SACP. How the process unfolds will depend on the policies of a post-apartheid government and on the union movement's decisions about its political role in a democratic society.

In its brief five years, Cosatu has shown itself capable of reaching great heights. How the federation resolves the challenges outlined above will have long-term implications for the future of the union movement and the country as a whole.

Index

A

D

E

F

G

General Workers Union see GWU
GFWBF, 18
Glass and Allied Workers Union, 25-26
Godongwane, Enoch, 144
Godsell, Bobby, 225-226, 234, 238, 286, 388, 411, 438
Goldfields, 230, 237-238
Golding, Marcel, 81, 227-228, 233-234, 238, 401-402, 413
Gomomo, John, 26, 352, 367, 409, 429
Gona, Fred, 367
Gordon, Max, 9
Government,
    attitude to Cosatu, 72, 127, 185, 191-192
    attitude to trade unions, 12, 16, 21, 24, 27, 127, 138, 148, 173, 185, 193-194, 262, 288, 464
    defiance campaign, 408-410
    negotiations with Cosatu, 335, 338, 346-350, 420
    registration of unions see Trade unions, registration
    relations with ANC, 347, 350, 420, 425, 462
Gqweta, Robert, 59
Gqweta, Thozamile, 28, 35
Great Miners' Strike see Strikes, Great Miners' Strike
Gumede, MP, 71, 125, 133
Gush, Peter, 227
Gwala, Harry, 346
Gwala, Jabulani, 20, 113
GWIU, 304
GWIU see also Gawu
GWU, 19, 30, 39, 103, 111
    unity talks, 34, 37-39, 41-42
GWU see also TGWU; WPGWU
Gwusa, 28, 37-39, 41-42, 216
Gxanyana, Mandla, 51, 349

H

Hadebe, GST, 133
Hani, Chris, 94
Harwu, 147, 197, 202, 204, 397-399, 401
Health and safety see NUM; Trade unions, health and safety
Hemson, Dave, 20
Hermanus, May, 153
Hlalele, Lebogang, 234

Mwasa, 39
Mwusa, 102
Mxenge, Victor, 89

N

Naawu, 25, 103, 112, 199
Nactu, 311-312, 344, 419
    AAC, 294-295, 297, 300
    anti-LRA campaign, 325-326, 386-387, 389-391, 414-415
    formation, 157-159
    political profile, 158-159, 218
    relations with Cosatu, 159, 281, 284, 290-291, 311-312, 319-325,
        344, 352, 414-415, 456
Nactu see also Azactu; Cusa
Nafcoc, 74, 122
Naidoo, Jay, 6, 59, 64-66, 73-75, 94-95, 99, 106-107, 112, 134,
    218-219, 245, 285, 296, 304-306, 312-313, 340-341, 348, 353, 362,
    367, 386, 405, 408, 435, 438
Naidoo, Jay (Ccawusa), 169, 398, 400
Nala, June-Rose, 20
Natal violence, 162, 331-342, 365-366, 425-426
National African Chamber of Commerce see Nafcoc
National Automobile and Allied Workers Union see Naawu
National Council of Trade Unions see Nactu
National Education Crisis Committee see NECC
National Education, Health and Allied Workers Union see Nehawu
National Federation of Workers see NFW
National Iron, Steel and Metal Workers Union see Nismawu
National Manpower Commission see NMC
National Sugar Refining and Allied Industries Employees Union
        see NSRAIEU
National Unemployed Workers Coordinating Committee see NUWCC
National Union of Brick and Allied Workers, 130
National Union of Furniture and Allied Workers see NUFAW
National Union of Laundry, Cleaning and Dyeing Workers
        see NULCDW
National Union of Metalworkers of South Africa see Numsa
National Union of Mineworkers see NUM
National Union of Namibian Workers see NUNW
National Union of Printing and Allied Workers see Nupawo
National Union of Railwayworkers see NUR

South African Transport Service see Sats
Soweto Civic Association, 62-63
Soweto uprising see South Africa, 1976 Soweto unrest
Soweto Youth Congress see Soyco
Soyco, 45
State of emergency see South Africa, dates and state of emergency
Stayaways, 14, 36, 44-45, 87-89, 120, 150, 273-275, 302, 332, 426-427
Stayaways 1986, 122-127, 136, 140-143, 454
Stayaways 1987, 188-190
Stayaways 1988, 283-285, 287-289
Stayaways 1989, 389-391, 404
Stayaways see also Mass mobilisation
Strike violence, 11-12, 18, 22, 81-82, 85, 162, 175-183, 227-229, 231, 233, 364, 417-418, 424
Strikes, 7, 10-12, 17-18, 22-25, 28, 77-85, 136-138, 155, 170, 183-185 248, 263-264, 305-306, 416-418, 424-425, 428, 441-442, 454
    Great Miners' Strike, 224-239
    illegal, 11, 24, 228, 264
    legal, 24, 29, 83, 169-171, 226-230, 234, 264, 318
    mine, 11-12, 18, 78-82, 224-239
    OK Bazaars strike, 168-171
    siyalala la, 83-85, 228
Sweet, Food and Allied Workers Union see SFAWU

T

T&LC, 12-13
Tambo, Oliver, 94, 329
Tawu, 19, 114
Teachers union see Sadtu
Textile and Allied Workers Union see Tawu
Textile Workers Industrial Union see TWIU
TGWU, 18, 102, 129, 200, 217, 282
    mergers, 111, 197, 199-202
TGWU see also GWU
Thabethe, Elizabeth, 356, 374-375
Thanda, Reginald, 382
Thate, Pule, 245, 397
Thathe, David, 220
Theron, Jan, 23, 111
Thibedi, Kaiser, 398
Thibedi, TW, 8

U

X

Y

Z